Windows Phone 8 in Action

Windows Phone 8 in Action

TIMOTHY BINKLEY-JONES
ADAM BENOIT
MASSIMO PERGA
MICHAEL SYNC

MANNING
SHELTER ISLAND

For online information and ordering of this and other Manning books, please visit www.manning.com. The publisher offers discounts on this book when ordered in quantity. For more information, please contact

Special Sales Department
Manning Publications Co.
20 Baldwin Road
PO Box 261
Shelter Island, NY 11964
Email: orders@manning.com

Manning Publications Co.
20 Baldwin Road
PO Box 261
Shelter Island, NY 11964

Development editor: Susan Conant
Copyeditor: Corbin Collins
Proofreader: Melody Dolab
Typesetter: Marija Tudor
Cover designer: Marija Tudor

ISBN: 9781617291371
Printed in the United States of America
1 2 3 4 5 6 7 8 9 10 – MAL – 18 17 16 15 14 13

brief contents

contents

preface

We authors come from different backgrounds and locations, but we came together to write this book. Michael is a Silverlight MVP who lives in Singapore; Massimo lives in Europe and worked at Microsoft on the Windows Phone team; Adam lives in Canada and has published several applications in the Windows Phone store; and Timothy lives in the United States and has worked as technical proofreader for other Manning books on WPF and Silverlight. Amid this diversity, our shared passion for XAML and mobile applications brought us together to produce this book.

In 2012, nearly 700 million smartphones were sold across the globe. The world is quickly moving to a fully connected society, and smartphones like the Windows Phone are already playing a major role in how we access data, connect with our family and friends, and interact with the world around us. Smartphones are almost always with us, know where they are located, and are connected to the internet.

Your job as application developers is to create applications that can interact with our environment, sift through the data, and present a simplified view of the world to users overwhelmed with the complexities of the fast-paced, high-tech digital world. We hope our book gives you the knowledge you need to determine location, process sensor input, capture audio and video, and scrutinize data to build killer Windows Phone applications that integrate nicely with the operating system and native applications.

acknowledgments

We'd like to thank our family, friends, and coworkers for their support and advice, for being there when we needed someone to listen to half-formed ideas, and for understanding when we said, "I'd love to, but I have to work on the book." And none of this would have been possible without Microsoft and the support it provides to the development community.

We'd like to thank the following reviewers, who read the manuscript at various stages during development and provided invaluable feedback: Alex Lucas, Alex Tcherniakhovski, Avijit Das, Berndt Hamboeck, Dave Campbell, Fulvio Gabana, Gary Ewan Park, Jan Vinterberg, Michael Williams, Sebastian Aguilar, and Sergio Romero.

Thanks also to our technical proofreaders Tom McKearney and Gary Park, copyeditor Corbin Collins, and proofreader Melody Dolab for their careful editing of our work, which resulted in a much better book.

Finally, thanks to everyone at Manning, especially Marjan Bace, Michael Stephens, and our development editor Susan Conant, as well as our production team of Mary Piergies, Kevin Sullivan, Marija Tudor, and Janet Vail. Your guidance and support during the writing and production process were much appreciated.

about this book

This book is a hands-on guide to building mobile applications for Windows Phone 8 using XAML, C#, and HTML5. The Windows Phone 8 operating system is Microsoft's latest entry into the fiercely competitive mobile market. In this book we show how to build user interfaces that adhere to the Windows Phone design and how to use the Windows Phone Runtime and .NET APIs to access the sensors and integrate with built-in applications.

Windows Phone 8 is both a brand-new operating system built upon the Windows 8 kernel and an upgrade of Windows Phone 7. Microsoft replaced the Windows CE kernel that powered Windows Phone 7 with the same Windows 8 kernel that runs Windows 8 PCs and tablets. The Windows Runtime was adapted and modified for the phone. Microsoft migrated core features and APIs from Windows Phone 7, such as the XAML user interface framework, .NET APIs, fast application switching, launchers and choosers, and platform extensibility. This hybridization of Windows 8 and Windows Phone 7 means that two different APIs exist for some features, and in this book we cover the newer Windows Phone Runtime APIs instead of the Windows Phone 7 APIs.

Who should read this book

This book is written for C# and .NET developers who are familiar with XAML, Silverlight, or WPF development. This book doesn't teach you the subtleties of C# or XAML development. It avoids many of the more powerful features of XAML and the Model-View-ViewModel pattern used by many XAML developers. Instead, we keep the focus on the features and APIs that are unique to the phone and endeavor to make the content accessible to readers who aren't very familiar with Microsoft technologies.

Roadmap

This book has 3 parts, 18 chapters, and 2 appendixes. The three parts introduce Windows Phone 8, cover the core concepts of the phone, and discuss enhancements to XAML.

Part 1 is an introduction to Windows Phone, the development environment, and the SDK. This part walks you through creating your first application.

In chapter 1 you discover why Microsoft scrapped the Windows Mobile operating system in favor of a completely new smartphone platform. We compare Windows Phone 8 to Android and iOS development and introduce you to Visual Studio and the SDK tools you'll use when building applications.

In chapter 2 you build your first Windows Phone 8 project, which is a traditional Hello World application. We use the Hello World application to introduce you to touch events, application tiles, the application bar, several XAML controls, and the Windows Phone navigation model.

Part 2 examines the core Windows Phone platform and what makes developing for the phone different from developing for the desktop or the browser. We introduce concepts that are brand new to Windows Phone, as well as concepts that have been adapted to operate within the phone's limitations.

In chapter 3 you learn about fast application switching and fast application resume, Microsoft's names for the battery-saving technologies that allow a dormant application to be quickly restored when a user switches from a foreground application to a background application.

In chapter 4 you learn how to create background agents that run periodically. You also discover how to use alarms and reminders to interact with users even when your application isn't running.

In chapter 5 you read about how to use launchers and choosers to interact with built-in applications such as the Phone Dialer, Email, and the People Hub.

In chapter 6 you work with the phone's built-in contacts database and calendar.

In chapter 7 you store application data using local storage and a SQL database.

In chapter 8 you build an application that captures images from the phone's camera and allows a user to make simple modifications to the photos.

In chapter 9 you integrate an application with the built-in Pictures and Music + Video Hubs.

In chapter 10 you learn how to obtain data from the phone's hardware, including the accelerometer, compass, gyrometer, inclinometer, and orientation sensor.

In chapter 11 we cover networking topics such as determining connection status and subscribing to Push Notifications. Push Notifications provide the ability for an external application or web service to send messages and updates to a particular Windows Phone device.

In chapter 12 we examine three Speech APIs: text-to-speech, voice commands, and speech recognition.

Part 3 presents XAML features and controls used to build applications that match the look and feel of Windows Phone.

In chapter 13 you take a deep dive into the application bar, a new toolbar control for the Windows Phone 8 platform. You also learn how to use the `ContextMenu` control from the Windows Phone Toolkit, a Codeplex project from Microsoft.

In chapter 14 you learn the ins and outs of the `Pivot` and `Panorama` controls. The controls, unique to the Windows Phone, form the foundation of the Windows Phone user experience.

In chapter 15 you work with the `MediaElement` to play audio and video.

In chapter 16 you build a location-aware application using location services and the Maps API.

In chapter 17 you learn how to use the `WebBrowser` control to build an HTML5 and JavaScript application.

In chapter 18 you discover how to make money from your applications and publish them to the Windows Phone Store. You also learn how to work with the `AdControl`.

Code conventions and downloads

All source code and many programming elements in the book are in a `fixed-width font like this`, which sets it off from the surrounding text. In many listings, the code is annotated to point out the key concepts, and numbered bullets are used in the text to provide additional information about the code. We've tried to format the code so that it fits within the available page space in the book by adding line breaks and using indentation carefully. Sometimes, however, very long lines include line-continuation markers.

The source code presented in the book can be downloaded from the publisher's website at www.manning.com/WindowsPhone8inAction. The source code is organized into folders for each chapter, with subfolders for each project. The source code contains the completed sample projects for each chapter. Many of the samples make use of third-party libraries added via the NuGet package manager.

Software or hardware requirements

The Windows Phone Developer Tools, which Microsoft provides as a free download, are required to compile and execute the sample projects presented in this book. The Windows Phone Developer Tools install an express edition of Visual Studio 2012 configured with the phone development tools. If you already have a retail edition of Visual Studio 2012 installed on your computer, the phone development tools will be installed as a plug-in to the IDE. Windows Phone projects can be written in both C# and Visual Basic.

We use the express edition throughout the book for the screenshots and sample code. Code and user interface design features will work the same in the retail editions of Visual Studio 2012. You can download the Windows Phone Developer Tools from http://developer.windowsphone.com.

A physical Windows Phone isn't required. The Windows Phone Developer Tools include Windows Phone 8 emulators. With a few exceptions, the samples in this book will run in the emulator exactly as they would on a physical phone. The samples that make use of the compass and gyroscope do require a physical device. If you want to use a physical device, a Windows Store Developer Account is required to unlock your phone. Developer Accounts can be purchased for as little as $19.

The system requirements for the Windows Phone tools are as follows:

- Supported operating systems: Windows 8 64-bit client versions
- 6.5 GB of free disk space on the system drive
- 4 GB RAM
- 64-bit CPU

The Windows Phone 8 emulators should work on most recent computers. The emulators are Hyper-V virtual machines and require a computer capable of running Hyper-V. The Windows Phone emulators require the following:

- Supported operating systems: Windows 8 Pro edition
- A 64-bit CPU with Second Level Address Translation (SLAT)

Author Online

Your purchase of *Windows Phone 8 in Action* includes free access to a private web forum run by Manning Publications where you can make comments about the book, ask technical questions, and receive help from the authors and from other users. To access the forum and subscribe to it, point your web browser to www.manning.com/WindowsPhone8inAction. That page provides information on how to get on the forum once you're registered, what kind of help is available, and the rules of conduct on the forum.

Manning's commitment to our readers is to provide a venue where a meaningful dialog between individual readers and between readers and authors can take place. It's not a commitment to any specific amount of participation on the part of the authors, whose contribution to the AO remains voluntary (and unpaid). We suggest you try asking the authors some challenging questions, lest their interest stray!

The Author Online forum and the archives of previous discussions will be accessible from the publisher's website as long as the book is in print.

about the cover illustration

The figure on the cover of *Windows Phone 8 in Action* is captioned "L'Usurier," which means a money lender, or, perhaps more accurately, in 21st-century parlance, a banker. The dapper young man exudes confidence, no doubt stemming from his profession. The illustration is taken from a 19th-century edition of Sylvain Maréchal's four-volume compendium of regional dress customs and uniforms, published in France. Each illustration is finely drawn and colored by hand. The rich variety of Maréchal's collection reminds us vividly of how culturally apart the world's towns and regions were just 200 years ago. Isolated from each other, people spoke different dialects and languages. In the streets or in the countryside, it was easy to identify where people lived and what their trade, station in life, or rank in the army was just by their dress.

Dress codes have changed since then, and the diversity by region, so rich at the time, has faded away. It's now hard to tell the inhabitants of different continents apart, let alone different towns or regions. Perhaps we've traded cultural diversity for a more varied personal life—certainly for a more varied and fast-paced technological life.

At a time when it's hard to tell one computer book from another, Manning celebrates the inventiveness and initiative of the computer business with book covers based on the rich diversity of regional life of two centuries ago, brought to life by Maréchal's pictures.

Part 1

Introducing Windows Phone

Welcome to *Windows Phone 8 in Action*, where you'll learn all about building applications for Microsoft's newest mobile operating system. This book is divided into three parts; part 1 introduces you to the Windows Phone and the Windows Phone SDK and walks you through creating your first application.

In chapter 1 you'll discover why Microsoft scrapped the Windows Mobile operating system in favor of a completely new smartphone platform. We compare Windows Phone to Android and iOS development and introduce you to Visual Studio and the other tools in the Windows Phone SDK you'll use when building applications.

In chapter 2 you'll build your first Windows Phone project, which is a traditional Hello World application. We use the Hello World application to introduce you to touch events, application tiles, the application bar, and the Windows Phone navigation model. You'll also learn tricks to style common controls to match the Windows Phone design and how to control the software keyboard. Finally, we introduce you to the Windows Phone Toolkit, a CodePlex project from Microsoft that includes additional user interface controls.

1 A new phone, a new operating system

This chapter covers

- Introducing Windows Phone 8
- Understanding the hardware platform
- Porting applications from other mobile operating systems
- Developing for Windows Phone

Windows Phone 8 is more than a new operating system. It's an operating system, powerful hardware platform, and collection of web services combined into one great experience for the busy individual, as shown in figure 1.1. Phone consumers demand the most from their phones as they balance work and life and use their phones to manage their busy lifestyles. Windows Phone 8 was designed to let users tailor the phone experience to their individual needs so that they can get tasks done faster and get back to the important aspects of their lives.

The Windows Phone 8 operating system is Microsoft's latest entry into the fiercely competitive mobile market. Windows Phone 8 is both an upgrade of the Windows Phone 7 operating system and a slimmed-down version of Windows 8, Microsoft's latest desktop and tablet operating system. With the release of Windows

Figure 1.1 A variety of screen shots from Windows Phone 8: Starting with the Start Screen at bottom center and moving clockwise, you can see the Application List, Office Hub, People Hub, Email application, and Lock Screen.

Phone 7 in October 2010, Microsoft re-imagined what a mobile operating system should be and completely changed the rules on how to build mobile applications. With the release of Windows 8, Microsoft has redefined how to build and market applications for touch-enabled desktop, laptop, and tablet computers. By bringing together Windows Phone 7 and Windows 8 into a single phone platform, Microsoft is ensuring a consistent foundation for touch-enabled application development, regardless of form factor.

In this chapter we present the motivation behind this revolution in the Microsoft OS for mobile devices. We detail how Windows Phone 8 differs from other mobile operating systems so that you can assess the capabilities of the new platform and understand how existing designs and code can be ported. We describe the various hardware specifications common to the different Windows Phone 8 devices so that developers can confidently target equipment that will always be available. And we introduce the developer tools that you'll use throughout the book to build applications targeted at the Windows Phone.

1.1 Rebooting the Windows Phone platform

Microsoft has been building operating systems for mobile devices and phones for more than a decade. One of the earliest versions was Pocket PC 2000, running on palm-sized devices such as the Hewlett-Packard Jornada and the Compaq iPAQ. These early devices weren't smartphones but were portable computers or PDAs targeted for business users and didn't initially include phone hardware or network connectivity. Users interacted with these devices using a stylus on a single-point touch screen and an awkward hardware input panel. Pocket PC 2000 was initially built on Windows CE 3.0 and later added the first version of the .NET Compact Framework. Device manufacturers often created custom builds of the operating system tightly coupled to specific hardware on a single device—making operating system upgrades impossible for most users.

Until Windows Phone 8, the most recent versions of Microsoft's operating system for mobile devices were Windows Mobile 6, Windows Phone 6.5, and Windows Phone 7.x. Windows Mobile 6 was built on Windows CE 5 and includes the .NET Compact Framework 2.0 SP1. Windows Mobile 6 came in three editions: Standard, Professional, and Classic. Windows Phone 7.x was built on Windows CE, the .NET Compact Framework, and Silverlight. Prior to Windows Phone 8, there were two releases of Windows Phone 7: 7.0 and 7.1/7.5. A third release of Windows Phone 7, version 7.8, was released shortly after the release of Windows Phone 8 and includes a few Windows Phone 8 features back-ported to the older operating system.

NOTE For the remainder of the book, when we use the term *Windows Phone* without a version number, we're referring to Windows Phone 8. We'll use *Windows Mobile, Windows Phone 6.5, or Windows Phone 7.x* to refer to older versions of the phone operating system.

Mobile phones have evolved rapidly and incredibly in the past several years. Once intended solely for business users, mobile phones are now predominately consumer devices and in many cases have replaced land-line services to become the user's only phone. Smartphones now include music players, cameras, global positioning systems, compasses, and accelerometers. Single-point touch screens that required a stylus have been replaced with multipoint touch screens that work with your fingertips. Awkward hardware input panels have been replaced with software input panels and optional hardware keypads (although at the time of this writing, none of the available Windows Phone 8 devices includes a hardware keypad).

Apple led the smartphone revolution with the release of the iPhone in June 2007 and the introduction of the App Store in July 2008. Google followed with the introduction of the Android OS and Android Market, since renamed Google Play, in October 2008. Since then, Microsoft has seen declines in Windows-powered device market share as consumers and manufacturers turned to smartphones running new mobile operating systems.

But phone hardware and mobile operating systems aren't all that have changed in the last decade. It's now an online world where users are in nearly constant contact with friends, coworkers, family, high school buddies they haven't seen in 20 years, and random followers they've never met. Applications that once worked only with local copies of documents and data are now interacting with services running in the cloud. And with all this online presence and exposure, security has become extremely important. It's no longer acceptable to give software full access to hardware or to data stored in the file system.

Application development platforms and paradigms have changed as well. With the rise of web applications, a whole new style of application development came into power. Rich interactive applications are the norm, complete with animations, dynamic transitions, and cool graphics. User interfaces are no longer built by developers but are created by designers who use a whole different set of tools.

Microsoft set out to build a new Windows Phone operating system designed to meet the demands of the altered smartphone market. The company realized it would need a new operating system, backed by a reliable hardware platform, to compete with Apple and Android.

1.2 Windows Phone foundations

Every application developer must understand the hardware and software platforms on which their code will run. This is true whether you're building desktop applications, web services, or mobile applications. When building Windows Phone applications, you should understand the hardware specifications and know how much memory you can expect to be installed as well as the supported screen resolutions. Windows Phone provides a unique look and feel that developers should respect when designing user interfaces. You should also know how to use or extend the features of built-in applications and services. In this section we talk about the Windows Phone hardware specifications, user interface look and feel, native applications, and the platform APIs you'll use to build your own applications.

1.2.1 Hardware specs

With the redesign of the operating system, Microsoft has taken the opportunity to define clear hardware specifications for Windows Phone 8 devices. All devices must meet the minimum hardware requirements.

Windows Phone 8 devices come in one of three screen resolutions: 800 * 480 (WVGA), 1280 * 768 (WXGA), and 1280 * 720 (720p). For the most part, you don't have to worry about the different screen resolutions because XAML applications are automatically scaled to fit the screen. WXGA screens are scaled by a factor of 1.5, and 720p screens are scaled by a factor of 1.6. A common scaled resolution allows the same user interface to be reused across different Windows Phone devices. But you do need to know that even at the scaled resolution, a 720p screen is slightly taller than the WVGA/WXGA screens, as shown in figure 1.2.

All Windows Phone devices provide the user with at least a four-point multitouch experience. The operating system provides a *software-based input panel* (SIP) to enable text input for devices without a physical keyboard. Phone manufacturers can add additional user input mechanisms, such as a landscape or portrait physical keyboard, but extra hardware can't add extra features to standard typing. The touch screen is capacitive to give the best experience possible on a mobile device.

Windows Phone devices come with an accelerometer, a proximity sensor, a light sensor, an optional compass, and an optional gyrometer. Developers access the raw data

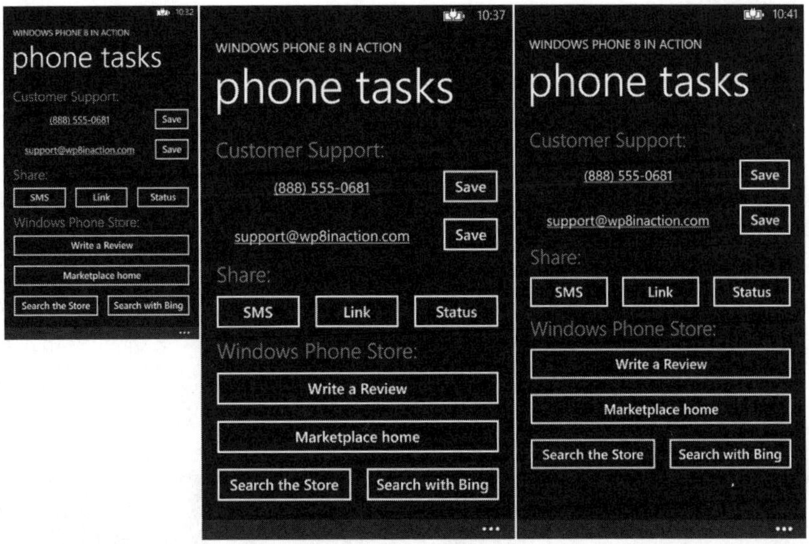

Figure 1.2 The three screen resolutions of Windows Phone 8: 800 * 480 (WVGA) on the left, 1280 * 768 (WXGA) in the center, and 1280 * 720 (720p) on the right. All three images are running the sample application you'll build in chapter 5. Notice how the 720p image has extra space at the bottom of the screen due to the different scale factor.

from each sensor or use wrapper APIs such as `Motion`, `Inclinometer`, or `OrientationSensor`, which wrap up multiple sensors into a simple-to-use interface. The operating system detects when a device has been rotated from portrait to landscape orientation. The sensors can also be used as an input mechanism for controlling an application or game. The sensors are covered in more detail in chapters 10 and 16.

The Windows Phone hardware specifications also include the following:

- GPS receiver to enable location-aware applications
- Rear-facing camera having a minimal resolution of 5 megapixels
- Optional low-resolution, front-facing camera
- GPU supporting DirectX 9 acceleration
- Dual-core Snapdragon S4 processor
- Minimum of 512 MB of RAM and 4 GB of Flash storage
- Optional expandable memory in the form of a microSD slot

The Windows Phone hardware specifications require certain hardware buttons to be present. Many of these keys aren't exposed to developers, and applications can't detect when they're pressed (you'll learn how to access the camera button in chapter 8). The physical buttons that are mandatory for all Windows Phone devices are the following:

- Volume Up
- Volume Down
- Back

- Start
- Search
- Camera
- Power On/Off

Minimum hardware specifications have simplified the task of developing a Windows Phone application. These common hardware specifications have allowed Microsoft to create several different emulator images that cover most of the possible user interactions with the device so that you can test most experiences in your emulator.

Microsoft defined clear hardware specifications to ensure that users and developers have the same experience on every device. Microsoft also designed a new user interface to provide a clean look and feel.

1.2.2 A new user interface

Windows Phone has completely redesigned the user interface, moving from an icon-centric style to the new graphical interface previously developed for the Zune HD media player. Microsoft designers spent some time looking for a proper way to present content and realized an intuitive style already existed. Signage and typography in railway and metro stations, shown in figure 1.3, are concise ways to present information to people coming from different cultures. Why not port this concept to Windows Phone?

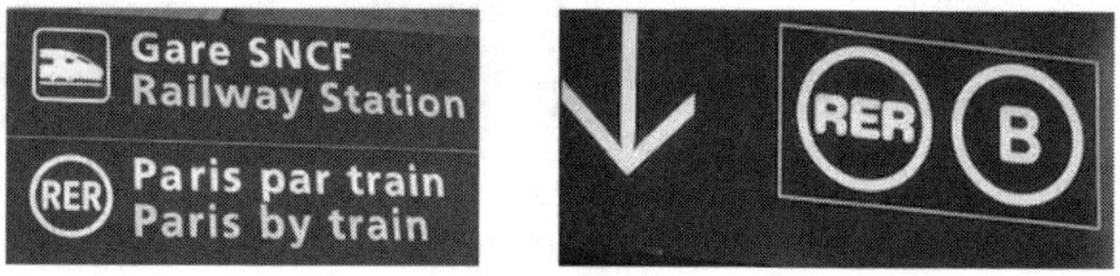

Figure 1.3 Common signs in railways and airports. On the left are icons integrated with text, whereas on the right only icons are used.

The second pillar of the user interface is full-touch support. The success of devices implementing a full-touch user interface is due to the immediacy provided by this natural way of interacting with applications. Concise indications and full-touch support play an important role in developing applications because you must align with these concepts when you design your user interface.

One well-known defect of the applications written for Windows Mobile was the lack of a common user experience. We've seen applications aligned with the template generated by Visual Studio but implemented with a user interface built to match the iPhone user experience. This is confusing to the user, and you should make every effort to match your creations to the Microsoft design language adopted by the native Windows Phone applications.

Last but not least, when developing your application you want to target as many users or customers as possible. Globalizing an application means making it right not only in terms of functionality but also in terms of its contents. We strongly recommend avoiding expressions or icons that don't have a global meaning. Also remember that your application will be inspected by Microsoft prior to publishing it to the Store. Store guidelines specify what content can and can't be presented through a Windows

Phone application. You can find the Windows Phone Store guidelines at http://mng.bz/Fefo.

1.2.3 User experience

Understanding the user experience of the Windows Phone is important for building an application that feels like it belongs on the phone. The built-in applications, called *hubs*, establish the look and feel of the device and provide integration and extensibility points for third-party applications.

> **NOTE** All the standard applications and hubs that ship on a real Windows Phone are available in the Windows Phone emulators that are installed with the developer tools.

The hubs are built with two new UI controls named `Panorama` and `Pivot`. You can read more about using the XAML versions of `Panorama` and `Pivot` in chapter 14.

START SCREEN

The *Start Screen* is the home screen for Windows Phone. It's the screen displayed when the phone is started. When the user presses the Windows button, they're brought back to the Start Screen. A user can pin their favorite applications, games, and contacts to the Start Screen so they can launch them quickly.

The images displayed on the Start Screen (shown in figure 1.4) are called *tiles*. Tiles can be dynamic, displaying information relevant to an application. The tile for the Weather Channel application updates with the latest weather conditions. Other tiles are badged when notifications are ready to be viewed. The tiles for Email display a count of new mail messages. Tile images, text, and format are provided by the developer.

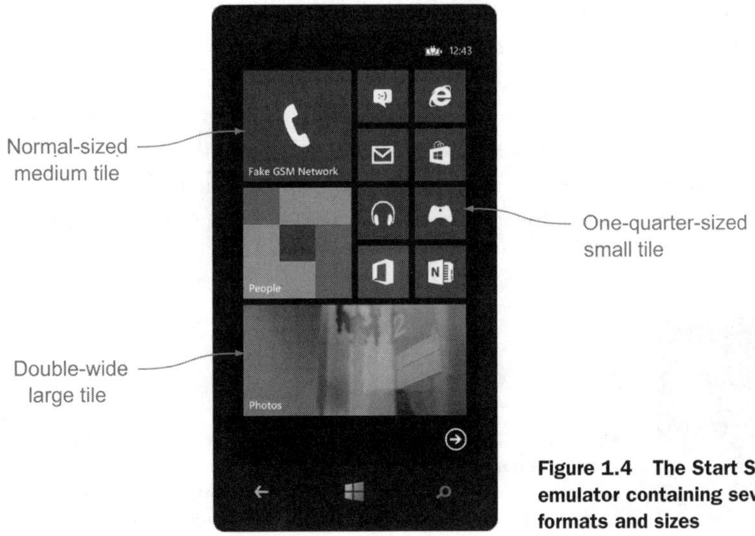

Figure 1.4 The Start Screen from the emulator containing several tiles of various formats and sizes

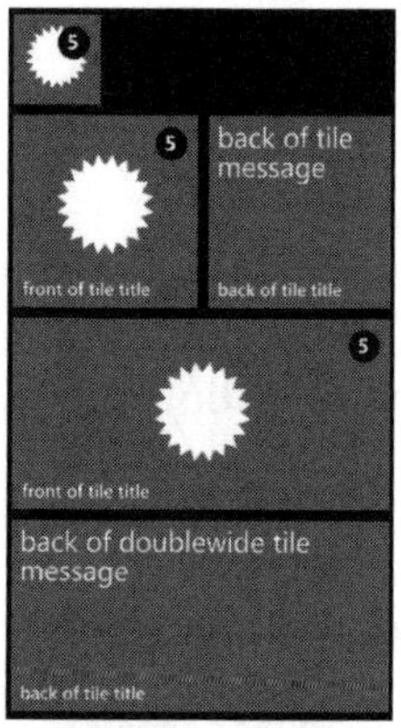

Figure 1.5 The three different sizes of a Flip tile. At the top of the image is the small-sized Flip tile showing only the background image and count badge. The front and back of both the normal-sized and double-wide-sized tiles are also shown—displaying the tile title, background image, count badge, and back-of-tile message.

Applications can pin multiple tiles to the Start Screen, each launching to a different spot within the application. Tiles can be updated from code running on the phone or remotely using the Microsoft Push Notification Service. Tiles are displayed in one of three formats: Flip, Iconic, or Cycle. Each of the tile formats can be one-quarter size, normal size, or double-wide size.

Flip tiles display a title, a count, and a background image on the front of the tile. The count is shown as a small badge in the upper-right corner. The back displays a message, as well as a title and image, but doesn't display the count. The operating system periodically animates the tile by flipping from front to back, then back to front, showing the user both sides of the tile. If the application hasn't assigned any properties for the back of the tile, the tile is never flipped over. The small version of the tile doesn't display a title and doesn't flip. You can see the different-sized Flip tiles in figure 1.5. If a Flip tile doesn't specify a background image, the background of the tile is filled with the accent color from the system-wide theme chosen by the user.

Iconic tiles have only a single side, which displays a title, icon, and count. Small and normal-sized tiles display the icon on the left side, with the count occupying the right side, as shown in figure 1.6. Small versions of the tile don't display the title. The icon and count are shown in the lower-right corner of double-wide tiles. Double-wide iconic tiles also display a message. The message shown on the large tile is specified in three parts, comprising a header and two rows of text. Iconic tiles can specify the background fill color, and if a color isn't specified, the accent color from the system-wide theme is used.

Figure 1.6 Three different sizes of an iconic tile. Both the small and normal-sized tiles display the icon and the count centered in the tile. The double-wide tile moves the icon and count to the corner to make room for three rows of text.

Cycle tiles cycle through a number of different background images. Up to nine different images can be specified. The current image runs in a panning animation that slowly moves the image from the bottom of the tile to the top. The transition between images, shown in figure 1.7, is also animated, quickly scrolling the next image into view. Cycle tiles display both a title and a count, with the count shown as a badge in the upper-right corner of the tile. The small Cycle tile doesn't cycle but rather shows a static image. The small tile also doesn't display a title.

Figure 1.7 A Cycle tile caught in transition from one image to another

Tiles are designed for WXGA resolution and are scaled by the operating system for WVGA and 720p displays. Tile sizes are 159 * 159 for one-quarter-sized tiles, 336 * 336 for normal tiles, and 691 * 336 for double-wide tiles.

APPLICATION LIST

The *Application List* (figure 1.8) is where all native and third-party applications appear. It doesn't matter whether the application is built using XAML or Direct3D, or if it's a native application built by Microsoft, a device vendor, or a mobile carrier. The developer determines the application title and icon that are shown in the Application List.

Unlike Start Screen tiles, Application List images are static and don't animate or display counts. The image is determined at compile time and can't be dynamically updated by the application. Application list icons are 100 * 100 pixels. The system theme accent color will show through any transparent pixels in the application's icon. The user can pin an application to the Start Screen or uninstall it from the context menu shown when the user taps and holds the application's tile or icon.

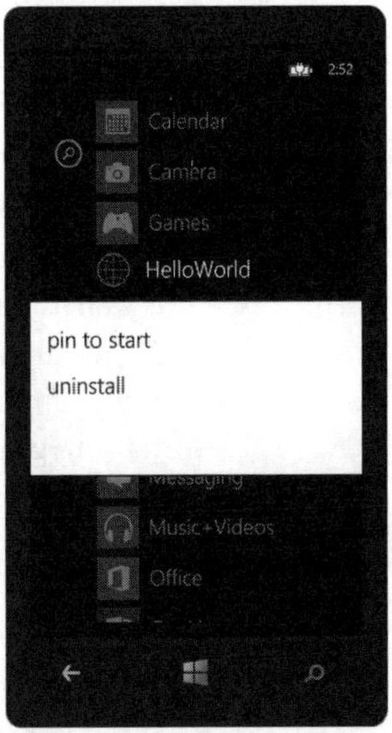

Figure 1.8 The Application List showing the tap-and-hold menu through which the user can uninstall an application or pin it to the Start Screen

GAMES HUB

If your project is declared to be a game, it'll be listed in the *Games Hub* instead of the Application List. The Games Hub is divided into three areas:

- The Collection view lists the games installed on the device.
- The Spotlight view displays news from Xbox Live.
- The Xbox view provides access to the user's Xbox gamer profile and Xbox Friends.

The game developer declares the title and icons displayed in the Collection view in the same manner that Application List images and titles are declared.

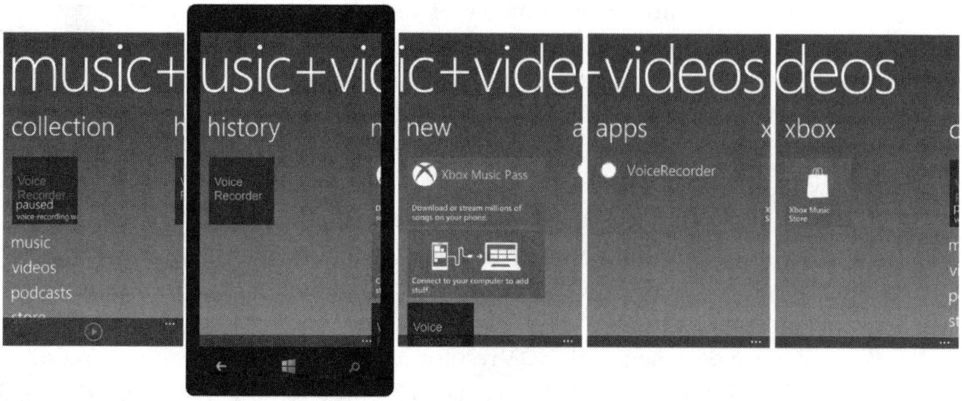

Figure 1.9 The Music + Videos Hub showing the Collection, History, New, Apps, and Xbox views

MUSIC + VIDEOS HUB

The Music + Videos Hub is the central place where you can find all music, video, and podcast activity on the device. The Music + Videos Hub is divided into five areas, as shown in figure 1.9:

- The Collection view is the central point for playing music, videos, and podcasts, as well as a link to the Windows Phone and Xbox Music Stores.
- The History view contains the list of music, videos, playlists, artists, and podcasts that you recently played. This includes media played by third-party applications that integrate with the Hub.
- The New view contains the list of new music, videos, or podcasts that you synced to the phone or downloaded from the Windows Phone or Xbox Music Stores. Third-party applications can add items to the New view.
- The Apps view contains the list of Music + Videos Hub applications that are installed on the device. Third-party media applications are listed here.
- The Xbox view displays artists and other content offered by the Xbox Music Store.

The Music + Videos Hub provides a few integration points to third-party applications. You can read more about the Music + Videos Hub in chapter 9.

PHOTOS HUB

The Photos Hub, shown in figure 1.10, is where you can see all of your photos from different sources. All photos you take with the phone, sync from the computer, download from the internet, or open in email are included in the Photos Hub. The Photos Hub is integrated with Outlook.com and Facebook, and all photos you upload to those websites are displayed in the Photos Hub as well. It also shows the latest photos of your friends on Facebook.

The Photos Hub can be extended by third-party applications that implement photo editing or sharing features. Extending the Photos Hub is described in chapter 9.

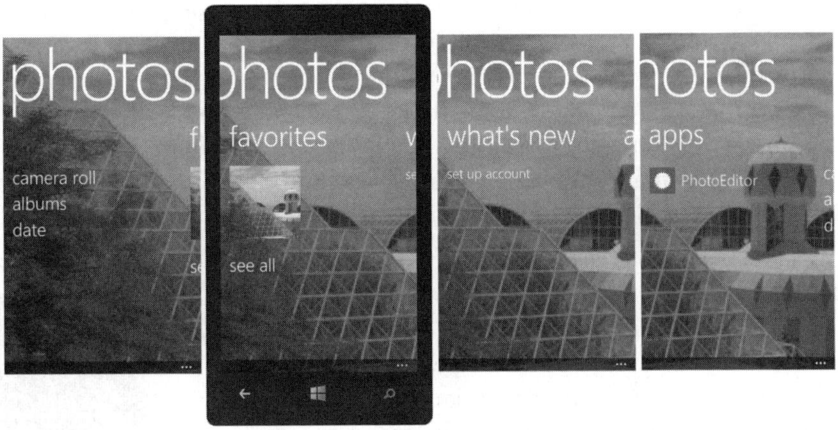

Figure 1.10 The Photos Hub showing the Collections, Favorites, What's New, and Apps views

PEOPLE HUB

The People Hub is the contacts application for Windows Phone. Here's where you find your contacts, along with their phone numbers and addresses. The People Hub also displays the latest status and activity obtained from Outlook.com, Facebook, Twitter, and other social networks. Third-party applications can read data directly from the contacts database and can read and write contacts data with *launchers* and *choosers*, which are introduced in the next section. Third-party applications can also create their own contact stores that are integrated into the People Hub. You'll learn more about working with built-in and custom contact stores in chapter 6.

Understanding Windows Phone's hubs and how they can be extended is key for building applications that enhance user productivity and that are integrated with the operating system. Third-party integrated applications and extensions are built on top of the features exposed in the platform APIs and frameworks.

1.2.4 Platform APIs and frameworks

At its core the Windows Phone 8 operating system is Windows 8—not the full-blown Windows 8 you run on your desktop, but pieces of the Windows 8 kernel and the Windows Runtime designed to run on mobile devices and tablets equipped with ARM processors. Because of this shared lineage, Windows Phone 8 includes a subset of the Windows Runtime, Win32, and .NET APIs found in Windows 8.

In addition to being built on top of the Windows 8 kernel, Windows Phone 8 inherits the features and APIs introduced in Windows Phone 7. This hybridization of Windows 8 and Windows Phone 7 means that in some places two different APIs exist for the same set of features. One example is the Isolated Storage APIs from Windows Phone 7 and the Local Storage APIs from the Windows Runtime. Other examples include the Networking and Sockets API and the APIs for the accelerometer, gyroscope, and other sensors. Throughout the book we try to indicate where we use APIs that have alternate implementations.

Like Windows Store applications on Windows 8, Windows Phone applications run in a sandbox and can't communicate with other processes or read from the file system. These security measures limit the ability to integrate with native applications and databases. To ease these limitations, native applications also expose various integration points. These integration points come in the form of *launchers*, *choosers*, and *extensions*. The platform also provides access to network APIs so that applications can use web services external to the device. Finally, facilities such as location and notification services are available to third-party developers.

LAUNCHERS

Launchers allow your code to activate a native or built-in application. Data can be passed to the launched application. When the native application is launched, your application is deactivated. Launchers are provided to activate the phone dialer, media player, web browser, and other native applications. Launchers are the only way to initiate a phone call or send an SMS message; see figure 1.11. Launchers are covered in depth in chapter 5.

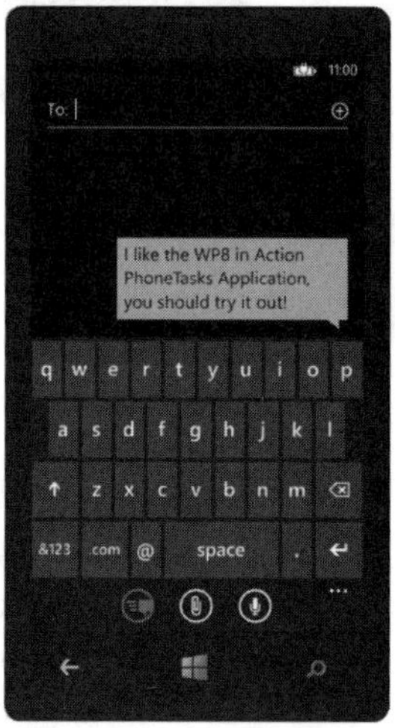

Figure 1.11 The sample application you'll build in chapter 5 uses a launcher to send an SMS text message.

CHOOSERS

Choosers return data to an application. Choosers are provided to retrieve email addresses, phone numbers, physical addresses, and photographs. Choosers also launch a native application, resulting in the deactivation and/or termination of your application. Choosers are also covered in chapter 5.

EXTENSIONS

Extensions allow an application to integrate their features seamlessly into a native application. For example, the Photos Hub allows photo-editing applications to be launched from its Apps list and from the Share and Apps menus, as shown in figure 1.12. The Music + Videos Hub allows applications to appear in its Apps list.

ASSOCIATIONS

Associations allow one application to open another application, even if the second application is built and distributed by another third party. Associations come in two forms: file associations and URI associations. *File associations* are used so that your application is opened when the

Figure 1.12 The Photo Editor application you'll build in chapter 9 extends the Photos Hub.

user opens a file with an extension you've registered with the operating system. The file might have come from an email attachment, been downloaded from the internet, or located on an external SD card. *URI associations* allow your application to launch, or be launched by, another application using a registered URI protocol. You'll learn more about URI associations in chapter 11.

NETWORKING

Windows Phone provides HTTP and sockets network communication. HTTP communication is implemented in the `WebClient`, `HttpWebRequest`, and `HttpWebResponse` classes found in the `System.Net` namespace. TCP and UDP communications are implemented with the `Socket` class in the `System.Net.Sockets` namespace in the .NET API or with the `StreamSocket` and `DataGramSocket` classes in the `Windows.Networking.Sockets` namespace in the Windows Phone Runtime API.

NOTIFICATIONS

The Microsoft Push Notification Service provides an API where a phone user can subscribe to a set of custom events. The notification events are defined by third-party applications and must be sent from a dedicated web service implemented by the application developer. Notifications are displayed to the phone user either on the application's tile in the Start Screen, at the top of the screen as a toast notification (figure 1.13), or within the running application.

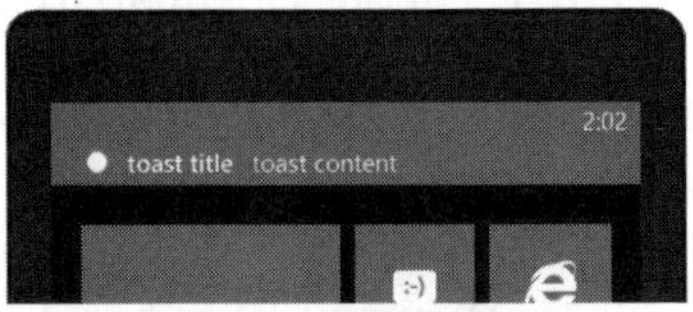

Figure 1.13 A toast notification appears at the top of the screen and displays a title and a message.

A toast notification is made up of a title and short message. The user can dismiss the notification by flicking to the right. The user can tap the toast to launch the application. The application developer can define a custom launch URI as part of the toast. We show how to build a notification application in chapter 11.

LOCATION

The Location service uses data from the wireless and cellular networks and GPS to allow you to create location-aware applications. Calls to the location cloud service are abstracted behind the `Geolocator` class in the `Windows.Devices.Geolocation` namespace found in the Windows Phone Runtime API. In chapter 16 we show how to use `Geolocator` in an application that uses location and maps.

CUSTOM WEB SERVICES

Beyond providing access to business application data or social networks, custom web services can be used to overcome some of the limitations of phones. If you have a suite of applications that share data, you can use a web service to share the data among them.

1.2.5 The Dev Center and the Windows Phone Store

The Dev Center is the portal where Windows Phone developers can find the tools and resources for building and selling applications and games. The Dev Center is where you can download the developer tools. You can also find sample code, tutorials, and documentation. If you need advice on a tricky problem, you can submit a question to the developer forums in the Dev Center. The Dev Center is located at http://developer.windowsphone.com.

Before you can deploy and debug your application on a real phone or publish your application to the Windows Phone Store, you must purchase a $99 yearly subscription to the Dev Center. Depending on what you're building, you may consider waiting to purchase a Dev Center subscription until your application is nearly complete, using the emulator to build and test your application. MSDN subscribers receive a Dev Center subscription as part of their MSDN subscription.

> **TIP** College students receive free Dev Center subscriptions through the *DreamSpark* program. DreamSpark is a Microsoft program providing students with free copies of retail development tools and servers. You can learn more about DreamSpark at http://dreamspark.com.

Once the application has been developed, it must go through an approval process run by Microsoft before it can be published to the Windows Phone Store. This ensures that the application conforms to Microsoft requirements for a Windows Phone application. Microsoft's requirements are detailed in the document App Certification Requirements for Windows Phone available from the Dev Center and MSDN at http://mng.bz/Fefo. More details about the Dev Center and submitting an application to the Windows Phone Store are provided in chapter 18.

1.3 Comparing Windows Phone to other mobile platforms

This book is written primarily for developers who have some experience working with C# and XAML. We focus on the features and APIs that have been introduced specifically for the phone or have been modified to fit the phone's unique characteristics.

If you already use WPF, Silverlight, or XAML to develop applications, you know they've matured rapidly over the last few years. Silverlight's success as a lightweight application framework demonstrates how XAML is ideal to use as the application framework on the mobile device. XAML is rich in features and has been proven with browser and desktop applications. You'll find many familiar features and tools in Windows Phone.

If you've used Direct3D to build games for the Windows Desktop, then Windows Phone is one more platform. Developers can easily build and port games for the new devices. Windows Phone introduces a new game development model by integrating XAML with Direct3D, which is beyond the scope of this book.

If you're not already a XAML developer, don't despair. The appendixes include a quick primer for XAML and an introduction to the Model-View-ViewModel (MVVM) pattern used by many XAML developers. And Manning has published several books on C# and Silverlight, which you can find in their catalogue at http://mng.bz/44nv.

> **NOTE** You can develop games for the Windows Phone 8 operating system with XNA Game Studio, but XNA Game Studio can only build Windows Phone 7.1 projects. The Windows Phone 8 operating system will run both Windows

Phone 7.1 and Windows Phone 8 applications. Windows Phone 7.1–style applications and games aren't covered in this book.

But what if you're coming to Windows Phone from some other background? How does the Windows Phone differ from Windows Store applications on Windows 8, for example? Where do you begin when porting your iOS or Android application? In this section we get you started with Windows Phone development by identifying similarities with and differences from other application platforms.

1.3.1 Windows 8

Although Windows 8 Store applications have a great deal in common with Windows Phone 8 applications, there are also differences in the two platforms. Significant portions of the .NET and Windows Runtime APIs have been implemented for Windows Phone, enabling sharing of concepts and code across both platforms.

One area where the two platforms differ is that of building user interfaces. You can build user interfaces for Windows 8 Store applications using C# with XAML, C++ with XAML, C++ with Direct3D, or JavaScript with HTML. Windows Phone applications are limited to C# with XAML or C++ with Direct3D.

On Windows 8, XAML controls exist in `Windows.UI.Xaml` and related namespaces, which are new to Windows 8. On Windows Phone 8, XAML controls exist in the same `System.Windows` and related namespaces used by WPF and Silverlight. That being said, the names of the classes and controls that exist in Windows 8 XAML also exist in Windows Phone 8 XAML—such as `Grid`, `TextBox`, `UserControl`, and so on. The similarities may allow you to share code. The differences—in the XAML markup, for example—may be problematic.

Problems with sharing XAML aren't quite as severe as you may think. The screen sizes and interaction models available to a Windows 8 Store application are significantly different from those available to a Windows Phone application. If you adhere to the UI design principles established for each platform, you should end up with different user interfaces.

1.3.2 Apple iOS

At first glance, you might think there's little in common between developing applications for an iOS device and the Windows Phone. On the iOS platform you use *Xcode* and Objective-C to write native applications; on the Windows Phone you use *Visual Studio* and C# (or Visual Basic) to write managed applications. It's our opinion that programming languages and frameworks are tools in a developer's tool belt, and good developers make use of several languages and frameworks. If you look beyond the languages and development environments, many of the same fundamental concepts exist on both platforms.

Apple and Microsoft both provide free development tools, complete with device simulators. Each platform has a set of style guides that applications should adhere to, and each also requires a fee-based subscription in order to deploy an application to a device. Each platform has a certification process and application store.

BUILDING YOUR INTERFACE

One thing to keep in mind when porting an iOS application is the differences in the user interface guidelines. You shouldn't build an application with an iOS look and feel for the Windows Phone. An iOS application ported to Windows Phone will have a different look and feel, user-interaction model, and workflow. Don't use chrome and icons from iOS.

Is your application built with controls from *UIKit* or does it use *OpenGL ES*? The XAML framework offers many of the controls and widgets provided by UIKit. On the other hand, OpenGL developers will use Direct3D to build applications. You can also mix application-style widgets from XAML with Direct3D-type graphics.

You'll build your XAML applications using Visual Studio and Blend. Your views will be built using XAML, an XML-based markup language. XAML can be coded by hand in Visual Studio's text editor or with the visual editors in Visual Studio and Blend. The core XAML Framework along with the Windows Phone Toolkit provide most of the controls you'll need when building an application.

If your iOS application uses Core Animation, you'll use the animation and storyboard classes from the `System.Windows.Media.Animation` namespace. Learn to use Blend's storyboard editor if you're doing anything beyond simple animations.

XAML applications are navigation-style applications, driven by the `NavigationService`. The `NavigationService` is similar to the `UINavigationController` provided by the iOS framework and is used to move between different pages or views. The difference is that all XAML applications use the `NavigationService`, even the simplest one-page applications.

INTERACTING WITH NATIVE APPLICATIONS

Like the iOS SDK, Windows Phone provides limited access to the phone dialer, SMS text application, and email. On iOS, the phone dialer is accessed via the `tel` URL; on Windows Phone you use the `PhoneCallTask`. `MFMessageComposeViewController` and `MFMailComposeViewController` are replaced by `SmsComposeTask` and `EmailComposeTask`.

The iOS SDK provides access to the address book with several classes in the Address Book and Address Book UI frameworks. On Windows Phone, read-only access to the address book is exposed via classes in the `Microsoft.Phone.UserData` namespace. Developers can also interact with the contacts database via a few launchers and choosers. You can prompt the user to choose a phone number, email address, or physical address with `PhoneNumberChooserTask`, `EmailAddressChooserTask`, and `AddressChooserTask`. You can prompt the user to save a phone number, email address, or contact with `SavePhoneNumberTask`, `SaveEmailAddressTask`, and `SaveContactTask`. You can read more about launchers and choosers in chapter 5 and access to the contacts database in chapter 6.

USING THE SENSORS

Like the iPhone, the Windows Phone has an accelerometer, compass, and camera. Some Windows Phones also have a gyroscope, compass, and/or proximity sensor. The

Windows Phone APIs provide access to all these sensors. Using the `Camera-CaptureTask`, you can launch the camera UI and manipulate a photo taken by the user. You can take direct control of the camera by using the `PhotoCamera`, `Photo-CaptureDevice`, or `WebCamera` APIs. Working with the camera is covered in chapter 8.

The Windows Phone complement to `UIAccelerometer` is either the `Microsoft.Devices.Accelerometer` class or the `Windows.Devices.Sensors.Accelerometer` class. The `Compass` class is the Windows Phone equivalent to `CLHeading`. Motion-detection features available by the Core Motion framework are provided by the `Gyroscope` and `Motion` classes in the .NET API or the `Gyrometer`, `OrientationSensor`, and `Inclinometer` classes in the Windows Phone Runtime API. We show how to use the accelerometer, compass, and gyroscope, shown in figure 1.14, in chapter 10.

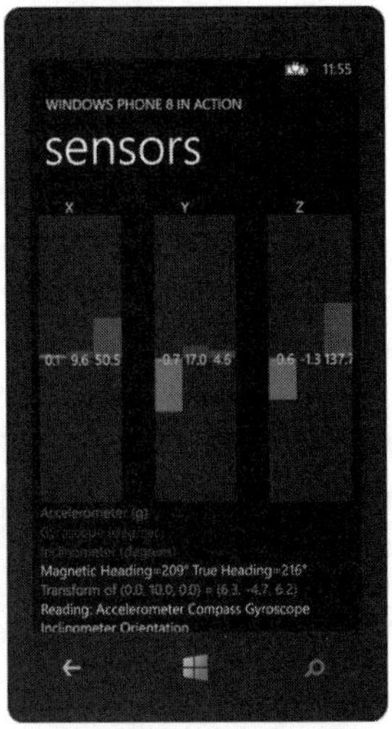

Figure 1.14 In chapter 10 you'll build applications that use the accelerometer, compass, and gyroscope.

STORING DATA

An iOS application can store its data in user defaults, on the file system, or in a database. The iOS SDK makes use of SQLite for local database management.

Windows Phone does provide limited access to the file system. An application can only write files to local storage and has no access to any other part of the file system. Local storage is similar to an iOS application's Documents folder.

Another way to store data is with the `IsolatedStorageSettings` class. This class is similar to the `NSUserDefaults` class in the iOS framework. It's intended to be used to store lightweight data objects and is ideal for storing user preferences. One difference between `NSUserDefaults` and `IsolatedStorageSettings` is that `IsolatedStorage-Settings` isn't global, and settings can't be shared between different applications.

Applications can store data in a Microsoft SQL Server Compact Edition (SQL CE) database using the LINQ to SQL framework. SQL CE is a lightweight database engine designed to run on mobile devices. The database files are written to a special folder in local storage and can't be shared with other applications. Chapter 7 demonstrates how to use each of the data storage options in your applications.

MEDIA

The iPhone uses the iPod software to play audio and video files. The iOS SDK's Media Player framework allows developers to access the library of music and videos and play them inside their applications. The Windows Phone uses Xbox Music for its media library, shown to users in the Music + Videos Hub. Applications can play audio and video files with the `MediaPlayerLauncher` class. Developers can also access the media library using the classes in the `Microsoft.Xna.Framework.Media` namespace. The `MediaPlayer` class can be used to play songs, whereas the videos are played with the `VideoPlayer` class.

XAML applications can use the XNA Media framework, but XAML also has its own media controls in the `System.Windows.Media` namespace. The `MediaElement` control supports audio and video playback. The `MediaStreamSource` class can be used to manipulate audio and video playback or implement custom media containers.

The Windows Phone equivalent to iOS's `AVAudioRecorder` class is the `Microsoft.Xna.Framework.Audio.Microphone` class.

Your application can integrate into the Music + Videos Hub on the phone. Your application can be listed in the hub's Apps list, as shown in figure 1.15, and media played by your application can be shown in the hub's History page.

You can read about working with media, the microphone, and the Music + Videos Hub in chapters 9 and 15.

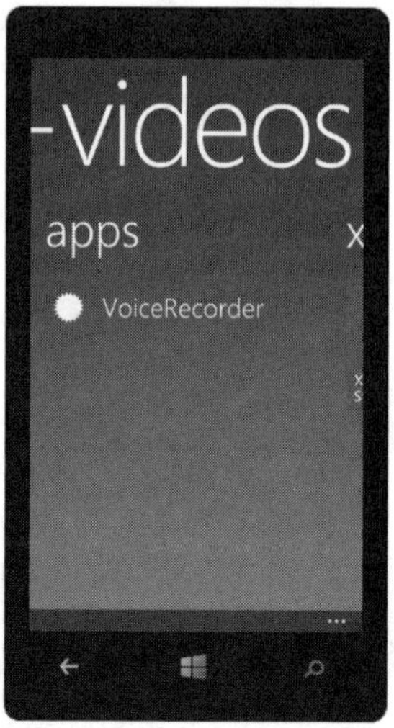

Figure 1.15 In chapter 9 you'll build VoiceRecorder, an application that integrates with the Music + Videos Hub.

NETWORKING

The iOS SDK offers several classes to enable network programming. A developer can choose to program using raw sockets or higher-level protocols such as HTTP and FTP. Windows Phone offers sockets and HTTP support. You perform HTTP communication using the `HttpWebRequest`, `HttpWebResponse`, and `WebClient` classes in the `System.Net` namespace. Sockets programming is performed using classes in the `Windows.Networking.Sockets` namespace.

Microsoft has also built a notification service to allow web services to push notifications to a phone. Developers host their own web service or other application. The application service sends notifications to Microsoft's Push Notification web service, which forwards notifications to a user's phone. Interaction with the notification service is covered in chapter 11.

As you can see, there are many differences between the iOS and the Windows Phone. There are also a number of similarities, and developers should be able to port most applications to the Windows Phone.

1.3.3 Android

Android is another mobile operating system that's capturing the hearts and minds of consumers and developers. Like the iPhone, there are many differences and many similarities between Android and Windows Phone. Like Windows Phone, Android runs on a number of different devices from a number of different manufacturers. Unlike Microsoft, Google hasn't dictated the hardware specifications to the manufacturers, and developers must design and test on several hardware configurations.

Android and Microsoft both provide free development tools complete with device emulators. But Microsoft requires a fee-based subscription in order to deploy an application to a device and certifies each application before making the application available in the application store.

RUNTIME ENVIRONMENT

Windows Phone applications run in the .NET Common Language Runtime (CLR). The CLR is a virtual machine much like the Dalvik virtual machine that runs on Android. Applications are packaged in XAP files, which is a ZIP archive of the assemblies and resources in the application bundle.

Windows Phone places restrictions on the types of applications that can run on the phone. Android allows for background services and UI-less broadcast receivers to run on the phone. Though Windows Phone offers limited support for background operations with background agents, there's no counterpart to broadcast receivers. Windows Phone doesn't have system alarms or triggers that can directly start an idle application. Windows Phone applications can be started when the user responds to alarms, reminders, or notifications.

The Android runtime does limit access to certain features with manifest permissions. Windows Phone uses a similar security model by requiring capabilities to be declared in the application manifest.

BUILDING YOUR INTERFACE

Android activities are loosely related to pages in a XAML application. Each page of an application has a unique address, and the operating system will use a page's URL to navigate to the page when restarting an application. Developers can use a page's URL when creating tiles. Android programmers declare user interfaces with layout XML files. Windows Phone user interfaces are declared using XAML, which are also XML files. If your application makes use of the Android `MapView`, you'll want to read about using the `Maps` control in chapter 16.

INTERACTIONS WITH OTHER APPLICATIONS

Android applications interact with built-in and third-party applications by dispatching *Intents*. Windows Phone applications interact with native applications via launchers, choosers, and URL associations. Windows Phone allows third-party applications to interact with other third-party applications only via URL associations, and developers can't create new launchers or choosers.

Android applications can replace, enhance, or eavesdrop on another application by handling the same Intents. Windows Phone doesn't allow third-party applications to replace any launchers or choosers. You can enhance the Pictures Hub and the Music + Videos Hub by implementing the required extensibility points.

Android applications share data by exposing and using content providers. On Windows Phone, there's no way to expose your data to other applications, and other applications can't use your data. The only exception to this rule is if your application implements a custom contact store.

You can read about the available launchers and choosers in chapter 5 and custom contact stores in chapter 6.

STORING DATA

An Android application can store its data in shared preferences, in the file system, or in a database. Android uses SQLite for local database management.

Windows Phone does provide limited access to the file system. An application can only write files to local storage and has no access to any other part of the file system. You can't read another application's files, and other applications can't read your application's files.

Another way to store data is with the `IsolatedStorageSettings` class. This class is similar to `SharedPreferences` in the Android framework. It's intended to be used to store lightweight data objects and is ideal for storing user preferences. One difference between `SharedPreferences` and `IsolatedStorageSettings` is that `IsolatedStorageSettings` isn't global, and settings can't be shared between different applications.

Window Phone applications can store data in a Microsoft SQL CE database using the LINQ to SQL framework. SQL CE is a lightweight database engine designed to run on mobile devices. The database files are written to a special folder in local storage and can't be shared with other applications. Chapter 7 demonstrates how to use each of the data storage options in your applications.

MEDIA

Android uses the OpenCORE library to play and record audio files and to play video files. OpenCORE's `MediaPlayer` class is used to play audio, whereas the `VideoView` widget is used to play video. Windows Phone applications use the `MediaPlayerLauncher` class to play audio and video files. Developers can also access the media library using the classes in the `Microsoft.Xna.Framework.Media` namespace. The `MediaPlayer` class can be used to play songs, whereas videos are played with the `VideoPlayer` class.

Windows Phone applications can use the XNA Media framework, but XAML also has its own media controls in the `System.Windows.Media` namespace. The `MediaElement` control supports audio and video playback. The `MediaStreamSource` class can be used to manipulate audio and video playback or implement custom media containers.

The Windows Phone equivalent to Android's `MediaRecorder` class is the `Microsoft.Xna.Framework.Audio.Microphone` class. You can read about working with media, the microphone, and the Music + Videos Hub in chapters 9 and 15.

NETWORKING

Android provides a variety of networking options, starting with raw sockets and extending through HTTP. Windows Phone offers sockets and HTTP support. You perform HTTP communication using the `HttpWebRequest`, `HttpWebResponse`, and `WebClient` classes in the `System.Net` namespace. Sockets programming is performed using classes in the `Windows.Networking.Sockets` namespace from the Windows Phone Runtime API.

Android networking applications can use the `ConnectivityManager` class to determine the status of the device's network connection. To check the network status of a Windows Phone, you use the `NetworkInterface` class in the `Microsoft.Net.NetworkInformation` namespace.

In many ways, the Android platform is more like the Windows Mobile platform. Applications have fewer restrictions and can replace core features of the operating system. Manufacturers can change the look and feel of the operating system. Developers must build for a wider range of hardware configurations. A certain set of Android applications can't be ported to Windows Phone because of the limitations enforced by the operating system.

1.4 The Windows Phone Developer Tools

To build great applications, you need great development tools. Microsoft's Visual Studio and Expression Blend fit the description. Visual Studio 2012 Express for Windows Phone joins the list of no-cost Express developer tools provided by Microsoft, and a no-cost version of Expression Blend 4 is available. All these tools have been packaged together and are distributed as the *Windows Phone SDK*, which can be freely downloaded from the Dev Center at http://developer.windowsphone.com.

1.4.1 Visual Studio for Windows Phone

The Windows Phone Developer Tools install an Express Edition of Visual Studio 2012 configured with the phone development tools. If you already have a retail edition of Visual Studio 2012 installed on your computer, the phone development tools will be installed as a plug-in to the IDE. Windows Phone projects can be written in C# and Visual Basic. Direct3D applications, Windows Phone Runtime Components, and native libraries can be written in C++.

We use the Express Edition throughout the book for the screen shots and sample code. Code and user interface design features will work the same in the retail editions of Visual Studio 2012.

You can launch the IDE by opening the Start menu and clicking Microsoft Visual Studio Express 2012 for Windows Phone in the Microsoft Visual Studio Express folder. Figure 1.16 shows the Visual Studio IDE.

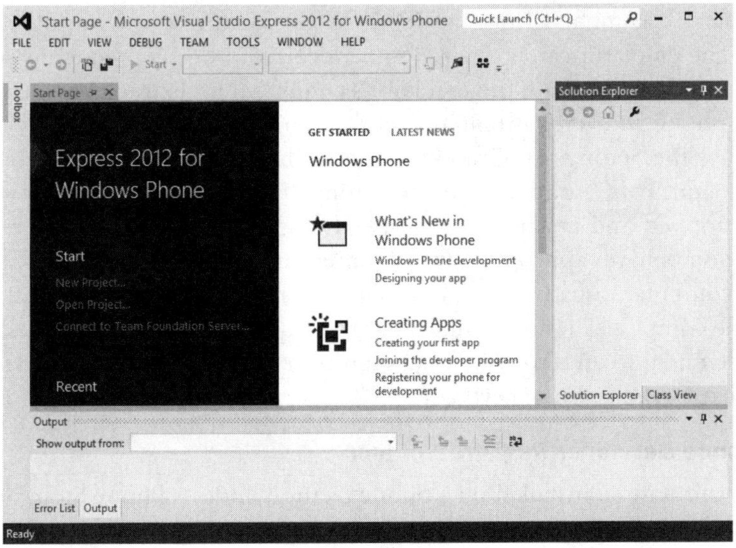

Figure 1.16 Visual Studio Express 2012 for Windows Phone

1.4.2 Blend for Visual Studio

Visual Studio has cool features, but it's not so friendly for the user interface designers on your team. Microsoft has created a tool for designers called *Blend for Visual Studio*. Originally part of the Expression Studio suite, a no-cost edition of Blend has been provided for creating Windows Phone applications. Blend allows the designer to create user interfaces without writing a single line of code.

Blend for Visual Studio can create the same XAML projects as Visual Studio. A designer can edit the same solution, project, and code files that a developer edits in Visual Studio. We occasionally cover Blend features in the book, but our focus is on using Visual Studio.

1.4.3 Windows Phone emulator

The Windows Phone 8 emulator is a Hyper-V virtual machine and has the same system requirements as Hyper-V. Hyper-V runs only on the 64-bit version of the Windows 8 Pro operating system. Hyper-V requires 4 GB or more of RAM. Hyper-V requires a CPU with virtualization extensions and BIOS that supports (and has enabled) hardware-assisted virtualization, Second Level Address Translation, and hardware-based Data Execution Prevention. System requirements are listed in the MSDN documentation at http://mng.bz/yyUx.

Four different Windows Phone 8 emulator configurations are installed with the Windows Phone Tools—one for each of the three possible screen resolutions (WVGA, WXGA, and 720p) and a second WVGA emulator constrained to 512 MB to enable testing low-memory scenarios.

> **NOTE** The Windows Phone Tools also install an emulator for Windows Phone 7.1. The Windows Phone 7.1 emulator isn't a Hyper-V virtual machine and has a different set of requirements.

The emulators are launched from inside Visual Studio when you run or deploy an application. The emulator can be resized to better fit your development environment. You can also use the buttons on the emulator's command toolbar to change the orientation of the phone and verify orientation changes in your application.

You can use the Settings application found in the Application List to change the emulator's default configuration. But the settings revert to their defaults when the emulator is stopped and restarted. You'll need to change the settings to verify that your application behaves appropriately with different configurations and locales.

If your computer uses a true multitouch monitor, the emulator will register touches to the computer monitor. Otherwise, the emulator simulates touches with the mouse. The emulator can also switch between using the SIP and treating your computer's keyboard as a hardware keyboard.

1.4.4 Windows Phone Developer Registration tool

Applications can only be installed on a phone by the Windows Phone Store or a Company Hub. Limited exceptions are made for phones registered to developers who have

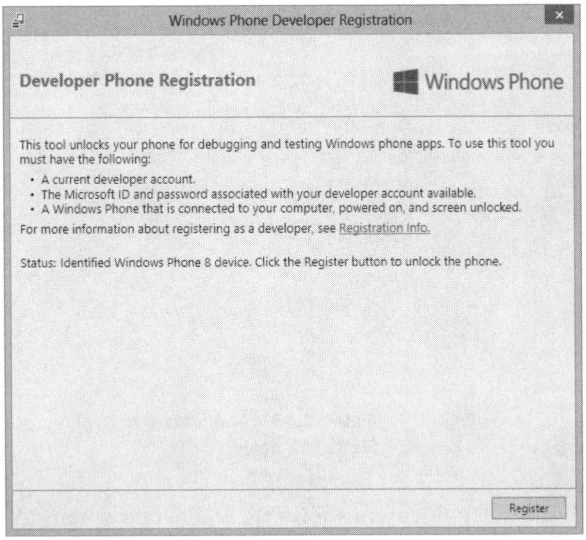

Figure 1.17 Windows Phone Developer Registration tool

subscriptions to the Dev Center. Dev Center subscriptions aren't free. You can purchase one from the developer portal at http://developer.windowsphone.com. Windows Phone applications can't be distributed as standalone packages. To develop your own application, you need to enable your device to allow the deployment of XAP files.

Once your account has been verified by the Dev Center, you can launch the Windows Phone Developer Registration tool from the Windows Phone Developer Tools folder in your Start menu. This tool, shown in figure 1.17, will prompt you to enter your Dev Center credentials and select a connected phone. You need to plug the device into your PC and have your PC connected to the internet in order to connect to Microsoft's registration servers.

A maximum of three phones can be registered to a single account, and a maximum of 10 developer applications can be installed on a phone at the same time. If you reach the installed application limit, you must uninstall one or more developer applications before you can deploy a new application from Visual Studio. Occasionally your phone registration will expire, and you'll receive an error when attempting to deploy an application to a device. You'll then need to reregister the phone with the registration tool.

You can also use the Windows Phone Developer Registration tool to unregister a phone. If you need to unregister a phone, but don't have it available because it's been lost or broken, you can unregister the device from your Dev Center account's Profile page, accessed through your browser at https://dev.windowsphone.com/en-us/Account/Devices.

1.4.5 XAP Deployment tool

To support testing applications by nondeveloper team members, you can deploy the executable binary of a Windows Phone application (the XAP file) to the emulator or to

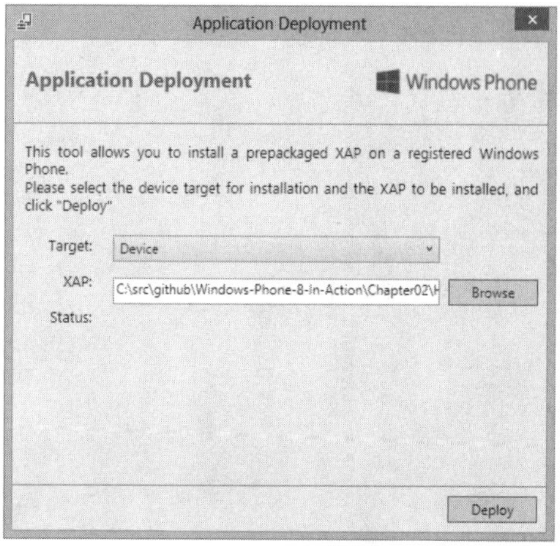

Figure 1.18 Application to deploy a binary (XAP) file to the device

a registered phone using the XAP Deployment tool. The XAP Deployment tool, shown in figure 1.18, is launched from the Start menu > Windows Phone Developer Tools folder. Select the target device and the XAP file, and then click Deploy.

When the deployment is complete, you can start the application from the Application List. You can uninstall an application from the Application List as well. Tap and hold the application's icon until the context menu appears, and select the uninstall option.

1.4.6 *Isolated Storage Explorer tool*

Most applications require some form of data storage—from user preferences and user-created data to local caches of data stored in a cloud application or web service. Each application is allotted its own storage sandbox on the phone, isolated from all other applications and from the operating system. Isolated storage is empty when an application is first deployed to the emulator or a device. During execution, many applications store data and settings in isolated storage.

While testing and debugging an application, developers may want to examine the files written to local storage or maybe even write data files to local storage to facilitate testing. The Isolated Storage Explorer tool (ISETool) is included in the Windows Phone 8 SDK to enable these scenarios. The ISETool allows a developer to take a snapshot of an application's local storage, copying the files from the phone to a desktop folder. You can also use the ISETool to copy files from the desktop to an application's local storage folder. The ISETool lists the files in a local storage folder, as shown in figure 1.19.

The ISETool requires the application's product `Guid`. The product `Guid` is generated by the Visual Studio project templates and is declared in a project's application manifest file, called WMAppManifest.xml. You'll learn more about the application manifest in chapter 2. We show how to use ISETool to populate a read-only database in chapter 7.

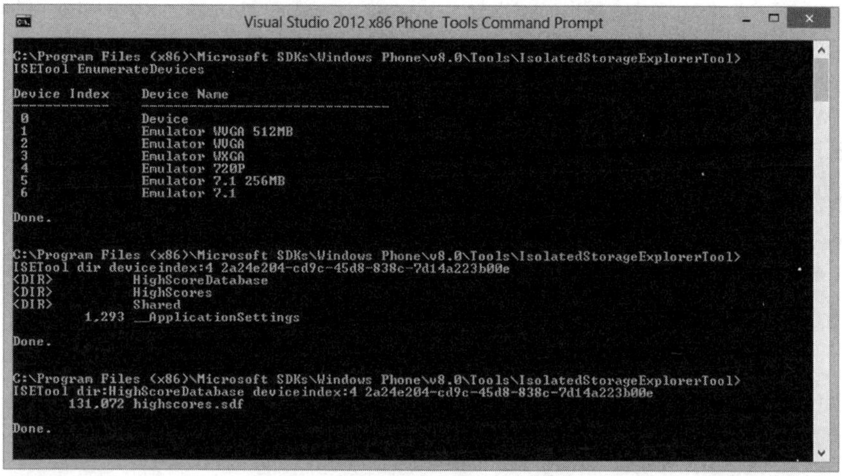

Figure 1.19 Using the Isolated Storage Explorer Tool to list the files in isolated storage in the emulator

1.4.7 The Simulation Dashboard

Inside Visual Studio, in the Tools menu, you'll find a tool called the Simulation Dashboard that comes in handy when working with the emulator. The Simulation Dashboard, shown in figure 1.20, provides tools to alter network connectivity, lock the screen, and display a reminder.

You'll use the Simulation Dashboard in chapter 3 when you learn how to detect when the screen is obscured and how to write applications that continue to run when the screen is locked. You'll also use the Simulation Dashboard in chapter 11.

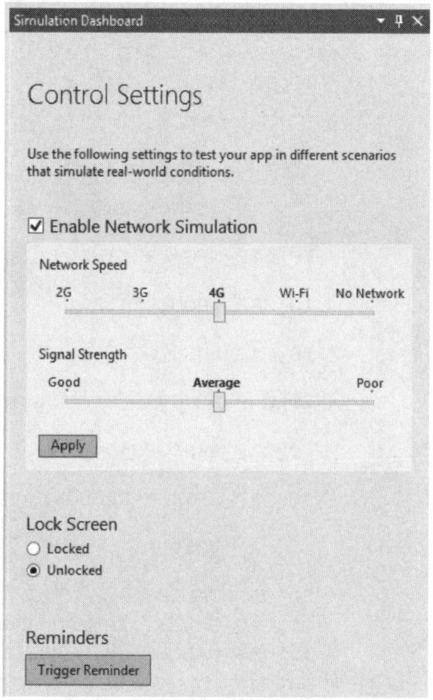

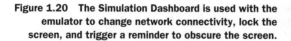

Figure 1.20 The Simulation Dashboard is used with the emulator to change network connectivity, lock the screen, and trigger a reminder to obscure the screen.

1.5 Declaring capabilities and requirements

Windows Phone is all about security sandboxes and user disclosure. Security capabilities are one facet of the operating system's security model, and a Windows Phone application must declare which capabilities or features of the operating system it uses. Hardware requirements are another form of disclosure, and applications must declare the need for optionally installed hardware so that the Windows Store doesn't sell software that won't run on a customer's device. The capabilities used by and the hardware required by an application are declared in the application's manifest file.

When an application is submitted to the store, the certification process inspects the compiled code and updates the manifest with the discovered capabilities. Table 1.1 details the set of capabilities that can be listed in the manifest.

Table 1.1 Security capabilities

Capability ID	Description
ID_CAP_APPOINTMENTS	Access appointment data from the calendar
ID_CAP_CONTACTS	Access contact data from the address book
ID_CAP_IDENTITY_USER	Access user information
ID_CAP_ISV_CAMERA	Access the Camera API and the raw image stream
ID_CAP_LOCATION	Use location services
ID_CAP_MAP	Use mapping features
ID_CAP_MEDIALIB_AUDIO* ID_CAP_MEDIALIB_VIDEO ID_CAP_MEDIALIB_PHOTO ID_CAP_MEDIALIB_PLAYBACK*	Access the media library
ID_CAP_MICROPHONE	Record with the microphone
ID_CAP_NETWORKING*	Use network services
ID_CAP_NFC_PROXIMITY	Use near field communication (NFC) services
ID_CAP_PHONEDIALER	Initiate phone calls
ID_CAP_PUSH_NOTIFICATION	Receive push notifications
ID_CAP_REMOVABLE_STORAGE	Read from the SD card
ID_CAP_SENSORS*	Use the accelerometer
ID_CAP_SPEECH_RECOGNITION	Use speech recognition and text-to-speech services
ID_CAP_VOIP	Use voice over IP (VoIP) services
ID_CAP_WALLET ID_CAP_WALLET_PAYMENT_INSTRUCTIONS ID_CAP_WALLET_SECURE_ELEMENT	Use the wallet

* These capabilities are included by default in new projects.

The manifest file created by the Visual Studio project templates automatically declares only a few capabilities. The developer can remove any capabilities that aren't required for the application and should add any missing capabilities. During marketplace certification, the list provided by the developer is deleted and replaced by a list of capabilities detected by the certification tools. The assembly is examined for calls to the secured APIs, and when one is found, the matching capability is reinstated to the manifest. If a required capability isn't listed in the manifest, the secured API will throw an `UnauthorizedAccessException`. When an application is downloaded from the store, the list of capabilities used by an application is displayed to the user, allowing the user to make an informed decision before purchasing the application.

Because security capabilities tell the operating system that your application needs access to certain APIs to operate correctly, hardware requirements are used to tell the operating system that your application won't run unless the specified hardware is installed on a device. Hardware requirements are listed in the application manifest using the identifiers listed in table 1.2.

Table 1.2 Hardware requirements

Requirement ID	Description
`ID_REQ_FRONTCAMERA`	Requires a front-facing camera to run
`ID_REQ_GYROSCOPE`	Requires a gyroscope to run
`ID_REQ_MAGNETOMETER`	Requires a compass to run
`ID_REQ_NFC`	Requires a proximity sensor to run
`ID_REQ_REARCAMERA`	Requires a rear-facing camera to run

You need to specify hardware requirements only if your application won't function without the hardware. If the hardware is optional—your application will function, but in a reduced capacity—don't list the requirement in the application manifest. For example, if you list `ID_REQ_NFC` in your application manifest, users will be unable to purchase your application if their device doesn't have a proximity sensor or NFC chip installed. If using NFC is only a small part of your application, and it works perfectly well without NFC, then you'll miss out on potential sales if you include `ID_REQ_NFC` in your application's manifest.

1.6 Summary

This chapter has introduced the Windows Phone platform. Windows Phone 8 is both an upgrade of the Windows Phone 7 operating system and a slimmed-down version of the Windows 8 kernel. Developers moving to Windows Phone from desktop applications must learn to work with the Windows Phone Developer Tools. Windows Phone 8 is locked down pretty tight, and many types of applications can't be ported to it.

You'll see in the next chapter how easy it is to create Windows Phone applications. We hope the ease of development mitigates the lack of advanced functionality that many developers have come to expect from Windows-based platforms.

If you haven't already done so, go ahead and download and install the Windows Phone 8 SDK from http://developer.windowsphone.com and move on to the next chapter. It's time to code!

2 Creating your first Windows Phone application

This chapter covers

- Creating your first application
- Handling touch events
- Navigating between pages
- Pinning secondary tiles

Now that you have the necessary background on the Windows Phone platform and the Windows Phone Developer Tools, it's time to get down to business and start programming. You'll start by building a Hello World project. For developers experienced with Visual Studio, simple Hello World projects may seem unduly remedial. But Windows Phone projects have several unique settings and features that you need to understand to build applications and games. The Hello World project in this chapter is designed to highlight these aspects of Windows Phone development.

In addition to the controls shipped as part of the Windows Phone SDK, we'll look at a few of the controls that are available in the Windows Phone Toolkit. The Windows Phone Toolkit is an open source project hosted on CodePlex. Microsoft uses the Windows Phone Toolkit project to share new controls and components with the development community.

You'll build a Hello World application and explore a few of the phone-specific extensions to XAML. XAML applications have several project properties unique to Windows Phone. Two of these properties define the icons used in the phone's Start Screen and Applications List. Other properties determine the titles shown next to the Start and Application List icons. You'll learn how to use the Visual Studio project templates to generate a new application and how to use the item templates to generate a new page for your application. You'll also learn how to deploy the application to the emulator or a physical device and use the debugger to step through code.

TIP If you're new to XAML development, read the primer on XAML in appendix A.

In most ways, building a XAML application for the phone is the same as building a Silverlight application for the browser, a WPF application for the desktop, or a XAML application for the Windows 8 Runtime, but there are some minor differences. You'll see some of the differences as you build your application. The Hello World application that you'll create is shown in figure 2.1.

The application displays a title, draws a globe, and prompts the user to enter a name. When the user taps the text box's action icon, the application navigates to a greeting page. You'll start building your application by creating a new Silverlight project.

Figure 2.1 The *Windows Phone 8 in Action* Hello World application. The screen on the left is shown when the application starts, and the screen on the right is shown when the user taps the text box's action icon.

2.1 Generating the project

To start the Hello World application, you use the Windows Phone App project template in Visual Studio. The Windows Phone App project template is one of several project templates installed with Visual Studio. Table 2.1 lists the available project templates.

Open Visual Studio and create a new project by choosing File > New Project. Figure 2.2 shows the New Project dialog for the Hello World application. Select the *Windows Phone App* project template and name the project *HelloWorld.*

Table 2.1 Windows Phone project templates*

Project template	Description
Windows Phone App	A basic application skeleton with a single page.
Windows Phone Databound App	An application demonstrating page navigation, databound list controls, and the MVVM pattern.
Windows Phone Class Library	A simple library for creating reusable components.
Windows Phone Panorama App	An application demonstrating a databound `Panorama` control and the MVVM pattern. The `Panorama` control is covered in chapter 14.
Windows Phone Pivot App	An application demonstrating a databound `Pivot` control and the MVVM pattern. The `Pivot` control is covered in chapter 14.
Windows Phone XAML and Direct3D App	An application that mixes managed XAML with native Direct3D graphics. The Direct3D portion of the application is written in C++.
Windows Phone HTML5 App	An application that uses the `WebBrowser` control to display a user interface written in HTML and JavaScript. HTML5 Apps are covered in chapter 17.
Windows Phone Audio Playback Agent	A library containing an application's background audio logic. Audio Playback Agents are covered in chapter 9.
Windows Phone Audio Streaming Agent	A library containing an application's background streaming audio logic.
Windows Phone Scheduled Task Agent	A library containing an application's background processing logic. Scheduled Tasks Agents are covered in chapter 4.

* Each of the project templates listed here is available for both C# and Visual Basic projects.

After you click OK, you're prompted with a dialog asking you to pick the target operating system version. This dialog can be confusing because it lists the Windows Phone SDK versions and not the operating system versions. If you're building an application that targets older devices running the Windows Phone 7.5 operating system, choose Windows Phone OS 7.1 from the drop-down. After you click OK, a new Visual Studio solution and project are created. The IDE opens MainPage.xaml in the editor, and you're ready to begin.

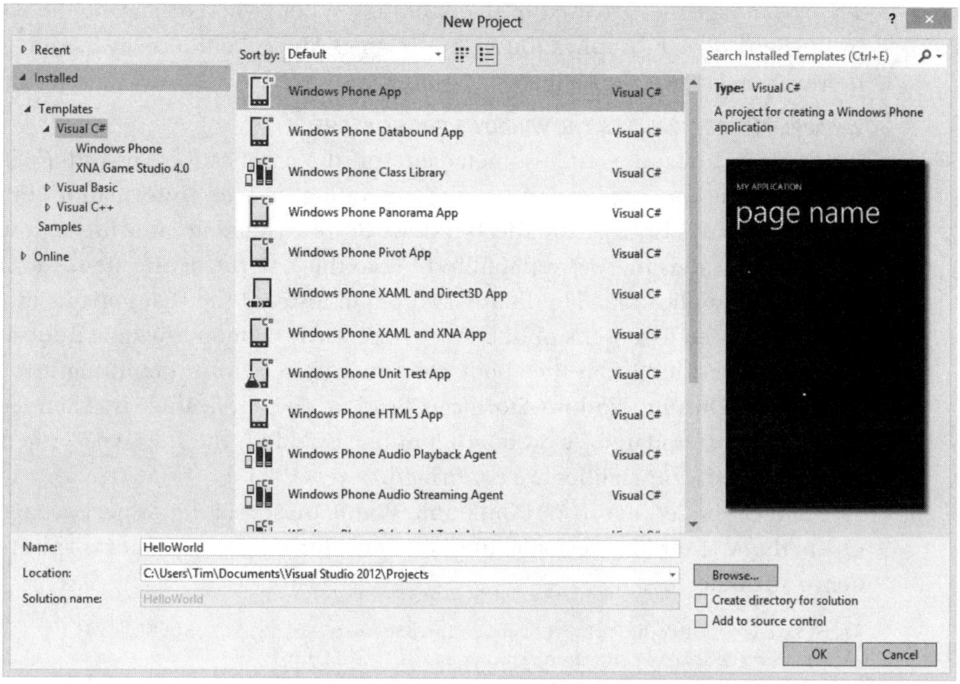

Figure 2.2 Visual Studio's New Project dialog box shows the available C# Windows Phone project templates.

Before you start work, let's take a look at what Visual Studio created. Figure 2.3 shows the new project in the Solution Explorer.

The project structure mirrors that of a regular .NET Framework project with Properties and References folders, App.xaml, MainPage.xaml, AppManifest.xml, and AssemblyInfo.cs. Along with the references to the .NET and Windows Phone assemblies, a few additional files are present:

- WMAppManifest.xml
- ApplicationIcon.png
- FlipCycleTile*.png
- IconicTile*.png
- LocalizedStrings.cs
- AppResources.resx

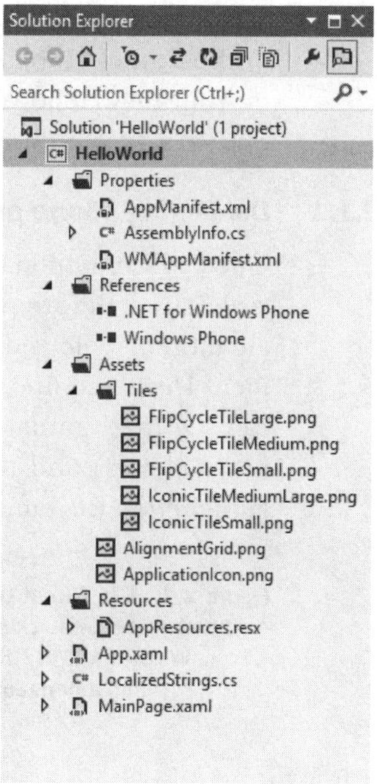

Figure 2.3 Project files and folders in the Solution Explorer

The PNG image files are used by the operating system when displaying the application in the Start Screen, Application List, or Games Hub. We'll look at the image files in more depth later in the chapter.

WMAPPMANIFEST.XML AND THE WINDOWS PHONE STORE

WMAppMainfest.xml contains metadata for the application, providing important details about the application to the operating system. Information in WMAppManifest.xml is also used by the Windows Store to validate and list an application. Visual Studio adds the WMAppManifest file to the XAP file deployment package when it builds an application. The final WMAppManifest.xml file that appears in the package downloaded to a user's phone won't necessarily contain the same information the developer specified when they built the application before submitting it to the Windows Store. During Windows Store certification, the application is examined, and its manifest file is updated. A product identifier is added, the hub type or genre is set, and the security capabilities are confirmed.

Many of the settings in WMAppManifest.xml are set via the project property pages. Open the WMAppManifest.xml file and look for the `App` element, specifically the `Genre` attribute:

```
<App xmlns="" ProductID="{10408c51-ec5c-43b6-b196-3f11505591cd}"
    Title="HelloWorld" RuntimeType="Silverlight"
    Version="1.0.0.0" Genre="apps.normal"
    Author="HelloWorld author" Description="Sample Description"
    Publisher="HelloWorld"
    PublisherID="{022cce02-8389-4f02-b74b-48f6b7544d37}">
```

Genre can be Apps.Normal or Apps.Games

The `Genre` attribute declares whether the application appears in the Application List or the Games Hub.

Your new Hello World project is ready to be built and deployed to the emulator or a phone. Visual Studio's Debugger is used to debug running Windows Phone applications.

2.1.1 Debugging phone projects

Once you've built a project, you'll be able to debug it both in the emulator and on a real device. Before starting a debug session, you'll want to confirm that the appropriate target is selected in the Target Deployment Device combo box. In figure 2.4, you can see that Emulator WVGA 512MB is the target device, and the application will be launched in the emulator.

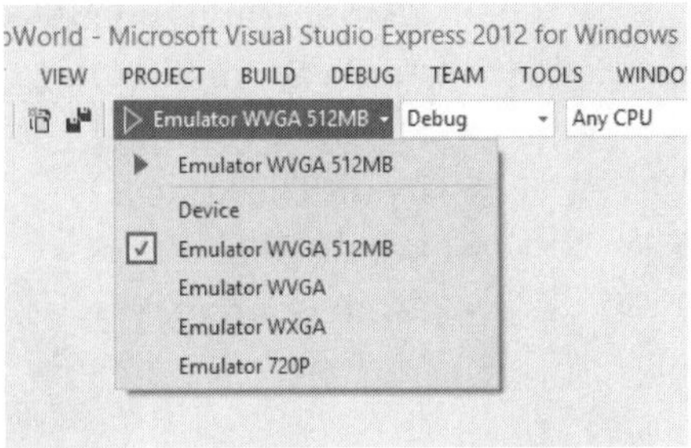

Figure 2.4 The Target Deployment Device selector showing the default deployment target (Emulator WVGA 512MB), the list of all the emulators, and a connected Windows Phone device

The first time you launch an application in the emulator, it takes some time to boot and initialize the emulator prior to starting the application. Once the application has been launched, you'll be able to debug and interact with it in the emulator. You can keep the Windows Phone emulator running between debugging sessions.

> **TIP** An application can detect whether it's running in the emulator by checking the value of the `Microsoft.Devices.Environment.DeviceType` static property. If the value is `DeviceType.Emulator`, the application is running in the emulator.

Prior to launching an application on a real device, the phone must be plugged in to the USB port and connected to your computer. And before you can deploy and debug an application on a real phone, you must register your phone with the Developer Registration tool. The Developer Registration tool is introduced in chapter 1.

SOURCE CODE BREAKPOINTS AND DEBUGGING

When the application is being debugged, it automatically stops on the breakpoints you've set in the source code. You can add or remove breakpoints during the execution as you would in any other desktop or Silverlight project. The debugger remains attached to the emulator even when your application isn't running. This feature lets you debug scenarios such as launching from a secondary tile, which you'll learn how to do later in the chapter. When you're finished, you can stop debugging in the IDE.

Visual Studio allows you to install or deploy the project on the device without starting a debugging session. Right-click the project name in the Solution Explorer and select Deploy from the menu. The application will be copied to the target device or emulator and can be launched from the Applications List on the phone. When the application is launched, Windows Phone adds a few custom steps to the startup process that aren't found in Silverlight or WPF applications.

2.1.2 Application startup

Like any other Silverlight or WPF application, the entry point is a `System.Windows.Application`-derived class found in App.xaml. All phone applications are XAML navigation applications. In your phone application, the `App` class creates an instance of `PhoneApplicationFrame`, which is used as the `RootVisual`. Behind the scenes, the application host calls the `NavigationService` directly to navigate to MainPage.xaml during initial launch. When an application is reactivated, the application host navigates to the active page's XAML—see chapter 3 for more details on application launching and activation.

RENAMING MAINPAGE.XAML

All this magic navigation is well and good; the application starts, and `MainPage` is automatically loaded. What happens when you decide to rename MainPage.xaml? Because the XAML filename doesn't have to match the name of the C# class that it contains, changing the name of `MainPage` is a two-step process. Fortunately, Visual Studio's refactoring features make this a simple operation. In the Solution Explorer, right-click

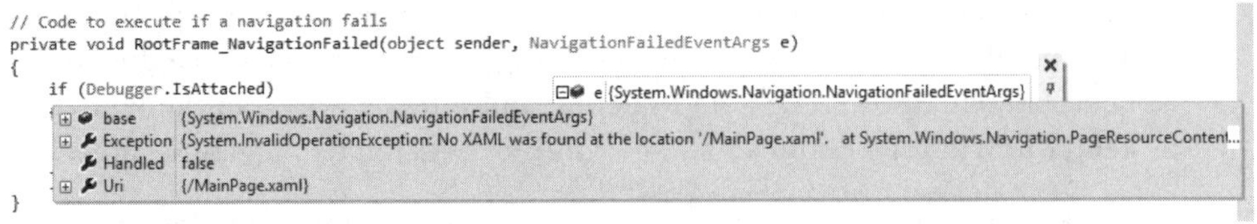

// Code to execute if a navigation fails
private void RootFrame_NavigationFailed(object sender, NavigationFailedEventArgs e)
{
if (Debugger.IsAttached)
e {System.Windows.Navigation.NavigationFailedEventArgs}
base {System.Windows.Navigation.NavigationFailedEventArgs}
Exception {System.InvalidOperationException: No XAML was found at the location '/MainPage.xaml'. at System.Windows.Navigation.PageResourceContent...
Handled false
Uri {/MainPage.xaml}
}

Figure 2.5 **`NavigationFailedEventArgs` properties after renaming MainPage.xaml**

MainPage.xaml, choose Rename, and change the filename to HelloPage.xaml. Renaming MainPage.xaml will also cause MainPage.xaml.cs to be renamed to HelloPage .xaml.cs. Open HelloPage.xaml.cs, select the `MainPage` text in the class definition, and choose Rename from the Refactor menu, specifying `HelloPage` as the new name.

When you debug the application now, the `App.RootFrame_NavigationFailed` event handler is called. Figure 2.5 shows the `NavigationFailedEventArgs` properties sent to the event handler.

Even though you renamed MainPage.xaml, the application is still configured to use MainPage.xaml as the startup URI. The startup URI is declared in the WMAppManifest.xml file as the `NavigationPage` attribute of the `Task` named `_default`. As with a number of other WMAppManifest.xml settings, you can set the Navigation page using the project property editor or by editing the default task URI in the XML file. Open WMAppManifest.xml, update the URI attribute, and then save and run the application:

```
<Tasks>
  <DefaultTask  Name="_default"
    NavigationPage="HelloPage.xaml"/>
</Tasks>
```

In this section you created a new Windows Phone application project and examined the files created by the project template. You learned that a `PhoneApplicationFrame` is the root visual for the application and that the operating system uses the navigation framework to load the Startup page. Now that the application is running and you've customized the name of the Startup page, you'll customize the page contents.

2.2 Implementing Hello World

The project template created a default main page for your application, which you renamed to HelloPage.xaml. In this section you'll add a second page to the application that will display a greeting message. The second page will employ a pair of `TextBlock` controls as well as a `RichTextBox`. You're also going to customize `HelloPage` by drawing a globe and asking the user to input their name.

First, we'll take a closer look at the page created for you by the project template.

2.2.1 Customizing the Startup page

The Windows Phone App project template created the Startup page with several elements meant to match the page design to the Microsoft design language described in

Microsoft's *Design Library for Windows Phone.* The design library, found in the Windows Phone Dev Center at http://dev.windowsphone.com/en-us/design/library, details the expected look and feel of phone applications. The following listing shows the XAML markup added by the project template for `HelloPage`'s content.

Listing 2.1 `HelloPage`'s content as created by the project template

```
<Grid x:Name="LayoutRoot"
      Background="Transparent">
    <Grid.RowDefinitions>
        <RowDefinition Height="Auto" />
        <RowDefinition Height="*" />
    </Grid.RowDefinitions>
    <!--TitlePanel contains the name of the application and page title-->
    <StackPanel x:Name="TitlePanel"
                Grid.Row="0"
                Margin="12,17,0,28">
        <TextBlock x:Name="ApplicationTitle"
                   Text="MY APPLICATION"
                   Style="{StaticResource PhoneTextNormalStyle}" />
        <TextBlock x:Name="PageTitle"
                   Text="page name"
                   Margin="9,-7,0,0"
                   Style="{StaticResource PhoneTextTitle1Style}" />
    </StackPanel>
    <!--ContentPanel - place additional content here-->
    <Grid x:Name="ContentPanel"
          Grid.Row="1"
          Margin=”12,0,12,0”>
    </Grid>
</Grid>
```

❶ **LayoutRoot Grid control with two rows**

❷ **TitlePanel with two TextBlocks**

❸ **ContentPanel for all other markup**

The page's root layout panel is a `Grid` control that has been split into two rows ❶. The first row contains `TitlePanel` ❷, which stacks two `TextBlock` controls for the application and page titles. The remainder of the page is allocated to the `ContentPanel` ❸. Figure 2.6 shows HelloPage.xaml as created by the project template.

Figure 2.6 HelloPage.xaml's `TitlePanel` in the Visual Studio Designer

BEST PRACTICES FOR APPLICATION AND PAGE TITLES

Application and page titles aren't required by the design guidelines or store certification, but you should follow several rules when using them. The application title should be the name of the application and should be in all uppercase characters. The page title should be in all lowercase characters and should describe the data or features displayed on the page. The titles shouldn't scroll or wrap; when the title doesn't fit on the screen, the text should appear truncated. If the title panel appears on the main page, it should appear on all pages to provide the user with a consistent experience.

In HelloPage.xaml, update the application title to *WINDOWS PHONE 8 IN ACTION* and the page title to *hello world*:

```
<TextBlock x:Name="ApplicationTitle"
                  Text="WINDOWS PHONE 8 IN ACTION"
                  Style="{StaticResource PhoneTextNormalStyle/>
<TextBlock x:Name="PageTitle"
                  Text="hello world"
                  Margin="9,-7,0,0"
                  Style="{StaticResource PhoneTextTitle1Style}" />
```

The title `TextBlock` controls have their `Style` properties set to a static resource. The style resources used here aren't found anywhere in your project—they're styles injected into your application by the XAML framework so that your application can adhere to the user interface theme chosen by the user. Theme resources are also used in the root `PhoneApplicationPage` element to set the font and foreground color properties for the page:

```
FontFamily="{StaticResource PhoneFontFamilyNormal}"
FontSize="{StaticResource PhoneFontSizeNormal}"
Foreground="{StaticResource PhoneForegroundBrush}"
```

ORIENTATION PROPERTIES

`PhoneApplicationPage` also has a couple of orientation properties: `Orientation` and `SupportedOrientations`. The `Orientation` property specifies whether the current orientation is portrait or landscape. The `SupportedOrientations` property declares which orientations are supported by the page. The visual designer supports both portrait and landscape and allows you to quickly switch between the two layouts, as shown in figure 2.7.

Windows Phone presents a status bar at the top edge of the screen in portrait layout. In landscape layout, the status bar is anchored to the edge opposite the Start button as it moves to the left or right, depending on the direction in which the user rotates the phone. The status bar displays the signal strength, battery, current time, and other indicators. Screen designs should account for the space occupied by the status bar, which varies depending on the screen resolution of the device. Applications can hide the status bar with the `SystemTray.IsVisible` attached property. The project template sets this attached property to `True`. You can provide more room for your application's content and hide the status bar by setting the property's value to `False`.

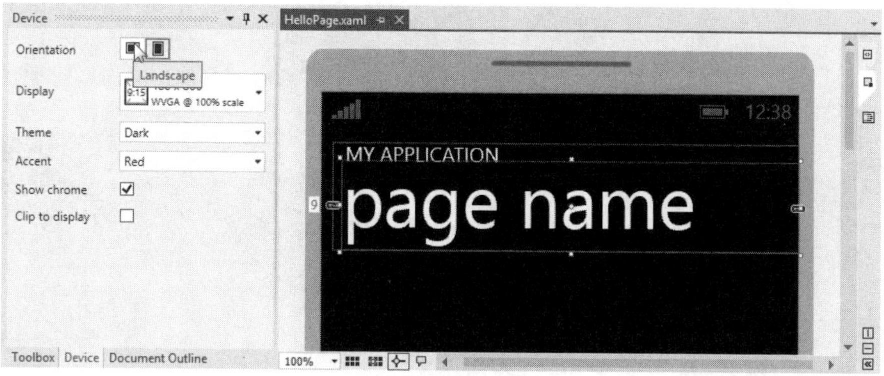

Figure 2.7 Use the device panel to switch between portrait and landscape layouts. The device panel also provides controls for changing the theme, accent color, and device resolution.

> **NOTE** Before you choose to hide the status bar in your application, you should know that many users consider the status bar an essential element and dislike applications that hide it.

You're making good progress. You've gotten your hands dirty with XAML and started customizing your application. Along the way, you've learned how to ensure your application fits into the system look and feel. Your next step is to add a globe and text box to the application content panel.

2.2.2 *Adding application content*

Remember that you want the first page of the application to display a globe and prompt the user to enter a name. These visual elements will be added to the `ContentPanel` `Grid` control that was created by the project template, as shown in the next listing. You'll start by dividing the `ContentPanel` into two rows, with one row using two-thirds of the panel, and the second using the remaining third.

Listing 2.2 Drawing the globe

```
<Grid x:Name="ContentPanel" Grid.Row="1" Margin="12,0,12,0">
    <Grid.Resources>
        <SolidColorBrush x:Key="GlobeBrush"
             Color="{StaticResource PhoneAccentColor}" />
    </Grid.Resources>
    <Grid.RowDefinitions>
        <RowDefinition Height="2*" />
        <RowDefinition Height="1*" />
    </Grid.RowDefinitions>
    <Canvas Width="200" Height="200" VerticalAlignment="Center"
        Background="{StaticResource PhoneBackgroundBrush}" >
        <Ellipse Width="200" Height="200"
            Stroke="{StaticResource GlobeBrush }"
            StrokeThickness="10" />
```

❶ GlobeBrush is static resource

❷ Binding to theme brush

```
        <Ellipse Width="100" Height="200"
            Canvas.Left="50"
            Stroke="{StaticResource GlobeBrush }"
            StrokeThickness="5" />
        <Path Data="M 100,0 100,200"
            Stroke="{StaticResource GlobeBrush }"              ❸ Binding to GlobeBrush
            StrokeThickness="5" />
        <Path Data="M 0,100 200,100"
            Stroke="{StaticResource GlobeBrush }"
            StrokeThickness="5" />
        <Path Data="M 30,40 A 100,50 0 0 0 170,40"
            Stroke="{StaticResource GlobeBrush }"
            StrokeThickness="5" />
        <Path Data="M 30,160 A 100,50 0 0 1 170,160"
            Stroke="{StaticResource GlobeBrush }"
            StrokeThickness="5" />
    </Canvas>
</Grid>
```

The globe is drawn using Silverlight's `Ellipse` and `Path` drawing primitives. These are two examples of the drawing primitive classes found in the `System.Windows.Shapes` namespace. The sphere of the globe and the two arced meridians are drawn with ellipses. The straight meridian and the three parallels are drawn with paths. The drawing canvas is centered in the first row of the `ContentPanel`.

> **TIP** To improve an application's performance, Microsoft recommends that complex XAML graphics be captured in a PNG or JPG and displayed with an `Image` control.

Each of the shapes has its `Stroke` property bound ❸ to a static resource you create named `GlobeBrush` ❶. `GlobeBrush` has its `Color` property bound to another static resource named `PhoneAccentColor`. The canvas has its `Background` bound to a static resource named `PhoneBackgroundBrush` ❷. `PhoneBackgroundBrush` and `PhoneAccentBrush` are other examples of the system theme resources that the Windows Phone injects into a XAML application. The Visual Studio System Resource picker, shown in figure 2.8, is accessed from the System Resource option in a property's Advanced Options menu.

In this section, you added XAML markup to draw a globe and bind the globe elements to system brushes to enable theme support. You still need to add UI controls to implement the remaining requirement, which is to navigate to the Greeting page and display the user's name. First, you need to create the Greeting page.

2.2.3 Adding the Greeting page

The second page of your application will display a greeting to the user, using the name typed into the main page. Add the new page by selecting Project > Add New Item and then choosing the *Windows Phone Portrait Page* item template. Name the file GreetingPage.xaml. The Portrait Page item template is one of several item templates

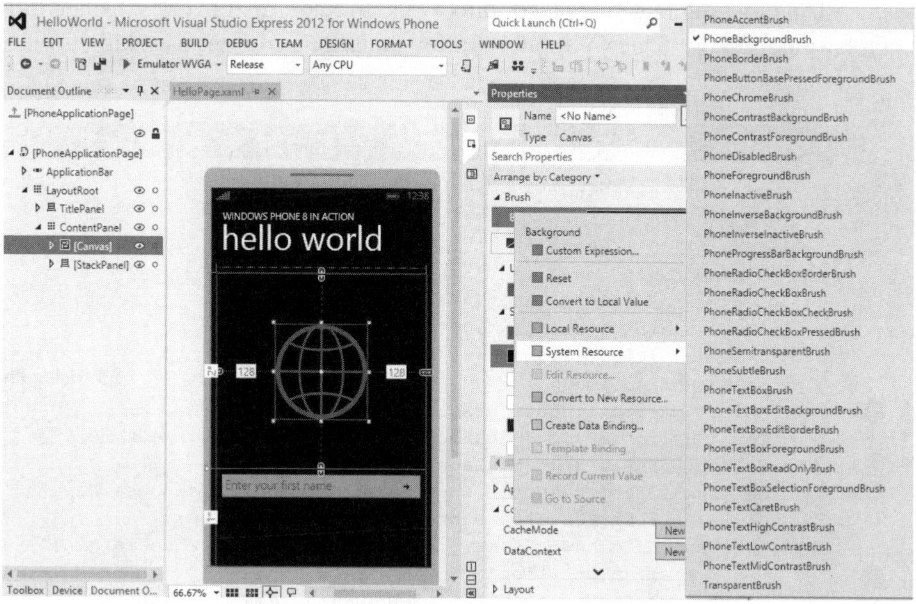

Figure 2.8 Visual Studio's System Resource menu shown when clicking the Advanced option button that appears on the right edge of most properties in the property editor. The first item in the menu is the name of the property, which in this screen shot is Background.

that ship with the Windows Phone Developer Tools. Table 2.2 lists the Windows Phone page item templates.

Table 2.2 Windows Phone page item templates

Page template	Description
Windows Phone Portrait Page	A basic application page with title and description fields. The `Orientation` and `SupportedOrientations` properties are set to `Portrait`.
Windows Phone Landscape Page	An application page identical to a Portrait page, except that the `Orientation` and `SupportedOrientations` properties are set to `Landscape`.
Windows Phone User Control	A starting point for creating reusable XAML-based controls.
Windows Phone Panorama Page	Adds an application page with the `Panorama` control as its only content element.
Windows Phone Pivot Page	Adds an application page with the `Pivot` control as its only content element.

The new Greeting page contains controls for the application and page title. Following the same steps described for the Hello page, change the application title to *WINDOWS PHONE 8 IN ACTION* and the page title to *greetings*.

The Greeting page uses a couple of `TextBlocks` and a `RichTextBox` control to display the message. The XAML markup for the page's content panel is shown in the following listing.

Listing 2.3 GreetingPage's content

```
<Grid x:Name="ContentPanel"
      Grid.Row="1"
      Margin="12,0,12,0">
    <Grid.RowDefinitions>
        <RowDefinition Height="72" />
        <RowDefinition Height="100" />
        <RowDefinition Height="*" />
    </Grid.RowDefinitions>
    <TextBlock Margin="{StaticResource PhoneMargin}"
        Text="Hello" Style="{StaticResource PhoneTextLargeStyle}" />
    <TextBlock x:Name="helloMessage" Grid.Row="1"
        Margin="{StaticResource PhoneMargin}" Text="name goes here"
        Style="{StaticResource PhoneTextExtraLargeStyle}" />
    <RichTextBox Grid.Row="2" Margin="{StaticResource PhoneMargin}"
        VerticalAlignment="Top">
        <Paragraph FontSize="{StaticResource PhoneFontSizeNormal}">
            Welcome to</Paragraph>
        <Paragraph FontSize="{StaticResource PhoneFontSizeMedium}"
            Foreground="{StaticResource PhoneAccentBrush}" >
            <Italic>Windows Phone 8 in Action</Italic>
        </Paragraph>
        <Paragraph FontSize="{StaticResource PhoneFontSizeNormal}">
            Written by Timothy Binkley-Jones, Adam Benoit,
            Michael Sync, and Massimo Perga.</Paragraph>
    </RichTextBox>
</Grid>
```

❶ Using PhoneMargin

❷ TextBlock for user's name

❸ Read-only RichTextBox

Start by dividing the content panel into three rows, specifying fixed heights for the first two rows. In the first row place a `TextBlock` containing the text "Hello." Use the `PhoneMargin` resource ❶ to align the controls with the `TextBlocks` in the title panel. Add a second `TextBlock` and give it the name `helloMessage` ❷. You'll use this `TextBlock` to display the name of the user. Add a `RichTextBox` ❸, which you'll use to display formatted text. On Windows Phone, the `RichTextBox` is read-only.

SYSTEM THEME RESOURCES IN THE GREETINGPAGE

What's interesting in listing 2.3 is the use of system theme resources. Using the theme style gives you compatibility with the user experience guidelines and is a good starting point to keep consistency between your application and the rest of the Windows Phone ecosystem. The available theme text styles are as follows:

- `PhoneTextAccentStyle`
- `PhoneTextContrastStyle`
- `PhoneTextExtraLargeStyle`
- `PhoneTextGroupHeaderStyle`
- `PhoneTextHugeStyle`

- `PhoneTextLargeStyle`
- `PhoneTextNormalStyle`
- `PhoneTextSmallStyle`
- `PhoneTextSubtleStyle`
- `PhoneTextTitle1Style`
- `PhoneTextTitle2Style`
- `PhoneTextTitle3Style`

When you use the theme text styles, you're assured that your text will match the theme colors chosen by the user. Three different title styles, a group header style, and five different-sized text styles are defined. There are also styles defined for subtle, accent, and contrast text. Figure 2.9 displays the text styles in both the dark and light themes.

The `PhoneTextContrastStyle`'s `color` matches the theme's background, and text drawn with it won't be visible unless the background has been changed. In figure 2.9, the contrast text is placed inside a `Border` control whose background is drawn with the `PhoneContrastBackgroundBrush`.

You now have the two pages in your Hello World application set up and ready to go. If you run the application now, you'll see the Hello page with the nice globe. But other than look at the globe, you can't do anything in the application yet. You still need to add input controls to capture the user's name. You also need something the user can use to navigate to the Greeting page. Let's take a look at how you interact with the user.

Figure 2.9 Theme text styles shown in the dark and light themes

2.3 Interacting with the user

XAML for Windows Phone provides most of the core user input controls that are available to Silverlight for the browser. The input controls have been modified and restyled to work in a touch-only environment and have new events that are raised when the user touches the screen. To maintain compatibility with Silverlight for the browser, the Windows Phone controls also provide mouse-related events and automatically promote touch events into mouse events. Unless you're specifically looking for touch events, you work with the input controls in nearly the exact same way you do when building browser applications.

There will be situations where you want to work with the touch events and gestures. Raw touch events are decomposed into *start*, *delta*, and *stop* events. *Touch gestures* combine several raw touch events into well-known gestures such as Tap, Double Tap, Hold, Pinch, Pan, and Flick. In this section you'll learn how to capture Tap and Double Tap gestures to change the color of the globe. First, let's take a closer look at how a text box operates on Windows Phone.

2.3.1 Touch typing

The Hello World application uses a `PhoneTextBox` control for text entry. The `PhoneTextBox` control is part of an external library that isn't included in the Windows Phone SDK, called the Windows Phone Toolkit. The toolkit is available for free from CodePlex (http://phone.codeplex.com) and can be added to your project with the NuGet Package Manager. You can also download a zip file that includes the full source code along with a sample application.

USING THE WINDOWS PHONE TOOLKIT

The Windows Phone Toolkit is packaged in a single assembly called Microsoft.Phone.Controls.Toolkit.dll. You need to add a reference to this assembly before

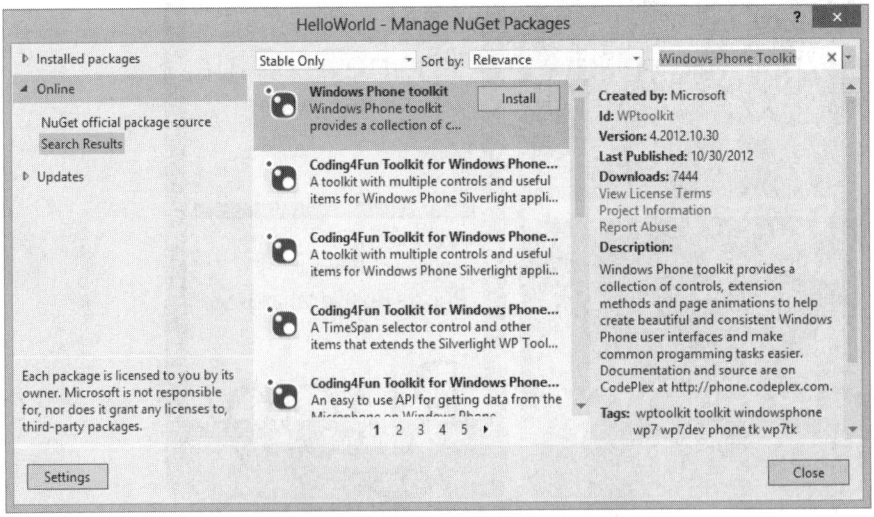

Figure 2.10 Add a reference to the Windows Phone Toolkit with the Manage NuGet Packages dialog.

using any of the toolkit's components. To add a reference to a NuGet package such as the Windows Phone Toolkit, click Project > Manage NuGet Packages. When the Manage NuGet Packages dialog appears, type *Window Phone Toolkit* in the Search Online input control and press Enter. A list of matching packages is shown in figure 2.10. Select the toolkit package from the list and click Install.

When working with toolkit components in XAML, you need to include an XML namespace declaration at the top of your page:

```
xmlns:toolkit="clr-namespace:Microsoft.Phone.Controls;
➥ assembly=Microsoft.Phone.Controls.Toolkit"
```

Now you're ready to add the `PhoneTextBox` to the `ContentPanel` of HelloPage.xaml. Because you'll need to reference the `PhoneTextBox` from code when you display the greeting message, give it the name `nameInput`:

```
<toolkit:PhoneTextBox Grid.Row="1" x:Name="nameInput"
   VerticalAlignment="Top" InputScope="Text"
   Hint="Enter your first name" ActionIcon="/Assets/next.png" />
```

The `PhoneTextBox` extends the normal `TextBox` control with a `Hint` and an `ActionIcon`, as shown in figure 2.11. The `Hint` is a watermark that displays when the field is empty. The `ActionIcon` represents a button that can be clicked to execute some code. You'll wire up the `ActionIcon` to an `ActionIcon-Tapped` event handler later in the chapter. The next.png file is one of the icons that comes from the Windows Phone SDK, which are installed to C:\Program Files\Microsoft SDKs\Windows Phone\v8.0\Icons. On 64-bit Windows, the SDK is installed in C:\Program Files (x86). Right-click the Add the Assets folder in the Solution Explorer and select Existing Item from the Add menu. Navigate to the SDK Icons folder and pick the next.png file from the Light folder. Make sure the Build Action is set to Content.

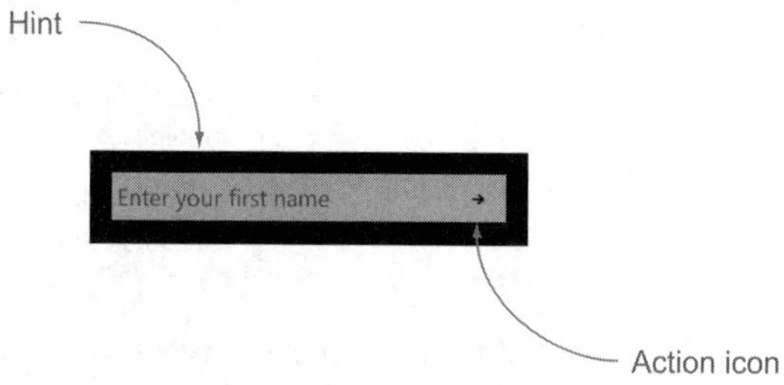

Figure 2.11 The PhoneTextBox from the Windows Phone Toolkit. The PhoneTextBox extends a normal TextBox with a hint watermark and an action icon.

When the user touches inside the `PhoneTextBox`, the onscreen keyboard is displayed if the device doesn't have a physical keyboard. The `InputScope` property can be used to control which software input panel is displayed to the user.

CONTROLLING THE KEYBOARD WITH INPUT SCOPE

Windows Phone devices have been designed to be fully touch-enabled, and a physical keyboard isn't present on many models. When a `TextBox` has the focus on a device that doesn't have a physical keyboard in use, a virtual keyboard or software input panel (SIP) is displayed. By default, the `TextBox` invokes a SIP with the standard QWERTY keyboard layout and doesn't provide text correction or suggestions. A number of different keyboard layouts are available, each one tailored to a specific task.

Input scope names are defined by the `InputScopeNameValue` enumeration. Table 2.3 lists a few of the input scope names that are useful to Windows Phone applications.

Table 2.3 Common input scopes

Input scope name	Description
`Chat`	A QWERTY keyboard layout with text suggestions and an emoticons key. Automatic correction isn't enabled.
`EmailNameOrAddress` `EmailSmtpAddress`	A QWERTY keyboard with @ and .com keys. Text suggestions and automatic correction aren't enabled.
`Maps`	A QWERTY keyboard layout with text suggestions and a customized Enter key. Automatic correction isn't enabled.
`NameOrPhoneNumber`	A QWERTY keyboard layout with a semicolon key and access to the 12-key number pad. Text suggestions and automatic correction aren't enabled.
`TelephoneNumber`	12-key number pad with * and #.
`Search`	A QWERTY keyboard layout with a customized Enter key. Text suggestions and automatic correction aren't enabled.
`Text`	A QWERTY keyboard layout with text suggestions and automatic correction enabled.
`Url`	A QWERTY keyboard layout with a .com key and a customized Enter key. Text suggestions and automatic correction aren't enabled.

Table 2.3 is only a partial list of input scopes. For a full list, see the MSDN documentation for the `InputScopeNameValue` enumeration at http://mng.bz/p9zM.

When developing your application, you should choose the most appropriate keyboard layout for your `TextBox` controls. If your `TextBox` accepts standard text phrases, you should consider using one of the layouts that provide suggestions and/or automatic correction. If your application automatically performs work or navigation once the user has input some text, you might want to use one of the layouts that provide a customized Enter key, which suggests some action will occur when Enter is pressed. If you have an input field that accepts only numbers, you might consider using the `Number` input scope. More than 60 different values are defined in the `InputScopeNameValue` enumeration. See the MSDN documentation for the full list and how each one affects the `TextBox`. We recommend that you always specify an `InputScope`, even if you only use the `Text` input scope that you've used here. The `Text` input scope provides word-correction features that aren't available with the default input scope.

The onscreen keyboard also exposes clipboard copy-and-paste operations. `TextBox` automatically supports the clipboard, and your application doesn't need to do anything special to enable clipboard operations. Developers can programmatically copy text to the system clipboard to share with other applications. Before we show how to copy text to the clipboard, let's look at how touch gestures are supported. Your application can listen for `Tap` gestures and perform custom actions in response to gesture events.

2.3.2 Touch gestures

The Windows Phone defines the touch gestures Tap, Double Tap, Hold, Pan, Pinch, and Flick. The Windows Phone SDK exposes three gesture events:

- `Tap`
- `DoubleTap`
- `Hold`

To demonstrate how touch gestures can be used in an application, you'll change the color of the globe when it's tapped by the user. Changing the color of the globe can be accomplished by changing the color of the brush used to draw the globe's ellipse and path graphics. Remember that you bound all the graphic elements to the static resource named `GlobeBrush`. To access the brush resource from code, you need to define a field and then initialize the field with the `SolidColorBrush` that's stored in the `ContentPanel`'s resource dictionary:

```
using System.Windows.Media;
...
SolidColorBrush globeBrush;
public HelloPage()
{
    InitializeComponent();
    globeBrush = (SolidColorBrush)ContentPanel.Resources["GlobeBrush"];
}
```

Before you implement the `Tap` and `DoubleTap` event handlers, you need to add a couple of fields to enable color changes. The first is an array of colors, and the second is an index of the current color:

```
Color[] colors = new Color[] { Colors.Red, Colors.Orange,
    Colors.Yellow, Colors.Green, Colors.Blue, Colors.Purple };
int colorIndex = 0;
```

ENABLING TAP AND DOUBLETAP EVENTS

Hook up the `Tap` and `DoubleTap` events to the canvas panel containing the globe:

```
<Canvas Width="200" Height="200" VerticalAlignment="Center"
    Background="{StaticResource PhoneBackgroundBrush}"
    Tap="Canvas_Tap" DoubleTap="Canvas_DoubleTap">
```

In the `Tap` event handler, you want to assign the `globeBrush`'s `Color` property to the next color in the `colors` array. Don't forget to check the index and reset it to the beginning of the array:

```
private void Canvas_Tap(object sender,
    System.Windows.Input.GestureEventArgs e)
{
    colorIndex++;
    if (colorIndex >= colors.Length)
        colorIndex = 0;
    globeBrush.Color = colors[colorIndex];
}
```

In the `DoubleTap` event handler, you reset the brush color to the accent color provided by the system theme. The accent color can be obtained from the application resources:

```
private void Canvas_DoubleTap(object sender,
    System.Windows.Input.GestureEventArgs e)
{
    globeBrush.Color = (Color)App.Current.Resources["PhoneAccentColor"];
}
```

If your application requires gestures beyond Tap and Hold, you'll need to process the raw manipulation events raised by the XAML controls. The `UIElement` class exposes `ManipulationStarted`, `ManipulationDelta`, and `ManipulationCompleted` events when a user touches, moves, and releases their finger from the screen. Converting manipulation events into gestures is beyond the scope of this book.

Now that you've learned about gestures, let's discuss how to copy text to the system clipboard. Your application will copy text to the clipboard when a toolbar button is pressed.

2.3.3 Adding a toolbar button

Windows Phone provides a built-in toolbar and menu control called the *application bar*. For your Hello World application, you need to add an application bar with three buttons to GreetingPage.xaml. The three buttons are labeled *ok*, *copy*, *pin*:

```
<phone:PhoneApplicationPage ... >
    <phone:PhoneApplicationPage.ApplicationBar>
        <shell:ApplicationBar >
            <shell:ApplicationBarIconButton Text="ok"
                IconUri="/Assets/AppBar/check.png" />
            <shell:ApplicationBarIconButton Text="copy"
                IconUri="/Assets/AppBar/save.png" />
            <shell:ApplicationBarIconButton Text="pin"
                IconUri="/Assets/AppBar/share.png" />
        </shell:ApplicationBar>
  </phone:PhoneApplicationPage.ApplicationBar>
```

The application bar markup is added as a child element of the `PhoneApplication-Page` element. In the application bar, you're using a few more of the icons from the Windows Phone SDK, which are installed to C:\Program Files\Microsoft SDKs\Windows Phone\v8.0\Icons\Dark. Create a project folder called AppBar within the folder called Assets and add the check.png, save.png, and share.png files to the folder. For each of the images, set the Build Action to Content. You'll read more about the application bar in chapter 13.

Like any other buttons, `ApplicationBarIconButtons` raise a `Click` event when the user taps them. You'll register for the `Click` event on the copy button and implement the event handler. Update the button's markup to declare the event handler:

```
<shell:ApplicationBarIconButton Text="copy"
    IconUri="/Assets/AppBar/save.png"
    Click="copyButton_Click" />
```

Add the event handler in GreetingPage.xaml.cs:

```
private void copyButton_Click(object sender, EventArgs e)
{
    string message = string.Format("Hello {0}!", helloMessage.Text);
    Clipboard.SetText(message);
}
```

The event handler constructs a message by concatenating the word *Hello* and the text in the `helloMessage` `TextBlock`. The greeting message is then copied to the `Clipboard` and is ready to be pasted into some other application.

The Model-View-ViewModel pattern

Many, but not all, XAML developers use the Model-View-ViewModel pattern (MVVM) to separate user interface markup and logic from application logic. The separation of UI and application logic promoted by MVVM is made possible with XAML's data binding, value converter, and commanding features. Input and `TextBlock` controls are bound to model objects, which often implement the `INotifyPropertyChanged` interface. Values are converted to strings using converter classes that implement `IValueConverter`. Click event handlers are eschewed in favor of command objects implementing the `ICommand` interface.

Though MVVM separates UI and business logic, it introduces complexity. We've intentionally avoided using the complexity of the MVVM pattern in the sample applications in the book. We've also avoided binding trivial properties, such as messages displayed in a `TextBlock`, and have placed a great deal of our application logic in the page code-behind. MVVM is a great pattern that's well suited for XAML applications, but one criticism of MVVM is that it's overkill for simple applications.

This is a book about Windows Phone, not XAML, but we've included an appendix where you can learn more about MVVM. The bits of XAML we use in the sample applications are intended to highlight the features of the Windows Phone SDK.

In this section you learned how to receive typed text from the user, respond to touch gestures, and use the system application bar to display a toolbar button. You implemented a click handler for one of the toolbar buttons, but the other two buttons don't perform any work. The unimplemented buttons will be used to navigate between the two pages, which we cover in the next section.

2.4 Page navigation

A phone application is a modified version of a XAML navigation application. XAML navigation applications are composed of a navigation frame and one or more pages that interact with the `NavigationService`. The `NavigationService` interacts with the operating system to maintain a journal or history of pages visited by the user. In this section you'll add navigation to the Hello World application.

2.4.1 Navigating to another page

Page navigation is the process that takes the user from one page to another. One example occurs when the user taps a button to open a new page and then, after completing some work, taps another button to come back to the main page. Navigation is managed by the `NavigationService` class. The `NavigationService.Navigate` method is called to move to a new page. When `Navigate` is called, the current page is placed on the navigation stack, and a new instance of the target page is generated. The `NavigationService.GoBack` method removes the current page and restores the previous page that's on the navigation stack.

ADDING PAGE NAVIGATION TO HELLO WORLD

You'll now add page navigation to your Hello World application. Starting in HelloPage.xaml, add an `ActionItemTapped` event handler to the `PhoneTextBox`:

```
<toolkit:PhoneTextBox Grid.Row="1" x:Name="nameInput"
   VerticalAlignment="Top" InputScope="Text"
   Hint="Enter your first name" ActionIcon="/Assets/next.png"
   ActionIconTapped="nameInput_ActionIconTapped" />
```

You want to navigate to `GreetingPage` when the icon is pressed, so you need to add code to the event handler:

```
void nameInput_ActionIconTapped(object sender, RoutedEventArgs e)
{
    this.NavigationService.Navigate(
        new Uri("/GreetingPage.xaml", UriKind.Relative));
}
```

You access the `NavigationService` via the `PhoneApplicationPage`'s `NavigationService` property. The `Navigate` method accepts a `Uri`, which in this case is the name of the file containing the page you want to load. You construct the `Uri` using `UriKind.Relative` because it's part of the same XAP file.

Reopen GreetingPage.xaml and generate the click event handler for the OK application bar button:

```
<shell:ApplicationBarIconButton Text="ok"
    IconUri="/Assets/AppBar/check.png"
    Click="navigateBackButton_Click" />
```

You implement the handler by calling the `GoBack` method:

```
void navigateBackButton_Click(object sender, EventArgs e)
{
    this.NavigationService.GoBack();
}
```

Now press F5, or choose Debug > Start Debugging, and debug the application. You've linked your two pages using only two lines of code. Press the action icon and see the second page appear. When you press the OK button, the main page appears again.

It's worth noting that you use the `GoBack` method instead of the `Navigate` method to return to MainPage.xaml. When you call `GoBack`, the current page is removed from the page stack. If you'd used `Navigate`, a new page would've been added on top of the

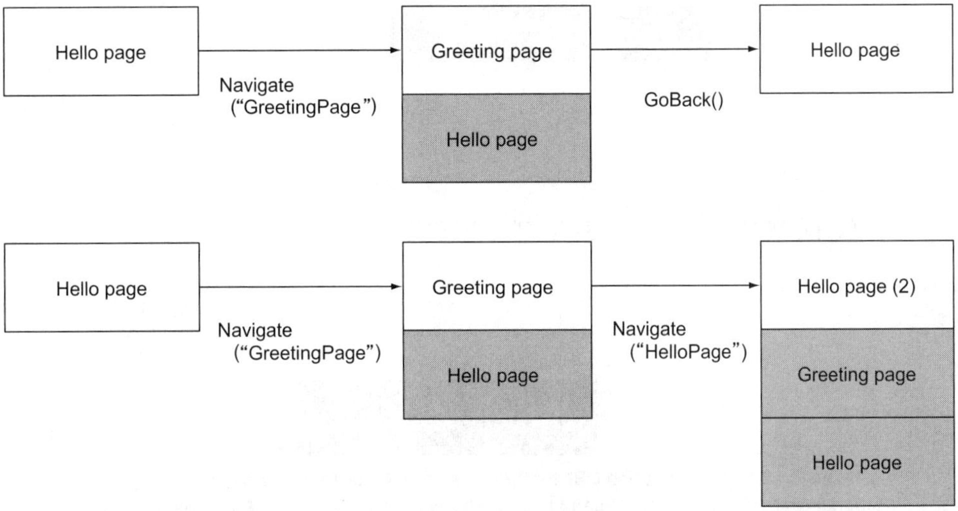

Figure 2.12 The navigation page stack resulting from `GoBack` (top) and `Navigate` (bottom) method calls—the white boxes represent the visible page, whereas the shaded boxes are the pages in the background.

page stack. Depending on the scenario you want to achieve, you can choose the approach most appropriate for your application, but you must be aware of the consequences. Both cases are illustrated in figure 2.12.

EXAMINING THE PAGE STACK

Let's examine the two scenarios presented in figure 2.12. In the top sequence the navigation uses `GoBack` to return to `HelloPage`, so the page stack is reduced. In the sequence on the bottom, the navigation uses `Navigate` to navigate to `HelloPage`, and a new page is added on top of the page stack and made visible.

You should watch out for a couple of gotchas when navigating with the `NavigationService`. If you pass in an invalid or misspelled filename to the `Navigate` method, or if you forget the leading / character, the `NavigationService` will raise the `NavigationFailed` event. A `NavigationFailed` event is also raised if you call `GoBack` when the `NavigationService`'s `CanGoBack` property returns `false`. By default the `NavigationFailed` event is handled in App.xaml.cs in the `RootFrame_NavigationFailed` method generated by the project template.

Your Hello World application now moves from one page to another, and the Greeting page starts up as expected. How do you get the user-entered name from the Hello page to the Greeting page? The XAML navigation framework provides features to enable passing data into a newly launched page.

2.4.2 Passing parameters between pages

In the preceding example you concentrated on navigation between pages but didn't pass any information to the Greeting page. In theory, pages should be as self-contained as possible in order to maintain isolation between the pages, but it can be useful to pass

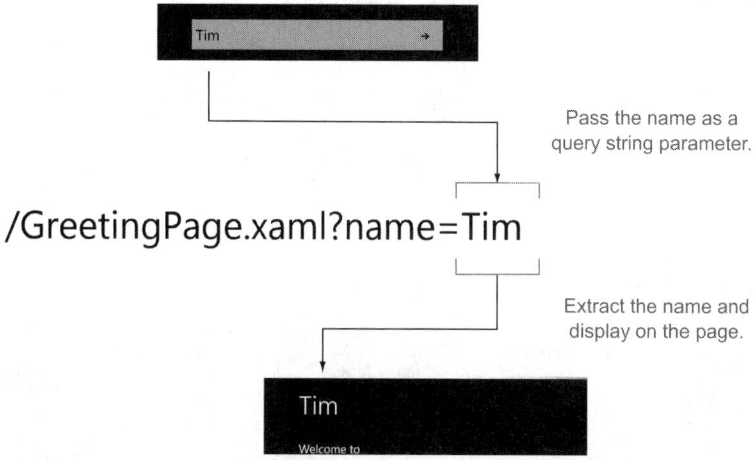

Figure 2.13 The navigation URI to the `GreetingPage` includes a query string parameter. The parameter is used to pass the name entered in the `PhoneTextBox` from `MainPage` to `GreetingPage`. `GreetingPage` extracts the passed value and displays it in a `TextBlock`.

parameters when navigating. You could choose to use some form of global data or data cached in the `App` class instead of passing data, but you should consider passing parameters in the `Uri` much as you would pass data to a constructor. As you'll learn later in the chapter, the operating system can call your page directly without ever constructing an instance of your main page.

In your sample main page, the user enters a name into a `TextBox` control named `nameInput` whose `Text` property will be used as a parameter passed to `GreetingPage`. `GreetingPage` will set the text block having the name `helloMessage` with the parameter passed by `HelloPage`. Two changes are required in your code to pass a parameter: `HelloPage` must pass the parameter value to `GreetingPage` via the navigation `Uri`, and `GreetingPage` must extract the parameter value from the query string. This process is shown in figure 2.13.

BUILDING A URI WITH A PARAMETER

When you first added page navigation to the application, you created a URI with the hardcoded name of the Greeting page in the `nameInput_ActionIconTapped` method. You could choose to hardcode the parameters as well, but now you have more magic strings in your code. What if you change the name of the Greeting page or change the name of the parameters passed in the query string? You'll move `Uri` construction code into a static method of the `GreetingPage` class next. Modify the `Uri` to pass a parameter in the same manner that you would if you were adding fields to a standard HTTP query string:

```
public static Uri BuildNavigationUri(string name)
{
    return new Uri("/GreetingPage.xaml?name=" + name, UriKind.Relative);
}
```

Update the nameInput_ActionIconTapped method in HelloPage.xaml.cs to call the new factory method, passing along the name entered by the user. The parameter value is obtained from the nameInput control:

```
NavigationService.Navigate(
     GreetingPage.BuildNavigationUri(nameInput.Text));
```

The data passed via the navigation Uri can be retrieved from the target page's NavigationContext property. The NavigationContext class has a single property named QueryString, which is an IDictionary<string, string> mapping parameter names to values.

You'll use the NavigationContext in the code-behind for GreetingPage.xaml. The appropriate time to access the query string is after the page navigation has completed. The navigation framework calls the PhoneApplicationPage.OnNavigatedTo virtual method when navigation is complete. In the sample application, you override OnNavigatedTo and obtain the parameter value by using the string "name" as a key into the QueryString. You set the returned value into the Text property of helloMessage:

```
protected override void OnNavigatedTo (NavigationEventArgs e)
{
    helloMessage.Text =
        this.NavigationContext.QueryString ["name"];
}
```

OnNavigatedTo is one of the virtual methods defined by PhoneApplicationPage that are called when navigation events occur. OnNavigatedFrom and OnNavigatingFrom are two other methods you can use to determine when the current page is changing.

In this section we've shown you how to use code to navigate between the pages of an application. Other activities, such as the user pressing the hardware Back key, can cause navigation changes in your application. Every Windows Phone is equipped with a hardware Back key. Its effect in an application is equivalent to calling the NavigationService.GoBack method.

2.4.3 Changing the Back key behavior

When the Back key is pressed, the navigation framework automatically performs a GoBack operation. The Back key behavior can be interrupted, for example, to avoid moving off a page that has unsaved changes. To interrupt the automatic GoBack, the PhoneApplicationPage class provides an event named BackKeyPress. You'll see this event in action by wiring it to an event handler in your GreetingPage class. Edit GreetingPage.xaml by adding an attribute to the PhoneApplicationPage tag:

```
BackKeyPress="Page_BackKeyPress"
```

Add the event handler to GreetingPage.xaml.cs. This example prompts the user with a confirmation message:

```
using System.ComponentModel;
...
void Page_BackKeyPress (object sender, CancelEventArgs e)
```

```
{
    MessageBoxResult result = MessageBox.Show(
        "Press OK to return to the previous page.",
        "WP8 in Action", MessageBoxButton.OKCancel);
    if (result == MessageBoxResult.Cancel)
        e.Cancel = true;
}
```

If the user taps the Cancel button in the message box, you set the `CancelEventArgs.Cancel` property to `true`. This cancels the default behavior of the Back key. Failing to add this statement or setting `e.Cancel` to `false` would have maintained the default behavior, which is to move to the previous page or terminate the application if no other pages are in the page stack.

NOTE "App certification requirements for Windows Phone" (http://mng.bz/Fefo) details appropriate application behavior when working with the Back key. Specifically, when the Back key is pressed while the main page is visible, the application must exit.

Navigation relies on URI and query strings to navigate to specific locations within an application. You can also use navigation strings to allow a user to launch to a specific location within your application with application tiles.

2.4.4 Navigating with tiles

Chapter 1 introduced you to Live Tiles, the dynamic images an application can pin to the Start Screen. Windows Phone users can pin an application's tile to the Start Screen. Applications can also create secondary tiles that navigate directly using a deep-link URI or a specific location in an application. Figure 2.14 shows the application and secondary tiles for the Hello World application.

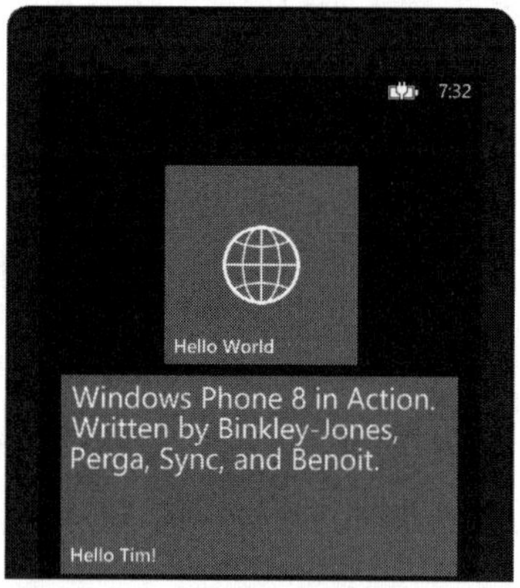

Figure 2.14 Application and secondary tiles for Hello World

When the user taps the application tile for Hello World, the application is launched, and the `NavigationService` is called with the URL `/HelloPage.xaml`. When the user taps the secondary tile, the application is launched and the application host passes the URL associated with the secondary tile to the `NavigationService`. When you built the `GreetingPage`, you added a pin button to the application bar. Add a click handler to the pin button and implement the code in the following listing to create a secondary tile.

Listing 2.4 Pinning a secondary tile

```
private void pinButton_Click(object sender, EventArgs e)
{
   var tileData = new FlipTileData
   {
```

```
        SmallBackgroundImage = new
           Uri("/Assets/Tiles/FlipCycleTileSmall.png", UriKind.Relative),
        BackgroundImage = new
           Uri("/Assets/Tiles/FlipCycleTileMedium.png", UriKind.Relative),
        WideBackgroundImage = new
           Uri("/Assets/Tiles/FlipCycleTileLarge.png", UriKind.Relative),
        BackTitle = string.Format("Hello {0}!", helloMessage.Text),
        BackContent = "Windows Phone 8 in Action",
        WideBackContent = "Windows Phone 8 in Action. Written by
        ➥ Binkley-Jones, Perga, Sync, and Benoit.",
    };
    ShellTile.Create(BuildNavigationUri(helloMessage.Text), tileData, true);
}
```

The `FlipTileData` class has several properties that set the image and text shown on the front side and flip side of the tile. The image properties are set to the `Uri` containing the path to three images created in the /Asset/Tiles project folder by Visual Studio. The `Create` method of the `ShellTile` class is used to create the new tile. Specify the `Uri` to the Greeting page, passing the same parameters specified by `HelloPage`. When `ShellTile.Create` is called, the application exits, and the Start Screen is launched, showing the new secondary tile to the user.

Tile types and properties

You learned in chapter 1 that tiles are displayed on the Start Screen in one of three formats: Flip, Iconic, or Cycle. Each of the tile formats can be one-quarter size, normal size, or double-wide size.

Flip tiles display a title, a count, and a background image on the front of the tile. The back of a Flip tile displays a message as well as a title and image but doesn't display the count. Flip tile properties are specified through the properties of the `FlipTileData` class: `BackBackgroundImage`, `BackContent`, `BackgroundImage`, `BackTitle`, `Count`, `SmallBackgroundImage`, `Title`, `WideBackBackgroundImage`, `WideBackContent`, and `WideBackgroundImage`.

Iconic tiles have only a single side, which displays a title, icon, and count. Iconic tile properties are specified through the properties of the `IconicTileData` class: `BackgroundColor`, `Count`, `IconImage`, `SmallIconImage`, `Title`, `WideContent1`, `WideContent2`, and `WideContent3`.

Cycle tiles display a title and count and cycle through up to nine different background images. Cycle tile properties are specified through the properties of the `CycleTileData` class: `Name`, `Count`, `CycleImages`, `SmallBackgroundImage`, and `Title`.

The `FlipTileData` class is one of three different tile data classes that can be used to pin secondary tiles. The other two are `CycleTileData` and `IconicTileData`. These classes all have different properties that are relevant to the three types of Live Tiles you learned about in chapter 1.

In this section you implemented the final requirement for your Hello World application—navigating to a second page and displaying a greeting to the user. You learned about the `NavigationService` and how to use query string parameters to pass data between pages. And you learned how to use tiles to navigate directly to the Greeting page from the Start Screen.

2.5 Summary

The Windows Phone Developer Tools help you build many different kinds of applications. Project templates are provided for simple projects and class libraries as well as list, pivot, panorama, HTML5, and XAML with Direct3D projects. You can read more about panorama and pivot applications in chapter 14 and HTML5-based applications in chapter 17.

The Windows Phone application framework makes it easy to align your application with the system theme and style. The framework injects resources into applications so they can match the system theme (light versus dark, accent color) and the look and feel (fonts, colors, sizes). The visual designers and property editors in Visual Studio expose theme resources.

XAML has been extended for Windows Phone with components built specifically for the platform. New navigation frame, page control, and application bar components are a few of the additions. Other existing controls have been modified to work on the phone. The chapters in part 3 of this book look at these new and modified components.

System capabilities must be declared in order to use many of the core phone APIs. The phone APIs provide access to the native applications, services, sensors, and media features of the phone. In part 2 of this book, you'll read about how to use the phone APIs. In the next chapter, you'll learn how Windows Phone implements application multitasking and how to design an application to handle lifecycle events.

Part 2

Core Windows Phone

Now that you understand the Windows Phone platform and how to use Visual Studio and the other tools in the Windows Phone SDK, it's time to learn the low-level details of how to build mobile applications. Part 2 of this book introduces concepts that are brand new to Windows Phone, as well as concepts that have been adapted to operate within the phone's limitations.

We start in chapter 3 with a discussion of fast application switching and fast application resume, Microsoft's names for the battery-saving technologies that allow a dormant application to be quickly restored when a user switches from a foreground application to a background application. Chapter 4 introduces technologies, such as background agents, that allow your application to work even when it's not running. Chapter 5 shows how to use launchers and choosers to interact with built-in applications such as the phone dialer, email, and the People Hub. Chapter 6 describes how to work with the phone's built-in contact and appointment databases, and chapter 7 explains how to store your own application data.

Chapters 8 and 10 show how to read data from the phone's hardware including the camera, accelerometer, compass, and gyroscope, whereas chapter 9 discusses how to integrate your app with the Photos and Music + Video Hubs. Chapter 11 introduces push notifications, a service that enables an external application or web service to send messages and updates to particular Windows Phone devices. Part 2 wraps up in chapter 12 with a discussion of the Speech API, which you can use to interpret spoken commands and convert text to speech.

3 Fast application switching and resume

This chapter covers

- Fast application switching
- Responding to lifetime events
- Fast application resume

Like any other operating system, an application on the Windows Phone starts up, runs for a while, and in the normal course of things, eventually exits. In other multitasking operating systems, an application can be moved to the background when the user switches applications. While in the background, the application will continue to run in lower-priority time slices. The Windows Phone OS is a multitasking operating system, but puts limitations on background operations. When a user switches applications, the running application is paused, and system resources are disconnected from the process so they can be freed up for foreground applications. A dormant application might eventually be terminated if the operating system needs to allocate additional resources to the foreground application.

Applications can't run in the background, but Windows Phone offers several options for the developer to build applications that require multitasking features. *Fast application switching* and *fast application resume* provide dormant applications the tools for quickly returning to full operation, giving the user the impression that the application continued to run. Background agents, covered in chapter 4, provide the mechanisms applications use to perform tasks even when applications aren't running.

The multitasking limitations imposed on applications may seem severe to developers looking to build the next killer mobile application. Microsoft has imposed these limitations to ensure that the user has the best overall experience possible. Background tasks aren't allowed to affect or slow down foreground applications, nor are they allowed to perform tasks that would quickly drain the phone's battery.

In this chapter you'll create a sample application that demonstrates how to build applications that support fast application switching and resume.

3.1 Fast application switching

Fast application switching is the term coined by Microsoft's Windows Phone team to describe the process that pauses a running application when the user switches to another application. The paused application usually remains in memory but can't execute any code. The application will resume running when the user switches back to the application, making it the foreground application once again.

An application may be paused via one of many scenarios:

- The user presses the Windows or the Search button.
- The user chooses to reply to a newly received text message.
- The user chooses to respond to a newly received toast notification.
- The user presses the Camera button.
- The user locks the phone, or the idle timeout expires.
- The application shows a launcher or chooser.

When the user backs out of the application, it's shut down normally. In all other situations, the user can restart an application with the Back button or by selecting it with the Task Switcher UI. If the application supports fast application resume (which we cover later in this chapter), an application can even be restarted from the Start Screen or Application List. Upon restart, the application should return to the state it was in before being paused, giving the user the impression that the application continued to run.

An application can also be obscured. *Obscuration* occurs when the operating system covers part of an application in favor of another application's UI. An application may be obscured when any of the following happens:

- The user receives a new phone call.
- The user returns to a phone call that was active before an application started.
- The user receives a new toast notification.
- The Lock Screen is enabled and the application has disabled idle detection mode.
- An alarm or reminder is triggered.
- An application uses the `PhoneCallTask` launcher.
- The user activates the Task Switcher.

Pausing and obscuration interfere with the normal flow of an application. Your application should be designed to react to interruptions by appropriately responding to the application lifetime events.

3.1.1 Understanding lifetime events

The Windows Phone class libraries expose operating system lifetime events, with several events defined on a few different classes. Table 3.1 describes each of the lifetime events and where the event is implemented in the framework.

Table 3.1 Application lifetime events

Event	Purpose	Implementation
`Launching`	Notifies the application that it's being started from scratch	`PhoneApplicationService.Launching`
`Closing`	Notifies the application that it's being terminated as part of a normal application exit	`PhoneApplicationService.Closing`
`Activated`	Notifies the application that it's being resumed from a dormant or tombstoned state	`PhoneApplicationService.Activated`
`Deactivated`	Notifies the application that it's being paused to allow another process to execute	`PhoneApplicationService.Deactivated`
`Obscured`	Notifies the application that it's losing focus in favor of an overlay	`PhoneApplicationFrame.Obscured`
`Unobscured`	Notifies the application that it's regaining focus	`PhoneApplicationFrame.Unobscured`

An application begins life when the user taps the application's icon in the Application List. The application host constructs an instance of the `Application` class, raises the `Launching` event, and then constructs and navigates to the default Navigation page. At this point the application is running, solving user problems, and generally making life easier. In the normal course of activity, the user presses the Back button to exit the application, and then the operating system navigates away from the application and raises the `Closing` event. The launching-running-closing workflow can be seen in figure 3.1 as the straight-line path between Start and End.

While running, an application will likely receive other lifetime events. When the `Obscured` event is raised, the application transitions to an obscured state. The application remains running, but its user interface is partially or completely hidden. When the user interface is uncovered, the `Unobscured` event is raised, and the application returns to the normal running state.

Deactivation is triggered when the operating system pauses an application in order to execute another process. The `Deactivated` event is raised to notify the application that it's transitioning to the dormant state. In the *dormant state,* the application remains in memory, with all processing and threads stopped, to facilitate a fast restart when the user switches between applications. When the user returns to the application, the `Activated` event is raised, and the application returns to the normal running state.

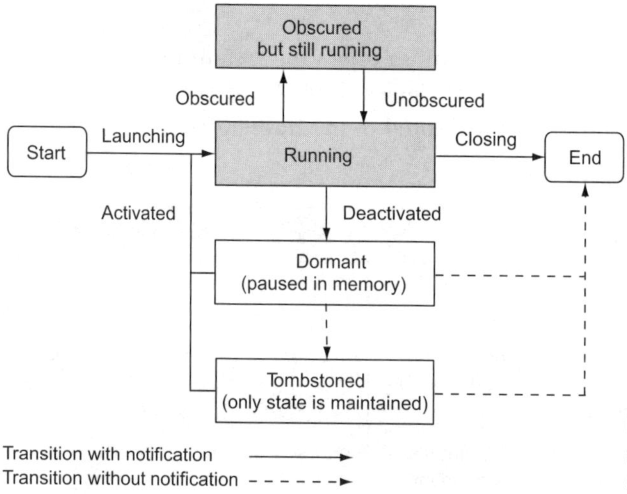

Figure 3.1 Application lifetime states and the actions that trigger state transition

A dormant application might also transition to a tombstoned state. When an application is *tombstoned*, no notification is given, the application is removed from memory, and almost all of its resources are freed up for other applications to use. The only application resources that are maintained in memory are those items that have been stored in one of two `State` dictionaries provided by the Windows Phone framework specifically for tombstoning scenarios. When the user navigates back to the application, the application host constructs a new instance of the `Application` class, raises the `Activated` event, and then constructs and navigates to the previously focused page. It's the application's responsibility to save application data to the `State` dictionaries and to read and restore data after reactivation.

When an application is dormant or tombstoned, the operating system may decide to terminate the application and end its life. When terminated, the application and any saved state are removed from memory. An application isn't notified when being transitioned to the end state.

In this chapter you'll build an application that handles each of the lifetime events. You'll add code to handle the `Launching`, `Activated`, `Deactivated`, `Obscured`, and `Unobscured` events. You'll start your sample application in the usual way—by creating a new project.

3.1.2 *Creating the Lifetime sample application*

The Lifetime sample application will handle each of the lifetime events. The sample code demonstrates how to distinguish between returning from a dormant state and a tombstoned state. You'll learn how to store application data in the `State` dictionaries and how to recover the data when returning from a tombstoned state. Finally, we show how to design an application capable of running when the phone is locked.

The Lifetime application records the time when each of the lifetime events is raised, displaying the times on the screen. Moving beyond the lifetime events, we explore other interesting moments in the Lifetime application such as construction and navigation. Figure 3.2 shows the Lifetime sample application.

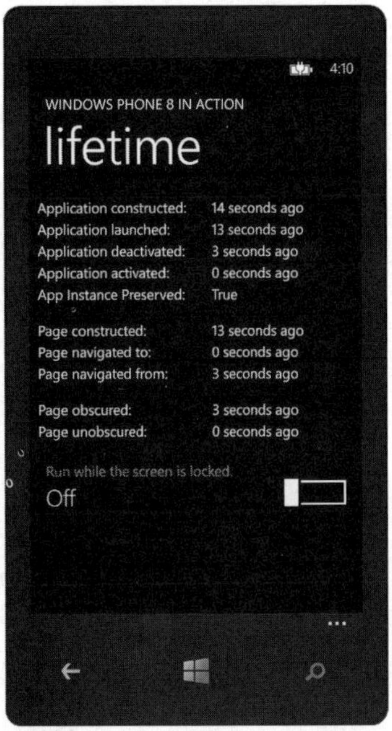

Figure 3.2 The Lifetime sample application

Create a new project using the Windows Phone App template and name the project *Lifetime*. The Visual Studio Windows Phone App project template automatically creates lifetime event handlers for the `PhoneApplicationService` events in App.xaml.cs. Events handlers aren't created automatically for the `PhoneApplicationFrame` events. A `PhoneApplicationService` instance is declared in App.xaml, and the `Launching`, `Closing`, `Activated`, and `Deactivated` events are wired up to methods generated in App.xaml.cs. The following listing shows the App.xaml markup and the corresponding event handlers in App.xaml.cs.

Listing 3.1 Generated application lifetime event handlers

```
<Application.ApplicationLifetimeObjects>
    <shell:PhoneApplicationService
        Launching="Application_Launching"
        Closing="Application_Closing"
        Activated="Application_Activated"
        Deactivated="Application_Deactivated"/>
</Application.ApplicationLifetimeObjects>

private void Application_Launching(object sender, LaunchingEventArgs e){}
private void Application_Activated(object sender, ActivatedEventArgs e){}
private void Application_Deactivated(object sender,
    DeactivatedEventArgs e){}
private void Application_Closing(object sender, ClosingEventArgs e){}
```

An application isn't considered correct if `PhoneApplicationService` events aren't handled. The handlers must be both declared in the XAML and implemented in the code-behind, at least as generated by the Visual Studio wizard.

The main page for the Lifetime sample application displays how many seconds ago a particular lifetime event occurred. The sample application will record the occurrence time of each of the lifetime events, along with a few other interesting events. The sample application displays these times as the number of seconds since the event was raised. The information for each event is displayed with two `TextBlocks`, the first displaying a label and the second displaying the number of seconds since the event.

To organize all the controls, you'll divide the ContentPanel into several rows and columns, as shown in the following listing.

Listing 3.2 Defining the ContentPanel's layout

```
<Grid x:Name="ContentPanel" Grid.Row="1" Margin="12,0,12,0">
    <Grid.RowDefinitions>
        <RowDefinition Height="30" />
...
        <RowDefinition Height="*" />
    </Grid.RowDefinitions>
    <Grid.ColumnDefinitions>
        <ColumnDefinition Width="250" />
        <ColumnDefinition Width="*" />
    </Grid.ColumnDefinitions>
</Grid>
```

❶ Declare 11 rows

❷ Declare 2 columns

First, you divide the Grid into 11 rows ❶ and two columns ❷. We've omitted the declaration of most of the rows for the sake of space; the rows not shown should be assigned a Height of 30 just like the first row. Whereas most of the rows and the first column are assigned a fixed height or width, the last row and last column fill the remainder of the page's available space.

As you work through the chapter, you'll add several TextBlock controls to MainPage.xaml. You'll add the first few controls in the next section when you display the number of seconds elapsed since the MainPage was constructed. Because the number of seconds continuously changes, the application should update the user interface once every second.

3.1.3 *Updating the user interface*

The sample application will use a DispatchTimer to update the user interface once every second. A DispatcherTimer raises a Tick event once per a specified time interval. The DispatcherTimer executes the event handler on the UI thread, making it ideal for updating the user interface. Add the code in the following listing to MainPage.xaml.

Listing 3.3 Using a DispatcherTimer to update the user interface

```
using System.Windows.Threading;

DispatcherTimer timer;

public MainPage()
{
   InitializeComponent();
   timer = new DispatcherTimer();
   timer.Tick += timer_Tick;
   timer.Interval = TimeSpan.FromMilliseconds(1000);
   timer.Start();
}
```

❶ Raise the Tick event once per second

```
void timer_Tick(object sender, EventArgs e)
{
   UpdateUserInterface();
}

void UpdateUserInterface()
{
}
```

The `DispatcherTimer` is constructed in the `MainPage` constructor and configured to raise the `Tick` event once per second ❶. The `timer_Tick` event handler calls a method named `UpdateUserInterface`, which is responsible for updating the user. You'll add code to the `UpdateUserInterface` method as you progress through the chapter.

With the sample application project created and the initial framework in place, you're ready to start investigating each of the lifetime events, starting with the `Launching` event.

3.2 Launching the application

You learned about application startup in chapter 2. During normal application startup, an instance of `App` and an instance of `MainPage` are constructed, and the application host calls the `NavigationService` directly to navigate to MainPage.xaml. In addition to constructing these two objects, the `PhoneApplicationService` raises the `Launching` event. In this section we'll look at how to detect when an application is launched.

3.2.1 Construction

The sample application captures when the `App` and `MainPage` instances are constructed and shows the times in the user interface. The construction times are stored in properties in each of the two classes. You'll start the implementation by updating the class in App.xaml.cs to define and assign a property named `AppConstructedTime`. The property is defined as an automatic property with a private setter. The `AppConstructedTime` property is assigned to the current time in the `App` class constructor:

```
public DateTime AppConstructedTime { get; private set; }
public App()
{
    AppConstructedTime = DateTime.Now;
    ...
}
```

Next, add a similar property to the `MainPage` class. In addition to recording the construction time, record when the `OnNavigatedTo` method is called. These two times are stored in two fields named `pageConstructedTime` and `navigatedToTime`:

```
DateTime pageConstructedTime;
DateTime navigatedToTime;
```

Now, update the `MainPage` class constructor to assign the current time to the `pageConstructedTime` field:

```
public MainPage()
{
    InitializeComponent();
    pageConstructedTime = DateTime.Now;
...
}
```

The `navigatedToTime` field is assigned the current time in the overridden `OnNavigatedTo` method:

```
protected override void OnNavigatedTo(NavigationEventArgs e)
{
    navigatedToTime = DateTime.Now;
    base.OnNavigatedTo(e);
}
```

Remember that the timer runs once a second and calls the `UpdateUserInterface` method. The `UpdateUserInterface` method is responsible for updating the user interface with the time values stored in the `App` properties and the `MainPage` fields. `UpdateUserInterface` sets the time values into associated `TextBlock` controls. Before you edit the `UpdateUserInterface` method, you need to add a few controls to MainPage.xaml, as shown in the following listing.

Listing 3.4 UI controls showing construction times

```
<TextBlock Grid.Row="0" Text="Application constructed:" />
<TextBlock x:Name="appConstructed" Grid.Row="0" Grid.Column="1"
    Text="{Binding StringFormat='\{0:N0\} seconds ago'}" />
<TextBlock Grid.Row="5" Text="Page constructed:" />
<TextBlock x:Name="pageConstructed" Grid.Row="5" Grid.Column="1"
    Text="{Binding StringFormat='\{0:N0\} seconds ago'}" />
<TextBlock Grid.Row="6" Text="Page navigated to:" />
<TextBlock x:Name="navigatedTo" Grid.Row="6" Grid.Column="1"
    Text="{Binding StringFormat='\{0:N0\} seconds ago'}" />
```

In this code listing, you've added six `TextBlock` controls. Three of the `TextBlock`s are used as labels. The other three display the relevant elapsed time values and are named `appConstructed`, `pageConstructed`, and `navigatedTo`. These three controls are used by the `UpdateUserInterface` method:

```
public void UpdateUserInterface()
{
  DateTime now = DateTime.Now;
  pageConstructed.DataContext = (now - pageConstructedTime).TotalSeconds;
  navigatedTo.DataContext = (now - navigatedToTime).TotalSeconds;
  var app = (App)Application.Current;
  appConstructed.DataContext = (now - app.AppConstructedTime).TotalSeconds;
}
```

The `DataContext` properties of the `TextBlock` controls are assigned values calculated by the number of seconds elapsed between the current time and the time stored in the related variables in the `MainPage` and `App` classes.

Run the application and examine the values displayed on the screen. On first run, the screen should display construction and navigation times of 1 or 0 seconds ago. The left side of figure 3.3 shows the initial construction times. Press the Start button and launch another application. Using the Task Switcher or the Back button, switch back to the running instance of the sample application.

> **NOTE** The Task Switcher is launched in the emulator by pressing and holding the F1 key on your computer keyboard. If you're running the application on a real device, press and hold the Back button until the Task Switcher is shown.

Windows Phone maintained the application process in memory, and the `App` and `MainPage` classes don't need to be recreated when the application is restored. Once the sample application is restored and running, the screen should display construction times of several seconds ago, depending on how long you took to switch back to the application. The navigation time should reset to 0 again, because `OnNavigatedTo` is called when returning to the application. The right side of figure 3.3 shows the user interface after the restart.

In this section you added code to track when the `App` and `MainPage` classes are constructed. The classes are constructed when the application is first launched and aren't necessarily constructed when the application returns from dormancy. Later in the chapter, we show situations where the operating system tombstones an application, and the `App` and `MainPage` classes are constructed again when the application is reactivated.

Fortunately, the Windows Phone framework provides the lifetime events to determine when an application is created during initial launch and when the application classes are re-created upon application reactivation.

Figure 3.3 Lifetime application after initial construction (left) and restart (right)

3.2.2 First-time initialization

When a user taps an application's icon on the phone's Application List, a new instance of the application is launched. If an existing instance of the application is currently dormant, it's removed in favor of the new instance. Other triggers that create a new instance of an application include the user tapping an application or secondary tile in the Start Screen, tapping the details section of an alarm or reminder, and using the hub extension points. (See chapter 4 for details on alarms and reminders and chapter 9 for hub extension points.) Later in the chapter, you'll learn how to use fast application resume to prevent a dormant application from being replaced by a new instance.

The first time an application instance runs, the `Launching` event is raised. When a dormant application resumes, the `Launching` event isn't raised. Because the `Launching` event is raised only once in an application's lifetime, the *`Launching` event handler* makes an ideal method for performing application initialization tasks.

> **NOTE** "App certification requirements for Windows Phone" (http://mng.bz/Fefo) requires that the first page be shown in less than 5 seconds and must be responsive to user input in less than 20 seconds.

The Lifetime sample application doesn't have any initialization requirements other than to record the time when the `Launching` event is raised, which you capture in another automatic property of the `App` class. Open the App.xaml.cs file and add a new `LaunchedTime` property:

```
public DateTime LaunchedTime { get; private set; }
```

You assign the property's value in the `Launching` event handler. You learned earlier in this chapter that the event handler was automatically generated with the name `Application_Launching` by the project template. Find the generated method and assign the current time to the `LaunchedTime` property:

```
private void Application_Launching(object sender, LaunchingEventArgs e)
{
    LaunchedTime = DateTime.Now;
}
```

The `Application_Launching` method is where you might put additional code that should only run once in the lifetime of an application. Be careful when performing tasks inside the `Launching` event handler. The `Launching` event is raised before the `MainPage` is created and initialized. Work performed in the event handler increases the amount of time before the application is ready to receive user input. If the delay is too long, the operating system will terminate the application.

Now that you have the launch time recorded, you can update `MainPage` to display the value. Add another two `TextBlock` controls to MainPage.xaml:

```
<TextBlock Grid.Row="1" Text="Application launched:" />
<TextBlock x:Name="launched" Grid.Row="1" Grid.Column="1"
    Text="{Binding StringFormat='\{0:N0\} seconds ago'}" />
```

Add a line to `UpdateUserInterface` to copy the value from the `App` property to the `TextBlock` control named `launched`:

```
launched.DataContext = (now - app.LaunchedTime).TotalSeconds;
```

With this code in place, run the application. You have a new line in the user interface showing the launch time. At this point, showing the launch time doesn't seem interesting. The launch time is nearly exactly the same value as the construction times. When we discuss tombstoned applications later in the chapter, you'll see situations where the launch time is greater than the construction times.

Before we can discuss tombstoning, we need to talk about what happens when the operating system deactivates, and later reactivates, an application.

3.3 Switching applications

When the user leaves an application using the Start button, the operating system pauses the application, putting the application's process into a dormant state. Other actions that cause an application to go dormant include using launchers and choosers, tapping a notification, or using the Task Switcher to change to another application.

There are situations where a dormant application is terminated but remains on the Task Switcher's back stack. This process is called *tombstoning*. When the application enters a tombstoned state, its physical process is terminated to save system resources, but its state is maintained by the operating system in volatile memory. Powering off the device or exhausting the battery has the effect of losing all the states maintained in the memory.

In this section you'll add features to the Lifetime sample application that detect and handle going dormant and being tombstoned.

3.3.1 Going dormant

When an application is dormant, the operating system stops all running threads, unhooks sensors, and stops any timers. The application is kept in memory and placed on the top of the stack of applications shown in the Task Switcher, and is accessible using the Back button. Figure 3.4 shows the Task Switcher with the Lifetime application in the middle of the stack.

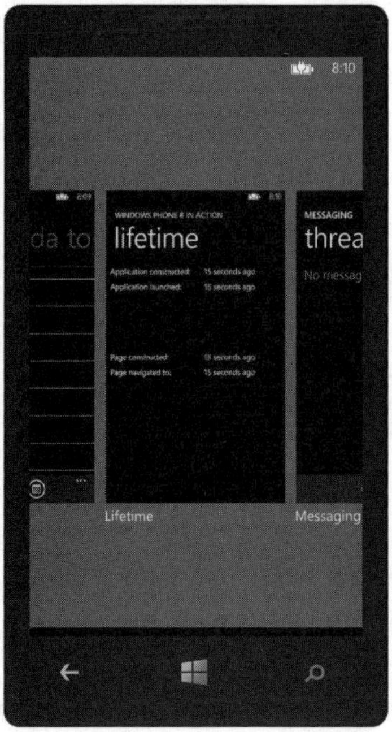

Figure 3.4 The dormant Lifetime application shown in the Task Switcher

Only a limited number of applications are kept in the back stack, including the currently running application. If there are already too many applications in the back stack when a new application is started, the dormant application at the bottom of the stack is terminated. Once terminated, the application is removed from memory, and any transient data used by the application is lost. The user can no longer navigate to the dormant application.

The operating system doesn't notify the dormant application when it's terminated. If you have any data that must be persisted to long-term storage, you must save it before or during deactivation. We discuss local long-term storage options in chapter 7.

ADDING THE DEACTIVATEDTIME PROPERTY

The sample application doesn't have any data-storage requirements, other than to capture the time when the `Deactivated` event is raised in a property of the `App` class. Open the App.xaml.cs file and add a new `DeactivatedTime` property:

```
public DateTime DeactivatedTime { get; private set; }
```

You assign the property's value in the `Deactivated` event handler that was generated by the project template. The event handler was generated with the name `Application_Deactivated`. Find the generated method and assign the current time to the `DeactivatedTime` property:

```
private void Application_Deactivated(object sender, DeactivatedEventArgs e)
{
    DeactivatedTime = DateTime.Now;
}
```

The `MainPage` class also offers a hook to catch when the application is losing focus. The `OnNavigatingFrom` and `OnNavigatedFrom` override methods are called even when the operating system is navigating away from a running application.

RECORDING THE TIME OF THE NAVIGATION EVENT

Your sample application will record when the `OnNavigatedFrom` method is called with a new `MainPage` field named `navigatedFromTime`:

```
DateTime navigatedFromTime;
```

Override the `OnNavigatedFrom` method and assign the new field with the current time. You only want to record the current time when navigating away from the application. You can determine whether the navigation target is external to your application by checking the `IsNavigationInitiator` property of the `NavigationEventArgs` parameter. The `IsNavigationInitiator` will be `false` if leaving the application:

```
protected override void OnNavigatedFrom(NavigationEventArgs e)
{
    if (!e.IsNavigationInitiator)
    {
        navigatedFromTime = DateTime.Now;
    }
    base.OnNavigatedFrom(e);
}
```

The `IsNavigationInitiator` will be `false` anytime you're leaving the application, including when the user is closing the application using the Back button.

DISPLAYING THE DEACTIVATION AND NAVIGATION TIMES IN THE UI

You need to show the new times in the user interface by adding four new `TextBlock` controls and modifying the `UpdateUserInterface` method. Open MainPage.xaml and add two `TextBlock` labels and two `TextBlock` controls named `deactivated` and `navigatedFrom`:

```
<TextBlock Grid.Row="2" Text="Application deactivated:" />
<TextBlock x:Name="deactivated" Grid.Row="2" Grid.Column="1"
    Text="{Binding StringFormat='\{0:N0\} seconds ago'}" />
<TextBlock Grid.Row="7" Text="Page navigated from:" />
<TextBlock x:Name="navigatedFrom" Grid.Row="7" Grid.Column="1"
    Text="{Binding StringFormat='\{0:N0\} seconds ago'}" />
```

Modify the `UpdateUserInterface` method in MainPage.xaml.cs to assign the `DataContext` properties:

```
if (navigatedFromTime != DateTime.MinValue)
    navigatedFrom.DataContext = (now - navigatedFromTime).TotalSeconds;
if (app.DeactivatedTime != DateTime.MinValue)
    deactivated.DataContext = (now - app.DeactivatedTime).TotalSeconds;
```

In this code snippet, you check whether the time values are equal to `DateTime.MinValue`. `DateTime.MinValue` is the default value for a `DateTime` variable, and you don't want to show a value on the screen if the variable still equals its default value.

TESTING THE APPLICATION

You're ready to run the application. At first launch you can see the new `TextBlock` controls, and they don't display any values because you haven't deactivated the application. Press the Start button, wait a few seconds, and press the Back button. When the application restarts, you should now see values displayed in the `deactivated` and `navigatedFrom` controls.

You have one more event to look at: the `Activated` event, which is raised when the application restarts and returns to action.

3.3.2 *Returning to action*

When an application is dormant, the user can return to it by tapping the Back button one or more times or by selecting the application in the Task Switcher. When a dormant application is reactivated, threads are restarted, and the `PhoneApplicationService` raises the `Activated` event. Because the application was never removed from memory, the `App` and `MainPage` instances are preserved and don't need to be reconstructed.

> **NOTE** Microsoft recommends that a dormant application be ready for user input within one second after being reactivated.

It's possible that a dormant application may never return to a running state. The operating system may terminate the application if other applications are started. If the user taps an application or secondary tile in the Start Screen or the application's icon in the

Application List, a new instance of the application will be launched, and the dormant instance will be lost forever, unless the application supports fast application resume.

RECORD AND DISPLAY THE TIME AT ACTIVATION

As with the other lifetime events, you need to record the time the event occurred in a property of the `App` class. Create a new property named `ActivatedTime` and assign the property value in the `Application_Activated` method:

```
public DateTime ActivatedTime { get; private set; }
private void Application_Activated(object sender, ActivatedEventArgs e)
{
    ActivatedTime = DateTime.Now;
}
```

Add two more `TextBlock` controls to MainPage.xaml to display the recorded time:

```
<TextBlock Grid.Row="3" Text="Application activated:" />
<TextBlock x:Name="activated" Grid.Row="3" Grid.Column="1"
    Text="{Binding StringFormat='\{0:N0\} seconds ago'}" />
```

Modify the `UpdateUserInterface` method to assign the `DataContext` property of the new `TextBlock` control:

```
if (app.ActivatedTime != DateTime.MinValue)
    activated.DataContext = (now - app.ActivatedTime).TotalSeconds;
```

Dormant applications maintain most of their application data and state. When dormant applications are reactivated, there's usually little work to do. There are situations—for example, when using the sensor APIs—when additional steps are required during activation. We identify these special scenarios in later chapters. You'll read about one such scenario when working with the camera in chapter 8.

We need to discuss one other reactivation process. In certain situations the operating system will tombstone a dormant application to free up system resources. A *tombstoned* application is a dormant application that has been terminated, while remaining on the Task Switcher back stack. Application developers need to write special code to save and restore application state during the tombstoning process.

3.3.3 *Tombstoning*

Windows Phone tombstones an application whenever system resources become scarce. To allow developers the ability to test tombstone recovery code, Microsoft provides an option in the project's properties to force the operating system to tombstone an application. Figure 3.5 shows the tombstone option.

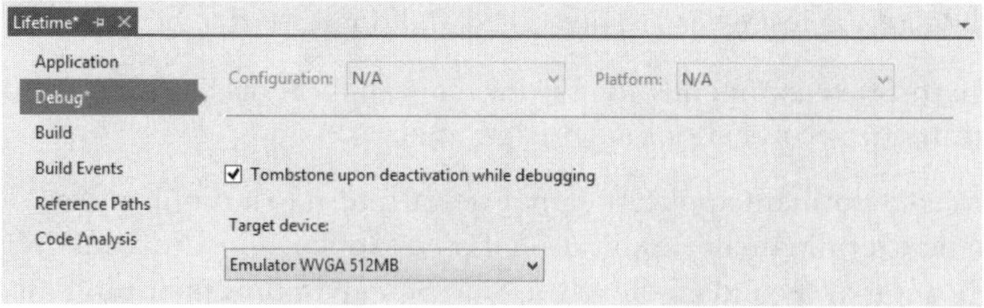

Figure 3.5 The tombstone debugging option in the Project Properties page

Enable tombstoning in the Lifetime sample project properties and debug the application. Debugging the application is important because the tombstone option doesn't apply when the application is run outside the debugger. The constructed and launched times should look normal. Press the Start button, wait a few seconds, and press the Back button. The times displayed in the user interface should look weird, as shown in figure 3.6. The construction and activated times look normal, but the launch time isn't right. Note that the deactivated and navigated from times are still at 0, even though you did navigate away from this page.

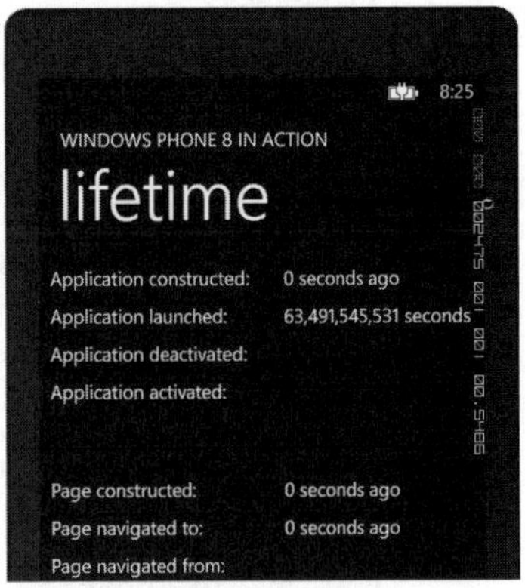

Figure 3.6 The Lifetime sample application after being reactivated from a tombstoned state. The weird value for the launched time is due to `LaunchedTime` defaulting to `DateTime.MinValue`.

Note that the construction times are 0 seconds ago. The operating system destroyed the instances of the `App` and `MainPage` classes that were in memory. When you pressed the Back button, new instances were created. You lost the values that had been stored in the `App` and `MainPage` properties. Some of these runtime values don't need to be saved, but others, like `DeactivatedTime`, `LaunchedTime`, and `navigatedFromTime`, are lost if you don't store them.

The Windows Phone application framework provides applications with two mechanisms for storing data that should be restored after tombstoning. The process to save and restore the state requires minimum work by the developer, detailed in this section.

RETURNING TOMBSTONED APPLICATIONS TO LIFE

When a dormant application is returned to life, the `PhoneApplicationService` raises the `Activated` event. The `Activated` event is also raised when a tombstoned application is returned to life. The `ActivatedEventArgs` class provides a `boolean IsApplicationInstancePreserved` property to allow developers the ability to distinguish between dormant and tombstoned reactivation. You'll show the value of this property on the user interface alongside the event times. You need to add a new `nullable boolean` property to the `App` class to record the `IsApplicationInstancePreserved` value provided by the event args. Assign a value to the new property in the `Application_Activated` method:

```
public bool? IsApplicationInstancePreserved { get; private set; }
private void Application_Activated(object sender, ActivatedEventArgs e)
{
    ActivatedTime = DateTime.Now;
    IsApplicationInstancePreserved = e.IsApplicationInstancePreserved;
}
```

Modify MainPage.xaml to add controls to display the value:

```
<TextBlock Grid.Row="4" Text="App Instance Preserved:" />
<TextBlock x:Name="instancePreserved" Grid.Row="4" Grid.Column="1" />
```

Modify the `UpdateUserInterface` method in MainPage.xaml.cs to assign the `Text` property of the `instancePreserved` `TextBlock`:

```
instancePreserved.Text = app.IsApplicationInstancePreserved.ToString();
```

Debug the application now and you should see a blank in the new control because the `nullable` `boolean` property defaults to `null`. Press the Start button to navigate away and then return to the application using the Back button. You should now see the word *False* in the `instancePreserved` `TextBlock`. If you run the application outside the debugger and perform the same steps, the `TextBlock` should display the word *True*.

METHOD 1: PERSISTING RUNTIME APPLICATION DATA

Now that you know how to detect when the application has been tombstoned, how do you save the `DeactivatedTime`, `LaunchedTime`, and `navigatedFromTime` values? The first facility for persisting application data is the `State` property exposed on the `PhoneApplicationService`. The *`State`* property is a dictionary of key-value pairs and will hold any object that can be serialized. Information should be placed into the `State` dictionary when the application is being deactivated. Modify the `Application_Deactivated` method to store the `DeactivatedTime` and `LaunchedTime` in the `State` dictionary:

```
private void Application_Deactivated(object sender, DeactivatedEventArgs e)
{
    DeactivatedTime = DateTime.Now;
    PhoneApplicationService.Current.State["DeactivatedTime"]
        = DeactivatedTime;
    PhoneApplicationService.Current.State["LaunchingTime"] = LaunchedTime;
}
```

Application data stored in the `State` dictionary can be restored in the `Activation` event handler. Update the `Application_Activated` method to restore the `Deactivated-Time` and `LaunchedTime` values. The following listing shows the new `Application_Activated` method.

Listing 3.5 Restoring tombstoned application data

```
private void Application_Activated(object sender, ActivatedEventArgs e)
{
    ActivatedTime = DateTime.Now;
    IsApplicationInstancePreserved = e.IsApplicationInstancePreserved;
    if (!e.IsApplicationInstancePreserved)            // 1 Was app tombstoned?
    {
        if (PhoneApplicationService.Current.State.
            ContainsKey("DeactivatedTime"))
        {
            DeactivatedTime = (DateTime)PhoneApplicationService.Current.   // 2 Restore DeactivatedTime
                State["DeactivatedTime"];
        }
        if (PhoneApplicationService.Current.State.
            ContainsKey("LaunchingTime"))
        {
```

```
                LaunchedTime = (DateTime)PhoneApplicationService.Current.       ❸ Restore
                    State["LaunchingTime"];                                        LaunchedTime
            }
        }
    }
```

The DeactivatedTime and LaunchedTime values should be restored only when recovering from a tombstoned state. You read from the State dictionaries only when IsApplicationInstancePreserved is false ❶. Ask the State dictionary whether it contains a value for the key DeactivatedTime. If the key exists, assign the value in the dictionary to the DeactivatedTime property ❷. Do the same check and assign operation for LaunchedTime ❸.

METHOD 2: PERSISTING RUNTIME APPLICATION DATA

The second facility for persisting runtime application data is another State dictionary provided by the PhoneApplicationPage. Because PhoneApplicationPage is the base class for MainPage, you can store MainPage's runtime data separate from the App class's runtime data. The only MainPage data you need to store is the navigatedFromTime. Update the OnNavigatedFrom method to store the navigatedFromTime right after assigning the variable:

```
protected override void OnNavigatedFrom(NavigationEventArgs e)
{
    if (!e.IsNavigationInitiator))
    {
        navigatedFromTime = DateTime.Now;
        State["NavigatedFromTime"] = navigatedFromTime;
    }
    base.OnNavigatedFrom(e);
}
```

The sample application writes data to the State dictionary during the OnNavigatedFrom method, but you don't have to wait until OnNavigatedFrom is called. The State dictionary can be accessed anytime during or after OnNavigatedTo and before or during OnNavigatedFrom. Objects stored in either of the State dictionaries must be serializable.

RESTORING RUNTIME APPLICATION DATA

The navigatedFromTime is restored in the OnNavigatedTo method. The new and improved OnNavigatedTo method is shown in the following listing.

Listing 3.6 Restoring navigatedFromTime

```
protected override void OnNavigatedTo(NavigationEventArgs e)
{
    navigatedToTime = DateTime.Now;
    var app = (App)Application.Current;
    bool appInstancePreserved =                                  ❶ Check for tombstone
        app.IsApplicationInstancePreserved ?? true;
    if (!appInstancePreserved && State.ContainsKey("NavigatedFromTime"))
    {
```

```
        navigatedFromTime = (DateTime)State["NavigatedFromTime"];
    }
    base.OnNavigatedTo(e);
}
```

Restore navigatedFromTime ❷

The only way to determine whether you're resuming from a tombstoned state is via the `IsApplicationInstancePreserved` property of the `ActivatedEventArgs` passed with the `Activated` event. You stored the `IsApplicationInstancePreserved` value in a property of the `App` class, which you use to determine whether the application is resuming from a tombstoned state ❶. If it was tombstoned, and the `State` dictionary contains the `NavigatedFromTime` key, then you assign the value stored in the dictionary to the `navigatedFromTime` field ❷.

NOTE In case you're not familiar with it, C#'s `??` operator, called the *null-coalescing operator*, is used to assign a default value to a variable. In listing 3.6, if the `app.IsApplicationInstancePreserved` property is `null`, the `appInstancePreserved` variable will be assigned the value after the `??` operator, which is `true` in this example.

Debug the application again, press the Start button, wait a few seconds, and press the Back button. The times displayed in the user interface should look almost normal this time. Note that the launching and navigated from times are farther in the past than the construction times. This is expected because the `App` and `MainPage` instances were re-created when the application was activated, but the launching and navigated from times were saved in the `State` dictionaries.

We've demonstrated a couple of procedures for saving a restore application and page state when the operating system reactivates your application. It's important that the save and restore routines execute reasonably quickly, because the operating system will kill any application that takes longer than 10 seconds to respond to `Activated` or `Deactivated` events.

The `Launching`, `Activated`, and `Deactivated` events are all notifications that the application is transitioning into or out of a running state. The last two events we'll look at, `Obscured` and `Unobscured`, are notifications that the application screen is partially or fully hidden, but that the application remains in the running state.

3.4 Out of sight

As you design applications for a phone, you must prepare for situations when the operating system will notify the user about an incoming call or a message. This situation is called *obscuration*, and in practice this is a partial or full coverage of an application made by a native application. Your application will also be obscured when an alarm or reminder is triggered and, in special circumstances, when the phone's Lock Screen is activated. In this section we'll examine how to detect when an application is obscured and then discuss the special circumstances surrounding the Lock Screen.

3.4.1 Obscuration

The event raised when the application gets covered is called `Obscured`, and the event raised when the application is again fully visible is called `Unobscured`. Both these events belong to the `PhoneApplicationFrame` class, and the developer has to explicitly add handlers for these events because they're not automatically generated by the Visual Studio wizard.

Many applications aren't affected by obscuration and can ignore the obscuration events. Other applications are more sensitive. An application that plays video may want to pause playback and then resume when the screen is no longer obscured. A game should pause game play and/or game timers so a user isn't penalized when the screen is inaccessible.

ADDING EVENT HANDLERS FOR OBSCURATION

The `App` class defines the only `PhoneApplicationFrame` instance as the static member variable called `RootFrame`. The following listing shows how to wire up and implement the event handlers in the `MainPage` class.

Listing 3.7 Adding `Obscured` and `Unobscured` event handlers

```
DateTime obscuredTime;                          ❶ Define new fields
DateTime unobscuredTime;

public MainPage()
{
    InitializeComponent();
    App.RootFrame.Obscured += RootFrame_Obscured;          ❷ Subscribe to events
    App.RootFrame.Unobscured += RootFrame_Unobscured;
...
}

void RootFrame_Obscured(object sender, ObscuredEventArgs e)
{
    obscuredTime = DateTime.Now;
}                                                          ❸ Update obscuration times

void RootFrame_Unobscured(object sender, EventArgs e)
{
    unobscuredTime = DateTime.Now;
}
```

Two new fields are added to the `MainPage` class ❶ to store the time when the `Obscured` and `Unobscured` events are raised. The events are wired up in the `MainPage` constructor ❷. The `App` class's `RootFrame` property is used to access the `PhoneApplicationFrame` instance. In each of the event handlers, the time is assigned to the appropriate field, and the user interface is updated to show the new times ❸.

We leave it as an exercise for the reader to modify `UpdateUserInterface` so that `obscuredTime` and `unobscuredTime` values are displayed in new user interface

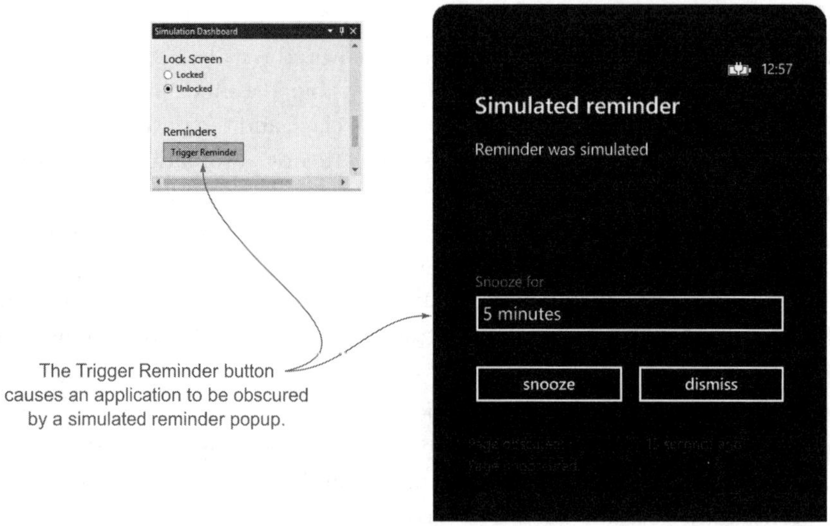

Figure 3.7 The sample application obscured by a reminder. The reminder was triggered using the Simulation Dashboard.

controls. *Hint:* You should add four `TextBlocks` to MainPage.xaml and assign their `Text` property in the `UpdateUserInterface` method. Once you've added the appropriate code to `UpdateUserInterface`, launch the application and observe the new behavior. To trigger an obscuration event in the emulator, you can either show the Task Switcher or use the Simulation Dashboard (see figure 3.7) to trigger a reminder or lock the screen. You read about the Simulation Dashboard in chapter 1.

In this section we've demonstrated how an application becomes dormant when the user presses the Start button. Another scenario that pauses a running application is when the phone is locked and the Lock Screen is activated. An application isn't required to go dormant when the phone is locked and may choose to remain running behind the Lock Screen.

3.4.2 Running behind the Lock Screen

All Windows Phones have a Lock button used to lock the phone and power off the device. A phone will also automatically lock after a specified timeout period in which the phone remains idle. The screen timeout duration is specified in the Lock Screen page of the Settings application. The phone is considered idle when the user hasn't tapped the touch screen.

When the phone is locked, the running application transitions to a dormant state. To see this in action, run the application and lock the screen using the Lock button on a physical device or the Simulation Dashboard with the emulator. When you unlock the screen, you'll find that the application was deactivated while the screen was locked and then reactivated when the screen was unlocked. Note that the `ActivatedTime` is reset to 0 seconds ago. This is a feature of the operating system intended to save battery life.

IDLE DETECTION MODE AND OBSCURATION

The `PhoneApplicationService` provides the `ApplicationIdleDetectionMode` property to allow applications to continue to run once the phone is locked. When an application wants to run under the Lock Screen, the `ApplicationIdleDetectionMode` property is assigned the value `IdleDetectionMode.Disabled`. Once idle detection mode is disabled, it can't be re-enabled. An attempt to re-enable idle detection will result in an exception.

> **NOTE** "App certification requirements for Windows Phone" places certain restrictions on applications that run behind the Lock Screen. Once the screen is locked, the application should no longer attempt to update the user interface and should disable all timers. The battery must be able to power the phone for 120 hours while the application is running under the Lock Screen.

An application is notified when the phone is locked via the `Obscured` event. The `Obscured` event handler passes an argument of type `ObscuredEventArgs`. `ObscuredEventArgs` contains a `boolean` property named `IsLocked`. When `IsLocked` is `true`, the application is running behind the Lock Screen.

LETTING USERS CHOOSE TO RUN THE APPLICATION BEHIND THE LOCK SCREEN

A good application will inform the user that it runs behind the Lock Screen. A better application will allow the user to choose whether the application runs behind the Lock Screen. Modify the Lifetime sample application to provide the user the ability to enable running behind the Lock Screen via a `ToggleSwitch` control. The `ToggleSwitch` is one of the controls left out of the Windows Phone SDK but implemented by the Windows Phone Toolkit introduced in the last chapter. The Windows Phone Toolkit is a set of user interface components that mimic controls seen in the native Windows Phone user interface but not provided with the SDK. The toolkit is available for free from CodePlex (http://phone.codeplex.com) and can be added to your project with the NuGet Package Manager. When working with toolkit components in XAML, you need to include an XML namespace declaration in your XAML page:

```
xmlns:toolkit="clr-namespace:Microsoft.Phone.Controls;
➥ assembly=Microsoft.Phone.Controls.Toolkit"
```

TOGGLESWITCH COMPARED TO TOGGLEBUTTON

The `ToggleSwitch` control is a component used to represent a choice to a user and is similar to the `CheckBox` and `RadioButton` controls, which derive from `ToggleButton`. The `ToggleSwitch` has a Boolean `IsChecked` property and raises `Click`, `Check`, `Indeterminate`, and `Uncheck` events. Even though `ToggleSwitch` has an interface similar to `ToggleButton`, it doesn't derive from `ToggleButton`.

One place where `ToggleSwitch` differs from `ToggleButton` is the lack of the `IsThreeState` property. The `ToggleSwitch.IsChecked` property can be set to a `null` value, and the `Indeterminate` event will be raised, but the user interface will look as if the `IsChecked` value is `false`.

Another difference between ToggleButton and ToggleSwitch is how the Content property is used. In a ToggleButton, the Content property is used for label text. In ToggleSwitch, the Content property is used as another way to render the IsChecked property. When the IsChecked property is true, the Content property displays the word *On*, which you can see in figure 3.8. The word *Off* is displayed when IsChecked is false or null.

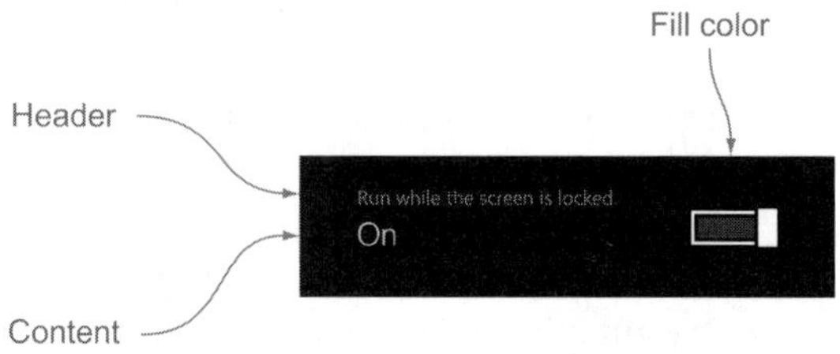

Figure 3.8 The ToggleSwitch control from the Windows Phone Toolkit

If the Content property is used to display On/Off, you might be wondering how you specify label text for a ToggleSwitch. The ToggleSwitch exposes the Header property to add label text to a ToggleSwitch. The switch's fill color is normally the color specified in the PhoneAccentBrush resource. The label text in the Header is normally rendered using the PhoneBorderBrush theme resource. The PhoneForegroundBrush theme resource is used to render the On/Off text in the Content. The ToggleSwitch provides the SwitchForeground property to allow the developer to specify a new color. The Foreground property controls the color of the On/Off text. Changing the Header text color isn't so easy.

ADDING TOGGLESWITCH TO MAINPAGE.XAML

Now that you know a little bit about the ToggleSwitch, add one to the ContentPanel in MainPage.xaml:

```
<toolkit:ToggleSwitch x:Name="lockscreen"
   Header="Run while the screen is locked." Grid.Row="10"
   Grid.ColumnSpan="2" Checked="lockscreen_Checked"/>
```

The ToggleSwitch's IsChecked property defaults to False. The Checked event is wired up to an event handler called lockscreen_Checked. Inside the event handler, set the ApplicationIdleDetectionMode to Disabled:

```
void lockscreen_Checked(object sender, RoutedEventArgs e)
{
    PhoneApplicationService.Current.ApplicationIdleDetectionMode
        = IdleDetectionMode.Disabled;
}
```

Because the ApplicationIdleDetectionMode property can't be re-enabled, a line of code is added to UpdateUserInterface to disable the ToggleSwitch when idle detection is disabled.

```
lockscreen.IsEnabled =
   PhoneApplicationService.Current.ApplicationIdleDetectionMode ==
      IdleDetectionMode.Enabled;
```

To adhere to the certification requirements restricting the use of timers while the phone is locked, the timer must be disabled in the `Obscured` event handler and re-enabled in the `Unobscured` event handler, as shown in the following listing.

Listing 3.8 Controlling the timer in adherence to the certification requirements

```
void RootFrame_Obscured(object sender, ObscuredEventArgs e)
{
    obscuredTime = DateTime.Now;
    if (e.IsLocked)                          ❶ Stop timer when
        timer.Stop();                          phone is locked
}

void RootFrame_Unobscured(object sender, EventArgs e)
{
    unobscuredTime = DateTime.Now;           ❷ Restart timer
    timer.Start();
}
```

The `IsLocked` property of the `ObscuredEventArgs` is set to `true` when the Lock Screen is enabled. Because the `Obscured` event can be triggered by a number of different scenarios, the `IsLocked` property is examined before stopping the timer ❶. When the unobscured event is triggered, the timer is restarted ❷.

To see how the new code changes the behavior of the Lifetime sample application, run the application and tap the new `ToggleSwitch`. Lock the phone, wait a few seconds, and unlock the phone. The user interface should show blanks for the `Deactivated` and `Activated` event times and show values for `Obscured` and `Unobscured` times.

Up to this point in the chapter, you've learned how to detect when your application is switched from the foreground to the background. The Lifetime sample application demonstrated the various events raised when an application is launched, deactivated, activated, or closed. We've shown you how and when to save application state and quickly recover when your application is switched back to the foreground using the Task Switcher or the Back button.

In the next section you'll learn how an application can quickly resume in those situations when the user re-launches the application from the Start Screen, Application List, or one of the various extension mechanisms provided by Windows Phone.

3.5 Fast application resume

Fast application switching does a pretty good job of balancing limited operating system resources with application performance. When a user navigates away from an application, the application is placed into a dormant mode and can be quickly reactivated, provided the user follows the necessary steps. But users often do their own thing and expect the application to work. This means a user may try to return to a dormant application using the Start Screen instead of the task switcher and will be frustrated when the application isn't in the same state it was when they left it.

You can experience this for yourself by launching the Lifetime sample application, pressing the Start button, switching to the application, and then re-launching the application by tapping its icon in the list. You should notice that all the application and page times have been reset to 0.

ENABLING FAST APPLICATION RESUME

Microsoft's solution to this frustrating user experience is *fast application resume.* When a dormant application supports fast application resume, the operating system will reactivate it instead of launching a brand-new instance. Applications generated by the Visual Studio project templates don't support fast application resume by default. Enabling fast application resume is simple and consists of setting the `ActivationPolicy` attribute of the `DefaultTask` element in the WMAppManifest.xml file. The file must be opened with the XML editor because the manifest editor doesn't provide access to the activation policy. To open the file with the XML editor, right-click the file in the Solution Explorer and select Open With from the context menu. Then select XML (Text) Editor from the list. Once you have the file open, add the `ActivationPolicy` attribute and set its value to `Resume`:

```
<Tasks>
   <DefaultTask Name="_default" NavigationPage="MainPage.xaml"
      ActivationPolicy="Resume" />
</Tasks>
```

After making this change in the Lifetime sample application, execute the previous workflow to launch, switch away, and re-launch the application. This time you should notice that application and pages times were not reset to 0. With fast application switching, the `Launched`, `Activated`, `Deactivated`, and `Closing` lifetime events are used by an application to properly handle switching scenarios. With fast application resume, an application uses navigation modes to properly handle resume scenarios.

3.5.1 *Navigation modes*

In chapter 2 you learned that Windows Phone applications are XAML navigation applications. Behind the scenes, the application host calls the *Navigation Service* directly to navigate to MainPage.xaml during initial launch, and when an application is reactivated, the application host navigates directly to the active page's XAML. Pages and other XAML controls detect navigation events through their `OnNavigatedTo`, `OnNavigatingFrom`, and `OnNavigatedFrom` methods. The event argument types sent to each of these methods (`NavigationEventArgs` and `NavigatingCancelEventArgs`) contain a property named `NavigationMode` of type `System.Windows.Navigation.NavigationMode`. The possible values of the `NavigationMode` property are listed in table 3.2.

Table 3.2 `NavigationMode` values

Navigation mode	Description
`Back`	Navigation initiated with the Back button or the Navigation Service's `GoBack` method. Also used when returning to a dormant application via the Back button or the Task Switcher.
`Forward`	Navigation initiated with the Navigation Service's `GoForward` method.

Table 3.2 `NavigationMode` values *(continued)*

Navigation mode	Description
`New`	Navigation initiated with the Navigation Service's `Navigate` method. Also used when the application is first launched or when a dormant application is re-launched to a new page or URI.
`Refresh`	Used when re-launching a dormant application to an already active page or URI.
`Reset`	Used when re-launching a dormant application via the Start Screen, Application List, or other extension mechanism.

When an application supports fast application resume, re-launching an application results in a two-step navigation process. First, the application receives a set of navigation events with the `NavigationMode` value of `Reset`. This informs the application that it's being restarted from a dormant state. The second step of the process depends on the currently active page and the URI used to launch the application, as shown in figure 3.9.

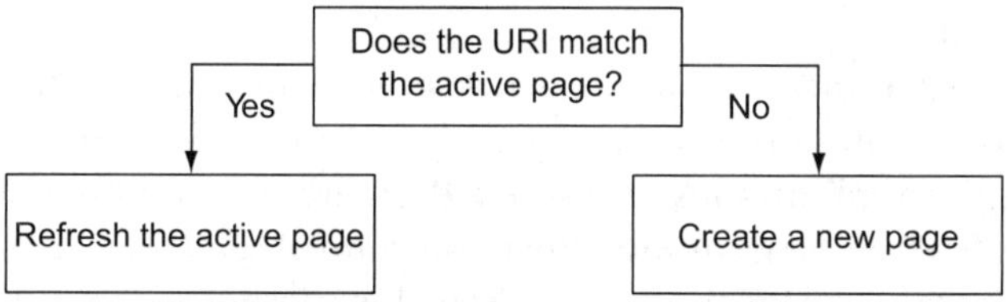

Figure 3.9 The default fast application workflow. If the launch URI matches the active page's URI, the active page is refreshed; otherwise a new page is created.

When the launch URI matches the URI of the active page, the application raises a set of navigation events with a `NavigationMode` of `Refresh`. This is the scenario in the Lifetime sample application. MainPage.xaml is the only page, and when launched from the application list, the launch URI is /MainPage.xaml. To examine the behavior when the launch URI doesn't match the active page, the Lifetime application needs to support alternative launch URIs.

3.5.2 *Resuming with an alternative URI*

The Hello World sample application in chapter 2 demonstrates how to pin a secondary tile to the Start Screen, which specified an alternative launch URI. The Lifetime application will implement a similar approach to launch MainPage.xaml with an alternative URI.

Open MainPage.xaml and add the following markup to create an `ApplicationBar` with a single button (or use the visual editor):

```
<phone:PhoneApplicationPage.ApplicationBar>
   <shell:ApplicationBar IsMenuEnabled="False" Mode="Minimized">
      <shell:ApplicationBarIconButton IconUri="/Assets/AppBar/favs.png"
         IsEnabled="True" Text="pin" Click="pin_Click"/>
   </shell:ApplicationBar>
</phone:PhoneApplicationPage.ApplicationBar>
```

Inside the button's click event handler, shown in the following listing, a new secondary tile will be created with a unique launch URI.

Listing 3.9 Pinning a secondary tile to the Start Screen

```
void pin_Click(object sender, EventArgs e)
{
   int count = ShellTile.ActiveTiles.Count();
   var tileData =  new FlipTileData
   {
       Title = "Lifetime",
       Count = count,
   };
   Uri launchUrl = new Uri(
      String.Format("/MainPage.xaml?context={0}",count),
      UriKind.Relative);
   ShellTile.Create(launchUrl, tileData, false);
}
```

❶ **Use count to create a unique URI**

You start by reading the count of active tiles from the `ShellTile ActiveTiles` collection. This number is used to create a new URI ❶ to MainPage.xml with a query string parameter named `context`.

After adding the button and the button's click event handler, start the sample application and tap the Pin button to add a secondary tile to the Start Screen. When the new tile is created, the application is placed in a dormant state, and the operating system navigates to the Start Screen, showing the newly pinned secondary tile. Tap the new secondary tile to re-launch the application. You should see the main page with page constructed time reset to 0 because a new instance of `MainPage` was created and existing instances of `MainPage` were cleared from the navigation stack. If you press the Start button and then press the secondary tile again, the application will re-launch, but this time the page constructed times shouldn't be reset because the URI matched the active page.

Up to this point, we haven't added any code to the sample application to support fast application resume. Between the operating system and code generated by the Windows Phone App project template, the application automatically supports a default resume workflow. Every application is different, and the resume workflow might need to be customized to provide a better user experience.

3.5.3 Customizing the resume experience

The default resume workflow provided by the operating system and generated code always navigates to the launch URI. This default workflow doesn't fix the frustrating user experience mentioned when we introduced fast application resume a few pages back. When returning to a dormant application using the primary tile or the icon in the Application List, a user expects the application to be in the same state it was in when they left it. If your application supports multiple launch URIs or internally navigates to multiple pages, the primary tile will cause your application to discard current state and re-launch the main page.

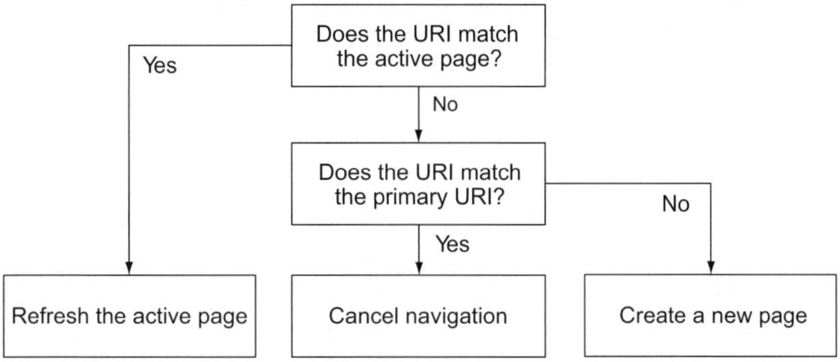

Figure 3.10 The customized fast application resume workflow for the Lifetime sample application. When the URI of the active page isn't /MainPage.xaml, and the launch URI is /MainPage.xaml, the navigation will be canceled.

CANCELING DEFAULT NAVIGATION

In this section you'll update the Lifetime application to cancel the default navigation when the user resumes the application using the primary tile. The new workflow is shown in figure 3.10.

When you created the sample application with the Windows Phone App project template, the App.xaml.cs file was generated with code to support the default fast application resume scenario. This support is implemented in the `CheckForResetNavigation` method, an event handler for the root frame's `Navigated` event. When the root frame receives a navigation event with a navigation mode value of `Reset` (when a dormant application is re-launched), the `CheckForResetNavigation` method wires up a new `Navigated` event handler to clear the navigation back stack.

To implement the customized workflow, the `CheckForResetNavigation` method in App.xaml.cs must wire up a new `Navigating` event handler, named `CancelNavigationAfterReset`, when the launch URI is /MainPage.xaml:

```
void CheckForResetNavigation(object sender, NavigationEventArgs e)
{
   if (e.NavigationMode == NavigationMode.Reset)
   {
       RootFrame.Navigated += ClearBackStackAfterReset;
       if (e.Uri.ToString() != "/MainPage.xaml")
          RootFrame.Navigating += CancelNavigationAfterReset;
   }
}
```

When a `Navigating` event is raised, the event handler can cancel the navigation by setting the event args' `Cancel` property to `true`. The `CancelNavigationAfterReset` event handler will set the `Cancel` property to `true` when the navigation mode is `New` and the target URI is equal to /MainPage.xaml:

```
void CancelNavigationAfterReset(object sender,
   NavigatingCancelEventArgs e)
{
```

```
        RootFrame.Navigating -= CancelNavigationAfterReset;
        if (e.NavigationMode == NavigationMode.New
            && e.Uri.ToString() == "/MainPage.xaml")
        {
            e.Cancel = true;
        }
    }
```

After updating `CheckForResetNavigation` and adding the implementation of the `CancelNavigationAfterReset` method, start the Lifetime application. Once it's running, press the Start button and tap the secondary tile to re-launch the application with a new URI. When the application restarts, confirm that the page constructed times are reset to 0. Press the Start button once again and make sure to use the primary tile or Application List icon to re-launch the application. This time the page constructed times shouldn't be reset, even though the application was launched with a URI different from that of the active page.

When designing the workflow for your own application, you should consider whether the application should support fast application resume and, if so, how the relaunch workflow should be customized. For each page in your application, consider what the user should experience when they leave the application and return to it from tiles on the Start Screen, Application List, or other extension mechanisms.

3.6 Summary

Throughout this chapter we've covered features of the Windows Phone that allow applications to appear to be continuously running when they're not. A continuously running application can pose a problem for a mobile device with limited resources. A running application might interfere with the power-management routines of the operating system and rapidly drain the battery. Runaway background applications steal processing power from foreground applications, resulting in a slow and unresponsive user experience.

Microsoft has designed the Windows Phone to provide the best user experience possible. The Windows Phone imposes limitations to ensure that applications can't intentionally or accidentally create performance or power problems for the user. One of these limitations prevents an application from running when it's not the foreground application.

You learned how to detect when your application is switched from the foreground to the background. The Lifetime sample application demonstrated the various events raised when an application is launched, deactivated, activated, closed, and resumed. We showed how and when to save application state and quickly recover when your application is switched back to the foreground.

You now know that a dormant background application can't perform any work. How can you create killer applications if they can't do any work in the background? The answer lies with the Scheduled Action Service. In the next chapter you'll create a new sample application to explore alarms, reminders, and background tasks—three different kinds of scheduled actions. Scheduled actions allow your application to alert the user or execute background work when your application isn't running.

4 Scheduled actions

This chapter covers

- Scheduling reminders
- Using the `DatePicker` and `TimePicker` controls
- Executing tasks with a background agent
- Integrating with the Lock Screen

You learned in the last chapter that a dormant application can't perform any work. How can you create killer applications if they can't do any work in the background? The answer lies with the Scheduled Action Service. In this chapter you'll create a sample application to explore alarms, reminders, and background tasks—three different kinds of scheduled actions. Scheduled actions allow your application to alert the user or execute background work when your application isn't running. Background agents are the mechanisms applications use to perform tasks when an application isn't running. You can use alarms and reminders to notify a user about important tasks and allow the user to easily restart an application.

As we acknowledge in chapter 3, the multitasking limitations imposed on applications may seem severe to application developers. Microsoft has imposed these limitations to ensure that the user has the best overall experience possible. Background tasks aren't allowed to affect or slow down foreground application, nor are they allowed to perform tasks that will quickly drain the phone's battery.

In this chapter you'll create a sample application named ScheduledActions, which uses the `ScheduledActionService` to schedule reminders and periodic tasks and implements an example background agent. The background agent will update the application's Live Tile, and ultimately the Lock Screen, with information about upcoming reminders.

4.1 Working on a schedule

A great number of use cases require an application to perform work on a periodic basis. This work may entail reminding the user that an online auction is about to close so they can log on and ensure they're the top bidder. Another example might be a CRM application that checks in with a web service to download new sales leads to the device.

Windows Phone empowers developers to build these types of applications with scheduled actions and the *Scheduled Action Service*. Scheduled actions are named actions that have beginning and expiration times. Once a scheduled action is registered, the Scheduled Action Service will execute the action at the appropriate time.

Two forms of scheduled actions are provided: notifications and tasks. *Notifications* consist of alarms and reminders and are displayed to the user at the appropriate time. The user can dismiss or snooze a notification and can tap the content of the notification to launch the application that created it. A *scheduled task* is nothing more than a request that the Scheduled Action Service launch an application's background agent, allowing the application to perform background processing.

In this section you'll create a new sample application that you'll use throughout the remainder of this chapter. The completed sample application is shown in figure 4.1.

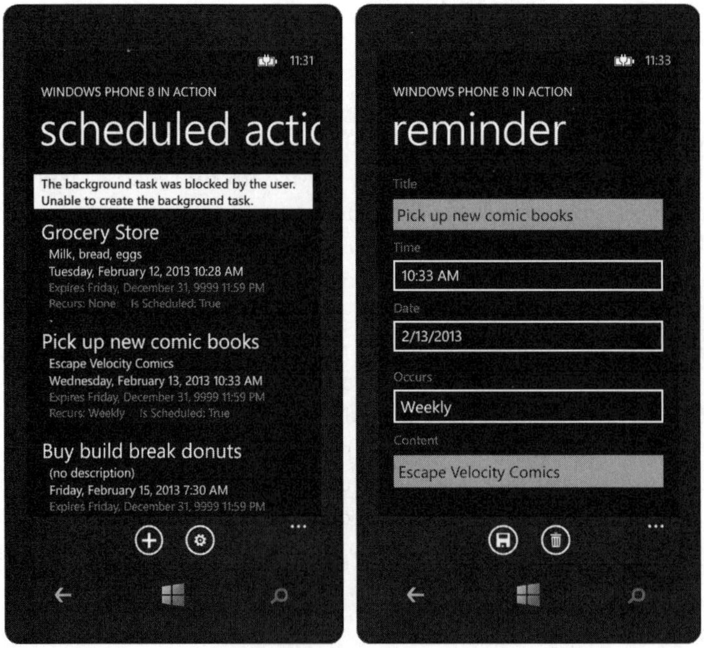

Figure 4.1 The `ScheduledActions` sample application showing three reminders and a status message indicating that the user disabled the application's background agent

The sample application will create, update, and delete scheduled actions. Later in the chapter, you'll add a background agent to the application that will monitor upcoming reminders and update the application's Live Tile and the phone's Lock Screen.

Create the new sample application using the Windows Phone App project template, name the project *ScheduledActions*, and be sure to select version 8.0 as the target operating system. Open up MainPage.xaml in the editor so that you can add the basic user interface elements displayed by the application. Start by dividing the `ContentPanel` `Grid` control into two rows:

```
<Grid x:Name="ContentPanel" Grid.Row="1" Margin="12,0,12,0">
    <Grid.RowDefinitions>
        <RowDefinition Height="Auto" />
        <RowDefinition Height="*" />
    </Grid.RowDefinitions>
</Grid>
```

You'll use the first row to display messages about the background agent later in the chapter. Add a `LongListSelector` to the second row of the `ContentPanel` (you'll add controls to display details of each notification to the `DataTemplate` later):

```
<phone:LongListSelector x:Name="notificationList" Grid.Row="1">
    <phone:LongListSelector.ItemTemplate>
        <DataTemplate>
            <StackPanel Margin="12">
            </StackPanel>
        </DataTemplate>
    </phone:LongListSelector.ItemTemplate>
</phone:LongListSelector>
```

The application displays two buttons in the `ApplicationBar`, and each button displays an image. The images used for the application bar must be added to the project. The easiest way to add images to the project is by using the application bar button property editor, because it adds the images automatically when you pick an image for the application bar button. The property editor is shown in figure 4.2.

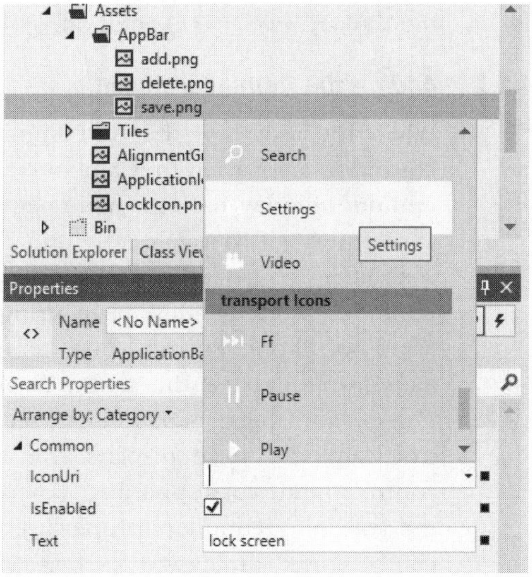

Figure 4.2 Adding an icon with the property editor. Icons included in the Windows Phone SDK appear in the popup selection list. Once an icon is selected, it's added to the /Assets/AppBar project folder.

The following listing shows the `ApplicationBar` markup for MainPage.xaml as well as the click event handlers that are called when the buttons are tapped.

Listing 4.1 `ApplicationBar` markup and click event handlers

```
<phone:PhoneApplicationPage.ApplicationBar>
   <shell:ApplicationBar >
      <shell:ApplicationBarIconButton Text="add"
         IconUri="/Assets/AppBar/add.png"
         Click="AddReminder_Click" />
      <shell:ApplicationBarIconButton Text="lock screen"
         IconUri="/Assets/AppBar/feature.settings.png"
         Click="Settings_Click" />
    </shell:ApplicationBar>
</phone:PhoneApplicationPage.ApplicationBar>
```

❶ Button image

❷ Click event handler

```
void AddReminder_Click(object sender, EventArgs e)
{
   NavigationService.Navigate(
         new Uri("/ReminderPage.xaml", UriKind.Relative));
}

void Settings_Click(object sender, EventArgs e)
{
}
```

❸ Show the reminder page

Listing 4.1 adds two buttons to the application bar. Each button uses one of the images ❶ provided by the Windows Phone SDK that's copied into your project. Each button wires up its `Click` event ❷ to an event handler in the code-behind. For the time being, add an empty implementation for `Settings_Click` to MainPage.xaml.cs. When the user taps the Add Reminder button, the application displays a new page where the user can enter the details for the reminder. The new page will be named ReminderPage.xaml and is displayed using the `NavigationService` ❸ from inside the `AddReminder_Click` method.

4.1.1 Adding the Reminder page

When the user taps the Add Reminder button, or later when they tap an existing reminder displayed on the main page, the application will navigate to a new page where the user can edit, save, and delete a reminder. Add the new page using the Windows Phone Portrait Page template and give the page the name *ReminderPage.xaml*. In figure 4.3, you can see that the Reminder page displays five input controls and corresponding labels for the various reminder properties. The controls used are `TextBox`, `TimePicker`,

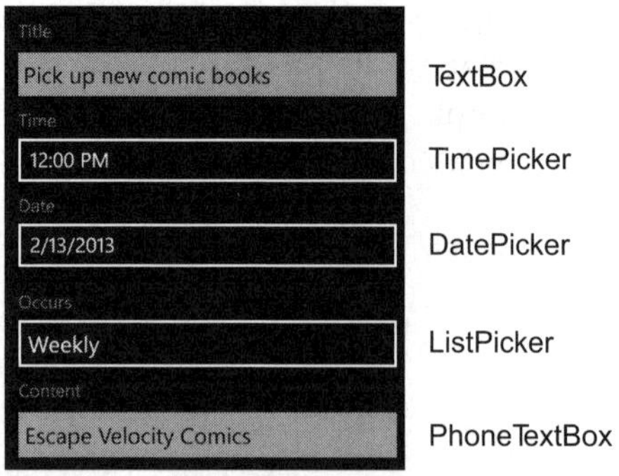

Figure 4.3 The controls used on the `ReminderPage` to edit the reminder properties. A `TextBlock` is used for the `TextBox`'s label, but the labels for the other four controls are provided through their `Header` properties.

DatePicker, ListPicker, and PhoneTextBox. All but TextBox come from the Windows Phone Toolkit.

You read about using the Windows Phone Toolkit in chapter 2. Remember that you need to use the NuGet package manager to add a reference to the toolkit before using any of its components. To add a reference to a NuGet package such as the Windows Phone Toolkit, select Project > Manage NuGet Packages. Once the Manage NuGet Packages dialog appears, type *Windows Phone Toolkit* in the Search Online input control, select the toolkit package from the search results list, and click Install.

Because ReminderPage.xaml is using toolkit components, an XML namespace declaration must be added at the top of the file:

```
xmlns:toolkit="clr-namespace:Microsoft.Phone.Controls;
➥ assembly=Microsoft.Phone.Controls.Toolkit"
```

Once the toolkit reference is added to the project, you're ready to add the input controls to the content panel of ReminderPage.xaml, as shown in the following listing.

Listing 4.2 XAML markup declaring the ContentPanel for the Reminder page

```
<StackPanel x:Name="ContentPanel"                       ❶ ContentPanel is a StackPanel
        Grid.Row="1" Margin="12,0,12,0">
    <TextBlock Style="{StaticResource PhoneTextSubtleStyle}" Text="Title" />
    <TextBox x:Name="titleBox" InputScope="Text" MaxLength="63"
        Text="{Binding Title, Mode=TwoWay}" />

    <toolkit:TimePicker x:Name="timePicker" Header="Time"
        Value="{Binding BeginTime, Mode=OneTime}" />        ❷ Bind DatePicker
    <toolkit:DatePicker x:Name="datePicker" Header="Date"      and TimePicker
        Value="{Binding BeginTime, Mode=OneTime}" />           to BeginTime

    <toolkit:ListPicker x:Name="listPicker" Header="Occurs"
        SelectedItem="{Binding RecurrenceType, Mode=TwoWay}">
    </toolkit:ListPicker>

    <TextBlock Style="{StaticResource PhoneTextSubtleStyle}"
        Text="Content" />
    <toolkit:PhoneTextBox x:Name="contentBox" MaxLength="256"
        InputScope="Text" AcceptsReturn="False" TextWrapping="Wrap"
        Hint="Enter your notes or description"
        Text="{Binding Content, Mode=TwoWay}" />
</StackPanel>
```

Start by changing the ContentPanel from a Grid to a StackPanel ❶. The page has five input controls: a TextBox, a TimePicker, a DatePicker, a ListPicker, and a PhoneTextBox. Each of these controls is bound to a property of the reminder object that will be edited by the page. Note that both the TimePicker and DatePicker are bound to the same property ❷. In order to keep the two controls from interfering with each other, the binding mode OneTime is specified in the Binding markup.

The Reminder page also needs a couple of application bar buttons to allow the user to save and delete a reminder. Add the following markup to ReminderPage.xaml:

```
<phone:PhoneApplicationPage.ApplicationBar>
```

```
    <shell:ApplicationBar >
       <shell:ApplicationBarIconButton Text="save"
          IconUri="/Assets/AppBar/save.png" Click="Save_Click" />
       <shell:ApplicationBarIconButton Text="delete"
          IconUri="/Assets/AppBar/delete.png" Click="Delete_Click" />
    </shell:ApplicationBar>
</phone:PhoneApplicationPage.ApplicationBar>
```

Because you're probably not familiar with the three different toolkit picker controls, the next couple of sections take a deeper look into how they work.

4.1.2 DatePicker and TimePicker

The native Windows Phone calendar application uses a couple of unique controls for picking date and time. The Windows Phone Toolkit provides managed implementations of these pickers with the `DatePicker` and the `TimePicker` controls. These two picker controls, shown in figure 4.4, are both composed of a button that displays the current value and a secondary page with scrolling selectors.

Both picker controls expose a `DateTime` property named `Value`. When you declare dates or times in XAML, the string is converted using the `TimeTypeConverter` class, which expects an English format. The pickers raise a `ValueChanged` event when the `Value` property is changed.

Keep in mind a couple of caveats when using the `DatePicker` and `TimePicker` controls. The first centers on the checkmark and delete icons that appear on the application bar of the secondary picker pages. The application bar requires icons to be in files shipped in the application's XAP file. You may have noticed that a new folder named Toolkit.Content was added to your project when you added the NuGet reference to the Windows Phone Toolkit. The folder contains four images, but only two of them are necessary for the date and time pickers. The necessary files are named ApplicationBar.Check.png and ApplicationBar.Cancel.png, respectively, for the checkmark and delete icons.

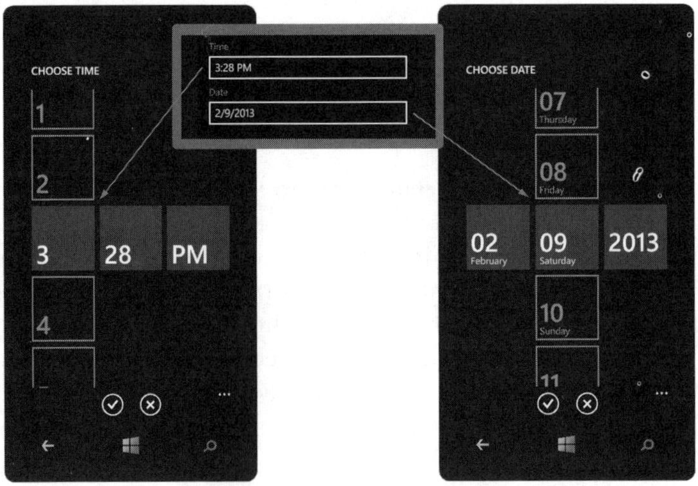

Figure 4.4 Time and date pickers provided by the Windows Phone Toolkit. The left image contains the page shown to the user when a `TimePicker` is tapped, and the right image is the corresponding page for the `DatePicker`.

The second caveat stems from how the picker controls display their secondary selector pages. When the user taps the picker, the control navigates to the secondary page. This means the page hosting the picker control is pushed onto the navigation stack, and the `OnNavigatedFrom` method override will be called. When the user returns from the selector page, the host page's `OnNavigatedTo` method override is called. You need to make sure any code you place in the page's navigation methods responds correctly when the picker's secondary pages are displayed and dismissed.

With the `DatePicker` and `TimePicker` controls, you can add features to your application so it behaves like the native phone applications. Native applications also use another type of picker to expose lists of choices to the user.

4.1.3 Making choices with the ListPicker

In other applications written for other platforms, you might use a `ComboBox` control to display a list of choices and allow the user to pick one of them. The version of `ComboBox` that comes with the Windows Phone isn't intended to be used by developers. Instead of a `ComboBox`, you should use the `ListPicker` control found in the Windows Phone Toolkit, as shown in figure 4.5.

The `ListPicker` control works differently depending on how many items are in the list that it manages. If the list has five or fewer items, the picker expands in place and displays all five items. This means you might need to put the `ContentPanel` of the

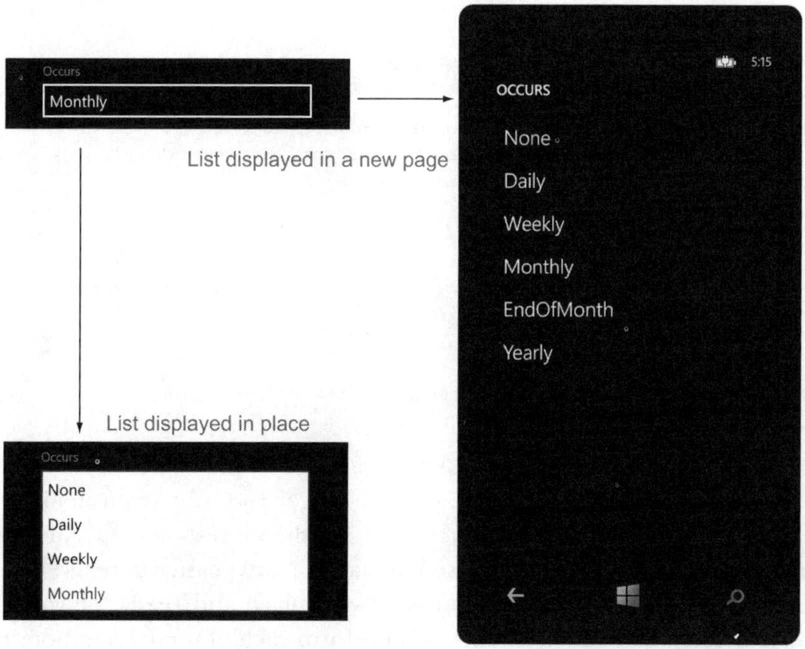

Figure 4.5 The `ListPicker` displays a list when tapped. If the list contains five or fewer items, the control is expanded in place. If the list contains more than five items, the list is shown on a new page.

page into a `ScrollViewer`—otherwise the bottom of the control might be expanded off the bottom edge of the screen.

When the list has more than five items, the `ListPicker` displays the list in a full-screen secondary page. Like the date and time pickers, the list picker will trigger navigation events when the full mode list is displayed and dismissed.

The `ListPicker` for the sample application displays six items. Each item represents one of the recurrence options available for a reminder. The six items come directly from the `RecurrenceInterval` enumeration defined in the namespace. The following snippet uses the `Enum.GetValues` method to build an array of all the possible `RecurrenceInterval` values, which is used as the `ItemsSource` of the `ListPicker`:

```
using Microsoft.Phone.Scheduler;

public ReminderPage()
{
   InitializeComponent();
   RecurrenceInterval[] values = (RecurrenceInterval[])
         Enum.GetValues(typeof(RecurrenceInterval));
   listPicker.ItemsSource = values;
}
```

Because six items are displayed in the list, the `ListPicker` displays the list using a full-mode secondary page. By default, the text used to display the full-mode list may be too small and too crowded. Providing a custom item template for a full mode list is a good idea, as shown in the following listing.

Listing 4.3 Implementing a custom full-mode item template

```
<toolkit:ListPicker x:Name="listPicker" Header="Occurs"
         SelectedItem="{Binding RecurrenceType, Mode=TwoWay}">
   <toolkit:ListPicker.FullModeItemTemplate>
      <DataTemplate>
         <Grid>
            <TextBlock Text="{Binding}"
               Margin="{StaticResource PhoneTouchTargetOverhang}"
               Style="{StaticResource PhoneTextLargeStyle}" />
         </Grid>
      </DataTemplate>
   </toolkit:ListPicker.FullModeItemTemplate>
</toolkit:ListPicker>
```

❶ Give items more room

❷ Make items larger

The `DataTemplate` used as the `FullModeItemTemplate` is simple, containing a single `TextBlock` inside a `Grid`. To provide enough finger room between items in the list, the margin uses the `PhoneTouchTargetOverhang` theme resource ❶. Another theme resource, `PhoneTextLargeStyle`, is used to make the text easier to read ❷.

The sample application's skeleton is now in place and ready for you to create, update, and delete scheduled actions. You perform each of these operations using the Scheduled Action Service.

4.2 Introducing the Scheduled Action Service

The Scheduled Action Service is implemented as a singleton by the `ScheduledActionService` class, which is found in the `Microsoft.Phone.Scheduler` namespace. The class provides methods for adding, updating, and removing scheduled actions. Scheduled actions are retrieved from the service either as a list or individually by name. Scheduled actions can only be seen and modified by the application that created them. The Scheduled Action Service doesn't expose actions created by other applications.

Scheduled actions are defined by the `ScheduledAction` class, which is the base class for both the `ScheduledNotification` class and the `ScheduledTask` class. These last two classes are base classes for other scheduled action classes we'll look at later in the chapter. Table 4.1 describes each of the properties exposed by the `ScheduledAction` class.

Table 4.1 `ScheduledAction` properties

Property name	Description
`BeginTime`	The `DateTime` when the action will be triggered for the first time. `BeginTime` must represent some point in the future when the action is scheduled.
`ExpirationTime`	The `DateTime` after which the action will no longer be triggered. `ScheduledNotification`s that have been snoozed by the user won't be triggered after the expiration time has passed. The expiration time defaults to `DateTime.MaxValue`. `ExpirationTime` must be greater than `BeginTime` when the action is scheduled.
`IsScheduled`	A read-only property, `IsScheduled` is `true` if the `ScheduledAction` will be invoked at some point in the future. `IsScheduled` is `false` if the user disables a task or dismisses a nonrecurring notification, or when the action's `ExpirationTime` has passed. Recurring notifications remain scheduled when the user dismisses the notification.
`Name`	A unique identifier for the `ScheduledAction`.

The sample application displays every scheduled notification registered with the Scheduled Action Service. The application invokes the `GetActions` method, which returns a collection of actions. The collection of actions is then displayed in the `LongListSelector` you added to MainPage.xaml. The code to retrieve the actions is added to the `OnNavigatedTo` method of `MainPage` and is shown in the following listing.

Listing 4.4 Building a list of notifications

```
using Microsoft.Phone.Scheduler;

protected override  void OnNavigatedTo(NavigationEventArgs e)
{
    List<ScheduledAction> items = new List<ScheduledAction>();
    var notifications = ScheduledActionService.
```

```
        GetActions<ScheduledNotification>()           ❶ Get alarms and reminders
        .OrderBy((item) => item.BeginTime);
    foreach (ScheduledNotification notification in notifications)
    {
        ScheduledAction item =                                  ❷ Use instance
            ScheduledActionService.Find(notification.Name);       returned by Find
        items.Add(item);
    }
    notificationList.ItemsSource = items;
}
```

First, create a new `List` variable to contain the alarms and reminders that will be displayed in the user interface. Obtain a collection of notifications from the Scheduled Action Service by calling the `GetActions` method. `GetActions` is a generic method and expects the calling code to declare which type of scheduled action is to be returned. The sample application could display both alarms and reminders, so the code invokes `GetActions` with the `ScheduledNotification` ❶ type, the base class for both the `Alarm` and `Reminder` classes. The notifications collection is sorted by the `BeginTime` property using the `OrderBy` extension method. Obtain another reference to the notification by calling the `Find` method ❷ with the name of the target item. Add each item returned by `Find` to the items list. Finally, assign the items list to the `LongListSelector`'s `ItemSource` property.

> **TIP** The Scheduled Action Service has an odd behavior—the notifications returned by `GetActions` are cached clones. Calling `GetActions` returns the cached instances. If an action's state has changed, such as when an alarm is shown to and dismissed by the user, the cached copy isn't updated. When the `Find` method is called, the cache is updated and the most recent state of the action is available. The code in listing 4.4 calls `Find` to force an update of the cache.

When you created MainPage.xaml in section 4.1, you added a `DataTemplate` to the `LongListSelector` but only declared an empty `StackPanel` inside the template. You need to add user interface components to display the properties of the scheduled notifications that were added to the `LongListSelector`. The following listing contains the fully declared `DataTemplate`.

Listing 4.5 Displaying a notification in the `LongListSelector`

```
<DataTemplate>                                              ❶ Add TextBlocks
   <StackPanel Margin="12">                                   to StackPane
      <TextBlock Text="{Binding Title}"
                 Style="{StaticResource PhoneTextLargeStyle}" />
      <TextBlock Text="{Binding Content}"
                 Style="{StaticResource PhoneTextNormalStyle}" />
Format fields with ❷ <TextBlock Text="{Binding BeginTime, StringFormat='\{0:f\}'}"
StringFormat             Style="{StaticResource PhoneTextSmallStyle}" />
      <TextBlock Text="{Binding ExpirationTime,
      ➥ StringFormat='Expires  \{0\:f}'}"
                 Style="{StaticResource PhoneTextSmallStyle}" />
```

```
        <StackPanel Orientation="Horizontal">
            <TextBlock Text="{Binding RecurrenceType,
            ➥ StringFormat='Recurs: \{0\}'}"
                    Style="{StaticResource PhoneTextSmallStyle}" />
            <TextBlock Text="{Binding IsScheduled,
            ➥ StringFormat='Is Scheduled: \{0\}'}"
                    Style="{StaticResource PhoneTextSubtleStyle}" />
        </StackPanel>
    </StackPanel>
</DataTemplate>
```

The `DataTemplate` contains several `TextBlock` instances ❶, each one displaying a different `ScheduledAction` property. The `TextBlocks` are styled using theme resources provided by the XAML framework. Some of the `TextBlocks` make use of the `StringFormat` binding markup ❷ to display in a more user-friendly format.

You now have a user interface that will display scheduled notifications to the user. At this point, the user interface remains blank, because there are no scheduled notifications to display. You need to implement the code to create some alarms and reminders.

4.2.1 Scheduling a reminder

Scheduled notifications are alarms and reminders that are registered with the operating system. Due to limitations imposed by the Windows Phone operating system, an application can't directly notify the user unless the application is running. With a scheduled notification, an application can schedule an alarm or a reminder and know that the user will be notified at the appropriate time, even if the application isn't running.

Scheduled notifications are implemented in two related classes, `Alarm` and `Reminder`. Both the `Alarm` and `Reminder` classes are derived from the `ScheduledNotification` class. As mentioned earlier, `ScheduledNotification` derives from `ScheduledAction`. `ScheduledNotification` extends its base class with additional properties called `Content` and `RecurrenceType`.

The `Content` property allows the application a place to display a message to the user when the notification is triggered. The `Content` property is a string with a maximum length of 256 characters.

The `RecurrenceType` property allows an application to create notifications that are triggered more than once. The recurrence patterns defined in the Scheduler API include daily, weekly, monthly, and yearly patterns. A notification is triggered at the appropriate time interval after the `BeginTime`. For example, if the recurrence pattern is daily, and the `BeginTime` is specified as 8:00 a.m. Monday, July 4, the notification will be triggered every day at 8:00 a.m. until the `ExpirationTime` has passed.

> **NOTE** The ScheduledActions sample application you build here will create only reminders. Creating alarms follows a similar pattern. We leave it as an exercise for you to add alarms to the project.

The ScheduledActions sample application defines a button allowing the user to create a `Reminder`. Figure 4.6 shows how a reminder would appear to a user. For comparison,

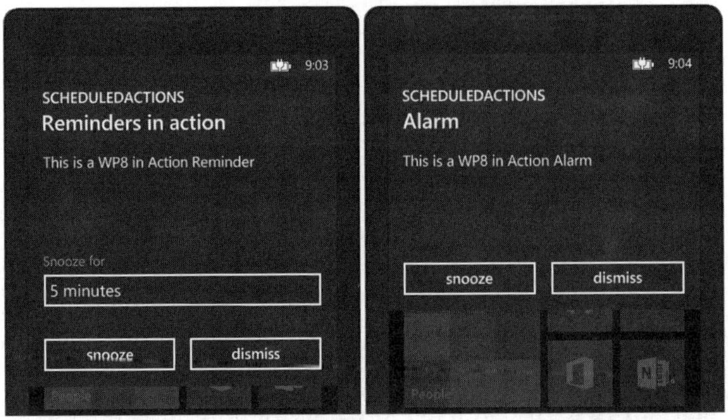

Figure 4.6 A reminder and an alarm as displayed to the user. Reminders can display a custom title and allow the user to choose a custom snooze interval. Alarms display only a stock title.

we show an alarm on the right side of the figure. When the user taps the title or content of a notification, the operating system will launch the host application's main page.

The observant reader will notice that a `Reminder` displays a custom title, whereas an `Alarm` always displays *Alarm* as the title. The title displayed by the `Reminder` is specified using the `Title` property. Another difference between `Alarms` and `Reminders` is that `Reminders` can specify a `NavigationUri` property, whereas `Alarms` have a `Sound` property.

The `Alarm.Sound` property is a `Uri` to any supported audio file located in the application's installation folder. The sound file must be added to the project with its build action property set to `Content`.

The `Reminder.NavigationUri` property is used by the operating system when the user taps the title or content of a `Reminder`. The operating system will launch the host application but will use the `NavigationUri` instead of the default page as the starting page.

A user of the sample application creates a new reminder by tapping the Add Reminder button on the main page application bar. Earlier in the chapter, you implemented the Add Reminder button's click event handler to use the `NavigationService` to navigate to ReminderPage.xaml. Although you've created the UI for the Reminder page and set up the controls to data bind to a `Reminder` object, you haven't created a `Reminder` object. The following listing shows how a `Reminder` is created in the Reminder page's `OnNavigatedTo` method.

Listing 4.6 Creating a reminder

```
Reminder reminder;                                          ❶ Create member field

protected override void OnNavigatedTo(NavigationEventArgs e)
{
   if (e.NavigationMode == NavigationMode.New)              ❷ Only create reminder when navigating forward
   {
      reminder = new Reminder(Guid.NewGuid().ToString());
```

```
        reminder.Title = "Reminder";
        reminder.BeginTime = DateTime.Now;
        reminder.NavigationUri = new Uri(
           "/MainPage.xaml?reminder=" + reminder.Name,
           UriKind.Relative);
        this.DataContext = reminder;
    }
}
```

❸ Set default values

A new member field ❶ is needed to keep track of the reminder object being edited by the page. Remember that the three picker controls will cause `OnNavigatedTo` to be called when their secondary pages are dismissed, so you need to create a `Reminder` object only when the `NavigationMode` is `New` ❷. `Reminders` must have unique names, and you start by constructing a new `Reminder` with a name built from a `Guid`. Assign the `BeginTime` property to the current time, assign the `Title` property ❸ to a default value, and fill in the `NavigationUri`. Set the newly constructed reminder object to the page's `DataContext` to enable binding to all the controls created earlier.

When a reminder is displayed to the user and they click the reminder title, the application will be launched with the specified navigation URI. Our sample doesn't define a special page and doesn't perform any special processing when receiving an URI. Your application may choose to display the reminder details in a special page or trigger other customized application logic when it receives a `Reminder`'s navigation URI.

When the user is finished editing the reminder, they tap the Save button on the application bar. In response to the click event, the code-behind schedules the reminder with the Scheduled Action Service and dismisses the page. The click event handler implementation is shown in the following listing.

Listing 4.7 Saving the reminder

```
using System.Windows.Input;

void Save_Click(object sender, EventArgs e)
{
   TextBox textInput = FocusManager.GetFocusedElement() as TextBox;
   if (textInput != null)
      textInput.GetBindingExpression(TextBox.TextProperty).UpdateSource();

   if (string.IsNullOrWhiteSpace(reminder.Title))
      reminder.Title = "(no title)";
   if (string.IsNullOrWhiteSpace(reminder.Content))
      reminder.Content = "(no description)";

   DateTime date = datePicker.Value.Value;
   DateTime time = timePicker.Value.Value;
   reminder.BeginTime = new DateTime(date.Year, date.Month,
         date.Day, time.Hour, time.Minute, time.Second);

   try
   {
```

❶ Supply default values

❷ BeginTime built from date and time controls

```
        ScheduledActionService.Add(reminder);
        NavigationService.GoBack();
    }
    catch (InvalidOperationException ex)
    {
        MessageBox.Show(ex.Message);
    }
}
```

❸ Save reminder

❹ Display error to user

Before registering the reminder with the `ScheduledActionService`, a few of its properties need to be validated or adjusted. If the user left either the `Title` or `Content` properties blank, the properties are assigned a default value ❶. A new `DateTime` value is constructed using the month, day, and year from the `DatePicker` and the hour, minute, and second from the `TimePicker` ❷. The reminder is registered with the `ScheduledActionService` using the `Add` method ❸, and the page is dismissed with a call to `NavigationService.GoBack`. The call to the `ScheduledActionService` is wrapped in a try/catch statement so that the user is notified ❹ and has a chance to fix any errors.

The begin time must be manually constructed because the `Reminder` object doesn't notify the binding engine when its `BeginTime` is changed and the two picker controls get out of sync. This step wouldn't be necessary if the `Reminder` object were wrapped with another object that raised property change notifications, or if you were using a ViewModel that adhered to the Model-View-ViewModel pattern.

> **TIP** You might wonder what the first few lines of listing 4.7 do. The `TextBox` control has an interesting quirk when updating bound data. It tries to be efficient with data-binding updates and may not have updated the bound field when the `Save_Click` event handler was called. In this listing you check to see if the currently focused control is a `TextBox`. If it is, ask for the `BindingExpression` object connected to the control's `Text` property and use the `BindingExpression`'s `UpdateSource` method to ensure the value is copied from the `TextBox` to the reminder.

You now know how to create scheduled notifications. Creation is only one of the create, update, and delete operations provided by the `ScheduledActionService`. The next operation we examine is updating or editing an existing notification.

4.2.2 Editing a notification

Once created, `ScheduledNotifications` can be modified by an application. Notifications are modified using the `Replace` method provided by the `ScheduledActionService`. The `Replace` method accepts an instance of `ScheduledNotification`, and the notification's `Name` property identifies which `ScheduledNotification` is to be replaced. The `ScheduledActionService` overwrites the saved notification with the values specified in the passed-in notification.

The sample application allows a user to edit an existing reminder by tapping one in the list displayed on the main page. With a few minor changes, the Reminder page can be reused to both add and edit reminders. First, you need to subscribe to the `SelectionChanged` event raised by the `LongListSelector`:

```
<phone:LongListSelector x:Name="notificationList" Grid.Row="1"
      SelectionChanged="NotificationList_SelectionChanged">
```

The implementation of the `NotificationList_SelectionChanged` method needs to retrieve the tapped or selected reminder and then send identifying information to the Reminder page. Query string parameters should be used to send information between pages. The following listing shows how to send the selected reminder's `Name` property to the Reminder page.

Listing 4.8 Sending a reminder's Name to the Reminder page

```
void NotificationList_SelectionChanged(object sender,
      SelectionChangedEventArgs e)
{
   ScheduledNotification notification =
         notificationList.SelectedItem as ScheduledNotification;
   if (notification != null)                                        ← 1 Do no work if nothing is selected
   {
      NavigationService.Navigate(new Uri("/ReminderPage.xaml?name="
            + notification.Name, UriKind.Relative));                ← 2 Navigate to the Reminder page
   }
}
```

Before doing any work, the event handler asks the `LongListSelector` for the currently selected item. If the `LongListSelector` doesn't have a selected item ❶, the event handler doesn't perform any work. When a scheduled notification is selected, its `Name` property is added to the URI used to navigate to ReminderPage.xaml, and the `NavigationService` is used to navigate to the new page ❷.

At this point the Reminder page doesn't know what to do with the name passed in the query string. The reminder page's `OnNavigatedTo` method needs to be changed to look for and use the value passed in the `name` parameter, as shown in the following listing.

Listing 4.9 Using the `name` parameter to find an existing reminder

```
protected override void OnNavigatedTo(NavigationEventArgs e)
{
   if (e.NavigationMode == NavigationMode.New)
   {
      if (NavigationContext.QueryString.ContainsKey("name"))        ← 1 Look for name parameter
      {
         string name = NavigationContext.QueryString["name"];
         reminder = (Reminder)ScheduledActionService.Find(name);   ← 2 Use name to find reminder
      }
      else
      {
         reminder = new Reminder(Guid.NewGuid().ToString());
         reminder.Title = "Reminder";
         reminder.BeginTime = DateTime.Now;
         reminder.NavigationUri = new Uri(
```

```
            "/MainPage.xaml?reminder=" + reminder.Name,
            UriKind.Relative);
      }
      this.DataContext = reminder;
   }
}
```

The code is changed by adding a new `if/else` statement, placing the previously existing `Reminder` construction code into the `else` block. The `if` statement condition checks for the key "name" in the `QueryString` dictionary ❶. If the "name" key exists, then the corresponding value is read and used in a call to the `Find` method of the `ScheduledActionService` ❷. The found reminder is used as the data context, and all the controls show values from the existing reminder.

Another minor change is required in the `Save_Click` method. The existing code only knows how to add new reminders. The `Replace` method must be used when updating already existing scheduled notifications. The new code is shown in the following listing.

Listing 4.10 Saving an edited reminder using `Replace`

```
void Save_Click(object sender, EventArgs e)
{
   ...
   try
   {
      if (ScheduledActionService.Find(reminder.Name) != null)    ❶ Does reminder already exist?
         ScheduledActionService.Replace(reminder);               ❷ Call Replace for existing reminders
      else
         ScheduledActionService.Add(reminder);
      NavigationService.GoBack();
   }
   ...
}
```

As with the `OnNavigatedTo` method, a new if/else block is added, with the existing code placed into the `else` block. A call to the `Find` method is used as the condition ❶ for the `if` statement, and a call to the `Replace` method is placed inside the `if` block. ❷.

When you created the Reminder page, you created two `ApplicationBar` buttons. You've implemented only one of the buttons. The second button allows the user to delete a notification.

4.2.3 Deleting a notification

The Delete Reminder button on the Reminder page isn't yet implemented. `Reminders` and all other forms of `ScheduledActions` are deleted with the `Remove` method of the `ScheduledActionService`. The `Remove` method accepts the name of the scheduled action to remove. The sample application removes a reminder in the Delete button's click event handler, as shown in the following code.

```
void Delete_Click(object sender, EventArgs e)
{
```

```
    if (ScheduledActionService.Find(reminder.Name) != null)
        ScheduledActionService.Remove(reminder.Name);
    NavigationService.GoBack();
}
```

Because the Reminder page might be editing a brand-new reminder, you first check that the current reminder exists by calling the scheduled action service's `Find` method. If the reminder does exist, the `Remove` method is called with the reminder's name.

Once created, a `ScheduledNotification` will be managed by the `ScheduledActionService` until the application removes the notification or the application is uninstalled. `ScheduledNotifications` are also removed if Visual Studio's Rebuild Solution option is used to build the project. A user can now use the sample application to create reminders for all the important events in their busy life. To make life even easier, and so that they can spend less time messing with their phone, the application should display details about upcoming reminders in its Live Tile. But the application can't update its Live Tile unless it's running. What you need is a way to update the Live Tile even when the application isn't running. What you need is a background agent.

4.3 Creating a background agent

Sometimes an application needs to run in the background to be useful. The Windows Phone allows an application to execute certain kinds of tasks in the background. Background tasks include playing or streaming audio as well as custom tasks that execute periodically. Background processes are called *background agents*. In this section we show how to create a scheduled task agent to perform work periodically in the background, even when the application isn't running. (We look at audio background agents in chapter 9 when building an application that integrates with the Music + Videos Hub.)

The ScheduledActions background agent will update the application's Live Tile, and ultimately the Lock Screen, with information about upcoming reminders. The number of remaining reminders left in the day is displayed as a count on the front of

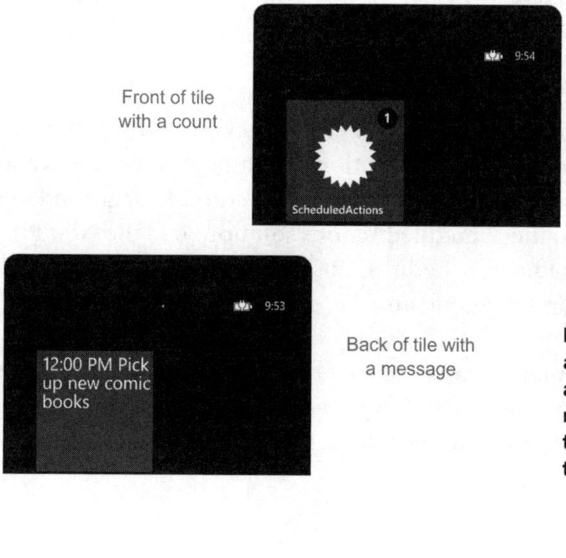

Figure 4.7 Screenshots showing the front and back of the ScheduleActions application's Live Tile. The front of the tile reports that there's one more reminder today, whereas the back of the tile shows the time and title of the next reminder.

the tile, whereas the time and title of the next reminder is shown on the back of the tile. Figure 4.7 demonstrates the front and the back of the application's Live Tile.

An application's scheduled task agent can run two types of scheduled tasks, both of them represented by classes derived from `ScheduledAction`. The first type of scheduled task executes once every half hour and is defined by the `PeriodicTask` class. The second type of background process is defined by the class named `ResourceIntensiveTask`. Resource-intensive tasks execute only if the device is plugged in and fully charged, connected to Wi-Fi or a computer, and screen locked. Both `PeriodicTask` and `ResourceIntensiveTask` are derived from `ScheduledTask`, which is derived from `ScheduledAction`.

Scheduled tasks aren't necessarily run exactly 30 minutes apart. The Scheduled Action Service coordinates the timing and execution of scheduled tasks. Waking up the device and powering on the sensors and radios is an expensive process. The Scheduled Action Service will power up once, execute all scheduled tasks, and power down. This is one of the methods employed by the Windows Phone to maximize battery life.

An application schedules a `ScheduledTask` with the `ScheduledActionService` using a process similar to scheduling a `ScheduledNotification`. An application can schedule only one `PeriodicTask` and one `ResourceIntensiveTask`. Unlike a `ScheduledNotification`, the user isn't notified when a `ScheduledTask` is triggered. Instead, the operating system notifies the host application through a `ScheduledTaskAgent`. `ScheduledTaskAgents` are defined in background agent projects.

Scheduled task agents are limited in the types of work they can do. They aren't allowed to access the camera, radio, accelerometer, compass, or gyroscope. Scheduled task agents can't add new scheduled actions or new background file transfers or show launchers or choosers. A complete list of unsupported APIs and restrictions is in Microsoft's SDK documentation on MSDN at http://mng.bz/ETjT.

You're going to create a `ScheduledTaskAgent` that executes a `PeriodicTask`. Periodic tasks and resource-intensive tasks differ only in the schedule they run on and the amount of time they're allowed to execute.

4.3.1 Background agent projects

The ScheduledActions sample application needs a background agent to execute a periodic task that scans all scheduled notifications and updates the application's Live Tile with information about upcoming reminders. To add a background agent, you need to add a new project to the ScheduledActions solution. Use the New Project Wizard and select the Windows Phone Scheduled Task Agent project template. Name the new project NotificationsUpdateAgent and be sure to select the Add to Solution option in the wizard.

The new project will contain a single source code file named ScheduledAgent.cs. Open ScheduledAgent.cs and find the class named `ScheduledAgent`. The generated `ScheduledAgent` class is derived from the `ScheduledTaskAgent`. `ScheduledTaskAgent` is one of three classes derived from the base BackgroundAgent class. The other background agent classes are used for playing audio files and are covered in more depth in chapter 9.

The next step is to reference the new background agent project in the ScheduledActions project. Using the Add Reference dialog, add a project reference to the NotificationsUpdateAgent project from the ScheduledActions project. In addition to adding the project reference, you need to update the WMAppManifest.xml file in the ScheduledActions project so that it contains a new ExtendedTask element:

```
<ExtendedTask Name="BackgroundTask">
    <BackgroundServiceAgent Specifier="ScheduledTaskAgent"
        Name="NotificationsUpdateAgent"
        Source="NotificationsUpdateAgent"
        Type="NotificationsUpdateAgent.ScheduledAgent" />
</ExtendedTask>
```

Add the ExtendedTask element to the Tasks element immediately following the DefaultTask element.

Along with generated diagnostic code, the newly added ScheduledAgent contains a method named OnInvoke, which is called by the Windows Phone framework to inform the agent that a ScheduledTask has been triggered. The agent will be passed to the triggered ScheduledTask object. The same background agent can execute both periodic tasks and resource-intensive tasks.

4.3.2 Executing work from the background agent

You're building a background agent to update the application's Live Tile. The tile will be updated by code in the ScheduledAgent class generated by the project template. Open the ScheduledAgent.cs file and add a new method named UpdateDefaultTile to look for any ScheduledNotifications that will occur during the remainder of the day and update the application's Live Tile. The method implementation is shown in the following listing.

Listing 4.11 Updating a Live Tile

```
using System.Linq;
using Microsoft.Phone.Shell;

public void UpdateDefaultTile()
{
   DateTime now = DateTime.Now;
   DateTime endOfDay =
      new DateTime(now.Year, now.Month, now.Day, 23, 59, 59);

   var notifications = ScheduledActionService                      // 1 Filter and sort notifications
      .GetActions<ScheduledNotification>()
      .Where((item) => item.BeginTime > now && item.BeginTime < endOfDay)
      .OrderBy((item) => item.BeginTime);

   int count = notifications.Count();
   ScheduledNotification nextNotification = notifications.FirstOrDefault();
```

```
    string message = null;
    if (nextNotification != null)
        message = string.Format("{0:t} {1}",
        nextNotification.BeginTime, nextNotification.Title);

    ShellTile defaultTile = ShellTile.ActiveTiles.First();       <-- ❷ Get primary Live Tile
    StandardTileData tileData = new StandardTileData
    {
        Count = count,
        BackContent = message
    };                                                            ❸ Update count and message
    defaultTile.Update(tileData);                              <--
}
```

In order to find only those notifications remaining in the current day, the current date is used to construct `endOfDay` with the time set to 11:59:59 p.m. The `endOfDay` variable is used in a LINQ expression that filters and orders the list of notifications returned by the `GetActions` method ❶. With the list ordered, the `FirstOrDefault` LINQ extension method is used to retrieve the upcoming notification. If there's an upcoming notification, a message is constructed using its `BeginTime` and `Title`. The `ShellTile` static property `ActiveTiles` returns the primary Live Tile and any other tile pinned to the Start Screen. The primary Live Tile is always in the list and is always the first one in the list ❷. A new instance of `StandardTileData` is constructed, and its `Count` and `BackContent` properties are assigned. The primary tile is updated with a call to the `Update` method ❸.

The `UpdateDefaultTile` method needs to be called from the agent's `OnInvoke` method:

```
protected override void OnInvoke(ScheduledTask task)
{
    UpdateDefaultTile();
    NotifyComplete();
}
```

With the scheduled task agent implemented and ready to do work, you need something that will trigger the background agent. Scheduled task agents are triggered by `ScheduledTasks`. In the next section you'll learn how to create a `PeriodicTask` from within the ScheduledActions application.

4.3.3 Scheduling a PeriodicTask

As with `ScheduledNotifications`, a `PeriodicTask` is scheduled with the Scheduled Action Service. Periodic tasks are instantiated, have their properties set, and are scheduled by invoking the `Add` method. `ScheduledTask` extends `ScheduledAction` by adding a `Description` property. The `Description` property is shown to the user in the background tasks settings application. The `ScheduledTask` doesn't define the code that's executed when the task is triggered—that code is defined by the background agent.

The sample application schedules the periodic task when the application is launched. You learned in the last chapter that the `PhoneApplicationService` raises a

Launching event when a new instance of an application is launched by the operating system. The App class generated by the project template contains a Launching event handler named Application_Launching. Open App.xaml.cs and modify the Application_Launching event handler to create a new PeriodicTask, as detailed in the following listing.

Listing 4.12 Creating a PeriodicTask

```
using Microsoft.Phone.Scheduler;

private void Application_Launching(object sender, LaunchingEventArgs e)
{
    PeriodicTask updateTask;
    try
    {
        updateTask = new PeriodicTask("NotificationUpdateTask");
        updateTask.Description = "A background agent responsible for
        ➥ updating the ScheduledActions' Live Tile and the lock screen.";
        ScheduledActionService.Add(updateTask);
    }
    catch (InvalidOperationException)
    {
        AgentStatus += "Unable to create the background task.";
        updateTask = null;
    }
}
```

❶ Assign description

❷ Report failure

Creating a PeriodicTask should feel familiar to you by now, because PeriodicTasks, Alarms, and Reminders are all forms of ScheduledActions. A Guid isn't included in the task's name, because the application will only create a single PeriodicTask. Assign the Description property with text that describes the work performed by the background task ❶. The call to the Add method is surrounded by a try/catch block to catch any exceptions that might be thrown, particularly when the user has permanently disabled background tasks for applications. If an exception is thrown, report the failure ❷ by assigning the AgentStatus property.

NOTE We're using the += operator to append messages to AgentStatus. You'll append other messages to the AgentStatus string in the following sections.

You haven't yet defined the AgentStatus property used in listing 4.12. Add a new automatic property to App.xaml.cs named AgentStatus:

```
public string AgentStatus { get; private set; }
```

In order to display the agent status on the screen, add another TextBlock to MainPage.xaml's ContentPanel. Place the TextBlock inside a Border and use the contrast background and styles to make the status messages stand out:

```
<Border Grid.Row="0"
    Background="{StaticResource PhoneContrastBackgroundBrush}">
```

```
    <TextBlock x:Name="agentMessage" TextWrapping="Wrap"
       Style="{StaticResource PhoneTextContrastStyle}"  />
</Border>
```

Next, add a line to MainPage's OnNavigatedTo method to assign the TextBlock's Text property:

```
agentMessage.Text = ((App)Application.Current).AgentStatus;
```

No message is displayed to the user when the periodic task is successfully created. Once created, the task will continue to execute twice an hour until its ExpirationTime. Unlike alarms and reminders, a scheduled task expires after two weeks.

4.3.4 Scheduled tasks expire after two weeks

By default, tasks are created with a maximum expiration time of 14 days in the future. The developer can schedule a task with a shorter expiration time. Any attempt to specify an expiration time more than two weeks in the future will result in an exception. The two-week limit requires the application to continuously reschedule the task to ensure that it'll be running as expected. This limitation also ensures that unused applications aren't draining device resources.

A good practice is to reschedule the task every time the application is launched. Update the Application_Launching method so that it looks for and removes any previously scheduled periodic task. Add the following snippet to the Application_Launching method, right before the try/catch block:

```
updateTask = ScheduledActionService.
    Find("NotificationUpdateTask") as PeriodicTask;
if (updateTask != null)
{
    if (updateTask.ExpirationTime < DateTime.Now)
        AgentStatus += "The background task was expired. ";
    ScheduledActionService.Remove(updateTask.Name);
}
```

Before removing the previously scheduled task, the snippet checks the expiration time. If the expiration time is in the past, the user is notified that the existing task has expired.

A few different types of applications have background agents that are automatically rescheduled. The operation system will automatically reschedule a background agent if it updates the application's Live Tile and the tile is pinned to the Start Screen or if the application has been chosen by the user to update the Lock Screen. Resource-intensive background agents of a Photos Hub extension application also get automatically updated if they upload photos and the user has enabled them in the Photos + Camera Settings page. You can read more about Photos Hub extension applications in chapter 9.

Even though the sample application might be automatically rescheduled, it's a good idea to programmatically renew the agent in case the Live Tile isn't pinned. Two-week expiration dates aren't the only things that prevent a periodic task from executing on schedule. The user can choose to disable your application's periodic task.

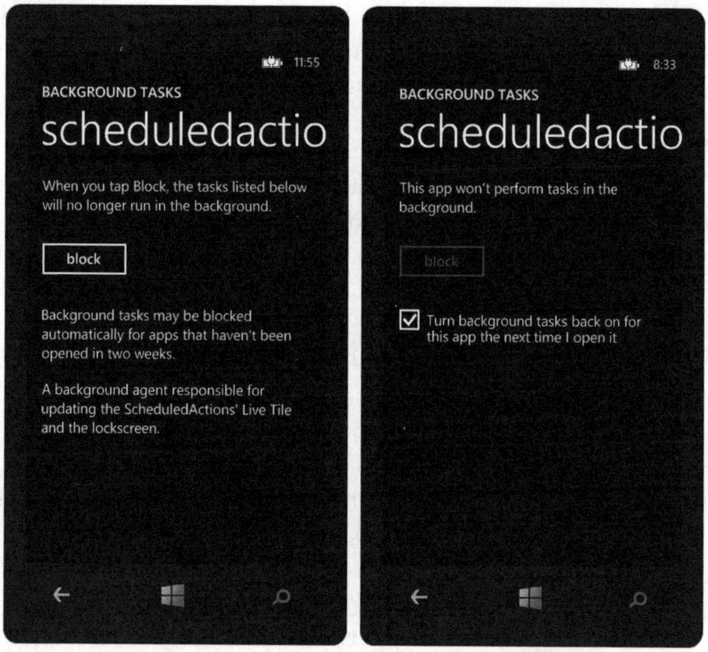

Figure 4.8 The Background Tasks page of the Settings application displays the periodic task's description and allows a user to disable the task. In the image on the right, the user has disabled the periodic task but will allow the application to recreate the task the next time it runs.

4.3.5 User-disabled tasks

`PeriodicTasks` can be disabled by the user in the Settings application. Figure 4.8 shows a screenshot of the Background Tasks page of the Settings application. If you examine the figure, you'll see how the text assigned to the `Description` property is shown to the user.

When the user has checked the Turn Back On option, the application will be allowed to remove and recreate the periodic task. If the option isn't checked, the Scheduled Action Service will throw an exception when attempting to recreate the task. An application can detect whether the user has disabled a task using the `IsEnabled` property. Add a check to the `Application_Launching` method to set the `AgentStatus` if the task has been disabled. The new code should be added inside the statement checking for `null`:

```
if (updateTask != null)
{
    if (!updateTask.IsEnabled)
        AgentStatus += "The background task was disabled by the user. ";
...
}
```

Only periodic tasks can be disabled. Resource-intensive tasks are listed in the Advanced page of the Background Tasks Settings application. The user can see the list of resource-intensive tasks but can't disable them.

4.3.6 When things go awry

Earlier in the chapter you learned that a background agent notifies the operating system that work was successfully completed using the `NotifyComplete` method. In a perfect world, the scheduled agent would always succeed, but we don't live in a perfect world. When the background agent fails to complete its work, it should call the `Abort` method.

The `Abort` method informs the Scheduled Action Service that the agent is unable to continue working. When the agent aborts, the Scheduled Action Service sets the `IsScheduled` property of the associated `ScheduledTask` to `false` and ceases to trigger the agent.

Other scenarios will also cause the background agent to fail. Background agents are limited to 11 MB of memory, and when a background process exceeds the memory quota, it's terminated. Periodic tasks are limited to 25 seconds of execution time and are terminated if the `NotifyComplete` method isn't called before the time limit is reached. An unhandled exception will also terminate the background agent. The exit status of the background agent is reported by the `LastExitReason` property of the scheduled task. The `LastExitReason` property returns one of the values in the `AgentExitReason` enumeration. The possible agent exit reasons are listed in table 4.2.

Table 4.2 Values of the `AgentExitReason` enumeration

Name	Description
`Aborted`	The background agent called the `Abort` method. The scheduled task's `IsScheduled` property has been set to `false`.
`Completed`	The background agent called the `NotifyComplete` method.
`ExecutionTimeExceeded`	The background agent failed to call `NotifyComplete` before its allocated time limit expired. Periodic tasks have a time limit of 25 seconds.
`MemoryQuotaExceeded`	The background agent attempted to allocate more than 11 MB of memory.
`None`	The background agent has not run.
`Other`	An unknown error occurred.
`Terminated`	The background agent was terminated early by the operating system due to conditions unrelated to the agent.
`UnhandledException`	The background agent failed to handle an exception produced during execution.

The host application should examine the `LastExitReason` property of its periodic tasks and at a minimum report the error condition to the user; you're going to implement error reporting in the sample application. The sample application reports agent errors through the `AgentStatus` property. Add the following snippet to the `Application_Launching` method, inside the check for the `null` statement:

```
if (updateTask.LastExitReason != AgentExitReason.Completed
    && updateTask.LastExitReason != AgentExitReason.None)
{
    AgentStatus += string.Format("The background task failed to complete
    ➥ its last execution at {0:g} with an exit reason of {1}. ",
       updateTask.LastScheduledTime, updateTask.LastExitReason);
}
```

You ignore the `Completed` and `None` exit reasons. All other exit reasons result in a message that reports the exit reason and the last time the background agent was scheduled to run.

The notification sample is nearly complete. Each time the application starts up, the `PeriodicTask` that triggers the background agent is renewed, and its `ExpirationTime` is reset to a full two weeks. The application also handles various error conditions that may occur, displaying status information to the user. At this point you should launch the application in different circumstances and get a feel for how the background agent might be affected. Disable the background task, either with or without the Turn Back On option checked. What status messages do you see when you restart the application?

Unless you're patient and waited half an hour or more, you probably haven't seen the background agent execute. Fortunately, Microsoft has provided an API to trigger early execution of background agents to enable developers to test them.

4.3.7 Testing background agents

In normal situations a periodic task is called only every 30 minutes. Resource-intensive tasks are scheduled even less predictably. Can you imagine having to wait half an hour for your background agent to trigger before you could debug and step through your code? The `ScheduledActionService` class provides the `LaunchForTest` API to give the developer control over when background agent execution is triggered.

The `LaunchForTest` method accepts the name of the `ScheduledTask` and a `TimeSpan` value describing how soon the task should be triggered. The `LaunchForTest` method can be used by either the host application or by the scheduled agent. Add a call to `LaunchForTest` to the end of the `Application_Launching` method of the sample application:

```
if (updateTask != null)
    ScheduledActionService.LaunchForTest(updateTask.Name,
       TimeSpan.FromSeconds(3));
```

Debug the application again, and a breakpoint in `OnInvoke` should be hit within a few seconds.

`LaunchForTest` will execute only when an application is deployed to a device using the Windows Phone SDK tools. When debugging your project with a background agent, the debugger will continue to run even after the application has stopped. This allows your agent to be debugged even when the application isn't running.

There's one more feature to add to the ScheduledActions sample application: updating the Lock Screen.

4.4 Updating the Lock Screen

The Windows Phone 8 Lock Screen provides simple important information at a glance. Phone users can peek quickly at their phone and continue on with their busy lives. Applications can participate in the Lock Screen in several ways: by being a wallpaper provider, a detailed notification provider, or a quick status provider.

In this section you'll update the ScheduledActions sample application so that it provides both quick and detailed status to the Lock Screen. You'll also allow the user to quickly launch the Launch Screen Settings application from the sample application. Figure 4.9 shows how a user can select the ScheduledActions application as a Lock Screen provider and what the notifications look like.

Surprisingly, you don't have to make any changes to the ScheduledActions code to enable the reporting of detailed and quick status. The Lock Screen reads the detailed status from an application's Live Tile—specifically the `BackContent` property. The

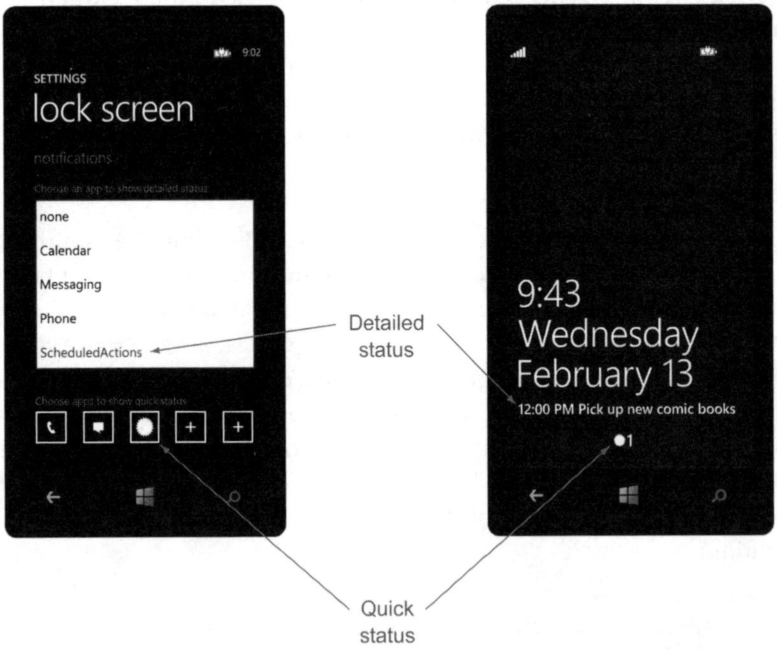

Figure 4.9 In the left-hand image, the user has selected the ScheduledActions application as the detailed status provider and the third quick status provider. The image on the right demonstrates how both detailed and quick status appear on the Lock Screen.

quick status is also read from the Live Tile, from the `Count` property. The Scheduled-Actions application and background agent already update the Live Tile. Even though no code changes are required, a few changes to the project are necessary. First, a quick status icon must be added to the project, and then the WMAppManifest.xml file needs a couple of changes.

The quick status icon is a normal image file sized at 38 * 38 pixels. This book's sample code (found at www.manning.com/binkley/) contains a file named LockIcon.png placed in the project's Assets folder, which is a scaled-down copy of the FlipCycleTile-Small.png file generated by the project template.

Open the WMAppManifest.xml file with the XML editor and look for the tile template child element of the `PrimaryToken` element. Update the `DeviceLockImageURI` element to contain the path to the quick status icon file:

```
<PrimaryToken TokenID="ScheduledActionsToken" TaskName="_default">
   <TemplateFlip>
      ...
      <DeviceLockImageURI IsRelative="true"
            IsResource="false">Assets\LockIcon.png</DeviceLockImageURI>
   </TemplateFlip>
</PrimaryToken>
```

Unless you changed the project's tile template, the sample project uses `TemplateFlip` for its tile template element.

While you have the WMAppManifest.xml file open, you need to add two more elements. Both elements are named `Extension` and are children of the `Extensions` element. If the `Extensions` element isn't in WMAppManifest.xml, add it immediately after the `Tokens` element:

```
<Extensions>
   <Extension ExtensionName="LockScreen_Notification_IconCount"
      ConsumerID="{111DFF24-AA15-4A96-8006-2BFF8122084F}"
      TaskID="_default" />
   <Extension ExtensionName="LockScreen_Notification_TextField"
      ConsumerID="{111DFF24-AA15-4A96-8006-2BFF8122084F}"
      TaskID="_default" />
</Extensions>
```

The extension element with `ExtensionName` `LockScreen_Notification_IconCount` tells the operating system that the application *extends* the Lock Screen and provides quick status notifications. The `LockScreen_Notification_TextField` extension element signals that the application provides status notifications. The `ConsumerID` attribute identifies the application or feature being *extended*—in this case, the Lock Screen.

> **NOTE** A third Lock Screen extension named `LockScreen_Background` is used to signal that an application provides wallpaper or background images for the Lock Screen.

With the new icon and the WMAppManifest.xml changes in place, the Scheduled-Actions application is now a Lock Screen provider. Once the application is installed, the user can open the Launch Screen Settings application and choose Scheduled-Actions to provide details and/or quick status notifications. To make it easier for the user to find the Settings application, an application can provide a button to launch the Settings application directly. You added a button to MainPage.xaml early in the chapter, along with a `Click` event handler. Open MainPage.xaml.cs, find the event handler, and add the following implementation:

```
using Windows.System;

void Settings_Click(object sender, EventArgs e)
{
   Launcher.LaunchUriAsync(new Uri("ms-settings-lock:"));
}
```

The `Launcher` class, found in the `Windows.System` namespace, is a service that runs native or third-party applications, as well as launches the appropriate application for any particular file. In the preceding snippet, we're using `ms-settings-lock:`, which is a registered URI, to launch the built-in Lock Screen Settings application. In the next chapter you'll learn how to launch other built-in applications. In chapter 11 you'll learn how to register a custom URI and use the `Launcher` class to launch your own applications.

4.5 Summary

In this chapter you learned how to use the Scheduled Action Service to implement features normally found in background applications. The Scheduled Action Service allows an application to schedule alarms and reminders, notifying the user at important points in time and providing a quick link back into the application. The Scheduled Action Service is also used to schedule work with periodic and resource-intensive tasks. Scheduled tasks are used to trigger an application's background agent to perform work even when the application isn't running in the foreground.

We looked at a few more controls from the Windows Phone Toolkit. The date and time pickers can be used to provide the same user experience found in native Windows Phone applications like Alarms and Calendar. You also learned how to use the `ListPicker` instead of a combo box control when providing the user with a list of options to choose from.

Limitations of the operating system prevent applications from directly accessing features in native applications such as the Phone Dialer, Email, Calendar, and Contact database. In the next chapter you'll learn how to use launchers and choosers to integrate with the native applications. You'll also learn how to use the User Data API to read from the Calendar and the Contacts database.

5 Launching tasks and choosers

This chapter covers

- Using the phone APIs
- Displaying apps with launchers
- Retrieving data with choosers
- Reading calendar appointments

A modern mobile phone does more than make phone calls. It allows you to send SMS text messages and emails. Phone numbers and email addresses are stored in the phone's contact list. Appointments and meetings are viewed using the Calendar application. Music and videos are played from the phone's media library. And don't forget about the ever-present camera. Windows Phone developers access these mobile phone features via the Tasks API.

The Windows Phone security model doesn't allow third-party applications to directly access the native applications and data stores provided by the operating system. Access to native applications is exposed through a variety of classes available in the Tasks API.

In this chapter we explore the Tasks API. You'll learn how to ask for contact and appointment data stored in the phone's People Hub and Calendar application. You'll also use tasks to access the native phone applications. To demonstrate how to use the Tasks API, you'll build an application that uses several different tasks to initiate phone calls, emails, and text messages.

5.1 The Tasks API

Phone tasks allow your code to interact with the native or built-in applications—the Phone Dialer, Media Player, Messaging, Contacts, Web Browser, Camera, and Windows Store. You'll build an application called PhoneTasks with a sample About page that uses tasks to contact customer support, share news about the application, add application reviews, and purchase a trial application.

NOTE The "App certification requirements for Windows Phone" (http://mng.bz/Fefo) specifies that every application provide easily discoverable technical support contact information.

Figure 5.1 The PhoneTasks application with hyperlinks and buttons for launching native applications

To begin the PhoneTasks application project, create a new Windows Phone application. The user interface is built using hyperlinks and buttons. As you implement the application, you'll show or launch the appropriate phone task from click event handlers in the page code-behind. The final PhoneTasks application is shown in figure 5.1.

The `ContentPanel` markup for the PhoneTasks project's main page is shown in the following listing. Open MainPage.xaml and copy the XAML markup into your project. As you add the various `Button` and `HyperlinkButton` controls, create corresponding empty `Click` event handlers in MainPage.xaml.cs.

Listing 5.1 Markup for the PhoneTask application's main page

```
<StackPanel x:Name="ContentPanel" Grid.Row="1" Margin="12,0,12,0">
   <TextBlock Text="Customer Support:"
      Style="{StaticResource PhoneTextGroupHeaderStyle}" />
   <StackPanel Orientation="Horizontal">
      <HyperlinkButton x:Name="supportPhoneLink" Width="325"
         Content="(888) 555-0681" Click="SupportPhoneLink_Click"
         Margin="{StaticResource PhoneTouchTargetOverhang}" />
      <Button x:Name="SavePhoneButton" Content="Save"
         Click="SavePhone_Click" />
   </StackPanel>
   <StackPanel Orientation="Horizontal">
```

Change ContentPanel to StackPanel ❶

Style labels as header text ❷

```
        <HyperlinkButton x:Name="supportEmailLink" Width="325"
            Content="support@wp8inaction.com" Click="SupportEmailLink_Click"
            Margin="{StaticResource PhoneTouchTargetOverhang}" />      ❸ Leave room for touches
        <Button x:Name="saveEmailButton" Content="Save"
            Click="SaveEmail_Click" />
    </StackPanel>
    <TextBlock Text="Share:"
        Style="{StaticResource PhoneTextGroupHeaderStyle}" />
    <Button Content="Share via Text Message" Click="ShareSms_Click" />
    <TextBlock Text="Windows Phone Store:"
        Style="{StaticResource PhoneTextGroupHeaderStyle}" />
    <Button Content="Write a Review" Click="Review_Click" />
    <Button x:Name="homePageButton" Content="Buy this application"
        Click="HomePage_Click" />
    <StackPanel Orientation="Horizontal">
        <Button Content="Search Marketplace" Click="Search_Click" />
        <Button Content="Search Bing" Click="BingSearch_Click" />
    </StackPanel>
</StackPanel>
```

Start by changing the `ContentPanel` from a `Grid` into a `StackPanel` ❶. Add the first of three header labels by creating a `TextBlock` and styling it with the theme resource called `PhoneTextGroupHeaderStyle` ❷. Use the customer support email address and phone numbers as the `Content` for two `HyperlinkButtons`. Use the theme resource called `PhoneTouchTargetOverhang` ❸ to ensure that each hyperlink has enough space around it to accommodate the thickness of a fingertip. Finally, add several `Buttons`, with which the user will initiate one of the phone tasks. Run the application now and confirm that the user interface appears as you'd expect.

The phone tasks are found in the `Microsoft.Phone.Tasks` namespace of the `Microsoft.Phone` assembly. Tasks don't share a common base class or interface, but every task implements a `Show` method. When the `Show` method is called, your application is deactivated and possibly terminated. Tasks are launched with the `Show` method because they're only *shown*. Your application can't use tasks to do anything. The tasks require the user to initiate all actions. Make sure to perform any necessary work before calling the `Show` method—for example, if you're calling `Show` from the user interface thread. If you block or otherwise tie up the UI thread, the `Deactivated` event will queue up until the UI thread is free. If the user returns to your application before `Deactivated` is fired, your application will appear to hang.

Tasks come in two forms: launchers and choosers. Launchers are fire-and-forget; they show the task and don't return any data. Choosers show the task and return data to your application when it's reactivated.

5.2 Launchers

Launchers are tasks that allow your code to activate a native or built-in application. Table 5.1 describes each of the launcher classes provided in the `Microsoft.Phone.Tasks` namespace. Data is passed to the launched application via properties set in the task. When the launcher's `Show` method is called, your application is deactivated.

Table 5.1 Windows Phone launchers

Launcher	Description
`ConnectionSettingsTask`	Launches the Airplane Mode, Bluetooth, Cellular, or Wi-Fi page of the Settings application.
`EmailComposeTask`	Launches the Email application and sends an email.
`MapDownloaderTask`	Launches the Maps Settings application. The user can choose to download map data to their device.
`MapsDirectionsTask*`	Launches the Maps application showing driving directions between two locations.
`MapsTask*`	Launches the Maps application centered on a location.
`MapUpdaterTask`	Launches the Map Settings application and checks for map data updates. The user can choose to download any updated content.
`MarketplaceDetailTask`	Launches the specified application's home page in the Marketplace Hub.
`MarketplaceHubTask`	Launches the Store Hub.
`MarketplaceReviewTask`	Launches an application's Review page in the Store Hub.
`MarketplaceSearchTask`	Launches the Search page in the Store Hub and searches for the specified keywords.
`MediaPlayerLauncher`	Launches the media player and plays the specified media.
`PhoneCallTask`	Launches the phone dialer with the specified phone number and places a phone call.
`SearchTask`	Launches the Bing application with the specified query.
`ShareLinkTask`	Launches the Post a Link page found in Internet Explorer. The user picks which social networks to share the link with.
`ShareMediaTask*`	Launches the Share page found in the Photos Hub. The user picks which Photos Hub extension application is used to share the specified photo or video.
`ShareStatusTask`	Launches the Post a Message page in the People Hub.
`SmsComposeTask`	Launches the Messaging application and sends a text message.
`WebBrowserTask*`	Launches Internet Explorer with the specified web address.

* `MapsDirectionsTask` and `MapsTask` are covered in chapter 16. `ShareMediaTask` is covered in chapter 9. `WebBrowserTask` is covered in chapter 17.

`PhoneCallTask`, `EmailComposeTask`, and `SmsComposeTask` are contact tasks. Use these tasks if your application is some form of contact-management application or if any of your data contains phone numbers or email addresses. For this example you'll use them in the PhoneTasks application to provide links to customer support.

`ShareLinkTask` and `ShareStatusTask` are social networking tasks. Use these tasks to allow users of your application to post links and status messages to Windows Live,

Facebook, Twitter, or LinkedIn. Using the social networking tasks is similar to using the other launchers, and we don't cover them in this book. You can see an example of how to use them in the PhoneTasks application that's available with the book's sample source code, which is slightly different than the application you build in this chapter.

The Windows Store or Marketplace tasks provide integration with the Store Hub. You'll use them in your PhoneTasks application to give users quick access to the Review and Buy Store pages and to search for other applications in the portfolio.

You'll start the PhoneTasks application implementation by using `PhoneCallTask` to call customer support.

5.2.1 Placing a phone call

`PhoneCallTask` shows the Phone Dialer, prompting the user to dial a phone number specified by the application. The user must initiate the phone call; the application can't dial a phone call directly. `PhoneCallTask` has a `PhoneNumber` property and a `DisplayName` property.

> **TIP** Using the `PhoneCallTask` requires the `ID_CAP_PHONEDIALER` capability to be declared in WMAppManifest.xml.

Figure 5.2 shows how the user is prompted when `PhoneCallTask Show` is executed. The dialer screen overlays the top portion of the application, and the remainder of the screen is disabled. Unlike all other tasks, `PhoneCallTask` doesn't pause or terminate the application but only obscures it. The application is notified via the `PhoneApplicationFrame Obscured` event. If the user clicks Call, the in-call screen overlays the running application.

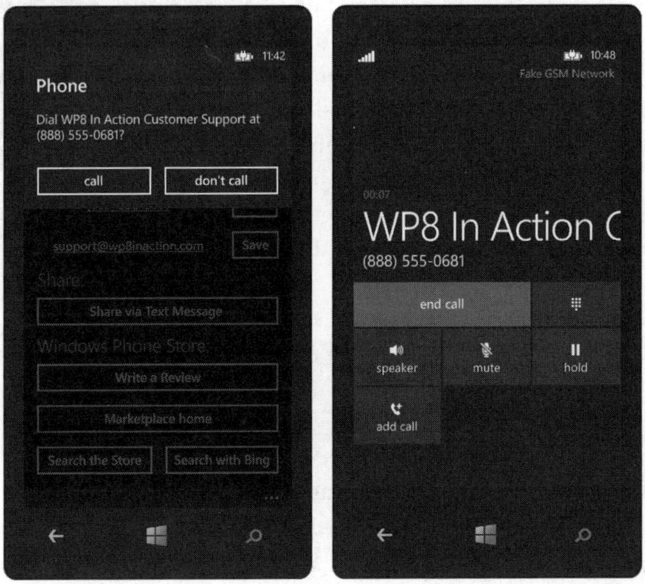

Figure 5.2 Phone dialer and in-call overlays

The in-call overlay presents the DisplayName if the phone number doesn't match an existing contact. When a phone number matches an existing contact, the data in the contact record is shown instead of the specified DisplayName. The user may return to the running application by tapping below the in-call overlay, which generates a PhoneApplicationFrame Unobscured event. The user may also take another action that results in the deactivation of your application. The following listing shows how to use PhoneCallTask.

Listing 5.2 Launching the Phone Dialer with PhoneCallTask

```
using Microsoft.Phone.Tasks;                                    // 1 Declare namespace
void SupportPhoneLink_Click(object sender, RoutedEventArgs e)
{
    PhoneCallTask task = new PhoneCallTask()                    // 2 Construct and initialize task
    {
        PhoneNumber = (string)supportPhoneLink.Content,
        DisplayName = "WP8 In Action Customer Support"
    };
    task.Show();
}
```

The PhoneCallTask class is defined in Microsoft.Phone.Tasks, so you add a using directive ❶ for the namespace at the top of the file. Implement the SupportPhoneLink_Click event handler by constructing a PhoneCallTask ❷ with object initializers for the PhoneNumber and DisplayName properties. The Show method is called to prompt the user to place the phone call.

The PhoneNumber property is required. If PhoneNumber isn't set, PhoneCallTask.Show will return immediately without performing any work, and the dialer screen won't be displayed to the user. The user's only options are to dial or not to dial, and the user can't change the phone number. The DisplayName property isn't required—if not specified, the in-call screen will display only the phone number. When the PhoneNumber property isn't a valid phone number, an error message is displayed to the user after they press the Call button, as shown in figure 5.3.

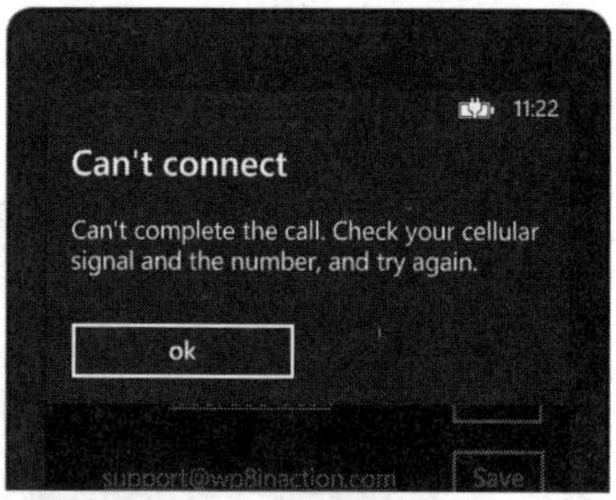

Figure 5.3 Error message displayed when an invalid phone number is specified

Some users prefer to interact with customer support via email instead of a phone call. For the next example, you'll use EmailComposeTask to allow these users to send an email.

5.2.2 *Writing an email*

The EmailComposeTask shows the Email application, prompting the user to send an email specified by the application to a specified email address. The user must initiate the send; your application can't send an email message directly. EmailComposeTask has `To`, `CC`, `Subject`, and `Body` properties. The following listing shows how to construct the `EmailComposeTask`.

Listing 5.3 Composing an email with `EmailComposeTask`

```
void SupportEmailLink_Click(object sender, RoutedEventArgs e)
{
    EmailComposeTask task = new EmailComposeTask()
    {
        To = (string)supportEmailLink.Content.ToString(),
        Subject = "WP8 in Action PhoneTasks Application",
        Body = "Support Issue Details:"
    };
    task.Show();
}
```

❶ Construct and initialize task

Implement the `SupportEmailLink_Click` event handler by constructing an `Email-ComposeTask` ❶ with object initializers for the `To`, `Subject`, and `Body` properties. The `Show` method is called to launch the Email editor.

> **NOTE** The Email application isn't accessible in the emulator, and when the `EmailComposeTask` is shown in the emulator, the user is shown an error message.

All the properties are optional. The Email application will launch with a new empty email when nothing is supplied. The `To` and `CC` properties can be one or more names or email addresses, separated with a semicolon. The Email application will attempt to match the `To` and `CC` values to contacts in the address book after the user taps Send. Once in the Email editor, the user can alter, delete, or replace any of the values passed in from your application.

The last contacts-related launcher we'll look at is the `SmsComposeTask`.

5.2.3 *Texting with SMS*

The `SmsComposeTask` shows the Messaging application, prompting the user to send a message specified by your application to a particular name or phone number. The user must initiate the send because your application can't send a text message directly. `Sms-ComposeTask` has `To` and `Body` properties.

You'll use the `SmsComposeTask` to provide the user a means to send information and news about the application to contacts in their address book, a form of high-tech word-of-mouth advertising.

Figure 5.4 shows the Messaging application as the user sees it when `SmsComposeTask.Show` is executed.

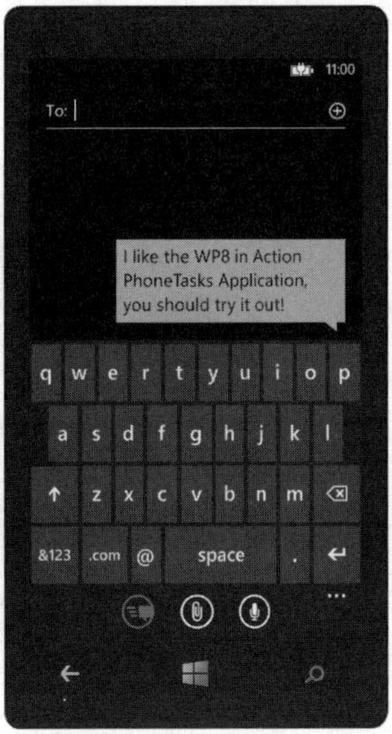

Figure 5.4 Messaging application

An SmsComposeTask is constructed in the ShareSms_Click event handler with object initializers for the Body property. The Show method is called to launch the Messaging application:

```
void ShareSms_Click(object sender, RoutedEventArgs e)
{
    SmsComposeTask task = new SmsComposeTask()
    {
        Body = "I like the WP8 in Action
        ➥ PhoneTasks Application, you should try it out!",
    };
    task.Show();
}
```

Both the To and Body properties are optional. The Messaging application will launch with a new empty message when neither is supplied. The To property can be one or more names or phone numbers, separated with a semicolon. The Messaging application will attempt to match the To values to contacts in the address book after the user taps Send. Once in the Messaging editor, the user can alter, delete, or replace the To and Body values passed in from your application.

As with other tasks, the user can return to your application by tapping the Back button. The user can return without sending the text. The user may also send the text and then choose to perform other actions without ever returning to your application. With the contacts features of the About page implemented, you're ready to implement the Marketplace tasks.

5.2.4 Working with the Windows Phone Store

The Windows Phone Store Hub, shown in figure 5.5, is where users go to download, review, and purchase applications for the Windows Phone. Three different tasks are available to launch the Store Hub from third-party applications. The tasks begin with *Marketplace* because the storefront in Windows Phone 7 was named Windows Phone Marketplace and was renamed to Windows Phone Store in Windows Phone 8.

Figure 5.5 The Windows Phone Store Hub

The MarketplaceHubTask launches the Store Hub to either the applications or music portal. The other two tasks, MarketplaceReviewTask and MarketplaceDetailTask, launch the Store Hub directly to an application's site within the Store. Let's take a closer look at each task, starting with MarketplaceHubTask.

MARKETPLACEHUBTASK

The first store task we'll discuss is the MarketplaceHubTask. This task launches the Windows Phone Store Hub. MarketplaceHubTask has a single ContentType property. Even though you're not adding the MarketplaceHubTask to the sample application, the task is launched with the Show method:

```
MarketplaceHubTask task = new MarketplaceHubTask()
{
    ContentType = MarketplaceContentType.Applications
};
task.Show();
```

The ContentType property must be set to one of the MarketplaceContentType enumeration values—Applications or Music. ContentType defaults to MarketplaceContentType.Applications.

In the sample application there is no need to launch the Store Hub start pages, but you do want to launch the Store's Create a Review feature. MarketplaceReviewTask lets you do that.

MARKETPLACEREVIEWTASK

Reviews are a big part of the Windows Phone Store. The Windows Phone Store will grow to tens or hundreds of thousands of applications. Good reviews help consumers find your great application amid a sea of mediocre competitors. With the MarketplaceReviewTask, Microsoft has made it easy to encourage users to create reviews for your application.

To wire up the review feature to the About page, you'll implement the Click handler for the Review button:

```
void Review_Click(object sender, RoutedEventArgs e)
{
    MarketplaceReviewTask task = new MarketplaceReviewTask();
    task.Show();
}
```

MarketplaceReviewTask doesn't have any public properties. The task determines the appropriate product ID from the running application, so when you call Show, the correct page in the Store is shown.

Offering more than the Review page, the Store allows you to direct the user to an application's home page with the MarketplaceDetailTask.

MARKETPLACEDETAILTASK

An application's home page in the Windows Phone Store provides all the details, screenshots, and reviews for an application. It's also where a user goes to purchase an application or download a trial. In your About page, you'll offer a link to your

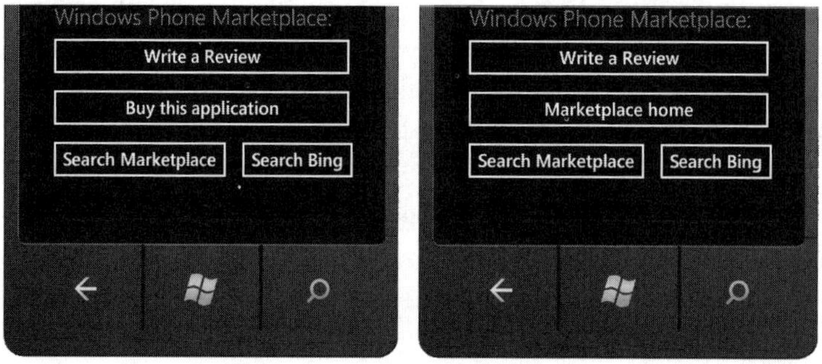

Figure 5.6 The home page button's content in trial and licensed modes

application's Store home page. When the application runs under a trial license, you want to show the user a Buy button, as shown in figure 5.6.

The following listing uses the `IsTrial` API to update the home page button's text.

Listing 5.4 Using `IsTrial` to customize the home page button's text

```
using Microsoft.Phone.Marketplace;
protected override void OnNavigatedTo(NavigationEventArgs e)
{
    LicenseInformation licenseInfo = new LicenseInformation();
    if (licenseInfo.IsTrial)
        homePageButton.Content = "Buy this application";
    else
        homePageButton.Content = "Marketplace home";
    base.OnNavigatedTo(e);
}
```

❶ Is app using trial license?

❷ Update button's content

The license check code is added to the `OnNavigatedTo` override because it's possible for the application to be licensed while it's deactivated. Start by creating an instance of `LicenseInformation` class and checking for a trial license ❶. When running under a trial license, the button text encourages the user to buy the application ❷.

Next, you need to implement the `HomePage_Click` event handler:

```
void HomePage_Click(object sender, RoutedEventArgs e)
{
    MarketplaceDetailTask task = new MarketplaceDetailTask();
    task.Show();
}
```

`MarketplaceDetailTask` has two properties: `ContentIdentifier` and `ContentType`. The `ContentType` property defaults to `MarketplaceContentType.Applications`, which is the only valid value for this task. `ContentIdentifier` defaults to `null`, which indicates that the task should use the product identifier of the currently running application.

`MarketplaceDetailTask` also lets you display the home page for any application, if you know its `ContentIdentifier`. Your application can provide links to all the applications published by you, because you're likely to know those IDs. Another option for showing the user all your applications is with a Store search.

MARKETPLACESEARCHTASK

Our About page uses the `MarketplaceSearchTask` to search for related applications. The search is defined with a set of search terms, which for this application is "Windows Phone 8 in Action":

```
void Search_Click(object sender, RoutedEventArgs e)
{
    MarketplaceSearchTask task = new MarketplaceSearchTask()
    {
        SearchTerms = "Window Phone 8 in Action",
        ContentType = MarketplaceContentType.Applications
    };
    task.Show();
}
```

Implement the `Search_Click` event handler by constructing a `MarketplaceSearchTask` with object initializers for the `SearchTerms` and `ContentType` properties. The `Show` method is called to launch the marketplace.

Searching with Bing is an alternative to searching the Windows Phone Store. The Tasks API includes a task to launch a Bing search.

5.2.5 Searching with Bing

The last task you'll use in the PhoneTasks sample application is `SearchTask`. `SearchTask` launches the Bing Search application with a specified search query. The PhoneTasks application uses `SearchTask` to search for "Windows Phone 8 in Action" on Manning's website:

```
void BingSearch_Click(object sender, RoutedEventArgs e)
{
    SearchTask task = new SearchTask()
    {
        SearchQuery = "Windows Phone 8 in Action site:manning.com"
    };
    task.Show();
}
```

The search query is constructed using the `site` operator defined in the Bing Query Language. The Bing Query Language is documented on MSDN at http://mng.bz/6NXP.

If the `SearchQuery` property is a `null` or empty string, the `Show` method returns immediately and doesn't launch the Bing Search application.

The `PhoneTasks` application is nearly finished. The remaining buttons allow the user to save the support phone number and email address to the contacts database. Saving data to contacts requires the user to choose which contact to update. For this you need choosers.

5.3 Choosers

Choosers are a category of Windows Phone tasks that return task status and data to an application. Each chooser displays a native application user interface and either saves data to the native application or returns data from the native application. Table 5.2

describes the choosers available in the Microsoft.Phone.Tasks namespace. Because applications may be terminated when a task is shown, there's no guarantee the user will ever return to your application with the chosen data.

Table 5.2 Windows Phone choosers

Chooser	Description
AddressChooserTask	Launches the Choose a Contact page in the People Hub and returns a physical address of the user's choosing
AddWalletItemTask	Launches the Wallet application prompting the user to add an application-provided item to the wallet
CameraCaptureTask*	Launches the Camera application and returns a photo the user takes
EmailAddressChooserTask	Launches the Choose a Contact page in the People Hub and returns an email address of the user's choosing
PhoneNumberChooserTask	Launches the Choose a Contact page in the People Hub and returns a phone number of the user's choosing
PhotoChooserTask*	Launches the Photos application and returns a picture of the user's choosing
SaveContactTask	Launches the New Contact page in the People Hub, prompting the user to edit and save a new contact
SaveEmailAddressTask	Launches the Choose a Contact page in the People Hub, prompting the user to add an email address to the contact of the user's choosing
SavePhoneNumberTask	Launches the Choose a Contact page in the People Hub, prompting the user to add a phone number to the contact of the user's choosing
SaveRingtoneTask	Launches the Ringtones application, prompting the user to save an audio file from the application's storage as a ringtone

*CameraCaptureTask and PhotoChooserTask are covered in chapter 8.

AddressChooserTask, EmailAddressChooserTask, and PhoneNumberChooserTask return data chosen by the user. SaveContactTask, SaveEmailAddressTask, SavePhoneNumberTask, and SaveRingtoneTask don't return any data; they only return status information. Data and status information are returned to your application via the TaskEventArgs parameter of the chooser's Completed event handler.

5.3.1 Completed events

Choosers, like all tasks, are launched with the Show method. When Show executes, your application is deactivated and possibly tombstoned. Upon activation, the

Windows Phone framework raises the chooser's `Completed` event. Because the completed event is called when a tombstoned application is restarted, `Completed` events should be treated specially.

Chooser instances should be declared as instance fields of the `PhoneApplicationPage`. To enable callbacks when recovering from tombstoning, `Completed` event handlers must be wired up in the `Page` constructor or `Loaded` event handler. When the event handler is added in a page constructor, the event handler is called immediately after the constructor, before the `Loaded` event. But if the event handler is added in the `Loaded` event, the `Completed` event is called immediately after the `Loaded` event.

You'll use `SavePhoneNumberTask` and `SaveEmailAddressTask` to finish the PhoneTasks application.

5.3.2 Saving a phone number

One feature of the PhoneTasks application allows the user to save the customer support phone number to the contacts database. Once the phone number is saved, the feature is hidden. The feature will be implemented with `SavePhoneNumberTask`. When the chooser launches, the user is prompted to select a new or existing contact and is then presented with the Edit Phone Number screen shown in figure 5.7.

At this point, the user can change the phone number or return to the application without saving the number (or start a completely different application, never returning to PhoneTasks). The following listing shows the code added to MainPage.xaml.cs

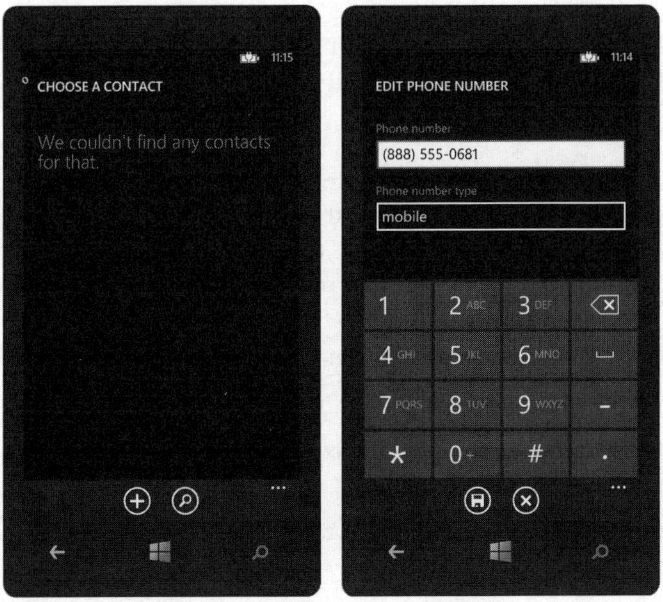

Figure 5.7 Saving an application-supplied phone number

for creating an instance field and adding the completed event handler in the constructor.

Listing 5.5 Wiring up the completed event handler

```
SavePhoneNumberTask savePhoneNumberTask = new SavePhoneNumberTask();    <-- Add field for task
public MainPage()
{
    InitializeComponent();
    savePhoneNumberTask.Completed += savePhoneTask_Completed;    Add completed event handler
}
void savePhoneTask_Completed(object sender, TaskEventArgs e)
{
    if (e.TaskResult == TaskResult.OK)
        SavePhoneButton.Visibility = Visibility.Collapsed;    (1) Confirm save and hide button
}
```

You only want to hide the SavePhoneButton when the returned status is TaskResult.OK (1). Hide the button by changing its Visibility property to Visibility.Collapsed.

Implement the SavePhone_Click event handler. The phone number you're asking the user to save comes from the SupportPhoneLink control:

```
void SavePhone_Click(object sender, RoutedEventArgs e)
{
    savePhoneNumberTask.PhoneNumber = (string)supportPhoneLink.Content;
    savePhoneNumberTask.Show();
}
```

Saving the customer support email address is the only remaining feature left to implement. You'll use SaveEmailAddressTask to complete PhoneTasks.

5.3.3 Saving an email address

The last feature of the PhoneTasks application lets the user save the customer support email address to the contacts database. As with the phone number, you'll hide the feature when the email address is saved. When the SaveEmailAddressTask chooser launches, the user is prompted to select a new or existing contact and is then shown the Edit Email address screen shown in figure 5.8.

Because this is another chooser, you need to add an instance field to the class:

```
SaveEmailAddressTask saveEmailAddressTask = new SaveEmailAddressTask();
```

Wire up the Completed event handler in the constructor and implement the event handler:

```
saveEmailAddressTask.Completed += saveEmailTask_Completed;
void saveEmailTask_Completed(object sender, TaskEventArgs e)
{
    if (e.TaskResult == TaskResult.OK)
        saveEmailButton.Visibility = Visibility.Collapsed;
}
```

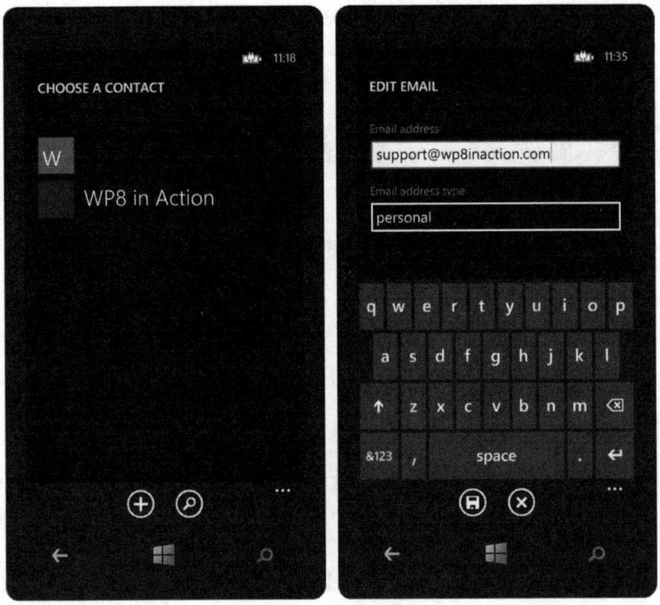

Figure 5.8 Saving an application-supplied email address

Implement the `SaveEmail_Click` event handler. The email address you're asking the user to save comes from the `SupportEmailLink` control:

```
void SaveEmail_Click(object sender, RoutedEventArgs e)
{
    saveEmailAddressTask.Email = (string)supportEmailLink.Content;
    saveEmailAddressTask.Show();
}
```

You've finished adding Windows Phone tasks to the PhoneTasks application, but we've not quite finished looking at chooser tasks. Before we move on to the next chapter, the next section discusses saving ringtones and choosing physical addresses, phone numbers, and email addresses.

5.3.4 Saving a ringtone

A *ringtone* is the sound played when a phone receives an incoming call, voice mail, text message, or email message. Ringtones are implemented with regular audio files that are installed on the phone. Windows Phone supports ringtones that are either M4R, MP3, or WMA audio files. To qualify as a ringtone, the audio file must be less than 40 seconds long and smaller than 30 MB. Ringtones must not have digital rights management (DRM) protection.

NOTE A ringtone-saving application is included with the book's sample code, which is available from the book's website at www.manning.com/binkley/.

The `SaveRingtoneTask` enables the development of applications that install custom ringtones. Custom ringtone audio files are read from the application install folder or local storage, which means your application must either include the ringtones in its XAP file or download them into local storage before installing them with `SaveRingtoneTask`. The following listing demonstrates how to install a custom ringtone.

Listing 5.6 Saving a ringtone with `SaveRingtoneTask`

```
void SaveRingtone_Click(object sender, EventArgs e)
{
    SaveRingtoneTask task = new SaveRingtoneTask()
    {
        DisplayName = "ringtones in action",
        IsoStorePath = new Uri("isostore:/Shared/Transfers/ringtone.wma"),
    };
    task.Completed += saveRingtoneTask_Completed;
    task.Show();
}
```

The `SaveRingtoneTask` is used like all the other choosers. The task is constructed, its properties are set, the `Completed` event is hooked, and the `Show` method is called. The `DisplayName` property is optional and, if not set, will default to the name of the audio file. The `IsoStorePath` property is required and must be a `Uri` using either the `appdata` or `isostore` schema. In this listing, you're referencing an audio file that was downloaded to local storage.

Once the chooser's user interface is displayed, the user can change the display name of the ringtone. The chooser UI is shown in figure 5.9. The chooser user interface is shown only if the audio file specified in the `IsoStorePath` is found at the given path and is an M4R, MP3, or WMA file. If the audio file is longer than 40 seconds or larger than 30 MB, the `Error` property in the `TaskEventArgs` returned to the `Completed` event handler will hold a `FormatException`.

`SaveRingtoneTask`, along with `SaveContactTask`, `SavePhoneNumberTask`, and `SaveEmailAddressTask`, displays a native user interface and allows data from a third-party application to be sent to a native application. These four tasks return status information to the calling application.

The next set of chooser tasks you'll learn about send data from the native applications to third-party applications. Your application can use these choosers to obtain a phone number, email address, or street address.

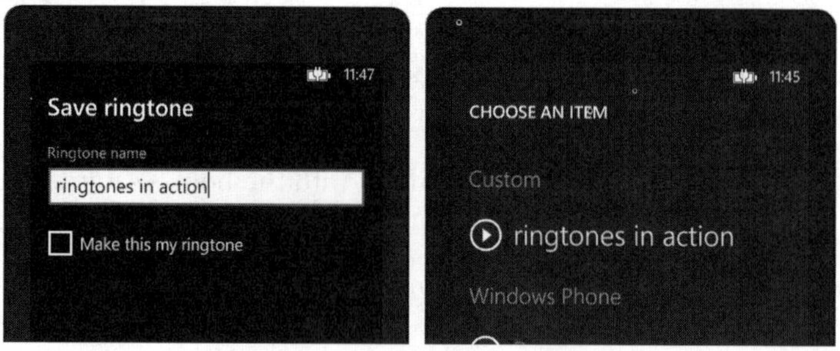

Figure 5.9 Saving a ringtone (left) and selecting a custom ringtone for a contact (right)

5.3.5 Choosing a phone number

PhoneNumberChooserTask retrieves a phone number from the contacts database, prompting the user to choose a phone number with the built-in contacts user interface. The PhoneNumberChooserTask.Completed event uses the PhoneNumberResult event args. The following listing shows how to use PhoneNumberResult.

Listing 5.7 Retrieving the phone number from PhoneNumberChooserTask

```
void phoneChooser_Completed(object sender, PhoneNumberResult e)
{
    if (e.Error != null)                                          ❶ Check for exceptions
       chooserResult = e.Error.Message;
    else if (e.TaskResult == TaskResult.Cancel)          ❷ User canceled
        chooserResult = "user canceled";
    else if (e.TaskResult == TaskResult.None)
        chooserResult = "no result";
    else if (e.TaskResult == TaskResult.OK)              ❸ Use selected phone number
        chooserResult = string.Format( "Phone Number for {0}\r\n{1}",
            e.DisplayName, e.PhoneNumber);
}
```

In this listing, chooserResult is a string field. Completed event handlers should check the Error property on the event args parameter ❶. If Error isn't null, an exception occurred during the choose operation. If the user presses the Back button to return to the application without selecting a phone number, a TaskResult.Cancel status is returned ❷, and the PhoneNumber property will be null. When the user completes the task, TaskResult.OK is returned, and the PhoneNumber property ❸ contains the selected value.

When your application requires an email address instead of a phone number, use EmailAddressChooserTask.

5.3.6 Choosing an email address

EmailAddressChooserTask retrieves an email address from the contacts database using the built-in contacts user interface. Your application depends on user interaction to choose the email address. The difference between EmailAddressChooserTask and PhoneNumberChooserTask lies in the type of result object passed to the Completed event handler. EmailAddressChooserTask uses EmailResult, which provides an Email property:

```
if (e.TaskResult == TaskResult.OK)
    chooserResult = string.Format("Email Address for {0}\r\n{1}",
        e.DisplayName, e.Email);
```

The last chooser we'll explore is the AddressChooserTask.

5.3.7 Choosing a street address

A physical address can be retrieved from the contacts database using the AddressChooserTask task. As with the other chooser tasks, the user is prompted to select an address with a built-in user interface. The `AddressChooserTask` returns an `AddressResult` object passed to the `Completed` event handler. The `Address` property of `AddressResult` provides the physical address in the form of a `string`:

```
if (e.TaskResult == TaskResult.OK)
    chooserResult.Text = string.Format("Street Address for {0}\r\n{1}",
        e.DisplayName, e.Address);
```

`AddressChooserTask` rounds out the list of choosers discussed in this chapter. In chapter 6 you'll read directly from the contacts database to retrieve more than a phone number, email address, or physical address. Even though using contacts choosers is limited, you should consider using them instead of reading directly from the contacts database. Choosers use the built-in user interface, saving the developer the work required to build a custom UI. Choosers provide the same consistent UI that phone users see when working in the People Hub.

5.4 Summary

The phone's security sandbox doesn't allow applications to share data directly. You can share data with the built-in native applications using launchers and choosers. Launchers and choosers provide a programmer the means to initiate phone calls, emails, and text messages and to read and write data to the contacts database. Marketplace tasks provide rich integration with the Windows Phone Store.

You haven't seen the last of launchers and choosers. In chapter 8 you'll use the `CameraCaptureTask` and `PhotoChooserTask` as we explore the Windows Phone's camera support for media. In chapter 9 you'll learn how to share photos and video with the `ShareMediaTask`. In chapter 16 you'll use the `MapsDirectionsTask` and the `MapsTask`. In chapter 17 you'll learn about the `WebBrowserTask` when you integrate your applications with Internet Explorer.

Remember that executing a launcher or chooser will deactivate, and potentially tombstone, your application. When the user finishes the task and returns to your application, the operating system reactivates your application. Be sure to code defensively and test that your application handles tombstoning and reactivation properly when returning from a launcher or chooser.

What should you do if your application requires more than phone numbers, email addresses, and physical addresses? The UserData API exposes nearly all the data stored in the contact database. In addition to granting read-only access to contact information, third-party applications can register a custom contact store. The UserData and ContactStore APIs are the topic of the next chapter.

6 Contacts and calendars

This chapter covers

- Searching for contact data
- Reading calendar appointments
- Creating a custom contact store
- Adding custom contacts

A modern mobile device is much, much more than a conveniently wireless telephone. For many people, the phone has replaced their appointment book and telephone directory. Phone numbers and email addresses are stored in the phone's contact list. Appointments and meetings are viewed using the Calendar application. Windows Phone developers access these mobile phone features via the UserData APIs.

As we discussed in chapter 5, the Windows Phone security model doesn't allow third-party applications to directly access the native data stores provided by the operating system. Access to native data stores, specifically the contacts and calendar data stores, is exposed through the `Contacts` and `Appointments` classes found in the UserData API.

In this chapter we'll explore the UserData and ContactStore APIs. You'll learn how to read contact and appointment data stored in the phone's People Hub and

Calendar application. You'll create a custom contact list, and you'll build an application to demonstrate how to use the UserData and ContactStore APIs. In the first half of the chapter, you'll build features that search for contacts and appointments in the native data stores. After that, you'll create a custom contact store and add features to add, edit, and delete contacts owned by the application.

In chapter 5 you learned how to use a chooser to prompt the user to pick an address or phone number from the native contact store. Even though using the contacts choosers is limited to phone numbers, email addresses, and physical addresses, you should consider using them instead of reading directly from the contacts database. Choosers use the built-in user interface, saving the developer the work of building a custom UI. They also provide the same consistent UI that phone users see when working in the People Hub.

> **TIP** The sample application built in this chapter displays contacts and appointments from the phone's People Hub and Calendar. When the phone emulators start up, the contact and calendar data stores are empty. Before starting this chapter, you should create a few contacts and appointments.

What are you to do if your application requires more than phone numbers, email addresses, and physical addresses? The UserData API exposes nearly all the data stored in the contacts database.

6.1 UserData APIs

Windows Phone aggregates contacts and calendar data from multiple service providers and social networks. Contacts from Windows Live, Facebook, Twitter, LinkedIn, and email accounts all appear in the People Hub. Appointments from each of the user's accounts are displayed in the Calendar application. The UserData API exposes a read-only view of the data that appears in the People Hub and the Calendar application.

> **NOTE** Users are notified that an application reads contacts and appointments data when they download the application from the Windows Phone Store. The Store doesn't tell them how an application will use the data. Applications that use the UserData API should respect the user's privacy and inform them how the data will be used. If the data is sent over the network, you should tell the user.

The UserData API consists of the classes and enumerations found in the `Microsoft.Phone.UserData` namespace. The two topmost classes are `Appointments` and `Contacts`, which provide the methods used to search through the calendar and contacts databases. Another important class is the `Account` class, used to identify the source of the data. Many of the classes in the `UserData` namespace have an `Account` property that identifies which service provided the contact or appointment data.

The `Account` class has two properties, called `Name` and `Kind`. The `Name` property displays the name value entered by the user when the account was first created in the

Settings application. The `Kind` property is of type `StorageKind` and will have one of the enumeration values listed in table 6.1.

Table 6.1 The kind of accounts exposed by the UserData API

`StorageKind` value	Description
`Phone`	Contact or appointment was created on the phone and isn't associated with any service provider
`Windows Live`	Contact or appointment data synchronized with a Windows Live account
`Outlook`	Contact or appointment data synchronized with a Microsoft Outlook account
`Facebook`	Contact data synchronized with Facebook
`Other*`	Contact and appointment data synchronized with some other service provider

* Later in this chapter, you'll build a custom contact store of your own that has the `StorageKind` type of `Other`.

To demonstrate how to work with the UserData API, you'll build a new sample application. Shown in figure 6.1, the application contains a `Pivot` control with two `PivotItems`—one for searching contacts and the other for searching appointments. The `Pivot` control is analogous to a tab control, and we cover it in depth in chapter 14.

To start building this application, open Visual Studio, select File > New Project, choose the Windows Phone App project template, and name the project *ContactsInAction*. You're starting with the basic application instead of the Windows Phone Pivot Application template. You're not using the Pivot Application Template because you

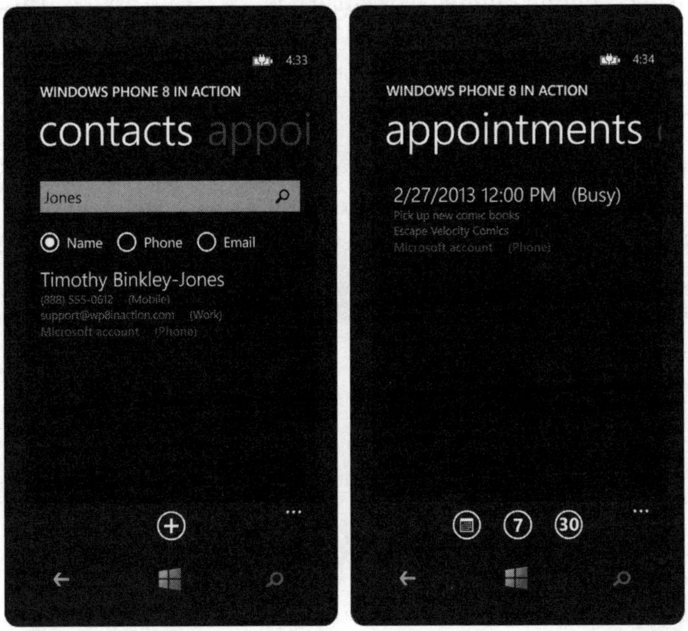

Figure 6.1 The ContactsInAction sample application. On the left is the contact-search pivot displaying the results of a search for all contacts with the name *Jones*. On the right is the appointments search pivot displaying an upcoming appointment.

don't need sample Model-View-ViewModel code generated for you. This project uses the Windows Phone Toolkit, so go ahead and use the NuGet Package Manager to add a reference to the toolkit assembly.

The MainPage.xaml file generated by the Windows Phone App project template isn't going to work here—you need to delete it from the project. Create a new page using the Project > Add New Item menu option. From the New Item dialog choose the Windows Phone Pivot Page item template and name the new page *MainPage.xaml*. If you look at the new MainPage.xaml file, you'll see a `Pivot` control containing two empty `PivotItems`. In the sample project, you'll add the controls shown in figure 6.1 to the `PivotItems`. You can read more about the `Pivot` control in chapter 14.

Just like the Hello World sample application in chapter 2, this ContactsInAction sample application uses the Windows Phone Toolkit. Use the NuGet package manager to add a reference to the toolkit and add the toolkit's namespace to the top of MainPage.xaml.

```
xmlns:toolkit="clr-namespace:Microsoft.Phone.Controls;
➥ assembly=Microsoft.Phone.Controls.Toolkit"
```

The first `PivotItem` contains controls to allow the user to search for a contact by name, phone number, or email address.

6.1.1 Searching for contacts

Contact records are discovered by executing a search against the contacts data store. The UserData API provides the `Contacts` class as the façade providing access to all of the service provider's contacts data. You can perform five different types of searches. A search can return all the data available in the data store. You can restrict searches to look for specific names, phone numbers, or email addresses. A search can also return the contacts that the user has pinned to the Start Screen.

> **TIP** Use of the Contacts API requires the `ID_CAP_CONTACTS` capability to be declared in WMAppManifest.xml.

The sample application allows the user to enter search terms, specify a search type, and then execute the search. The contact-search user interface is implemented in the contact `PivotItem`. The XAML markup for contact search is shown in the following listing.

Listing 6.1 XAML markup for the contact `PivotItem`

```
<phone:PivotItem Header="contacts">                    <-- ❶ Re-label first item
   <Grid>
      <Grid.RowDefinitions>
         <RowDefinition Height="Auto" />
         <RowDefinition Height="Auto" />
         <RowDefinition Height="*" />
      </Grid.RowDefinitions>
      <toolkit:PhoneTextBox Grid.Row="0" x:Name="filterBox"
         InputScope="Text" Hint="Enter a search term"
         ActionIcon="/Assets/search.png"
         ActionIconTapped="searchContacts_ActionItemTapped" />
```

```
        <StackPanel Grid.Row="1" Orientation="Horizontal">
            <RadioButton x:Name="nameSearch" Content="Name"
                IsChecked="True" />
            <RadioButton x:Name="phoneSearch" Content="Phone" />
            <RadioButton x:Name="emailSearch" Content="Email" />
        </StackPanel>
        <phone:LongListSelector x:Name="contactsList" Grid.Row="2" >
            <phone:LongListSelector.ItemTemplate>
                <DataTemplate/>
            </phone:LongListSelector.ItemTemplate>
        </phone:LongListSelector>
    </Grid>
</phone:PivotItem>
```

❷ Radio buttons to specify search kind

❸ Display results

You start the code listing by changing the header ❶ of the first `PivotItem` from *item1* to *contacts*. Add several controls to the `PivotItem`, starting with a `PhoneTextBox`, which allows the user to input the search term and execute the search. The `PhoneTextBox`'s `ActionItemTapped` event is handled by a method called `searchContacts_ActionItemTapped`, which you'll implement in the following pages. Add three `RadioButton` controls ❷ to allow the user to specify the kind of search to execute—name, phone number, or email. Add a `LongListSelector` control to display the results of the search ❸. The `contactList`'s `ItemTemplate` property is an empty `DataTemplate` to start with, and you'll be adding controls to display details about the resulting contact records.

Searches are executed using an asynchronous pattern with the `SearchAsync` method of the `Contacts` class. Results are returned via a completed event named `SearchCompleted`. `SearchAsync` accepts a search term and a filter type. Allowable values for the filter type are `None`, `PinnedToStart`, `EmailAddress`, `PhoneNumber`, and `DisplayName`. These values are defined by the `FilterKind` enumeration. Like many other methods that follow the older .NET asynchronous pattern, `SearchAsync` also accepts a state object that calling code can use to pair method calls to completed events.

Before implementing the `searchContacts_ActionItemTapped` method, you need to declare and construct an instance of the `Contacts` class. Add a field to the `MainPage` class to hold the `Contacts` instance, as well as a `using` statement:

```
using Microsoft.Phone.UserData;
Contacts contacts = new Contacts();
```

With the contacts instance created, you're ready to search the contacts data store. The following listing implements the `searchContacts_ActionItemTapped` method where you perform the search.

Listing 6.2 Searching for a contact

```
void searchContacts_ActionItemTapped(object sender, RoutedEventArgs e)
{
    FilterKind filterKind = FilterKind.DisplayName;
    if (phoneSearch.IsChecked.Value)
        filterKind = FilterKind.PhoneNumber;
    else if (emailSearch.IsChecked.Value)
        filterKind = FilterKind.EmailAddress;
```

❶ Specify type of search

```
    string filter = filterBox.Text;
    contacts.SearchAsync(filter, filterKind, null);     <-- 2 Execute search
}
```

First, determine the type of search to perform by looking at the radio buttons ❶. If a radio button is checked, use the corresponding `FilterKind` enumeration value. Next, retrieve the search term from the `TextBox` before finally calling the `SearchAsync` method ❷.

Phone number searches look for an exact match of all of the digits in the search term. *Email searches* match the search term to the user name or user name and domain name. *Display name searches* match the search term with the contact's first or last name using a *starts with* algorithm.

> **NOTE** The sample application doesn't use `None` or `PinnedToStart`, two of the five possible `FilterKind` values. Searches conducted with the `None` value will ignore the search term and return all contacts in the data store. The search term is also ignored by `PinnedToStart` searches, which return all the contacts that have Live Tiles pinned to the Start Screen.

Search results are returned to the application via the `SearchCompleted` event. Event handlers are passed an instance of the `ContactsSearchEventArgs` class, which exposes properties containing the search term, the `FilterKind` value, and the state object specified in the call to `SearchAsync`. The `ContactsSearchEventArgs` also has a `Results` property, which is a collection containing contacts that match the search term.

You're now ready to implement your own `SearchCompleted` event handler. Start by hooking the `SearchCompleted` event from the `Contacts` class. Wire up the `SearchCompleted` event to the `contacts_SearchCompleted` method in the constructor for the `MainPage` class:

```
contacts.SearchCompleted += contacts_SearchCompleted;
```

Now implement the event handler:

```
void contacts_SearchCompleted(object sender, ContactsSearchEventArgs e)
{
   contactsList.ItemsSource = e.Results.ToList();
}
```

The event args `Results` property is of type `IEnumerable<Contact>`, which means you convert the results to a list before you can assign the result to the `ItemsSource` property of the `LongListSelector` control.

The `Contact` class contains more than a dozen different properties and one method. `CompleteName`, `DisplayName`, and `IsPinnedToStart` are the only properties that aren't collections. The remaining properties are collections of `Strings`, `DateTimes`, or more complex objects. Table 6.2 details the complex classes found in the `UserData` namespace that are used by the `Contact` class.

Table 6.2 Contact-related classes

Class	Description
`CompleteName`	The first, middle, and last name of the contact. Nickname, title, and suffix are also provided.
`ContactAddress`	Contains a physical address for the contact in the form of a `CivicAddress` instance. Also contains an `AddressKind` property that specifies whether the address is a home or work address.
`ContactCompanyInformation`	Contains the company name and location as well as job title of the contact.
`ContactEmailAddress`	Contains an email address for the contact. Also contains an `EmailAddressKind` property that specifies whether the email address is for a personal or work account.
`ContactPhoneNumber`	Contains a phone number for the contact. Also contains a `PhoneNumberKind` property that specifies whether the phone number is for home, work, a mobile, a fax, or another type of device.

All the classes in this table except `CompleteName` contain an `Accounts` collection specifying the source of the data.

If you run the application now, you won't see any `Contact`-related data. You haven't yet declared any user interface elements to display the `Contact`. The following listing details the `ItemTemplate` XAML markup to display some of the data available for a contact.

Listing 6.3 Displaying contact properties with a `DataTemplate` and data binding

```
<DataTemplate>
   <StackPanel>
      <TextBlock Text="{Binding DisplayName}"
            Style="{StaticResource PhoneTextLargeStyle}" />
      <StackPanel Orientation="Horizontal">
         <TextBlock Text="{Binding PhoneNumbers[0].PhoneNumber}"
               Style="{StaticResource PhoneTextSmallStyle}" />
         <TextBlock Text="{Binding PhoneNumbers[0].Kind,
         ➥ StringFormat='(\{0\})'}"
               Style="{StaticResource PhoneTextSmallStyle}" />
      </StackPanel>
      <StackPanel Orientation="Horizontal">
         <TextBlock Text="{Binding EmailAddresses[0].EmailAddress}"
               Style="{StaticResource PhoneTextSmallStyle}" />
         <TextBlock Text="{Binding EmailAddresses[0].Kind,
         ➥ StringFormat='(\{0\})'}"
               Style="{StaticResource PhoneTextSmallStyle}" />
      </StackPanel>
      <StackPanel Orientation="Horizontal">
         <TextBlock Text="{Binding Accounts[0].Name}"
               Style="{StaticResource PhoneTextAccentStyle}" />
```

1 First phone number in collection

2 Data binding with StringFormat

```
            <TextBlock Text="{Binding Accounts[0].Kind,
            ➥ StringFormat='(\{0\})'}"
                   Style="{StaticResource PhoneTextAccentStyle}" />
        </StackPanel>
    </StackPanel>
</DataTemplate>
```

The user interface declared in the code listing isn't pretty. There are several `TextBlocks` stacked on top of each other, each showing their own bit of data. Each `TextBlock` is bound to one of the properties of the `Contact` object. For each of the collections shown in the template, only the first item is displayed, using index syntax in the binding expression ❶. You make use of the `StringFormat` feature available in XAML's data-binding syntax ❷.

Run the application now, input a search term, pick a search type, and execute the search by tapping the button. If a matching contact is found, you should see available contact details displayed on the screen. If you pick the Name radio button and leave the search term blank, all contacts visible to the application will be returned. Contact data is only part of the information available through the UserData API. Calendar appointments are also exposed via the UserData API.

6.1.2 Reviewing appointments

Calendar records are discovered by executing an asynchronous search against the appointments data store. The UserData API contains the `Appointments` class, which is the façade providing access to each service provider's calendar data. Searches are defined in terms of a date range and can be restricted to a specified `Account`.

> **TIP** Use of the Appointments API requires the `ID_CAP_APPOINTMENTS` capability to be declared in WMAppManifest.xml.

Your sample application allows the user to search for all appointments within a specified date range. The three supported date ranges are all appointments for today, all appointments in the next 7 days, and all appointments in the next 30 days. The user will specify the data range via three buttons displayed on an `ApplicationBar` visible only when the second `PivotItem` in your application is selected. The XAML markup for the application bar is shown in the following listing.

Listing 6.4 The appointments pivot application bar markup

```
<phone:PhoneApplicationPage.Resources>
   <shell:ApplicationBar x:Key="appointmentsAppBar">
      <shell:ApplicationBarIconButton Click="searchAppointments_Click"
         IconUri="/Assets/AppBar/feature.calendar.png" Text="today" />
      <shell:ApplicationBarIconButton Click="searchAppointments_Click"
         IconUri="/Assets/AppBar/search7.png" Text="7 days" />
      <shell:ApplicationBarIconButton Click="searchAppointments_Click"
         IconUri="/Assets/AppBar/search30.png" Text="30 days" />
   </shell:ApplicationBar>
</phone:PhoneApplicationPage.Resources>
```

❶ Added to page's resource dictionary

Because you want the application bar to show up only when the appointment's `Pivot-Item` is selected, you define the application bar as a static resource in the page's resource dictionary ❶. You'll need to copy the icon files into your Assets/Appbar folder and include them in the project. The icon file for the first button comes from the Windows Phone SDK. The other two can be found in the book's sample source code, which can be downloaded from http://manning.com/binkley.

The application bar is enabled when the user taps the second pivot item. An application can listen for selected item changes via the `SelectionChanged` event. Subscribe to the event in MainPage.xaml:

```
<phone:Pivot Title="WINDOWS PHONE 8 IN ACTION"
      SelectionChanged="Pivot_SelectionChanged">
```

In the event handler, called `Pivot_SelectionChanged`, check the `Pivot` control's `SelectedIndex` property. *If the selected index is 1*, then you need to assign the application bar resource to the page's `ApplicationBar` property:

```
void Pivot_SelectionChanged(object sender, SelectionChangedEventArgs e)
{
   Pivot pivot = (Pivot)sender;
   if (pivot.SelectedIndex == 1)
      ApplicationBar = (ApplicationBar)Resources["appointmentsAppBar"];
   else
      ApplicationBar = null;
}
```

If the selected index isn't 1, the `ApplicationBar` property is set to `null`. With the search button in the application bar, the markup for the second `PivotItem` contains nothing but a `LongListSelector`:

```
<phone:PivotItem Header="appointments">
   <Grid>
      <phone:LongListSelector x:Name="appointmentsList">
         <phone:LongListSelector.ItemTemplate>
            <DataTemplate/>
         </phone:LongListSelector.ItemTemplate>
      </phone:LongListSelector>
   </Grid>
</phone:PivotItem>
```

The `PivotItem` header is changed from *item2* to *appointments.* A `LongListSelector` is added to display the list of matching appointments returned from the search. The `LongListSelector`'s `ItemTemplate` is left empty for now.

The `Appointments` class provides the `SearchAsync` method and uses the same asynchronous pattern that the `Contacts` class uses. Results are returned via a completed event named `SearchCompleted`. There are four overrides of the `SearchAsync` method. The overrides all accept different combinations of start date, end date, account, and maximum number of items to be returned. Each of the `SearchAsync` overrides also accepts a state object that calling code can use to pair method calls to completed events.

The `SearchAsync` method limits the number of appointments returned. When you use an override of the `SearchAsync` method that doesn't specify the number of items, the search will be performed using the value defined in the DefaultMaximumItems field of the Appointments class, which is 100 items.

Before implementing the searchAppointments_Click method, you need to declare and construct an instance of the Appointments class. Add a field to the MainPage class to hold the Appointments instance:

```
Appointments appointments = new Appointments();
```

With the appointment instance created, you're ready to search the calendar data store. The following listing implements the searchAppointments_Click method where you perform the search.

Listing 6.5 Searching for appointments

```
void searchAppointments_Click(object sender, RoutedEventArgs e)
{
    DateTime start = DateTime.Today;
    DateTime end = DateTime.Today.AddDays(1).AddSeconds(-1);
    if (sender == ApplicationBar.Buttons[1])
        end = end.AddDays(7);
    else if (sender == ApplicationBar.Buttons[2])
        end = end.AddDays(30);
    appointments.SearchAsync(start, end, null);
}
```

❶ Start search with today's date

❷ Adjust end date

❸ Execute search

First, set the start date using DateTime.Today, which will cause the start time to be 12:00 a.m. Set the end date to be 11:59:59 p.m. by adding one day to Today and then subtracting one second ❶. Adjust the end date by adding either 7 or 30 days, depending on which application bar button was tapped, comparing the sender to the buttons in the application bar's Buttons collection ❷. Finally, call the SearchAsync method ❸.

Search results are returned to the application via the SearchCompleted event, which passes an instance of the AppointmentsSearchEventArgs class. The AppointmentsSearchEventArgs class exposes StartTimeInclusive, EndTimeInclusive, and the state object specified in the call to SearchAsync. AppointmentsSearchEventArgs also has a Results property, which is a collection containing appointments that fall within the specified date range, up to the specified number of items returned.

You're now ready to implement your own SearchCompleted event handler. Start by hooking the SearchCompleted event from the Appointments class. Wire up the SearchCompleted event to the appointments_SearchCompleted method in the constructor for the MainPage class:

```
appointments.SearchCompleted += appointments_SearchCompleted;
```

Now implement the event handler:

```
void appointments_SearchCompleted(object sender,
    AppointmentsSearchEventArgs e)
{
    appointmentsList.ItemsSource = e.Results.ToList();
}
```

The `Appointment` class defines several properties providing details about the appointment. Table 6.3 lists each of the `Appointment` properties.

Table 6.3 Appointment properties

Name	Description
`Account`	Details about which service provider is the source of the data.
`Attendees`	A collection of `Attendee` records representing people who were invited to the event. The `Attendee` class has `DisplayName` and `EmailAddress` properties.
`Details`	A `string` value describing the appointment.
`EndTime`	A `DateTime` value.
`IsAllDayEvent`	`True` if the appointment is flagged as an all-day event.
`IsPrivate`	`True` if the appointment is flagged as private.
`Location`	A `string` describing the location of the appointment.
`Organizer`	The `Attendee` record representing the person who created the appointment.
`StartTime`	A `DateTime` value.
`Status`	An `AppointmentStatus` enumeration with the value `Busy`, `Free`, `OutOfOffice`, or `Tentative`.
`Subject`	A string describing the subject of the appointment.

Your next step in the sample application is to create a simple user interface that will display a few of the properties from the appointment. The appointment UI will be added to the `appointmentsList_ItemTemplate`. Because the `appointmentsList` contains `Appointment` instances in its `ItemsSource` collection, you can use data binding to display appointment details with the `appointmentsList_ItemTemplate`. The following listing implements the appointment user interface.

Listing 6.6 Displaying an appointment

```
<DataTemplate>
   <StackPanel Margin="{StaticResource PhoneMargin}">
      <StackPanel Orientation="Horizontal">
         <TextBlock Text="{Binding StartTime, StringFormat='\{0:g\}'}"
               Style="{StaticResource PhoneTextLargeStyle}" />
         <TextBlock Text="{Binding Status, StringFormat='(\{0\})'}"
               Style="{StaticResource PhoneTextLargeStyle}" />
      </StackPanel>
      <TextBlock Text="{Binding Subject}"
            Style="{StaticResource PhoneTextSmallStyle}" />
      <TextBlock Text="{Binding Location}"
            Style="{StaticResource PhoneTextSmallStyle}" />
      <StackPanel Orientation="Horizontal">
         <TextBlock Text="{Binding Account.Name}"
```

Format StartTime with a standard format ❶

Add parentheses around Status ❷

```
                Style="{StaticResource PhoneTextAccentStyle}" />
            <TextBlock Text="{Binding Account.Kind, StringFormat='(\{0\})'}"
                Style="{StaticResource PhoneTextAccentStyle}" />
        </StackPanel>
    </StackPanel>
</DataTemplate>
```

You're displaying the `Appointment` with the same crude technique you used when displaying contact information. Stack several `TextBlocks`, one on top of the other, and then use data binding and string formatting to set their `Text` properties. This time use a `StringFormat` expression to display `StartTime` using *g*, ❶ which is the *General Date Short Time Format*. `StringFormat` is also used to place parentheses around the `Status` ❷ and `Account.Kind` values.

With the user interface declared, you're now ready to run the application and search for appointments. After checking to make sure you have appointments—if you're running on the emulator, you'll need to create a few by hand in the Calendar application—launch the application and tap each of the application bar buttons on the appointment pivots.

> **TIP** When calling `SearchAsync`, be sure to check the start and end dates passed to the method. No error is raised if the end date is before the start date, and an empty list is returned.

By now you've learned how to use choosers to add phone numbers, email addresses, and physical addresses. You've also learned how to read contact data using the UserData API. But what if your application's use cases require creating and managing lists of contacts? No worries—there's one more API that lets you build and manage a custom contact store.

6.2 Providing Custom Contacts

The Launchers, Choosers, and UserData APIs aren't the only APIs that can read and write contact information. The Windows Phone also offers the ContactStore API for those applications that need to manage their own contacts. Throughout the remainder of the chapter, you'll learn how to create a custom contact store and how to add contacts to it. To demonstrate how to add contacts, and to show how custom contacts are exposed to other applications through the UserData API, you'll add a new page to the ContactsInAction sample application. The new page is shown in figure 6.2.

A custom contact store is represented to application code via the `ContactStore` class, found in the `Windows.Phone.PersonalInformation` namespace. The `ContactStore` class implements a variety of methods for creating, deleting, and managing a contact store. These methods are described in table 6.4.

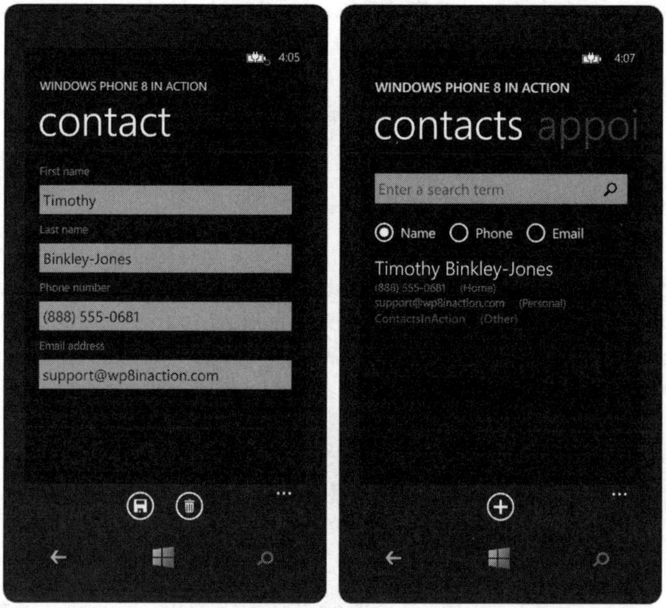

Figure 6.2 On the left is the screen you'll build to add new contacts to a custom contact store. On the right you see how a custom contact appears in the contacts search pivot item.

Table 6.4 ContactStore methods

Name	Description
`CreateContactQuery`	Creates a new query that specifies the fields to be returned and the sort order to be used to retrieve contact records.
`CreateOrOpenAsync`	Opens the application's one and only contact store. If the contact store doesn't exist, it's created.
`DeleteAsync`	Deletes the application's one and only contact store.
`DeleteContactAsync`	Deletes the specified contact from the contact store.
`FindContactByIdAsync`	Retrieves a contact from the contact store using the phone-assigned contact ID.
`FindContactByRemoteIdAsync`	Retrieves a contact from the contact store using an application-assigned contact ID.
`GetChangesAsync`	Retrieves a list of IDs for contacts that have been created, modified, or deleted.
`LoadExtendedPropertiesAsync`	Retrieves custom properties added to the contact store.
`SaveExtendedPropertiesAsync`	Adds or updates the custom properties attached to the contact store.

The `ContactStore` class has a single instance property called `RevisionNumber`. The `RevisionNumber` property changes each time a contact is added, updated, or removed. `RevisionNumber`, combined with the `GetChangesAsync` method, is particularly useful when you allow a contact store to be edited with the People Hub and you need to synchronize the changes with a remote database.

Before going any further, add a new page to the ContactsInAction sample application, using the Windows Phone Portrait Page template. Name the new page *ContactPage*. You'll need to add code to navigate to this new page.

6.2.1 Navigating to the Add Contact page

The ContactPage is launched via an application bar button. The button appears on an application bar that's specific to the contact search pivot on MainPage.xaml. Using the same technique used to declare the application bar for the appointment search pivot, add a new application bar resource to the MainPage resource dictionary:

```
<phone:PhoneApplicationPage.Resources>
   <shell:ApplicationBar x:Key="contactsAppBar" >
      <shell:ApplicationBarIconButton Click="addContact_Click"
            IconUri="/Assets/AppBar/add.png" Text="add"  />
   </shell:ApplicationBar>
...
</phone:PhoneApplicationPage.Resources>
```

The Add button uses an icon from the Windows Phone 8 SDK, shown in figure 6.3. Make sure it's added to the project.

Figure 6.3 The Add icon from the Windows Phone SDK

When the user taps the button, the `addContact_Click` event handler is called, which is where you add code to navigate to the new contact page:

```
void addContact_Click(object sender, EventArgs e)
{
   NavigationService.Navigate(
         new Uri("/ContactPage.xaml", UriKind.Relative));
}
```

The application bar is activated when the contact search pivot is selected. Update the `Pivot_SelectionChanged` event handler to assign the page's `ApplicationBar` property to the new application bar instance from the resource dictionary:

```
void Pivot_SelectionChanged(object sender, SelectionChangedEventArgs e)
{
   Pivot pivot = (Pivot)sender;
   if (pivot.SelectedIndex == 1)
      ApplicationBar = (ApplicationBar)Resources["appointmentsAppBar"];
   else
      ApplicationBar = (ApplicationBar)Resources["contactsAppBar"];
}
```

Now that the ContactPage is in place and can be launched with a tap on the Add button, you're ready to create a custom contact store.

6.2.2 *Creating a contact store*

You have a few different options when creating a contact store. You can create a read-only store that's only updatable by your application, or you can create a contact store that can be added to and edited by the built-in People Hub. When we first introduced the UserData API, we mentioned that not all properties visible in the People Hub are visible through the UserData API—for example, contact stores with a `StorageKind` of `Other`. When you create a contact store, you specify whether all the contact properties are accessible to other applications via the UserData API or only a limited number of properties.

> **Working asynchronously**
>
> To keep the OS working smoothly, Microsoft designed the Windows Phone Runtime APIs to make heavy use of asynchronous operations. Microsoft has a vested interest in making sure that all applications perform work on background threads, leaving the UI thread as responsive as possible. To this end, they force developers to write asynchronously as well.
>
> Fortunately, asynchronous support was built deep into the .NET Framework and exposed with the `async` and `await` keywords. When the compiler encounters the `await` keyword, it generates a bunch of code behind the scenes to implement the messy callback interaction that you'd otherwise have to code by hand. This greatly simplifies asynchronous programming, allowing you to write asynchronous code as if it were synchronous.
>
> For years the .NET Framework has used an asynchronous model centered on the `Task` and `Task<TResult>` classes. A different model is used by the Windows Phone Runtime centered on the `IAsyncInfo` interface and its derivatives. If you stick to using the `async` and `await` keywords, you probably don't need to worry about this difference. If you find yourself in a situation where the difference is important, you can use the extension methods on the `WindowsRuntimeSystemExtensions` class to convert from `Task` to `IAsyncInfo`, and from `IAsyncInfo` to `Task`.

An application creates a new contact store using the static method `CreateOrOpenAsync` from the `ContactStore` class. There are two forms to the `CreateOrOpenAsync` method: a no-parameter version, which creates a read-only, limited-access data store, and a version that accepts options for system access mode and application access mode. Initially, the ContactsInAction sample application creates a contact store from within the `OnNavigatedTo` method using the default options. The new `ContactStore` instance is assigned to a field of the `ContactPage` class:

```
using Windows.Phone.PersonalInformation;
ContactStore store;
protected override async void OnNavigatedTo(NavigationEventArgs e)
{
   store = await ContactStore.CreateOrOpenAsync();
}
```

CreateOrOpenAsync uses the new async/await pattern to simplify async programming, and the OnNavigatedTo method must be declared as an asynchronous method with the async keyword.

> **TIP** If you create a contact store with one set of options and then call CreateOrOpenAsync with a different set of options at some point in the future, an exception will be thrown.

With a new, albeit empty, page in place where the user can enter contact data and a newly created custom contact open and ready for use, you're ready to add new contacts to the contact store.

6.2.3 Adding a contact to the contact store

You add contacts to a contact store by creating a StoredContact object and updating its fields. The StoredContact object can't be created by itself because the StoredContact constructor requires a ContactStore instance. If you don't have a ContactStore instance available, an alternative approach is to create a ContactInformation object, fill in its values, and then create a StoredContact from it when the ContactStore instance is present.

Before a contact can be created by the sample application, a user interface needs to be created (shown in figure 6.4) that allows a user to specify first and last names, a phone number, and an email address.

Figure 6.4 The ContactPage uses TextBoxes to gather first and last names, a phone number, and an email address from the user.

Open ContactPage.xaml and add the markup in the following listing for a data entry form.

Listing 6.7 The XAML markup for the data entry form

```
<StackPanel x:Name="ContentPanel" Grid.Row="1" Margin="12,0,12,0">    <- Change ContentPanel to StackPanel
   <TextBlock Text="First name"
         Style="{StaticResource PhoneTextSmallStyle}" />
   <TextBox x:Name="firstNameInput" InputScope="PersonalGivenName" />
   <TextBlock  Text="Last name"
         Style="{StaticResource PhoneTextSmallStyle}" />
   <TextBox x:Name="lastNameInput" InputScope="PersonalSurname" />    <- 1 TextBoxes each use different input scope
   <TextBlock Text="Phone number"
         Style="{StaticResource PhoneTextSmallStyle}" />
   <TextBox x:Name="phoneInput" InputScope="TelephoneNumber" />       <-
   <TextBlock Text="Email address"
         Style="{StaticResource PhoneTextSmallStyle}" />
   <TextBox x:Name="emailInput" InputScope="EmailSmtpAddress" />
</StackPanel>
```

The data entry form consists of a series of TextBlocks and TextBoxes stacked one on top of another inside a StackPanel. Different InputScopes are assigned to each

TextBox to match the type of data to be captured by each ❶. For example, the TextBox used to capture a phone number is assigned the TelephoneNumber input scope.

Once the user has input some names and numbers, they tap a button on the application bar. The application bar contains two buttons: one to save a contact and one to delete a contact. Add the following application bar declaration:

```
<phone:PhoneApplicationPage.ApplicationBar>
   <shell:ApplicationBar>
      <shell:ApplicationBarIconButton Click="Save_Click"
            IconUri="/Assets/AppBar/save.png" Text="save"  />
      <shell:ApplicationBarIconButton Click="Delete_Click"
            IconUri="/Assets/AppBar/delete.png" Text="delete" />
   </shell:ApplicationBar>
</phone:PhoneApplicationPage.ApplicationBar>
```

Each of the buttons triggers an event handler. The Delete button is handled by the Delete_Click method. For the time being, implement an empty Delete_Click method. A new contact is added from the Save_Click method, shown in the following listing, which handles the Add button's click event.

Listing 6.8 Saving a new contact

```
async void Save_Click(object sender, EventArgs e)
{
   StoredContact contact = new StoredContact(store);          ❶ Pass contact store to constructor

   IDictionary<string, object> properties =                    ❷ Get known properties collection
            await contact.GetPropertiesAsync();
   contact.GivenName = firstNameInput.Text;
   contact.FamilyName = lastNameInput.Text;
   properties[KnownContactProperties.Email] = emailInput.Text;            ❸ Use keys to set
   properties[KnownContactProperties.Telephone] = phoneInput.Text;        email address, phone number

   await contact.SaveAsync();
   NavigationService.GoBack();                                 ❹ Add new contact
}
```

A new StoredContact object is created by calling the StoredContact constructor. The constructor requires a valid ContactStore, so the instance referenced by the store field is passed in ❶. Unlike the UserData Contact class, StoredContact doesn't have explicit properties for most of the contact data, the exception being a handful of properties to get and set the name. There's no Addresses property returning a collection of address objects or PhoneNumbers property returning a collection of phone number objects. Instead, the most common or well-known contact properties are accessed as key-value pairs stored in a dictionary. This collection of well-known properties is retrieved using the GetPropertiesAsync method ❷. When setting values into the properties dictionary, use the constants defined by the KnownContactProperties class ❸. The new contact record is added to the contact store by calling the SaveAsync method of the StoredContact class ❹. Once the contact is saved, GoBack is called to close the ContactPage and return to MainPage.

The `KnownContactProperties` class contains nearly three dozen key values. Example keys beyond the `Email` and `Telephone` constants used earlier include `Birthdate`, `Children`, `JobTitle`, `Notes`, and `Url`. There are also nine phone number keys, three email keys, and three address keys. The `Address`, `WorkAddress`, and `OtherAddress` keys should be used with a `ContactAddress` object. Consult the MSDN documentation for a full list of `KnownContactProperties` keys. Only known properties can be added to the dictionary returned by `GetPropertiesAsync`. If your version of a contact record includes uncommon or custom properties, you can add them to the dictionary returned by the `GetExtendedPropertiesAsync` method of the `StoredContact` class.

Now you're ready to run the application and add a contact. Be sure to add a phone number and an email address. After you add the contact, execute a search from the search pivot. Your new contact should appear in the list. What's missing? The phone number and email address are blank, as shown in figure 6.5. To verify that the number and email address were added, open the People Hub and look at the contact you created.

The information is missing because the contact store was created with *limited application access*, which is the default setting when a contact store is created using the no-parameter version of `CreateOrOpenAsync`. This includes UserData API searches from the application that created the contact store.

To demonstrate how an application can create a contact store with read/write system access and read-only application access, open ContactPage.xaml.cs and change the code to use the two-parameter version of `CreateOrOpenAsync`. The two parameters are of type `ContactStoreSystemAccessMode` and `ContactStoreApplicationAccessMode`. `ContactStoreSystemAccessMode` controls whether or not the People Hub can add, modify, and remove contacts. `ContactStoreApplicationAccessMode` controls whether or not the UserData API hides most of the contact data. The

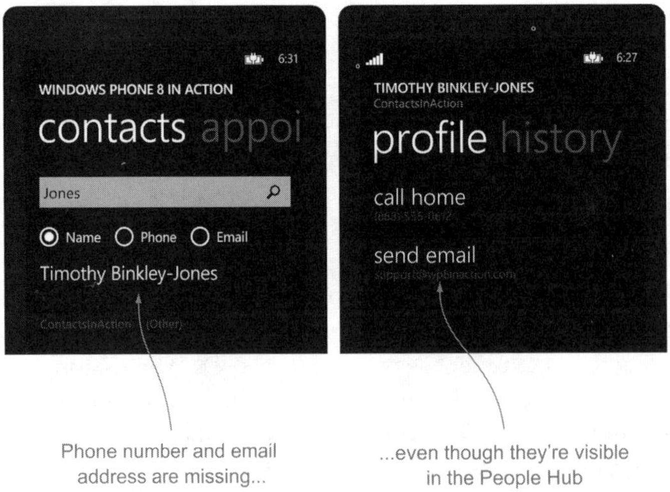

Figure 6.5 When a contact store is created with the limited, read-only access mode, the UserData API will hide most of the contact data, even though this data is visible from within the People Hub.

no-parameter version of `CreateOrOpenAsync` uses `ContactStoreSystemAccessMode.ReadOnly` and `ContactStoreApplicationAccessMode.LimitedReadOnly`. Change the code to call the two-parameter version of `CreateOrOpenAsync` with `ContactStoreSystemAccessMode.ReadWrite` and `ContactStoreApplicationAccessMode.ReadOnly`:

```
protected override async void OnNavigatedTo(NavigationEventArgs e)
{
   store = await ContactStore.CreateOrOpenAsync(
                  ContactStoreSystemAccessMode.ReadWrite,
                  ContactStoreApplicationAccessMode.ReadOnly);
}
```

Once a contact store is created, it must be opened with the same access modes used to create it—otherwise an `ArgumentException` is thrown by the `CreateOrOpenAsync` method. Because you've already created a contact store and are now opening it with different parameters, you must delete the existing contact store. You can do that by uninstalling the application from the phone or performing a rebuild-all in Visual Studio. After uninstalling or rebuilding, run the application again and re-add a contact. Switch to the contacts pivot and execute a search. This time, the phone number and email address should appear on the screen.

To demonstrate that the contact store is read/write, open the People Hub and add a new contact. When the Create Contact In screen appears, choose the ContactsInAction application from the list (shown in figure 6.6) and add names, addresses, and phone numbers for the new contact. Switch back to the sample application and execute a search one more time. The new contact should appear in the list and should show ContactsInAction in the `Account.Name` field.

Figure 6.6 When a custom contact store is created with read/write system access, a user can choose the contact store when adding new contacts in the People Hub.

A user can also use the People Hub to seamlessly edit and delete contacts from your contact store, giving the impression that your contact store is built right into the phone. Editing and deleting a contact can be done directly in the sample application using the ContactStore APIs.

6.2.4 *Updating an existing contact*

The sample application already has a data entry form for editing a contact's first and last names, email address, and phone number. This form was built for adding new contacts but can be reused to edit an existing contact. You're now going to update the application to use the search result list as a mechanism for choosing which contact to edit. When a user taps a ContactsInAction contact in the search results list, the contact's given and family names are sent to the ContactPage. The `LongListSelector`'s `ItemTemplate` uses a `StackPanel` as the layout container, used to detect when the user taps a contact. The following snippet wires up the StackPanel's Tap event to an event handler named stackPanel_Tap:

```
<phone:LongListSelector.ItemTemplate>
   <DataTemplate>
      <StackPanel Tap="stackPanel_Tap">
```

On a phone the search results list probably displays contacts owned by several different contact stores, but the ContactsInAction application can edit or update only the contacts it manages. Therefore, the event handler is required to examine the contact selected by the user and do nothing when the selected contact belongs to another application. The UserData API exposes who owns a contact through the Account class. The following listing shows how the Account.Name property is used to determine whether the contact should be edited.

Listing 6.9 Navigating to the contact page to edit a contact

```
void stackPanel_Tap(object sender, System.Windows.Input.GestureEventArgs e)
{
   StackPanel layout = (StackPanel)sender;
   Contact contact = (Contact)layout.DataContext;
   Account firstAccount = contact.Accounts.First();
   if (firstAccount.Kind == StorageKind.Other
         && firstAccount.Name == "ContactsInAction")
   {
      string uri = string.Format(
         "/ContactPage.xaml?givenName={0}&familyName={1}",
         contact.CompleteName.FirstName,
         contact.CompleteName.LastName);
      NavigationService.Navigate(new Uri(uri, UriKind.Relative));
   }
}
```

❶ Edit only application's contacts

❷ Pass names in query string

Cast the sender to a StackPanel and then cast its DataContext to a UserData Contact object. The first Account in the contact's Accounts collection is retrieved. This example ignores the situation when a contact has more than one Account, as happens when the user has used the People Hub to link two or more contact records together. The Account's Kind and Name properties are examined ❶, and when they match StorageKind.Other and "ContactsInAction", respectively, the contact's first and last names are added to the ContactPage URL as query string parameters ❷, and the ContactPage is launched.

Now that the MainPage is sending contact information, the ContactPage needs to be modified to extract the information from the query string and use it to find and load a StoredContact from the contact store. The following snippet shows new code added to the OnNavigatedTo method in ContactPage.xaml.cs:

```
protected override async void OnNavigatedTo(NavigationEventArgs e)
{
   ...
```

```
    if (NavigationContext.QueryString.ContainsKey("givenName") &&
        NavigationContext.QueryString.ContainsKey("familyName"))
    {
        string givenName = NavigationContext.QueryString["givenName"];
        string familyName = NavigationContext.QueryString["familyName"];
        FindAndLoadContact(givenName, familyName);
    }
}
```

Reading `StoredContacts` from a `ContactStore` differs from reading `Contacts` from the UserData API. The UserData API returns all fields but allows you to specify a filter. The ContactStore allows you to specify which fields you desire but doesn't accept a filter. The desired fields are specified by constructing and manipulating a `ContactQueryOptions` object. The `ContactQueryOptions` object has two properties: a collection of property keys named `DesiredFields` and an `enum` property named `OrderBy`.

The `OrderBy` `enum` is of type `ContactQueryResultOrdering` and has three possible values:

- `SystemDefault`
- `GivenNameFamilyName`
- `FamilyNameGivenName`

The `OrderBy` property defaults to `SystemDefault`. The `SystemDefault` ordering is defined by the operating system but doesn't match the ordering the user chooses in the People Hub settings.

By default the `DesiredFields` collection contains `DisplayName`, `FamilyName`, `GivenName`, `MobileTelephone`, `Email`, and a few other fields. It's a good idea to tailor this list to pull only the data you need for a specific view, and in the sample application only `GivenName`, `FamilyName`, `Telephone`, and `Email` are needed.

Once the `ContactQueryOptions` are configured to your application's needs, the next step is to retrieve a `ContactQueryResult` from the `ContactStore` via the `CreateContactsQuery` method. `CreateContactsQuery` is one of the few contact store methods that is *synchronous*. Although the `ContactQueryResult` class contains the word *Result*, it isn't a result but an object used to retrieve results. Results of a query are retrieved via `GetContactsAsync`, which comes in two forms. The first override of `GetContactsAsync` accepts no parameters and returns every contact in the contact store. The second version of `GetContactsAsync` accepts a starting index and maximum number of contacts and is ideal for retrieving small sets of data for display in a paging or scrolling user interface.

The whole process—create options, create the query result, and get contacts—is demonstrated in the `FindAndLoadContact` implementation, shown in the following listing.

Listing 6.10 Finding and loading an existing contact

```
StoredContact contact;                          <-- ❶ New field to reference contact

async void FindAndLoadContact (string givenName, string familyName)
{
```

```
   ContactQueryOptions options = new ContactQueryOptions();
   options.DesiredFields.Clear();
   options.DesiredFields.Add(KnownContactProperties.GivenName);
   options.DesiredFields.Add(KnownContactProperties.FamilyName);
   options.DesiredFields.Add(KnownContactProperties.Email);
   options.DesiredFields.Add(KnownContactProperties.Telephone);

   ContactQueryResult query = store.CreateContactQuery(options);
   IReadOnlyList<StoredContact> contacts = await query.GetContactsAsync ();

   contact = contacts.First(item =>
       item.GivenName == givenName &&
       item.FamilyName == familyName);

   IDictionary<string, object> props = await contact.GetPropertiesAsync();
   firstNameInput.Text = contact.GivenName;
   lastNameInput.Text = contact.FamilyName;
   if(props.ContainsKey(KnownContactProperties.Email))
      emailInput.Text = (string)props[KnownContactProperties.Email];
   if(props.ContainsKey(KnownContactProperties.Telephone))
         phoneInput.Text = (string)props[KnownContactProperties.Telephone];
}
```

❷ Remove all default fields and add desired fields

❸ Use LINQ expression to filter

Before implementing the `FindAndLoadContact` method, a new field is added ❶ to the `ContactPage` class to track the reference to the contact being edited. The first step in the method is to create a `ContactQueryOptions` instance, clear out the default `DesiredFields`, and add in only the four fields ❷ used in the sample application user interface. The options are then used to create a `ContactQueryResult`, which in turn is used to retrieve a list of `StoredContacts`. Because the contact store doesn't accept a filter, the method uses a LINQ expression ❸ to find the first contact record matching the specified `givenName` and `familyName` values. The matching contact's properties are then copied into the `TextBoxes` that compose the user interface.

NOTE Matching on only a first and last name isn't sufficient for identifying a contact in a real-world application. A contact list may have several contacts with the same names.

One last little change to `ContactPage` is required to support editing a contact. The `Save_Click` method currently creates a brand-new `StoredContact`. The method needs to be changed to check whether a contact already exists and, if not, create the new `StoredContact`. Replace the first line of the `Save_Click` method with the `if` statement shown in the following code snippet:

```
async void Save_Click(object sender, EventArgs e)
{
   if(contact == null)
      contact = new StoredContact(store);
   ...
}
```

You should now be able to run the ContactsInAction application, search for a contact in the main page, tap an existing ContactsInAction contact in the list, and edit the contact in the contact page. The final contact-management feature that needs to be implemented in the sample application is deleting a contact.

6.2.5 Deleting a contact

Users generally get annoyed when an application allows them to create content but doesn't allow them to delete it. This may be doubly true for a contact-management application. Imagine if you couldn't delete the pesky friend-of-a-friend who is always asking you to help them move. Deleting a `StoredContact` from a custom contact store is simple: you call the `DeleteContactAsync` method with the internal ID of the contact to remove:

```
async void Delete_Click(object sender, EventArgs e)
{
   if (contact != null)
       await store.DeleteContactAsync(contact.Id);
   NavigationService.GoBack();
}
```

The event handler in the preceding snippet is wired to the Delete button found on the application bar for the ContactPage. The Delete button uses the icon shown in figure 6.7. The user experience pattern is similar to that of native applications: before you can delete an item, you must first edit the item. Notice that the event handler first checks to see whether the contact field references an existing contact. Whether it does or not, the `NavigationService` is instructed to return to the main page.

Figure 6.7 The delete icon from the Windows Phone SDK

You're finished with the ContactsInAction sample application. This also concludes our coverage of the UserData and ContactStore APIs. Although we mixed up the two APIs in a single application, it's unlikely that you'd do so in a real application. Reading custom contacts from the UserData API has limitations, such as not being able to read the contact ID and not being able to read hidden data when the contact store is created with limited application access.

6.3 Summary

Even though the phone's security sandbox prevents one application from reading and writing data from another application, there are a few situations where limited amounts of data can be shared. A third-party application can read directly from the contact and appointment stores using the UserData APIs. The UserData APIs expose more than a contact's phone number, email address, and street address. The UserData API opens up the entire database, including full name, birthday, employer data, family members, and websites.

Your own applications can create a custom contact store and let users see, and possibly edit, the application's private data in the native People Hub. When created with the appropriate settings, other third-party applications can read your application's contacts through the UserData API.

The UserData APIs also provide access to calendar data—something not possible with launchers and choosers. A third-party application can search for appointments that fall within a given date range or come from a specific service provider.

Now that you know how to read data directly from the contact and calendar data stores, you might be tempted to write your own user interfaces to display this information. Carefully consider the user interfaces that you build and which of the APIs you use in your applications. The launchers and choosers you learned about in chapter 5 provide a user experience that exactly matches that of the native applications. Even if your application requires full access to the data exposed by the UserData APIs, consider using the chooser tasks when prompting the user to select a phone number or email address. Once you have the phone number, you can search against the contacts data to retrieve any other data required by your application.

Custom contact stores are one way an application can store data on the phone. In the next chapter you'll learn about other methods for storing data. The new Windows Runtime includes a completely new mechanism for reading and writing data to files on the hard disk or the equivalent flash memory used in a phone. Other data-storage mechanisms include writing data to a database hosted in a built-in version of SQL Server Compact Edition.

7 Storing data

This chapter covers

- Working with application settings
- Saving files in local storage
- Database operations
- Upgrading databases

Most applications require some form of data storage—from user preferences and user-created data to local caches of data stored in a cloud application or web service. Some of the data storage concepts discussed in this chapter will be familiar to .NET Framework developers because they're limited versions of the same storage technologies that have existed in the .NET Framework for many years. Other concepts are new to the Windows Runtime, and this may be your introduction to them. In this chapter you'll learn about the differences between the storage APIs in the .NET Framework and the storage APIs provided in the Window Phone SDK. For starters, the Windows Phone security model limits storage available to third-party applications to the local storage sandbox.

Each application is allotted its own sandbox on the phone, isolated from all other applications and from the operating system. The application's sandbox is

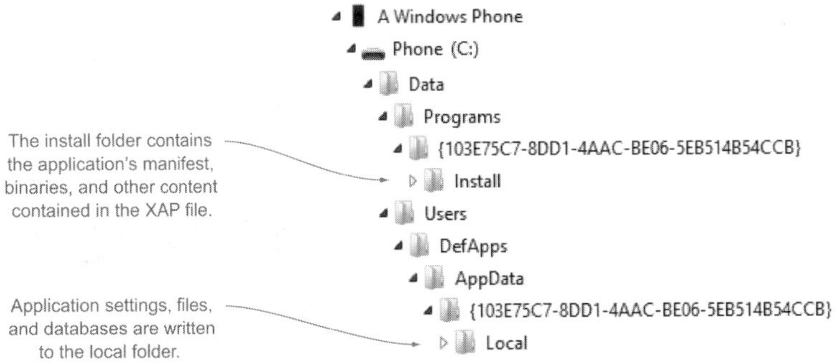

Figure 7.1 Application file system overview

separated into two folders, as shown in figure 7.1. The first folder, often referred to as *appdata* or the *install* folder, contains the installed application files. The second folder, called the *local* folder, `IsolatedStorage`, or *isostore*, stores files created or downloaded by the application.

Developers access the local folder with the .NET Framework class `IsolatedStorageSettings` from the `System.IO.IsolatedStorage` namespace or with the Windows Runtime classes `StorageFolder` and `StorageFile` from the `Windows.Storage` namespace. Developers can also use a relational database in the form of SQL Server Compact Edition, accessed via the LINQ to SQL framework found in the `System.Data.Linq` namespace. `IsolatedStorageSettings` provides a simple mechanism for storing data, removing the burden of messing with `FileStreams`. `Windows.Storage` exposes a more robust API for manipulating directories and files.

Windows Phone file system restrictions

Developers using the .NET Framework are used to accessing long-term storage with classes from the `System.IO` namespace including `File`, `FileInfo`, `Directory`, `DirectoryInfo`, `Path`, `FileStream`, and others. Because of the Windows Phone sandbox, many of these classes have been removed or have been changed to throw `MethodAccessExceptions` when used by applications and games. Silverlight developers should be aware that shared site settings and storage have been removed from `IsolatedStorage` for Windows Phone. Without access to the storage device, or shared site storage files, applications can't share local data with other applications.

The size of isolated storage in Silverlight for the browser applications is controlled by a quota. The quota is initially limited to 1 MB. The application can request quota increases, which must be approved by the user. Isolated storage for Windows Phone applications is effectively unlimited. The quota limit defaults to the maximum long value, and an exception is thrown if you call the `IncreaseQuotaTo` method.

To demonstrate using the `IsolatedStorage`, `StorageFolder`, `StorageFile`, and LINQ to SQL APIs, you'll build a sample application that reads and writes data using application settings, local storage files, and a relational database.

In the next section, you'll prepare a sample application that will interact with the three different data repositories you'll create later in the chapter.

7.1 Creating the High Scores sample application

The sample application, shown in figure 7.2, manages a list of high scores for a fictional game. It contains an application bar button for adding a randomly generated score, as well as a button for deleting the entire HighScore table. The sample application only shows high scores; you're not going to build a real game in this chapter.

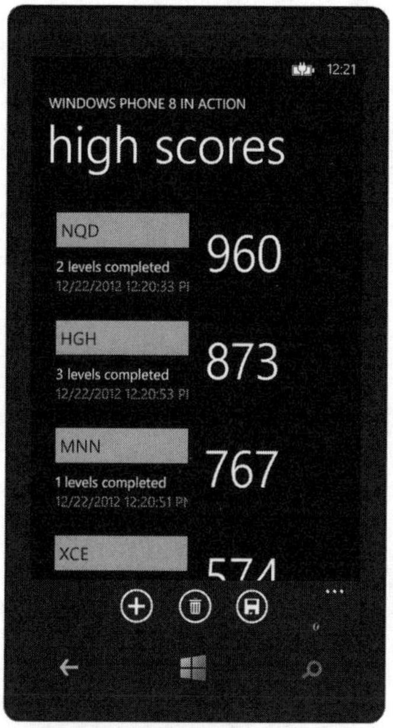

Figure 7.2 The High Scores sample application

First, you'll build the sample application and implement add and delete functionality without worrying about storing the high scores list. You'll then implement reading and writing the high scores list using a few simple repository methods. Start your sample application by creating a new Windows Phone App project in Visual Studio. Name the new project *DataStorage.*

The first thing you'll implement is a class to represent the high scores. Create a new class named `HighScore` and add properties for `Name`, `Score`, `LevelsCompleted`, and `Date`:

```
public class HighScore
{
    public HighScore() { Date = DateTime.Now; }
    public string Name { get; set; }
    public int Score { get; set; }
    public int LevelsCompleted { get; set; }
    public DateTime Date { get; set; }
}
```

The properties are all simple automatic properties, and the `Date` field is initialized in the class constructor.

7.1.1 Displaying the high scores list

High scores are displayed to the user using a `LongListSelector` on the main page of the application. The following listing shows the MainPage XAML markup for the content panel.

Listing 7.1 Displaying high scores

```
<Grid x:Name="ContentPanel" Grid.Row="1" Margin="12,0,12,0">
    <phone:LongListSelector x:Name="HighScoresList" Margin="0,0,-12,0">
        <phone:LongListSelector.ItemTemplate>
            <DataTemplate>
```

```
                <Grid Margin="12">
                    <Grid.ColumnDefinitions>
                        <ColumnDefinition />
                        <ColumnDefinition />
                    </Grid.ColumnDefinitions>                  ❶ Divide into 2 columns and 3 rows
                    <Grid.RowDefinitions>
                        <RowDefinition />
                        <RowDefinition />
                        <RowDefinition />
                    </Grid.RowDefinitions>
                    <TextBlock Text="{Binding Name}"
                        Style="{StaticResource PhoneTextLargeStyle}" />
Bind TextBlocks to  ❷  <TextBlock Grid.Row="1"
HighScore properties    Text="{Binding LevelsCompleted,
                        ➥ StringFormat='\{0\} levels completed'}"
                    Style="{StaticResource PhoneTextNormalStyle}" />
                    <TextBlock Grid.Row="2" Text="{Binding Date}"
                        Style="{StaticResource PhoneTextSubtleStyle}" />
                    <TextBlock Grid.Column="1"
Score spans             Grid.RowSpan="3"
3 rows ❸                VerticalAlignment="Center"
                        Text="{Binding Score}"
                        Style="{StaticResource PhoneTextTitle1Style}" />
                </Grid>
            </DataTemplate>
        </phone:LongListSelector.ItemTemplate>
    </phone:LongListSelector>
</Grid>
```

The LongListSelector consumes the entire content panel. Define the data template to be a Grid divided into two columns and three rows ❶. Several TextBlocks are arranged inside the Grid and are bound to properties of the HighScore object ❷ displayed in the LongListSelector. The Name, Date, and LevelsCompleted values are stacked in the first column, and the Score value is shown in a larger font, spanning all three rows ❸ of the second column.

Add two buttons to the application bar for adding new scores and clearing the entire list. Add the following application bar markup to MainPage.xaml:

```
<phone:PhoneApplicationPage.ApplicationBar>
    <shell:ApplicationBar>
        <shell:ApplicationBarIconButton Click="add_Click"
            IconUri="/Assets/AppBar/add.png" Text="add" />
        <shell:ApplicationBarIconButton Click="clear_Click"
            IconUri="/Assets/AppBar/delete.png" Text="clear" />
    </shell:ApplicationBar>
</phone:PhoneApplicationPage.ApplicationBar>
```

As with many of the applications in this book, you're using icons from the Windows Phone SDK, and if you use the property editor, the icons will automatically be added to your project.

You'll add the ApplicationBarIconButton Click events soon, but first you need to create a collection to hold the high scores list in the page's code-behind file.

Listing 7.2 Creating a collection of HighScores

```
using System.Collections.ObjectModel;
ObservableCollection<HighScore> highscores;                ❶ Define field for collection

public MainPage()
{
    InitializeComponent();
    this.Loaded += MainPage_Loaded;                        ❷ Wire up loaded event handler
}

void MainPage_Loaded(object sender, RoutedEventArgs e)
{
    highscores = new ObservableCollection<HighScore>();    ❸ Assign collection to list control
    HighScoresList.ItemsSource = highscores;
}
```

An `ObservableCollection` is used to hold all the high scores. The collection is defined as a field in the `MainPage` class ❶ and is instantiated in the `MainPage_Loaded` event handler, which is wired up in the `MainPage` constructor ❷. Finally, the collection is assigned to the `ItemsSource` property ❸ of the `LongListSelector` you named `HighScoresList`.

7.1.2 Managing the high scores list

Now that you have the collection created in the code-behind and displayed with XAML markup, you need to implement the logic for adding and clearing the list of high scores. A new `HighScore` is created with random values when the user presses the Add application bar button. The following listing details how a `HighScore` is generated and added to the collection.

Listing 7.3 Adding a HighScore with random values

```
Random random = new Random();                              ❶ Class-level random number generator
void add_Click(object sender, EventArgs e)
{
    int score = random.Next(100, 1000);                    ❷ Generate random values
    int level = random.Next(1,5);
    string name = string.Format("{0}{1}{2}", (char)random.Next(65,90),
        (char)random.Next(65,90), (char)random.Next(65,90));
    var highscore = new HighScore { Name = name, Score = score,
        LevelsCompleted = level };

    bool added = false;

    for (int i = 0; i < highscores.Count; i++)             ❸ Insert into sorted collection
    {
        if (highscores[i].Score < highscore.Score)
        {
            highscores.Insert(i, highscore);
            added = true;
            break;
        }
    }
```

```
    if (!added)
        highscores.Add(highscore);
}
```

A new HighScore is generated with the help of the Random class ❶, a pseudo-random number generator that you place in a new field named random. Define the add_Click event handler, and generate random values for the score, the level, and three characters that make up the name ❷. The random values are used to construct a new HighScore object. Insert the score into the highscores collection using an insertion-sort technique ❸.

Clearing the list is much easier. Inside the Click event handler, call the Clear method on the collection:

```
void clear_Click(object sender, EventArgs e)
{
    highscores.Clear();
}
```

The shell of the sample application is now complete. You can run the application, add a few high scores, and clear the list. When you exit the application and restart, the high scores list is empty once again. Because the topic of this chapter is data storage, the sample is far from complete. The application should be storing the high scores list and reloading the list when the application restarts.

Throughout the rest of this chapter, you'll look at three different methods for storing data: application settings, local storage files, and LINQ to SQL. Before we examine the details of each method, you should abstract the data layer from the user interface using a high scores repository.

7.1.3 Defining a high scores repository

You now have a working application, but the application doesn't store the list of high scores. To hide the details of the data storage implementation, you'll create a high scores repository to load, save, and clear the list of high scores. In this section you'll define the new repository type and modify the sample application to use the methods to access the high scores data.

Add a new class to the project using Visual Studio's Add New Item feature. Name the class HighScoreSettingsRepository. The new class declares Load, Save, and Clear methods, which you'll implement in the next section:

```
public class HighScoreSettingsRepository
{
    public List<HighScore> Load(){ return new List<HighScore>(); }
    public void Save(List<HighScore> highScores) {}
    public void Clear(){}
}
```

Now you're ready to update the MainPage class to use the repository. MainPage should initialize the high scores collection from the repository during construction. MainPage should also call the Save method when new HighScores are generated and the Clear method when the collection is cleared. Start by declaring a new member field for the repository and constructing a new instance:

```
HighScoreSettingsRepository repository = new HighScoreSettingsRepository ();
```

Now update the code in the loaded event handler to load the `highscores` list from the repository:

```
void MainPage_Loaded(object sender, RoutedEventArgs e)
{
    var results = repository.Load();
    highscores = new ObservableCollection<HighScore>(results);
    HighScoresList.ItemsSource = highscores;
}
```

The best time to save the list of high scores is after adding a new `HighScore` to the collection. Add the following line of code to the end of the `add_Click` method:

```
repository.Save(highscores.ToList());
```

The repository's `Clear` method should be called when the `ObservableCollection` is cleared. Add a call to the `Clear` method to the end of the `clear_Click` method:

```
repository.Clear();
```

With the call to the `Clear` method, all the repository functionality has been wired up. Wired up—but not yet implemented. To implement the first of three different repository implementations, you need to learn how to store data with application settings.

7.2 Storing data with application settings

Application settings provide a convenient API to store user preferences, application state, or other forms of data. They can store both simple and complex objects using key-value pairs. Application settings are accessed through a static property on the `IsolatedStorageSettings` class. The property, called `ApplicationSettings`, returns an instance of the `IsolatedStorageSettings` class. `IsolatedStorageSettings` implements a `Dictionary` interface with each setting paired with a unique key.

Objects placed in the settings dictionary must be serializable. When objects aren't serializable, an exception will be thrown when the settings are written to the storage device. Application settings are stored in a file written to local storage, as shown in figure 7.3.

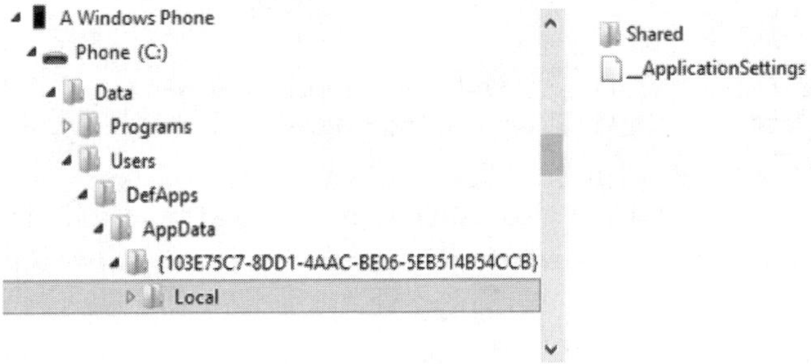

Figure 7.3 Application settings are written to a file in the local storage folder.

> **NOTE** Any action that clears local storage will remove the file, and application settings will be lost. Such actions include uninstalling an application and using the Rebuild Solution command in Visual Studio.

`IsolatedStorageSettings` can be found in the `System.IO.IsolatedStorage` namespace, and you need to add a `using` statement to any code file that makes use of application settings.

Start by implementing the `Load` method for the new repository. Within the `Load` method, declare a list of `HighScore` objects and call the `IsolatedStorageSettings` method `TryGetValue` to initialize the list:

```
public List<HighScore> Load()
{
    List<HighScore> storedData;
    if (!IsolatedStorageSettings.ApplicationSettings.
        TryGetValue ("HighScores", out storedData))
    {
        storedData = new List<HighScore>();
    }
    return storedData;
}
```

If a key-value pair doesn't exist in application settings, `TryGetValue` will return `false`, and you'll create an empty list so that you always return a valid collection.

Next, implement the `Save` method. Add the list of high scores to application settings using the `Item` property of the dictionary:

```
public void Save(List<HighScore> highScores)
{
    IsolatedStorageSettings.ApplicationSettings ["HighScores"] = highScores;
    IsolatedStorageSettings.ApplicationSettings.Save();
}
```

Values placed in the application settings dictionary aren't immediately written to disk. The values are usually saved when the application hosting the settings is terminated. Writes can be forced using the `Save` method.

Implement the `Clear` method by making a call to the settings class's `Remove` method. The `Remove` method will clear out the `HighScores` key but will leave all other application settings data intact. You can also force a write of the data by calling the `Save` method:

```
public void Clear()
{
    IsolatedStorageSettings.ApplicationSettings.Remove("HighScores");
    IsolatedStorageSettings.ApplicationSettings.Save();
}
```

The `IsolatedStorageSettings` class also implements a `Clear` method. The `Clear` method will remove every key-value pair stored in the settings dictionary. You could've used the `Clear` method because you only have a single key-value pair, but using the `Clear` method wouldn't be appropriate in any applications using multiple key-value pairs.

Your repository implementation is complete, and you can now use the settings repository in your application. Run the application, add a few high scores to the list, and exit with the Back button. Restart the application, and this time you should see the high scores reloaded and displayed in the user interface. Saving data to application settings is simple and only requires a serializable object to be stored in the settings dictionary. When your application requires a more complex data model, you should consider writing the data to files in local storage.

7.3 Serializing data to local storage files

Access to the file system is restricted on the Windows Phone. Instead of accessing the file system with the `Directory` and `File` classes found in the `System.IO` namespace, Windows Phone developers use `StorageFolder` and `StorageFile` found in the `Windows.Storage` namespace. `Windows.Storage` provides the basic file system APIs for managing files and directories. Windows Phone applications aren't allowed to use the traditional `System.IO` classes for managing files and directories, nor are they allowed to see the file system outside the sandbox. A few of the file system methods provided by the `StorageFolder` class are described in table 7.1.

Table 7.1 File system management methods provided by `Windows.Storage`

Method	Description
`CreateFileAsync`	Asynchronously creates a new empty file in the storage folder and returns a `StorageFile`
`CreateFolderAsync`	Asynchronously creates a new folder
`DeleteAsync`	Asynchronously deletes a folder
`GetFileAsync`	Asynchronously gets a file from the storage folder and returns a `StorageFile`
`GetFolderAsync`	Asynchronously gets a child folder from the storage folder and returns a `StorageFolder`

You may have noticed that all the methods in table 7.1 work asynchronously. In the past, working with asynchronous methods was a nasty business, with spaghetti code spread across various invoker and callback methods. Code written for Windows Phone 8 can use the new `async` and `await` keywords to keep the code clean.

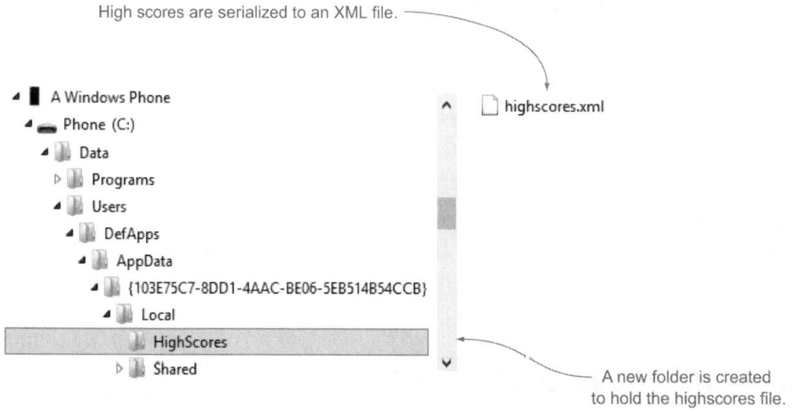

Figure 7.4 High scores are written to an XML file located in a new folder in local storage.

You're going to create a high scores repository that reads and writes data to an XML file using the `Windows.Storage` APIs. As shown in figure 7.4, the data file will be named HighScores.xml and stored in a new folder named HighScores.

Add a new class to the sample application project and call it `HighScoreFileRepository`. The new class will have nearly the same interface as the `HighScoreSettingsRepository`, with one notable change to the `load` method. The `HighScoreSettingsRepository` will load high scores asynchronously. In the application settings repository you built in the last section, the list of high scores was implicitly serialized by the framework. In the file storage repository, you're responsible for serializing the list. To help with serialization, you'll use the `XmlSerializer`.

7.3.1 Serializing high scores with the XmlSerializer

The `XmlSerializer` class is found in the `System.Xml.Serialization` namespace. The assembly containing the `XmlSerializer` class isn't automatically added to the project references by the Windows Phone App project template. To use `XmlSerializer` you must manually add an assembly reference to `System.Xml.Serialization.dll`.

You'll use `XmlSerializer` in both the `LoadAsync` and `Save` methods of the new `HighScoreFileRepository` class. The implementation of the `LoadAsync` method is shown in the following listing.

Listing 7.4 Loading scores from a file

```
using System.Threading.Tasks;
using System.Xml.Serialization;
using Windows.Storage.Streams;
using System.IO;

public async Task<List<HighScore>> LoadAsync()      <-- (1) Mark method with async
{
   List<HighScore> storedData;
   try
   {
```

```
        StorageFolder localFolder = ApplicationData.Current.LocalFolder;
        StorageFolder scoresFolder = await
             localFolder.GetFolderAsync("HighScores");
        StorageFile scoresFile = await
             scoresFolder.GetFileAsync("highscores.xml");

        using (IRandomAccessStreamWithContentType randomAccess
                = await scoresFile.OpenReadAsync())
        {
            XmlSerializer serializer = new
                XmlSerializer(typeof(List<HighScore>));
            storedData = (List<HighScore>)serializer
                .Deserialize(randomAccess.AsStreamForRead());
        }
    }
    catch (FileNotFoundException ex)
    {
        storedData = new List<HighScore>();
    }
    return storedData;
}
```

❷ Look for file in subfolder

❸ Deserialize list

❹ Create empty list

The method is named `LoadAsync`, instead of `Load`, to follow the naming conventions established by Microsoft where asynchronous methods have *Async* appended to the end of their name. The `async` keyword ❶ is required on a method declaration whenever it uses the `await` keyword. A reference to the application's local storage folder is retrieved through the `LocalFolder` property of the singleton `ApplicationData` instance. Using the local folder instance, the code searches for a subfolder named HighScores and then a file named highscores.xml ❷, retrieving references to each using the `GetFolderAsync` and `GetFileAsync` methods, respectively.

The `await` keyword is placed before the calls to `GetFolderAsync` and `GetFileAsync`. When the compiler sees the `await` keyword, it generates a bunch of code to set up an asynchronous call. When the `LoadAsync` method is executed, execution is stopped, and control is yielded to the caller. Once the asynchronous method following the `await` keyword completes, the next line of code in `LoadAsync` is executed. Because there are three uses of `await` in `LoadAsync`, the code is stopped three different times before finally opening the file and loading the high scores. Without the `await` keyword and the compiler's support for asynchronous programming, the `LoadAsync` method would have been implemented with four or five separate methods.

Once the file is opened via `OpenReadAsync`, its data is read by `XmlSerializer`. An `XmlSerializer` class is created, and the `Deserialize` method is used to read the persisted list and assign it to the return variable ❸. `OpenReadAsync` returns an instance of `IRandomAccessStreamWithContentType`, which is a WinRT concept. `XmlSerializer` doesn't know how to use WinRT concepts, so the `AsStreamForRead` extension method is used to convert `IRandomAccessStreamWithContentType` to a `Stream` that can be used by the serializer.

The first time the application runs, the local folder will be empty, and `GetFolderAsync` will throw a `FileNotFoundException`. If the folder, and subsequently the file, doesn't exist, it means that there's no high scores data to return. If no data exists, an empty list is returned, constructed in the `catch` block ❹.

It's interesting to note that although the method is declared as returning a `Task`, the code returns a `List`. This is another example of how the compiler simplifies asynchronous programming. Behind the scenes, the compiler is adding code to construct the `Task` instance and return it to the caller.

What if the HighScores directory doesn't exist? You know that it won't exist the first time you run the application. The directory must be created by your code. The file repository's `Save` method, shown in the following listing, will create the directory if it doesn't exist.

Listing 7.5 Saving high scores to a file

```
public async Task Save(List<HighScore> highscores)
{
   StorageFolder localFolder = ApplicationData.Current.LocalFolder;
   StorageFolder scoresFolder = await localFolder
         .CreateFolderAsync("HighScores",                          ❶ Create directory
         CreationCollisionOption.OpenIfExists);

   StorageFile scoresFile = await scoresFolder
         .CreateFileAsync("highscores.xml",                        ❷ Create or
         CreationCollisionOption.ReplaceExisting);                    overwrite file

   using (IRandomAccessStream randomAccess
         = await scoresFile.OpenAsync(FileAccessMode.ReadWrite))
   {
      using (IOutputStream output = randomAccess.GetOutputStreamAt(0))
      {
         XmlSerializer serializer = new
               XmlSerializer(typeof(List<HighScore>));
         serializer.Serialize(                                     ❸ Serialize list
               output.AsStreamForWrite(), highscores);
      }
   }
}
```

If the directory doesn't exist, such as the first time the application runs, the `Save` method adds a new directory to the root of local storage. The code uses `CreateFolderAsync` with the `OpenIfExists` option ❶. A new highscores.xml file is created with the `CreateFileAsync` method. When called with the `ReplaceExisting` option, `CreateFileAsync` ❷ creates a new file, or overwrites an existing file, and returns an unopened `StorageFile`. The file is opened asynchronously, and an output stream suitable for writing data is retrieved. The output stream will be used to write data to the file and should be closed when it's no longer needed. You place the code using the stream inside a `using` block, which will automatically call `close` and clean up the file handle for you. The list of high scores is written to the XML file using the `Serialize` method of the `XmlSerializer` class ❸. The `AsStreamForWrite` extension method is used to convert the WinRT `IOutputStream` instance to a .NET Framework `Stream` instance usable by the `XmlSerializer`.

7.3.2 Deleting files and folders

The last repository method you need to implement is `Clear`. The file repository implements `Clear` by deleting the HighScores folder. Deleting the folder deletes the file as well:

```
public async Task Clear ()
{
   StorageFolder localFolder = ApplicationData.Current.LocalFolder;
   StorageFolder scoresFolder = await localFolder
         .GetFolderAsync ("HighScores");
   await scoresFolder.DeleteAsync();
}
```

Once created, the HighScores.xml file and the HighScores folder will continue to exist in local storage. Files and folders in local storage are deleted when a user uninstalls an application, but they remain unchanged when a user upgrades an application to a new version.

The final step before running the application is to update the `MainPage` class to declare and instantiate a `HighScoreFileRepository`:

```
HighScoreFileRepository repository = new HighScoreFileRepository();
```

You should remove or comment out the `HighScoreSettingsRepository` that was added earlier in the chapter. You also need to update the `MainPage_Loaded` event handler, marking it as `async` and calling `LoadAsync` with the `await` keyword:

```
async void MainPage_Loaded(object sender, RoutedEventArgs e)
{
   var results = await repository.LoadAsync();
   highscores = new ObservableCollection<HighScore>(results);
   HighScoresList.ItemsSource = highscores;
}
```

The file repository demonstrates file and directory management within local storage available to an application. Some data models match nicely with a file-based storage solution. Other data models work better with a relational database solution.

7.4 Working with a database

Windows Phone ships with a built-in relational database engine, allowing applications to store data in a local database. The built-in database engine is a version of SQL Server Compact Edition. The bad news is that you can't use raw SQL to interact with the database. The data access API for working with local databases is LINQ to SQL.

> **NOTE** LINQ to SQL for Windows Phone only works with local databases. If your application needs to work with a remote database, you should consider using the OData API. You can learn more about OData at www.odata.org.

LINQ to SQL is an *object-relational mapping* (ORM) technology that was introduced with version 3.5 of the .NET Framework for desktop and server applications. Applications work with objects defined in a programming language, whereas relational databases work with tables, records, and fields defined by the database schema. An ORM is responsible for mapping the objects in the application with rows and fields in a database table. In the sample application, you work with `HighScore` objects. LINQ to SQL will transform `HighScore` objects into rows in the HighScore table of your database, and rows in your database into `HighScore` objects.

The LINQ to SQL libraries contain the following namespaces:

- `System.Data.Linq`
- `System.Data.Linq.Mapping`
- `Microsoft.Phone.Data.Linq`
- `Microsoft.Phone.Data.Linq.Mapping`

The `System.Data.Linq` and `System.Data.Linq.Mapping` namespaces contain a subset of the LINQ to SQL APIs that are found in the desktop libraries. The `Microsoft.Phone.Data.Linq` and `Microsoft.Phone.Data.Linq.Mapping` namespaces contain phone-specific extensions to LINQ to SQL.

Throughout the remainder of this chapter, you'll learn how to modify your sample application to use a local database. You'll learn how to read and write high scores data to the local database using LINQ expressions. And you'll learn how to create and delete databases and work with read-only databases that are included in the application's XAP deployment package.

First, you need to learn how to define your database schema using LINQ to SQL classes and attributes.

7.4.1 Attributing your domain model

The Windows Phone implementation of LINQ to SQL allows two different methods of defining a local database schema. The first method, covered in this section, uses attributes attached to the classes defined in your code. The second method, which is beyond the scope of this book, uses XML files to define the mapping.

LINQ to SQL provides attribute classes to define tables, columns, and indexes. One-to-one, one-to-many, and many-to-many relationships between tables are also declared using attributes. The LINQ to SQL attributes supported by Windows Phone are listed in table 7.2.

Table 7.2 LINQ to SQL attributes

Attribute	Description
`Association`	Declares an association between two classes, resulting in a relationship between two tables in the database.
`Column`	Declares a column in a table and maps the fields of an object to the column. The `Column` attribute has several properties that are used to describe the column.
`Index`	Declares an index for a table. Multiple indexes can be declared for the same table. The `Index` attribute is found in the `Microsoft.Phone.Data.Linq.Mapping` namespace.
`Table`	Declares a table in the database and identifies the type of object stored in the table. The database table name can be customized with the attribute's `Name` property.

With the `Table`, `Column`, `Index`, and `Association` attributes, you can create an entire database schema. You can create a multicolumn index by providing a comma-separated list of names for the `Columns` property.

The sample High Scores application is fairly simple and can be implemented using a single database table. Start the implementation by adding a few attributes to the existing `HighScore` class. The new `HighScore` code is shown in the following listing.

Listing 7.6 Updating the `HighScore` class

```
using System.Data.Linq.Mapping;                          ❶ Use mapping
using Microsoft.Phone.Data.Linq.Mapping;                   namespaces
[Table]
[Index(Columns="Score")]                           ❷ Define index
public class HighScore
{
    public HighScore() { Date = DateTime.Now; }
    [Column] public string Name { get; set; }
    [Column] public int Score { get; set; }
    [Column] public int LevelsCompleted { get; set; }
    [Column] public DateTime Date { get; set; }
    [Column(IsPrimaryKey = true, IsDbGenerated = true)]   ❸ Create
    public int Id { get; set; }                             primary key
}
```

Add `using` statements for the namespaces ❶ `System.Data.Linq.Mapping` and `Microsoft.Phone.Linq.Mapping` so you can easily use the `Table`, `Index`, and `Column` attributes. Start defining the database schema by adding the `Table` attribute to the `HighScore` class. Also add the `Index` attribute ❷ to the `HighScore` class, declaring a database index using the `Score` column. Add a `Column` attribute to each of the fields in the `HighScore` class. Create a new `Id` field ❸, declaring that the field is the primary key for the table and that its value is created by the database.

The attributed `HighScore` class defines how the HighScore table will be built in the database. Each row in the table will be mapped to a `HighScore` object by LINQ to SQL. You may be wondering how LINQ to SQL combines all tables to define the database and how you access the tables from code. The database itself is represented by LINQ to SQL with the data context.

7.4.2 *Defining the data context*

Each LINQ to SQL database is represented by a custom data context implementation. The data context is the API used to access data in the database. It defines the tables, caches reads, and tracks changes to objects. The data context knows what has changed and performs the appropriate SQL update statements. Your code tells the data context when to add a new object or delete an existing object, and the data context issues the appropriate insert or delete commands. Changes, insertions, and deletions are queued up in memory until LINQ to SQL is asked to submit the changes to the database, which happens when the `SubmitChanges` method is called. The data context performs all changes using transactions.

Later in the chapter, you'll look at how to use the data context in create, read, update, and delete (CRUD) operations. First, let's look at how to define a data context for your HighScores database. Each custom data context is derived from the DataContext base class found in the System.Data.Linq namespace. In this sample application, you'll create a new class named HighScoresDataContext and derive it from the DataContext class:

```
using System.Data.Linq;
public class HighScoresDataContext : DataContext
{
    public Table<HighScore> HighScores;
    public HighScoresDataContext(string path) : base(path) { }
}
```

For each table that should be created in the database, there must be a matching field in the DataContext class. The field will be of type Table<T>, where T is the LINQ to SQL attributed class that will be stored in the table. In the sample application, you have only one table to hold HighScore objects, so your data context defines a Table<HighScore> field.

The only other change you make to the HighScoresDataContext class is to implement a constructor. The constructor will accept a connection string and pass it along to the base class. The connection string can provide database details such as the filename of the database, the maximum size of the database, the read/write mode used to open the database file, and other options. Sample connection strings are shown in table 7.3.

Table 7.3 Sample database connection strings

Connection string	Description
/file1.sdf	Open the database located in the local storage file named file1.sdf. Open the database in read/write mode.
isostore:/file1.sdf	Same as /file1.sdf.
/folder1/file1.sdf	Open the database located in local storage in the folder called folder1, in the file called file1.sdf.
datasource='appdata:/file1.sdf';mode=read only	Open the database located in the application's install folder, in the file called file1.sdf. Open the database in read-only mode.
datasource='/file1.sdf'; max database size=512	Open the database located in the local storage file called file1.sdf. Allow the database to grow to 512 megabytes.

For a complete list of connection string parameters, see the local database connection strings for Windows Phone documentation on MSDN at http://mng.bz/3dVS.

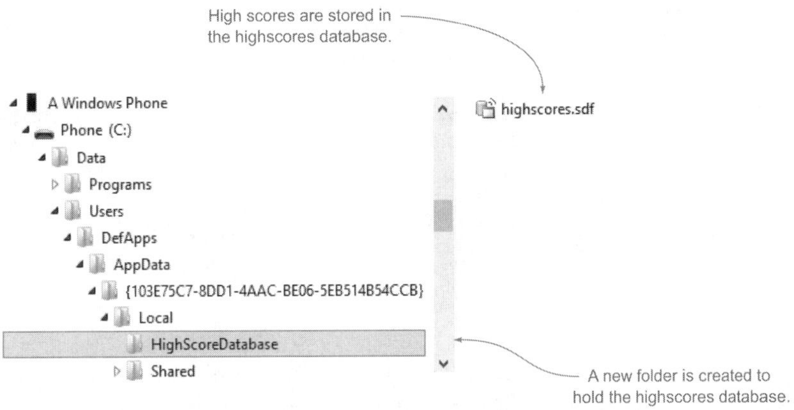

Figure 7.5 High scores are written to a database located in a new folder in local storage.

The simplest connection string requires only a filename. The `DataContext` class will look in the root folder of the application's local storage for a file with the given name. Database files can exist in folders other than the root folder. Read-only database files can also be read from the application's installation folder using the *appdata:* prefix. The default maximum value for a database is 32 MB.

Now that you have a data context class and have defined database mapping attributes on the `HighScore` class, you're ready to create the database.

7.4.3 Creating the database

At this point you've defined your database schema and data context and are ready to use the database in your High Scores sample application. You'll be loading and saving high scores using the same repository pattern you've been using throughout this chapter. You're going to add a new repository class to your project. Name the new class `HighScoreDatabaseRepository` and implement empty `Load`, `Save`, and `Clear` methods.

Your new repository class will use a `HighScoresDataContext` to read and write high scores to a database file in local storage. As shown in figure 7.5, the database file will be named highscores.sdf and will be placed in a folder named HighScoreDatabase.

Before you create the database, you declare the data context as a field in the repository and instantiate it in an `Initialize` method. The following listing details the repository class definition and `Initialize` method.

Listing 7.7 Creating the HighScores database

```
using Windows.Storage;

public class HighScoreDatabaseRepository
{
    HighScoresDataContext db;
    public async Task Initialize()
    {
        StorageFolder localFolder = ApplicationData.Current.LocalFolder;
```

```
            StorageFolder scoresFolder = await localFolder
                .CreateFolderAsync("HighScoreDatabase",
                CreationCollisionOption.OpenIfExists);          ❶ Create folder in local storage

            db = new HighScoresDataContext(
                @"isostore:/HighScoreDatabase/highscores.sdf"); ❷ Instantiate data context

            if (!db.DatabaseExists())
            {                                                   ❸ Create database file
                db.CreateDatabase();
            }
        }
    }
```

Before you create a new data context, ensure that the HighScoreDatabase folder exists by calling `CreateFolderAsync` ❶. Instantiate a new `HighScoresDataContext` object, specifying a file named highscores.sdf in the HighScoreDatabase folder ❷. Check whether the file has been created using the `DatabaseExists` method. If the database doesn't yet exist, ask the data context to create one ❸.

Because of the `Initialize` method, the database repository differs from the settings and file repositories implemented earlier in the chapter. The `Initialize` method must be called before the repository is used, and the best place to make the call is in the `MainPage_Loaded` event handler:

```
HighScoreDatabaseRepository repository = new HighScoreDatabaseRepository();
async void MainPage_Loaded(object sender, RoutedEventArgs e)
{
   await repository.Initialize();
   var results = repository.Load();
   highscores = new ObservableCollection<HighScore>(results);
   HighScoresList.ItemsSource = highscores;
}
```

You're now ready to implement the remaining repository methods. The `Load`, `Save`, and `Clear` methods will use database create, read, update, and delete (CRUD) operations provided by the data context.

7.4.4 CRUD operations

Usually, when working with databases, the developer has to keep track of which items are new, which have been updated, and which have been deleted. LINQ to SQL frees the developer from these tedious bookkeeping tasks. The data context tracks which objects have been updated and issues the appropriate update statements when changes are submitted. New objects are created in the normal fashion (using the `new` keyword) and are inserted into the table. To delete an object, the developer removes the object from the table.

READING DATA

We're getting ahead of ourselves—before you can work with objects loaded from a database, you must first be able to read them from the database. Your `HighScoreDatabaseRepository` class reads high scores from the database when the application calls the Load method. The LINQ to SQL table is a queryable collection, which allows you to use LINQ expressions to retrieve data from the table:

```
public List<HighScore> Load()
{
    var highscores = from score in db.HighScores
                     orderby score.Score descending
                     select score;
    return highscores.ToList();
}
```

In the Load method, you query the HighScore table using a LINQ expression built with the integrated query language. Select HighScore objects and sort them in a descending order of score. Then convert the collection to a list and return.

Behind the scenes, the LINQ to SQL framework converted the LINQ expression into a true SQL select statement. The SQL statement was sent to the SQL Server CE database, which returned a result set. LINQ to SQL then transformed the result set into a collection of HighScore objects. The list of high scores was returned to the application and displayed in the user interface as it was when you used application settings and local storage files.

CREATING NEW HIGH SCORES

The user of the application creates a new high score by tapping the Add button. The button's click handler creates a new HighScore object, inserts it into the list of high scores, and then asks the repository to save the list. LINQ to SQL tracks HighScore objects that it creates, but it doesn't automatically track objects created by application code. A new object can be added to the list of tracked objects using either the InsertOnSubmit or InsertAllOnSubmit methods provided by the Table class.

The InsertOnSubmit method accepts a single object. The new object will be added to the internal list of tracked objects and will be added to the database the next time the SubmitChanges method is called. InsertAllOnSubmit works with a collection of new objects.

The HighScoreDatabaseRepository doesn't provide a mechanism for registering new objects with the repository, and you don't need to change the interface. Instead, you can add logic to the Save method to detect when unmanaged objects have been added to the collection:

```
public void Save(List<HighScore> highScores)
{
    var newscores = highScores.Where(item => item.Id == 0);
    db.HighScores.InsertAllOnSubmit(newscores);
    db.SubmitChanges();
}
```

You detect when a HighScore object is new by looking at the value of the Id field. You added the Id field to the HighScore class because the database required a primary key, and you declared that the field's value would be generated by the database. This means that objects with a field value of zero have never been added to the database. Use a regular LINQ Where expression to find new HighScore objects in the list. Once you've identified new objects, use the `InsertAllOnSubmit` method to register them as new objects with the LINQ to SQL table.

Wrap up your implementation of the `Save` method by calling `SubmitChanges` on the `DataContext`. The `DataContext` will generate SQL insert statements for any new records. After the new scores are submitted to the database, LINQ to SQL reads the generated `Id` values and updates the `HighScore` objects so that their `Id` fields won't be zero.

Note that if you'd changed a value in an existing field, the changes would also have been submitted to the database with a SQL update statement. We'll take a close look at how LINQ to SQL updates changed data later in this chapter. First, let's look at how to delete data.

DELETING DATA

The sample application allows the user to reset the list of high scores by tapping the Clear button. The button's click handler calls the repository's `Clear` method. LINQ to SQL tracks `HighScore` objects that it reads from the database, but it doesn't automatically know when to remove an object from the database. An object can be removed from the database using either the `DeleteOnSubmit` or `DeleteAllOnSubmit` methods provided by the `Table` class.

When deleting a single object, use the `DeleteOnSubmit` method. The deleted object will be added to the internal list of tracked objects and will be removed from the database the next time the `SubmitChanges` method is called. `DeleteAllOnSubmit` works with a collection of objects.

The `HighScoreDatabaseRepository` assumes that `Clear` will delete all high scores records. Your implementation of the `Clear` method reads all the high scores from the `HighScores` table and then calls `DeleteAllOnSubmit` to delete every high score:

```
public void Clear()
{
    var scores = from score in db.HighScores
                 select score;
    db.HighScores.DeleteAllOnSubmit(scores);
    db.SubmitChanges();
}
```

When the `SubmitChanges` method is called, the appropriate SQL `delete` statements are generated and sent to the database.

The `HighScoreDatabaseRepository` is now fully implemented. Run the application and add a few new high scores. Exit and restart the application, and you should see the high scores reloaded from the database and displayed in the user interface. Clear the list and restart the application, and you should see a blank screen.

Now that the basic create, read, and delete operations are working, let's take a closer look at how LINQ to SQL implements update operations.

UPDATING DATA

By default the database context stores two instances of each object. The first object is returned as part of the query, and the second object is an unchanged internal copy. It uses the internal copy to determine when an object has been changed. When the `Submit` method is called, LINQ to SQL walks through each object it knows about and compares it to the internal copy. If the two objects differ in any way, LINQ to SQL generates a SQL update expression to store the changes.

> **NOTE** If you're not making changes to a database, you can improve performance by setting the `DataContext`'s `ObjectTrackingEnabled` property to `false`. When object tracking is false, the `DataContext` doesn't generate internal copies of tracked objects.

In order to demonstrate how to update objects with LINQ to SQL, you'll add an editing feature to your sample application. You'll allow the user to edit the name associated with the `HighScore` object, as shown in figure 7.6.

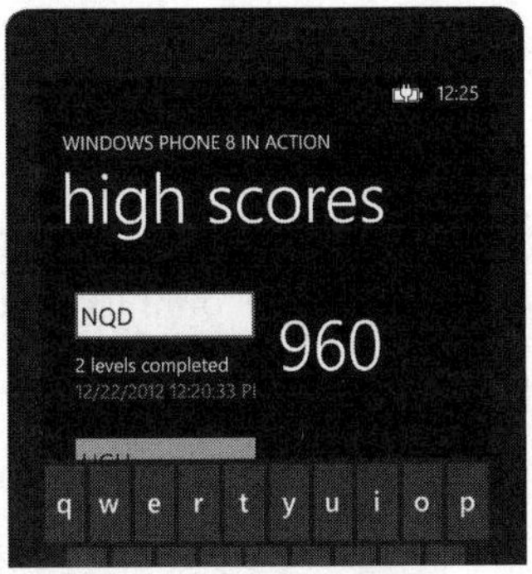

Figure 7.6 Editing the name associated with a high score

The user will edit the name with a standard `TextBox` control. In MainPage.xaml, replace the `TextBlock` that displays the name with a `TextBox`:

```
<TextBox Text="{Binding Name, Mode=TwoWay}" />
```

Add an application bar button that the user can tap to force a save of changes:

```
<shell:ApplicationBarIconButton Click="save_Click"
    IconUri="/Assets/AppBar/save.png" Text="save" />
```

Implement the `save_Click` event handler. Inside the event handler, you call the repository's `Save` method as you do when a new high score is generated:

```
using System.Windows.Input;
void save_Click(object sender, EventArgs e)
{
    var nameInput = FocusManager.GetFocusedElement() as TextBox;
    if (nameInput != null)
        nameInput.GetBindingExpression(TextBox.TextProperty)
            .UpdateSource();
    repository.Save(highscores.ToList());
}
```

You may wonder what the first few lines of the snippet do. The `TextBox` control has an interesting quirk when updating bound data. It tries to be efficient with data-binding updates and may not have updated the `HighScore`'s `Name` field when the `save_Click` event handler is called. In this snippet, you get the `TextBox` that has focus and ask for the `BindingExpression` object connected to the control's `Text` property. You use the `BindingExpression`'s `UpdateSource` method to ensure the name is copied from the `TextBox` to the `HighScore` object before you call the `Save` method.

You don't need to change the repository's `Save` method implementation. LINQ to SQL maintains an internal copy of the changed `HighScore` object. When the

SubmitChanges method is called, LINQ to SQL figures out which high scores have been updated and saves the changed objects to the database.

Developers can help the database context use fewer resources by using objects that implement the INotifyPropertyChanged interface. When serving up an object that reports it's own changes, LINQ to SQL doesn't generate an internal copy of the object. Instead it adds an event handler that listens to the PropertyChanged event. When the PropertyChanged event is raised, LINQ to SQL records the change internally. Then when the SubmitChanges method is called, the DataContext uses the list of changed objects to generate the appropriate SQL update expressions.

LINQ to SQL uses the underlying LINQ framework to provide powerful capabilities when working with collections and databases. Though describing the full features of LINQ is beyond the scope of this book, there are a couple more LINQ features you should understand. LINQ expressions are used to search for records in the database. We'll look at a couple simple alternative query expressions before discussing how to use precompiled query expressions to improve application performance.

7.4.5 Searching for data

The High Scores sample application uses a single query expression to return an ordered list of every high score in the database. What if you wanted a list of the scores for the third level in your fictional game? If you were writing a traditional SQL expression, you'd add a where clause comparing the LevelsCompleted column with the value 3. LINQ to SQL allows you to use a similar technique:

```
var highscores = from score in db.HighScores
                 orderby score.Score descending
                 where score.LevelsCompleted == 3
                 select score;
```

In this snippet a where clause has been added to the LINQ expression. Note that this where clause uses C# comparison operators. You'll add support for this scenario to the HighScoreDatabaseRepository by altering the Load method declaration to accept a level number:

```
List<HighScore> Load(int level = 0);
```

Here you're using C# optional argument syntax to specify a default value for the level argument. You set the default level value to zero, which means return all levels. When the level isn't zero, you should return only the high scores for the requested level. This is accomplished by using a where clause in the LINQ expression. Update the database repository's Load method, as shown in the following listing.

Listing 7.8 Loading scores for specific levels

```
public List<HighScore> Load(int level = 0)        <-- 1 Update arguments list
{
    IEnumerable<HighScore> highscores;
    if (level == 0)
    {
```

```
        highscores = from score in db.HighScores
                     orderby score.Score descending
                     select score;
    }
    else
    {
        highscores = from score in db.HighScores
                     orderby score.Score descending
                     where score.LevelsCompleted == level
                     select score;
    }
    return highscores.ToList();
}
```

❷ Default query

❸ Query including specified level

Begin updating the `Load` method in the `HighScoreDatabaseRepository` by adding the `level` argument ❶. Wrap the existing query ❷ with an `if` statement, executing the default query when the requested level has the value of zero. Execute a query containing a `where` expression ❸ when a specific level is requested.

Because your application always uses the same two queries, you can improve performance a bit by compiling the queries once and using compiled queries in your `Load` method.

7.4.6 Compiling queries

When LINQ to SQL encounters a query expression, the framework parses the expression, turning LINQ syntax into a SQL statement. This parsing must be performed every time the query is executed. To minimize the performance hit of constantly reparsing the same expression, LINQ provides a mechanism to compile an expression once and reuse it over and over.

Compiled LINQ expressions are represented in code with the `Func<TResult>` class. The `Func` class is a form of `Delegate`, representing a reference to a method that returns the type specified with the `TResult` generic type parameter. There are several variations of the `Func` class, allowing for anywhere from zero to four parameters.

You need two compiled queries, which means you need two member `Func` fields to represent them:

```
Func<HighScoresDataContext, IOrderedQueryable<HighScore>> allQuery;
Func<HighScoresDataContext, int, IQueryable<HighScore>> levelQuery;
```

The first compiled query represents the search for all high scores and is a `Func` class that accepts one argument, a `HighScoresDataContext`, and returns an `IOrdered-Queryable`, which is an ordered collection of `HighScore` objects. The second compiled query represents the search for the high scores for a specified level and is a `Func` class that accepts two arguments: the data context and the specified level.

The queries are compiled using the `CompiledQuery` utility class found in the `System.Data.Linq` namespace. This class is part of the LINQ to SQL implementation and provides a `Compile` method. You compile the two queries in the `HighScoreData-`

baseRepository constructor, which you'll have to create. The allQuery Func is generated with the following code snippet:

```
allQuery = System.Data.Linq.CompiledQuery.Compile(
    (HighScoresDataContext context) =>
        from score in context.HighScores
        orderby score.Score descending
        select score);
```

The second compiled query is generated with a similar expression, but includes a level argument and a where clause in the query:

```
levelQuery = System.Data.Linq.CompiledQuery.Compile(
    (HighScoresDataContext context, int level) =>
        from score in context.HighScores
        orderby score.Score descending
        where score.LevelsCompleted == level
        select score);
```

With the newly compiled queries at your disposal, you can simplify the Load method. The new Load method implementation uses the allQuery and levelQuery Func objects instead of inline LINQ expressions:

```
if (level == 0)
{
    highscores = allQuery(db);
}
else
{
    highscores = levelQuery(db, level);
}
```

If you think using a compiled query looks like calling a method, you're right. Compiled queries are instances of a Func, and the Func class is a form of a delegate. Delegates are references to methods.

7.4.7 Upgrading

When you're building applications and databases, it's rare that the data model is perfectly designed before the first release. Applications evolve, either because of new features that weren't thought of during initial design or because existing features didn't quite solve the problems the application was built to solve. What do you do when you need to change the database schema for an existing database when the user installs a new version of your application?

Database upgrade algorithms usually involve a series of SQL statements that alter and drop tables and columns in the database. The database support in Windows Phone doesn't allow SQL statements to be issued directly against the database. The Windows Phone LINQ to SQL implementation supports a few database upgrade scenarios. These scenarios are focused on additions to the database schema. New tables can be added to the database. New columns and indexes can be added to existing tables. New associations between tables can also be added to the database schema.

To demonstrate updating an existing database, let's pretend that version 1.0 of your application has already been released and users have installed the application on their phones. In version 1.1 of the application, you'll add a field to the `HighScore` class, which corresponds to adding a column to the database used to store the sample application data. When the user upgrades from version 1.0 to 1.1 of your application, the data stored in the application's local storage folder is left intact. The first time version 1.1 of the application runs, it executes code to upgrade the database created by version 1.0 of the application.

To see the upgrade code in action, make sure you run the application and create the database before making the modifications described in this section. Once you have an existing database, open the `HighScore` class and add a new `Difficulty` field:

```
[Column] public string Difficulty { get; set; }
```

Database updates are performed using the `DatabaseSchemaUpdater` class found in the `Microsoft.Phone.Data.Linq` namespace. To create instances of `DatabaseSchemaUpdater`, an extension method named `CreateDatabaseSchemaUpdater` has been added to the `DataContext` class. The following listing details how to create and execute an update.

Listing 7.9 Upgrading an existing database

```
if (!db.DatabaseExists())
{
    db.CreateDatabase();
}
else
{
    var updater = db.CreateDatabaseSchemaUpdater();
    if (updater.DatabaseSchemaVersion == 0)
    {
        updater.AddColumn<HighScore>("Difficulty");
        updater.DatabaseSchemaVersion = 1;
        updater.Execute();
    }
}
```

❶ **Standard database creation**
❷ **Check schema version**
❸ **Update schema and version**

The database upgrade code is added to the `HighScoreDatabaseRepository`'s constructor in an `else` block following the check for database existence ❶. The updater is created with a call to `CreateDatabaseSchemaUpdater`. Examine the current version of the database ❷. When the database is at version 0, you know it was created by version 1.0 of the application and that you need to add the new column to the HighScore table. The column is added with the `AddColumn` method ❸. Change the database version to the value `1`. When all the changes are complete, commit the changes to the database with the `Execute` method. The `Execute` method applies all the requested changes in a single transaction.

Debug the application and step through the database update code. If the database exists and is at version 0, the new column will be added to the HighScore table. If you

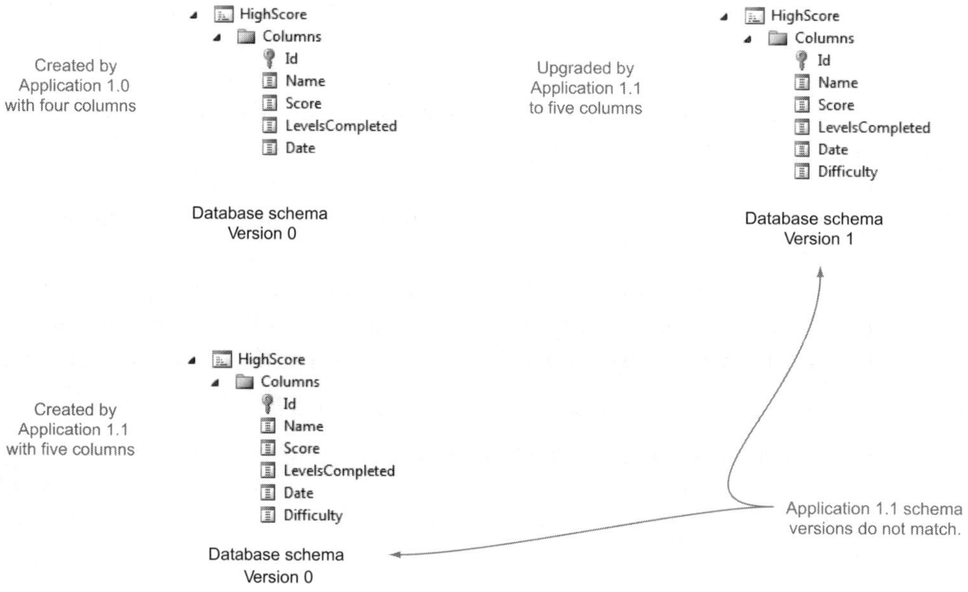

Figure 7.7 Database schema as created and upgraded by the application

exit the application and run it a second time, the database will be at version 1 and the upgrade code will be skipped.

There's a small problem with updating databases. The versioning scheme is an extension to LINQ to SQL specific to Windows Phone. The core LINQ to SQL code doesn't understand versioning, and databases are always created with a schema version of 0. As shown in figure 7.7, version 1.1 of your application also creates a database with a schema version of 0. A database upgraded by version 1.1 of the application will have a schema version of 1.

To demonstrate the problem, uninstall the High Score sample application (or use the Rebuild Solution option in Visual Studio). The first time you run the application, the database will be created at version 0, but this time version 0 contains the `Difficulty` column. Exit the application and run it again. The database update code will try to execute but will generate an exception because the `Difficulty` column already exists.

How can you fix this problem? You can use the `DatabaseSchemaUpdater` to set the schema version immediately after you create the database. Before you change the version 1.1 code that creates and upgrades the database, back up and start the process over. Comment out the `difficulty` field in the `HighScore` class and the `else` block with the upgrade code in the `HighScoreDatabaseRepository` constructor. Uninstall the application from the phone so that the current database is deleted. Deploy and run the code so that a database with schema 0 is created.

Now you're ready to fix the database's create and update code in version 1.1. The new code is shown in the following listing.

Listing 7.10 A better database upgrade implementation

```
if (!db.DatabaseExists())
{
    db.CreateDatabase();
    DatabaseSchemaUpdater updater = db.CreateDatabaseSchemaUpdater();
    updater.DatabaseSchemaVersion = 1;
    updater.Execute();
}
else
{
    DatabaseSchemaUpdater updater = db.CreateDatabaseSchemaUpdater();
    int databaseSchemaVersion = updater.DatabaseSchemaVersion;
    if (databaseSchemaVersion == 0)
    {
        updater.AddColumn<HighScore>("Difficulty");
        updater.DatabaseSchemaVersion = 1;
        updater.Execute();
    }
}
```

❶ Newly created database is version 1

❷ Upgrade if database not version 1

Change the database creation code to record version 1 in `DatabaseSchemaVersion` ❶. When the version of the schema is 0, upgrade ❷ the database by adding the `Difficulty` column and changing the database version to 1.

Run the application, and your database with schema version 0 should be upgraded to schema version 1. Run the application a second time, and the update code should find the schema version of 1. Now uninstall the application and redeploy it. The first time you run the application after deploy, you create the database with a schema version of 1. The next time you run the application, the updater reports version 1, and the new code decides that there's no work to perform.

We're nearly finished with our coverage of LINQ to SQL. The one other feature of LINQ to SQL that's unique to Windows Phone concerns deploying and using a read-only reference database.

7.4.8 Adding a read-only database to your project

Not all applications require writable databases, and some databases are intended for read-only scenarios. Consider a database that contains ZIP codes and tax rates for a CRM application or a dictionary of words for a word scramble game. Read-only databases can be included in your XAP deployment package in the same way that audio files, icons, and other content files can be included.

Read-only databases can be used directly from the application install folder and don't need to be copied into local storage. The connection string that's supplied to the `DataContext` allows you to specify the application installation folder as the location for a database file. How do you create the database file to begin with? One solution may be to create a Windows Phone project specifically to generate the database.

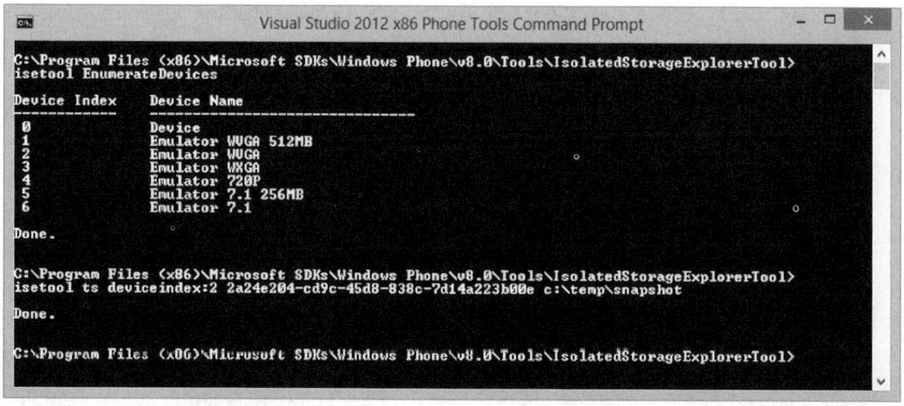

Figure 7.8 Taking a snapshot with the Isolated Storage Explorer. Before taking the snapshot, the devices are enumerated, and the appropriate device index is used in the subsequent invocation of ISETool.

The database generator project would share the data model classes along with the data context. The data model and data context could be placed in a shared assembly project or could be directly used in both projects using linked files.

The database generator project would call the data context's `CreateDatabase` method to create the database file. Once created, the database generator would create objects and insert them into the appropriate `Table` objects. When the database is fully created, the application can exit.

For the next step, you need the product ID from the generator project's WMAppManifext.xml file. The manifest file resides in the project's Properties folder. Find and open the file and look for the product ID:

```
<App xmlns="" ProductID="{c81a71a5-6f9f-4999-bc30-8f7cd48e1909}"
```

Fire up the Isolated Storage Explorer tool introduced in chapter 1. For this task, you'll take a snapshot of local storage, which will copy all the files in local storage to a location on your computer's hard drive. Figure 7.8 shows the results of downloading a snapshot to the C:\temp\snapshot folder.

Once the snapshot is copied, you can find the SDF file and copy it into your project by clicking Visual Studio Project > Add Existing Item. Mark the file's build action as Content, and it'll be included in the application's XAP file.

Now when your application is deployed, the database will also be deployed. When the application is running, the reference database can be opened with the following connection string:

```
datasource='appdata:/file1.sdf';mode=read only
```

One advantage of a read-only database is apparent when working with a large dataset. A dictionary of words could easily be stored in an XML file and loaded into memory. Loading large datasets into memory becomes impractical, if not impossible, when the database size approaches 100 MB. Using LINQ to SQL, an application can query for and load only a subset of the database, reducing the memory footprint required by the application.

7.5 Summary

In this chapter we presented three solutions for storing application data in the Windows Phone file system. You now know how to store application data between runs of an application. Simple sets of data can be stored in application settings using `IsolatedStorageFile`. Documents, text files, and binary data can be written to files using the `Windows.Storage` APIs provided by WinRT. The last alternative involves relational databases, SQL Server CE, and LINQ to SQL.

LINQ to SQL is a broad subject, and many topics require more detail than we can provide in this book. For more depth on LINQ to SQL, see the MSDN documentation. There are also several books devoted entirely to the subject.

We also showed how to use the Isolated Storage Explorer tool to copy data from a phone, specifically for generating read-only databases. The ISETool can also be used to load data into local storage, which is ideal for restoring a test device to a known state, allowing for the execution of specific test cases.

Some of the data storage concepts discussed in this chapter should be familiar to .NET Framework developers, because they're limited versions of the same storage technologies that have existed in the .NET Framework for many years. Other concepts, specifically those found in WinRT, are likely new to you unless you've already learned how to build Windows Store applications for Windows 8. In the next chapter you'll learn how to use the `PhotoChooserTask`, the `CameraCaptureTask`, and the `PhotoCamera` classes to develop camera-based applications.

8 Working with the camera

This chapter covers

- Working with the photo and camera choosers
- Taking pictures with the camera hardware
- Editing pictures
- Saving pictures to isolated storage

You're reading this book because you want to build mobile applications. To build a useful mobile application, you need to understand how most mobile users use their phones. Do they only use their phones for talking and sending text messages? No. A lot of mobile users use their devices for listening to music or the radio, watching videos, and taking photos. As mobile developers, we need to know how to integrate multimedia into our applications to let users do what they want to do in better and more efficient ways. In this chapter, you'll learn how to integrate the phone camera into your application and let the user capture photographs and include them in your application.

You may remember that we skipped the `PhotoChooserTask` and `CameraCaptureTask` in chapter 5 when we covered launchers and choosers. Both of these tasks are related to the camera, and we explain them in detail in this chapter. The `PhotoChooserTask` allows your application to prompt the user to pick a picture from the Photos Hub to load into the application. The `CameraCaptureTask` allows your application to use the built-in camera application to take a picture for use in your application.

TIP The Windows Phone emulator doesn't contain any photographs when it's turned on. But the first time the Photos Hub application is opened, it generates a photo album named 8 with a number of sample pictures. Before working through the samples in this chapter, open the Photos Hub so that you have some pictures to work with.

Working with the built-in camera application is great, but some applications need access to the underlying camera hardware and video stream. In addition to the two choosers, the Windows Phone SDK provides several different camera-related APIs. The .NET API for Windows Phone provides the `PhotoCamera`, which offers basic features for taking still photographs and is available only to managed code. A second class called `PhotoCaptureDevice`, introduced in Windows Phone 8 as part of the Windows Phone Runtime, works with both managed and native code. A third set of APIs extends `PhotoCaptureDevice` but are available only to native code. In this chapter you'll build a sample application demonstrating how to use both choosers and the `PhotoCamera` API to capture a picture. Once the picture is captured, you'll add a simple image-editing feature and save the picture to local storage.

Let's get started with the sample application, which you'll name PhotoEditor.

8.1 Starting the PhotoEditor project

PhotoEditor will capture a photograph using a few different APIs. The user will be able to pick a photograph from their media library using `PhotoChooserTask`. The user will also be able to take a picture using the built-in camera application with `CameraCaptureTask`. We show how to use the `PhotoCamera` API to turn the PhotoEditor into a custom camera application.

After you learn how to load or capture pictures, you'll put the *edit* in PhotoEditor by implementing a simple feature that places a stamp on a photograph. The sample application with a stamp can be seen in figure 8.1.

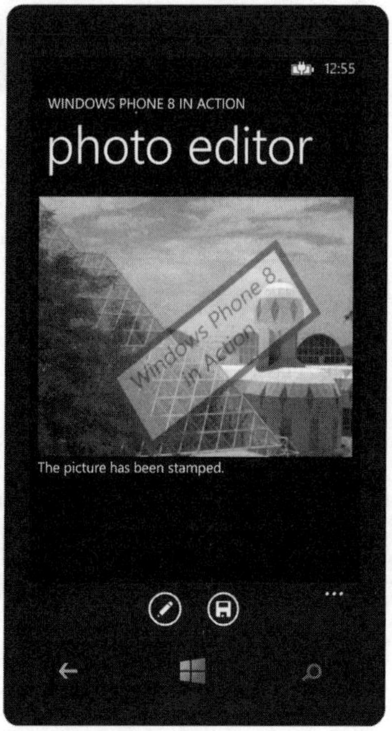

Figure 8.1 The PhotoEditor sample application

After stamping a picture, the user will be able to save the edited picture to local storage. In addition to routines to save the picture, you'll also create routines to reload the picture from a file in local storage.

Start the PhotoEditor application by creating a new project from the Windows Phone App project template. Name the project *PhotoEditor*. Once the project is created, open MainPage.xaml and add the following markup to the `ContentPanel Grid` control:

```
<Grid x:Name="ContentPanel" Grid.Row="1" Margin="12,0,12,0">
    <Grid.RowDefinitions>
        <RowDefinition Height="360" />
        <RowDefinition Height="*" />
    </Grid.RowDefinitions>
    <Rectangle x:Name="photoContainer" Fill="Gray" />
    <TextBlock x:Name="imageDetails" Grid.Row="1" TextWrapping="Wrap"
        Text="Choose an image source from the menu."/>
</Grid>
```

The `ContentPanel` is divided into two rows. The first row contains a `Rectangle` control called `photoContainer`. You'll render the selected picture image in this `Rectangle` using an `ImageBrush`. Later you'll use the `Rectangle` to display the live stream from the `PhotoCamera`. The second row contains a `TextBlock` that's used to provide the user with instructions, information about the image, and error messages. The second row is automatically sized, taking up all the space not consumed by the 360-pixel-high first row.

Now that you have the skeleton of the project ready, let's discuss how to load a picture into the `photoContainer Rectangle` using one of the two camera tasks.

8.2 Working with the camera tasks

All Windows Phones have at least one built-in camera. Microsoft's minimum hardware specification requires a camera with a flash. Many phones have a second front-facing camera. The Windows Phone class library contains two chooser tasks that provide limited access to the camera or, more specifically, to pictures taken by the camera or that exist in the media library.

> **NOTE** Only photographs are accessible via the chooser tasks. The chooser classes don't allow you to access videos from the camera.

The chooser tasks are `PhotoChooserTask` and `CameraCaptureTask`. Let's first look at choosing from the media library with `PhotoChooserTask`.

8.2.1 Choosing a photo with PhotoChooserTask

All phone users are familiar with how to take a picture with their mobile devices—taking pictures is a part of their daily phone usage. But as programmers, knowing how to take a photo with the phone isn't enough. `PhotoChooserTask` allows an application to launch the built-in Photo Chooser application.

You need to know how to use the camera from your code and how to integrate it with your custom application. That's what you'll learn in this section. `PhotoChooserTask` lets users select photos from the phone's media library with the built-in Photo Chooser. Photo Chooser has a navigation button that can take you to the camera application. `PhotoChooserTask` is handy for applications that allow a user to choose a photograph and use it somewhere in the application. One example is adding a picture to a user's profile. Table 8.1 describes the members of `PhotoChooserTask`.

Table 8.1 PhotoChooserTask members

Name	Type	Description
`Show`	Method	Shows the Phone Chooser application
`ShowCamera`	Property	Gets or sets whether the user is presented with a button for launching the camera during the photo-choosing process
`Completed`	Event	Occurs when a chooser task is completed

`PhotoChooserTask`'s `Show` method launches the built-in Photo Chooser application. When the `Show` method executes, your application is moved to the background as the operating system switches to the Photo Chooser application. Photo Chooser (shown in figure 8.2) opens to a list of albums that the user has created in the phone. There are two default albums, Camera Roll and Sample Pictures, in the emulator, but the user may have more in a real phone device. Note that Camera Roll is the default album that stores all photos taken by using the phone camera.

Figure 8.2 A screenshot of the built-in Photo Chooser application with Camera button

The `ShowCamera` property must be set to `true` if you want to show the camera icon in the application bar. When the camera icon is shown, the user has the option to take a new picture. It's always a best practice to set the `ShowCamera` property to `true`, because the user may want to take a new photo right away instead of selecting one from the photo albums.

Add an `ApplicationBar` menu item to show the `PhotoChooserTask` in your `PhotoEditor` application:

```
<phone:PhoneApplicationPage.ApplicationBar>
    <shell:ApplicationBar IsVisible="True" IsMenuEnabled="True">
        <shell:ApplicationBar.MenuItems>
            <shell:ApplicationBarMenuItem Text="choose photo"
                Click="Choose_Click" />
        </shell:ApplicationBar.MenuItems>
    </shell:ApplicationBar>
</phone:PhoneApplicationPage.ApplicationBar>
```

The `ApplicationBarMenuItem` displays the text *choose photo*. The click event handler for the menu item constructs a `PhotoChooserTask` and sets the `ShowCamera` property to `true`:

```
using Microsoft.Phone.Tasks;
void Choose_Click(object sender, EventArgs e)
{
    var task = new PhotoChooserTask ();
    task.ShowCamera = true;
    task.Completed += chooserTask_Completed;
    task.Show();
}
```

The `Completed` event is wired up to the `chooserTask_Completed` event handler. Recall from chapter 5 that when the `Show` method is called, your application is paused and placed in the Task Switcher's back stack. When the user completes the chooser operation, the operating system navigates back to your application. The `Completed` event handler is called when the application resumes operation in the foreground. The `Completed` event will be raised when the user selects a photo from the photo library, takes a new photo, or uses the Back button to navigate back to the application. The following listing shows how to handle the `Completed` event and display the selected photo in the image control.

Listing 8.1 Displaying the selected photograph

```
using Microsoft.Phone;
using System.Windows.Media;
using System.Windows.Media.Imaging;

private WriteableBitmap currentImage;                          ❶ Field to hold chosen photo
void chooserTask_Completed(object sender, PhotoResult e)
{
    if (e.TaskResult == TaskResult.OK)
    {
        currentImage = PictureDecoder.DecodeJpeg(e.ChosenPhoto);   ❷ Photo stream in e.ChosenPhoto
        photoContainer.Fill = new
            ImageBrush{ ImageSource = currentImage };              ❸ Display image with brush
        imageDetails.Text = string.Format("Image from {0}\n",
            sender.GetType().Name);
        imageDetails.Text += string.Format("Original filename:\n{0}",
            e.OriginalFileName);
    }
    else
    {
        photoContainer.Fill = new SolidColorBrush(Colors.Gray);
        imageDetails.Text = e.TaskResult.ToString();
    }
}
```

First, you need a new `WriteableBitmap` field named `currentImage` ❶ in which you store the photograph shown in the `photoContainer Rectangle` control. It's a best practice to check the `TaskResult` property to determine whether the chooser task completed `OK` or the task was canceled. The `PhotoResult` class defines two properties,

Figure 8.3 The left-hand image is a screen shot showing a successful result from the PhotoChooserTask displayed to the user. A gray box is shown with the message "Cancel" when a result other than `OK` is returned, such as when the user presses the Back button.

`ChosenPhoto` and `OriginalFileName`. `ChosenPhoto` contains the selected picture's data in a `Stream`. Pass the image stream to the `DecodeJpeg` method of the helper class called `PictureDecoder` ❷. The `PictureDecoder` class is found in the `Microsoft.Phone` namespace. The `DecodeJpeg` method builds a `WriteableBitmap`. Use the `WriteableBitmap` as the source for an `ImageBrush`, and the brush is used as the `Fill` for the `photoContainer` ❸. Then build a message informing the user that the picture came from the `PhotoChooserTask` and had the filename specified in the `OriginalFileName` property.

When the `TaskResult` isn't `OK`, clear the `photoContainer` by setting the `Fill` property to a `SolidColorBrush` and display the `TaskResult` value in the `image-Details` `TextBlock`. The successful and unsuccessful results are shown in figure 8.3.

Run the application, select the Choose Photo menu item, and pick a photo. The photo you choose should be shown in the application when the `PhotoChooserTask` completes. Next, we look at how to use the `CameraCaptureTask`.

8.2.2 Taking photos with CameraCaptureTask

`CameraCaptureTask` is another useful task that allows developers to launch the built-in Camera application. Unlike `PhotoChooserTask`, it allows you to open the camera directly from an application without requiring the user to perform additional steps. Shown in figure 8.4, the Camera application in the emulator shows a placeholder gray screen with a moving colored block. You can take a photo in the emulator by clicking anywhere within the placeholder image. We recommend you use a physical device to test this task.

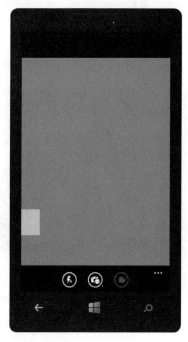

Figure 8.4 The Camera application in the emulator. A colored square moves along the border of the screen while the camera is active. When a picture is snapped, the result is the same image—a field of gray with a colored box along the edge.

The `CameraCaptureTask` doesn't have any properties and only implements the `Show` method. Show the Camera application by calling the `Show` method from the click event of a new menu item you add to MainPage.xaml:

```
<shell:ApplicationBarMenuItem Text="capture photo" Click="Capture_Click" />
```

The following snippet shows how to use `CameraCaptureTask`:

```
void Capture_Click(object sender, EventArgs e)
{
    var task = new CameraCaptureTask ();
    task.Completed += chooserTask_Completed;
    task.Show();
}
```

You subscribe to the `Completed` event to receive the photo stream from the camera and call the `Show` method to launch the camera. For the `Completed` event, you can use the same event handler method that you used in the `PhotoChooserTask` sample.

Deploy the updated application to your phone, run the application, and choose the capture photo menu option. Hold the phone in landscape orientation, snap a picture, and tap the Accept button. When the task completes, you should see your new photo displayed in the `photoContainer`. Select the capture photo menu option again, but this time hold your phone in portrait orientation when you snap the picture. When the task returns this time, the new picture is displayed with the top of the photo right side up in the `photoContainer Rectangle`, as shown in figure 8.5. Take a few more pictures, rotating the camera into different orientations. Each time the picture should appear in the `photoContainer` right-side up. When the Windows Phone processes the picture, it knows how to adjust the picture based on the phone's orientation. It's important to

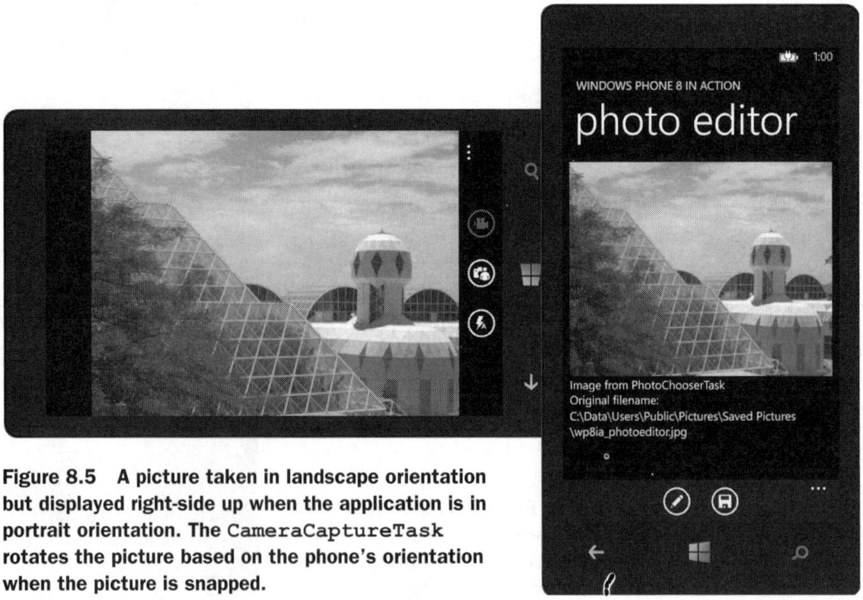

Figure 8.5 A picture taken in landscape orientation but displayed right-side up when the application is in portrait orientation. The `CameraCaptureTask` rotates the picture based on the phone's orientation when the picture is snapped.

recognize this behavior because you'll need to implement your own rotation logic later in the chapter.

Before you learn how to process pictures, you need to learn how to control the camera.

8.3 Controlling the camera

When Windows Phone was first released, the only way to access the camera was with `CameraCaptureTask`. The Windows Phone SDK 7.1 introduced APIs allowing programmatic access to the camera hardware. The `PhotoCamera` class allows a developer access to the image data as it's captured by the camera hardware. The `CameraButtons` class allows applications to detect when the user has pressed or released the Camera button built in to every phone.

> **TIP** Applications that use the `PhotoCamera` class must include the `ID_CAP_ISV_CAMERA` capability in their application manifests. You should include the `ID_REQ_REARCAMERA` and/or the `ID_REQ_FRONTCAMERA` requirements if your application would be useless without a camera.

As we've mentioned, every Windows Phone has a built-in primary camera, and some also have a front-facing camera. `PhotoCamera` supports both cameras, allowing the developer to specify which camera to use when constructing an instance of `PhotoCamera`. The camera is specified with either the `Primary` or `FrontFacing` values defined in the `CameraType` enumeration. The following snippet demonstrates how to construct a `PhotoCamera` that reads from the front-facing camera:

```
if(PhotoCamera.IsCameraTypeSupported(CameraType.FrontFacing))
    camera = new PhotoCamera(CameraType.FrontFacing);
```

The `PhotoCamera` class provides a static method named `IsCameraTypeSupported`, which is used to determine whether the phone has a front-facing camera. Developers should check whether a front-facing camera is installed before trying to access it.

The `PhotoCamera` class provides access to the live preview image picked up by the camera lens. The camera buffers the preview image into arrays of raw image data. The preview buffer is accessed via three different methods, each providing the raw image data in a different format:

- `GetPreviewBufferArgb32` returns image data in the same 4-byte ARGB structure used by Silverlight.
- Luminance and chrominance information, as defined by the YCbCr color model, is returned through the `GetPreviewBufferYCbCr` method.
- The `GetPreviewBufferY` method returns luminance information only.

The `GetPreviewBuffer` methods are useful for a variety of real-time image processing and augmented reality applications. The sample application won't perform any sophisticated image processing and displays an unaltered preview image prior to capturing the image when the user presses the Camera button. Microsoft includes APIs designed for this scenario, which we demonstrate in the next section.

A few steps are required to prepare the PhotoEditor application to use the `PhotoCamera`. You need to add a new menu item allowing the user to pick the live camera as the source of an image. You also need to add a `Click` event handler responsible for creating and initializing a `PhotoCamera`. Add the menu item to the application bar declared in MainPage.xaml.cs:

```
<shell:ApplicationBarMenuItem Text="custom camera" Click="Camera_Click" />
```

When the user taps the Custom Camera menu item, the application will show a live preview image in the `photoContainer`, as shown in figure 8.6. The preview image continues to be shown until the user either presses the menu item a second time or captures a snapshot with the Camera button. You'll start with the `Click` event handler, shown in the following listing.

Choose custom camera again to close camera. Use the hardware shutter button to take a picture.
2 supported resolutions.
Current resolution: 2560,1920
Preview resolution: 640,480

Figure 8.6 The custom camera feature showing a live preview

Listing 8.2 The camera `Click` event handler

```
using Microsoft.Devices;
PhotoCamera camera;                                    ❶ Class level field
void Camera_Click(object sender, EventArgs e)
{                                                      ❷ Is camera
    if (camera == null)                                  already in use?
    {
        currentImage = null;
        imageDetails.Text = string.Format("Choose custom camera again to
        ➥ close camera. Use the hardware Camera button to
        ➥ take a picture.\n");
        InitializeCamera();
    }
    else
    {
        CleanUpCamera();
        photoContainer.Fill = new SolidColorBrush (Colors.Gray);
        imageDetails.Text = "Choose an image source from the menu.";
    }
}
```

You need a new class-level field to reference the instance of the `PhotoCamera` ❶ you create when the user clicks the Custom Camera menu item for the first time. If the field is `null`, you prepare the application by clearing the current image, displaying a message to the user, and initializing the camera. If the camera is already in use ❷, the user has tapped the menu item a second time to cancel the Custom Camera operation, and you clean up the camera and clear the `photoContainer`. We'll look at the `CleanUpCamera` method later, but let's look at `InitializeCamera` now. You may want to create empty placeholder methods in your code so that the project compiles.

The `InitializeCamera` method is where you hook up interesting events and capture the preview buffer so you can display a viewfinder to the user. You'll enhance the

InitializeCamera method in later sections, but you start the method's implementation here by constructing a new instance of PhotoCamera:

```
void InitializeCamera()
{
    camera = new PhotoCamera(CameraType.Primary);
    camera.Initialized += camera_Initialized;
}
```

The first camera-related event you wire up is the Initialized event. A PhotoCamera instance isn't fully ready for use when the constructor completes. The PhotoCamera class raises the Initialized event once it's completely ready.

A fully initialized PhotoCamera is able to report which resolutions are supported when previewing images and capturing pictures. Supported resolutions are reported in the AvailableResolutions property. A developer can determine the resolution of the preview buffer with the PreviewResolution property. The Resolution property not only reports the current resolution but also allows the developer to specify which of the available resolutions should be used to capture a photograph.

You'll display the PreviewResolution and Resolution values to the user once the camera is initialized. The following listing implements the camera_Initialized event handler.

Listing 8.3 Reading supported resolutions in the Initialized event

```
void camera_Initialized(object sender, CameraOperationCompletedEventArgs e)
{
    Dispatcher.BeginInvoke(() =>
    {
        imageDetails.Text += string.Format("{0} supported resolutions.\n",
            camera.AvailableResolutions.Count());
        imageDetails.Text += string.Format("Current resolution: {0}\n",
            camera.Resolution);
        imageDetails.Text += string.Format("Preview resolution: {0}\n",
            camera.PreviewResolution);
    });
    camera.Initialized -= camera_Initialized;
}
```

❶ Update on UI thread

❷ Unwire event

The Initialized event handler isn't called on the UI thread. Because your code updates the user interface, use the Dispatcher ❶ to execute your code on the UI thread. After updating the user interface, you don't need to capture Initialized events and unsubscribe the event handler ❷.

Now that you know about the PhotoCamera, how can you use it in your PhotoEditor application? You already display pictures in the photoContainer Rectangle using an ImageBrush. You can turn the photoContainer into a camera viewfinder using a VideoBrush.

8.3.1 Painting with the VideoBrush

The VideoBrush class, an implementation of the Brush class, is designed to paint video instead of a solid color, gradient color, or image. The Windows Phone SDK

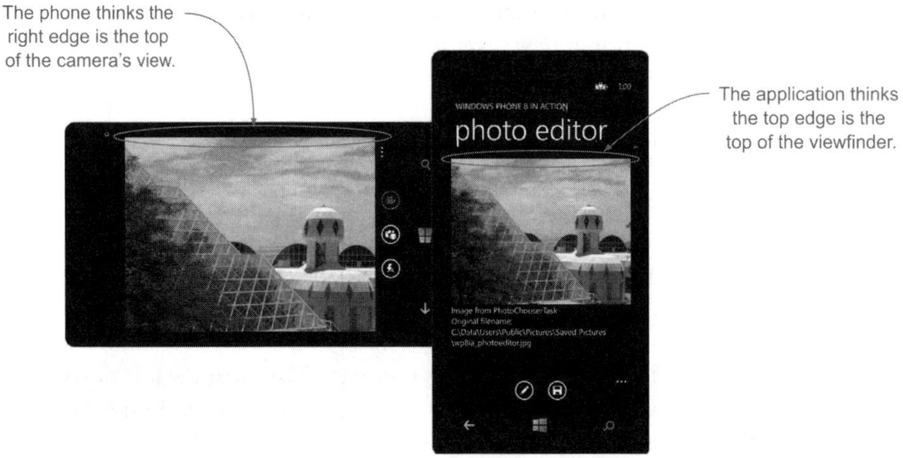
The phone thinks the right edge is the top of the camera's view.
The application thinks the top edge is the top of the viewfinder.
WINDOWS PHONE 8 IN ACTION
photo editor

Figure 8.7 The phone is designed to treat the right edge as the top of the camera's view. When an application displays a raw camera feed in a portrait orientation, it must transform the image by 90 degrees.

contains an extension method named `SetSource` to enable painting the camera's preview buffer with a `VideoBrush`. To see a `PhotoCamera`-driven `VideoBrush` in action, add the following code to the end of the `InitializeCamera` method:

```
var brush = new VideoBrush();
brush.SetSource(camera);
brush.RelativeTransform = new RotateTransform
    { CenterX = 0.5, CenterY = 0.5, Angle = camera.Orientation };
photoContainer.Fill = brush;
```

The `SetSource` extension method used here is defined in the `CameraVideoBrushExtensions` class and is found in the `Microsoft.Devices` namespace.

As shown in figure 8.7, the camera is constructed to treat the right edge of the phone as the top of the camera's picture, meaning the live camera feed is rotated 90 degrees from the application's portrait orientation. To solve the orientation problem with the preview buffer, you rotate the `VideoBrush` using a `RotateTransform`. The camera tells you the amount of mismatch with the `Orientation` property, which you use as the source of the `RotateTransform`'s `Angle` property.

> **TIP** `RotateTransform` is one of several transform classes you can use to manipulate XAML elements and controls. If you're unfamiliar with XAML's transform classes, you can read more about them in the book *Silverlight 5 in Action* by Pete Brown (Manning Publications, 2012) or from the MSDN article titled "Transforms," found at http:/mng.bz/tZjv.

Run the application now and select the custom camera option. You should see the photo container turn into a viewfinder. Pick up the phone and move it around. The image in the viewfinder updates in real time. Now all you need is the ability to capture the picture.

8.3.2 Snapping a photo

When using the built-in camera application, the user presses the camera's Camera button to capture a picture. Applications that use the `PhotoCamera` to capture pictures should also use the Camera button. The Camera button is exposed to the developer with events on the static `CameraButtons` class.

> **TIP** When working in the emulator, the computer keyboard can be used to mimic the hardware buttons, including the camera buttons. F6 triggers a half press of the Camera button. F7 registers a full press of the Camera button.

The `CameraButtons` class provides three events named `ShutterKeyHalfPressed`, `ShutterKeyPressed`, and `ShutterKeyReleased`. In the built-in Camera application, a half press of the Camera button focuses the camera, and a full press snaps the picture. You'll use the `ShutterKeyPressed` event in your application as the trigger to capturing a picture. Add the following line of code to the `InitializeCamera` method, right before the `VideoBrush` code you added in the last section:

```
CameraButtons.ShutterKeyPressed += cameraButtons_ShutterKeyPressed;
```

The `ShutterKeyPressed` event is handled by the `cameraButtons_ShutterKeyPressed` method. The only responsibility of the event handler is to start the process that snaps the picture and captures the image in a JPEG image stream. The capture process is started with a call to `PhotoCamera`'s `CaptureImage` method:

```
void cameraButtons_ShutterKeyPressed (object sender, EventArgs e)
{
    camera.CaptureImage();
}
```

The process that captures the picture raises four events, called `CaptureStarted`, `CaptureImageAvailable`, `CaptureThumbnailAvailable`, and `CaptureCompleted`. `CaptureStarted` is raised first, and `CaptureCompleted` is raised once the capture process has completed. In between these two events, `CaptureImageAvailable` and `CaptureThumbnailAvailable` are raised, providing the calling application the opportunity to save either a full resolution or thumbnail copy of the captured image.

The PhotoEditor application is only interested in the `CaptureImageAvailable` and `CaptureCompleted` events. Wire up two new event handlers in the `InitializeCamera` method:

```
camera.CaptureImageAvailable += camera_CaptureImageAvailable;
camera.CaptureCompleted += camera_CaptureCompleted;
```

First, we look at the `CaptureImageAvailable` event handler, which you'll name `camera_CaptureImageAvailable`. The event handler is passed an instance of the `ContentReadyEventArgs` class, which provides the image stream containing the image captured by the camera:

```
void camera_CaptureImageAvailable (object sender, ContentReadyEventArgs e)
{
    Dispatcher.BeginInvoke(() =>
    {
```

```
            currentImage = PictureDecoder.DecodeJpeg(e.ImageStream);
            photoContainer.Fill = new ImageBrush{ ImageSource = currentImage };
            imageDetails.Text = "Image captured from PhotoCamera.";
        });
    }
```

The `CaptureImageAvailable` event isn't raised on the UI thread, so use the `Dispatcher` to execute your user interface update code on the UI thread. Decode the image stream by calling the `DecodeImage` method you created earlier in the chapter. The captured image is displayed in the `photoContainer` control.

When the picture capture process is complete, you need to clean up the camera. Perform the camera cleanup in the `CaptureCompleted` event handler, as shown in the next listing.

Listing 8.4 Checking for errors in the `CaptureCompleted` event handler

```
void camera_CaptureCompleted (object sender,
    CameraOperationCompletedEventArgs e)
{
    if (!e.Succeeded)                                      <-- ❶ Check for errors
    {
        photoContainer.Fill = new SolidColorBrush (Colors.Gray);
        imageDetails.Text = "Camera capture failed.\n"
            + e.Exception.Message;                         <-- ❷ Display exception's message
    }
    CleanUpCamera();
}
```

An instance of the `CameraOperationCompletedEventArgs` class is passed into the event handler. Your code checks the `Succeeded` property ❶ to determine whether the image capture process completed as expected. If the operation failed, clear the `photo-Container` and display the message ❷ from the `Exception` property.

In the PhotoEditor application, only use the `PhotoCamera` when the user has selected the custom camera menu option. Once the user has snapped a picture, you need to clean up all registered event handlers and dispose of the camera:

```
void CleanUpCamera()
{
    CameraButtons.ShutterKeyPressed -= cameraButtons_ShutterKeyPressed;
    camera.CaptureImageAvailable -= camera_CaptureImageAvailable;
    camera.CaptureCompleted -= camera_CaptureCompleted;
    camera.Dispose();
    camera = null;
}
```

The `CleanUpCamera` method nearly completes your custom camera feature. Run the application, choose the custom camera, and snap a picture. You should see the picture ready for use shortly after pressing the Camera button.

Deploy the updated application to your phone, run the application, and choose the Custom Camera menu option. Hold the phone in landscape orientation and snap a picture with the Camera button. When the capture operation completes, you should

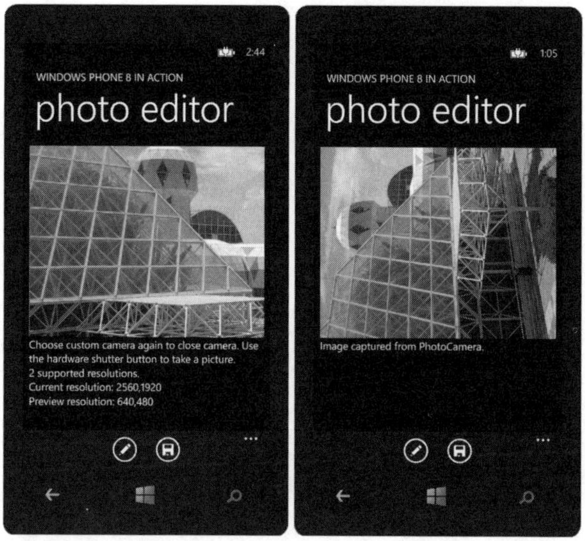
WINDOWS PHONE 8 IN ACTION
photo editor
Choose custom camera again to close camera. Use the hardware shutter button to take a picture.
2 supported resolutions.
Current resolution: 2560,1920
Preview resolution: 640,480
WINDOWS PHONE 8 IN ACTION
photo editor
Image captured from PhotoCamera.

Figure 8.8 Orientation problems when using `PhotoCamera`. On the left is the picture as it appeared in the viewfinder with the phone held in portrait orientation. When the photograph was snapped and the image was copied into the photo container, it appeared rotated with the top of the image toward the left side of the phone, as shown on the right.

see your new photo displayed in the `photoContainer`. Select the Custom Camera menu option again, but this time hold your phone in portrait orientation when you snap the picture. When the capture completes this time, the new picture is displayed with the top of the photo sideways, as shown in figure 8.8. The important thing to note is that the image stream that returns from the camera doesn't respect the orientation of your application. We show you how to handle the orientation of a picture in the next section.

8.3.3 Handling picture orientation

In figure 8.8, the orientation of the photograph doesn't match the orientation of the application. The photo stream that returns from the camera doesn't know or care about the orientation of your application. The picture's orientation will be based on how the user holds the phone while taking the picture. You can't ask your user to hold the phone in a specific position; they'll hold the phone however they like. All you can do is adjust the orientation of the photo before showing it in your application.

The camera writes metadata about the picture to the stream along with the image data. The image data and metadata are in the *Exchange Image File Format* (Exif). Exif has an attribute you can read to determine the orientation of the photo. `PhotoCamera` returns `Stream`, and you need a way to extract the Exif data from the stream. In this example you'll use ExifLib by Simon McKenzie, an open source Exif library that can be downloaded with the NuGet package manager. To add a reference to a NuGet package such as the ExifLib, select Project > Manage NuGet Packages. Once the Manage NuGet Packages dialog appears, type *exif* in the Search Online input control and press Enter. Select the ExifLib package from the list and click Install.

Before you think about how to modify the orientation, you need to figure out the default orientation of the photo that you get from the camera and how the orientation

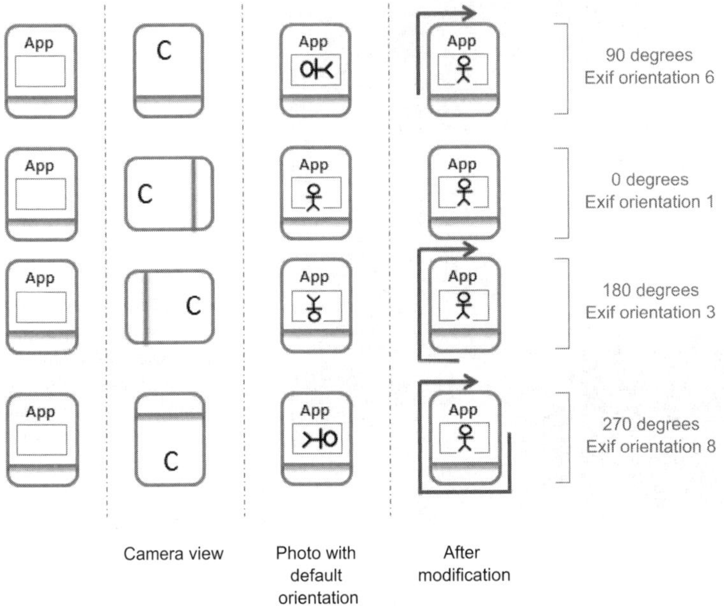

Figure 8.9 Different ways of holding the camera produce different photo output and Exif orientation values.

is different from the application's orientation. The Exif specification (which can be downloaded from http://www.exif.org/specifications.html) defines eight possible orientation values for a picture. Figure 8.9 shows the possible combinations of application and camera orientation, along with the corresponding Exif orientation value.

The figure shows four different ways of holding the camera and the output. The first column illustrates that your sample application is always in a portrait orientation. The second column shows the different ways of holding the phone. The third column displays the output photo from the camera. As you can see, the default orientation of a photo will be different depending on how the user holds the phone. The last column shows how many degrees you need to rotate the photo to get an orientation that matches the application, along with the related Exif orientation value.

The code that performs the desired modifications shown in the figure is implemented in two steps. The first step extracts the orientation from the image, and the second performs the rotation. The following listing demonstrates how to use the ExifLib library to extract the orientation value.

Listing 8.5 Extracting the Exif orientation value from the image stream

```
using ExifLib;                                          <- Use Exif library
using System.IO;
ushort GetExifOrientation(Stream imageStream)
{
   try
   {
```

```
        using(ExifReader reader = new ExifReader(imageStream))
        {
            ushort orientation;
            if (reader.GetTagValue(ExifTags.Orientation, out orientation))   // ❶ Read orientation
            {
                return orientation;
            }
        }
    }
    catch (ExifLibException) { }          // ❷ Exception thrown when Exif data isn't found
    return 1;
}
```

Read the orientation from the Exif formatted stream ❶. An `ExifReader` constructor accepts the image stream. Extract the orientation, in the form of an `unsigned short integer`, by calling the `GetTagValue` method with the `ExifTags.Orientation` value. The `ExifReader` constructor will throw an exception ❷ if the image stream doesn't contain Exif data, and in this case you ignore the error and return an orientation value of 1.

Once you know the Exif orientation, you need to rotate the original photo, and it's easy to create a new photo with the correct orientation based on the original photo. The `WriteableBitmap` class provides direct access to the pixel-level information of bitmaps. The image data is accessed through the `Pixels` property, a one-dimensional array of pixels laid out in a row-first pattern. The `PixelWidth` and `PixelHeight` properties are used to determine how many rows and columns of pixels exist in the two-dimensional image. The first row of pixels resides in the `Pixels` array from index 0 to `PixelWidth` -1. The second row of pixels resides in the `Pixels` array from index `PixelWidth` to 2 * `PixelWidth` -1. The following listing shows how to read the pixels from the original photo and copy them to the right position in the new bitmap image.

Listing 8.6 Copy pixels from original bitmap to new bitmap

```
WriteableBitmap RotateBitmap(WriteableBitmap source,
    int width, int height, int angle)
{
    var target = new WriteableBitmap(width, height);     // ❶ Create empty bitmap
    int sourceIndex = 0;
    int targetIndex = 0;
    for (int x = 0; x < source.PixelWidth; x++)
    {
        for (int y = 0; y < source.PixelHeight; y++)
        {
            sourceIndex = x + y * source.PixelWidth;
            switch (angle)                                 // ❷ Determine target location
            {
                case 90:
                    targetIndex = (source.PixelHeight - y - 1)
                        + x * target.PixelWidth;
                    break;
                case 180:
                    targetIndex = (source.PixelWidth - x - 1)
                        + (source.PixelHeight - y - 1) * source.PixelWidth;
                    break;
```

```
                case 270:
                    targetIndex = y + (source.PixelWidth - x - 1)
                        * target.PixelWidth;
                    break;
Copy pixels 3   }
            target.Pixels[targetIndex] = source.Pixels[sourceIndex];
        }
    }
    return target;
}
```

The RotateBitmap method accepts four parameters: the source bitmap, the width and height of the new bitmap, and the angle the bitmap should be rotated. The method starts off by creating a new WriteableBitmap with the specified width and height ❶. Loop through each pixel in the source bitmap, calculating the index of the source pixel and the index in the target bitmap where you'll copy the pixel. Depending on the rotation angle ❷, calculate the target index using one of three different expressions. Finally, copy the pixels ❸ from the source bitmap to the target bitmap.

NOTE For more information, read the MSDN documentation for the Windows Phone version of WriteableBitmap, available at http://mng.bz/c3HK.

RotateBitmap accepts a WriteableBitmap. The ContentReadyEventArgs passed to the camera_CaptureImageAvailable method provides a Stream. Currently the camera_CaptureCompleted method uses PictureDecoder.DecodeJpeg to convert the stream to a WriteableBitmap. Wrap the call to the DecodeJpeg and RotateBitmap methods in a new DecodeJpeg method. The code for the new method is shown in the following listing.

Listing 8.7 Decoding the image stream

```
WriteableBitmap DecodeJpeg(Stream imageStream)
{
    WriteableBitmap source = PictureDecoder.DecodeJpeg (imageStream);
    imageStream.Position = 0;                                    ❶ Reset stream position
    ushort orientation = GetExifOrientation(imageStream);

    switch (orientation)
    {
        case 3:
            return RotateBitmap(source, source.PixelWidth,
                    source.PixelHeight, 180);
        case 6:
            return RotateBitmap(source, source.PixelHeight,      ❷ Swap width and height
                    source.PixelWidth, 90);
        case 8:
            return RotateBitmap(source, source.PixelHeight,
                    source.PixelWidth, 270);
        default:
            return source;                                       ❸ Skip RotateBitmap
    }
}
```

The new DecodeJpeg method accepts an image stream. The first step is to convert the image stream into a WriteableBitmap using the PictureDecoder helper class. The image stream position is then reset to the beginning ❶, and GetExifOrientation is called to extract the orientation value. Use the orientation value to determine the degree of rotation, calling RotateBitmap if necessary. When rotating the image by 90 or 270 degrees, you're swapping the width and height ❷. When the angle is 0, don't call RotateBitmap ❸.

Using the new DecodeJpeg method, you can update the camera_CaptureImageAvailable method to rotate the captured photos. In the event handler, replace the call to PictureDecoder.DecodeJpeg with the following snippet:

```
currentImage = DecodeJpeg(e.ImageStream);
```

1:57
WINDOWS PHONE 8 IN ACTION
photo editor
Choose custom camera again to close camera. Use the hardware shutter button to take a picture.
2 supported resolutions.
Current resolution: 2560,1920
Preview resolution: 640,480

Figure 8.10 When the PhotoEditor is running in custom camera mode and the user switches away from and then returns to the application, the viewfinder is blank.

The code is now ready to run. Launch the application and snap a few more pictures, checking to see that the pictures all appear right-side up in the application. Now try one more thing: launch the application and select the Custom Camera menu option. With the camera enabled and the viewfinder active, press the Start button to switch to the Start Screen and then use the Back button to navigate back. You might notice that the viewfinder is no longer active when returning from fast application switching, as shown in figure 8.10. This is one of those situations we told you about in the "Returning to action" section of chapter 3, where additional work is required to support fast application switching.

8.3.4 Supporting fast application switching

Developers who use PhotoCamera need to understand how fast application switching impacts their application code. Because the camera hardware is a shared resource, the operating system disconnects the camera when an application is sent to the background in favor of another task. When the application is restored to the foreground, the camera isn't automatically restored.

Camera-based applications should clean up camera resources when they're moved into the background. In chapter 3, you learned that an application can detect when it's entering a dormant state by using the Deactivated event or the OnNavigatedFrom override in their user interface pages. The PhotoEditor application uses the OnNavigatedFrom method:

```
protected override void OnNavigatedFrom(NavigationEventArgs e)
{
    if (camera != null)
```

```
    {
        CleanUpCamera();
        State["customCamera"] = true;
    }
}
```

The PhotoEditor only uses the camera when the user has selected the Custom Camera menu option. In this situation, the camera field isn't `null`, and you call the `CleanUpCamera` method to unwire the event handlers and dispose of the camera. You also add a `customCamera` key to the page's `State` dictionary as a flag you'll see when the application is restarted.

The `OnNavigatedTo` method is called once the application is restarted and `MainPage` is reloaded. Your code looks for the `customCamera` flag in the `State` dictionary. If the flag is found, remove it and initialize the camera:

```
protected override void OnNavigatedTo(NavigationEventArgs e)
{
    if(State.ContainsKey("customCamera"))
    {
        State.Remove("customCamera");
        InitializeCamera();
    }
}
```

Run the application and perform the application switching steps you used earlier. This time, the viewfinder should be reactivated when switching back to the PhotoEditor. Speaking of editing, you haven't implemented any editing features. Let's look at one now.

8.4 Image editing

The PhotoEditor application edits pictures by stamping them with the text "Windows Phone 8 in Action" surrounded by a border (shown in figure 8.11). It's not much fun to edit an image unless you can also keep the changes, so allow the user to save the stamped picture to a file.

Figure 8.11 A picture stamped with "Windows Phone 8 in Action"

The two new features are accessed with application bar buttons added to MainPage.xaml to enable editing and saving images loaded or captured within the application:

```
<shell:ApplicationBarIconButton IconUri="/Assets/AppBar/edit.png"
    Text="edit" Click="Edit_Click" />
<shell:ApplicationBarIconButton IconUri="/Assets/AppBar/save.png"
    Text="save" Click="Save_Click" />
```

The images for the buttons come from the icons library installed with the Windows Phone SDK. You'll implement the `Edit_Click` and `Save_Click` event handlers later in the chapter. For now, you'll want to create empty implementations so that your code will compile and run.

To implement the stamp, you may think you need to design a complex algorithm to access the raw image data and alter the appropriate pixel values. Instead, you'll use a feature of the XAML Framework that draws a XAML `UIElement` over the top of the image contained within the `WriteableBitmap`. This feature lets you define the stamp using a `TextBlock` and a `Border` control as the first element in MainPage.xaml's `ContentPanel`:

```
<Border x:Name="photoStamp" Height="125" Width="300" Opacity="0.5"
    HorizontalAlignment="Left" VerticalAlignment="Top"
    Background="White" BorderBrush="Red" BorderThickness="10">
    <TextBlock Text="Windows Phone 8 in Action" Foreground="Red"
        Style="{StaticResource PhoneTextLargeStyle}"
        TextWrapping="Wrap" TextAlignment="Center" />
</Border>
```

The `Border` is named `photoStamp` and defined with a `BorderThickness` of `10`. The `Border` is drawn with a red outline and a white background. Inside the `Border` is a `TextBlock` that draws red text. The `Border` is given an `Opacity` of `0.5` so that the picture shows through the stamp. The `Grid` control draws elements in the order in which they're added in XAML, and you want to make sure you add the `photoStamp` element as the first child of the `ContentPanel` so that it's hidden by the `photoContainer` `Rectangle` control.

Adding a `UIElement` to a XAML page is simple enough. Rendering the same element into a `WriteableBitmap` is also simple.

8.4.1 Rendering XAML elements

The `WriteableBitmap` class exposes a method named `Render`. The `Render` method draws a XAML `UIElement` over the top of the image contained within the `WriteableBitmap`. You already have the stamp declared as a `UIElement` (it's a `Border` control). Now you need to make a call to `Render` from the `Edit_Click` method in MainPage.xaml.cs. The `Edit_Click` method, shown in the following listing, is the event handler for the Edit button you added to the application bar.

Listing 8.8 Adding a stamp to the current image

```
void Edit_Click(object sender, EventArgs e)
{
    if (currentImage != null)
    {
        currentImage.Invalidate();
        var transform = new CompositeTransform          <-- (1) Resize photoStamp
        {
            ScaleX = currentImage.PixelWidth / ContentPanel.ActualWidth,
            ScaleY = currentImage.PixelHeight / ContentPanel.ActualHeight,
            Rotation = -35,
            TranslateX = 100 *
                currentImage.PixelWidth / ContentPanel.ActualWidth,
            TranslateY = 400 *
                currentImage.PixelHeight / ContentPanel.ActualHeight,
```

```
        };
        currentImage.Render(photoStamp, transform);
        currentImage.Invalidate();
        imageDetails.Text = "The picture has been stamped.";
    }
}
```

❷ Draw stamp

WriteableBitmap's Render method accepts a UIElement and a Transform. The UIElement that you use is the photoStamp you added to MainPage.xaml. The transform is used to position the element within the bitmap. You'll scale, rotate, and translate the photoStamp element using a CompositeTransform ❶. Even though the image is displayed on the screen at about 480 pixels wide, the bitmap may be much wider. You scale the stamp so that it appears approximately the same size as it does in the ContentPanel. You rotate the stamp by 35 degrees. The stamp is translated so that it appears in the lower-right corner of the image. You make a call to the bitmap's Invalidate method to ensure the image is properly updated on the screen ❷. Finally, you update the message displayed to the user.

Additional Camera APIs in the Windows Phone SDK

We'd like to mention a couple of other camera APIs that are included in the Windows Phone SDK but aren't covered in this book. The CaptureDevice .NET API was first introduced with Silverlight 4 for the browser, providing access to the web cameras and microphones attached to a host computer. The same CaptureDevice API is implemented in Windows Phone 8 devices, allowing developers access to the video camera and microphone built into a Windows Phone device. You can read more about the CaptureDevice API in *Silverlight 5 in Action* by Pete Brown (Manning Publications, 2012) or from the CaptureDevice API documentation on the MSDN website.

The Windows Phone Runtime also includes a video-capture API named AudioVideoCaptureDevice. This API is an alternative to the CaptureDevice that provides access to the raw image stream that's inaccessible with CaptureDevice. AudioVideoCaptureDevice also allows you to record only audio or only video.

Run the application now, choose your favorite image, and press the Edit button. If all goes well, you should see a cool stamp enhancing (or at least obscuring) your favorite picture. The only problem is that you can't save your incredible work of art. You need to wire up the Save button to an event handler so you don't lose any of your hard-earned edits.

8.4.2 Saving an image to local storage

The Windows Phone SDK includes a static class called Extensions, defined in the System.Windows.Media.Imaging namespace. The Extensions class provides two extension methods for the WriteableBitmap class, called LoadJpeg and SaveJpeg. The following listing demonstrates how to use SaveJpeg to store the picture displayed in the PhotoEditor application to local storage.

Listing 8.9 Saving an image to local storage

```
using Windows.Storage;                                  ❶ Include Storage namespace
async void Save_Click(object sender, EventArgs e)
{
   if (currentImage != null)
   {

      StorageFolder localFolder = ApplicationData.Current.LocalFolder;
      using (Stream imageStream = await localFolder
            .OpenStreamForWriteAsync("custom-photo.jpg",
               CreationCollisionOption.ReplaceExisting))
      {
         currentImage.SaveJpeg(imageStream, currentImage.PixelWidth,     ❷ Write image to file
            currentImage.PixelHeight, 0, 100);
      }
      imageDetails.Text = "Image saved with filename:\ncustom-photo.jpg";
   }
}
```

Start by adding a `using` statement for the `Windows.Storage` namespace ❶ where the `StorageFolder` class is found. After checking whether there's a current image, get the local storage folder and create a new file named custom-photo.jpg using the `OpenStreamForWriteAsync` extension method. `OpenStreamForWriteAsync` is defined in the `WindowsRuntimeStorageExtensions` class, provided to ease mixing Windows Phone Runtime storage concepts with .NET `Streams`. A real application would probably use a filename entered by the user instead of the hardcoded filename used here. Send the file stream to the `SaveJpeg` method ❷, passing the picture's width and height.

The `SaveJpeg` method declares two other parameters called `orientation` and `quality`. The `orientation` parameter isn't used and should be set to zero. The `quality` parameter allows you to trade image quality for file size. The permitted range of quality values is `0` to `100`. Smaller values will result in smaller files, with a trade-off of reduced image quality.

The `SaveJpeg` method makes saving captured or edited pictures easy. Loading pictures is equally easy.

8.4.3 *Loading an image from local storage*

Now that you're saving an image to a file in isolated storage, how do you reload the image back into the application? You already have all the tools you need to load a JPEG file into memory. You'll use `IsolatedStorageFile` to open a file stream and `PictureDecoder` to read the file stream and load the image into a `WriteableBitmap`. Next, you'll add a new menu item to the application bar in MainPage.xaml to allow the user to load an image:

```
<shell:ApplicationBarMenuItem Text="open custom photo"
    Click="Open_Click" />
```

The menu item's `Click` event is handled by a method called `Open_Click` in MainPage .xaml.cs. The following listing shows the implementation of the `Open_Click` method.

Listing 8.10 Loading an image from local storage

```
async void Open_Click(object sender, EventArgs e)
{
   try
   {
      StorageFolder localFolder = ApplicationData.Current.LocalFolder;
      using (Stream imageStream = await localFolder                          ❶ Open file
            .OpenStreamForReadAsync("custom-photo.jpg"))
      {
         currentImage = PictureDecoder.DecodeJpeg (imageStream);             ❷ Decode image stream
         photoContainer.Fill = new ImageBrush{ImageSource = currentImage};
      }
      imageDetails.Text = "Image loaded from filename:\ncustom-photo.jpg";
   }
   catch (FileNotFoundException)
   {
      photoContainer.Fill = new SolidColorBrush (Colors.Gray);               ❸ Clear screen
      imageDetails.Text = "Image not found!";
   }
}
```

Start by getting a reference to the local storage folder, opening the file custom-photo.jpg ❶, and getting a reference to the image stream. `OpenStreamForReadAsync`, another extension method found in the `WindowsRuntimeStorageExtensions` class, returns the image stream. The image stream is passed to the `DecodeJpeg` method ❷, and the resulting `WriteableBitmap` is used as the `photoContainer`'s `Fill` brush. If the file doesn't exist, a `FileNotFoundException` is thrown by the `OpenStreamForReadAsync` method. In the catch handler, the `photoContainer` is cleared with a solid gray brush ❸.

Run the application and choose the New menu option to load the image you saved in the last section. Pretty cool! You're finished with the PhotoEditor application for now. In the next chapter, you'll update the PhotoEditor to integrate with the Photos Hub.

8.5 Summary

We started the chapter with two Windows Phone built-in chooser tasks that were left out of the previous discussion on launchers and choosers. The first built-in task is the `PhotoChooserTask`, which allows the application developer to launch the phone's photo selector application from code so that users can select photos from the media library. Another task is the `CameraCaptureTask`, which can be used to open the phone camera from your application programmatically. We then showed how to use the `PhotoCamera` API to access the camera directly instead of using the native camera application exposed via the `CameraCaptureTask`. You learned how to use a `VideoBrush` to render the camera's viewfinder in your application and how to listen for

Camera button events to trigger the capture of a picture. We showed you how to use the `WriteableBitmap` class to render XAML UI elements into the bitmap when you implemented the stamping feature of the sample application. And you learned how to read and write files to local storage.

The sample application is fairly limited. Real applications wouldn't hardcode filenames but would allow the user to enter a filename of their own. We're certain that few people are interested in placing a *Windows Phone 8 in Action* stamp on their pictures. But if you allowed the user to create custom stamps with their own messages, colors, and symbols, you might have an appealing application.

We're not finished with the PhotoEditor sample application. In the next chapter you'll learn how to integrate the PhotoEditor into the Photos Hub. When viewing a picture in the Photos Hub, the user will be able to launch the PhotoEditor. You'll also update the PhotoEditor to load pictures from the camera roll.

You'll also learn about a method for accessing the microphone using the XNA Framework. You'll build a VoiceRecorder application to create .wav files and store them in local storage. We'll also show you how to integrate the VoiceRecorder with the Music + Videos Hub.

9 Integrating with the Photos and Music + Videos Hubs

This chapter covers

- Loading and saving pictures in the media library
- Viewing and sharing photos
- Recording voice with the microphone

Windows Phone contains several built-in applications, including the Phone Dialer, Email, Camera, Bing search, Photos Hub, and Music + Videos Hub. In chapters 5 and 8 you learned how to use launchers and choosers and the `PhotoCamera` class to interact with the built-in applications. Most of these interactions consisted of sample applications launching the built-in applications. In this chapter you're going to learn how to make the Photos Hub and Music + Videos Hub launch your application.

The built-in applications use navigation URLs to launch your application and pass information. The Photos Hub uses extensibility features to display a list of applications in the hub panorama, as well as in various menus displayed throughout the hub. When viewing a picture, the user can choose to share, edit, or view the picture with your application. In this chapter you're going to extend the PhotoEditor sample application from chapter 8 to use Photo Extensibility for Windows

Phone. Along the way, you'll learn to use the `MediaLibrary` from the XNA Framework to read and write pictures to the phone's picture albums.

The other built-in application you'll learn to extend is the Music + Videos Hub, which lets the user play or watch several different types of audio and video. Music and audio may be stored in the phone media library, but they may also be stored in third-party applications or streamed from the internet. Applications that play audio report information to the Music + Videos Hub, which displays information to the user in the pages of the hub's panorama control.

In this chapter you'll build a sample application that records voice using the phone's microphone and saves the recording to a wave file in local storage. The sample application will report information about the voice recording to the Music + Videos Hub, and the user will then be able to play the voice recordings from the Music + Videos Hub. We also show you how to create and use a background agent to play the voice recordings even when the application isn't running in the foreground.

We have a lot to cover, so let's get started with updating the PhotoEditor sample application to read and save pictures in the media library.

9.1 Working with pictures in the media library

You're going to continue working with the PhotoEditor application you created in the last chapter. When you last left the PhotoEditor, the user was able to edit pictures and save them to local storage. The Photos Hub is where you want to save pictures, because this is where the user expects to see all pictures on the device. The `MediaLibrary` class provides the API you need to save pictures to the Photos Hub.

The `MediaLibrary` class from the XNA Framework provides access to songs, playlists, and pictures in the device's media library. The media library plays a huge role in Windows Phone because it's useful when you want to integrate your applications with the phone's built-in applications.

The `MediaLibrary` class has six properties, and we categorize them into pictures and audio/videos. We cover only picture-related properties in this section.

9.1.1 Exposing pictures

The two picture-related classes in the `MediaLibrary` namespace are `Picture` and `PictureAlbum`. Each `Picture` class instance provides information about a picture via the `Name`, `Date`, `Height`, `Width`, and `Album` properties. Picture albums are containers for pictures and other picture albums. The collection of pictures in a `PictureAlbum` is accessed through the album's `Pictures` property. The other `PictureAlbums` contained in the album are exposed with the `Albums` property. You can also retrieve the parent `PictureAlbum` via the `Parent` property.

`Pictures` and `PictureAlbums` are exposed by several properties of the `MediaLibrary` class. Table 9.1 lists the picture-related properties of the `MediaLibrary`.

Table 9.1 MediaLibrary properties that expose pictures

Property name	Description
`Pictures`	A single collection of `Picture` objects representing every picture in the Camera Roll, Saved Pictures, and Sample Pictures albums.
`RootPictureAlbum`	The root of the picture album hierarchy. This is the `PictureAlbum` parent of the Saved Pictures, Camera Roll, Sample Pictures, and Favorite Pictures albums.
`SavedPictures`	A collection of `Picture` objects representing every picture in the Saved Pictures album.

Let's talk about the `RootPictureAlbum` property of `MediaLibrary`. `RootPictureAlbum` provides everything (including photo albums) from the root folder. To better understand the differences between the `Pictures` and `RootPictureAlbum` properties, look at the portable device folder, shown in figure 9.1. This folder is added to your desktop system when you plug a real phone into your computer's USB port. On the phone, the root folder is named Pictures, and this is what `RootPictureAlbum` returns. Usually there aren't any pictures in the root folder, but it may have two or more default folders.

The Camera Roll folder is the default location where all photos that the user has taken with the phone's camera are stored automatically. The Sample Pictures folder is created by Windows Phone the first time the Photos Hub is launched, and the Saved Pictures folder is the default place where a user saves all images from the internet or an application.

NOTE In the Photos Hub, the user is able to view photos from SkyDrive, Facebook, and other social networking sites, but those aren't stored on the device. Social networking photos can be saved to the Saved Pictures folder on the phone by tapping the Save to Phone menu item in the application bar while viewing the photo.

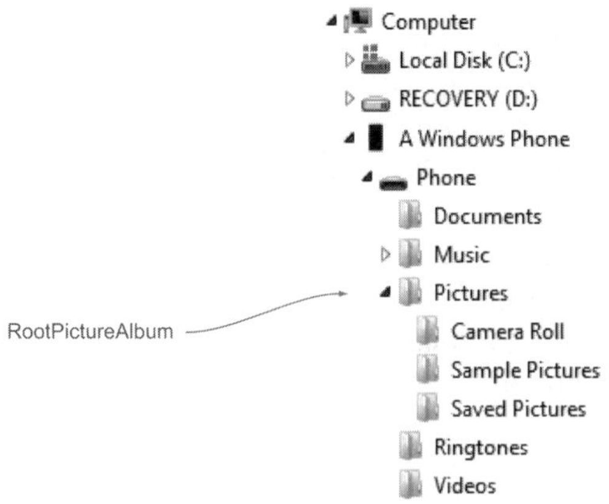

Figure 9.1 Phone picture albums in the Windows File Explorer. A portable device folder is added to the computer node in the File Explorer hierarchy. The Pictures library shown in File Explorer is equivalent to the `RootPictureAlbum` property of the `MediaLibrary` class.

The Pictures property of the MediaLibrary returns the collection of pictures that have been stored in the media library. Due to the integration with Facebook, Windows Live, and other photo-providing applications, more pictures may be visible in the Photos Hub than are reported by the MediaLibrary. MediaLibrary doesn't provide any information about online photos that haven't been saved to the device yet. You can query all other photos that have been taken with the phone camera, downloaded, or synced from computers.

The last picture-related MediaLibrary property is SavedPictures. SavedPictures returns the collection of pictures stored in the Saved Pictures album. This is a convenient property, saving you the hassle of navigating the album hierarchy from RootPictureAlbum. The Saved Pictures album is also the only album in the MediaLibrary that an application can use when saving pictures.

9.1.2 Saving pictures to the media library

In chapter 8 you learned how to save a picture to a file in local storage. An edited photo seems out of place in local storage. All the other pictures on the phone are stored in the Photos Hub and synchronized with the Windows Phone software on the PC. Now that you have a good understanding of the MediaLibrary, we can talk about how to save photos in the Photos Hub.

> **TIP** Use of the MediaLibrary requires the ID_CAP_MEDIALIB_PHOTO capability to be declared in WMAppManifest.xml.

Launch Visual Studio and open the PhotoEditor project. Find the Save_Click method in MainPage.xaml.cs and update the code to match the following listing.

Listing 9.1 Saving a picture to the media library

```
using Microsoft.Xna.Framework.Media;          // ❶ Add using statement
void Save_Click(object sender, EventArgs e)
{
   if (currentImage != null)
   {
      using(var stream = new MemoryStream())
      {
         currentImage.SaveJpeg(stream, currentImage.PixelWidth,   // ❷ Save image to memory stream
         currentImage.PixelHeight, 0, 100);
         stream.Seek(0, 0);
         var library = new MediaLibrary();
         Picture p = library.SavePicture("customphoto.jpg", stream);   // ❸ Save image to SavedPictures album
         imageDetails.Text = string.Format(
           "Image saved to media ibrary.\r\nFilename:\r\ncustomphoto.jpg");
      }
   }
}
```

Before you can use the MediaLibrary class, declare that you're using the Microsoft.Xna.Framework.Media namespace ❶. Alter the method to save the image in a

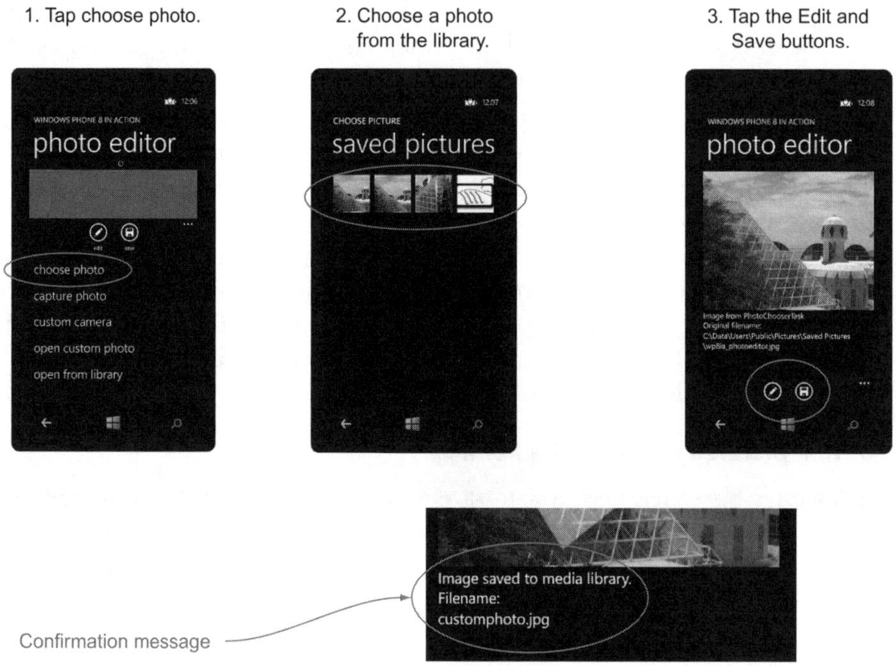

Figure 9.2 Selecting, editing, and saving a photo in the sample application

MemoryStream instead of a stream attached to a StorageFile ❷. Create a MediaLibrary instance and call the SavePicture method ❸, passing in the memory stream. The MediaLibrary doesn't care whether a picture with the name customphoto.jpg already exists. Pictures won't be overwritten, and two pictures will be created. When shown in Windows File Explorer on the PC, the duplicate copies are named customphoto(1).jpg, customphoto(2).jpg, and so on.

Once you've implemented the new Save_Click code, you can run the sample project from Visual Studio. Use the Choose Picture menu option to select one of the existing pictures in the Photos Hub. Once the picture is displayed in the PhotoEditor application, click the Edit button followed by the Save button (see figure 9.2). The application should display the message "Image saved to media library" if the photo was saved successfully. You can then go the Photos Hub and check the Saved Pictures album, where you'll see the new image.

Adding pictures to the Photos Hub is one form of integration with the Photos Hub. We'll look at other methods later in the chapter. First, let's look at how to read a picture from the library.

9.1.3 Retrieving a picture from the media library

Retrieving a list of all pictures from the media library is easy: instantiate a MediaLibrary instance and use the Pictures property. The Pictures property returns a collection of `Picture` objects representing every picture in the Camera Roll, Sample Pictures, and Saved Pictures albums. If you only want a collection from the Saved Pictures album, use the `SavedPictures` property instead.

The `Picture` class not only provides image details through the `Name`, `Date`, `Width`, and `Height` properties, but also provides access to the stream of bytes that compose the image contained in the picture file. The `Picture` class provides access to two image streams: the full-size image and a small thumbnail image. These two image streams are accessed via the `GetImage` and `GetThumbnail` methods respectively.

Update the PhotoEditor application to open and edit a picture from the media library. Open MainPage.xaml and add a new menu item to the `ApplicationBar`:

```
<shell:ApplicationBarMenuItem Text="open from library"
    Click="OpenFromLibrary_Click" />
```

The new menu item is wired up to a click event handler called `OpenFromLibrary_Click`. Open MainPage.xaml.cs and add the implementation for the new event handler. The `OpenFromLibrary_Click` implementation is shown in the following listing.

Listing 9.2 Reading a picture from the media library

```
using Microsoft.Xna.Framework.Media.PhoneExtensions;
void OpenFromLibrary_Click(object sender, EventArgs e)
{
    var library = new MediaLibrary();
    var pictures = library.SavedPictures;
    var picture = pictures.FirstOrDefault(                  ❶ Find
        item => item.Name == "customphoto.jpg");              customphoto.jpg
    if (picture != null)
    {
Get image   using (var stream = picture.GetImage())
stream ❷    {
            currentImage = PictureDecoder.DecodeJpeg(stream);
        }
        photoContainer.Fill = new ImageBrush{ ImageSource = currentImage };
        imageDetails.Text = string.Format(
            "Image from Album: {0}\r\nPicture name: {1}",
            picture.Album, picture.GetPath());
    }
    else
    {
Clear ❸     photoContainer.Fill = new SolidColorBrush(Colors.Gray);
container   imageDetails.Text = "Choose an image source from the menu.";
    }
}
```

Start by obtaining a collection of all pictures in the Save Pictures album. Iterate over the collection and find the first picture named customphoto.jpg ❶. After you find it, use the `PictureDecoder` class to convert the stream returned from `Picture.GetImage` ❷ into a `WriteableBitmap`. Update the user interface, filling the `photoContainer` and displaying the name of the picture's album and the full path to the picture's file. Retrieve the path to the picture's file using the `GetPath` extension method from the `MediaLibraryExtensions` class. If a picture isn't found, fill the user interface with a gray rectangle ❸.

You now know how to load an image from the `MediaLibrary` from within your sample application. In the next section you extend the Photos Hub so that a user can open the picture in your sample application directly from the Photos Hub.

9.2 Editing and sharing from the Photos Hub

The Photos Hub, shown in figure 9.3, is where a user can see all their photos that have been taken with the phone, synced from the computer, and downloaded from the internet or email. The Photos Hub is integrated with Windows Live and Facebook, and all photos uploaded to those websites are displayed in the Photos Hub as well.

The apps list is shown only when the user has installed applications that extend the Photos Hub. Let's see how you can register the PhotoEditor sample application as a Photos Hub extension.

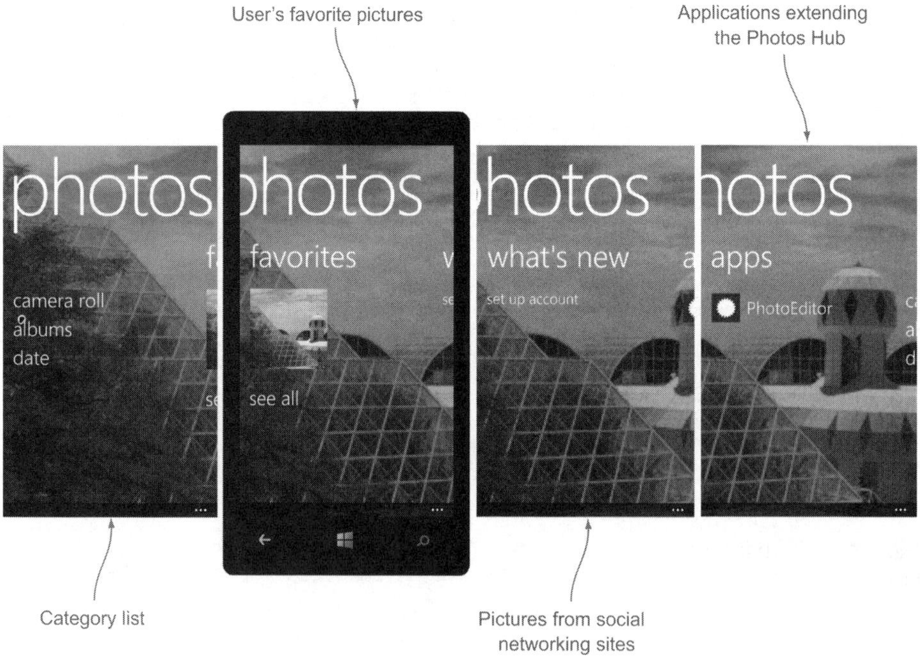

Figure 9.3 Four different sections of the panorama can be seen in this Photos Hub. The first image presents a list of categories. The second shows the pictures the user has identified as their favorites. The third is a running list of new pictures added to the user's social networks. The last image shows the apps list, which provides a list of applications registered as Photos Hub extensions.

9.2.1 Extending the Photos Hub

The app picker in the Photos Hub is extended with a feature known as *Photo Extensibility for Windows Phone*. The advantage of Photo Extensibility is that users don't need to leave the Photos Hub to use your application. It's already integrated inside the Photos Hub, and the user can use it directly from the Photos Hub. Applications register with the Photos Hub by including an `Extension` element in the WMAppManifest.xml file found in the project's Properties folder:

```
<Extensions>
  <Extension ExtensionName="Photos_Extra_Hub"
    ConsumerID="{5B04B775-356B-4AA0-AAF8-6491FFEA5632}"
    TaskID="_default" />
</Extensions>
```

The `Extension` element is placed inside the `Extensions` element, immediately after the `Tokens` element. The `Extension` element has three attributes called `ExtensionName`, `ConsumerID`, and `TaskID`. The `ConsumerID` field is the unique ID of the application that's being extended, and the unique ID representing the Photos Hub is {5B04B775-356B-4AA0-AAF8-6491FFEA5632}, which is detailed in the Photo Extensibility documentation on MSDN. The `TaskID` is the name of the task in your application that should be navigated to when the user taps the application in the Apps page of the Photos Hub. In Windows Phone, the only supported `TaskID` is the task called `_default`. We talk about an application's default task in chapter 2.

> **NOTE** The default manifest editor in Visual Studio doesn't support the extensibility options. To add an `Extension` element to WMAppManigest.xml, you need to open the file with the XML editor by right-clicking the file in the Solution Explorer and choosing Open With from the menu.

The `ExtensionName` is defined by the application being extended. The Photos Hub defines three extensions named `Photos_Extra_Hub`, `Photos_Extra_Viewer`, and `Photos_Extra_Share`. `Photos_Extra_Hub` is the name of the Apps page extension. The other two extensions allow an application to participate in the edit and share pickers, which are available when viewing a single picture in the Photos Hub.

Open the WMAppManifest.xml file for the PhotoEditor and add a `Photos_Extra_Hub` extension element. Rebuild the PhotoEditor application and deploy it to your Windows Phone device or emulator. Launch the Photos Hub and look for the PhotoEditor in the list on the Apps page. Tapping PhotoEditor will launch the application using the normal startup routine.

Extending the apps picker is the first of three extension points exposed by the Photos Hub. The second extension point you're going to implement in the PhotoEditor is `Photos_Extra_Viewer`, which lets an application extend the photo viewer.

9.2.2 Extending the photo viewer

One of the cool things about Windows Phone is that it allows developers to register a picture-related application (such as PhotoEditor) as an extension to the Windows

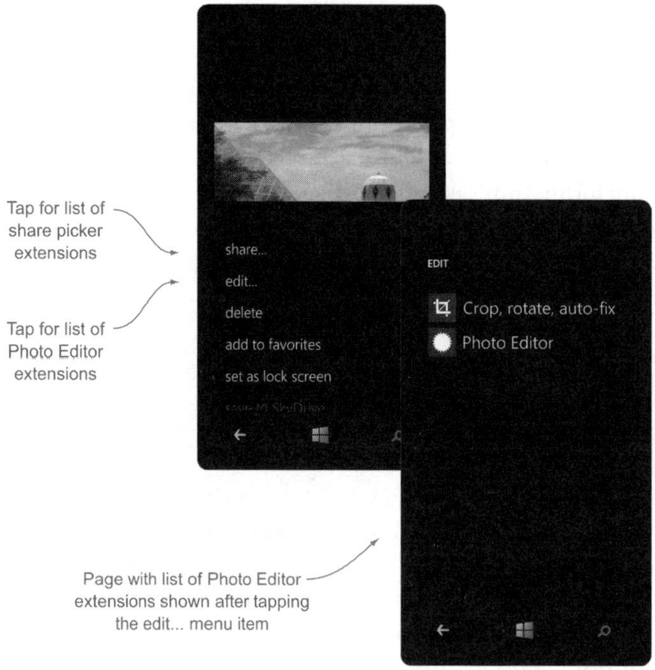

Figure 9.4 The photo viewer page showing installed Photos_Extra_Image_Editor applications

Phone built-in photo viewer application. This enables a user viewing photos to use your application directly from the photo viewer. Figure 9.4 shows the photo viewer displaying Share and Edit menu items when the user opens an individual photo. If the user taps one of these menu items, they're taken to the list of photo extensibility applications installed on the device.

When the user taps the application's name in the picker, the application is launched and is expected to display the selected picture.

Now it's time to turn the PhotoEditor application into a photo viewer extension. Add an `Extension` element with the name `Photos_Extra_Viewer` to the WMAppManifest.xml file:

```
<Extension ExtensionName="Photos_Extra_Image_Editor"
    ConsumerID="{5B04B775-356B-4AA0-AAF8-6491FFEA5632}"
    TaskID="_default" />
```

Once you've rebuilt and deployed the application to a Windows Phone device, launch the Photos Hub and choose a photo. Expand the application bar's menu and select the Apps menu item to see the list of photo viewer applications. You should see your PhotoEditor sample application in the list.

DETERMINING WHICH PICTURE THE USER IS VIEWING

When the photo viewer launches your application, it passes a token identifying the selected photo. The token is passed as a query string parameter in the navigation URI. The token can then be passed to the XNA `MediaLibrary` to retrieve the corresponding

Picture object. Let's see how to use the token in your sample application, as detailed in the next listing.

Listing 9.3 Using the Photos Hub token to display the selected photo

```
protected override void OnNavigatedTo(NavigationEventArgs e)
{
   if(State.ContainsKey("customCamera"))
   {
      State.Remove("customCamera");
      InitializeCamera();
   }
   IDictionary<string, string> queryStrings =          ❶ Get query strings
      NavigationContext.QueryString;                      sent on URI

   string action = null;
   if (queryStrings.ContainsKey("Action"))
      action = queryStrings["Action"];

   string token = null;
   if (queryStrings.ContainsKey("FileId"))          ❷ Extract
      token = queryStrings["FileId"];                  token value

   if (!string.IsNullOrEmpty(token))
   {                                                        ❸ Get picture
      MediaLibrary mediaLib = new MediaLibrary();             from media
      Picture picture = mediaLib.GetPictureFromToken(token);  library
      currentImage = PictureDecoder.DecodeJpeg(picture.GetImage());
      photoContainer.Fill = new ImageBrush { ImageSource = currentImage };
      imageDetails.Text = string.Format("Image from {0} action.\n
      ➥ Picture name:\n{1}\nMedia library token:\n{2}",
         action, picture.GetPath(), token);
   }
}
```

You're updating the OnNavigatedTo method in MainPage.xaml.cs that you created in the last chapter. Get the query string parameters sent to the application from the QueryString property of NavigationContext ❶. Check whether a token was passed from the Photos Hub ❷ in the FileId parameter. If it was, save the value in the token variable. Get the picture from MediaLibrary by using the token that you received ❸. Display the image in the photoContainer control and update the message displayed in the imageDetails TextBlock. You also display the value of the "Action" parameter, which in the case of Photos_Extra_Image_Editor extensions is EditPhotoContent.

You can easily debug applications that are launched by the Photos Hub. Start the application with the debugger in the normal fashion. Visual Studio maintains a debug session for your application, even though it may not be running, so when the Photos Hub launches PhotoEditor, the debugger reattaches to the application. Try this for yourself by placing a breakpoint in the OnNavigatedTo method and performing the following steps:

1 Press the Start button on the phone or emulator to return to the Start Screen.
2 Tap the Photos Hub tile to fire up the Photos Hub.

3 Find a picture you'd like to edit.
4 Select Edit from the application bar menu.

A photo viewer extension is typically an application that displays or edits a picture. The last Photos Hub extension we'll discuss is for applications that share pictures with social networking, messaging, or other web-based applications.

9.2.3 Sharing pictures from your Photos Hub extension

The Windows Phone Photos Hub has built-in support for sharing pictures with social-networking applications, text messaging, email, and SkyDrive. Third-party developers can register a picture-sharing application as an extension to the Photos Hub. This lets the user activate your application from the Share menu that appears from several locations in the Photos Hub, one of which is shown in figure 9.4. The Share menu activates the share picker, which displays all applications registered as `Photos_Extra_Share` extensions. You'll now turn the PhotoEditor application into a share picker extension. The first step is to add an `Extension` element with the name `Photos_Extra_Share` to the WMAppManifest.xml file:

```
<Extension ExtensionName="Photos_Extra_Share"
    ConsumerID="{5B04B775-356B-4AA0-AAF8-6491FFEA5632}"
    TaskID="_default" />
```

When the Photos Hub launches a sharing application, it passes the pictures token to the application. As with an edit picker application, a share picker extension receives the pictures token in the query string parameter named `FileId`. Share picker applications receive `ShareContent` in the `Action` query string parameter. Because the PhotoEditor application already looks for and handles `Action` and `FileId` query string parameters, you need make no further change in the sample code.

This wraps up the PhotoEditor application you've been working on for a chapter and a half. The application integrates with the camera and the Photo Chooser and extends the Picture Hub. But the Picture Hub isn't the only application that provides extension points. The next application you learn how to extend is the Music + Videos Hub.

9.3 Playing and recording with the Music + Videos Hub

You'll first learn about the Music + Videos Hub from an end-user point of view. Then you'll see how to develop an application that integrates with this hub.

The Music + Videos Hub is the central place where you can find all music, videos, and podcast activity on the device. You launch the Music + Videos Hub from its tile on the Start Screen or from its icon in the Application List. Let's take a look at the architecture of this hub. It's divided into the five sections shown in figure 9.5:

- *Collection*—The central view for playing music, videos, podcasts, and radio, and for accessing the marketplace.
- *History*—Contains the list of music, videos, playlists, artists, and podcasts that the user has recently played.

Figure 9.5 The five different sections of the Music + Videos Hub. The first image is the list of media collections in the media library. The second lists the media recently played by the user. Newly downloaded media is shown in the third section. The app picker lists applications that extend the Music + Videos Hub. The last section contains links to the Xbox Music Store.

- *New*—Contains the list of new music, videos, or podcasts that have recently been synced to the phone or downloaded from the store. This list is updated when media is added to the device or when the user creates an object in a Music + Videos application.
- *Apps*—Contains the list of applications installed on the device that integrate with the Music + Videos Hub.
- *Xbox*—Contains links to Xbox companion apps such as Xbox SmartGlass and links to content available from the Xbox Music Store.

When you're developing for the Music + Videos Hub application, keeping these five sections in mind is crucial.

To demonstrate how to integrate with the Music + Videos Hub, you need a new sample application. The application will use the phone's microphone to record voice recordings. You may use this feature to create a pronunciation training program that helps users record their voice and practice until they can pronounce properly. People who like to learn languages may find such a program useful.

When a new file is recorded, your application will create an item in the new section of the Music + Videos Hub. The application will also allow the user to play their recordings, which will create items in the Music + Videos History view. Because the sample application integrates with the Music + Videos Hub, it'll be shown in the apps list. When the user taps any of the items you add to the history, new, or apps section, your application will be launched by the Music + Videos Hub.

Start by creating a new Windows Phone App project named VoiceRecorder (shown in figure 9.6). The media and microphone APIs you'll use are in the XNA Framework, which is part of .NET for Windows Phone and so is automatically referenced by your project.

> **TIP** Use of the microphone requires the `ID_CAP_MICROPHONE` capability to be declared in WMAppManifest.xml

There's one incompatibility between XNA and XAML: The two frameworks use different event systems. To record voice data, you need to use the XNA event system. That means you need to pump the XNA dispatcher to get the microphone events to fire. We'll first take a look how to enable the XNA Framework events in a XAML application.

Figure 9.6 The VoiceRecorder sample application

9.3.1 *Enabling XNA Framework events*

XNA Framework events are dispatched by the `Update` method of the `FrameworkDispatcher` class. In XNA Game projects, the `FrameworkDispatcher` is called automatically by the XNA Framework. The XAML Framework doesn't automatically call XNA's `FrameworkDispatcher`. Because you're using XNA's `Microphone` class in a XAML project, you have to call `FrameworkDispatcher.Update` manually to dispatch messages that are in the XNA Framework's message queue.

The `Update` method must be called several times each second to properly process each event. An efficient method for dispatching an XNA event is to place the call to `Update` inside the `Tick` event handler of a `DispatchTimer` object. Add a new `DispatchTimer` field called `xnaTimer` to the `App` class in App.xaml.cs, and include a few necessary namespaces:

```
using System.Windows.Threading;
using Microsoft.Xna.Framework;
DispatcherTimer xnaTimer;
```

Initialize the field in the App constructor, wiring up the `Tick` event with a lambda expression:

```
xnaTimer = new DispatcherTimer{ Interval = TimeSpan.FromMilliseconds(16) };
xnaTimer.Tick += (sender, e) => FrameworkDispatcher.Update();
xnaTimer.Start();
```

The lambda expression makes a call to the `Update` method. The `Tick` event is raised every 16 milliseconds, or about 60 times per second. That's all you need to do to enable XNA events in a XAML project. With this bit of housekeeping done, you can move on to the user interface.

9.3.2 Building the user interface

Figure 9.7 The Stop and Record application bar buttons in the VoiceRecorder sample application

Your sample application will have two application bar buttons to start and stop recording, shown in figure 9.7. When the user taps the Record button, the application will start recording from the microphone. The user taps the Stop button to stop the recording. The sample application will store the voice recording in local storage and add the filename to the playlist. The user can tap the Play button to play the recorded audio file.

The following listing shows the markup for the application bar and the content panel that you need to add to MainPage.xaml.

Listing 9.4 Adding controls to MainPage.xaml

```
<phone:PhoneApplicationPage.ApplicationBar>
    <shell:ApplicationBar>
        <shell:ApplicationBarIconButton Text="record"
            IconUri="/Assets/AppBar/record.png"
            Click="record_Click" />
        <shell:ApplicationBarIconButton Text="stop"
            IconUri="/Assets/AppBar/stop.png"
            Click="stopRecord_Click" />
    </shell:ApplicationBar>
</phone:PhoneApplicationPage.ApplicationBar>
...
<Grid x:Name="ContentPanel" Grid.Row="1" Margin="12,0,12,0">
    <phone:LongListSelector x:Name="recordingList">
        <phone:LongListSelector.ItemTemplate>
            <DataTemplate>
                <StackPanel Orientation="Horizontal" Margin="12">
                    <Button Click="play_Click" Tag="{Binding Title}"
                        Background="Black">
                        <Image Source="/Assets/transport.play.png" />
                    </Button>
                    <TextBlock Text="{Binding Title}"
                        VerticalAlignment="Center"
                        FontSize="{StaticResource PhoneFontSizeLarge}" />
               <TextBlock Text="{Binding Date,
[CA] StringFormat='Recorded: \{0:g\}'}"
                  FontSize="{StaticResource PhoneFontSizeNormal}" />
                </StackPanel>
            </DataTemplate>
        </phone:LongListSelector.ItemTemplate>
    </phone:LongListSelector>
```

❶ Start and Stop recording buttons

❷ Add Play button to template

```
    <TextBlock x:Name="recordingMessage" Text="Recording..."
        Visibility="Collapsed" HorizontalAlignment="Center"
        VerticalAlignment="Center"
        Foreground="{StaticResource PhoneAccentBrush}"
        FontSize="{StaticResource PhoneFontSizeLarge}" />

</Grid>
```

(3) Hidden recording message

The ApplicationBar contains two buttons to start and stop a recording (1). The buttons use custom images, which you can find in the book's sample source code. You'll implement the button click handlers later in the chapter, but you might want to create empty implementations so your code will compile. The main part of the user interface is built using a LongListSelector to display each voice recording stored in local storage. The LongListSelector's ItemTemplate displays the name of each recording and the date and time when the file was recorded. The template also places a Button (2) next to each item in the list. The button is used to start and pause playback of the recording. You use data binding to store the filename in the button's Tag property. The button displays an image from the Windows Phone SDK image library.

The listing declares a TextBlock containing the message "Recording..." that's initially hidden (3). The TextBlock will be shown to the user when the application is actively recording from the microphone, as shown in figure 9.8. The message is hidden once recording stops.

Figure 9.8 The Play button and recording message as displayed in the VoiceRecorder user interface

Once you've added the required controls in XAML, you need to initialize the microphone. The microphone is represented by the XNA Framework class called Microphone. The Microphone is a singleton and is accessed through the static Default property. Before using the Microphone class, you need to set the BufferDuration property and wire up the BufferReady event in the MainPage constructor:

```
public MainPage()
{
    InitializeComponent();

    Microphone.Default.BufferDuration = TimeSpan.FromSeconds(1);
    Microphone.Default.BufferReady += microphone_BufferReady;
}
```

While recording, the Microphone stores audio data in an internal buffer. When the buffer is full, the Microphone raises the BufferReady event. The BufferDuration field specifies how much audio will fit into the buffer. Expressed another way, the BufferDuration determines the TimeSpan between each BufferReady event.

There's one last bit of supporting code you need before you can start recording audio with the Microphone. You need a simple class to hold the title and recording date. Create a new class named VoiceRecording with Title and Date properties:

```
public class VoiceRecording
{
    public string Title { get; set; }
    public DateTime Date { get; set; }
}
```

The `LongListSelector`'s `ItemsSource` property must be initialized in the `MainPage` constructor to a new `ObservableCollection` of `VoiceRecording` objects:

```
using System.Collections.ObjectModel;
recordingList.ItemsSource = new ObservableCollection<VoiceRecording>();
```

With the new class in place, you're ready to move on to the main feature of the sample application—recording audio with the `Microphone`.

9.3.3 *Recording audio*

The `Microphone` raises the `BufferReady` event once after recording audio for the duration specified in the `BufferDuration` property. In the `BufferReady` event handler, audio data should be copied from the `Microphone` into a storage location. In the sample application, this audio data is temporarily copied into a `byte` array and then written to a `MemoryStream`. Add two new fields to the `MainPage` class for the `byte` array and the `MemoryStream`:

```
using System.IO;
MemoryStream audioStream = null;
byte[] audioBuffer = null;
```

The `BufferReady` event is an XNA Framework event and is raised by the `FrameworkDispatcher`. In the event handler, you get the data from the microphone and write that data to the `MemoryStream`:

```
void microphone_BufferReady(object sender, EventArgs e)
{
    int count = Microphone.Default.GetData(audioBuffer);
    audioStream.Write(audioBuffer, 0, count);
}
```

The `Microphone`'s `GetData` method copies data into the `audioBuffer` `byte` array and returns the number of bytes written. Use the count of bytes written to the buffer when writing to the `audioStream`.

The `BufferReady` event isn't triggered until the user starts recording with the microphone. The user starts a recording by tapping the Record button in the user interface. The Record button is wired to the `record_Click` method, detailed in the following listing.

Listing 9.5 Recording with the `Microphone`

```
void record_Click(object sender, EventArgs e)
{
    if (Microphone.Default.State == MicrophoneState.Stopped)
    {
```

```
            recordingList.IsEnabled = false;
            recordingMessage.Visibility = Visibility.Visible;
            audioStream = new MemoryStream();
            audioBuffer = new byte[Microphone.Default.
                GetSampleSizeInBytes(TimeSpan.FromSeconds(1))];
            Microphone.Default.Start();
        }
    }
```

❶ Display recording message

❷ Allocate temporary storage

The Microphone has a property named State that you check to determine whether the microphone is already on. If not, start the microphone. When the microphone is recording, the recordingList LongListSelector is disabled, and the recording message in shown to the user ❶. The user can't select or play any existing recordings while the current track is being recorded. The temporary byte array and MemoryStream are allocated ❷ before you start recording. Recording is started by calling the Start method of the singleton Microphone instance.

Recording continues until the user taps the Stop button and triggers the stopRecord_Click event handler. The following listing shows the implementation of the stopRecord_Click event handler.

Listing 9.6 Stopping the recording

```
async void stopRecord_Click(object sender, EventArgs e)
{
    if (Microphone.Default.State == MicrophoneState.Started)
    {
        Microphone.Default.Stop();
        string filename = await WriteFile();
        audioBuffer = null;
        audioStream = null;
        recordingMessage.Visibility = Visibility.Collapsed;
        recordingList.IsEnabled = true;
        recordingList.ItemsSource.Add(new VoiceRecording
            { Title = filename, Date = DateTime.Now });
    }
}
```

❶ Write audio data to file

❷ Add recording to ListBox

Before you do any work in the stopRecord_Click method, check whether the microphone's state is Started. After the microphone has been stopped, write the contents of the MemoryStream to a file in local storage ❶ and clean up the temporary variables. The recording list is re-enabled, and the recording message is hidden once again. Create a new VoiceRecording instance and add it to the items displayed in the LongListSelector ❷.

The listing calls through to a method named WriteFile to save the audio data in a file. The audio data recorded by the Microphone is stored in raw PCM data format. To make the raw PCM data into a real audio file, you must wrap the audio data with a media container. In this application, you're using a wave file container format. A *wave file* is merely a header block followed by the audio data. The following listing shows the implementation of the WriteFile method.

Listing 9.7 Saving audio data to isolated storage

```
using System.Threading.Tasks;
using Windows.Storage;
async Task<string> WriteFile()
{
    StorageFolder localFolder = ApplicationData.Current.LocalFolder;
    StorageFile file = await localFolder.CreateFileAsync(
        "voice-recording.wav",
        CreationCollisionOption.GenerateUniqueName);          ❶ Generate unique filename

    using (Stream fileStream = await file.OpenStreamForWriteAsync())
    {
        using (var writer = new BinaryWriter(fileStream))
        {
            writer.Write(new char[4] { 'R', 'I', 'F', 'F' });
            writer.Write((Int32)(36 + audioStream.Length));        ❷ Write wave header
            writer.Write(new char[4] { 'W', 'A', 'V', 'E' });
            writer.Write(new char[4] { 'f', 'm', 't', ' ' });
            writer.Write((Int32)16);

            writer.Write((UInt16)1);
            writer.Write((UInt16)1);
            writer.Write((UInt32)16000);
            writer.Write((UInt32)32000);
            writer.Write((UInt16)2);
            writer.Write((UInt16)16);
            writer.Write(new char[4] { 'd', 'a', 't', 'a' });
            writer.Write((Int32)audioStream.Length);               ❸ Write MemoryStream to the file
            writer.Write(audioStream.GetBuffer(), 0,
                (int)audioStream.Length);
            writer.Flush();
        }
    }
    return file.Name;
}
```

Start by getting a reference to the local storage folder and creating a new file. Generate a new filename ❶ by specifying the `GenerateUniqueName` value of the `CreationCollisionOption` enumeration. `GenerateUniqueName` tells `CreateFileAsync` to append a number in parentheses to the end of the desired file. Next, open a .NET `Stream` for the file and create a `BinaryWriter`. Use the `BinaryWriter` to write the wave header ❷ and `WaveFormatEx` information. Write the PCM data stored in the `MemoryStream` to the end of the file ❸.

> **NOTE** Details of the wave header and the PCM format are beyond the scope of this book. You can read more about wave files on MSDN at http://mng.bz/6Xe9.

In listing 9.7 you added the newly saved voice recording to the display. You should be displaying all the voice recordings saved in local storage. You'll now create a new method called `DisplayRecordingNames` to read the names of all the recordings and add them to the recordingList. Override MainPage's OnNavigatedTo method and add a call to the new method. The DisplayRecordingNames implementation is shown in the following listing.

Listing 9.8 Displaying stored recordings

```
protected override async void OnNavigatedTo(NavigationEventArgs e)
{
    await DisplayRecordingNames ();
}

async Task DisplayRecordingNames ()
{
    StorageFolder folder = ApplicationData.Current.LocalFolder;
    IReadOnlyList<StorageFile> files = await folder.GetFilesAsync();
    foreach (StorageFile file in files)
    {
        recordingList.ItemsSource.Add( new VoiceRecording
            { Title = file.Name, Date = file.DateCreated });
    }
}
```

1 Get all filenames in root folder

2 Display recording information

After opening the storage device, get a list of every StorageFile in the root folder **1**. Loop over the list, retrieving the filename and the date the file was created, adding each recording to the LongListSelector **2**. The results are shown in figure 9.9.

If you run the VoiceRecorder application now, you'll be able to press the Record button and speak into the phone. Your voice will be recorded, and when you press Stop the recording will be saved into a wave file in isolated storage. The next feature you'll implement is playing the voice recording.

Figure 9.9 The sample application displaying several recordings in the LongListSelector

9.3.4 *Playing audio*

In addition to providing the Microphone class to record audio, the XNA Framework provides classes to play audio files. The two classes you're going to use in the VoiceRecorder application are SoundEffect and SoundEffectInstance. The SoundEffect class represents an audio file or stream. The SoundEffectInstance wraps the SoundEffect, allowing the developer to start, pause, and stop playback of a SoundEffect.

The SoundEffect class can work with and decode several different types of media containers and audio formats, including wave and PCM. A SoundEffect is initialized using a stream containing the audio file. The following listing demonstrates how to open a file stream, initialize a `SoundEffect`, create a `SoundEffectInstance`, and start playback.

Listing 9.9 Playing the recorded voice

```
SoundEffectInstance audioPlayerInstance = null;          ❶ Declare audio player field
async void PlayFile(string filename)
{
    StorageFolder localFolder = ApplicationData.Current.LocalFolder;
    using (Stream fileStream = await
                localFolder.OpenStreamForReadAsync(filename))   ❷ Open audio file
    {
        var soundEffect = SoundEffect.FromStream(fileStream);
        audioPlayerInstance = soundEffect.CreateInstance();      ❸ Create Sound-EffectInstance
        audioPlayerInstance.Play();
    }
}
```

Add a new field to the `MainPage` class ❶ to hold the currently playing voice recording. Create a new method named `PlayFile` that's responsible for opening and playing an audio file. The method opens the file stream in read-only mode ❷. The file stream is used to create a new `SoundEffect` using the static `FromStream` method ❸. The `audioPlayerInstance` field is assigned to the `SoundEffectInstance` class returned from the `CreateInstance` method. Start playback using the `Play` method of the `SoundEffectInstance`.

The `PlayFile` method accepts a filename from the calling code. In this case, the calling code is the `Click` event handler for the Play button declared in the `ListBox ItemTemplate`. The event hander code is detailed in the following listing.

Listing 9.10 Handling `Click` events for the Play button

```
void play_Click(object sender, EventArgs e)
{
    if (audioPlayerInstance != null &&
        audioPlayerInstance.State == SoundState.Playing)
    {
        audioPlayerInstance.Pause();
    }
    else
    {
        var button = (Button)sender;
        string filename = (string)button.Tag;
        PlayFile(filename);
    }
}
```

When the user taps the Play button in the `ListBox`, you examine the `State` property to see whether the audio player is currently playing an audio file. If so, stop playback by calling the `Pause` method and exit the event handler. If the audio player isn't busy, you get the filename from the `Tag` property of the `Button` control. The `Button` control is sent to the event handler in the `sender` property. Remember that in listing 9.4 you bound the Button's Tag property to the filename in the LongListSelector ItemTemplate. You send the retrieved filename to the PlayFile method.

You've now created a simple voice recorder for Windows Phone. Run the application, and you should see a list of voice recordings. Tap the Play button next to one of the recordings, and you should hear that recording play through the phone's speaker or headphones. Applications that play audio files—music tracks in particular—should consider extending the Music + Videos Hub.

9.4 Playing recorded audio in the Music + Videos Hub

In section 9.2 of this chapter you learned that the Photos Hub enables extensions with Extension elements in the WMAppManifest.xml file. The Music + Videos Hub doesn't work with Extension elements when figuring out which applications to display in the apps list. How can you make the VoiceRecorder sample application show up in the apps list? The answer is simple.

The App element in the WMAppManifest.xml file includes an attribute named HubType. When the HubType attribute is set to 1, your application will be shown in the apps list of the Music + Videos Hub.

> **NOTE** Updating the HubType attribute in WMAppManifest.xml is used for development and testing. When an application is submitted to the Windows Phone Store, the certification process automatically determines the HubType and overwrites WMAppManifest.xml accordingly.

Certain requirements must be met when creating a Music + Videos Hub application, which we cover later in the section. Here's an example of an App element:

```
<App xmlns=""
     ProductID="{ dbf1198b-6030-495a-bc4c-0abcc8e2d521}"
     Title="VoiceRecorder" RuntimeType="Silverlight"
     Version="1.0.0.0" Genre="apps.normal"
     Author="VoiceRecorder author"
     Description="Sample description"
     Publisher="VoiceRecorder"
     PublisherID="{8ff41791-6c68-4370-a64d-c6dad1b4f1dc}"
     HubType="1" >
```

When you play any kind of media from a Music + Videos Hub application, you need to integrate with the built-in Music + Videos Hub. That means that your application needs to meet the following requirements:

- *Now Playing*—When you play any media from your application, the media's details should be displayed in the Now Playing list in Music + Videos Hub.
- *History*—Once the media track has finished playing in your application, you need to add the media's details to the History view.
- *New*—When the user adds new media to your application, such as creating a new voice recording or purchasing a new song through the application, that media's details should be added in the New view list in the hub.

Microsoft established the Music + Videos requirements to ensure a consistent user experience for all media applications.

9.4.1 Fulfilling Music + Videos Hub requirements

The Windows Phone class library provides the `MediaHistoryItem` and `MediaHistory` classes that you can use to fulfill these three requirements. The certification guidelines say that any application using the `MediaHistoryItem` and `MediaHistory` classes is considered to be a Music + Videos application. We'll look first at creating a `MediaHistoryItem`, as shown in the following listing.

Listing 9.11 Creating a `MediaHistoryItem`

```
using Microsoft.Devices;
using System.Windows.Resources;
MediaHistoryItem createMediaHistoryItem(string fullFileName,
    bool smallSize)
{
    string imageName = smallSize ? "Assets/artwork173.jpg"
                                 : "Assets/artwork358.jpg";
    StreamResourceInfo imageInfo = Application.GetResourceStream(
        new Uri(imageName, UriKind.Relative));
    var mediaHistoryItem = new MediaHistoryItem
    {
        ImageStream = imageInfo.Stream,
        Source = "",
        Title = fullFileName
    };
    mediaHistoryItem.PlayerContext.Add("vrec-filename", fullFileName);
    return mediaHistoryItem;
}
```

1. Load image from content
2. Properties must not be null
3. Identity data added to context

The Music + Videos Hub requires media artwork when displaying media items. In this example, the artwork is coming from a file named either artwork173.jpg or artwork358.jpg that's been added to the project using a build action of `Content`. You use the `GetResourceStream` API to load the file and get access to its image stream ❶. The `MediaHistoryItem` class has three properties that must be assigned a value ❷. The `Source` property isn't used by the hub but is still required to have a non-null value. The `Title` property contains the name of the media and is displayed in the hub with the artwork.

The Windows Phone certification requirements define specific rules about the images used in the `MediaHistoryItem`. The images must be JPEGs. The tile image must include your application title or logo. The Now Playing image must be 358 pixel * 358 pixels in size. The History and New item images must be 173 pixels * 173 pixels in size.

One other `MediaHistoryItem` property is `PlayerContext` ❸, which is a dictionary of strings that can be used by an application to identify the media item. The entries placed in `PlayerContext` are returned to the application when the user selects the media item in the hub.

The MediaHistory class is what you use to integrate with the Music + Videos Hub. There's only one instance of the MediaHistory class, which is accessed via the Instance property. An application updates the Now Playing information in the hub via MediaHistory's NowPlaying property. The best time to update the NowPlaying property in your sample application is in the PlayFile method, right after SoundEffectInstance.Play is called:

```
MediaHistory.Instance.NowPlaying = createMediaHistoryItem(filename, false);
```

When using the NowPlaying property, the artwork should be a 358 * 358 pixel image. When creating media artwork, you should be careful to keep the overall size of the image file under the value specified by MediaHistoryItem.MaxImageSize, which is about 16 KB.

The NowPlaying property can also be used by your application to retrieve the information about the last media item it was playing. This may be handy if the user has exited your application and restarts it sometime in the future. You can restart the last item played. NowPlaying will only return the last MediaHistoryItem played by your application. It won't return media history for items added by other applications.

When your application has finished playing a media item, it should update the recently played list. The sample application isn't implemented to detect when the SoundEffect class finished playing, so you're going to cheat and update the recently played list right after you call SoundEffectInstance.Play:

```
MediaHistory.Instance.WriteRecentPlay(
    createMediaHistoryItem(filename, true));
```

Using the WriteRecentPlay API will cause a new tile to appear in the Music + Videos Hub History view. Your artwork for the recent play tile should be 173 * 173 pixels.

When your application acquires a new media item, it should update the New item list. You acquire new media items when the user has finished a recording, and the new file is written to local storage. Update the WriteFile method and add a call to WriteAcquiredItem:

```
MediaHistory.Instance.WriteAcquiredItem(
    createMediaHistoryItem(fullFileName, true));
```

Using the WriteAcquiredItem API will cause a new tile to appear in the Music + Videos Hub New view, as shown in figure 9.10. Your artwork for the new item tile should be 173 * 173 pixels.

Run the application, create a voice recording, and play it back. Switch to the Music + Videos Hub, and you should see a listing in both the New items list and the History list. It's expected that when you tap the listing in the hub, the VoiceRecorder application will be launched, and the selected recording will be played. Let's take a look at how to determine when your sample application is launched by the Music + Videos Hub.

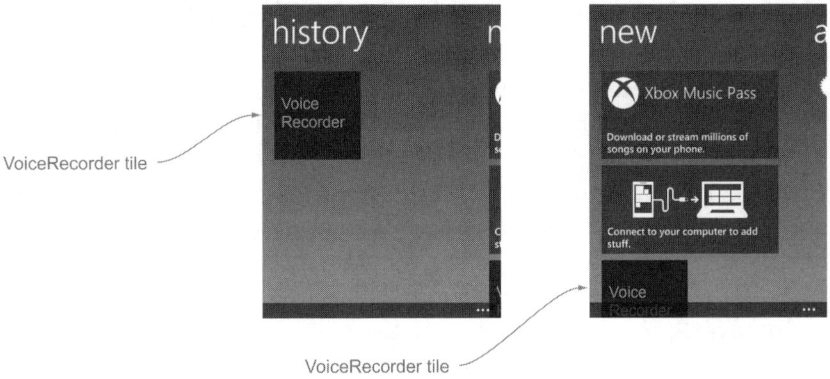

Figure 9.10 When using the MediaHistory methods, tiles representing an application's media files are displayed in the Music + Videos Hub.

9.4.2 *Launching from the Music + Videos Hub*

When the user taps the tile representing your media items in the History or New view in the Music + Videos Hub, your application will be launched and the `MediaHistoryItem`'s `PlayerContext` values will be sent to your application as query string parameters. You can read the query string parameters from the `NavigationContext`'s `QueryString` property in the `OnNavigatedTo` override method:

```
protected override await void OnNavigatedTo(NavigationEventArgs e)
{
    await DisplayRecordingNames();
    IDictionary<string, string> queryStrings =
        NavigationContext.QueryString;
    if (queryStrings.ContainsKey("vrec-filename"))
    {
        PlayFile(queryStrings["vrec-filename"]);
    }
}
```

Remember that in listing 9.11 you saved the voice recording filename in the `MediaHistoryItem`'s `PlayerContext` dictionary with the `vrec-filename` key. In `OnNavigatedTo` you check whether the query string contains a parameter named `vrec-filename`. If the parameter is present, you pass the parameter's value to the `PlayFile` method.

In this section you've learned how to integrate an application with the Music + Videos Hub, which is the single access point for all media on the Windows Phone. Applications that play or create media should consider using the `MediaHistory` class to report now-playing and history information. When a foreground application plays audio files, playback stops once the user switches to another application. Windows Phone applications can use background agents to continue playing audio files when the user switches tasks.

9.5 Playing recorded audio with a background agent

Background agents, introduced in chapter 4, enable an application to execute tasks and perform work even when their host application isn't running. The Windows Phone SDK provides two background agents exclusively for playing audio. The background audio agents and their supporting classes are defined in the `Microsoft.Phone.BackgroundAudio` namespace. The `AudioPlayerAgent` allows applications to play local or remote audio files. The `AudioStreamingAgent` can be used to play audio streamed to the device. In this section you add an `AudioPlayerAgent` to the VoiceRecorder application to enable background playing of the recorded audio.

`AudioPlayerAgents` are created using the Windows Phone Audio Playback Agent project template. Add a new audio playback project to the Visual Studio solution containing the VoiceRecorder project and name the new project VoiceRecorderPlaybackAgent. Using the Add Reference dialog, add a project reference to the VoiceRecorderPlaybackAgent project from the VoiceRecorder project.

The project template created one class named `AudioPlayer` in the VoiceRecorderPlaybackAgent project. Derived from `AudioPlayerAgent`, the `AudioPlayer` class is generated with four overrides called `OnPlayStateChanged`, `OnUserAction`, `OnError`, and `OnCancel`. Before we talk about each of these overrides, let's discuss how the foreground application communicates with the background agent.

Applications communicate with the background agent through the `BackgroundAudioPlayer` class. `Playback` is controlled using the `Play`, `Pause`, and `Stop` methods. The audio player also provides `FastForward`, `Rewind`, `SkipNext`, and `SkipPrevious` methods. Playback progress can be read with `PlayerState`, `Position`, and `BufferProgress` properties.

Now that you have a background audio agent, you need to update the VoiceRecorder to use the `BackgroundAudioPlayer` instead of a `SoundEffectInstance` to play and pause audio files. The application tells the `BackgroundAudioPlayer` which audio file to play using the `Track` property. Open MainPage.xaml.cs, find the `PlayFile` method, and replace the code that opens the file stream and uses the `SoundEffect` class and the `audioPlayerInstance` field with the code in the following snippet:

```
using Microsoft.Phone.BackgroundAudio;
void PlayFile(string filename)
{
    Uri fileUri = new Uri(filename, UriKind.Relative);
    BackgroundAudioPlayer.Instance.Track = new AudioTrack(
        fileUri, filename, "Windows Phone 7 in Action", null, null, null,
        EnabledPlayerControls.Pause);
    BackgroundAudioPlayer.Instance.Play();
...
}
```

Once the track is specified, you ask the background agent to play the voice recording by calling the `BackgroundAudioPlayer`'s `Play` method. Access the singleton instance of the `BackgroundAudioPlayer` using the static `Instance` property.

The Track property is of type AudioTrack, and you construct a new AudioTrack by specifying the URI to the voice recording's location in local storage along with the title and artist. You use the filename as the track's title and the string "Windows Phone 8 in Action" as the track's artist. You also specify that only the Pause button should be enabled in the Universal Volume Control (UVC).

The host application isn't the only process that controls background audio playback. Background audio agents automatically integrate with the UVC. Normally, the UVC allows the user to fast forward, rewind, skip previous, and skip back. When you created the AudioTrack, you specified that only the Pause button should be enabled, and the UVC for the VoiceRecorder (shown in figure 9.11) disables the Rewind/Skip Previous and Fast Forward/Skip Next buttons.

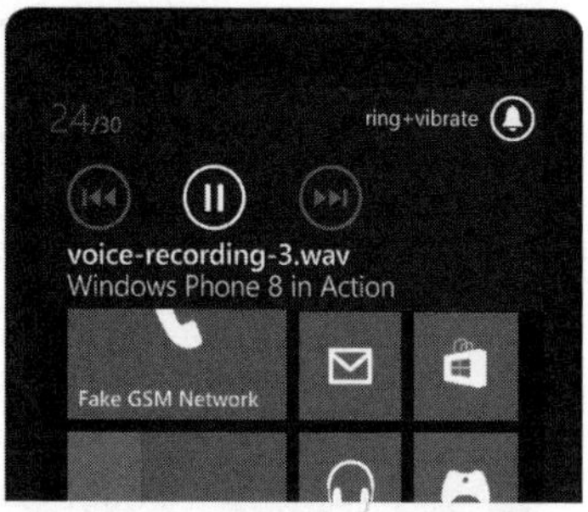

Figure 9.11 Voice recordings in the Universal Volume Control

Remember that the user can pause the voice recording within the VoiceRecorder application by pressing the Play button during playback. You need to replace the pause code in the play_Click method so that it also uses the BackgroundAudioPlayer instead of the audioPlayerInstance field:

```
private void play_Click(object sender, EventArgs e)
{
    if (BackgroundAudioPlayer.Instance.PlayerState == PlayState.Playing)
    {
        BackgroundAudioPlayer.Instance.Pause();
    }
    ...
}
```

The BackgroundAudioPlayer reports the current playback state through the PlayerState property and the PlayState enumeration. The PlayState enumeration defines a dozen different states, including Playing, Paused, and Stopped. In this code, if the state is Playing, you call the Pause method.

Note that calling the Play or Pause methods from the foreground applications doesn't result in the voice recording playing. When the foreground application calls Play, Pause, or the other playback control methods, a message is sent to the background agent. It's the responsibility of the background agent to handle the foreground requests. The BackgroundAudioPlayer delivers messages to the background agent with the OnUserAction override method.

The OnUserAction method is sent information about the action to be performed through a UserAction enumeration value. Possible actions include Stop, Pause, Play, SkipNext, SkipPrevious, FastForward, Rewind, and Seek. The VoiceRecorder sample application uses only Play and Pause, so those are the only actions your background agent will support.

The `AudioPlayer` class generated by the project template contains a default implementation of `OnUserAction`. Open the AudioPlayer.cs file and review the generated code. When the user action is `Play` or `Pause`, the corresponding method on the passed-in `BackgroundAudioPlayer` instance is invoked. Calling the `Play` methods from the background application does cause the audio file playback to start or continue. You learned in chapter 4 that the `NotifyComplete` method is called by a background agent to inform the operating system that it has successfully completed its work.

Use the `OnPlayStateChanged` override method to detect when the audio track has finished or stopped. `OnPlayStateChanged` will be called with `Stopped` and then with `Shutdown` when the user picks a song from the music library. `OnPlayStateChanged` is called with `TrackEnded` once the audio track finishes.

You've now created a simple voice recorder for Windows Phone. There are a lot of ways that you can improve this application to end up with a more professional voice recorder. This is an example—we'll leave those improvements for you.

9.6 Summary

You started the chapter by updating the PhotoEditor sample application introduced in chapter 8. You learned about the Pictures and Music + Videos Hubs. You now understand that those hubs are the applications where all photos, songs, videos, and podcasts are stored in your phone. We analyzed the Photos Hub from both the end-user and developer perspectives. You registered the PhotoEditor application as an extension of Photos Hub with Photo Extensibility for Windows Phone.

We explored recording voice using the Windows Phone microphone and extending the Music + Videos Hub. Any application that plays audio files should consider making use of audio background agents for playing or streaming while other applications are running in the foreground. In the next chapter you'll learn how to use the phone sensors, such as the accelerometer and the gyroscope.

10 Using sensors

> ***This chapter covers***
> - Understanding Sensor API design
> - Interpreting sensor data
> - Using sensors in the emulator
> - Moving with the motion sensor

You can build cool applications by combining sensors with other features of the phone. Applications may respond to a user shaking the device by randomly selecting an object or clearing the screen. Games can use the device's movement as an input mechanism, turning the whole phone into a game controller. Another class of applications augments the real world with computer-generated information. Augmented reality apps can show you the location of friends nearby in relation to your current location. Astronomy applications determine the position of your device and identify the stars in the night sky. A tourist application may be able to identify nearby landmarks.

All these applications require sensor input from the physical world. The phone's accelerometer, compass, and gyrometer sensors capture input from the real world and serve the data to applications through the Windows Phone SDK's Sensor API. When combined with location data from the phone's Location Service, stunning augmented-reality applications are possible. We discuss the Location Service in chapter 16.

Dealing with raw data from the sensors can be tricky—for example, when you're trying to calculate which direction a device is pointed in. The `Inclinometer` and `OrientationSensor` classes take input from each of the other sensors, perform several complex calculations, and provide data related to motion and a device's relative position in the real world.

To gain a good understanding of the raw data returned by the various sensors, you're going to build a sample application that presents data on the screen. The first part of the chapter covers the `Accelerometer`, `Compass`, and `Gyrometer` classes to demonstrate what data they return, how they're similar, and how they differ. The latter half of the chapter covers the `Inclinometer` and `OrientationSensor` classes and how they're wrappers around the three other sensors.

Before we dive into the sample application, we introduce the common Sensor API that's the foundation for the sensors exposed by the Windows Phone SDK.

10.1 Understanding the Sensor APIs

Although the `Accelerometer`, `Compass`, `Gyrometer`, `Inclinometer`, and `OrientationSensor` Sensor APIs each return different types of data, they each implement the same pattern for reporting their data. Over the next several pages, you'll learn techniques that are useful for reading data from any of the sensors. We show you these techniques as you build the foundation of the sample application. The classes and interfaces that compose the Sensor API are found in the `Windows.Devices.Sensors` namespace.

> **NOTE** In the Windows Phone 8 SDK there are two separate Sensor APIs. The APIs found in `Microsoft.Devices.Sensors` were originally part of the Windows Phone 7 SDK and have been brought forward to Windows Phone 8. The second Sensor API, found in the `Windows.Devices.Sensors`, comes from the Windows 8 Runtime that the Windows Phone shares with the Windows 8 operating system. If you intend to share code between Windows Phone and Windows 8 applications, you should consider using the Windows 8 Sensor API. The Windows Phone 7 Sensor API isn't covered in this book.

Even though the `Accelerometer`, `Compass`, `Gyrometer`, `Inclinometer`, and `OrientationSensor` don't share a common base class, they all have a number of identical properties, methods, and events. These common members are described in table 10.1.

Table 10.1 Common sensor class members

Member	Type	Description
`GetCurrentReading`	Method	Returns a read-only object containing the currently available sensor data.
`GetDefault`	Method	A static factory method that returns a sensor instance.

Table 10.1 Common sensor class members *(continued)*

Member	Type	Description
`MinimumReportInterval`	Property	A read-only value specifying the smallest value that can be passed set in the `ReportInterval` property.
`ReadingChanged`	Event	An event raised whenever the current reading changes.
`ReportInterval`	Property	Specifies how often the sensor reads new data. The data returned by the `GetCurrentReading` will change only once during every time interval.

An application obtains the current sensor reading by calling the `GetCurrentReading` method. Alternatively, an application can subscribe to the `ReadingChanged` event to receive a sensor reading only when the sensor has new data. The `GetCurrentReading` method may be called even when the sensor isn't ready, but the value returned may be `null`.

> **NOTE** If the `ID_CAP_SENSORS` capability isn't present in the WMAppManifest .xml file, calls to `GetDefault` for any sensor will result in an `Unauthorized-AccessException`.

Each of the sensor classes defines a static method named `GetDefault`. The `Get-Default` method allows a developer to determine whether the sensor hardware is installed on a particular device and whether the sensor is available to the application. If the device doesn't have a particular sensor installed and available, the `GetDefault` method for the missing sensor returns `null`.

The Sensor API handles fast application switching on its own. Developers don't need to unhook the sensors when the application is switched from the foreground. Unlike the camera, sensors automatically resume and don't provide an explicit restore method. When the application is resumed, the sensors and events are reconnected, and data starts to flow again. Before you learn how to work with the data flowing from the sensors, you need to understand how the sensors report data in three dimensions.

10.1.1 Data in three dimensions

Each of the sensors reports data relative to the x, y, z coordinate system defined by the Windows Phone device. The device's coordinate system is fixed to the device and moves as the phone moves. The x axis extends out the sides of the device, with positive x pointing to the right side of the device and negative x pointing to the left side of the device. The y axis runs through the top and bottom of the device, with positive y pointing toward the top. The z axis runs from back to front, with positive z pointing out the front of the device. Figure 10.1 shows the x, y, and z axes from three different views of a phone.

The coordinate system used by the sensors doesn't necessarily match the coordinate system used by other APIs. One example is the coordinate system used by XAML.

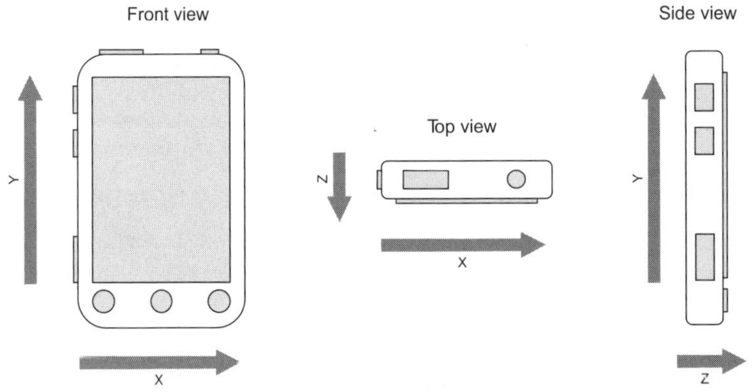

Figure 10.1 The x, y, z coordinate system as defined by a Windows Phone

In portrait mode XAML, the y axis points in the opposite direction, with positive y pointing out the bottom of the device.

Now that you understand the coordinate system used by the sensors, let's take a closer look at reading data from the sensors.

10.1.2 Reading data with events

Each of the sensors supports an event-driven interaction model with the `ReadingChanged` event. The `ReadingChanged` event sends an event args class instance to an event handler, where the type of event args class varies with each sensor. The `Accelerometer` sends an `AccelerometerReadingChangedEventArgs`, the `Compass` sends a `CompassReadingChangedEventArgs`, and so on.

The `ReadingChanged` event handler is called on a background thread. If the event handler updates the user interface, the update logic must be dispatched to the UI thread. The following code snippet shows an example that handles the `ReadingChanged` event from the `Gyrometer` sensor:

```
void sensor_ReadingChanged(object sender,
    GryometerReadingChangedEventArgs e)
{
    GryometerReading reading = e. Reading;
    Dispatcher.BeginInvoke(() =>
    {
        // add logic here to update the UI with data from the reading
        ...
    }
}
```

The Sensors sample application you'll build in this chapter doesn't use the `ReadingChanged` event. Instead, the sample application will poll for data using the `GetCurrentReading` method.

10.1.3 Polling for data

An application doesn't need to wait for the sensor to raise an event to ask for data. Each sensor exposes data through the `GetCurrentReading` method. The

`GetCurrentReading` method can be called whenever the application data determines it needs new data. For example, the reading may be initiated from a button click, a timer tick event, or a background worker:

```
if (compassSensor != null)
{
    CompassReading reading = compassSensor.GetCurrentReading();
    if (reading != null)
    {
        // add logic here to use the data from the reading
        ...
    }
}
```

You'll read sensor data from a timer tick event in the sample application. Before we can show you the sensors in action, you need to create a new project and prepare the application to display sensor data.

10.2 Creating the sample application

Open Visual Studio and create a new Windows Phone App called Sensors. The sample application will read values from the `Accelerometer`, `Compass`, `Gyrometer`, `Inclinometer`, and `OrientationSensor`. The sample application, shown in figure 10.2, displays a set of colored bars for data from the `Accelerometer`, `Gyrometer`, and `Inclinometer`. Each set of bars displays sensor readings for the x, y, and z coordinates. At the bottom of the screen, the application displays a legend and informational messages about the sensors, as well as readings from the `Compass` and `OrientationSensor`.

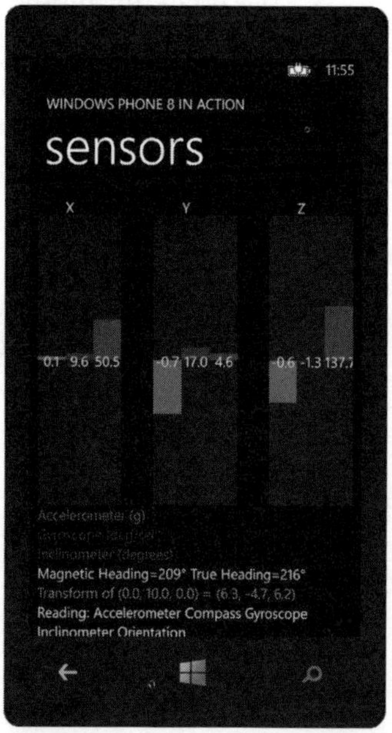

Figure 10.2 The Sensors sample application displays bars representing the x, y, and z values reported by the `Accelerometer`, `Gyrometer`, and `Inclinometer`.

When a sensor's value is positive, a bar will be drawn to scale above the effective zero line. A negative sensor value results in a bar drawn below the zero line. Because the range of possible values differs between each sensor, the height of the bar is transformed from the sensor's value into a pixel height using a scaling factor. We talk more about each sensor's range of values throughout the chapter.

First, you'll create a reusable control to display the positive and negative bars.

10.2.1 Creating a reusable Bar control

To simplify the sample application, you'll build a reusable control that allows you to set a scale factor and a sensor value. When the scale or value properties change, the control should draw the appropriate positive or negative bar and display the value with a label. The `Bar` control will be implemented using the Windows Phone User Control item template, accessed via the Project > Add New Item menu. Name the new item *Bar*. The XAML markup for the new control is shown in the following listing.

Listing 10.1 Markup for the `Bar` control

```
<Grid x:Name="LayoutRoot">
    <Grid.RowDefinitions>
        <RowDefinition Height="1*" />
        <RowDefinition Height="1*" />
    </Grid.RowDefinitions>
    <Rectangle x:Name="positiveBar" VerticalAlignment="Bottom" />
    <Rectangle x:Name="negativeBar" Grid.Row="1" VerticalAlignment="Top" />
    <TextBlock x:Name="label" VerticalAlignment="Center"
        Grid.RowSpan="2" Text="0" TextAlignment="Center" />
</Grid>
```

1 Divide control into two rows

2 Center label

The grid is divided into two halves **1** with each half containing a `Rectangle`. The first `Rectangle` displays positive values, and the other displays negative values. A label is placed in the middle **2** to show the bar's value. Figure 10.3 demonstrates what the control will look like for a `Bar` with a scale value set to `2.0` and a current value set to `-1.0`.

Pages that host a `Bar` control need the ability to set different fill colors for the `Rectangles`. Add a new property named `BarFill` to the Bar.xaml.cs code behind file:

```
using System.Windows.Media;
public Brush BarFill
{
    get { return positiveBar.Fill; }
    set
    {
        positiveBar.Fill = value;
        negativeBar.Fill = value;
    }
}
```

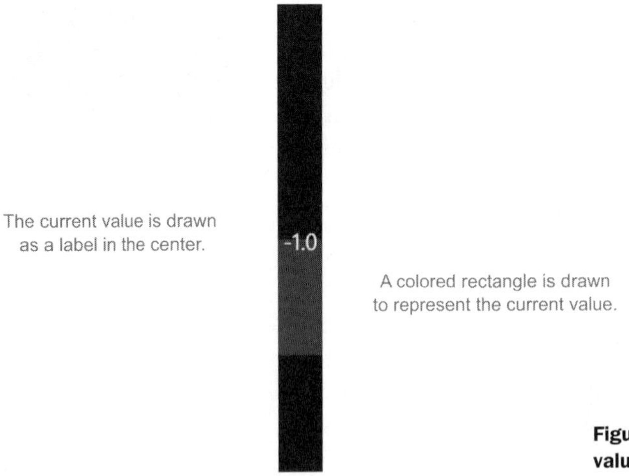
The current value is drawn
as a label in the center.
-1.0
A colored rectangle is drawn
to represent the current value.

Figure 10.3 A `Bar` control with a scale value of `2.0` and a current value of `-1.0`

The setter for the `BarFill` property assigns the specified `Brush` to both the `positiveBar` and `negativeBar` `Rectangles`.

> **NOTE** If you were building a reusable XAML control, the `BarFill` property and the other properties would be dependency properties. The control would declare template parts and would provide XAML markup as the default template. See Pete Brown's book *Silverlight 5 in Action* (Manning Publications, 2012) for more details on building reusable XAML controls.

Next, you create properties to set the scale and value for the bar. Because you don't know the full range of values, you need the caller to tell the control how to scale the value to the height of the rectangles. Let's say you need the bar to display a value between `2` and `-2`, and the `Bar` control is 200 pixels high. A value of `2` would require the positive bar to be 100 pixels high, whereas a value of `-1` would require the negative bar to be 50 pixels high. The following listing details how the bar height is calculated using the `Scale` and `Value` properties.

Listing 10.2 Calculating bar height with the `Scale` and `Value` properties

```
private double scale;
public double Scale
{
    get { return scale; }
    set
    {
        scale = value;
        Update();                          // 1 Recalculate when properties change
    }
}
private double barValue;
public double Value
{
    get { return barValue; }
    set
    {
        barValue = value;
        Update();
    }
}
private void Update()
{
    int height = (int)(barValue * scale);                 // 2 Calculate height of bar
    positiveBar.Height = height > 0 ? height : 0;
    negativeBar.Height = height < 0 ? height * -1 : 0;    // 3 Invert negative height
    label.Text = barValue.ToString("0.0");
}
```

Both the `Scale` and the `Value` properties are implemented with backing fields and simple getters and setters. Inside the setter of each property, you call the `Update` method ❶ to recalculate the height of the bar rectangles and update the user interface. Inside the `Update` method you multiply the `scale` and `barValue` fields ❷, and the resulting value is the number of pixels high the bar should be drawn. If the calculated height value is greater than `0`, the `positiveBar`'s `Height` is updated to the new value. If the calculated height value is less than `0`, you invert the calculated value ❸ before assigning the `negativeBar`'s height. Finally, you use the `ToString` method with a formatting string to set the label's `Text` property.

Now that you have a `Bar` control, you can create the sample application's user interface. You need to add an XML namespace to MainPage.xaml so that you can use your new bar control:

```
xmlns:l="clr-namespace:Sensors"
```

You're now ready to use the `Bar` control in the MainPage's XAML markup. You need to design the MainPage to have three `Bar` controls for each sensor, for a total of nine `Bar` controls.

10.2.2 Designing the main page

In figure 10.2, notice that MainPage.xaml is divided into three rows and several columns. The markup for the `ContentPanel` of MainPage.xaml is shown in the following listing.

Listing 10.3 Markup for MainPage.xaml

```
<Grid x:Name="ContentPanel" Grid.Row="1" Margin="12,0,12,0">
  <Grid.RowDefinitions>
    <RowDefinition Height="25" />
    <RowDefinition Height="400" />
    <RowDefinition Height="*" />
  </Grid.RowDefinitions>
  <Grid.ColumnDefinitions>
    <ColumnDefinition Width="40" />
    <ColumnDefinition Width="40" />
    <ColumnDefinition Width="40" />
    <ColumnDefinition Width="48" />
    <ColumnDefinition Width="40" />
    <ColumnDefinition Width="40" />
    <ColumnDefinition Width="40" />
    <ColumnDefinition Width="48" />
    <ColumnDefinition Width="40" />
    <ColumnDefinition Width="40" />
    <ColumnDefinition Width="40" />
  </Grid.ColumnDefinitions>
  <TextBlock Text="X" Grid.Column="1" />
  <TextBlock Text="Y" Grid.Column="5" />
  <TextBlock Text="Z" Grid.Column="9" />
  <l:Bar x:Name="accelX" Grid.Row="1" Grid.Column="0"
    BarFill="Red" Scale="100" />
  <l:Bar x:Name="accelY" Grid.Row="1" Grid.Column="4"
    BarFill="Red" Scale="100" />
  <l:Bar x:Name="accelZ" Grid.Row="1" Grid.Column="8"
    BarFill="Red" Scale="100" />
  <l:Bar x:Name="gyroX" Grid.Row="1" Grid.Column="1"
    BarFill="Blue" Scale="1.111111" />
  <l:Bar x:Name="gyroY" Grid.Row="1" Grid.Column="5"
```

❶ 11 columns

❷ 3 bars for each sensor

```
    BarFill="Blue" Scale="1.111111" />
  <l:Bar x:Name="gyroZ" Grid.Row="1" Grid.Column="9"
    BarFill="Blue" Scale="1.111111" />
  <l:Bar x:Name="inclineX" Grid.Row="1" Grid.Column="2"
    BarFill="DarkGreen" Scale="1.111111" />
  <l:Bar x:Name="inclineY" Grid.Row="1" Grid.Column="6"
    BarFill="DarkGreen" Scale="2.222222" />
  <l:Bar x:Name="inclineZ" Grid.Row="1" Grid.Column="10"
    BarFill="DarkGreen" Scale="0.555556" />
  <StackPanel Grid.Row="2" Grid.ColumnSpan="11">
    <TextBlock Foreground="Red" Text="Accelerometer (g)" />
    <TextBlock Foreground="Blue" Text="Gyrometer (deg/sec)" />
    <TextBlock Foreground="DarkGreen" Text="Inclinometer (degrees)" />
    <TextBlock x:Name="heading" Foreground="Yellow" />
    <TextBlock x:Name="point" Foreground="Violet" />
    <TextBlock x:Name="messageBlock" TextWrapping="Wrap" />
  </StackPanel >
</Grid>
```

❸ **Legend and messages**

Start by dividing the `ContentPanel` into 3 rows and 11 columns ❶. The first row contains three `TextBlocks` serving as the titles for the x, y, and z coordinates. The second row shows three bars ❷ for each of the `Accelerometer`, `Gyrometer`, and `Inclinometer` sensors. The `Bar` controls are 400 pixels high, divided into positive and negative sections of 200 pixels each. Allowing for 3 columns for each sensor and 2 spacer columns, you need a total of 11 columns. The last row ❸ contains a legend and messages.

Each `Bar` control is assigned a `BarFill` color—red for `Accelerometer` readings, blue for `Gyrometer` readings, and dark green for `Inclinometer` readings. Each `Bar` control is also assigned a scale value. We describe how the scale factors were calculated in our detailed discussion of each sensor later in the chapter.

10.2.3 Polling sensor data with a timer

In the sample application the screen is updated with data from each of the different sensors. To simplify the logic, the application won't use the `ReadingChanged` events for the sensors and will use a polling method instead. A `DispatchTimer` will be used to update the user interface about 15 times a second. Add a `DispatchTimer` field:

```
using System.Windows.Threading;
DispatcherTimer timer;
```

The `timer` field is initialized inside the `MainPage` constructor. The timer ticks every 66 milliseconds, or about 15 times a second. The application will poll each of the sensors inside the `timer_Tick` method:

```
public MainPage()
{
    InitializeComponent();
    timer = new DispatcherTimer();
    timer.Tick += timer_Tick;
    timer.Interval = TimeSpan.FromMilliseconds(66);
    Start();
}
```

The timer is started in the `start_Click` method. When the timer is started, the application updates the message displayed in the `TextBlock` named `messageBlock` to let the user know which sensors have been started:

```
void Start()
{
    if (!timer.IsEnabled)
    {
        string runningMessage = "Reading: ";

        // Sensors will be initialized here

        timer.Start();
        messageBlock.Text = runningMessage;
    }
}
```

You'll add additional code to the `Start` method as you hook up the `Accelerometer`, `Compass`, `Gyrometer`, and other sensors later in the chapter.

You could run the application now to check that the form is laid out as you expect, but the application doesn't do anything interesting yet. You'll remedy that by adding in the `Accelerometer` sensor.

10.3 Measuring acceleration with the accelerometer

The accelerometer can be used in games and applications that use phone movement as an input mechanism or for controlling game play. The accelerometer tells you when the device is being moved. It can also tell you whether the device is being held flat, at an angle, or straight up and down.

The accelerometer measures the acceleration component of the forces being applied to a device. Note that acceleration due to gravity isn't reported by the sensor. Unless the device in is free fall, forces are always being applied to a device. The accelerometer reports numbers in terms of the constant g, which is defined as the acceleration due to Earth's gravity at sea level. The value of g is –9.8 m/s^2.

When a device is at rest lying on a table, the table is exerting a force on the device that offsets the pull of gravity. The accelerometer measures the acceleration of the force the table applies. When the device is falling, the accelerometer reports zero acceleration.

Now consider when you push the device along the surface of the table. Other forces are now in play, such as the force being applied by your hand and the force due to friction between the device and the table. The accelerometer measures all these forces. When a user shakes a phone, the x, y, and z acceleration values will rapidly change from one extreme to another in a random pattern.

TIP The `Accelerometer` class has a special event named `Shaken` that you can subscribe to if your application needs to know when the user shakes a device.

By examining the x, y, and z values of the accelerometer, and how they change from one reading to the next, you can determine whether the device is in motion and how the device is being held. Before we get into the details about exactly what the accelerometer measures and what the reported values mean, you'll hook up the sensor to the bars displayed in the user interface of the sample application.

10.3.1 Hooking up the sensor

The sample application you built in the previous section is designed to show how the data returned by the sensors changes as the user moves the phone. To see how the accelerometer data changes, you need to call the `GetCurrentReading` method of an `Accelerometer` instance and update the three `Bar` controls allocated for the accelerometer's x, y, and z values. Before you can hook up a sensor, you need to declare a member field to reference the `Accelerometer` instance:

```
using Microsoft.Devices.Sensors;
Accelerometer accelSensor;
```

In the `Start` method, initialize the field and set the `ReportInterval`. The `ReportInterval` is set to match the tick interval of the `DispatchTimer` used to trigger user interface updates. Add the following snippet right before the line in the `Start` method where the timer's `Start` method is called:

```
accelSensor = Accelerometer.GetDefault();
if (accelSensor != null)
{
   accelSensor.ReportInterval = 66;
   runningMessage += "Accelerometer ";
}
```

You're adding the string `"Accelerometer "` to the message displayed in the user interface, informing the user that the accelerometer was started. If the sensor isn't supported, `GetDefault` will return `null`.

The final step is to read the accelerometer data when the timer ticks and the `timer_Tick` event handler is called. You're going to isolate the code that reads the accelerometer data into a method named `ReadAccelerometerData`. The timer tick method calls the `ReadAccelerometerData` method, shown in the following listing.

Listing 10.4 Reading acceleration

```
void timer_Tick(object sender, EventArgs e)
{
    ReadAccelerometerData();
}
void ReadAccelerometerData()
{
    if (accelSensor != null)
    {
        AccelerometerReading reading = accelSensor.GetCurrentReading();
        if (reading != null)                                    <-- 1 Make sure data was read
        {
```

```
                accelX.Value = reading.AccelerationX;
                accelY.Value = reading.AccelerationY;
                accelZ.Value = reading.AccelerationZ;
            }
        }
    }
```

❷ **Update user interface**

First, check whether or not an accelerometer exists before getting the current `AccelerometerReading` value from the sensor. Also check that `GetCurrentReading` returned a valid value ❶. The acceleration reading reports acceleration values in the three directions of the phone's coordinate system. Update the `Bar` controls in the user interface with the x, y, and z properties reported by the acceleration vector ❷.

When you created the `Bar` controls for the accelerometer in MainPage.xaml, you set the `Scale` property to `100`. The `Bar` controls are 400 pixels high, allowing for positive and negative sections of 200 pixels each. The maximum value of the acceleration vector is ±2. Using this information, you can determine that the scale factor for the bar should be 100, or 200/2.

At this point, you should be able to run the application. If you run the application on a physical device, you should see the bars grow and shrink as you move the device about. Tilt it front to back or side to side, lay it down flat, or hold it upside down. You can mimic all these movements in the emulator using the Accelerometer Tool.

10.3.2 Acceleration in the emulator

With the Sensors sample application open in Visual Studio, run the application on the emulator. The emulator's default position is standing in portrait orientation, and the accelerometer reports an acceleration of –1 along the y axis. Open the Additional Tools windows using the Expander button on the emulator's control bar. The Accelerometer Tool, shown in figure 10.4, is found in the first tab of the Additional Tools window.

The Accelerometer Tool allows you to move the device by dragging the orange dot. The device can also be changed from the Portrait Standing orientation to Portrait

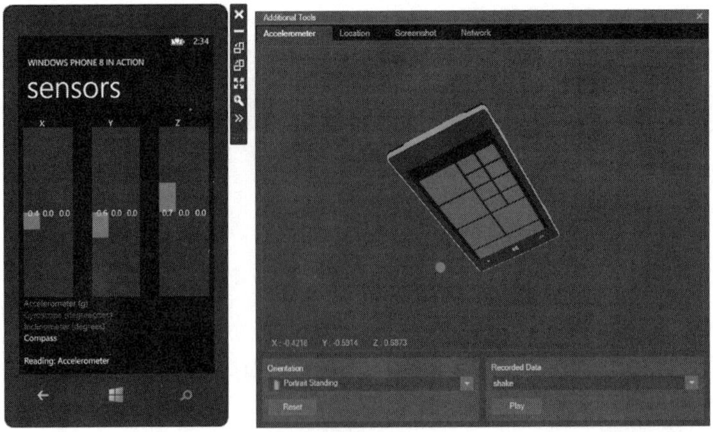

Figure 10.4 Controlling acceleration with the emulator's Accelerometer Tool

Flat, Landscape Standing, and Landscape Flat. The Accelerometer Tool also plays a canned script that mimics shaking the device.

With the Sensors application running in the emulator, you should see the bars grow and shrink as you move the device about with the orange dot. Play the Shake script and watch how the acceleration bars bounce up and down as the data changes. Now that you have a better idea of what numbers are reported by the accelerometer, let's take a closer look at exactly what the numbers mean.

10.3.3 Interpreting the numbers

The accelerometer sensor in the phone senses the acceleration due to forces applied to the phone but ignores the acceleration due to gravity. When a device is at rest lying on a table, the table is exerting a force on the device that offsets the pull of gravity. The accelerometer measures the acceleration of the force that the table applies to the device. When the device is falling, the accelerometer reports zero acceleration. Figure 10.5 demonstrates the values reported by the accelerometer when a phone is held in various positions.

If the number reported by the device is related to the force a surface exerts on the device, why is the number negative instead of positive? Remember that the number reported is in terms of g or gravity, and g equals –9.8 m/s^2, a negative number relative to the phone's coordinate system. When the accelerometer reports a `-1` (or a vector `1` pointing down), it means a vector with the value `9.8` pointing up. Table 10.2 lists the

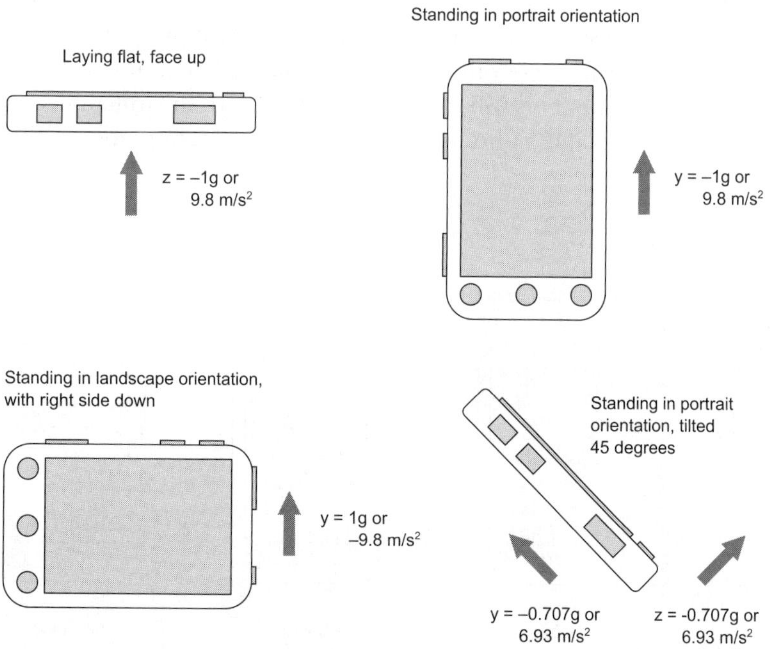

Figure 10.5 Acceleration from the forces on a device at rest. Each of the arrows represents the acceleration due to the force holding the device in the stated position.

approximate x, y, z values reported by the accelerometer when the device is at rest in various positions.

Table 10.2 Accelerometer readings with the device at rest

Position	X	Y	Z
In free fall	0g	0g	0g
Flat on back, lying on a surface	0g	0g	–1g or 9.8 m/s^2
Flat on face	0g	0g	1g or –9.8 m/s^2
Standing portrait, bottom is down	0g	–1g or 9.8 m/s^2	0g
Standing portrait, top is down	0g	1g or –9.8 m/s^2	0g
Standing landscape, left is down	–1g or 9.8 m/s^2	0g	0g
Standing landscape, right is down	1g or –9.8 m/s^2	0g	0g

When you move the device, you apply a force along the direction you want the device to move. The force causes the device to accelerate. Acceleration changes the velocity of the device, and it starts to move. Let's say your phone is resting flat, face up on the surface of a table, at point A. Now you give your device a modest push so that it slides along the surface to point B. The initial push is a moderate force in the positive x axis. After you release the device, allowing it to slide, your initial force stops, and the force due to friction begins to slow down the device until it stops moving. Figure 10.6 shows the values reported by the accelerometer in this scenario. The numbers are somewhat contrived, because real numbers will vary based on how hard the initial push is and the amount of friction between the phone and the surface it's resting upon.

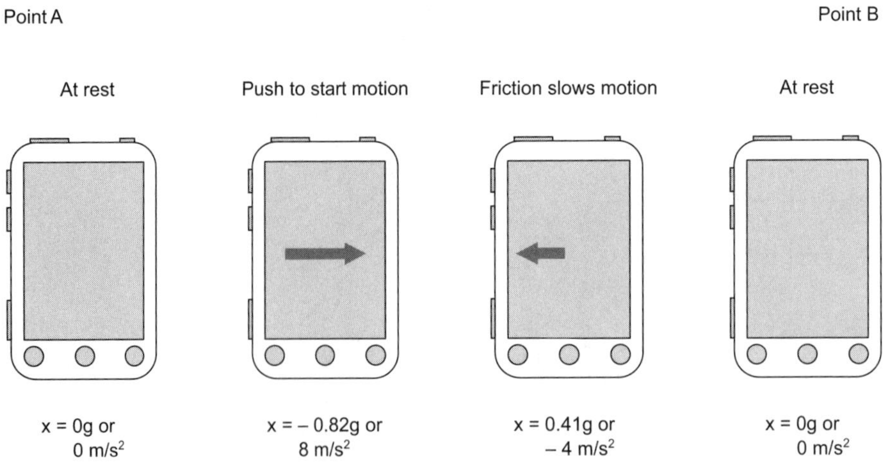

Figure 10.6 Acceleration due to the motion of sliding the device across a table

Again, note that the numbers reported by the accelerometer are opposite what you may expect. You push the device in the direction of the positive x axis, but the number reported is a negative value. Remember that the number reported is in terms of g or gravity, and g equals -9.8 m/s^2.

The figure demonstrates the forces involved in pushing a phone across a table. This is probably not something you do often. The same concepts can be applied when the device is moving in a user's hand. When motion begins, the user's hand is applying a force to the device in the direction of motion. When motion ends, the user's hand is applying force in the direction opposite the motion. When the user is moving the device, there may be a period between start and stop when the device is moving at a constant rate, and the acceleration in the direction of motion is zero.

By detecting changes in acceleration values, an application can determine when the device is being moved. The acceleration data can also tell you whether the device is being held flat, at an angle, or straight up and down. What the accelerometer can't tell you is which direction the device is pointed. If you need to know the direction the device is pointed, use the compass.

10.4 Finding direction with the compass

The compass is useful when an application needs to know which direction a device is pointed relative to the real world. The compass reports direction relative to the Magnetic North Pole. This information is useful for applications such as the astronomy application we mentioned earlier, where the application updates the display based on the direction the user is facing. The compass is also useful in motion-sensitive applications that need to know when a device is rotated.

The compass senses the strength and direction of the Earth's magnetic field. If the compass detects that a device is aligned with the Earth's magnetic field, then it knows that the device is pointed, or headed, north. If a device isn't aligned with the magnetic field, then the compass measures the device's *heading*—the angle between the magnetic field and the direction the device is pointed, as depicted in figure 10.7.

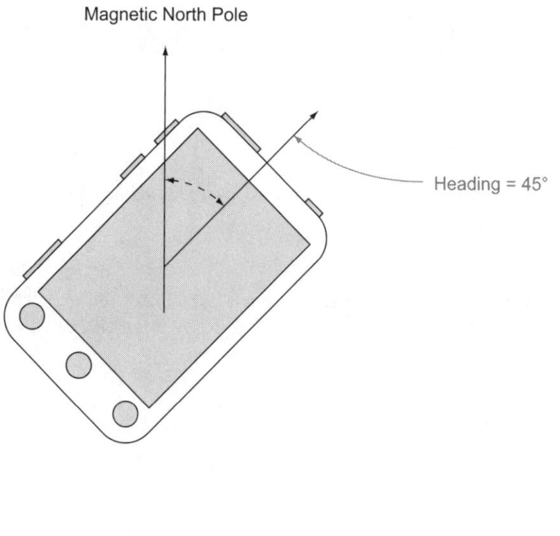

Figure 10.7 The compass measures the device's heading, which is the angle between magnetic north and the direction the device is pointed.

The compass reports information with the `CompassReading` structure. The device direction is read with the `HeadingMagneticNorth` and `HeadingTrueNorth` properties. Before we look closer at the difference between `HeadingMagneticNorth` and `HeadingTrueNorth`, you'll hook up the sensor to both values in the user interface of the Sensors application.

> **NOTE** The `System.Devices.Sensors.Compass` class in the Windows Phone Runtime reports only heading values. The Windows Phone 7 `Microsoft.Devices.Sensors.Compass` sensor decomposes the magnetic field into x, y, and z vectors and reports the magnitude of the vectors in microteslas (μT).

10.4.1 Hooking up the sensor

This section is going to look a lot like the section where you hooked up the accelerometer. You need to initialize the sensor in the `Start` method and create a method to read the sensor data. Start by defining a field in the `MainPage` class:

```
Compass compassSensor;
```

Initialize the sensor in the `Start` method. Before using the sensor, the code must first check whether the `Compass` is supported. If it isn't supported, `GetDefault` will return `null`, which is the case with the emulator. After initializing the sensor, you set the `ReportInterval`:

```
compassSensor = Compass.GetDefault();
if (compassSensor != null)
{
   compassSensor.ReportInterval = 66;
   runningMessage += "Compass ";
}
```

Create the `ReadCompassData` method in order to update the user interface with the sensor's current heading. The following listing contains the implementation of the `ReadCompassData` method. Don't forget to call the new `ReadCompassData` method from the `timer_Tick` event handler.

Listing 10.5 Reading Compass data

```
void ReadCompassData()
{
   if (compassSensor != null)
   {
      CompassReading reading = compassSensor.GetCurrentReading();
      if (reading != null)
      {
         heading.Text = string.Format(
            "Magnetic Heading={0:F0}° True Heading={1:F0}°",    ① Report heading values
            reading.HeadingMagneticNorth, reading.HeadingTrueNorth);
      }
   }
}
```

Figure 10.8 A screen shot of the heading `TextBlock` showing the `HeadingMagneticNorth` and `HeadingTrueNorth` properties. Note that the heading values differ by 7 degrees.

Start by retrieving the current `CompassReading` value from the sensor. The code updates the message displayed in the `TextBlock` ❶ near the bottom of the screen to show the values of the `HeadingMagneticNorth` and `HeadingTrueNorth` properties. Figure 10.8 shows how the message appears in the application.

Now you're ready to run the application. You must run the application on a physical device because the `Compass` isn't supported on the emulator.

> **NOTE** If an application requires that a phone have a compass to work correctly, the ID_REQ_MAGNETOMETER hardware requirement should be specified in the WMAppManifest.xml file. Specifying this requirement will prevent the application from being deployed to devices that don't have a compass, including the emulators included in the Windows Phone SDK.

When running the application, turn around and face a number of different directions. You should see the numbers grow and shrink between 0 and 360 degrees as you move the device about. Can you figure out where north is by interpreting the numbers reported in the `TextBlock` control? Does your device report different numbers for `HeadingMagneticNorth` and `HeadingTrueNorth`?

10.4.2 Interpreting the numbers

We mentioned that the compass works by sensing the Earth's magnetic field and measuring the angle between the magnetic field and the direction the device is pointed. We also mentioned that the Earth's magnetic field is aligned with the Magnetic North Pole. But the Earth's Magnetic North Pole isn't in the same location as the Earth's geographic North Pole. Not only are the two poles not in the same location, but the Magnetic North Pole is constantly moving about. Each year the Magnetic North Pole shifts approximately 25 miles.

As you may have guessed, the `HeadingMagneticNorth` property measures the device's heading relative to the Magnetic North Pole. The `HeadingTrueNorth` property measures the device's direction relative to the geographic North Pole. The difference between the two heading measurements is called *magnetic declination.*

Figure 10.9 illustrates magnetic declination for two different locations on the Earth's surface. For each location a line is drawn to the North Pole and the Magnetic North Pole. If the acute angle from the North Pole to the Magnetic North Pole is clockwise, then declination is positive. Conversely, a negative declination has a counterclockwise angle. The United States government's National Oceanic and Atmospheric Administration (NOAA) provides online tools to calculate magnetic declination at http://www.ngdc.noaa.gov/geomag-web/.

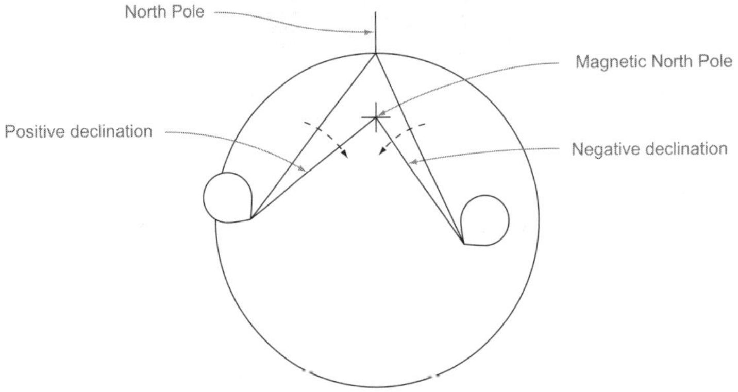

Figure 10.9 Examples of positive and negative declination for two different locations on the Earth's surface

The compass can't sense where the geographic North Pole is located and must calculate `HeadingTrueNorth` from declination values stored in a database. In order to look up the declination for a device, the compass must know the device's current location. If the device's location is unknown, the compass will report the same value for both heading properties.

> **TIP** An application that depends on `HeadingTrueNorth` can retrieve the device's current location by using the `Geolocator` class. You can ensure that the compass has recent location data by calling the `Geolocator`'s `Get-GeopostionAsync` method within the application. You'll read more about using the `Geolocator` class in chapter 16.

If the device has traveled a considerable distance since the last time its location was read or cached, the value reported by `HeadingTrueNorth` may not be accurate. The value reported by `HeadingMagneticNorth` may be inaccurate as well for a variety of different reasons. The Earth's magnetic field is relatively weak. This means that local environmental conditions will impact the magnetic field sensed by the compass. If the device is within a few feet of a normal magnet, for example, the compass will sense the magnetic field generated by the magnet.

The compass is useful when an application needs to know which direction the device is pointed relative to the real world. If the device is turned or rotated, an application can determine how much the device was turned by comparing the current heading with a previous heading. The compass isn't useful if your application needs to be notified while the device is turning. The gyrometer is ideal for applications that respond when the device is rotated.

10.5 Pivoting with the gyrometer

The gyrometer sensor reports how quickly the device is turning on one or more of its axes. The rotational velocity is reported in degrees per second, and when a device is rotated in a complete circle, it rotates 360 degrees. The values are reported with counterclockwise being the positive direction.

> **NOTE** The gyrometer is optional hardware for Windows Phones and isn't supported on many phones. If an application requires that a phone have a gyrometer to work correctly, the ID_REQ_GYROMETER hardware requirement should be specified in the WMAppManifest.xml file. Specifying this requirement will prevent the application from being deployed to devices that don't have a gyrometer, including the emulators included in the Windows Phone SDK.

The gyrometer only reports turning motion around an axis, and if the device is held still, the sensor reports values of zero. If the device is moved from point A to point B without any twisting motion, the gyrometer also reports zero.

The gyrometer reports values with the `GyrometerReading` struct. Rotational velocities are read from the `GyrometerReading` through the `AngularVeclocityX`, `AngularVelocityY`, and `AngularVelocityZ` properties that break absolute movement into rotation about the x, y, and z axes. You'll now hook up the gyrometer to the user interface in the sample application so you can see the numbers for yourself.

10.5.1 Hooking up the sensor

The Sensor APIs are intentionally similar, and hooking up the gyrometer in your sample application is nearly identical to hooking up the accelerometer and compass. You start by declaring a field to reference the `Gyrometer` instance:

```
Gyrometer gyroSensor;
```

You then construct and initialize the field in the `Start` method, as shown in the following listing.

Listing 10.6 Initializing the `Gyrometer` in the `Start` method

```
try
{
   gyroSensor = Gyrometer.GetDefault();
}
catch (System.IO.FileNotFoundException) { }      <-- (1) Surround with try-catch

if (gyroSensor != null)
{
   gyroSensor.ReportInterval = 66;
   runningMessage += "Gyroscope ";
}
```

When running in the emulator, the call to `Gyrometer`'s `GetDefault` method throws a `FileNotFoundException`, which is handled by the surrounding `try-catch` block (1).

As with the `Accelerometer` and `Compass` sensors, you create a new method to read the `Gyrometer`'s current reading and update the user interface. The new method is called ReadGyrometerData and is called from the timer_Tick method. The code for ReadGyrometerData is shown in the following listing.

Listing 10.7 Reading Gyrometer data

```
void ReadGyrometerData()
{
   if (gyroSensor != null)
   {
      GyrometerReading reading = gyroSensor.GetCurrentReading();   // 1 Get reading
      if (reading != null)
      {
         gyroX.Value = reading.AngularVelocityX;    // 2 Update user interface
         gyroY.Value = reading.AngularVelocityY;
         gyroZ.Value = reading.AngularVelocityZ;
      }
   }
}
```

Start by retrieving the current GyrometerReading value ❶ from the sensor. Then update the user interface with the x, y, and z angular velocity values ❷.

When you created the Bar controls for the Gyrometer in MainPage.xaml, you set the Scale property to 1.111111. The positive and negative bars are each 200 pixels. You assume the maximum rotation rate is a half spin once per second, or ±180 degrees per second. The scale of the Bar control is calculated at 1.111111 or 200/180.

What can you do to see the gyrometer bars move in the application? Let's get dizzy. Do you have a spinning office chair? If so, you can hold the device flat in your hand and spin back and forth in your chair. You should see the z-bar move up and down as you spin. Another example is to hold the device in your hand so that it's standing up in portrait mode. Now tilt the phone back until it's lying flat in your hand. You should see the x-bar move down and report a negative value. Tilt the phone back up, and the bar should move up and report a positive value.

You've seen how each of the hardware sensors is exposed by classes and structures in the Sensors API. The sensors each return individual sets of data that can be used in various ways to build interesting applications. Each of the sensors tells you different bits of information about how the device is held, how it's moving, and which direction it's pointed in. Correlating this information across sensors can be tricky and involves a solid understanding of physics, mathematics, and three-dimensional coordinate spaces. Fortunately, the Windows Phone SDK provides the Inclinometer and OrientationSensor classes to perform these calculations for you.

10.6 Wrapping up with motion

Unlike the other sensors we've covered so far in this chapter, the Inclinometer and OrientationSensor are not hardware based. These two classes are wrappers around the Accelerometer, Compass, and Gyrometer. Instead of sensing data from hardware, the Inclinometer and OrientationSensor consume data from the other sensors and perform some convenient number crunching.

The `Inclinometer` class reports the results of its data analysis in the `InclinometerReading` class. The `InclinometerReading` class reports `Yaw`, `Pitch`, and `Roll` values. The `OrientationSensor` class delivers data via the `OrientationSensorReading` class, which provides both a rotation matrix and a quaternion that can be used for coordinate mapping. We'll show how to use both the `InclinometerReading` and `OrientationSensorReading` classes to map coordinates as you finish off the Sensors sample application.

10.6.1 Hooking up the sensors

As with the `Accelerometer`, `Compass`, and `Gyrometer`, the `Inclinometer` and `OrientationSensor` instances are stored in member variables and initialized in the `start` method of the Sensors application's `MainPage` class. The following listing shows the member declarations and the code added to the `Start` method.

Listing 10.8 Initializing the `Inclinometer` and `OrientationSensor`

```
Inclinometer inclineSensor;                       ❶ Declare field
OrientationSensor orientationSensor;                 variables

void Start()
{
   ...
   inclineSensor = Inclinometer.GetDefault();                  ◁─┐
   if (inclineSensor != null)                                    │
   {                                                             │
      inclineSensor.ReportInterval = 66;                         ❷ Initialize fields
      runningMessage += "Inclinometer ";                         │ with GetDefault
   }                                                             │
                                                                 │
   orientationSensor = OrientationSensor.GetDefault();         ◁─┘
   if (orientationSensor != null)
   {
      orientationSensor.ReportInterval = 66;
      runningMessage += "Orientation ";
   }
   ...
}
```

The listing starts by declaring new fields ❶ to reference the sensor instances. Following the same pattern used for the other sensors in this chapter, instances of the sensors are retrieved by their respective `GetDefault` methods ❷. Before attempting to use a sensor instance, you check for `null` to determine whether the device supports the sensor. Set the `ReportInterval` property to `66` milliseconds to match the timer tick values.

Continuing with the pattern established earlier, two new read data methods are created and called from the `timer_Tick` method:

```
void timer_Tick(object sender, EventArgs e)
{
   ...
```

```
    ReadInclinometerData();
    ReadOrientationData();
}
```

The `Inclinometer` measures how far from a normal position a phone is titled or rotated, where normal is defined as lying flat, face up, with the top of the device pointed at the North Pole. In this position, the x axis points due east, the y axis points north, and the z axis points straight up. The numbers reported by the `Inclinometer` are properties of the `InclinometerReading` class called `PitchDegrees`, `RollDegrees`, and `YawDegrees`.

The next listing shows the implementation of the `ReadInclinometerData` method. The Sensors application displays inclinometer data in the third set of `Bar` controls you added to MainPage.xaml in section 10.2.2.

Listing 10.9 Displaying inclinometer data

```
void ReadInclinometerData()
{
    if (inclineSensor != null)
    {
        InclinometerReading reading = inclineSensor.GetCurrentReading();
        if (reading != null)
        {
            inclineX.Value = reading.PitchDegrees;
            inclineY.Value = reading.RollDegrees;      ❶ Update the Bar controls
            inclineZ.Value = reading.YawDegrees;
        }
    }
}
```

First, check whether an inclinometer exists before getting the current `InclinometerReading` value from the sensor and check that `GetCurrentReading` returns a valid value. Update the `Bar` controls in the user interface with the `Pitch`, `Roll`, and `Yaw` properties reported by the sensor ❶.

When you created the `inclineX`, `inclineY`, and `inclineZ` `Bar` controls for the inclinometer in MainPage.xaml, you set the `Scale` properties to `1.111111`, `2.222222`, and `0.555556`, respectively. The `Bar` controls are 400 pixels high, allowing for positive and negative sections of 200 pixels each. The value of the `PitchDegrees` property varies between –180 and 180 degrees. Dividing 200 by 180 gives a scale of 1.111111. The `RollDegrees` property varies between –90 and 90 degrees, resulting in a scale of 2.222222. The `YawDegrees` property varies between 0 and 360. Even though a negative value isn't possible, 360 is still used in the scale equation—therefore the scale is calculated using 200/360, resulting in 0.555556.

Where the inclinometer is useful for determining how much a device is tilted or rotated from a normal position, the `OrientationSensor` is useful for transforming a point in normal space to a point in the coordinate space of the phone. The following listing demonstrates how to use the `RotationMatrix` provided by `OrientationSensor` to transform the point (0,10,0) into a point in the phone's coordinate system.

Listing 10.10 Transforming a point with orientation data

```
using System.Windows.Media.Media3D;
...
static readonly Matrix3D pointMatrix = new Matrix3D(
            0, 0, 0, 0,
            0, 0, 0, 0,
            0, 0, 0, 0,
            0, 10, 0, 1);

void ReadOrientationData()
{
   if (orientationSensor != null)
   {
      OrientationSensorReading reading =
            orientationSensor.GetCurrentReading();
      if (reading != null)
      {
         SensorRotationMatrix srm = reading.RotationMatrix;
         Matrix3D rotationMatrix = new Matrix3D(
            srm.M11, srm.M12, srm.M13, 0,
            srm.M21, srm.M22, srm.M23, 0,
            srm.M31, srm.M32, srm.M33, 0,
            0, 0, 0, 0);

         Matrix3D bodySpaceMatrix = pointMatrix * rotationMatrix;
         point.Text = string.Format(
            "Transform of (0.0, 10.0, 0.0) = ({0:F1}, {1:F1}, {2:F1})",
            bodySpaceMatrix.OffsetX, bodySpaceMatrix.OffsetY,
            bodySpaceMatrix.OffsetZ);
      }
   }
}
```

❶ Matrix representing the point (0,10,0)

❷ Convert to Matrix3D

❸ Transform point with matrix multiplication

The listing begins with a `using` statement that includes the `System.Windows.Media.Media3D` namespace, the home of the `Matrix3D` struct used for point transformation. The sample point (0,10,0) is encoded into a `Matrix3D` struct and stored in a constant field of the `MainPage` class ❶. Next, the current `OrientationReading` is read from the `OrientationSensor` and its rotation matrix is converted from a `SensorRotationMatrix` into a `Matrix3D` ❷. The target point is transformed with matrix multiplication ❸, and the resulting point is displayed in the user interface.

Deploy the application to your device and run it. Start the sensor and examine the inclinometer values as you move your phone around. Don't forget to look at the point transformation message line and at how the coordinate point is transformed. Let's take a closer look at the readings reported by the `Inclinometer` and `OrientationSensor` classes and discuss how to interpret the numbers.

10.6.2 Interpreting the numbers

To understand the uses of the `Inclinometer` and the `OrientationSensor`, you need to understand the frame of reference, or coordinate system, for both the real world and the device. These two classes assume a real-world coordinate system where y points due north, z points straight up, and x points due east. When the device is lying flat, face up, with the top of the device pointing north, the device's frame of reference matches the real-world frame of reference. This is shown in figure 10.10.

The `Yaw`, `Pitch`, and `Roll` readings are all approximately zero, and the rotation matrix is the identity matrix. An object at point (0,10,0) in the world frame has the same coordinates in the device frame. The device's y axis is pointing north, and the x axis is pointing east.

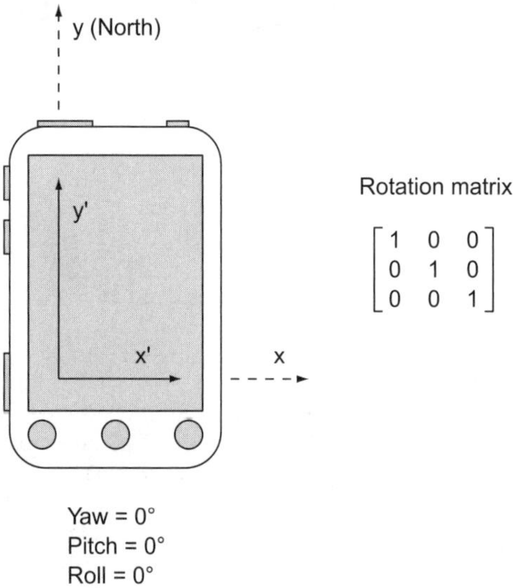

Figure 10.10 The device frame aligns with the world frame when the device is lying flat and pointed north.

When the device is rotated, its frame of reference no longer matches the real-world frame of reference. If the top of the device lying flat is rotated to point east, the device is considered to be rotated 270 degrees, and the inclinometer reading will have a `Yaw` reading of 270 degrees. The `Yaw`, or rotation about the z axis, is read as the counterclockwise angle between the two y axes, as shown in figure 10.11

Now the device's y axis is pointing east, and the x axis is pointing south. Again, consider an object at the coordinate (0,10,0) in the world frame. This same object will have the coordinates (–10,0,0) in the device frame.

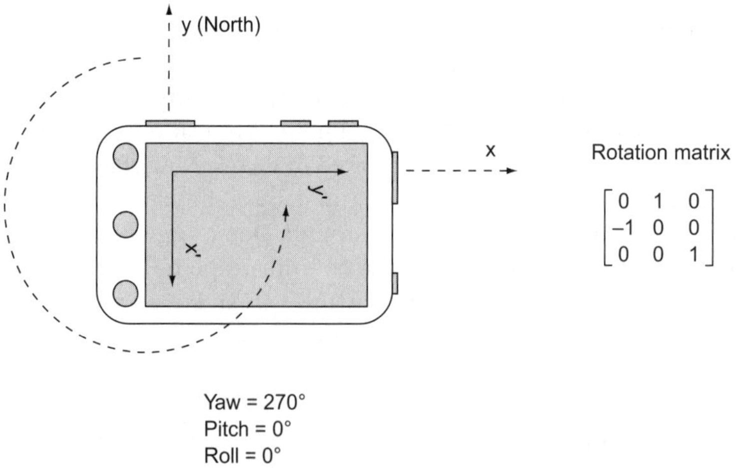

Figure 10.11 The device rotated 270 degrees around the z axis

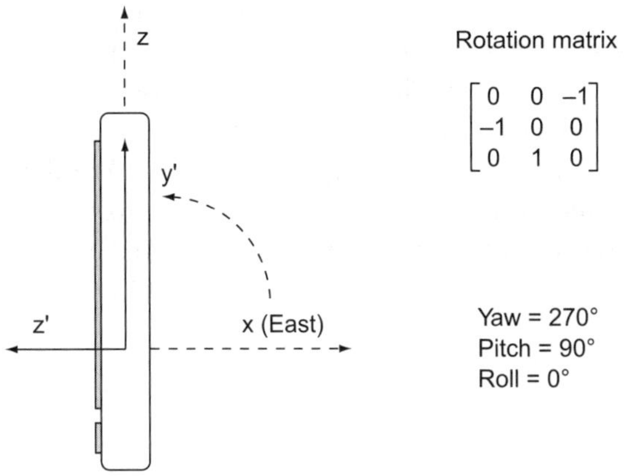

Figure 10.12 The device rotated 270 degrees around the z axis and 90 degrees around the x axis

With the top of the device still pointed east, raise the top of the device until it's in the standing portrait orientation, with the back of the device facing east, as shown in figure 10.12. In this case you've rotated the device frame about the x axis and changed the `Pitch` of the device. The inclinometer reading will still have a `Yaw` reading of 270 degrees but will now also have a `Pitch` reading of 90 degrees. The `Pitch`, or rotation about the x axis, is read as a counterclockwise angle.

Now the device's y axis is pointing up toward the sky, aligned with the world frame's z axis. The device's z axis is pointing to the west. The device's x axis is still pointing south. Again, consider an object at the coordinate (0,10,0) in the world frame. This same object will still have the coordinates (–10,0,0) in the device frame because changing the pitch didn't change the direction of the device's x axis.

When working with the `InclinometerReading`, you must remember that the `Yaw`, `Pitch`, and `Roll` values are order dependent. To translate a point in one frame of reference to a point in another frame of reference, you must apply `Yaw` first, followed by `Pitch`, and then by `Roll`.

Though we've referred to the `Inclinometer` and `OrientationSensor` classes as sensors, they're more services than sensors. They make use of a few different sources of data to provide a convenient service for detecting motion and position.

10.7 Summary

In this chapter we've covered three different hardware sensors and two classes that wrap the other sensors. The `Accelerometer` reports acceleration due to the forces acting on a device. The `Compass` reports the heading of the device relative to north. The `Gyrometer` reports the rotational velocity of the device. There aren't any sensors that report linear velocity or rotational acceleration. And there's no sensor that reports exactly how far a phone has moved.

The `Inclinometer` and `OrientationSensor` classes use data from the `Accelerometer`, `Compass`, and `Gyrometer` to perform a few complex calculations and provide the information necessary to convert device coordinates into real-world coordinates.

Application developers should consider mixing one or more sensors with the location service to build applications that mesh the real world with the digital world. Novel augmented-reality applications can be built to show the user the location of nearby landmarks or the position of constellations in the night sky.

In the next chapter we'll explore the networking features of the Windows Phone SDK. You'll learn how to determine network connection state and how to connect to web services. You'll also learn how to send notifications to a phone from a web service.

11 Network communication with push notifications

This chapter covers

- Detecting network information
- Pushing notifications
- Updating application tiles
- Using URL associations

With the advent of smartphones, the way in which most mobile users use their phones has dramatically changed. The phone has become our constant companion and keeps us connected with family, friends, and coworkers. We use the phone to read news, check email, tweet on Twitter, post and read updates on Facebook, and play games. Most of the applications you're using on your phone have one thing in common. Can you guess what it is? All of them access the network to retrieve the information stored in the cloud. Consuming resources from the network is crucial. As a developer of a mobile app, you need to understand how to efficiently consume network resources.

Networked applications need to know whether a network connection is available and, if so, what type of connection is enabled. We open this chapter by discussing how you can detect the network connection before consuming resources. We show how to detect whether the device is connected to a cellular data network or to a Wi-Fi access point or is in airplane mode.

To keep a user informed, applications need to retrieve updates from the internet, but how can they do that when they're not running? In chapter 4 you learned about background agents, which require code to be running on the phone periodically checking for updates. In this chapter we explore another technology: *push notifications*. As you'll learn in this chapter, with push notifications, code runs in a web service and updates are pushed to the phone. Notifications are used to update an application's tile or display a toast message to the user.

As we explore push notifications, you'll learn about the `HttpWebRequest` class that's useful for connecting to and sharing data over an HTTP connection, which is one type of network connection. The Windows Phone SDK also provides a `Socket` class that enables lower-level network communication with TCP and UDP.

To demonstrate push notifications and networking, you're going to build two related sample applications:

- A push notification simulator that will demonstrate how to detect network status and push notifications to a Windows Phone
- A push notification client that will register for and receive push notifications from the simulator

To enable pushing notifications from the simulator to the client, the simulator must have the channel URI established by the client. Normally a push notification client sends the channel URI to a web service, but because your simulator is another application, you'll use *URL associations* to communicate between applications. URL associations are custom protocols registered with the operating system used to launch an application. Any application can launch any other application as long as the registered protocol is known.

Both sample applications require a network connection. We open the chapter with a look at the network information classes and how to use them to detect network connectivity status.

11.1 Detecting network connectivity

Detecting network connectivity is a crucial task for mobile application developers because many of the more interesting mobile applications require access to network resources. Applications that use network capabilities should be aware of the status of the network connection and whether that network is using the cellular data network or a Wi-Fi network. Mobile applications must also adjust to changes in the network connection, which can change from no access to cellular data to Wi-Fi in a short period of time. The Windows Phone SDK contains a set of network information APIs unique to the Windows Phone in the `Microsoft.Phone.Net.NetworkInformation` namespace.

TIP Windows Phone 8 includes a feature named Data Sense, which tracks cellular data usage. Application developers can use the Data Sense APIs to detect if a user is nearing their data usage limits and, if so, choose to not perform network communication over a cellular network. Unfortunately, the Data Sense feature may not be installed if the mobile operator decides not to support it. You can read more about the Data Sense API on MSDN at http://mng.bz/5s69.

Before we look at `Microsoft.Phone.Net.NetworkInformation`, you'll create the Visual Studio project for your first sample application, the push notification simulator. You'll use the simulator application to demonstrate networking code. Using the Windows Phone App template, create a new project named NotificationSimulator. When creating the project, name the solution PushNotifications. The simulator sample application is built using a `Pivot` control. Delete MainPage.xaml and add a new `MainPage` using the Windows Phone Pivot Page item template. The first pivot in the application, shown in figure 11.1, contains a `TextBlock` used to display the network connection status and a `Button` to update the screen with the current status.

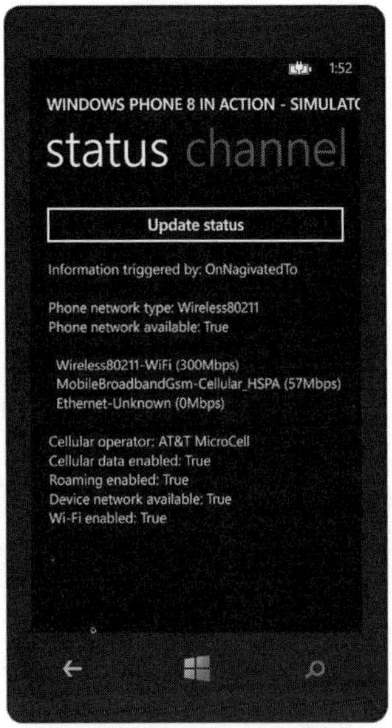

Figure 11.1 The networking sample application

The `TextBlock` will display a formatted string built from network and device information that you gather from a couple of APIs. Give the `TextBlock` the name `statusMessage`:

```
<phone:PivotItem Header="status">
    <StackPanel>
        <Button Click="Button_Click">Update status</Button>
        <TextBlock x:Name="statusMessage" />
    </StackPanel>
</phone:PivotItem>
```

This sample application will display the network availability in the `statusMessage` `TextBlock` whenever the application is activated or the button is tapped. Create a method called `LoadInformation` in MainPage.xaml.cs that will be called to gather up network information and display it in the user interface:

```
void LoadInformation(string trigger)
{
    string information = string.Format(
        "Information triggered by: {0}", trigger);
    statusMessage.Text = information;
}
```

Now call the `LoadInformation` method from the `OnNavigatedTo` method so that the network status is displayed whenever the page is activated:

```
protected override void OnNavigatedTo(NavigationEventArgs e)
{
    LoadInformation("OnNagivatedTo");
}
```

```
void Button_Click(object sender, RoutedEventArgs e)
{
  LoadInformation("Button click");
}
```

At this point, the sample application doesn't do anything interesting, other than display OnNavigatedTo or Button Click in the user interface. You'll liven up the application by displaying device settings to the user.

11.1.1 Reading device settings

The `Microsoft.Phone.Net.NetworkInformation` namespace was created specifically for the phone and has everything you need for reading network information. The namespace contains a few interesting classes called `NetworkInterface`, `DeviceNetworkInformation`, and `NetworkInterfaceInfo`. `DeviceNetworkInformation` provides several properties, listed in table 11.1, that report the current values of networking-related options specified in the settings application.

Table 11.1 Properties of DeviceNetworkInformation

Name	Description
`CellularMobileOperator`	Returns the name of the wireless service provider
`IsCellularDataEnabled`	Returns `true` if the cellular data network is available, `false` if airplane mode is enabled
`IsCellularDataRoamingEnabled`	Returns `true` if the data roaming option is set to roam, `false` if the option is set to not roam
`IsNetworkAvailable`	Returns `true` if any network connection is available
`IsWiFiEnabled`	Returns `true` if Wi-Fi network is enabled in the settings application, even if the device isn't connected to a Wi-Fi network

Update the NotificationSimulator sample application to display the properties of the `DeviceNetworkInformation` class. Start by adding a call to a new `LoadDeviceInformation` method in the `LoadInformation` method you created in section 11.1:

```
void LoadInformation(string trigger)
{
    string information = string.Format(
        "Information triggered by: {0}\n\n{1}",
        trigger, LoadDeviceInformation());
    statusMessage.Text = information;
}
```

The new `LoadDeviceInformation` method, shown in the following listing, returns a formatted string containing a description and value for each of the properties of the `DeviceNetworkInformation` class.

Listing 11.1 Reading `DeviceNetworkInformation` properties

```
using Microsoft.Phone.Net.NetworkInformation;
string LoadDeviceInformation()
{
    return string.Format("Cellular operator: {0}\n" +
        "Cellular data enabled: {1}\nRoaming enabled: {2}\n" +
        "Device network available: {3}\nWi-Fi enabled: {4}\n",
        DeviceNetworkInformation.CellularMobileOperator,
        DeviceNetworkInformation.IsCellularDataEnabled,
        DeviceNetworkInformation.IsCellularDataRoamingEnabled,
        DeviceNetworkInformation.IsNetworkAvailable,
        DeviceNetworkInformation.IsWiFiEnabled);
}
```

The message returned by `LoadDeviceInformation` is displayed on the screen by the `LoadInformation` method, as shown in figure 11.2.

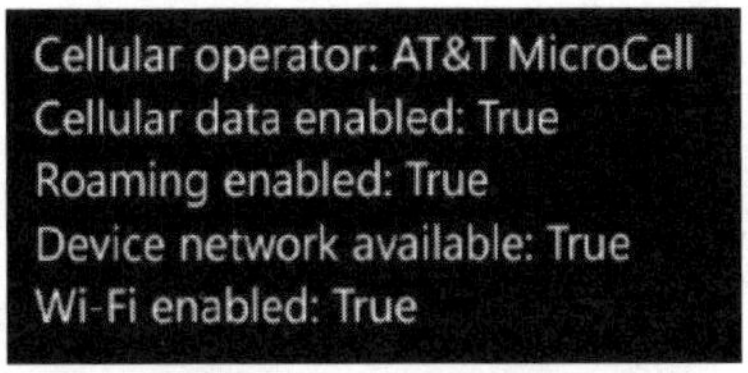

Figure 11.2 Device information as displayed in the sample application

The `DeviceNetworkInformation` class provides an event called `NetworkAvailabilityChanged` that reports network status changes such as connecting, disconnecting, and changing the roaming status. Register for this event in the `MainPage` constructor and use it as a trigger for updating the user interface:

```
public MainPage()
{
    InitializeComponent();
    DeviceNetworkInformation.NetworkAvailabilityChanged +=
        (sender, e) => LoadInformation(e.NotificationType.ToString());
}
```

You pass the value of the `NotificationType` property as the trigger parameter to `LoadInformation`. `NotificationType` is an enum with the value `InterfaceConnected`, `InterfaceDisconnected`, or `CharacteristicUpdate`. `DeviceNetworkInformation` tells you about the phone's network-related settings.

Next, we'll look at the `NetworkInterface`, which tells you not only whether a network is connected but the type of network you're connected to.

11.1.2 Using the NetworkInterface class

If you're coming from a Silverlight or .NET background, you may already be familiar with the `NetworkInterface` class in the `System.Net.NetworkInformation` namespace, used to determine network connectivity. The `Microsoft.Phone.Net.NetworkInformation` namespace provides a phone-specific implementation of the `NetworkInterface` class, also named `NetworkInterface`. The `NetworkInterface` class is inherited from the `System.Net.NetworkInformation.NetworkInterface` class, and both classes have a static method named `GetIsNetworkAvailable`. The phone's `NetworkInterface` class also provides an enum property named `NetworkInterfaceType`, which can be used to determine whether the current connection is on a cellular data or Wi-Fi network. Applicable values for `NetworkInterfaceType` are listed in table 11.2.

Table 11.2 List of network types

Member Name	Description
`None`	The device isn't connected to a network.
`Ethernet`	The device is connected to a wired Ethernet network. Usually this indicates the device is connected to a desktop computer and is sharing the desktop's network connection.
`Wireless80211`	The device is connected to a Wi-Fi network.
`MobileBroadbandGsm`	The device is connected to a GSM cellular network.
`MobileBroadbandCdma`	The device is connected to a CDMA cellular network.

The `NetworkInterfaceType` enumeration defines approximately 24 other network types that aren't used by the Windows Phone operating system. Only the five network types mentioned in table 11.2 are currently supported by the phone. If you're on a Wi-Fi network, the network type will be `Wireless80211`, and if you're using a cellular data network, the network type will be `MobileBroadbandGsm` or `MobileBroadbandCdma`.

Wire in the data returned from `NetworkInterface` into the user interface. Start by adding a new method called `LoadPhoneNetworkInformation`:

```
string LoadPhoneNetworkInformation()
{
    return string.Format(
        "Phone network type: {0}\nPhone network available: {1}\n",
        NetworkInterface.NetworkInterfaceType,
        NetworkInterface.GetIsNetworkAvailable());
}
```

It's important to know that calls to the `NetworkInterfaceType` property may take a long time to complete. When calling the property from your code, you should take extra care to not block the user interface thread. In your sample application you'll update the `LoadInformation` method so that it runs on a background thread. The following listing shows the new implementation of `LoadInformation`.

Listing 11.2 Loading network information on a background thread

```
using System.Threading;
void LoadInformation(string trigger)
{
   statusMessage.Text = "loading...";
   ThreadPool.QueueUserWorkItem((state) =>      ❶ Spin up background thread
   {
```

```
        string information = string.Format(
            "Information triggered by: {0}\n\n{1}\n{2}",
            trigger, LoadPhoneNetworkInformation(),
            LoadDeviceInformation());
        Dispatcher.BeginInvoke(() => statusMessage.Text = information);
    });
}
```

Update user interface ❷

The first change you implement is to display a loading message in the user interface. Wrap the existing code in an anonymous function and use the `QueueUserWorkItem` method to request that the `ThreadPool` class execute the function on a background thread ❶. Once the information string is built, use the `Dispatcher` to update the `statusMessage TextBlock` ❷ on the user interface thread. An example message returned by `LoadPhoneNetworkInformation` is displayed in figure 11.3.

Figure 11.3 Phone network information as displayed in the sample application

The `NetworkInformation` class reports information from only one of the available network interfaces. If you want to know the status of all of the network interfaces available to the device, there's another class you can use to list all network connections.

11.1.3 Listing all network connections

The last class we examine from the `Microsoft.Phone.Net.NetworkInformation` namespace is the `NetworkInterfaceInfo` class. Not only can you discover all the network interfaces on the devices, but `NetworkInterfaceInfo` provides more details about each of the interfaces than what are provided by the `NetworkInterface` class. The properties of `NetworkInterfaceInfo` are listed in table 11.3.

Table 11.3 `NetworkInterfaceInfo` properties

Property	Description
`Bandwidth`	Gets the speed of the network interface
`Characteristics`	Specifies whether the device is roaming
`Description`	Specifies the description of the network interface
`InterfaceName`	Specifies the name of the network interface
`InterfaceState`	Specifies whether the device is connected to a network
`InterfaceSubtype`	Specifies the underlying networking technology used by the interface, including GPRS, EVDO, 3G, HSPA, LTE, and others
`InterfaceType`	Specifies whether the interface is connected with Unknown, 80211, GMS, or CDMA.

To obtain the list of network interfaces, create an instance of the `NetworkInterfaceList` class. You do this in the sample application by adding one more load information method called `LoadNetworkInterfaceInfo` to display the details for each network interface, as shown in the following listing.

Listing 11.3 Loading information for all interfaces

```
using System.Text;
string LoadNetworkInterfaceInfo ()
{
   StringBuilder builder = new StringBuilder();
   NetworkInterfaceList list = new NetworkInterfaceList();
   foreach (NetworkInterfaceInfo networkInterface in list)      <-- 1 Iterate through list
   {
      builder.AppendFormat("  {0}-{1} ({2}Mbps)\n",
         networkInterface.InterfaceType,
         networkInterface.InterfaceSubtype,
         networkInterface.Bandwidth/1000);      <-- 2 Divide bandwidth by 1,000 to get Mbps
   }
   return builder.ToString();
}
```

The `NetworkInterfaceList` class implements `IEnumerable`, which enables iteration through the list ❶ using a `foreach` statement. For each of the network interfaces, a message is appended to a `StringBuilder` containing the interface type, subtype, and bandwidth. To convert the interface's bandwidth from Kbps to Mbps, divide `Bandwidth` by 1000 ❷. The contents of the `StringBuilder` are returned to the caller. The results can be seen in figure 11.4.

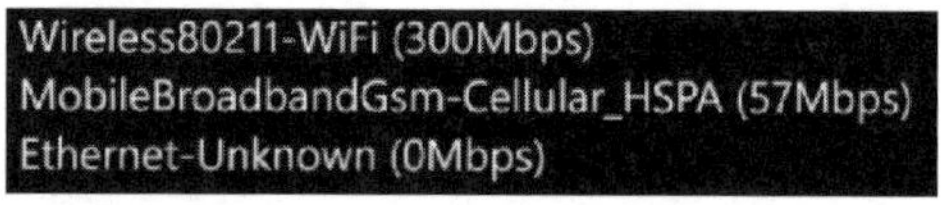

Figure 11.4 Network interface information as displayed in the sample application

Call the new method from the `LoadInformation` method:

```
string information = string.Format(
   "Information triggered by: {0}\n\n{1}\n{2}\n{3}",
   trigger,
   LoadPhoneNetworkInformation(),
   LoadNetworkInterfaceInfo(),
   LoadDeviceInformation());
```

Run the NotificationSimulator application and examine the data reported on the screen. Change your device's setting by turning on airplane mode or disabling Wi-Fi. Does the screen update as you expect? In the next section you'll add more features to the NotificationSimulator application as you learn how to push notifications to the phone.

11.2 Pushing notifications to a phone

Distributed application developers have two options when notifying phone users with updates and alerts. The first requires code on the phone to periodically pull data from a web service and can be implemented using background agents (which are covered in chapter 4). An alternative model is for a web service to push notifications to a phone. The Microsoft Push Notification (MPN) Service enables sending updates and alerts to a phone without an active agent running on the phone. MPN and Windows Phone support three different types of notifications.

In this section we explore the different types of notifications and how to use the MPN Service to send them. Before remote services can send a message to a phone, the user must register the phone with the Service, and we'll show you the API calls used for registration. You'll update the simulator application to send different types of push notifications.

11.2.1 Three types of notifications

Windows phone provides three types of push notifications you can use to send a notification from a web service to a Windows Phone. They are *toast*, *tile*, and *raw* notifications:

- *Toast* notifications are short messages displayed at the top of the screen.
- *Tile* notifications update an application's tile that's pinned to the Start Screen.
- *Raw* notifications are used to send custom content to a running application.

Notifications are sent only to phones that have subscribed to a *notification channel*. Notification channels are linked to specific applications. Raw notifications are displayed only if the client application implements custom code to display the content of the message. Let's take a closer look at what the user sees when toast and tile notifications are received by a phone.

VIEWING A TOAST NOTIFICATION

A toast notification is made up of a title and a short content message, as shown in figure 11.5. The user can dismiss the notification by flicking to the right and can tap the toast to launch the application. The application developer can define a custom launch URI as part of the toast.

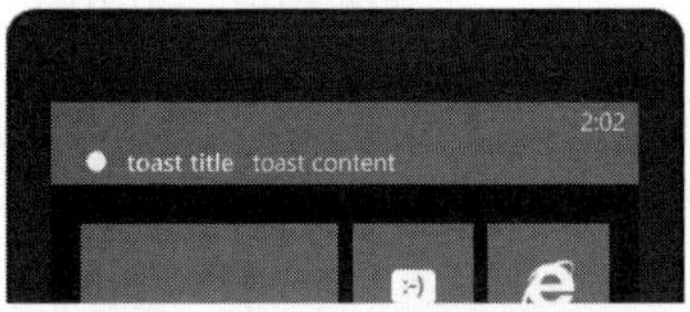

Figure 11.5 Toast notification

The toast is shown at the top of the screen only if the linked application isn't running. When the application is running, the application is notified of the toast through a custom event. You'll learn how to use both the launch URI and the notification event later in this chapter when you build the sample client application.

BRINGING TILES TO LIFE WITH TILE NOTIFICATIONS

A tile notification is used to update the primary Application Tile on the Start Screen of the phone. If an application isn't pinned to the Start Screen, tile notifications don't have any effect. We covered three different types of tiles in chapter 1, but let's review what you learned:

- Tiles display titles, images, messages, and counts on the front and back of a tile.
- Applications can pin multiple tiles to the Start Screen, each launching to a different spot within the application.

- Tiles can be updated from code running on the phone or remotely using MPN.
- Tiles are displayed in one of three formats: Flip, Iconic, or Cycle.
- Each of the tile formats can be one-quarter-size size, normal size, or double-wide size.

We showed how to update tiles from code in chapters 2, 3, and 4. In this chapter we show how to update tiles with a push notification.

11.2.2 Push notification workflow

Web services can't send notifications to any random Windows Phone. Users must first install an application on the phone, and application code is then required to open a notification channel. The Windows Phone supports a limited number of open channels, and there's no guarantee that an application will be able to open a new channel. Once the channel is opened, the application must forward the channel URI to its web service. Figure 11.6 shows the workflow for opening a notification channel and sending push notifications:

1. A push-enabled Windows Phone application is installed. When the application is run by the user, it opens a notification channel with the Microsoft Push Notification Service. The MPN Service returns a unique URI that a web service can use to push notifications to the phone.
2. Once the channel URI is returned to the application, the application sends the channel URI to the web service. The web service uses the channel URI when posting notifications to the MPN Service.
3. At some point in the future something interesting happens, and the web service constructs notification messages to be sent to each phone that has sent its channel URI to the web server. The web service uses `HTTP POST` to ask the MPN Service to send the notification to the phone's channel URI.
4. The MPN Service forwards the notification message to the phone identified by the channel URI.

Because this is a book about programming Windows Phone and not about web server programming, you're not going to build a web service. Instead, you'll add features to the NotificationSimulator sample application so that it simulates a web service by

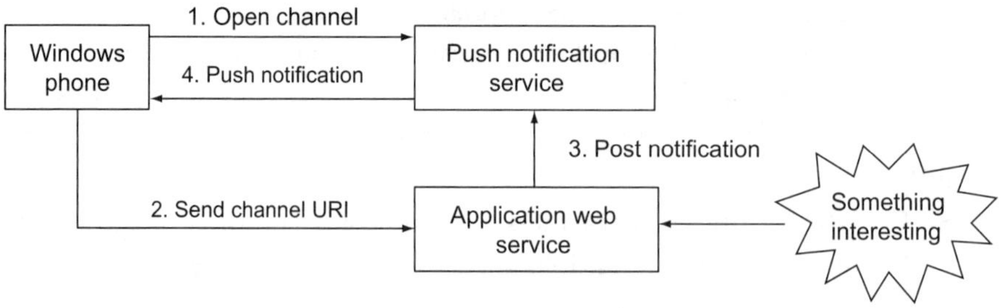

Figure 11.6 Push notification workflow

performing `HTTP POST` calls directly to the MPN Service. The NotificationSimulator application will be paired with a new NotificationClient application, which will open the notification channel.

11.2.3 Creating a push notification client

Create a new project in the PushNotifications solution using the Windows Phone App project template. You can see the completed client project in figure 11.7. The XAML markup for the main page contains a `StackPanel` control and an application bar. The following listing contains the markup for the `ContentPanel`.

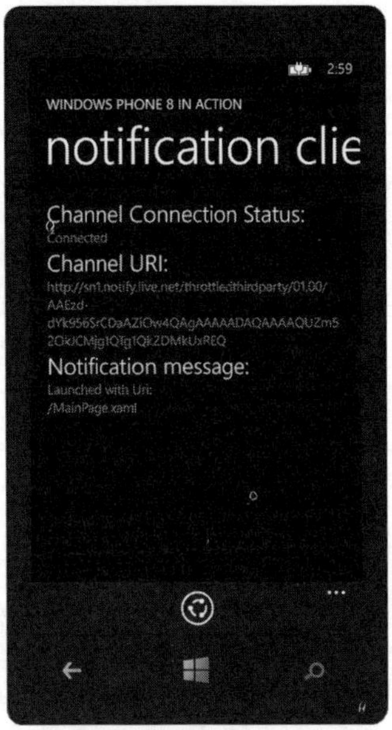

Figure 11.7 The completed notification client

Listing 11.4 The markup for MainPage.xaml's `Pivot` control

```
<Grid x:Name="ContentPanel" Grid.Row="1" Margin="12,0,12,0">
<StackPanel>
    <TextBlock Text="Channel Connection Status:"
      Style="{StaticResource PhoneTextTitle2Style}" />
    <TextBlock x:Name="channelStatus" Text="channel does not exist"
      TextWrapping="Wrap" Style="{StaticResource PhoneTextSmallStyle}"/>
    <TextBlock Text="Channel URI:"
      Style="{StaticResource PhoneTextTitle2Style}" />
    <TextBlock x:Name="channelUri" TextWrapping="Wrap"
      Style="{StaticResource PhoneTextSmallStyle}" />
    <TextBlock Text="Notification message:"
      Style="{StaticResource PhoneTextTitle2Style}" />
    <TextBlock x:Name="notificationMessage" Text="(no message)"      ❶ Display notification details
      TextWrapping="Wrap" Style="{StaticResource PhoneTextSmallStyle}"/>
  </StackPanel>
</Grid >
```

The application displays a simple user interface with several `TextBlocks`. The `TextBlocks` are used either for labels or to display the channel's connection status and the channel URI. The last `TextBlock` ❶ is used to display information from toast notifications that are received while the application is running.

The first time the user runs the application, push notifications aren't enabled. To enable the channel the first time the application is executed, and to reconnect on subsequent launches, you call a new method named `SetupChannel` inside the `MainPage` constructor:

```
public MainPage()
{
```

```
        InitializeComponent();
        SetupChannel();
    }
```

Before you can implement `SetupChannel`, you need to learn how to use the push notification APIs to open a notification channel.

11.2.4 Opening a notification channel

Push notification channels are created and opened through instances of the `HttpNotificationChannel` class, found in the `Microsoft.Phone.Notification` namespace. The `Microsoft.Phone.Notification` namespace contains other classes and enums used to support the methods and events defined by `HttpNotificationChannel`. We'll examine the supporting classes as you build the NotificationClient sample application.

When an `HttpNotificationChannel` is constructed, it's given a name. The channel name is used by the client when looking for already opened channels. In the MainPage.xaml.cs of the NotificationClient application, add a constant string for the channel name and a field to reference an opened notification channel:

```
using Microsoft.Phone.Notifications;
const string CHANNEL_NAME = "PushNotificationChannel";
HttpNotificationChannel channel;
```

Once a channel is constructed, it's opened using the `Open` method. Opening a channel isn't as easy as constructing the channel and calling the `Open` method. Applications must check whether an open channel already exists. `HttpNotificationChannel` provides a static `Find` method to allow application code to look for existing open channels. You use the `Find` method in the `SetupChannel` method implementation, shown in the following listing.

Listing 11.5 Finding and constructing channels

```
void SetupChannel()
{
    bool newChannel = false;
    channel = HttpNotificationChannel.Find(CHANNEL_NAME);
    if (channel == null)
    {
        channel = new HttpNotificationChannel (CHANNEL_NAME);    ❶ Create new channel
        newChannel = true;                                          if not found
    }
    channel.ConnectionStatusChanged += channel_ConnectionStatusChanged;
    channel.ChannelUriUpdated += channel_ChannelUriUpdated;
    channel.ErrorOccurred += channel_ErrorOccurred;
    if (newChannel)
    {
        channel.Open();
        channel.BindToShellTile();             ❷ Open and configure
        channel.BindToShellToast();               new channels
```

```
    }
    channelStatus.Text = channel.ConnectionStatus.ToString();
    if(channel.ChannelUri != null)
        channelUri.Text = channel.ChannelUri.ToString();
}
```

❸ **Update user interface**

Start by looking to see whether an open channel already exists and create a new `HttpNotificationChannel` ❶ only when an existing channel isn't found. After you have a channel instance, subscribe to the `ConnectionStatusChanged`, `ChannelUriUpdated`, and `ErrorOccurred` events. Open the channel with the `Open` method and configure ❷ the channel to receive tile and toast notifications by calling the two bind methods. If the bind methods aren't used, those types of notifications won't be sent to the phone. Though you bind them once while initializing your sample, a real application should provide user settings allowing the user to specify which types of notifications to enable independently. Update the user interface ❸ with the channel's connection status and URI, if one exists. When updated, the user interface will look something like figure 11.8.

Figure 11.8 The client's connections status and URI as displayed in the sample application

When the channel is first created, the MPN channel URI doesn't exist, and the channel URI is retrieved asynchronously from the MPN Service. You want to display the URI once it's set, so you subscribe to the `HttpNotificationChannel`'s `ChannelUriUpdated` event. The newly assigned URI is read from the `ChannelUri` property of the event's `NotificationChannelUriEventArgs` instance:

```
void channel_ChannelUriUpdated(object sender,
    NotificationChannelUriEventArgs e)
{
   Dispatcher.BeginInvoke(() => channelUri.Text = e.ChannelUri.ToString());
}
```

The channel class also exposes events called `ErrorOccurred` and `ConnectionStatusChanged`, which may be useful for troubleshooting notification connections. We leave it to you to implement the `ErrorOccurred` and `ConnectionStatusChanged` event handlers. Notification channels remain opened even when the application terminates, and it's important to call `HttpNotificationChannel`'s `Close` method when the application no longer wants to receive notification messages.

11.2.5 Looking for navigation parameters

When the application is launched from a toast notification, query string parameters are sent to the application. To fully demonstrate toast notifications, you should display the navigation URI to the user when the sample application is launched. The best place to obtain the navigation URI and update the user interface is inside the `OnNavigatedTo` method:

```
protected override void OnNavigatedTo(NavigationEventArgs e)
{
    notificationMessage.Text =
        string.Format("Launched with Uri:\n{0}", e.Uri);
}
```

The navigation URI is read from the `Uri` property of the `NavigationEventArgs` and is written to the `notificationMessage` `TextBlock`. You also use `notificationMessage` to display information from toast notifications received while the client application is running. Figure 11.9 displays the navigation URI from a toast sent by the notification simulator, a feature you'll add to the simulator later in the chapter.

Figure 11.9 The navigation URI from a toast notification as displayed in the sample application

11.2.6 In-app notifications

When toasts are sent while the application is running, the toasts don't appear in the normal spot in the UI. In fact, they won't appear at all unless the application explicitly handles the notification. Raw notifications are also completely lost unless the application is running and listening.

A running application can receive toast and raw notifications by subscribing to `ShellToastNotificationReceived` and `HttpNotificationReceived` respectively. We leave listening for raw notifications with the `HttpNotificationReceived` event as an exercise for the reader. To see `ShellToastNotificationReceived` events in action, subscribe to it in the `SetupChannel` method:

```
channel.ShellToastNotificationReceived +=
    channel_ShellToastNotificationReceived;
```

The payload of a toast notification contains three strings containing the toast's title, content, and navigation URI. These strings are read from the `Collection` property of the `NotificationEventArgs` instance passed to the `ShellToastNotificationReceived` event handler. The following listing shows how the sample application reads the notification data and updates the user interface.

Listing 11.6 Receiving toast notifications

```
void channel_ShellToastNotificationReceived(object sender,
    NotificationEventArgs e)
{
    string title, content, parameter;
    e.Collection.TryGetValue("wp:Text1", out title);
    e.Collection.TryGetValue("wp:Text2", out content);
    e.Collection.TryGetValue("wp:Param", out parameter);
```

❶ **Read notification payload**

```
    string message = string.Format("Toast notification received.\nTitle:"
        + " {0}\nContent: {1}\nParameter: {2}\n\n{3}",
        title, content, parameter, DateTime.Now);
    Dispatcher.BeginInvoke(() => notificationMessage.Text = message);
}
```

The `Collection` property is a dictionary mapping string to string, and you read payload data using the `TryGetValue` method ❶. The dictionary will only contain entries if the sending application provided data when it sent the notification. The key names are defined by an XML schema governing notifications. You'll see an example of the XML used to create notifications later in the chapter as you implement the NotificationSimulator.

You need to implement one last feature in the client application before moving back to the simulator: sharing the client's channel URI with the simulator application. One way to share information with the simulator application is to use the Installation Manager to launch it with a custom navigation URL.

11.3 Launching applications with the Installation Manager

In a normal push notification solution, the client would share the channel URI by sending it to a web service as part of a web request. Both the NotificationClient and the NotificationSimulator sample applications run on the Windows Phone, and the client needs to communicate to the simulator. The Windows Phone operating system enables an application to launch another application from the same publisher through the *Installation Manager*.

Throughout this book, you've seen examples where the operating system launches an application with a customized URL. Pinned tiles, reminders, and toast notifications are a few examples. URL associations allow any application to launch registered applications with a customized URL. The Installation Manager lets you use custom navigation URLs to launch other applications that you've published.

> **NOTE** Another technique where one application can launch another application uses URL associations and the `Windows.System.Launcher.LaunchUri-Asyc` API. URL associations have the advantage that any application can open a registered application whether or not it's from the same publisher. Several of the built-in applications can be launched using URI associations.

The Installation Manager is implemented by the `InstallationManager` class, found in the Windows Phone Runtime namespace `Windows.Phone.Management.Deployment`. In addition to launching other applications you've published, the Installation Manager allows you to determine which other applications are installed and when they were installed.

11.3.1 Using the same publisher ID

When Visual Studio creates a new project, it generates new product and publisher IDs. This means that your NotificationClient and NotificationSimulator probably have

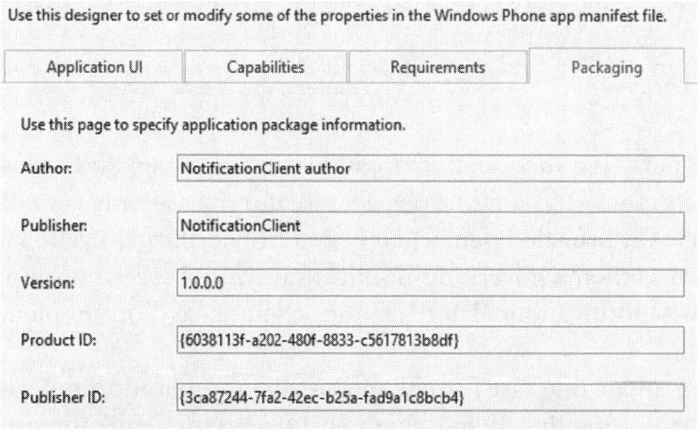

Figure 11.10 The Packaging tab of the manifest file editor. Publisher ID is shown at the bottom of the image. The NotificationClient and NotificationSimulator must have the same publisher ID to allow the client to launch the simulator using the Installation Manager.

different publisher IDs. You can verify this by opening the WMAppManifest.xml file and looking at the Packaging tab, shown in figure 11.10.

If the two projects don't have the same publisher ID, copy the publisher ID from the NotificationClient project and paste it into the NotificationSimulator's WMApp-Manifest.xml file. With both the client and the simulator using the same publisher ID, they're ready to share the channel URI.

11.3.2 Sharing the channel URI

In a normal push notification solution, the client would share the channel URI by sending it to a web service as part of a web request. Both the NotificationClient and the NotificationSimulator run on the Windows Phone, and the operating system prevents applications from sharing data—with the exception of sending data on a navigation URL. In this section you'll update the NotificationClient so that it launches the NotificationSimulator and sends its channel URI on the navigation URL. Start by adding an application bar with a button the user can tap to initiate sharing:

```
<phone:PhoneApplicationPage.ApplicationBar>
   <shell:ApplicationBar>
      <shell:ApplicationBarIconButton IconUri="/Assets/AppBar/share.png"
            IsEnabled="True" Text="share" Click="share_Click"/>
      </shell:ApplicationBar>
</phone:PhoneApplicationPage.ApplicationBar>
```

The share.png file used for the button comes from the Windows Phone SDK. In the button's `Click` event handler, use the Installation Manager to determine whether the NotificationSimulator is installed and, if so, build a navigation URL and launch the application. The implementation for the `Click` event handler is shown in the following listing.

Listing 11.7 Finding and launching the NotificationSimulator

```
using Windows.Phone.Management.Deployment;
using Windows.ApplicationModel;
```

1 Add namespaces

```
void share_Click(object sender, EventArgs e)
{
   IEnumerable<Package> packages =
         InstallationManager.FindPackagesForCurrentPublisher();
   Package simulator = packages.FirstOrDefault(
         item => item.Id.Name == "NotificationSimulator");
   if(simulator != null)
   {
      simulator.Launch("/MainPage.xaml?ClientChannelUri="
         + channelUri.Text);
   }
}
```

❷ Get list of packages

❸ Launch with a navigation URL

Before calling the Installation Manager, add using statements ❶ for `Windows.Phone.Management.Deployment`, where `InstallationManager` is found, and for `Windows.ApplicationModel`, where the `Package` class is found. A list of all applications is retrieved from the singleton Installation Manager instance through the static method called `FindPackagesForCurrentPublisher` ❷. A `Package` represents an application, exposing its product ID and the date it was installed and providing a mechanism for retrieving a thumbnail image of the application's icon. To launch the notification simulator, construct a navigation URL and call the `Launch` ❸ method of the `Package` class.

Now that the channel URI can be sent to the simulator, you need to update the NotificationSimulator application so that it reads the channel URI from the navigation URL. Open MainPage.xaml in the NotificationSimulator project and add a new `PivotItem` with a header value of `channel`:

```
<phone:PivotItem Header="channel">
    <StackPanel>
        <TextBlock Text="Enter the channel uri:" />
        <TextBox x:Name="channelUri" TextWrapping="Wrap" />
    </StackPanel>
</phone:PivotItem>
```

The `PivotItem` contains a `TextBlock` for a label and a `TextBox` to hold the channel URI. To load the sent channel URI into the `TextBox`, update the `OnNavigateTo` method:

```
protected override void OnNavigatedTo(NavigationEventArgs e)
{
   if (NavigationContext.QueryString.ContainsKey("ClientChannelUri"))
   {
      channelUri.Text = NavigationContext.QueryString["ClientChann-
     elUri"];
   }
   LoadInformation("OnNagivatedTo");
}
```

Now that the simulator application has the client's channel URI, you're ready to add code to NotificationSimulator to simulate a push notification service.

Figure 11.11 The NotificationSimulator

11.4 Simulating a Push Notification Service

Real solutions would have a web service built using ASP.NET, Node.js, or other server-side technology. This book isn't about those, so you're taking a shortcut and building a phone application that sends notifications to the MPN Service. The code shown for performing the web request is nearly identical to the code you may implement in an ASP.NET server-side implementation. The simulator application's user interface is shown in figure 11.11.

You'll update the NotificationSimulator project to include new screens to allow you to enter information for toast or tile notifications and tap a button to send the notification. The `Click` event handler code will call through to a new class, named `NotificationService`, which will issue a `HTTP POST` request to the MPN Service.

11.4.1 Issuing HTTP web requests

Windows Phone provides several ways to interact with web services, including those that expose SOAP and REST APIs. SOAP and REST web services have different designs and structures, but both communicate using HTTP, the same protocol used by traditional HTML web servers.

In this section, we introduce you to `HttpWebRequest`, a `System.Net` class you can use to communicate with HTTP servers such as MPN. The `HttpWebRequest` class isn't unique to Windows Phone and exists in both Silverlight and the desktop .NET Framework. `HttpWebRequest` allows you to control how the HTTP request is constructed and sent. For example, you can select the HTTP verb, set the timeout, add header values or cookies to the request, and manage credentials and certificates. Covering the full breadth and depth of the `HttpWebRequest` API is beyond the scope of this book, but you'll use it to POST notifications to the MPN.

There are three steps in sending a web request using the `HttpWebRequest` class. The first is to create the request and set the HTTP verb, URI, and headers. The second entails writing the body of the request. The final step is to read the web server's response. These three steps will be implemented with code you place into a new class called `NotificationService`. Add this new class to the NotificationSimulator project. The `NotificationService` class starts the process of sending a request in a method called `Post`, shown in the following listing.

Listing 11.8 Posting a notification using `HttpWebRequest`

```
void Post(Uri channel, string payload, string target,
    string interval)
{
    HttpWebRequest request =
        (HttpWebRequest)HttpWebRequest.Create(channel);
    request.Headers["X-NotificationClass"] = interval;
    request.Headers["X-MessageID"] = Guid.NewGuid().ToString();
    if (target.Length > 0)
        request.Headers["X-WindowsPhone-Target"] = target;
    request.Method = "POST";
    request.ContentType = "text/xml; charset=utf-8";
    request.BeginGetRequestStream(WriteCallback,
       new RequestStreamState{Request = request, Payload = payload });
}
```

1 Create custom headers

2 Asynchronously write body of request

Start by creating a new `HttpWebRequest` using the static `Create` method. Add custom web headers **1** defined by the MPN Service. The header named `X-Notification-Class` specifies how quickly the notification should be sent and is specific to each type of notification. The `X-MessageID` header is optional and is provided to allow the sending application to match web requests with web responses. The type of notification is identified with the header called `X-WindowsPhone-Target`. The target header is left blank for raw notifications, set to `toast` for toast, and set to `token` for tile notifications. After setting the HTTP verb, you start the second step in the request process by calling `BeginGetRequestStream` **2**.

`BeginGetRequestStream` is an asynchronous method that takes a callback method and a user-defined state object. When the web request is ready for the body to be written, the callback method executes, and the user-defined state object is passed in. Here's a custom state class named `RequestStreamState`:

```
class RequestStreamState
{
    public HttpWebRequest Request;
    public string Payload;
}
```

RequestStreamState allows you to pair the payload and the request object together so that they're both available to the WriteCallback method. The following listing shows the WriteCallback implementation.

Listing 11.9 Writing the payload to the request stream

```
using System.IO;
using System.Text;
void WriteCallback(IAsyncResult result)
{
    RequestStreamState state = (RequestStreamState)result.AsyncState;
    using (var stream = (Stream)state.Request.EndGetRequestStream(result))
    {
        byte[] messageBytes =
            Encoding.UTF8.GetBytes(state.Payload);          ❶ Convert payload to bytes
        stream.Write(messageBytes, 0, messageBytes.Length);
    }
    state.Request.BeginGetResponse(
        ReadCallback, state.Request);                       ❷ Asynchronously read response
}
```

The first thing you do in WriteCallback is pull the RequestStreamState out of the result. Next you get the Stream associated with the request by calling EndGetRequest-Stream. Before you write the payload to the stream, convert the string to a byte array ❶ using the GetBytes method of the Encoding class. The last step is to call BeginGet-Response ❷.

Following the .NET asynchronous pattern, BeginGetResponse takes a callback method and a user-defined state. The callback method is executed once the HTTP server has received your request and sent a response document. Your callback method is named ReadCallback, shown in the following listing, and you pass the original HttpWebRequest instance as the state object.

Listing 11.10 Receiving the response

```
void ReadCallback(IAsyncResult result)
{
    string message;
    HttpWebRequest request = (HttpWebRequest)result.AsyncState;
    try
    {
        HttpWebResponse response =
            (HttpWebResponse)request.EndGetResponse(result);
        message = string.Format(
            "Push request compeleted with:\n  {0}\n  {1}\n  {2}",
            response.Headers["X-NotificationStatus"],
            response.Headers["X-SubscriptionStatus"],            ❶ Look at response headers
            response.Headers["X-DeviceConnectionStatus"]);
    }
    catch (Exception ex)
    {
        message = string.Format("{0} pushing notification: {1}",
            ex.GetType().Name, ex.Message);
```

```
    }
    Deployment.Current.Dispatcher.BeginInvoke(() =>
        MessageBox.Show(message));
}
```

❷ **Display response message**

Listing 11.10 starts by casting the `AsyncState` property to `HttpWebRequest`. Call `EndGetResponse` to get the `HttpWebResponse` instance that represents the response document sent from the server. You read a few custom headers defined by the MPN Service and format a message with them ❶. When an exception occurs while reading the response, format an error message. Display the message ❷ using the `MessageBox` class. An example response message is shown in figure 11.12.

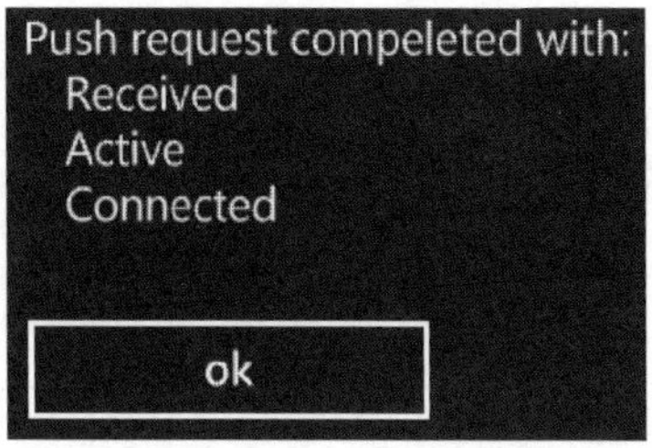

Figure 11.12 The message box displaying the MPN Service response

`HttpWebReponse` provides several other properties and methods not used in the sample application. The body content of the response can be read using `GetResponseStream`. The HTTP status code and description are returned by the `StatusCode` and `StatusDescription` properties.

Now that the `NotificationService` class is ready to push notifications, try sending a toast notification.

11.4.2 Sending toast notifications

The payload for a toast notification is a string containing a well-defined XML document. The XML document uses the `WPNotification` namespace (xmlns). The root element is `Notification`, with a single `Toast` element:

```
<?xml version="1.0" encoding="utf-8"?>
<wp:Notification xmlns:wp="WPNotification">
    <wp:Toast>
        <wp:Text1>your title</wp:Text1>
        <wp:Text2>your content</wp:Text2>
        <wp:Param>your parameter</wp:Param>
    </wp:Toast>
</wp:Notification>
```

The `Toast` element should contain three child elements called `Text1`, `Text2`, and `Param`. `Text1` is the toast's title, and the toast's content is placed in `Text2`. `Param` contains the launch URI used when the user taps a displayed toast notification.

> **NOTE** The Push Notification Service isn't the only way to display a toast notification to the user. A background agent can display a toast notification to the user using the `Show` method of the `ShellToast` class.

In your sample applications you'll send a toast with a launch URI containing two query string parameters. Add a new `PivotItem` to the simulator's MainPage.xaml to allow the user of the simulator to enter the title, content, and query string parameters for the toast. The markup for the new `PivotItem` is shown in the following listing.

Listing 11.11 Markup for entering a toast notification into the simulator

```
xmlns:toolkit="clr-namespace:Microsoft.Phone.Controls;
➥ assembly=Microsoft.Phone.Controls.Toolkit"                  ❶ Reference Windows Phone Toolkit
...
<phone:PivotItem Header="toast">                              ❷ Label pivot item
    <StackPanel>
        <TextBlock Text="Title:"  />
        <toolkit:PhoneTextBox x:Name="toastTitle" Hint="enter title" />
        <TextBlock Text="Content:"  />
        <toolkit:PhoneTextBox x:Name="toastContent" Hint="enter content" />
        <TextBlock Text="First query string value:"  />
        <toolkit:PhoneTextBox x:Name="toastValue1" Hint="enter value1" />
        <TextBlock Text="Second query string value:"  />
        <toolkit:PhoneTextBox x:Name="toastvalue2" Hint="enter value2" />
        <Button Content="Send toast" Click="sendToast_Click" />   ❸ Button to send toast
    </StackPanel>
</phone:PivotItem>
```

You're using the PhoneTextBox control from the Windows Phone Toolkit, so you need to include the toolkit namespace ❶ and use the NuGet Package Manager to download and reference the toolkit package. The new PivotItem is added and given the label toast ❷. Four pairs of TextBlocks and PhoneTextBoxes are stacked in the user interface. Each pair is a label and input control to capture the values to be sent in the toast. Finally, a Button ❸ is provided, which the user taps to send the toast notification. The Click event handler, called sendToast_Click, calls a new NotificationService method named SendToast:

```
void sendToast_Click(object sender, RoutedEventArgs e)
{
    Uri channel;
    if (Uri.TryCreate(channelUri.Text, UriKind.Absolute, out channel))
    {
        service.SendToast(channel, toastTitle.Text, toastContent.Text,
            string.Format("/MainPage.xaml?value1={0}&amp;value2={1}",
                toastValue1.Text, toastvalue2.Text));
    }
}
```

Inside sendToast_Click, the client's channel URI is read from the channelUri TextBox. The launch URI is constructed by concatenating the two query string values. You still need to create a new field of the MainPage class to hold the service reference:

```
NotificationService service = new NotificationService();
```

The new SendToast method formats the payload and calls the Post method:

```
public void SendToast(Uri channel, string title, string content,
    string launchUri)
{
   string payload = string.Format(ToastPayload, title, content, launchUri);
   Post(channel, payload, "toast", "2");
}
```

The payload XML string is constructed by using the `Format` method to replace placeholders in the constant `ToastPayload` string with the specified title, content, and launch URI. The `ToastPayload` constant, not shown here for space, contains the XML for a toast notification with placeholders in the appropriate places. The payload is passed to the `Post` method along with the channel URI, an `X-WindowsPhone-Target` string of `toast`, and an interval of `2` for the `X-NotificationClass` value.

Valid interval values for toast notifications are `2`, `12`, or `22`. A value of `2` indicates that the MPN Service should forward the notification immediately, whereas values of `12` and `22` indicate wait times of 450 seconds and 900 seconds, respectively.

11.4.3 Using notifications to update a tile

The payload for a tile notification is also a string containing a well-defined XML document. The XML document uses the `WPNotification` namespace with a `Notification` root element. Inside the `Notification` element is a single `Tile` element. The MPN Service supports the three different tiles formats available on the phone—Flip, Cycle, and Iconic. The tile notification XML for a Flip tile is shown in the following listing.

Listing 11.12 Payload XML format for a tile notification

```
<?xml version="1.0" encoding="utf-8"?>
<wp:Notification xmlns:wp="WPNotification">
   <wp:Tile ID="tile uri">                                   ❶ Optional ID attribute
      <wp:BackgroundImage>your image</wp:BackgroundImage>
      <wp:SmallBackgroundImage>your image</wp:BackgroundImage>
      <wp:WideBackgroundImage>your image</wp:BackgroundImage>
      <wp:Count Action="Clear">your badge count</wp:Count>   ❷ Optional Action attribute
      <wp:Title Action="Clear">your title</wp:Title>
      <wp:BackBackgroundImage Action="Clear">your back image
         </wp:BackBackgroundImage>
      <wp:WideBackBackgroundImage Action="Clear">your back image
         </wp:WideBackBackgroundImage>
      <wp:BackTitle Action="Clear">your back title</wp:BackTitle>
      <wp:BackContent Action="Clear">your back content</wp:BackContent>
      <wp:WideBackContent Action="Clear">your back content
         </wp:WideBackContent>
   </wp:Tile>
</wp:Notification>
```

The Flip tile XML format includes each of the 10 tile properties. The XML format for Cycle or Iconic tiles is similar, each listing the properties that are relevant for those tile types. `BackgroundImage`, `SmallBackgroundImage`, `WideBackgroundImage`, `Count`, and `Title` update the front of the tile, whereas `BackBackgroundImage`, `WideBackBackgroundImage`, `BackTitle`, `BackContent`, and `WideBackContent` update the back of the tile. The `Notification` element defines an optional ID attribute ❶ that can be used to update a secondary tile instead of the main application tile. Nine of the 10 tile properties define an optional `Action` attribute. When the `Action` attribute is set to `Clear` ❷, the corresponding tile property is set back to its default value.

You'll update the simulator's user interface with a new PivotItem for setting each of the six tile notification properties used for normal-sized tiles—ignoring the properties for small or doublewide tiles. The user interface for containing controls for each of the six properties doesn't fit nicely into a single screen. The tile notification PivotItem, shown in the following listing, uses a ScrollViewer that allows the user to scroll the form to see offscreen input controls.

Listing 11.13 XAML markup for sending a tile notification from the simulator

```
<phone:PivotItem Header="tile">
   <ScrollViewer>
      <StackPanel>
         <TextBlock Text="Title:"/>
         <toolkit:PhoneTextBox x:Name="tileTitle" Hint="enter title"/>
         <TextBlock Text="Badge Count:"/>
         <toolkit:PhoneTextBox x:Name="tileBadgeCount"
               Hint="enter a count" InputScope="Number"/>        ❶ Use number keyboard
         <TextBlock Text="Image:"/>
         <StackPanel Orientation="Horizontal">
            <RadioButton x:Name="tileDefaultImage" GroupName="tile"
               Content="default"/>
            <RadioButton x:Name="tileBlueImage" GroupName="tile"
               IsChecked="True" Content="Blue.png"/>                ❷ Pick background image
            <RadioButton x:Name="tileGreenImage" GroupName="tile"
               Content="Green.png"/>
         </StackPanel>
         <TextBlock Text="Back Title:"/>
         <toolkit:PhoneTextBox x:Name="tileBackTitle"
               Hint="enter back title"/>
         <TextBlock Text="Back Content:"/>
         <toolkit:PhoneTextBox x:Name="tileBackContent"
               Hint="enter back content"/>
         <TextBlock Text="Back Image:"/>
         <StackPanel Orientation="Horizontal">
            <RadioButton x:Name="tileBackNoImage" GroupName="backTile"
                Content="None"/>
            <RadioButton x:Name="tileBackBlueImage" GroupName="backTile"
               Content="Blue.png"/>
            <RadioButton x:Name="tileBackGreenImage" IsChecked="True"
               GroupName="backTile" Content="Green.png"/>
         </StackPanel>
         <Button Content="Send tile" Click="sendTile_Click"/>
      </StackPanel>
   </ScrollViewer>
</phone:PivotItem>
```

Start by declaring a new PivotItem that contains a StackPanel inside a ScrollViewer. Most of the user interface is built from pairs of TextBlocks and PhoneTextBoxes, allowing the user to enter the titles, count, and content values to be sent with the tile notification. The InputScope of the TextBox for entering the count value is set to Number ❶, to make it easier for the user. There are two groups of RadioButtons ❷ on the form for picking which image file should be used for the background images.

The last item added to the tile `PivotItem` is a `Button` the user taps to send the notification. The next listing details the implementation of the button's `Click` handler. After reading and translating values from the user interface, the `NotificationService` method named `SendTile` is called.

Listing 11.14 The `SendTile` `Click` handler

```
void sendTile_Click(object sender, RoutedEventArgs e)
{
    Uri channel;
    if (Uri.TryCreate(channelUri.Text, UriKind.Absolute, out channel))
    {
        string imagePath = tileDefaultImage.IsChecked.Value ?
            "/Assets/Tiles/FlipCycleTileMedium.png" :
            tileBlueImage.IsChecked.Value ? "/Assets/Tiles/Blue.png" :
            "/Assets/Tiles/Green.png";
        string backImagePath = tileBackNoImage.IsChecked.Value ? "" :
            tileBackBlueImage.IsChecked.Value ? "/Assets/Tiles/Blue.png" :
            "/Assets/Tiles/Green.png";
        int badgeCount;
        Int32.TryParse(tileBadgeCount.Text, out badgeCount);
        service.SendTile(channel, imagePath, badgeCount, tileTitle.Text,
            backImagePath, tileBackTitle.Text, tileBackContent.Text);
    }
}
```

❶ Convert count text to integer

First, the image `RadioButtons` are examined to determine which image should be sent in the notification. The NotificationClient application includes FlipCycleTileMedium.png, Blue.jpg, and Green.jpg files in the XAP file. For the sample included with this book's source code, Blue.png and Green.png are copies of FlipCycleTileMedium.png that have been given a solid background color. The value entered into the `tileBadgeCount` `TextBox` is converted from text to an integer with the `TryParse` method ❶. Send all six property values to `SendTile`.

The implementation of `SendTile`, shown in the following listing, isn't as straightforward as the implementation of `SendToast`.

Listing 11.15 Building the tile payload

```
const string Clear = "Action\"Clear\"";
public void SendTile(Uri channel, string tileId, string imagePath,
    int badgeCount, string title, string backImagePath,
    string backTitle, string content)
{
    string badgeCountAction = "", titleAction = "",
        backImagePathAction = "", backTitleAction = "", contentAction = "";
    if (badgeCount < 1) badgeCountAction = Clear;
    if (string.IsNullOrEmpty(title)) titleAction = Clear;
    if (string.IsNullOrEmpty(backImagePath)) backImagePathAction = Clear;
    if (string.IsNullOrEmpty(backTitle)) backTitleAction = Clear;
    if (string.IsNullOrEmpty(content)) contentAction = Clear;
    string payload = string.Format(TilePayload, imagePath,
        badgeCountAction, badgeCount, titleAction, title,
```

❶ Text for Action attributes

```
        backImagePathAction, backImagePath, backTitleAction, backTitle,
        contentAction, content);
    Post(channel, payload, "token", "1");
}
```

`SendTile` examines each of the properties to see whether it contains a valid value and, if not, sets the `Action` attribute of the related XML element to the value `Clear`. Define a constant string ❶ to use when formatting the payload XML string. The payload XML string is constructed by using the `Format` method to replace placeholders in the constant `TilePayload` string with the specified title, content, and launch URI. The `TilePayload` constant, not shown here for space, contains the XML for a tile notification, with placeholders in the appropriate places. The payload is passed to the `Post` method along with the channel URI, an `X-WindowsPhone-Target` string of `token`, and an interval of `1` for the `X-NotificationClass` value. Valid interval values for tile notifications are `1`, `11`, or `21`. A value of `1` indicates that the MPN Service should forward the notification immediately, whereas values of `11` and `21` indicate wait times of 450 seconds and 900 seconds, respectively.

Now you're ready to send some push notifications. Start by pinning the NotificationClient to the Start Screen. Next, run the NotificationClient sample application. Once the channel URI is displayed, tap the application bar button to launch the simulator, sending the channel URI from one application to the other. Once the simulator is running, switch to the channel pivot and verify that the channel URI was properly received. Now you can use the tile and toast pivots to send notifications.

11.5 Summary

In this chapter you looked at three different methods to enable communication between a Windows Phone application and a remote service. Push notifications allow a remote service to send messages to the user of an application, even when the application isn't running on the phone. Push notifications are a one-way communication from server to client. One-way communications from client to server are possible with the `HttpWebRequest` class. A client uses `HttpWebRequest` to send a request to the server and then reads the server's response. You used `HttpWebRequest` to send push notification request to the Microsoft Push Notification Service (MPN).

Push notifications provide a mechanism where a web service can indirectly communicate with a Windows Phone application, whether or not the application is running. Indirect communication isn't sufficient for many applications that require direct connections between the client and the web service. Some applications can use the `HttpWebRequest` class for direct connections initiated by the client, but it doesn't support server-initiated interactions. Applications whose network interaction requirements can't be satisfied by push notification or `HttpWebRequest` can use sockets to enable communication between client and server. Though not covered in this book, the Windows Phone Runtime enables socket programming with classes in the `Windows.Networking.Sockets` namespace.

In the next chapter you'll learn how to use the Speech APIs to accept commands from a user and to prompt the user with synthesized speech.

12 Using the Speech API

This chapter covers

- Using text-to-speech and speaking voices
- Using Speech Synthesis Markup Language (SSML)
- Using voice commands and speech recognition

Speech is a powerful thing. We spend our first years learning how to talk and continue to do it the rest of our lives. Speaking is the preferred way of interacting with each other and sharing information. This natural interaction, when extended to mobile devices, can become second nature to users.

As the processing power available in our everyday devices continues to increase, we'll see that talking to machines and receiving vocal responses are increasingly the norm. Microsoft recognizes this fact and has made a push to get variations of its speech technologies into multiple areas of our daily lives, including voice mail systems, PC and console gaming, automobiles, and now in our mobile devices.

With Windows Phone 7, Microsoft gave users the ability to perform basic operations using only their voices. These operations included calling and texting contacts, opening apps, and searching. Although these were useful, developers were left out of the fun and were forced to use third-party web services to enable speech features in their apps.

Windows Phone 8 opens up the speech capabilities of the operating system to developers and allows users to not just open an app but give it commands to perform actions. Once the app is open, it can accept additional commands and data via voice while prompting the user in a synthesized voice. These features can be combined to create apps that free the user from tedious typing and even from needing to look at the screen altogether.

In this chapter we look at the three major areas of the Speech API included in Windows Phone 8: text-to-speech, voice commands, and speech recognition. In this chapter you create a simple app that uses all three areas of the Speech API. First, you read back what you type using simple text-to-speech as well as Speech Synthesis Markup Language (SSML) using a chosen voice. You add the ability to tell the app to perform an action using voice commands. And you add speech recognition to set values.

About the samples

The text-to-speech samples in this chapter are best experienced using the emulator. Although we did test all samples on a device, the number of languages and voices installed on it were only a fraction of the 15 languages and 30 voices the emulator comes with. Some text-to-speech samples may appear to not work correctly if the language used isn't installed on the device.

Voice-command and speech-recognition samples, on the other hand, work much better on a device. The microphone on the device is better at picking out the user speech than a typical PC microphone. If using your computer, you may need to adjust your microphone settings and turn down any background noise to get consistent results.

12.1 Text-to-speech

When taking advantage of the Speech API, text-to-speech (TTS) is one of the simplest features to implement. It can make your app stand out from the crowd and simplify how the user interacts with it. The standardized voices also give your app the feeling that it's a part of the phone's OS.

Let's dive right into some code because adding TTS can be a three-liner. Obviously, you'll need more than this to make an app, but as far as speech is concerned, it's only three lines.

The first listing shows the creation of a new instance of a `SpeechSynthesizer` object. After checking that a `TextBox` contains text to be spoken, the phone speaks and displays it in a `MessageBox`.

Listing 12.1 Basic text-to-speech example code

```
using Windows.Phone.Speech.Synthesis;

private SpeechSynthesizer _speechSynthesizer = new SpeechSynthesizer();
private async void SayItButtonClick(object sender, RoutedEventArgs e)
{
```

Declare SpeechSynthesizer object

```
        try
        {
            if (!string.IsNullOrEmpty(PhraseTextBox.Text))          <-- Check for text to speak
            {
                await _speechSynthesizer.SpeakTextAsync(PhraseTextBox.Text);    <-- Call SpeakTextAsync, wait
                MessageBox.Show("Text read: '" + PhraseTextBox.Text + "'");     <-- to display MessageBox
            }
            else
            {
                MessageBox.Show("Phrase text is required.",
                                "Error",
                                MessageBoxButton.OK);          <-- Display MessageBox
            }                                                      if no text provided
        }
        catch (Exception ex)
        {
            MessageBox.Show(ex.Message,
                            "Exception", MessageBoxButton.OK);   <-- Catch and display
        }                                                            exceptions to user
    }
```

Notice how the `SayItButtonClick` event handler contains the `async` modifier, and the call to `SpeakTextAsync` is preceded by the `await` operator. This tells the system to wait for the asynchronous call to finish before moving on. The UI isn't locked, but any operations following the awaited call are delayed until the text is read. This is shown by the `MessageBox.Show` call made after the awaited call. Clicking thc button multiple times shows this behavior.

> **TIP** Use of text-to-speech requires that the `ID_CAP_SPEECH_RECOGNITION` capability be declared in WMAppManifest.xml.

12.2 Available speaking voices

One of the improvements from Windows Phone 7 is the addition of voices. In Windows Phone 8 you can specify the voice used to speak, and as a developer you have

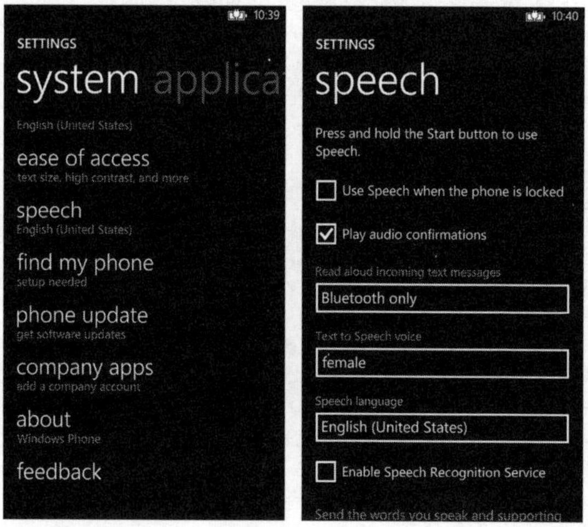

Figure 12.1 The Speech Settings pages

some control of the voice used in your apps. To explore the different voices available, in Settings find the Speech item under the System heading, as shown in figure 12.1.

In order to programmatically specify a voice, you must set the `SetVoice` property with a `VoiceInformation` object. The best way to get the needed `VoiceInformation` object is to use the `InstalledVoices` class and query its `All` property using LINQ.

Open Visual Studio and create a new Windows Phone App project. Copy the XAML in listing 12.2 into the `ContentPanel Grid` in the MainPage.xaml file. It demonstrates the UI that could be used to facilitate the selection of the language and voice of a programmatically selected speaking voice using two `ListBoxes`. When the `LanguagesListBox` selection is changed, it triggers the update of `VoicesListBox`.

Listing 12.2 `LanguagesListBox` and `VoicesListBox`

```
<StackPanel>
    <TextBlock Height="30"
        Text="Language"
        Foreground="{StaticResource PhoneAccentBrush}" />
    <ListBox Name="LanguagesListBox" Height="182"          LanguagesListBox
        ItemsSource="{Binding}"
        SelectionChanged=
            "LanguagesListBox_OnSelectionChanged" >
        <ListBox.ItemTemplate>
            <DataTemplate>
                <TextBlock Text="{Binding DisplayName}"
                    FontSize="{StaticResource
                    PhoneFontSizeMedium}"
                    Grid.Column="0"
                    Grid.Row="0"
                    Grid.ColumnSpan="2" />
            </DataTemplate>
        </ListBox.ItemTemplate>
    </ListBox>
    <TextBlock Height="30"
        Text="Voice"
        Foreground="{StaticResource PhoneAccentBrush}" />
    <ListBox Name="VoicesListBox" Height="176"             VoicesListBox
        ItemsSource="{Binding}"
        SelectionChanged="VoicesListBox_OnSelectionChanged" >
        <ListBox.ItemTemplate>
            <DataTemplate>
                <Grid Margin="10">
                    <Grid.RowDefinitions>
                        <RowDefinition Height="30"/>
                        <RowDefinition Height="30"/>
                    </Grid.RowDefinitions>
                    <Grid.ColumnDefinitions>
                        <ColumnDefinition Width="200"/>
                        <ColumnDefinition Width="*"/>
                    </Grid.ColumnDefinitions>
                    <TextBlock Text="{Binding DisplayName}"
                       FontSize=
                       "{StaticResource PhoneFontSizeMedium}"
```

```
                Grid.Column="0"
                Grid.Row="0"
                Grid.ColumnSpan="2"/>
            <TextBlock Text="{Binding Language}"
                FontSize=
                "{StaticResource PhoneFontSizeMedium}"
                Grid.Column="0"
                Grid.Row="1"/>
            <TextBlock Text="{Binding Gender}"
                FontSize=
                "{StaticResource PhoneFontSizeMedium}"
                Grid.Column="1"
                Grid.Row="1"/>
          </Grid>
        </DataTemplate>
      </ListBox.ItemTemplate>
    </ListBox>
    <TextBlock Height="30"
        Text="Phrase"
        Foreground="{StaticResource PhoneAccentBrush}" />
    <TextBox Height="116"
        Name="PhraseTextBox"
        Text="Windows Phone is awesome!"/>
    <StackPanel Orientation="Horizontal">
        <Button Content="Say It" Click="SayItButtonClick" />
    </StackPanel>
</StackPanel>
```

The `LanguagesListbox` is filled with languages for all installed voices. When the `SelectionChanged` event is triggered, the `VoicesListBox` is updated with the available voices in the selected language.

GETTING INSTALLED LANGUAGES

With the UI in place, let's look at how to get the list of languages installed on a Windows Phone 8 device. Because you're binding your results to a `ListBox`, you're going to create a property in MainPage.xaml.cs that uses LINQ to return an `IEnumerable` list of `CultureInfo` objects. To do this, you need to know what voices are available and get only the languages with installed voices. This gives you a place to reuse the list of voices installed. The following listing shows how to create properties that return lists of voices and languages installed on the phone.

Listing 12.3 Language and voice properties

```
using Windows.Phone.Speech.Synthesis;
using System.Globalization;

private IEnumerable<VoiceInformation> _availableVoices =
        InstalledVoices.All;                          <- Return collection of
private IEnumerable<CultureInfo> InstalledLanguages      VoiceInformation
{
    get
    {
```

```
            return _availableVoices.Select(
                            voice => new CultureInfo(voice.Language)
                        ).Distinct()
                        .ToList();
        }
}
```

Query availableVoices, select CultureInfo

Filter to unique CultureInfo objects

Transform results to List<CultureInfo>

Using LINQ, query the `_availableVoices` property you created and return a list of `CultureInfo` objects. Because each installed language has both male and female voices, you want to ensure you get only one entry by using the LINQ `Distinct` method. To bind this property to the `ListBox`, you need to set the `DataContext` in the constructor like this:

```
LanguagesListBox.DataContext = InstalledLanguages;
```

Use the `OnSelectionChanged` event of the languages `ListBox` to trigger the voices `ListBox` to be filled with the voices for the selected language. Because the languages in the `ListBox` are `CultureInfo` objects, you'll create a method that takes a `CultureInfo` object and updates the voices `ListBox` with the correct voices. In listing 12.4, you again use LINQ to query the `_availableVoices` property, and this time you get the `VoiceInformation` objects whose language matches the `CultureInfo` object passed. Then the order is set to ensure they're in a consistent order in the `ListBox`. You can use the `SelectionChanged` event to call this new method.

Listing 12.4 Updating voices `ListBox`

```
private SpeechSynthesizer _speechSynthesizer = new SpeechSynthesizer();
private List<VoiceInformation> _availableVoices = Installed-
     Voices.All.ToList();
private void LanguagesListBox_OnSelectionChanged(
                              object sender, SelectionChangedEventArgs e)
{
    UpdateVoicesListBox((CultureInfo)((ListBox)sender).SelectedItem);
}

private void UpdateVoicesListBox(CultureInfo info)
{
    VoicesListBox.DataContext =
        _availableVoices.Where(v => v.Language == info.Name)
        .OrderBy(v => v.Gender);
}
```

Cast sender and item, call method

Bind data with DataContext

Query availableVoices

Set order

You detect the language selected by casting the sender to a `ListBox` and then casting the selected item as a `CultureInfo` object. Pass this to the method you created to update the voices `ListBox`.

SETTING THE SELECTED VOICE

Finally, you can set the selected voice to be used by using the `SetVoice` method in the `SpeechSynthesizer` you created. In this example app there are two places the voice needs to be set: when the user selects a language and the voices `ListBox` is populated, and when the user selects a voice. The first has a `VoiceInformation` object readily available, and the second requires two casts to get the required `VoiceInformation` object.

The following listing shows how to check the type of an object and cast as required, getting the `VoiceInformation` object needed to set the voice of the `SpeechSynthesizer` object.

Listing 12.5 Setting voice used by the `SpeechSynthesizer`

```
private void SetVoice(object sender)
{
    if (sender is VoiceInformation)
    {
        _speechSynthesizer.SetVoice((VoiceInformation)sender);    <-- Cast object and set voice
    }
    else
    {
        _speechSynthesizer.SetVoice(
                (VoiceInformation)((ListBox)sender).SelectedItem);    <-- Cast SelectedItem and set voice
    }
}
```

The method is called in two places. For the first, use the `OnSelectionChanged` event of the voices `ListBox`, as shown in the following listing.

Listing 12.6 Setting voice when new voice is selected

```
private void VoicesListBox_OnSelectionChanged
                    (object sender, SelectionChangedEventArgs e)
{
    SetVoice(sender);
}
```

For the second place, add the following to the `UpdateVoicesListBox` method to set the voice to the first in the list:

```
SetVoice(VoicesListBox.Items[0]);
```

Now when you run the app, the text is spoken in the selected language and voice. The text in the example is in English, but selecting another language and voice will speak the text in an accent. Changing the provided text to another language and selecting the correct language will cause the text to be spoken correctly. Change the text to *Windows Phone es impresionante!* and choose any of the Spanish options. Try other languages to see what happens. Some sound correct, and others don't. Be sure you select an appropriate voice for the text you provide or you may get some unexpected results.

In this section we looked at how to add text-to-speech to your apps using the `SpeechSynthesizer` class. Then we examined how to specify the voice used to speak. This kind of implementation will cover the majority of cases where text-to-speech is required. In other cases, such as eBooks or poetry, a more advanced way of specifying what is spoken and how it's spoken is required. For this, Speech Synthesis Markup Language is available.

12.3 Speech Synthesis Markup Language

Speech Synthesis Markup Language (SSML) is an XML-based format for specifying what the speech synthesis says and how it's said. SSML is a W3C-recommended format for providing a standard way of sharing speech data between different systems. Microsoft's implementation is based on version 1.0, so any other system that supports 1.0 can use the same SSML source. This system could be a web service that provides speech data to client applications or SSML files stored on a web server. Applications running on different mobile or desktop operating systems could access and use the same data.

> **Note about code samples for SSML**
>
> The samples for the remaining sections don't create a complete sample app. They are, however, a part of the downloadable code for this chapter, where they're complete and functional.
>
> Please download the code samples to see these examples in action.

The `SpeechSynthesizer` object in Windows Phone 8 has two methods for processing SSML files and strings: `SpeakSsmlAsync` and `SpeakSsmlFromUriAsync`. The `SpeakSsmlAsync` method takes a string in the SSML format. Listing 12.7 shows how you could generate an XML string using `XDocument` from a data source. In this example, the document is generated by code but could as easily come from a database or other data source as mentioned.

Listing 12.7 Creating an SSML string with `XDocument`

```
using System.Xml.Linq;

public List<List<string>> GeneratePoem()                    <-- Generate poem
{
    List<List<string>> poem = new List<List<string>>();
    for (int i = 1; i <= 4; i++)
    {
        List<string> verse = new List<string>();
        for (int j = 1; j <= 4; j++)
        {
            string line = "Verse " + i + ", Line " + j;
            verse.Add(line);
        }
        poem.Add(verse);
    }
    return poem;
}

public string CreateSsmlWithXDocument(List<List<string>> poem )
{
    XNamespace xmlns =
          XNamespace.Get("http://www.w3.org/2001/10/synthesis");   <-- Override xmlns namespace
```

```
    XDocument ssmlDocument = new XDocument();

    XElement rootElement = new XElement(xmlns + "speak");          <-- Declare root element
    rootElement.SetAttributeValue("version", "1.0");
    rootElement.SetAttributeValue(XNamespace.Xmlns + "xsi",
            "http://www.w3.org/2001/XMLSchema-instance");
    rootElement.SetAttributeValue(
             XNamespace.Xml + "lang", "en-US");

    XElement voiceElement = new XElement("voice");
    voiceElement.SetAttributeValue("name",                          Declare voice
_speechSynthesizer.GetVoice().DisplayName);                     <-- and set it

    foreach (var verse in poem)                                  <-- Loop through
    {                                                                verses in poem
Declare p element --> XElement paragraphElement = new XElement("p");
        foreach (string line in verse)
        {                                                            Declare and
            paragraphElement.Add(new XElement("s", line));       <-- fill s element
        }
        voiceElement.Add(paragraphElement);                      <-- Add paragraph
    }                                                                element
Add voices --> rootElement.Add(voiceElement);
    ssmlDocument.Add(rootElement);     <-- Add root element
                                                                     Format as
    return ssmlDocument.ToString(SaveOptions.DisableFormatting);  <-- plain text
}
```

If your SSML is stored in local files or is from a web service, you'll use the `SpeakSsmlFromUriAsync` method. You create a `URI` object that points to the resource and passes it to the `SpeakSsmlFromUriAsync`. The following listing shows how to load an XML file.

Listing 12.8 Loading SSML from a file

```
using Windows.ApplicationModel;                          Set path to SSML-compliant
...                                                                        XML file
string path = Package.Current.InstalledLocation.Path +
                                        "\\SSMLExample.xml";           <--
Uri fileToRead = new Uri(path, UriKind.Absolute);        <-- Create URI object
await _speechSynthesizer.SpeakSsmlFromUriAsync(fileToRead);  from file path for #A
^-- Speak the SSML file contents
```

When calling `SpeakSsmlAsync` or `SpeakSsmlFromUriAsync`, use `await` to tell the phone to wait until it's finished speaking before moving on. This will cause a pause that is acceptable for short speech, but for something longer it may be undesirable. Be sure to test your app during development to ensure it behaves in an acceptable way.

Let's look at the different elements that make up an SSML document.

SSML ELEMENTS

SSML is a robust markup that contains only a handful of elements. Table 12.1 shows the elements that are most important when getting started with SSML. There are additional elements and attributes that are used to customize the output. We cover those later in this chapter but not in this table. You can read more about these additional items at http://mng.bz/0XB1.

Table 12.1 The most commonly used SSML elements

Element	Attribute	Description
`speak`	`version`	*Required.* Indicates the version of SSML 1.0 specification used to interpret the document markup. 1.0 is the current version.
	`xml:lang`	*Required.* Specifies the language of the root document. The value may contain either a lowercase, two-letter language code (such as `en` for English) or may optionally include an uppercase, country/region or other variation in addition to the language code (such as `zh-CN`).
	`xmlns`	*Required.* Specifies the URI to the document that defines the markup vocabulary (the element types and attribute names) of the SSML document. The current URI is http://www.w3.org/2001/10/synthesis.
`voice`	`gender`	*Optional.* Specifies the preferred gender of the voice that will speak the contained text. The allowed values are `male`, `female`, and `neutral`.
	`xml:lang`	*Optional.* Specifies the language that the voice must support. The value may contain either a lowercase, two-letter language code (such as `en` for English) or may optionally include an uppercase, country/region or other variation in addition to the language code (such as `zh-CN`).
	`variant`	*Optional.* An integer that specifies a preferred voice when more than one voice matches the values specified in any of the `xml:lang`, gender, or age parameters.
`p` and `s`	`xml:lang`	*Required.* Specifies the language of the root document. The value may contain either a lowercase, two-letter language code (such as `en` for English) or may optionally include an uppercase, country/region or other variation in addition to the language code (such as `zh-CN`).

The `xml:lang` attribute controls the language spoken and voice used when the file is interpreted. It can be set in several different elements depending on your intent. Setting it on the `speak` element will set the whole document to that language and voice. You can also set it on paragraph (`p`) or sentence (`s`) elements, but note that doing so will override the language set on any elements higher in the XML tree, including the `speak` element. This is useful if you need to read text in multiple languages or want to read some text with an accent. In the following listing, the `p` element is set to Italian, and the `s` elements are set to other languages. This English text is read by the phone in the voice matching the language specified.

Listing 12.9 p and s element examples

```
<!-- p and s element examples-->
<p xml:lang="it">
    <s>This is Italian, set by the paragraph element.</s>
<s xml:lang="de"> This is German </s>
    <s xml:lang="de"> Diese ist Deutsch </s>
    <s>This is still Italian</s>
</p>
```

- Set Italian voice (line 2)
- English text, Italian voice (line 3)
- English text, German voice (line 4)
- German text, German voice (line 5)
- English text, Italian voice (line 6)

The SSML element that gives the most control of the voice used is the `voice` element. It allows you to specify the language and the gender. Setting the `variant` attribute to `1` or `2` will select a voice, but you're not certain which gender voice you'll get. This is because there are two voices per language, male and female, but they're in no particular order.

The speaking voice can be modified by several elements to add some dramatic effect to the text being spoken. These elements aren't among the most commonly used (see table 12.1) but are useful nonetheless.

ADDITIONAL SSML ELEMENTS

Several SSML elements are used to change how the words are spoken. Inserting a pause is accomplished using the `break` element. With `break` you can specify the length of a break in seconds or milliseconds using the `time` attribute, or set the break to one of several preset values using the `strength` attribute. Setting `strength` to `none` removes the pause entirely—useful if the pause at the end of a sentence or between words is unnecessary.

The following listing shows how to set the voice in a conversational context, such as a spelling bee. Using the `break` and `prosody` elements, you can add some dramatic effect to how the phone speaks by changing the pitch and volume and inserting pauses into the spoken text.

Listing 12.10 Voice `gender`, `characters`, `break`, and `pitch` examples

```
<voice xml:lang="en" gender="female">
        <s>Spell dog.</s>
</voice>
<voice xml:lang="it" gender="male">
        <s>
                Dog.<break strength="weak"/>
                <say-as interpret-as="characters">
                        DOG
                </say-as>
                <break strength="weak"/> Dog.
        </s>
</voice>
<voice xml:lang="en" gender="female">
        <s>
                You are <break time="1.5s"/>
                <prosody pitch="+20000Hz" volume="x-loud">
                        Correct!
                </prosody>
        </s>
</voice>
```

- English female: "Spell dog"
- Italian male: "Dog," pauses, spells out
- Female pauses, exclaims: "Correct!"

Both listings 12.10 and 12.11 demonstrate use of the `say-as` element. The `say-as` element can also be used to read dates and times, cardinal and ordinal numbers, and phone numbers. Note that in the following listing, the date formats differ based on the language used. If the incorrect date format is provided, the phone will read out the numbers instead of reading them as a date.

Listing 12.11 say-as examples

Date, time in male British voice

```
<voice xml:lang="en-gb" gender="male">
        <!-- dates -->
        <s xml:lang="en-gb">
                Today is not
                <say-as interpret-as="date" format="mdy">
                        12-25-2020
                </say-as>
                        at
               <say-as interpret-as="time" format="hms12">
                        7:17am
               </say-as>
                        Or is it?
        </s>
```

Date, time in male American voice

```
        <s xml:lang="en-us">
                Today is not
                <say-as interpret-as="date" format="dmy">
                        12-25-2020
                </say-as>
                        at
                <say-as interpret-as="time" format="hms12">
                        7:17am
                </say-as>
                Or is it?
        </s>
```

Cardinal and ordinal numbers

```
        <s>
                We are <say-as interpret-as="cardinal">5</say-as> days in.
                It is the <say-as interpret-as="ordinal">5th</say-as> day.
        </s>
```

Phone number with automatic pause

```
        <s>
                Jenny Jenny, Who can I turn to?
                <say-as interpret-as="telephone" format="1">
                        867-5309
                </say-as>.
        </s>
</voice>
```

The prosody element allows you to change how things are said using its pitch, rate, and volume attributes. If a word is unpronounceable, the sub element is used to substitute a pronounceable word in its place. The following listing demonstrates both prosody and sub elements.

Listing 12.12 Speed, substitution, and voice variant examples

First American English voice

```
<voice xml:lang="en" variant="1">
        <s>
                The Itsy Bitsy
```

"$pld3r" replaced by "spider," spoken extra slowly

```
                <prosody rate="x-slow"><sub alias="spider">
                        $p1d3r
                </sub></prosody>
                crawled up the water spout
```

```
        </s>
        <s>
                Down came the rain and washed the
                <prosody rate="slow">Spider</prosody>       "Spider" spoken
                out.                                         faster
        </s>
</voice>                                                     Second American
<voice xml:lang="en" variant="2">                            English voice
        <s>
                Out came the sun and dried up all the rain
                <break strength="none" />                    Remove pause
        </s>                                                 with s element
        <s>
    so the Itsy Bitsy
                <prosody rate="fast">Spider</prosody>        "Spider" spoken fast
                went up the spout again.
        </s>
</voice>
<p>
        <s>                                                  Counting with
                <prosody volume="silent">0</prosody>         increasing volume
                <prosody volume="x-soft">1</prosody>
                <prosody volume="soft">2</prosody>
                <prosody volume="medium">3</prosody>
                <prosody volume="loud">4</prosody>
                <prosody volume="x-loud">5</prosody>
                <prosody volume="default">6</prosody>
        </s>
</p>
```

As you can see, there's a great deal of flexibility when creating SSML documents to mimic natural speech patterns. Because of this, it isn't always possible to know when a particular bit of text will be spoken. For this reason, the Windows Phone 8 implementation support bookmarks in the SSML document.

Bookmarks placed within your SSML document trigger an event that can be listened for and handled accordingly. Set the `name` attribute of the `mark` element such as `<mark name="bookmark1"/>` at the spot where you want to trigger an event, and attach your event handler to the `BookmarkReached` event. The bookmark name you assign can be found in the `Bookmark` property of the `SpeechBookmarkReachedEventArgs` object. In the following listing a `MessageBox` is displayed when a bookmark is reached.

Listing 12.13 BookmarkReached event example

```
_speechSynthesizer.BookmarkReached += _speechSynthesizer_BookmarkReached;   Set up event handler for SpeechSynthesizer
private void _speechSynthesizer_BookmarkReached(
        SpeechSynthesizer sender, SpeechBookmarkReachedEventArgs args)
{
    Dispatcher.BeginInvoke(() =>
                MessageBox.Show(args.Bookmark + " Reached"));   Display MessageBox
}
```

This bookmark functionality can be used to trigger words being highlighted, pages being turned, or other UI changes based on where in the SSML document the phone is. Figure 12.2 shows a `MessageBox` triggered by a `BookmarkReached` event as a simple example, but the possibilities are open for you to take advantage of the bookmark functionality to create more interactive apps.

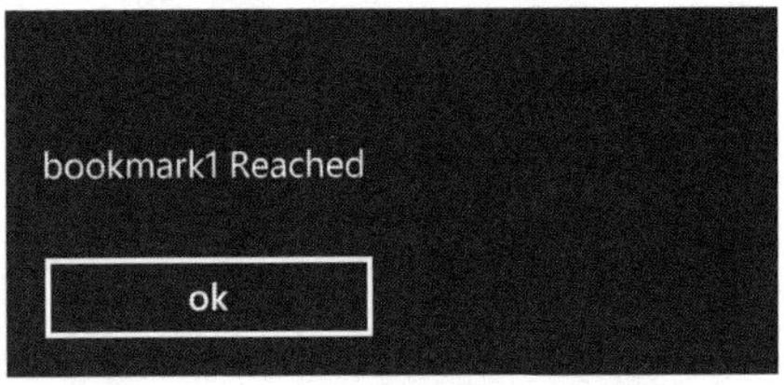

Figure 12.2 A `MessageBox` triggered by a `BookmarkReached` event

As you've seen, it's possible to implement speech patterns that are more natural using SSML on Windows Phone 8. Although providing text to the `SpeechSynthesizer` is a quick and easy way to provide verbal feedback to the user, applications such as educational apps with more advanced speech requirements will benefit from the time spent developing robust SSML documents or a web service to generate the required documents.

So far, you've seen how to enable your apps to talk to users. Next, you'll see how to verbally send commands directly to your app and open a new area of interactivity between your app and its users.

12.4 Voice commands

Voice commands allow the user to interact with your app from anywhere in the phone before the application is started. By providing interactivity like this, you encourage the use of your app by making access as simple as holding the Start button and telling the phone, and your app, what to do. At the core of this is the Voice Command Definition (VCD) file.

> **TIP** Use of voice commands requires the `ID_CAP_SPEECH_RECOGNITION`, `ID_CAP_MICROPHONE`, and `ID_CAP_NETWORKING` capabilities to be declared in WMAppManifest.xml.

12.4.1 The Voice Command Definition file

The Voice Command Definition (VCD) file is the document that contains the list of commands, action, prompts, and other information necessary for voice commands to work. Its XML format makes it easy to understand and work with. In its simplest form it may contain a few commands to navigate users to specific pages within your app. It can grow to be complex as you add phrase lists and support for additional languages.

The following listing shows a simple yet functional VCD file. With the optional words, dozens of variations of the same command can be condensed into a few lines.

Listing 12.14 Sample Voice Command Definition file

```
<?xml version="1.0" encoding="utf-8"?>

<VoiceCommands xmlns="http://schemas.microsoft.com/voicecommands/1.0">
  <CommandSet xml:lang="en-US" Name="EnglishCommands">
```

```
    <CommandPrefix>Speech Sample</CommandPrefix>
    <Example> set voice to Adam</Example>

    <Command Name="ListVoicesCommand">
      <Example> list voices </Example>
      <ListenFor> [and] list [all] [voices] </ListenFor>
      <ListenFor> [and] list [only] {gender} [voices] </ListenFor>
      <ListenFor> [and] list [all] {gender} [voices] </ListenFor>
      <Feedback> Listing Voices... </Feedback>
      <Navigate Target="VoicesList.xaml" />
    </Command>

    <PhraseList Label="gender">
      <Item>male</Item>
      <Item>female</Item>
    </PhraseList>

  </CommandSet>
</VoiceCommands>
```

Name of app as addressed at voice prompt

Commands phone listens for

Page in app commands will be sent to

PhraseLists static or dynamically generated

Note about code samples

The samples for the remaining sections don't create a complete sample app. They are, however, a part of the downloadable code for this chapter, where they are complete and functional.

Please download the code samples to see these examples in action.

To add a VCD file to a project, right-click the project name in the Solution Explorer. Click Add > New Item, as shown in figure 12.3. Choose Voice Command Definition, as shown in figure 12.4. Name it anything you want, but put it in the root folder of your project.

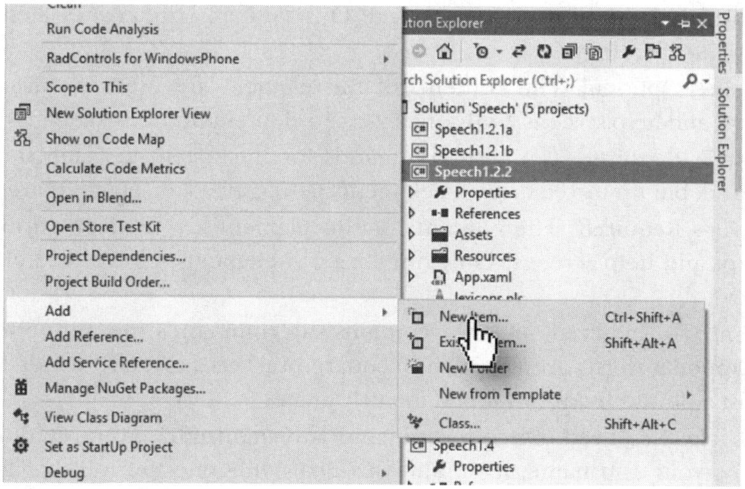

Figure 12.3 Adding a new VCD file to a project

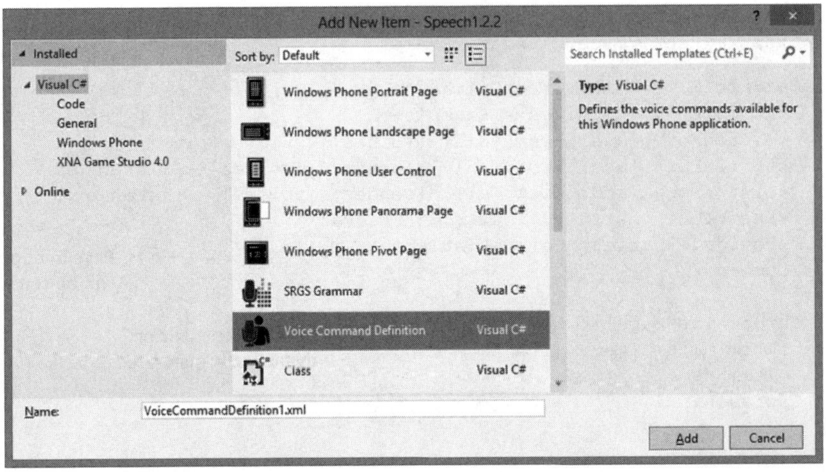

Figure 12.4 Choosing a VCD file

The structure of the VCD file is simple, with only 11 different elements. The following list contains key points about each. Both the preceding sample and the default template when adding a new VCD file to your project contain examples of all these elements in use. Although there aren't many of them, these elements provide the ability to create complex voice commands that account for the multiple ways a command can be given:

- `VoiceCommands`—Required. This is the root element of the document. Can contain as many `CommandSet` elements as required.
- `CommandSet`—Required. It's important for localization to have a `CommandSet` element for each language you want to support. The `xml:lang` attribute is used to specify the locale.
- `CommandPrefix`—Optional. If your app has a long or unpronounceable name, use this element to provide a different name to address your app by. If not set, the display name of your app is used. Only one `CommandPrefix` element per `CommandSet` is allowed.
- `Example`—Optional. The contents of this element are used on various voice prompt and help screens. Only one `Example` element per `CommandSet` is allowed.
- `Command`—Required. Contains commands for the system to listen for. One is required, but up to 100 `Command` elements per `CommandSet` element are allowed.
- `Example`—Required. The contents of this element are used on various voice prompt and help screens. Only one `Example` element per `Command` element is allowed.
- `ListenFor`—Required. This tag contains the commands the phone will listen for. Optional words are wrapped in square brackets (`[]`), and words to match against a phrase list are wrapped in curly braces (`{}`).
- `Feedback`—Required. Once a command is recognized, a confirmation screen displays your app name, icon, and this text. Only one `Example Feedback` per `Command` is allowed.

- `Navigate`—Required. Although the element is required, the `Target` attribute is not. Not setting the `Target` will send users to the default page within the app. Only one `Navigate` element per `Command` is allowed.
- `PhraseList`—Optional. Contains `Item` elements. Can be updated dynamically in code to stay up to date. Must have its `Name` attribute uniquely set. Can be an empty element, but we recommend that it contain at least one `Item element`.
- `Item`—Optional. Contain words or phrases to match command parameters against.

Optional words, phrase lists, and wildcards

Some words, like *and* and *to* are commonly used but can be considered optional in the context of giving commands. Commands like "Set Voice to Adam and Read" can also be said like "Set Voice, Adam. Read" and still have the same meaning. Because of this type of variation in speech patterns, you need to take into account all the ways your users may give commands. To make words in your `ListenFor` elements optional, wrap them in square brackets (`[]`). If the system doesn't detect the word, it won't cause any trouble.

The power of *optional words* can be shown with some simple math. The command `<ListenFor> [and] list [all] [voices] </ListenFor>` contains four optional words (you can say "Open" before the app name, plus the three optional words in the `ListenFor` element). Every optional word doubles the number of possible ways the phrase is said. $2^4 = 16$, so this represents 16 different ways this one command can be successfully interpreted.

Phrase lists, on the other hand, allow you to specify specific words or short phrases that the user can use. A simple list can have one or two entries, like the gender list in the example app, or they can be longer, like the voice list in the same app. To use a phrase list in a `ListenFor` element, wrap the name of the `PhraseList` element in curly braces (`{}`). In the example `<ListenFor> [and] list [all] {gender} [voices] </ListenFor>`, the phrase list being addressed is `gender` and is wrapped in curly braces. One additional place you can use phrase lists is within the `Feedback` element. The only gotcha with using it there is that all `ListenFor` elements within the command must use the phrase list. The sample app contains an example of this.

You can create as many phrase lists as you need, but keep in mind that you're limited to 2000 phrase items across all phrase lists in a `CommandSet` element. Be sure to remember this limit when updating phrase lists via code because you can reach this limit quickly if you're working with large datasets. Exceeding this limit will cause your application to throw a `System.Exception` when it tries to load the phrase list.

Wildcards give you the ability to detect additional input as part of the command. They look like `{*}` and are used with standard command words and phrase lists. The detected input is available with the rest of the input in the returned object.

Now that you have an understanding of the VCD file, let's look at how this file is used in an application.

12.4.2 Enabling voice commands

Once your voice commands are defined, you're ready to register them with the phone, which is how it knows that the app is capable of accepting voice commands. Without registering your VCDs, the only thing your user can do via voice is open the app and nothing more.

> **Note on emulator versus device**
>
> One notable point of frustration may be getting the emulator to successfully recognize what you're saying. The sensitivity of the microphone can be an issue. Even minor shuffling in the background may be enough to cause it to fail. Adjusting the microphone sensitivity and volume can help, but the room may still need to be fairly quiet. Once the application is deployed to a device, things will likely be completely different. The phone will recognize the commands every time, even with music playing in the background.
>
> Keep this in mind if you're experiencing issues with your commands not working consistently. If you don't have access to a device to test on, the emulator will work but may require adjusting your microphone and working in a quiet room.

The first step in enabling voice commands is to register the VCD file by calling the `InstallCommandSetsFromFileAsync` method of the `VoiceCommandService` class. This method takes a `URI` object as its only parameter. In order for the app to correctly register the file, you must use the `ms-appx://` prefix on the file path. Place this call inside a function with the `async` modifier, using the `await` operator on the call itself. You do this to ensure that the file is registered before you make any attempt to update the phrase list, because doing so would cause an error. Registering the VCD file is correctly implemented in the following listing.

Listing 12.15 Registering a VCD file

```
using Windows.Phone.Speech.VoiceCommands;
private async void RegisterVoiceCommands()
{
        await VoiceCommandService.InstallCommandSetsFromFileAsync(
                new Uri("ms-appx:///VoiceCommands.xml",
                UriKind.RelativeOrAbsolute));
       UpdatePhraseList("EnglishCommands", "voice");
}
```

You can place the `RegisterVoiceCommands()` call as the last item of the MainPage.xaml.cs constructor. Another approach is to place the call to `InstallCommandSetsFromFileAsync` in the `Application_Launching` event in `App.xaml.cs` instead. If you do, remember to add the `async` modifier to the `Application_Launching` event.

You detect when a voice command is used to open the app by looking at `NavigationContext.QueryString` for the key `"voiceCommandName"` using the `ContainsKey` method. If it exists, then the app was opened with a voice command,

and you then use a `Switch` (or an `If` block if you prefer) to execute code specific to the command. Data passed via voice commands is also found in `NavigationContext.QueryString` and can be used as needed. Table 12.2 shows the contents of the `NavigationContext.QueryString` array when a voice command is used to open the app. The commands and phrase lists referenced are defined in the VCD file in the sample app.

Table 12.2 Contents of the NavigationContext.QueryString array when a voice command opens the app

Key	Value
`voiceCommandName`	`"SetVoiceCommand"`
`reco`	`"start Speech Sample set voice to Adam read"`
`action`	`"read"`
`voice`	`"Adam"`

In table 12.2 we gave the command "Speech Sample, set voice to Adam. Read." In the VCD file, you defined the `SetVoiceCommand` command to listen for several variations of the same command using multiple `ListenFor` elements. The one that was recognized is this one: `[and] set [voice] [to] {voice} [and] {action}`. Comparing the command recognized to the table of values returned to the app shows both the `voice` and `action` phrase list items it recognized.

12.4.3 Phrase lists

As shown in listing 12.14, in a VCD file phrase lists let you specify lists of words and phrases to be detected in voice commands. Lists that don't change, such as gender, are best defined in the VCD file. If the phrase list changes or is unknown until runtime, then define it in the VCD file and update it in code.

You update a phrase list in two steps. As shown in listing 12.16, first create a `VoiceCommandSet` object from `VoiceCommandService.InstalledCommandSets` using the `CommandSet Name` as the key. Then, with the `VoiceCommandSet` object, call its `UpdatePhraseListAsync` method, passing the name of the phrase list to update and a list of strings to use. When you call this method, you're replacing the contents of the phrase list with new contents. If you need to keep the existing items, you need to include them in the list when updating.

Listing 12.16 Updating a phrase list

```
private async void UpdatePhraseList(string commandSetName,
                                     string phraseListName)
{
        List<string> voiceNames = new List<string>();
        foreach (VoiceInformation voice in _availableVoices)
        {
```

```
            string voiceName = voice.DisplayName.Split(' ')[1];
            voiceNames.Add(voiceName);
        }                                                        Get VoiceCommandSet
        VoiceCommandSet commandSet =                                    to update
            VoiceCommandService.InstalledCommandSets[commandSetName];  <--
Update phrase list
with list of strings -->
        await commandSet.UpdatePhraseListAsync(phraseListName, voiceNames);
    }
```

12.4.4 Localization

When discussing VCD files earlier in this section, we noted that the `CommandSet` is used to specify the locale. In listing 12.17, the `xml:lang` attribute of the only `CommandSet` element is set to `en-US`. If you were to set the locale of the phone or emulator to any other locale, none of the commands would work and your app wouldn't appear in the list of voice-enabled apps. For this reason it's important to include a `CommandSet` element setup for each region you require support for. In some countries you may need to support more than one language, such as the United States (English and Spanish) and Canada (English and French).

Listing 12.17 Sample VCD file

```
<?xml version="1.0" encoding="utf-8"?>

<VoiceCommands xmlns="http://schemas.microsoft.com/voicecommands/1.0">
  <CommandSet xml:lang="en-US" Name="EnglishCommands">        <-- Phone set to
    <CommandPrefix>Speech Sample</CommandPrefix>                  this language
    <Example> set voice to Adam</Example>
    ...
```

> **Translating commands to other languages**
>
> When creating voice commands in languages you don't speak, try to resist the urge to use an online translator. Every language has its own nuances and ways of saying things. Using one may lead to incorrect commands that make no sense to users. Instead, try to locate a native speaker of the language and have them provide you with the required translations. By asking friends, family, or other developers or searching online, you should be able to find good translations of your commands.

Because voice commands are triggered by the phone's operating system, users will see a number of screens. Some of these screens can be customized to be useful to users, and some can't. Let's look at these screens.

12.4.5 Voice UI screens

Windows Phone provides a number of screens related to speech that are a part of the phone's user experience. The first time you use voice commands, you're presented with the screen shown in figure 12.5, which informs you that to use some speech features you must agree to send some information to Microsoft, including the words it recognizes, contact names, and other data. If you accept, all features are enabled. If you decline,

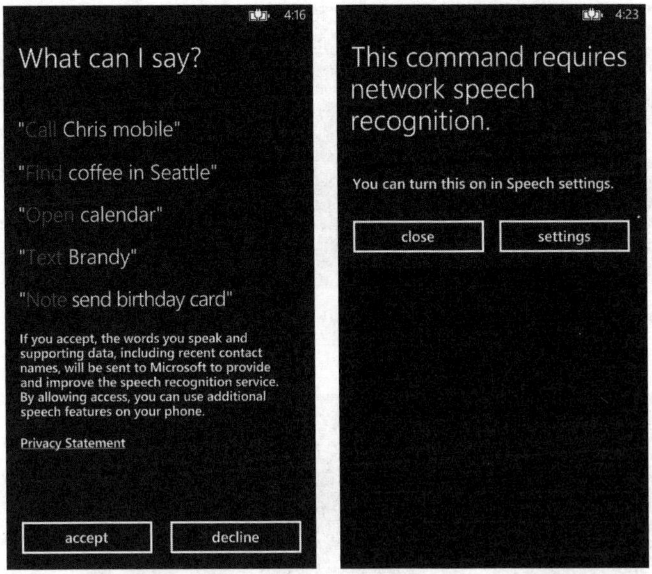

Figure 12.5 Permission voice UI screens

you'll still be able to use voice commands to call contacts and launch apps, but features such as texting, searching, and sending voice commands to apps aren't enabled. Attempting to use one of these features after saying no results in the error message also shown in figure 12.5. To use the features, tap the Settings button to open the Speech Settings page, and check the Enable Speech Recognition Service check box.

Figure 12.6 Voice prompt UI screens

Holding the Start button brings up the Listening prompt. Providing no speech or unrecognized speech results in a messages informing you of the problem, shown in figure 12.6. Successful recognition of your app name results in the Starting screen shown in figure 12.7. When you give your application a voice command, the screen displays the content you set in the feedback element if the command is recognized, as shown in figure 12.8. If you use

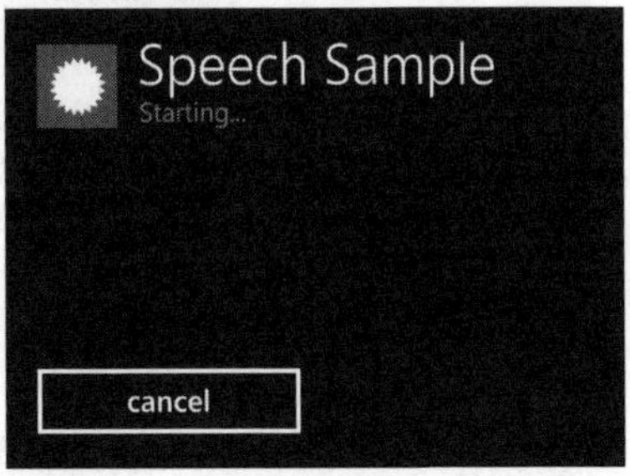

Figure 12.7 Opening app from voice prompt

Figure 12.8 Voice prompt command recognized

Figure 12.9 Voice Help screens

a phrase in a command and set the phrase set in the feedback element, the recognized phrase is displayed.

The last set of the voice-related screens, shown in figure 12.9, is the Help screens. At the voice prompt you can say, "What can I say?" or tap the question mark to bring up the "What can I say?" screen. This screen contains sample voice commands and a list of apps that support voice commands. The value you set in the `Example` element of the `CommandSet` element in the VCD file is displayed here. Tapping an app name brings up the "Did you know?" screen, shown in figure 12.10, which shows all examples found in the VCD file. A link to this page is also displayed when the app name is recognized but not the command (figure 12.9).

Figure 12.10 Voice Help screens for an application

Now that you know how to make the phone talk and are able to send commands to your application, it's time to look at speech recognition.

12.5 Speech recognition

Speech recognition for Windows Phone 8 gives you the ability to listen for and process verbal input from users. You can use this input to perform actions such as changing settings, triggering buttons, or almost anything else you can think of. In this section we'll look at speech grammars, speech recognizers with and without the system UI, and handling speech recognition results and errors.

> **TIP** Use of speech recognition requires that the `ID_CAP_SPEECH_RECOGNITION`, `ID_CAP_MICROPHONE`, and `ID_CAP_NETWORKING` capabilities be declared in WMAppManifest.xml.

Speech recognition within an app can be done with or without the speech recognition UI screens provided by the Windows Phone OS. In some apps using the provided screens is preferred because it helps retain a consistent feel between your app and the phone. In other apps where this isn't so important, you may decide to provide your own UI that follows the design of your app. The next listing shows a simple example of prompting the user for verbal input using the system-provided speech UI screens. Once the user says their phrase, the detected text is displayed to the user on screen and in a `MessageBox`.

Listing 12.18 Recognizing speech

```
using Windows.Phone.Speech.Recognition;
using System.Threading.Tasks;

SpeechRecognizerUI speechRecognizerUI = new SpeechRecognizerUI();
private async Task RecognizeSpeech()
{
    speechRecognizerUI.Settings.ListenText = "Say your phrase...";
    speechRecognizerUI.Settings.ExampleText = "What's going on?";
    speechRecognizerUI.Settings.ReadoutEnabled = false;
    speechRecognizerUI.Settings.ShowConfirmation = false;
    SpeechRecognitionUIResult recognitionResult =
            await speechRecognizerUI.RecognizeWithUIAsync();
    Dispatcher.BeginInvoke(
            delegate
                {
                    DetectedTextTextBox.Text =
                        recognitionResult.RecognitionResult.Text;
                });
    MessageBox.Show(recognitionResult.RecognitionResult.Text);
}
```

Text to display on voice prompt screen (ListenText, ExampleText)

Detected text isn't verbally repeated (ReadoutEnabled)

Confirmation screen isn't displayed (ShowConfirmation)

Prevent cross-thread exceptions when updating UI (Dispatcher.BeginInvoke)

By setting `ListenText`, `ExampleText`, `ReadoutEnabled`, and `ShowConfirmation` on the `SpeechRecognizerUI` object, you can customize the system speech UI screens with content useful to the user. To customize what the phone will listen for, you'll need to use speech grammars.

> **Note about code samples**
>
> The samples for the remaining sections do not create a complete sample app. They are, however, a part of the downloadable code for this chapter, where they are complete and functional.
>
> Please download the code samples to see these examples in action.

12.5.1 Grammars

Speech grammars are lists of words or phrases the speech recognizer uses to determine what you're saying. Some grammars require internet access to function because they're so large that they won't fit on the phone. Other grammars are defined by the application developer and contain only specific commands or phrases. This second kind of grammar can be generated by the application or defined in advance for use without requiring internet access.

Windows Phone provides three methods of adding grammars to the speech recognizer:

- `AddGrammarFromPredefinedType` is used to add one of the two predefined grammars described in the next section.
- `AddGrammarFromList` is used to add list of strings stored in an `IEnumerable<string>` object.
- `AddGrammarFromUri` is used to add grammars from a Speech Recognition Grammar Specification (SRGS) file stored either locally or remotely.

Once you've loaded a grammar, it's used when trying to recognize speech input. If you only load one, it will be the one used. If you load several grammars, you can use the `enabled` property to turn the use of specific grammars on and off. The following listing shows how to enable and disable grammars.

Listing 12.19 Turning a grammar on and off

```
private async Task AskForColor()
{
        speechRecognizerUI.Settings.ListenText = "Which color?";
        speechRecognizerUI.Settings.ExampleText =
                        @"'Red', 'Blue', 'Green', 'Yellow',
                        'Purple', 'Orange', 'Black', 'White'";
        speechRecognizerUI.Settings.ReadoutEnabled = false;
        speechRecognizerUI.Settings.ShowConfirmation = false;
        speechRecognizerUI.Recognizer.Grammars["voicesList"]
                                              .Enabled = false;
       speechRecognizerUI.Recognizer.Grammars["colorList"]
                                              .Enabled = true;
        SpeechRecognitionUIResult result = await
                        speechRecognizerUI.RecognizeWithUIAsync();

        SetColorFromCommand(result.RecognitionResult.Text);
}
```

Display text on voice prompt screen

Detected text isn't verbally repeated

Confirmation screen isn't displayed

Disable voicesList, enable colorList

Call method to use detected color

PREDEFINED GRAMMARS

There are two predefined grammars available as part of the Speech API. Both are too large to be stored on the phone and are found through the web service the phone calls to access them. The first one, the *Dictation* grammar, is a free text grammar that can understand the most varying text. The *webSearch* grammar is optimized for web searches.

Both grammars work best with short phrases and become less accurate the longer the input is. Utilizing either of these grammars requires that the user allow the Speech Recognition Service internet access. The user will be asked for permission by the phone at the screens in figure 12.5.

When using speech recognition, if you don't specify any grammars, the Dictation grammar is used by default. Because this requires the internet, if it isn't available, neither is speech recognition in your app, and the user will be told the phone can't access the network.

> **TIP** If you add a predefined grammar to the speech recognizer, it must be the only grammar. You can add either a Dictation or webSearch grammar, but not both, and no other type of grammar can be added.

The following listings show how the Dictation and webSearch grammars are loaded.

Listing 12.20 Adding Dictation grammar

```
speechRecognizerUI.Recognizer.Grammars.AddGrammarFromPredefinedType(
                    "defaultGrammar", SpeechPredefinedGrammar.Dictation);
```

Listing 12.21 Adding webSearch grammar

```
speechRecognizerUI.Recognizer.Grammars.AddGrammarFromPredefinedType(
                    "webSearchGrammar",
    SpeechPredefinedGrammar.WebSearch);
```

Using these kinds of grammars is perfect for applications that take notes or search, but some applications need to know only a smaller set of phases or words. For these cases there are list grammars.

LIST GRAMMARS

When you know the phrases your app needs to recognize, creating a list grammar is the best way to go. List grammars are defined on the phone and don't require internet access to work, making them available all the time.

> **TIP** You can add multiple list grammars to a speech recognizer as long as no predefined grammars are added to it. You can add multiple list and SRGS grammars to the same speech recognizer without issue.

List grammars are most useful when you have a list of items such as songs, movie titles, names, or places that you need recognized. If you can get the list into any `IEnumerable<string>` list, you can define it as a list grammar. The next listing shows a simple function that takes a key name and a list of strings and adds it to a `SpeechRecognizerUI` defined elsewhere. It can be used to load a list of strings as a list grammar.

Listing 12.22 Adding a list grammar

```
private void LoadListGrammar(string key, IEnumerable<string> listOfItems )
{
        speechRecognizerUI.Recognizer.Grammars.AddGrammarFromList(
                                                            key, listOfItems);
}
```

List grammars are the best choice when the data needed to build an `IEnumerable<string>` should be on the phone and an internet connection isn't required to create it. Predefined grammars require internet access to facilitate the recognition of input, whereas list grammars don't. Keep this in mind when creating voice-enabled apps because you can't guarantee internet access all the time. If you can avoid relying on internet access, it's best to do so, to avoid features that only work part of the time.

SPEECH RECOGNITION GRAMMAR SPECIFICATION

Speech Recognition Grammar Specification (SRGS) is an XML format for specifying grammar. It allows you to set up rules to specify the order of words, which lists to pick words from, and optional words. You can also define alternate words to use and alternate pronunciations of words.

Because covering SRGS would take an entire chapter unto itself, we don't go into any depth on this topic. MSDN provides extensive documentation on creating grammar with SRGS as well as a markup reference. For more information, see the following:

- *SRGS Grammar XML Reference*—http://mng.bz/N39n
- *How to Create a Basic XML Grammar*—http://mng.bz/sms3
- *Speech Recognition Grammar Specification Version 1.0*—http://mng.bz/gusU

Because it's likely that some list or SRGS grammars will be large and may take time to load, if you don't preload them, the first time the user uses speech recognition in your app the grammar will load and make the user wait while it does. You can avoid this by calling the `PreloadGrammarsAsync` method within the `Recognizer` property in your `SpeechRecognizer` object.

With an understanding of how to define what an app listens for, let's look at how to use this and prompt the user for input.

12.5.2 Speech recognizers

As a developer, you have two choices when you want to prompt the user for input: `SpeechRecognizer` and `SpeechRecognizerUI`. `SpeechRecognizerUI` provides the system voice prompt screens, as shown earlier (in section 12.4.5), but customized with contextual info you provide. Using this recognizer requires the least amount of setup and adds the advantage of making your app feel like it's a part of the system. `SpeechRecognizer` doesn't provide you with any UI screens to help your users know what's going on. It's up to you to provide an interface that's helpful to your users.

Several customization options are available in `SpeechRecognizerUI` to provide useful info and feedback to users. You access these settings, listed in table 12.3, via the `Settings` property of `SpeechRecognizerUI`.

Table 12.3 Properties for customizing user experience when using the `SpeechRecognizerUI`

Property	Description
`ListenText`	Gets/sets the heading text on the Listening screen. If not set, the default is "Listening."
`ExampleText`	Gets/sets the example text on the Listening screen. If not set, no example is displayed, although this may not be ideal.
`ShowConfirmation`	Gets/sets whether the Heard You Say screen is shown after successfully recognizing the input.
`ReadoutEnabled`	Gets/sets whether the recognized test is read back when the Heard You Say screen is displayed. Has no effect if `ShowConfirmation` is `false`.

If you're going to be creating your own user interface for voice prompts and other screens, you'll use the `SpeechRecognizer` class instead. Listing 12.23 shows an example of the use of the `SpeechRecognizer` class. It's similar to using `SpeechRecognizerUI` except no UI is displayed, and it's up to you to implement one for the user. It's a part of the downloadable code for this chapter.

Listing 12.23 `SpeechRecognizer` example

```
private async Task AskForColor()
{
        SpeechRecognizerUI speechRecognizerUi = new SpeechRecognizerUI();
        SpeechRecognizer speechRecognizer = speechRecognizerUi.Recognizer;
        speechRecognizer.Grammars.AddGrammarFromList(
                                           "colorList", _colorNames);

        PromptTextBox.Text = "Which color?";
        ExampleTextBox.Text =
             "'Red', 'Blue', 'Green', 'Yellow',
              'Purple', 'Orange', 'Black', 'White'";
        _speechSynthesizer.SpeakTextAsync( "Which color?");

        SpeechRecognitionResult result =
                        await speechRecognizer.RecognizeAsync();
        if ((int)result.TextConfidence <
                       (int)SpeechRecognitionConfidence.Medium)
        {
                Dispatcher.BeginInvoke(
                        () => PromptTextBox.Text =
                                    "Recognition Confidence too low.");
                _speechSynthesizer.SpeakTextAsync(
"Recognition Confidence too low. Please try again.");
                await AskForColor();
        }
```

Annotations: **Load list of colors** (AddGrammarFromList); **Prompt user for input** (ExampleTextBox); **Verbally prompt user for input** (SpeakTextAsync); **Wait for user input** (RecognizeAsync); **Verify SpeechRecognitionConfidence** (TextConfidence check); **If not high enough, tell user to try again** (low-confidence messages).

```
        else
        {
            SetColorFromCommand(result.Text);
            PromptTextBox.Text = "Color set to " + result.Text;
            _speechSynthesizer.SpeakTextAsync(
                                    "Color set to " + result.Text);
        }
}
```

Use detected input, provide feedback

As you can see, when using `SpeechRecognizer` you need to provide some visual or audible indicator so the user knows when to speak. By using `SpeechRecognizerUI`, you can skip that and use the voice UI screens and prompts discussed in the next section.

12.5.3 Prompts, confirmation, and choice screens

When you use the `SpeechRecognizerUI` class, one of the advantages is having a standardized user experience. This experience is provided by a set of standard pages your user will see and, if they've used voice on their phone before, recognize.

When using the built-in screens, the user will see four different screens. The Listening screen (figure 12.11) is shown when the `RecognizeWithUIAsync` method is called and the phone is waiting for the user to speak. It can be customized using the `ListenText` and `ExampleText` properties.

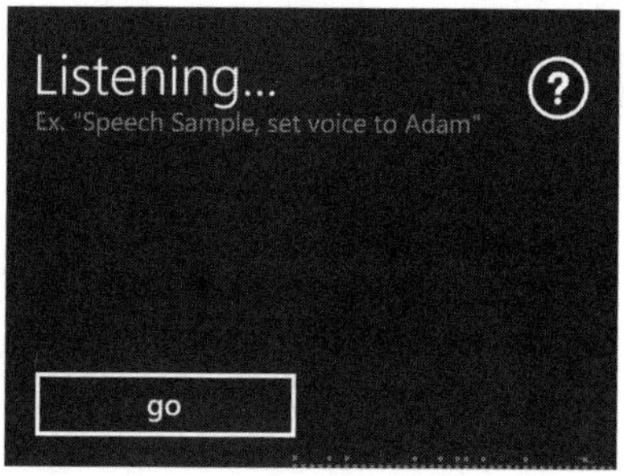

Figure 12.11 The Listening screen

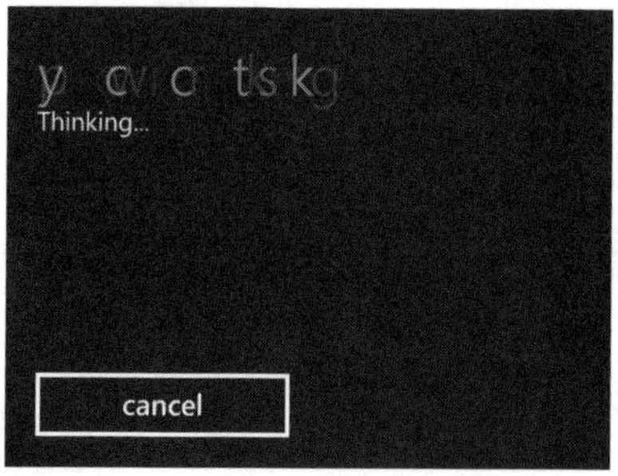

Figure 12.12 The Thinking screen

If you're using dictation or web search grammar, the Thinking screen (figure 12.12) is shown while the phone is calling its web service to retrieve recognition results.

The Heard You Say screen (figure 12.13) is shown when the `ShowConfirmation` property is set to `true`. The results can be read to the user as well if the `ReadoutEnabled` property is set to `true`.

Figure 12.13 The Heard You Say screen

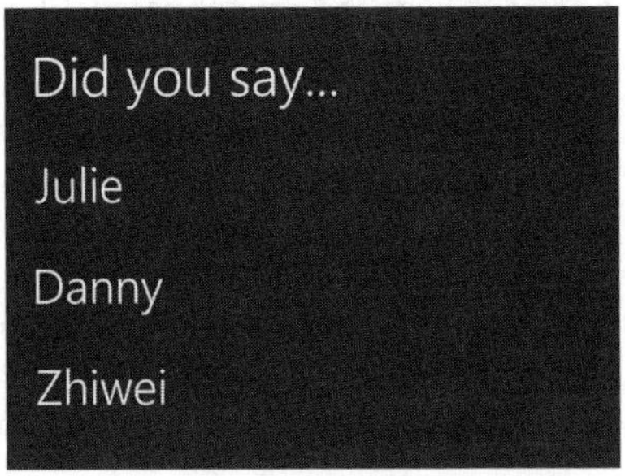

If the results match more than one item in a list or SRGS grammar, the Did You Say screen (figure 12.14) is shown, prompting the user for more input. If the ReadoutEnabled property is set to true, the phone will read out the possible matches.

Figure 12.14 The Did You Say screen

The Error screen (figure 12.15) is shown when the phone can't determine what was said. The header text says, "Sorry, didn't catch that." The screen allows the user to try again by tapping the Speak button.

Figure 12.15 The Error screen

Using these standard screens helps your app retain the feel of the operating system and, if configured correctly, provides everything the user needs to know about what your app is asking for. Once they provide the requested verbal input, you can access the detected results and use them as required. Let's take a look at how that's done.

12.5.4 Handling recognition results

When you use the `RecognizeWithUIAsync` or `RecognizeAsync` methods to recognize speech, you do so using the `await` operator because there's no event to listen for when the recognition is complete. You must await the results and immediately assign them to a results object.

If you use the `SpeechRecognizer` class, the results are returned as a `SpeechRecognitionResult` object. If you use a `SpeechRecognizerUI`, the results are a `SpeechRecognitionUIResult` object. Both contain all the same information, but the results in `SpeechRecognitionUIResult` are found one level deep in the `RecognitionResult` property.

After the `RecognizeAsync` or `RecognizeWithUIAsync` method returns with a successful result object, you'll find several properties with details of the recognized speech. The results object also contains a method called `GetAlternates` that returns a collection of speech-recognition objects in descending order of confidence. When accessing the returned collection, use the `ToList` method to make the contents useable. Table 12.4 shows the properties found in the `SpeechRecognitionResult` and `SpeechRecognitionUIResult` objects.

Table 12.4 Properties of `SpeechRecognitionResult` and `SpeechRecognitionUIResult`

Property	Description
`Details`	Contains additional info about the recognition results, including the `ConfidenceScore`.
`RuleName`	The SRGS rule element that was triggered to return the recognized phrase. If a list grammar is used, this property contains the key of the list grammar as a string.
`Semantics`	Contains a dictionary of the properties of a recognized phrase in an SRGS grammar.
`Text`	Contains a string of the recognized phrase.
`TextConfidence`	Contains a `SpeechRecognitionConfidence` enumeration value of `High`, `Medium`, `Low`, or `rejected`.

Once you have a result object, you should check the result to make sure it was understood by the speech-recognition system. You can use the `TextConfidence` property to verify that you have good results, as shown in listing 12.24. The best results come back as `High`, but `Medium` is still a good result. If you get `Low` confidence, you'll want to try again, as you would with rejected results.

Listing 12.24 Checking the `TextConfidence` property

```
SpeechRecognitionResult result =                Wait for input, store in result object
                  await speechRecognizer.RecognizeAsync();
if (result.TextConfidence < SpeechRecognitionConfidence.Medium)
{                                               Verify SpeechRecognition-
    FillUi(result);                             Confidence is high enough
    Dispatcher.BeginInvoke(() =>
        PromptTextBlock.Text =
            "Recognition Confidence too low.");
    _speechSynthesizer.SpeakTextAsync(
        "Recognition Confidence too low. Please try again.");
}                                               If not, tell user
else                                            to try again
{
    SetColorFromCommand(result.Text);
    PromptTextBlock.Text = "Color set to " + result.Text;
    FillUi(result);                             Defined elsewhere in project
    _speechSynthesizer.SpeakTextAsync("Color set to " + result.Text);
}
```

Annotations: "Defined elsewhere in project" (FillUi(result) in the if block); "Use detected input and provide feedback" (SetColorFromCommand, PromptTextBlock.Text, _speechSynthesizer.SpeakTextAsync in the else block).

Under normal circumstances, the input provided by the user will be detected and usable by your app. But sometimes something goes wrong, and you have to have to deal with those situations. In the next section we look at speech-specific error handling.

12.5.5 Handling errors

Errors occur when the unexpected happens and should be caught by wrapping your code in a `try-catch` block. Most errors generated by the speech synthesis engine are in HResult format with a code you can test for, although you may encounter managed exceptions. The exceptions in table 12.5 and the errors in table 12.6 represent only the ones generated by speech synthesis. Other areas of the Speech API generate additional errors, but handling them is the same, no matter where they're generated.

Table 12.5 Managed exceptions

Exception	Description
InvalidFormatException	An SSML prompt file referenced by a speech synthesizer has an invalid format.
InvalidOperationException	An operation is already in progress.
FileNotFoundException	An SSML prompt file referenced by a speech synthesizer can't be found.
UnauthorizedAccessException	A capability required by speech recognition hasn't been set.

Table 12.6 Error codes

Error	Error code	Description
SPERR_SYSTEM_CALL_INTERRUPTED	0x80045508	A speech operation was aborted by a system call—for example, fast app switching or an incoming phone call.
SPERR_WINRT_INTERNAL_ERROR	0x800455A0	Generic error that's not actionable by developers.
SPERR_WINRT_ALREADY_IN_LEX	0x800455A1	The word, pronunciation, or POS pair being added is already in lexicon.
SPERR_WINRT_NOT_IN_LEX	0x800455A2	The word doesn't exist in the lexicon.
SPERR_WINRT_UNSUPPORTED_PHONEME	0x800455B5	Unknown phoneme.
SPERR_WINRT_PHONEME_CONVERSION	0x800455B6	Can't convert the phonemes to the specified phonetic alphabet.
SPERR_WINRT_LEX_INVALID_DATA	0x800455B8	The lexicon data is invalid or corrupted.
SPERR_WINRT_UNSUPPORTED_LANG	0x800455BC	The requested language isn't supported.
SPERR_WINRT_STRING_TOO_LONG	0x800455BD	The string is too long.
SPERR_WINRT_STRING_EMPTY	0x800455BE	The string can't be empty.
SPERR_WINRT_NO_MORE_ITEMS	0x800455BF	When enumerating items, the requested index is greater than the count of items.

You can determine the type of error by comparing the HResult property of the exception object to known error codes. The returned error code is cast to an unsigned integer and compared to the known error codes. For the sake of readability, it's a good idea to declare known error codes as `uint` variables with descriptive names. You can declare these above the constructor with the other properties or within an error-handling function.

In listing 12.25, after declaring the integer property for the `SPERR_WINRT_STRING_TOO_LONG` error, you use an `if` block to check and display a message. Because mobile apps tend to be smaller, this may be an ideal solution. More complex applications may need a more robust error-handling system.

Listing 12.25 Checking an error code

```
const uint StringTooLongHResult = 0x800455BD;                    // SPERR_WINRT_STRING_TOO_LONG error
private async void SaySsml_Click(object sender, RoutedEventArgs e)
{
        try
        {
                // CODE                                           // Code causes error
        }
        catch (Exception ex)
        {
                if ((uint)ex.HResult == StringTooLongHResult)
                {
                        MessageBox.Show(ex.Message,
                                "SPERR_WINRT_STRING_TOO_LONG",
                                MessageBoxButton.OK);             // Check for exception, display MessageBox
                }
                else                                              // Catch all other exceptions
                {
                        MessageBox.Show(ex.Message,
                                    ex.GetType().ToString(),
                                            MessageBoxButton.OK);
                }
        }
}
```

Handling speech errors is like handling errors in general. How you do it elsewhere is likely to work for speech, as well as long as you're aware of the `HResult` error codes you may encounter. You can find a complete list of error codes relating to the Speech API at http://mng.bz/4j02.

12.6 Summary

To get speech up and running quickly, remember three important classes and their main functions: Use `SpeakTextAsync` in the `SpeechSynthesizer` class to talk to the user with minimal configuration. Register VCD files with the `InstallCommandSetsFromFileAsync` method in the `VoiceCommandService` class to enable sending voice commands to your app. Use the `RecognizeWithUIAsync` method in `SpeechRecognizerUI` to use speech recognition within your app. All three areas of speech are easy to use and can be added to an existing app in a few hours.

When deciding whether to add speech features to your application, start with which one would benefit your users the most. Providing verbal feedback or help prompts for the user brings your app to life. Launching commonly used functions within your app from the voice prompt speeds up repetitive actions and brings your application more into the daily lives of your user. Once in your app, continuing the speech abilities already in the phone's operating systems creates a continuous user experience that, if done right, will set your app apart from the pack.

Part 3

XAML for Windows Phone

Even though XAML for Windows Phone is similar to Silverlight for the browser, and by extension to Windows Presentation Foundation, there are new controls and concepts found only in the Windows Phone SDK. In part 3, you'll learn how to use new XAML features to build applications that match the look and feel of Windows Phone.

Although you've used the `ApplicationBar` and `Pivot` controls in sample applications throughout this book, this part takes a deep dive into these new controls. Chapter 13 explains features of the application bar that you haven't seen yet, such as dynamically enabling and disabling buttons and menu items, as well as learning how to display pop-up context menus. Chapter 14 shows you all the ins and outs of the `Pivot` control, and you'll also learn about the `Panorama` control, an essential ingredient for building hub-style user interfaces.

In chapters 15, 16, and 17 you'll work with the `MediaElement`, `Map`, and `WebBrowser` controls. You'll also learn how to use the Location Service and Map launchers to make a location-aware application. We wrap up the book in chapter 18 with a discussion on how to publish your application to the Windows Phone Store and earn revenue with advertisements and in-app purchases.

13 ApplicationBar and context menus

This chapter covers

- Working with the application bar
- Dynamically changing buttons
- Displaying a context menu

The Windows Phone comes with its own edition of the XAML framework found in WPF, Silverlight, and Windows 8. This means that if you know how to build XAML applications, you know how to build Windows Phone applications. By this point in the book, you've already used many of the XAML controls in the Windows Phone SDK. This chapter is the first of six chapters that take a closer look at XAML controls and discuss how to use them on the phone platform.

Windows Phone has redefined how an application displays a toolbar and menu. Applications use the new `ApplicationBar` control to show up to four shortcut icons for the most common operations on the page. If additional options are available but don't fit in the bar containing shortcuts, or a different level of granularity must be provided, developers can add textual menu items as well. In this chapter we cover how to create a basic menu that can be used in your applications.

We venture beyond the standard Windows Phone SDK and show how to implement a context menu with a set of controls from the Windows Phone Toolkit. The Windows Phone Toolkit `ContextMenu` mimics the tap-and-hold context menu behavior seen in many of the built-in phone applications.

You've used the `ApplicationBar` control throughout the book, including in several examples in earlier chapters, but your use of these controls was basic. In this chapter we take a deeper look at `ApplicationBar` and `Pivot` controls and introduce the `ContextMenu` control. We accomplish this with a sample application that demonstrates features of the application bar we haven't discussed, such as disabling buttons and menu items, dynamically adding and removing items, and using different display modes.

13.1 Working with the ApplicationBar

The `ApplicationBar` is the new toolbar and menu paradigm created for the Windows Phone. It provides a toolbar for buttons with an expandable menu. The application bar is always placed at the bottom of the screen in portrait orientation and on the side of the screen in landscape orientation (see figure 13.1). The application bar is usually associated with a page and isn't global to the application.

NOTE If you want to reuse the same application bar on multiple pages, you can declare an `ApplicationBar` as a resource in your project's App.xaml file and then assign it to a page's `ApplicationBar` property using the `StaticResource` markup extension.

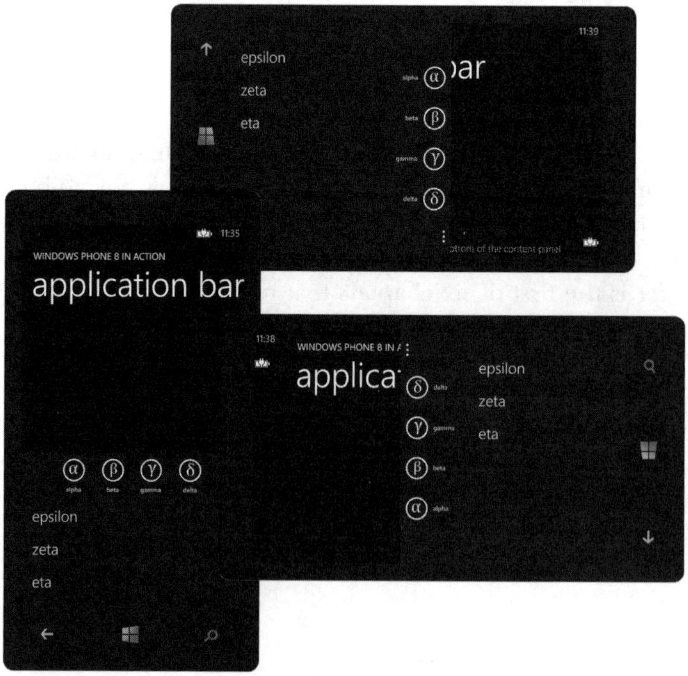

Figure 13.1 The application bar with expanded menu in portrait, landscape left, and landscape right orientations

The application bar is always positioned on the side of the screen where the Start button lives. Tapping the three dots at the edge of the application bar expands it to show the defined menu items. There are a maximum of 4 buttons and 50 menu items.

13.1.1 Building an application bar

We'll use a new sample application to demonstrate using an application bar in a XAML application. Create a new project, named ApplicationBar, using the Windows Phone App project template. Once the project is created, open up MainPage.xaml and add the markup declaring a new application bar. The following listing shows the XAML used to declare the application bar shown in figure 13.1.

Listing 13.1 Declaring application bar buttons and menu items

```
<phone:PhoneApplicationPage.ApplicationBar>
    <shell:ApplicationBar>
        <shell:ApplicationBar.MenuItems>
            <shell:ApplicationBarMenuItem Text="epsilon"
                Click="item_Clicked" />
            <shell:ApplicationBarMenuItem Text="zeta"
                Click="item_Clicked"/>
            <shell:ApplicationBarMenuItem Text="eta"
                Click="item_Clicked"/>
        </shell:ApplicationBar.MenuItems>
        <shell:ApplicationBarIconButton
            IconUri="/Assets/AppBar/alpha.png"
            Text="alpha" Click="item_Clicked" />
        <shell:ApplicationBarIconButton
            IconUri="/Assets/AppBar/beta.png"
            Text="beta" Click="item_Clicked" />
        <shell:ApplicationBarIconButton
            IconUri="/Assets/AppBar/gamma.png"
            Text="gamma" Click="item_Clicked"/>
        <shell:ApplicationBarIconButton
            IconUri="/Assets/AppBar/delta.png"
            Text="delta" Click="item_Clicked" />
    </shell:ApplicationBar>
</phone:PhoneApplicationPage.ApplicationBar>
```

❶ Create application bar

❷ Add menu items to collection

❸ Add buttons to content

An application bar is created as a property of the `PhoneApplicationPage` using XAML's property element syntax ❶. An application bar is represented by the `ApplicationBar` class, found in the `Microsoft.Phone.Shell` namespace, which is aliased in XAML as `shell`. The `ApplicationBar` contains two collection properties named `Buttons` and `MenuItems`. The `MenuItems` collection is populated by declaring `ApplicationBarMenuItem` objects inside the `MenuItems` element ❷. The `Buttons` collection is populated by declaring `ApplicationBarIconButton` objects as the content of the `ApplicationBar` ❸.

The `ApplicationBarIconButton` class exposes `IconUri`, `Text`, and `IsEnabled` properties. `IconUri` must be provided and is a relative `Uri` to an image file that's been added to the project with a build action of `Content`. We discuss image files later in the chapter. The `Text` property is also required.

NOTE The alpha.png, beta.png, gamma.png, and delta.png files used in listing 13.1 can be found in this book's sample code. You can download the sample code from Manning's website at www.manning.com/binkley.

The `ApplicationBarMenuItem` class has only `Text` and `IsEnabled` properties. The `Text` property is required, and a value must be specified when the menu item is declared.

`ApplicationBarIconButton` and `ApplicationBarMenuItem` both provide a `Click` event that can be wired up to an event handler in XAML. The `Click` events are basic event handlers and don't send a `RoutedEventArgs` or any other custom `EventArgs` type. If you need to know which button or menu item was clicked, you can use the event handler's `sender` parameter. In listing 13.1, the same `Click` event handler was wired up to each of the buttons and menu items. In the following listing, the `Click` event handler is implemented.

Listing 13.2 `Click` event handler for application bar items

```
void item_Clicked(object sender, EventArgs e)
{
    var button = sender as ApplicationBarIconButton;
    if (button != null)
    {
        MessageBox.Show(button.Text, "Button Clicked",
            MessageBoxButton.OK);
    }
    else
    {
        var menuItem = sender as ApplicationBarMenuItem;
        MessageBox.Show(menuItem.Text, "Menu Item Clicked",
            MessageBoxButton.OK);
    }
}
```

The click event handler first checks whether the sender is a button or a menu item. The value of the `Text` property is retrieved from the `sender`. A `MessageBox` informs the user that the application bar item was clicked. Like any other event, the XAML editor has features that can be used to automatically create the event handler in the code-behind file. This is one of the features supported by the Windows Phone Developer tools.

13.1.2 Tooling support

Visual Studio has good support for building an application bar with visual and property editors. The visual editor will display an application bar, complete with the appropriate icons, and will allow you to create and select the `ApplicationBar` and its buttons and menu items in the Document Outline panel, shown in figure 13.2. The property editor for the buttons, shown in figure 13.3, has a convenient icon selector that allows you to pick from local icons or one of the icons provided in the Windows Phone SDK. When you choose an SDK icon, Visual Studio automatically adds the icon file to the /Assets/AppBar folder in your project.

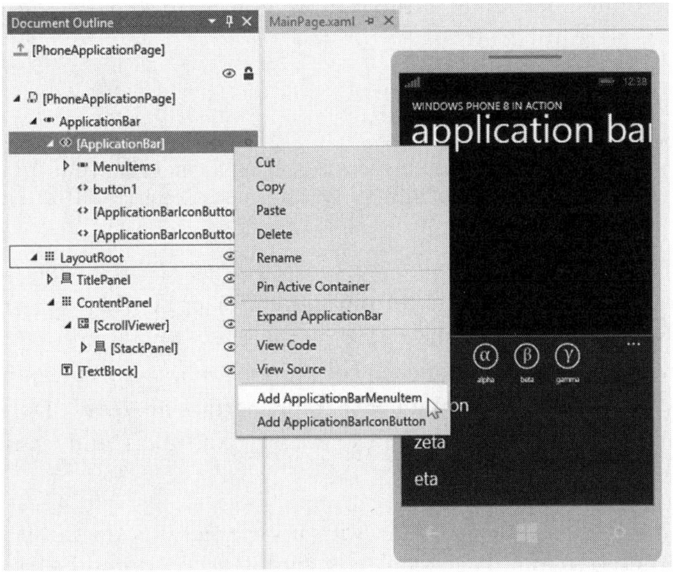

Figure 13.2 Visual Studio's designer support for the `ApplicationBar`. The `ApplicationBar`, or any of its menus or buttons, can be selected in the Document Outline.

The `ApplicationBar` and its button and menu item classes aren't `Framework-Elements` or even `DependencyObjects`. This means they don't participate in data binding, can't be located using the `FindName` API or the `VisualTreeHelper`, and don't appear in the visual tree. This also means that although you can apply an `x:Name` attribute to the buttons and menu items, and member fields will be generated for them, the fields won't automatically be wired up in `InitializeComponents`.

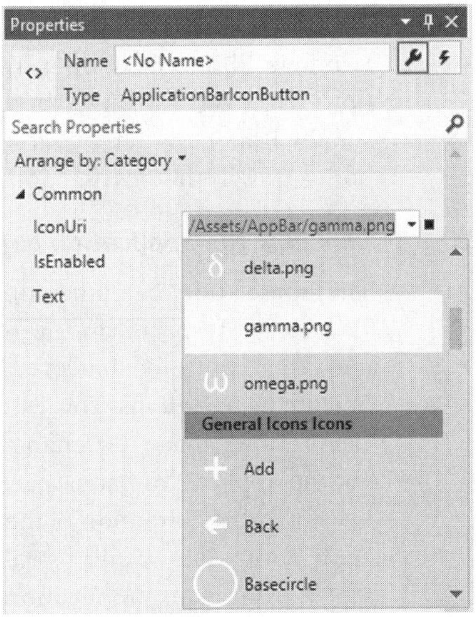

Figure 13.3 Visual Studio's property editor, displaying icons that already exist in the project and the stock icons that ship with the SDK. When a stock icon is selected, Visual Studio automatically copies the icon to the project.

You can use the `x:Name` attribute to get the member variables generated and then wire them up yourself in code-behind. First, add a name to the Alpha button and the Epsilon menu item:

```
<shell:ApplicationBarMenuItem x:Name="menuItem1"
    Text="epsilon" Click="item_Clicked" />
<shell:ApplicationBarIconButton x:Name="button1"
    IconUri="/icons/alpha.png" Text="alpha" Click="item_Clicked" />
```

Assign the generated member fields to the button and menu item instances, which you do in the MainPage constructor:

```
public MainPage()
{
    InitializeComponent();
    button1 = (ApplicationBarIconButton)ApplicationBar.Buttons[0];
    menuItem1 = (ApplicationBarMenuItem)ApplicationBar.MenuItems[0];
}
```

The `ApplicationBar` instance is accessed via the `ApplicationBar` property of your `MainPage` class. The property is inherited from the `PhoneApplicationPage` class and will be `null` unless you have added an `ApplicationBar` via XAML or code. Set your `button1` field to the first item in the `Buttons` collection. You must perform the cast to `ApplicationBarIconButton` because the `Buttons` property is an `IList`. Do the same thing for the `menuItem1` field, using the `MenuItems` collection and casting it to `ApplicationBarMenuItem`.

> **NOTE** Using a hardcoded index value to wire up the fields is fragile. If the buttons are reordered in MainPage.xaml, you could end up using the wrong button instance if the index value isn't changed in the code-behind.

In this section we've shown how to declare and build an application bar using the Windows Phone Developer Tools. You're probably asking yourself a couple of questions. How can I change the bar and its items while an application is running? How should I alter my screen designs to accommodate the application bar? We address both issues in the next section.

13.1.3 Changing the application bar appearance

The application bar takes up 72 pixels of space, and you need to account for that space in your page designs. You can claim more space by changing the application bar's opacity. In this situation, the application bar won't steal space from your application page but will still be visible floating above the page. Be careful because the semitransparent application bar may obscure your user interface. Figure 13.4 demonstrates how setting the `ApplicationBar.Opacity` property to 0.5 causes the application bar to obscure the page behind it.

Figure 13.4 Application page obscured by a semitransparent application bar

Another way to reclaim screen real estate from the application bar is to use minimized mode. In minimized mode, the application bar doesn't draw any buttons, as

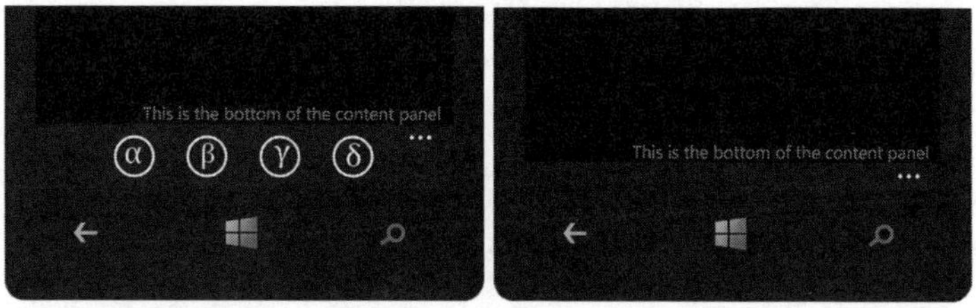

Figure 13.5 The application bar in default (left) and minimized mode (right)

shown in figure 13.5, and draws only the ellipses. When the user taps the ellipses, it expands to display the icon buttons and menu. You put the `ApplicationBar` in minimized mode by setting the `Mode` property to the `ApplicationBarMode.Minimized` enumeration value. Using the `ApplicationBarMode.Default` value returns the application bar to normal. `Minimized` mode only affects how the application bar is drawn in portrait layout. The application bar is always drawn full-size in landscape layout, even when the `Mode` property is set to `Minimized`.

The application bar contains an `IsVisible` property that you can use to show or hide the control while the application is running. This is useful if your application has a period of activity during which the application bar isn't required, but when that activity ends, you need to display the application bar. You can demonstrate this behavior by adding a `CheckBox` to your application that can be used to control the visibility of the `ApplicationBar`:

```
<StackPanel>
    <CheckBox Content="ApplicationBar.IsVisible" IsChecked="True"
        Click="appBarVisible_Clicked" />
</StackPanel>
```

In the click event handler, set the `IsVisible` property to be the `Checkbox`'s `IsChecked` value:

```
void appBarVisible_Clicked(object sender, RoutedEventArgs e)
{
    var checkBox = (CheckBox)sender;
    ApplicationBar.IsVisible = checkBox.IsChecked.Value;
}
```

Unlike XAML `UIElements`, visibility is specified using a Boolean instead of the `Visibility` enumeration.

The `ApplicationBar` also has an `IsMenuEnabled` Boolean property that controls whether the menu items are displayed when the bar is expanded. You may have some situations where you don't show the menu and other situations where you do.

13.1.4 Dynamically updating buttons and menu items

Individual buttons and menu items can be enabled or disabled at runtime using their `IsEnabled` properties. Add a `CheckBox` to demonstrate changing the `IsEnabled` property of your Alpha button:

```
<CheckBox Content="button1.IsEnabled" IsChecked="True"
    Click="button1Enabled_Clicked" />
```

The event handler for the check box sets the button's `IsEnabled` property to the `CheckBox`'s `IsChecked` value:

```
void button1Enabled_Clicked(object sender, RoutedEventArgs e)
{
    var checkBox = (CheckBox)sender;
    button1.IsEnabled = checkBox.IsChecked.Value;
}
```

Though not shown here, the same technique can be used with `ApplicationBar-MenuItems`. An example is available in this project's sample source code.

There may be situations where instead of disabling a button or a menu item, you'd rather remove the item from the application bar altogether. The `Buttons` and `Menu-Items` collections implement `IList`'s `Add`, `Remove`, and `Insert` methods, which you can use to add and remove items from the application bar. Use the same `CheckBox` technique to remove or add a button from the `Buttons` collection:

```
<CheckBox IsChecked="True" Content="Show button1"
    Click="button1Show_Checked" />
```

In the event handler, you insert the button at the beginning of the collection when the check box is checked. When it's unchecked, you remove the button from the collection:

```
void button1Show_Checked(object sender, RoutedEventArgs e)
{
    var checkBox = (CheckBox)sender;
    if (checkBox.IsChecked.Value)
        ApplicationBar.Buttons.Insert(0, button1);
    else
        ApplicationBar.Buttons.Remove(button1);
}
```

In this instance, you're inserting and removing a button that was created when the page was first loaded. You could choose to destroy the button and create a brand-new instance if necessary.

> **NOTE** Even though the `Buttons` collection's `Add` and `Insert` methods accept a parameter of type `object`, an exception will be thrown if anything other than an `ApplicationBarIconButton` instance is passed to the methods.

The user interface is updated as soon as the button is added or removed. You can use a similar technique to add and remove `ApplicationBarMenuItems`. The user doesn't see any changes to the menu until the application bar is expanded.

By default, the application bar is displayed in the current theme colors. If your application doesn't use the system theme, you'll likely want to change the application bar colors to match your application. The `ApplicationBar` class provides the `Back-groundColor` and `ForegroundColor` for this situation. The application bar will automatically apply the colors to the button icons if the icons are properly designed.

13.1.5 Designing button icons

Icons should be 48 * 48 and contain only white or transparent pixels. When the dark theme is active, the application bar displays your image pretty much as is. When the light theme is active, or you're using a custom foreground color, the application bar blends all non-transparent pixels with the foreground color. You shouldn't use colored icons, because your buttons will end up with odd-looking icons. The application bar will automatically draw the button's bounding circle. The icons shouldn't contain the bounding circle and should fit within it.

Text and icons for the button can be changed from code-behind. You may want to change the text and icon if you're toggling some state in your application. For example, an application that plays background music may offer a Mute button and change the text and icon once the user has enabled mute.

Change your sample application to toggle `button1` between Alpha and Omega. Update MainPage.xaml to hook up `button1` to a new event handler:

```
<shell:ApplicationBarIconButton x:Name="button1"
    IconUri="/icons/alpha.png" Text="alpha" Click="button1_Clicked" />
```

Change the text and icon in the event handler, as shown in the next listing. The event handler code will use the `button1` field and will also use icon files named alpha.png and omega.png.

Listing 13.3 Toggle button icon and text

```
void button1_Clicked(object sender, EventArgs e)
{
    if (button1.Text == "alpha")                          <-- Check current state
    {
        button1.Text = "omega";
        button1.IconUri =
            new Uri("/Assets/AppBar/omega.png", UriKind.Relative);   <-- Load icon from XAP package
    }
    else
    {
        button1.Text = "alpha";
        button1.IconUri =
            new Uri("/Assets/AppBar/alpha.png", UriKind.Relative);
    }
}
```

The application bar will update the buttons as soon as the changes are made in code. `ApplicationBarMenuItems` can also have their `Text` property updated in the code-behind. The new menu item text will be visible the next time the `ApplicationBar` is expanded.

When the `ApplicationBar` is expanded or collapsed, the `StateChanged` event is raised. The event sends an `ApplicationBarStateChangedEventArgs` instance to the event handler. This event args class exposes the `IsMenuVisible` Boolean property, which tells you whether the menu is visible. The `StateChanged` event is useful if you need to pause some activity in your application when the menu is shown and resume the activity when it's hidden. You may think this event handler would be the ideal place to update the `IsEnabled` property for all your menu items, but it's not. Any changes to the menu items in the event handler won't be seen by the user until the next time the application bar is expanded.

The `ApplicationBar` and `ApplicationBarIconButtons` can be updated in the `StateChanged` event handler, and these changes will be immediately reflected in the UI. For example, you may change the foreground and background colors when the menu is opened.

The application bar is the new menu and toolbar control for Windows Phone applications. You should use the application bar in place of a row of buttons to provide access to the most common features. Less-used features should be accessed via the application bar's menu. You can declare buttons and menu items in XAML or define them in the code-behind, and the application bar can dynamically update to match the state of the application.

`ApplicationBar` buttons aren't ideal for every situation. Often you need a menu that offers options specific to a particular item or context. In that scenario a context menu is the perfect paradigm.

13.2 ContextMenu

Earlier in the book we introduced the Windows Phone Toolkit, which is another set of user interface components that mimic controls seen in the native Windows Phone user interface but isn't provided with the SDK. `ContextMenu` is one of the controls left out of the SDK but implemented by the Windows Phone Toolkit. The toolkit is available for free from CodePlex (http://phone.codeplex.com) and can be added to your project with the NuGet Package Manager. You can also download a zip file that includes the full source code along with a sample application.

The Windows Phone Toolkit is packaged in a single assembly named Microsoft.Phone.Controls.Toolkit.dll. You need to add a reference to this assembly before using any of the toolkit components. When working with toolkit components in XAML, include an XML namespace declaration:

```
xmlns:toolkit="clr-namespace:Microsoft.Phone.Controls;
➥ assembly=Microsoft.Phone.Controls.Toolkit"
```

In the preceding section you learned how to create menu items on the application bar. Though this is a good place to put access to application-level features, sometimes you need a menu specific to a single object in the user interface. The Windows Phone Toolkit provides a context menu implementation you can use for these situations.

The `ContextMenu` and the related `ContextMenuService` provide the toolkit implementation of a context menu. A context menu is displayed when the user performs a tap-and-hold gesture on a user interface component. When the context menu is shown, it shrinks the page, giving the appearance that the menu pops out of the

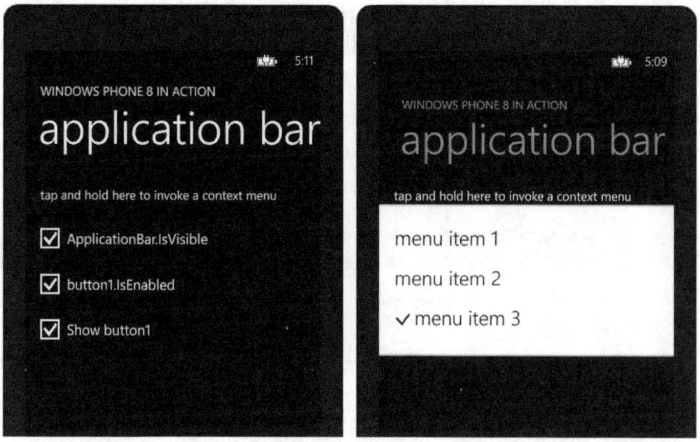

Figure 13.6 A context menu demonstrating the zoom effect and a complex menu item header

application. This zoom effect, shown in figure 13.6, is optional and is controlled by using the `IsZoomEnabled` property.

The `ContextMenuService` class provides the dependency properties that allow a `ContextMenu` to be declared in XAML using attached property syntax. The `ContextMenu` can be attached to any user interface element. The following listing demonstrates how to attach a `ContextMenu` to a `TextBlock`.

Listing 13.4 Adding a `ContextMenu` to a `TextBlock`

```
<TextBlock Margin="{StaticResource PhoneTouchTargetLargeOverhang}"
        Text="tap and hold here to invoke a context menu">
    <toolkit:ContextMenuService.ContextMenu>
        <toolkit:ContextMenu>
            <toolkit:MenuItem x:Name="contextMenuItem1"
                Header="menu item 1"
                Click="contextMenuItem_Click" />
            <toolkit:MenuItem x:Name="contextMenuItem2"
                Header="menu item 2"
                Click="contextMenuItem_Click" />
        </toolkit:ContextMenu>
    </toolkit:ContextMenuService.ContextMenu>
</TextBlock>
```

❶ Attached property

❷ Menu text declared with Header

Add a `ContextMenu` using attached property syntax ❶. Then add two `MenuItems`, providing each with a name and using the `Header` property to declare the menu text ❷. Wire up the `Click` event of both `MenuItems` to the same event handler, a method called `contextMenuItem_Click`:

```
void contextMenuItem_Click(object sender, RoutedEventArgs e)
{
    var menuItem = (MenuItem)sender;
    MessageBox.Show(menuItem.Name, "Menu Item Clicked",
        MessageBoxButton.OK);
}
```

The click event handler casts the `sender` property to a `MenuItem`. A `MessageBox` informs the user that the menu item was clicked. Individual menu items can be enabled or disabled at runtime using their `IsEnabled` properties.

The display of a `MenuItem` can be customized by declaring custom markup for the `Header` or by creating a `HeaderTemplate`. In the following listing, you create a `MenuItem` that displays a checkmark next to the menu item text.

Listing 13.5 A `MenuItem` with complex header content

```
<toolkit:MenuItem x:Name="contextMenuItem3" Click="contextMenuItem_Click">
    <toolkit:MenuItem.Header>                                    <-- (1) Property element syntax
        <StackPanel Orientation="Horizontal">
            <Path Margin="0,0,6,0"
                Data="M 3 23 L 12 33 L 24 17"
                Stroke="{StaticResource PhoneChromeBrush}"
                StrokeThickness="{StaticResource PhoneStrokeThickness}" />
            <TextBlock Text="menu item 3" />
        </StackPanel>
    </toolkit:MenuItem.Header>
</toolkit:MenuItem>
```

You declare the `Header` using property element syntax (1). The `Header` content is a horizontal `StackPanel` containing a `Path` and a `TextBlock`. The `Path` draws the shape of a checkmark and uses theme resources for the `Stroke` and `StrokeThickness` properties.

13.3 Summary

In this chapter you learned how to use the application bar as a toolbar and menu for your application. We showed how the Windows Phone Toolkit's context menu can display specific options to the user when a user interface element is selected. These controls help you build applications that match the design of the built-in applications such as the Email and Calendar applications.

In the next chapter we'll take our first look at the `Panorama` control, used to power the built-in Music + Videos and Office Hubs. We'll wrap up with a thorough examination of the `Pivot` control.

14 Panorama and pivot controls

This chapter covers

- Using panoramas
- Pivoting views
- Filtering data

The built-in Windows Phone applications provide a rich experience, allowing the user to use pan and flick gestures to quickly navigate their way through a large amount of data. Most of these applications are grouped into two categories: panorama applications and pivot applications. The People Hub, Photos Hub, and Music + Videos Hub are all panorama applications. The Messaging, Email, Phone, and Settings applications are all built with a `Pivot` control.

The `Panorama` control is used across the phone when the main screen of the application provides a rich graphical front end to quickly access favorite and recently used content. Items appearing in the panorama are links to other pages where the content is viewed or manipulated. The `Pivot` control is similar to a tab control, where discrete pages display different sets of data or settings to the user. The Email application is one example that uses a `Pivot` control to present separate pages for All, Unread, and Marked messages.

You've used `Pivot` controls throughout the book, including several examples in earlier chapters, but your use has been basic. In this chapter we take a deeper look at the `Pivot` control and introduce the `Panorama` control. We accomplish this through a couple of sample applications. The first sample application focuses on how to build a hub-like application using the `Panorama` control. Working with the `Pivot` control is the theme of the final sample application, concentrating on how to efficiently pivot between views in an application.

14.1 Improving the scenery with the Panorama control

One control unique to Windows Phone is the `Panorama` control, which is a long horizontal panel spread across several screens. The user pans left or right to change the viewport and move between the various screens in the control. The People Hub, the Photos Hub, and the Music + Video Hub are a few of the native applications that use a `Panorama` control. In this section you'll build a sample application, shown in figure 14.1, to demonstrate a few of the behaviors found only in the `Panorama` control.

A `Panorama` control should be used when you want to give a seamless flow to the contents in your application. The different viewports of the `Panorama` are each contained within a `PanoramaItem` control.

The `Panorama` control has three different visual layers that scroll at different rates as the user pans across the application. The background layer is stretched across the entire width of the control and moves at the slowest rate. The title layer moves a bit faster but makes sure that a portion of the title appears above the current `Panorama-Item`. The top layer contains the `PanoramaItem` controls and moves at the fastest rate.

You can add `Panorama` controls to an application using either the Windows Phone Panorama App project template or the Windows Phone Panorama Page item template.

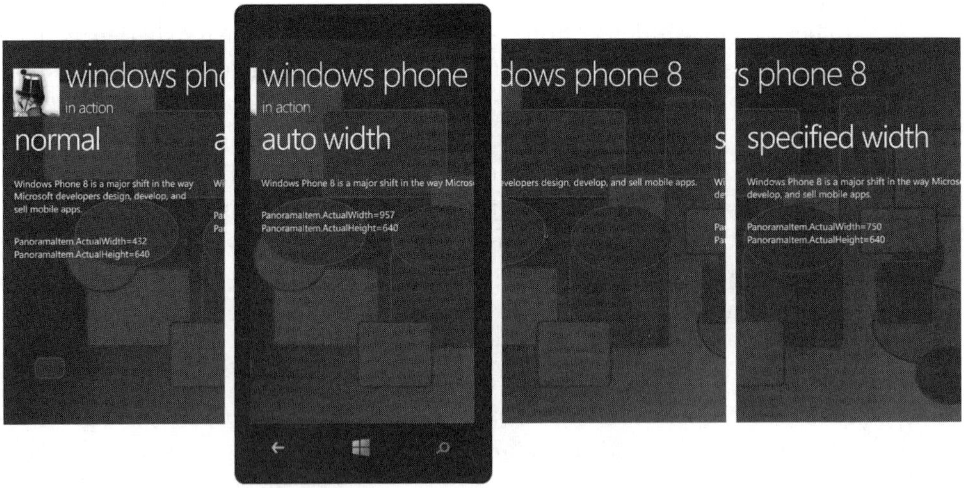

Figure 14.1 The sample Panorama application with three items

You're going to use the Windows Phone Panorama Page item template to embed a Panorama control in your application.

First, you need to create the sample project.

14.1.1 Building a panorama application

You're going to create a new project to demonstrate using a Panorama control in a XAML application. Create a new project named Panorama using the Windows Phone App template. You're not using the Windows Phone Panorama App template, because you don't need sample Model-View-ViewModel code generated for this sample application.

The MainPage.xaml file generated by the Windows Phone Application template isn't going to work for you, and you need to delete it from the project. Create a new MainPage.xaml by clicking Project > Add New Item. From the New Item dialog, choose the Windows Phone Panorama Page item template and name the new page MainPage.xaml. Once the page is created, open MainPage.xaml and take a look at the XAML markup created by the template, shown in the next listing.

Listing 14.1 Panorama markup created by the item template

```
<Grid x:Name="LayoutRoot">
    <phone:Panorama Title="my application">          <- 1 Declare Panorama
        <phone:PanoramaItem Header="item1">          | 2 Declare items
            <Grid/>
        </phone:PanoramaItem>
        <phone:PanoramaItem Header="item2">
            <Grid/>
        </phone:PanoramaItem>
    </phone:Panorama>
</Grid>
```

MainPage.xaml was created with a Grid as the LayoutRoot, with the Panorama control ❶ as its only child. The Panorama control was generated with two placeholder PanoramaItem controls ❷. The content for each of the PanoramaItems is an empty Grid control. Empty grids aren't exciting, so you'll add some content shortly. But first we need to discuss namespaces and assemblies.

The Panorama control lives in the Microsoft.Phone.Controls namespace, which is the same namespace and assembly that contains PhoneApplicationPage. Before you add some content to each of the item controls, you'll make some simple adjustments to the generated XAML. First, change the title of the Panorama control and give it a name:

```
<phone:Panorama x:Name="panorama" Title="windows phone 8 in action">
```

You also need to give each of the PanoramaItems their own names and titles:

```
<phone:PanoramaItem x:Name="panoItem1" Header="normal">
...
<phone:PanoramaItem x:Name="panoItem2" Header="auto width">
```

While you're at it, create a third `PanoramaItem`:

```
<phone:PanoramaItem x:Name="panoItem3" Header="specified width">
    <Grid/>
</phone:PanoramaItem>
```

Normally, every `PanoramaItem` would have a different set of content. In order to illustrate interesting behavior with the size of panorama items, you're going to place similar content in each `PanoramaItem`. You'll place a few text blocks in each item that will display a relatively long message, along with the width and height of the `PanoramaItem` control. The following listing details the XAML markup for the item content.

Listing 14.2 `PanoramaItem` content markup

```
<StackPanel Margin="12, 0">
   <TextBlock TextWrapping="Wrap"
              Margin="0,0,0,40">
           Windows Phone 8 is a major shift in the way Microsoft
           developers design, develop, and sell mobile apps.
   </TextBlock>
   <StackPanel Orientation="Horizontal">
      <TextBlock Text="PanoramaItem.ActualWidth=" />
      <TextBlock Text=
         "{Binding ActualWidth, ElementName=panoItem1}" />
   </StackPanel>
   <StackPanel Orientation="Horizontal">
      <TextBlock Text="PanoramaItem.ActualHeight=" />
      <TextBlock Text=
         "{Binding ActualHeight, ElementName=panoItem1}" />
   </StackPanel>
</StackPanel>
```

❶ Relatively long message

❷ Bind to item's width

❸ Bind to item's height

You replace the empty `Grid` in each of the `PanoramaItem` controls with a `StackPanel` control. Inside the `StackPanel`, create a `TextBlock` to display a message ❶ that's too long to fit on a single line. Tell the `TextBlock` to wrap the text when it can't display the text on one line. Create a pair of `TextBlock` controls to display the current width of the `PanoramaItem` control. Use element binding to display the `ActualWidth` property ❷ of the `PanoramaItem` control you named `panoItem1`. Display the height of the `PanoramaItem` using another pair of `TextBlock` controls, which you bind to the `ActualHeight` property ❸.

Repeat the same chunk of markup for the other two `PanoramaItem` controls. Make sure you change the element binding to `panoItem2` and `panoItem3` as appropriate. When you run the sample application now, it should look like figure 14.2.

Figure 14.2 The Panorama sample application with fixed-width items

If you drag your finger across the screen from right to left, the application will pan the screen and bring the second `PanoramaItem` into view, followed by the third `PanoramaItem`. You should notice that the title pans as well but at a different rate from the contents. You should also notice that the message text in each panel is wrapped across three lines and that each of the panels is a single screen wide.

Remember the Photos Hub we talked about in section 14.1? The second panel in the Photos Hub is wider than a single screen. Let's look at how to make your own `PanoramaItems` behave the same way.

14.1.2 Widen the view

When the `Panorama` control lays out its children, it automatically resizes each of the `PanoramaItem` controls to fill the remaining space on the screen. After subtracting space for the panorama title, the item header, and the overlap for the next item, a `PanoramaItem` control ends up 432 pixels wide and over 600 pixels high.

The `Panorama` control is designed so that `PanoramaItems` can have variable widths. When deciding how wide to size a `PanoramaItem` item, the `Panorama` control looks at the item's `Orientation` property. When the item's `Orientation` property is `Vertical`, the `Panorama` control sets the item's width to a single screen. The `Panorama` control allows the item to declare its own width when the `Orientation` property is set to `Horizontal`. The default value of the `Orientation` is `Vertical`, so all your item controls are sized to a single screen.

To see this behavior in action, change `panoItem2`'s `Orientation` property to `Horizontal` and restart the application:

```
<phone:PanoramaItem x:Name="panoItem2" Header="auto width"
    Orientation="Horizonatal">
```

Pan over to the Auto Width panel, and you should notice that the message text is now in a single line and the panel spans a couple of screens. Figure 14.3 shows the updated panel.

Figure 14.3 A wide `PanoramaItem` that calculates its own width

The `TextBlock` containing the message text prefers to display the message in a single line. When the `Panorama` layout routine asks the `PanoramaItem` for its preferred width, the `TextBlock`'s preferred size is reported back. The result is that the `PanoramaItem` has an `ActualWidth` of over 950 pixels. If the message text were longer, the panel would be wider; the longer the text, the wider the panel.

Infinitely wide panels are undesirable. As with any other layout scenario, you can control the width of a panel by setting either the `Width` or `MaxWidth` properties of the `PanoramaItem` control. Hardcode the width of `panoItem3` to 750 pixels:

```
<phone:PanoramaItem x:Name="panoItem3" Header="specified width"
    Orientation="Horizontal" Width="750" >
```

If you run the application now, you should see two lines of message text on the third panel. Once you're on the third panel, use the Start button to exit the application and return to it using the Back button. Now exit the application, change the project property so that the application is tombstoned upon deactivation, and restart the application. Scroll to the third panel, press the Start button, and once again return to it using the Back button. The application restores, but the selected panel is the first one instead of the third. Let's look at how you can restore the panel that was selected before the application was tombstoned.

14.1.3 Remembering where you are

Well-behaved applications remember their state when the user switches to another application, and they restore the state when the application is reactivated. Panorama applications are no different and should return the user to the correct `PanoramaItem` when the application is restarted.

The `Panorama` control exposes `SelectedIndex` and `SelectedItem` properties, but they're both read-only and can't be used to restore state. Instead, the `Panorama` control provides the `DefaultItem` property. Before you can use the `DefaultItem` property to restore user state on reactivation, you need to record which `PanoramaItem` control is selected.

When the user pans to a new item, the `Panorama` control fires the `SelectionChanged` event. Wire up the event in MainPage.xaml:

```
<phone:Panorama x:Name="panorama" Title="windows phone 8 in action"
    SelectionChanged="panorama_SelectionChanged">
```

Implement the event handler in MainPage.xaml.cs by saving the selected index to application settings:

```
using System.IO.IsolatedStorage;
void panorama_SelectionChanged(object sender,
    SelectionChangedEventArgs e)
{
    IsolatedStorageSettings.
        ApplicationSettings["selection"] = panorama.SelectedIndex;
}
```

Restore the selection in the `OnNavigatedTo` event handler, where you read the selected index from application settings, and use it to set the `DefaultItem` property:

```
protected override void OnNavigatedTo(NavigationEventArgs e)
{
    int selectedIndex;
    if (IsolatedStorageSettings.ApplicationSettings
        .TryGetValue("selection", out selectedIndex))
    {
        panorama.DefaultItem = panorama.Items[selectedIndex];
    }
}
```

Figure 14.4 Title alignment when the second item isn't the default (left) and when it is the default (right)

When the `DefaultItem` property is set in code, the `Panorama` immediately makes the specified `PanoramaItem` control the selected item. The change in selection isn't animated as it is when the user pans the screen. This could be disconcerting for the user if you have logic in your application that changes the `DefaultItem` based on non-panning activity, such as a button click.

There's one other idiosyncrasy with using the `DefaultItem` property: the `Panorama` title is lined up with the item that's specified as the default. Figure 14.4 illustrates how the title is lined up with the second `PanoramaItem` control when it's the default item.

When the normal panel is the default item, the Auto Width panel aligns with the letter s in the word Windows. When the Auto Width panel is the default, it aligns with the letter W in Windows. The default panel also is aligned to the left edge of the background image when a background is specified. You'll add a background image to your `Panorama` control next.

14.1.4 Adding a background

When we first described the `Panorama` control, we mentioned that there were three panning layers that moved at different speeds. You've seen only two of these layers in action so far because you haven't yet added a background to your application. The `Panorama Background` property is inherited from the `Control` class and is specified like the background of any other control.

The `Background` property is of type `Brush`. This means the background can be painted with a solid color or one of the gradient brushes. You can also use an `ImageBrush` or even a `VideoBrush`. Creating the `ImageBrush` in XAML is easy:

```
<phone:Panorama x:Name="panorama" Title="windows phone 8 in action"
    SelectionChanged="panorama_SelectionChanged">
    <phone:Panorama.Background>
        <ImageBrush ImageSource="Assets/PanoramaBackground.jpg" />
    </phone:Panorama.Background>
```

In this snippet you're telling the `ImageBrush` to use the file named PanoramaBackground.jpg. You can create your own background image or use the image we created for this sample, which you can download with this book's sample source code. You should add the file to the Assets folder of your project and select a build action of `Resource`, which will cause the image to be compiled into your assembly. This is the optimal option for `Panorama` backgrounds because the image is available as soon as the control is displayed. Background images can be loaded from the XAP file content or even from an internet location, but the user will experience a delay between when the `Panorama` control is displayed and when the background image first appears.

> **NOTE** For the best performance and user experience, choose a background image that's between 480 * 800 pixels and 1024 * 800 pixels.

All user interface elements pick up their look and feel from the system theme resources. This means that if the phone is set to the dark theme, the background will be black, and text displayed in the `Panorama` will be white. The text will be black and the background white when the user has chosen the light theme for their phone.

Unless you explicitly set the text color on the `Panorama` control, you must ensure that the default system text color is readable against your background image. The image in this PanoramaBackground.jpg example doesn't play well with black text. To remedy the situation, hardcode the `Panorama Foreground` property to `White`:

```
<phone:Panorama x:Name="panorama" Title="windows phone 8 in action"
    SelectionChanged="panorama_SelectionChanged"
    Foreground="White">
```

By setting the `Foreground` property, you're telling the `Panorama` control to ignore the system text color.

Now that you have a background image, you're nearly finished with your sample application. You have `PanoramaItems` with different widths and you restore the active panel when the application is re-launched. Before we move on to the `Pivot` control, let's take a deeper look at panorama titles.

14.1.5 Customize the title

When you look through the various built-in hubs on the phone, you'll notice that most use simple text for the panorama title. One notable exception is the Office Hub. Shown in figure 14.5, the Office Hub displays an image in the panorama title.

The `Title` property of the `Panorama` control is of type `Object` and is displayed with the data template specified in the `TitleTemplate` property. You aren't going to replace the template in this example because you're going to add a `Grid` control with an `Image` and two `TextBlocks`. The XAML markup for the new panorama title is shown in the following listing.

Figure 14.5 The Office Hub with an image in the panorama title

Listing 14.3 Adding an image and two title lines to the `Panorama` control

```
<phone:Panorama x:Name="panorama"
        Foreground="White"
        SelectionChanged="panorama_SelectionChanged">
    <phone:Panorama.Title>
        <Grid Margin="0,55,0,0">
            <Grid.ColumnDefinitions>
                <ColumnDefinition Width="Auto" />
                <ColumnDefinition Width="*" />
            </Grid.ColumnDefinitions>
            <Grid.RowDefinitions>
                <RowDefinition Height="Auto" />
                <RowDefinition Height="Auto" />
            </Grid.RowDefinitions>
            <Image Source="Assets/PanoramaLogo.png"
                Grid.RowSpan="2" Margin="12,36,12,0" />
            <TextBlock Grid.Column="1" Text="windows phone 8"
              FontSize="{StaticResource PhoneFontSizeExtraExtraLarge}" />
            <TextBlock Grid.Row="1" Grid.Column="1" Text="in action"
                FontSize="{StaticResource PhoneFontSizeLarge}" />
        </Grid>
    </phone:Panorama.Title>
```

1. **Use property element syntax**
2. **Divide into two rows and two columns**
3. **Add image**
4. **Add title lines**

Using XAML's property element syntax ❶, add a `Grid` control to the `Panorama.Title` property. Be sure to remove the `Title` attribute before adding the `Panoroama.Title` element. The `Grid` is divided into two rows and two columns ❷. Declare the `Image` control, placing it in the first two rows of the first column of the `Grid` ❸. The `Image` control will display the image in the file PanoramaLogo.png, which you add to the project with a build action of `Resource`. You can create your own logo image or use the image that's available in the book's sample source code. Add two `TextBlock` controls that display the title ❹. Bind the `FontSize` property of each control to a theme font-size resource.

Run the application and note the scrolling behavior of the new title. The image and two text lines scroll as a single unit when the user pans across the panorama. The continuous multilayer movement of the background, title, and content is unique to the `Panorama` control. Multilayer movement distinguishes the `Panorama` control from its counterpart, the `Pivot` control.

14.2 Pivoting around an application

The `Pivot` control is the Windows Phone equivalent of a `Tab` control. The `Pivot` control displays the title of each of its child `PivotItems` across the top of the control. The user can switch between items by tapping the titles or panning to scroll a new pivot into view. The main title displayed by the `Pivot` control is stationary and doesn't move.

Unlike the `Panorama` control, which loads every item when it's created, the `Pivot` control loads only the currently displayed page. When a user switches to another pivot item, the old item is unloaded and removed from the visual tree. We'll examine the events raised when `Pivot` switches between items.

Figure 14.6
The sample Pivot application with three pivots

To demonstrate the features of the `Pivot` control, you'll build a new sample application. Shown in figure 14.6, this application will contain three `PivotItems` implementing a pattern that's common in many pivot-based experiences. The first pivot item displays an unfiltered list of data. The second displays the same list but filtered to a subset of the data. The last pivot item allows the user to specify options or settings for the application.

`Pivot` controls can be added to an application using either the Windows Phone Pivot App project template or the Windows Phone Pivot Page item template. You're going to use the Windows Phone Pivot Page item template to embed a `Pivot` control in your application.

First, you need to create the sample project.

14.2.1 Building the sample application

You're going to create another new project to demonstrate using a `Pivot` control as the main page of an application. Create a new project named Pivot using the Windows Phone App template. You're starting with the basic application instead of the Windows Phone Pivot App template. You're not using the Pivot Application template because you don't need sample Model-View-ViewModel code generated for you.

The MainPage.xaml file generated by the Windows Phone Application template isn't going to work here, so you need to delete it from the project. Create a new MainPage.xaml by clicking Project > Add New Item. From the New Item dialog, choose the Windows Phone Pivot Page item template and name the new page MainPage.xaml. Once the page is created, open up MainPage.xaml and take a look at the XAML markup created by the template, shown in the following listing.

Listing 14.4 Pivot markup created by the item template

```
<Grid x:Name="LayoutRoot" Background="Transparent">
    <phone:Pivot Title="MY APPLICATION">                    ← ❶ Declaring Pivot
        <phone:PivotItem Header="item1">
            <Grid/>
        </phone:PivotItem>                            ❷ Declaring items
        <phone:PivotItem Header="item2">
            <Grid/>
        </phone:PivotItem>
    </phone:Pivot>
</Grid>
```

MainPage.xaml was created with a `Grid` as the `LayoutRoot`, with a `Pivot` control ❶ as its only child. The `Pivot` control was generated with two placeholder `PivotItem` controls ❷. The content for each of the `PivotItems` is an empty `Grid` control.

Before you add some content to each of the item controls, you'll make some simple adjustments to the generated XAML. First, change the title of the `Pivot` control and give it a name:

```
<phone:Pivot x:Name="pivot" Title="WINDOWS PHONE 8 IN ACTION">
```

You also need to give each of the pivot items their own name and title:

```
<phone:PivotItem x:Name="allDataItem" Header="all">
...
<phone:PivotItem x:Name="filteredDataItem" Header="filtered">
```

While you're at it, create a third `PivotItem` for the settings pivot:

```
<phone:PivotItem Header="settings">
    <StackPanel>
        <RadioButton x:Name="allDataOption" IsChecked="True"
            Content="Load all data at start up" />
        <RadioButton x:Name="asNeededOption"
            Content="Only load data when needed" />
    </StackPanel>
</phone:PivotItem>
```

Providing the user an option on the settings pivot implies that you need to save and reload the selected option when the application restarts. Save the option in the `OnNavigatedFrom` method override:

```
using System.IO.IsolatedStorage;
protected override void OnNavigatedFrom(NavigationEventArgs e)
{
    IsolatedStorageSettings.ApplicationSettings["loadAllData"]
        = allDataOption.IsChecked.Value;
}
```

Reload the save option in the `OnNavigatedTo` method override:

```
protected override void OnNavigatedTo(NavigationEventArgs e)
{
    bool loadAllData = false;
    IsolatedStorageSettings.ApplicationSettings
```

```
        .TryGetValue("loadAllData", out loadAllData);
    allDataOption.IsChecked = loadAllData;
    asNeededOption.IsChecked = !loadAllData;
}
```

Your sample application is off to a good start. You have three pivots, and your settings page remembers the options chosen by the user. You should also remember the currently selected `PivotItem` when the user switches away from and then back to your application.

14.2.2 Remembering the current selection

You should be a good citizen and restore the selected pivot when the user switches tasks, and be sure to return to the appropriate pivot when the application is reactivated. Add the following line to the `OnNavigatedFrom` method override:

```
State["selection"] = pivot.SelectedIndex;
```

You want your application to always start a new instance showing the first pivot item, so you'll store the selection in the `State` dictionary instead of application settings.

Restoring the selection isn't as straightforward as saving it. In some situations, the `Pivot` control won't allow the `SelectedIndex` to be modified before it's loaded. To prevent problems, you'll add your index restoration logic to an event handler wired up to the `Pivot` control's `Loaded` event:

```
<phone:Pivot x:Name="pivot" Title="WINDOWS PHONE 8 IN ACTION"
    Loaded="pivot_Loaded">
```

In the implementation of the event handler you check whether the `State` dictionary contains a selection and, if so, use it to change the current pivot:

```
void pivot_Loaded(object sender, RoutedEventArgs e)
{
    if(State.ContainsKey("selection"))
    {
        pivot.SelectedIndex = (int)State["selection"];
    }
}
```

When the `SelectedIndex` is changed from code, the user will see the normal animation as the `Pivot` control moves the related `PivotItem` to the foreground.

The user can now safely switch applications knowing that their pivot selection will be restored when they switch back to the application. At this point, there's no good reason to switch back because the application doesn't display any data.

14.2.3 Generating sample data

Your sample application is modeled after a class of data-browsing applications that use a `Pivot` control to move between different sets of filtered data. Without data, you're going to have a hard time demonstrating a filtering technique. For simplicity, your application is going to generate a sample dataset. In a real application the data set might come from a file, a database, or a web service. Add a new class file to the project and name it SampleData.cs. The following listing shows the implementation of the `SampleData` class.

Listing 14.5 Generating sample data with the `SampleData` class

```
public enum SampleCategory{ Even, Odd }
public class SampleData
{
    public string Name { get; set; }
    public int Value { get; set; }
    public SampleCategory Category { get; set; }
    public static IEnumerable<SampleData> GenerateSampleData()
    {
        var results = new List<SampleData>();
        var generator = new Random();
        for (int i = 1; i < 100; i++)
        {
            var value = generator.Next(1000);
            var data = new SampleData
            {
                Name = "data point " + i,
                Value = value,
                Category = value % 2 == 0 ?
                    SampleCategory.Even : SampleCategory.Odd,
            };
            results.Add(data);
        }
        return results;
    }
}
```

❶ Enum to distinguish odd from even

❷ Sample properties

❸ Generate 100 random data points

Within the SampleData.cs file you create a class named `SampleData` and an enum named `SampleCategory` ❶. The category enumeration value will be used later when you build the filter. The `SampleData` class has three properties for `Name`, `Value`, and `Category` ❷. You also created a static method that you can call to generate 100 random values ❸. As each data point is created, check whether the random value is even or odd and assign the appropriate category.

Update MainPage.xaml.cs by adding a field to hold the generated data and initialize the field in the class constructor:

```
IEnumerable<SampleData> data;
public MainPage()
{
    InitializeComponent();
    data = SampleData.GenerateSampleData();
}
```

Now that you have some data to display, you need something that will display data. A `ListBox` should do nicely—you'll add one to each `PivotItem`. Both `ListBoxes` will display data exactly the same way, and you can create a single `DataTemplate` that can be shared. The `DataTemplate`, shown in the following listing, will be added to the page's `Resources` dictionary, as the first child element of `PhoneApplicationPage`.

Listing 14.6 The DataTemplate used to display SampleData

```
<phone:PhoneApplicationPage.Resources>
    <DataTemplate x:Key="dataTemplate">
        <Grid Width="432">
            <Grid.RowDefinitions>
                <RowDefinition />
                <RowDefinition />                      ❶ Create 2 * 2 grid
            </Grid.RowDefinitions>
            <Grid.ColumnDefinitions>
                <ColumnDefinition />
                <ColumnDefinition />
            </Grid.ColumnDefinitions>
            <TextBlock Text="{Binding Name}"
                Style="{StaticResource PhoneTextLargeStyle}" />
            <TextBlock Grid.Row="1" Text="{Binding Category}"
                Style="{StaticResource PhoneTextSubtleStyle}" />
            <TextBlock Grid.RowSpan="2" Grid.Column="1"
                Text="{Binding Value}" HorizontalAlignment="Right"      ❷ Value spans two rows
                Style="{StaticResource PhoneTextExtraLargeStyle}" />
        </Grid>
    </DataTemplate>
</phone:PhoneApplicationPage.Resources>
```

The DataTemplate displays the SampleData using three TextBlock controls placed in a Grid. The Grid is divided into two rows and two columns ❶. Each of the three TextBlocks uses a different style defined in the system theme resources. The TextBlock displaying the value spans both rows in the second column ❷.

Now add the ListBoxes. In the first two PivotItems, replace the empty Grid control with a ListBox. Bind the ListBox's ItemTemplate to the DataTemplate you added:

```
<phone:PivotItem x:Name="allDataItem" Header="all">
    <ListBox x:Name="allDataList"
        ItemTemplate="{StaticResource dataTemplate}" />
</phone:PivotItem>
```

We show the XAML for only the first pivot, but you need to add the same markup to the filtered PivotItem, giving the ListBox the name filteredDataList.

Next, you need to load data into the ListBoxes. The pivot_Loaded method is a good place to do this. Add the following code to the bottom of the pivot_Loaded method:

```
if (allDataOption.IsChecked.Value)
{
    allDataList.ItemsSource = data;
    filteredDataList.ItemsSource = from d in data
                                   where d.Category == SampleCategory.Even
                                   select d;
}
```

If the user has selected to load all data at startup, you set the ItemsSource of the first ListBox to the data collection. Filter the data using a LINQ expression and set the result as the ItemsSource of the second ListBox. When you run the application now with the Load at Startup option, you'll see a list of 100 items in the first PivotItem and a list of even-valued data points in the second PivotItem.

You should notice a couple things. When the application first starts, the data in the first `PivotItem` appears after a slight delay. When you move between the pivots, the data appears instantaneously. The delay is due to waiting to set the `ItemsSource` property until after the `Pivot` is loaded. After the initial load, the data appears instantaneously because both `ListBoxes` are holding the data in memory as well as the UI elements needed to display the data. The data is held in memory, even if the user never visits the `PivotItem`.

Holding a large amount of data and user interface elements in memory could create performance and resource problems for an application. The `Pivot` control provides developers a set of events so that they can manage application resources and dynamically load and unload pages.

14.2.4 Dynamically loading pages

To enable developers to control when data is loaded and discarded, the `Pivot` control provides a series of events. Two events, called `LoadingPivotItem` and `LoadedPivotItem`, are raised when a `PivotItem` is gaining focus. Two complementary events, `UnloadingPivotItem` and `UnloadedPivotItem`, are raised when a `PivotItem` is losing focus. A fifth event, `SelectionChanged`, is used to determine which item is being selected and which item is losing selection.

The events are raised in the order shown in figure 14.7. Notice that the `SelectionChanged` event is raised after the new item begins loading but before the old item starts unloading.

The `LoadedPivotItem` and `UnloadedPivotItem` events are the perfect place to load and unload your data. Wire the `Pivot` control events to new event handlers in your code-behind:

```
<phone:Pivot x:Name="pivot" Title="WINDOWS PHONE 8 IN ACTION"
    Loaded="pivot_Loaded" LoadedPivotItem="pivot_LoadedPivotItem"
    UnloadedPivotItem="pivot_UnloadedPivotItem">
```

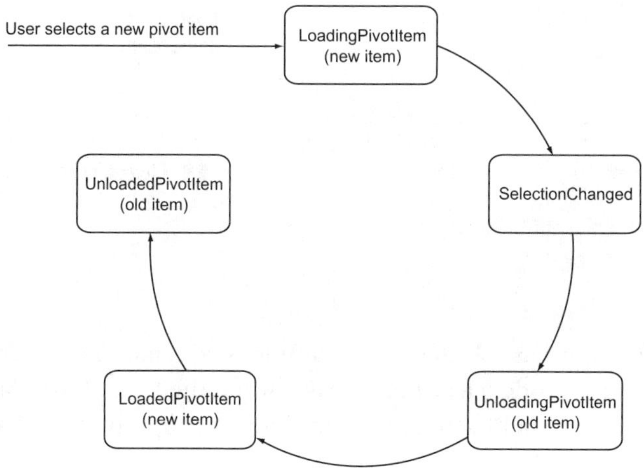

Figure 14.7 Pivot selection events

The following listing details the LoadedPivotItem event handler and how to load data into the ListBox.

Listing 14.7 Loading ListBox data in response to a LoadedPivotItem event

```
void pivot_LoadedPivotItem(object sender, PivotItemEventArgs e)
{
    if (e.Item == allDataItem && allDataList.ItemsSource == null)    ❶ Is data already loaded?
    {
        allDataList.ItemsSource = data;
    }
    else if (e.Item == filteredDataItem
        && filteredDataList.ItemsSource == null)
    {
        filteredDataList.ItemsSource =
            from d in data
            where d.Category == SampleCategory.Even
            select d;
    }
}
```

The LoadedPivotItem event passes a PivotItemEventArgs class, which exposes a single Item property. The Item property is a reference to the PivotItem that's currently being selected. Check whether the Item being loaded is the allDataItem and confirm that the allDataList doesn't currently contain data ❶. If all is well, set the ItemsSource property as you did when loading data during startup. Perform the equivalent check and set whether the current Item is the filtered PivotItem.

Unloading data when the user moves to another PivotItem follows a similar pattern. The UnloadedPivotItem event is handled by the pivot_UnloadedPivotItem method, shown in the following listing.

Listing 14.8 Clearing the ItemsSource property when an item is unloaded

```
void pivot_UnloadedPivotItem(object sender, PivotItemEventArgs e)
{
    if (!allDataOption.IsChecked.Value)           ❶ Load data as needed?
    {
        if (e.Item == allDataItem)
        {
            allDataList.ItemsSource = null;       ❷ Clear ListBox
        }
        else if (e.Item == filteredDataItem)
        {
            filteredDataList.ItemsSource = null;  ❷
        }
    }
}
```

First, check whether the user has selected the option to load data only as needed ❶. When in the only-as-needed mode, clear the ListBox when the PivotItem containing it is unloaded. Clear the ListBox by setting its ItemsSource property to null ❷.

Your sample application is now complete. Data is loaded and shown in two views, one of them filtering out all the odd data. The user can specify how you handle the data by listening for loaded and unloaded events raised by the `Pivot` control. You use the unloaded event handlers to clean up resources used by the `ListBox`es in the pivot items.

14.3 Summary

In this chapter you learned about controls that are new to Windows Phone and aren't available in other XAML implementations like Windows Runtime, Silverlight, and WPF. The `Panorama` and `Pivot` controls are found only in the Windows Phone SDK.

We showed how the `Panorama` control creates a unique user experience by employing three layers of movement when scrolling between items in the control. You built an application that uses a `Pivot` control to implement a data-filtering pattern common to many applications.

Applications can mix and match the controls presented in this chapter to build compelling applications. Many applications employ a `Panorama` control for the main page but use `Pivot` controls once the user drills into the content of the application. Panorama and pivot items can serve as the host container for a `ListBox`. `Pivot` controls often provide an application bar with buttons that let the user manage data displayed in the control.

We began our look at XAML controls in the last chapter, discussing the `ApplicationBar`, and continued in this chapter with the `Pivot` and `Panorama` controls. We're not finished looking at the controls available to the phone developer. In chapter 15 you use the `MediaElement` control that's part of the Windows Phone SDK, and we'll look at the `SmoothStreamingMediaElement`, which is part of the Smooth Streaming SDK open source library. We wrap up our coverage of XAML controls in chapters 16, 17, and 18 with a close look at the `Map`, `WebBrowser`, and `AdControl` controls.

15 Building a media player

This chapter covers

- Using the `MediaPlayerLauncher`
- Building a media player
- Working with local and web media

One of the more popular uses for a mobile phone is as a media player. Developers have a variety of different options when building applications that play media. In chapter 9 we showed you how to integrate with the Music + Videos Hub and to make use of the XNA Framework and the `BackgroundAudioPlayer` to play audio. In this chapter we look at the `MediaPlayerLauncher` and the XAML `MediaElement` control that can be used to play both audio and video from inside an application.

Both of these media players can play media files that are in the install or local storage folders and download and play media files located on the internet. With both players you can create a full-featured media player with a few lines of code. In this chapter you'll see how to launch the built-in Media Player application, providing your users with the common experience they're familiar with. Next, you'll implement a basic media player by using the `MediaElement` control, which gives you programmatic control over the experience that's not available when using the `MediaPlayerLauncher`. In this example you'll learn how to render different media

Figure 15.1 The MediaPlayback sample application

types supported by Windows Phone and how to control the playback. The media containers supported by Windows Phone through the `MediaElement` control include WAV, MP3, WMA, 3GP, 3G2, MP4, M4A, WMV, and M4V.

In this chapter you'll build a simple media player application. Figure 15.1 shows the application and the different features you'll build. We demonstrate how to play media that's distributed in the XAP file and installed as part of the application. We also discuss how to play media located on the internet or saved into the application's local storage.

The `MediaPlayerLauncher` and `MediaElement` classes' controls allow you to build custom media players for your audio and video content. Let's see how easy this is by starting with the `MediaPlayerLauncher` task.

15.1 Playing media with the MediaPlayerLauncher

Before we get to the meat of the application (a custom-built media player), let's look at the `MediaPlayerLauncher`. It's one of the phone tasks provided in the `Microsoft.Phone.Tasks` namespace that you read about in chapter 5. Phone tasks allow your code to interact with the native or built-in applications—Phone Dialer, Media Player, Messaging, Contacts, Web Browser, Camera, and so on. *Launchers* are a category of tasks that allow your code to activate a native or built-in application, sending it information such as the phone number to dial or the name of a media file to play. Data is passed to the launched application via properties set on the task. When the launcher's `Show` method is called, your application is deactivated, and the native application becomes the foreground application.

15.1.1 Creating the media player project

Before we discuss how to use `MediaPlayerLauncher` to play audio and video files, you'll build the skeleton user interface for your application. Start by creating a new project using the Windows Phone App project template and name the project MediaPlayback. Leave the main screen blank for the time being. The application will launch the native Media Player from three different application bar menu items to show the differences in playing media from the install folder, the local storage folder, and the internet. The application bar markup is shown in the following listing.

Listing 15.1 MediaPlayback's `ApplicationBar`

```
<phone:PhoneApplicationPage.ApplicationBar>
   <shell:ApplicationBar IsVisible="True" IsMenuEnabled="True">
      <shell:ApplicationBar.MenuItems>
         <shell:ApplicationBarMenuItem Text="video from install"
            Click="VideoFromInstall_Click" />
         <shell:ApplicationBarMenuItem Text="video from storage"
            Click="VideoFromStorage_Click" />
         <shell:ApplicationBarMenuItem Text="video from web"
            Click="VideoFromWeb_Click" />
      </shell:ApplicationBar.MenuItems>
   </shell:ApplicationBar>
</phone:PhoneApplicationPage.ApplicationBar>
```

No button, only menu items ❶

❷ Menu items launch video from different locations

The application bar doesn't contain any application bar buttons, so the only element is the `MenuItems` collection ❶. `ApplicationBarMenuItems` are used to load media content from different locations and sources, so each menu item invokes a different `Click` event handler. You'll implement the event handlers later in the chapter, but you may want to create empty implementations now so your code will compile. The install, storage, and web options demonstrate how to load media from the install folder, a web URL, or a file that has been saved in local storage ❷. Before you can play a video from the install folder, you'll add a video to your project.

15.1.2 Adding a video file to the project

The `MediaPlayerLauncher` can load files using relative or absolute URIs, including URIs representing a location within the install or local folders. Media files are saved into the install folder when the XAP package is installed to the emulator or device. This requires that media files be included in the Visual Studio project and compiled into the XAP package. To add a file to the project, click Project > Add existing item in Visual Studio. Once you've added the media file, you can set the Build Action property to either `Resource` or `Content`, as shown in figure 15.2. If you choose

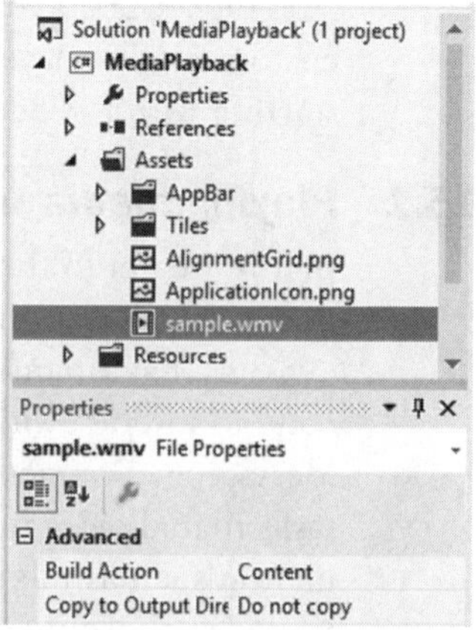

Figure 15.2 Adding sample.wmv to the Assets folder in the sample application project with the Build Action property set to `Content`

`Resource`, the file will be embedded into the assembly. In this chapter we assume that you've added a file named sample.wmv to the Assets folder and have set the build property to `Content`. You can record your own video or use the video we created for this sample, which you can download with this book's sample source code.

When a file is embedded into an assembly, this will increase the application's startup time, so use this option only for small media files. If you choose `Content`, the file will be added to the XAP package. In either case, the file increases the size of the deployment package. Any package larger than 20 MB will prevent the user from downloading the application from the Windows Phone Store with the cellular network, and users will be able to download your application only when connected to a Wi-Fi network. Application packages must not exceed a total of 225 MB.

There's one other thing you need to do with the sample video file before the project is ready to launch video files from the local storage folder: copy the video from the install folder into the local storage folder.

15.1.3 Copying an installed file to local storage

When an application is first deployed to a device, local storage is empty, and there's no automatic mechanism for prepopulating files. You have three options for placing files into local storage: create new files, copy files from the install file, or download files from the network. Because this application requires a file in local storage, you're going to add the code required to copy the embedded sample.wmv file from the install file to local storage (see figure 15.3).

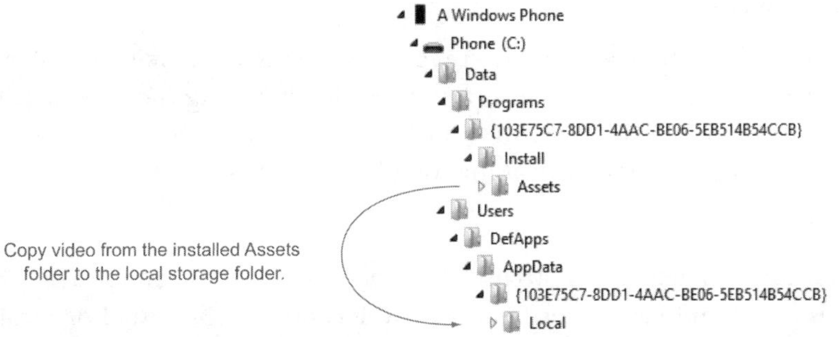

Figure 15.3 Copying sample.wmv from the install folder to the local storage folder

You'll add this to the code that's run when the application is launched. The following listing details the code added to `Application_Launching` event handler in App.xaml.cs.

Listing 15.2 Copying content files into isolated storage

```
using Windows.Storage;
using Windows.ApplicationModel;
async void Application_Launching(object sender, LaunchingEventArgs e)
{
```

```
    try
    {
        StorageFolder installFolder = Package.Current.InstalledLocation;
        StorageFolder assetsFolder =                                      // 1 Get Assets folder
            await installFolder.GetFolderAsync("Assets");
        StorageFile file = await assetsFolder.GetFileAsync("sample.wmv");

        StorageFolder localFolder = ApplicationData.Current.LocalFolder;
        StorageFile copiedfile = await file.CopyAsync(localFolder,        // 2 Copy file
            "sample.wmv", NameCollisionOption.FailIfExists);
    }
    catch (Exception ex){}        // 3 Ignore exception thrown if file already exists
}
```

Start by adding the async keyword to the method header. Next, get the StorageFolder instance representing the install folder from the current Package. Because sample.wmv was placed in the Assets folder in the project, it's installed into the Assets folder on the device, and you need to get the StorageFolder instance for the Assets folder ❶. Retrieve the StorageFile instance representing the sample.wmv video file. Get the local storage folder from the current ApplicationData object. Copy the video file using the CopyAsync method ❷, passing in the local storage folder and specifying the FailIfExists collision option. The exception thrown if the file already exists in local storage is caught and ignored ❸.

The sample application is ready to launch the built-in Media Player and show the sample video.

15.1.4 Launching the video

Like any other launcher task, MediaPlayerLauncher is used by constructing a new instance first, setting properties next, and then finally calling the Show method. The MediaPlayerLauncher class is defined in Microsoft.Phone.Tasks, so you'll add a using directive for the namespace at the top of MainPage.xaml.cs:

```
using Microsoft.Phone.Tasks;
```

The MediaPlayerLauncher has two useful properties: Location and Media. The Media property is a URI and can either be a relative location in the install or local storage folders or an absolute URI to a file located on the internet. The Media URI accepts only relative paths to files in the install or local storage folders and doesn't accept the appdata, isostore, or ms-appx protocols. The Location property is an enum type named MediaLocationType. The three MediaLocationType values are Install, Data, and None. None is specified when the target video file is located on the internet.

If the Media property isn't set, MediaPlayerLauncher.Show will throw an InvalidOperationException. A FileNotFoundException is thrown when a file can't be found with a relative URI. If all goes well, the video will start playing, and the user will be able to control playback by tapping the buttons presented on the screen, as you can see in figure 15.4.

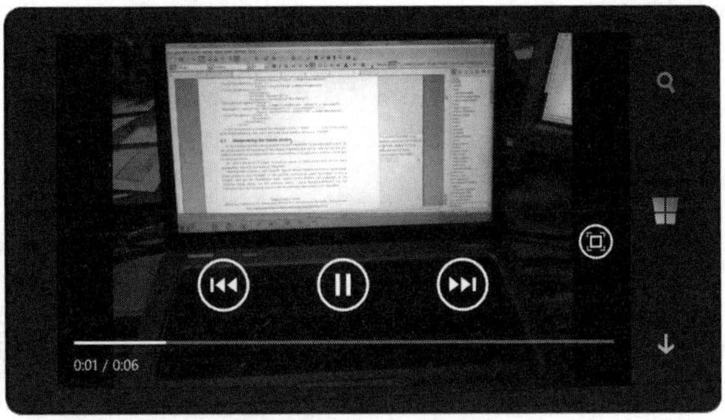

Figure 15.4 The sample video playing in the built-in Media Player application, launched by the `MediaPlayerLaucher` task. The video plays in landscape orientation with playback controls visible.

NOTE The `MediaPlayerLauncher` class defines two other properties named `Orientation` and `Controls` that appear to give the calling program some amount of control over how the media is displayed to the user. Unfortunately, these two properties have no effect on the media player—it's always displayed in landscape orientation with all controls visible.

To see this in action, implement the three `VideoFromXXX_Click` event handlers by constructing a `MediaPlayerLauncher` specifying a `Location` and a `Media` URI pointing to the sample.wmv file you added to the project. Once the properties are set, call the `Show` method. The three methods are nearly identical, differing only in the values assigned to the `Location` and `Media` properties. The method implementations are shown in the following listing.

Listing 15.3 Handling menu item clicks and launching the media player

```
void VideoFromInstall_Click(object sender, EventArgs e)
{
   var task = new MediaPlayerLauncher();
   task.Location = MediaLocationType.Install;
   task.Media = new Uri("Assets/sample.wmv", UriKind.Relative);
   task.Show();
}

void VideoFromStorage_Click(object sender, EventArgs e)
{
   var task = new MediaPlayerLauncher();
   task.Location = MediaLocationType.Data;
   task.Media = new Uri("sample.wmv", UriKind.Relative);
   task.Show();
}

void VideoFromWeb_Click(object sender, EventArgs e)
{
   var task = new MediaPlayerLauncher();
   task.Location = MediaLocationType.None;
   task.Media = new Uri(
      "http://www.windowsphoneinaction.com/sample.wmv");
   task.Show();
}
```

1 Video located in install folder

2 Video located in local storage

3 Video located on the internet

The first method launches the sample.wmv video located in the Assets subfolder in the install directory ❶. The second method specifies a `Location` value of `Data` ❷, instructing the media player to look for a file named samples.wmv in the local storage folder. To load a file from the internet, the `Location` value of `None` is used ❸.

If an error occurs while loading a web-based media file, such as if the file doesn't exist at the specified URI, the user is presented with an error message, as shown in figure 15.5. The application that launches the media player isn't notified of the error. Keep in mind that when the `MediaPlayerLauncher`'s `Show` method is called, your application will be deactivated and moved to the background.

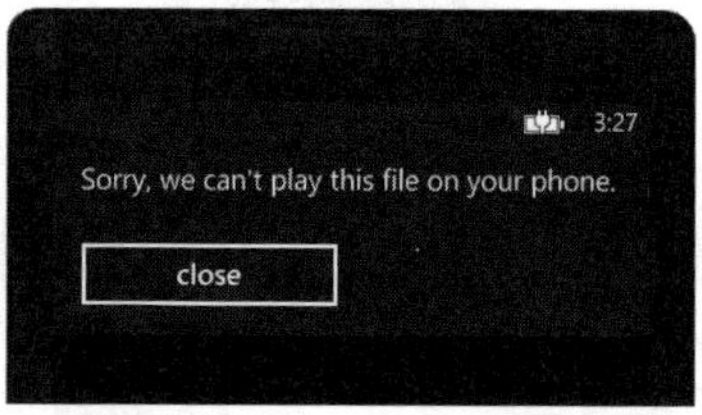

Figure 15.5 The error message displayed to the user when a file doesn't exist at the specified URI

You're now ready to run the sample application. Start the application, open the application bar, and tap one of the menu items. You should see your sample video playing. The videos located in the install and local storage folders should start nearly instantaneously. The web-based file might take longer to launch and play because the media player has to download the file before it can be played.

The `MediaPlayerLauncher` is a nice feature to add if you don't require any influence over the playback experience. When you do need to customize or otherwise control the playback experience, you can build your own media player with the `MediaElement`.

15.2 Building a media player with MediaElement

`MediaElement` is a user interface control that got its start in the Windows Presentation Foundation (WPF) framework. It's been part of the Silverlight framework since version 2 and is now available for Windows Phone. `MediaElement` for Silverlight isn't as full-featured as the WPF implementation, and the Windows Phone edition is even more limited. The media containers supported by Windows Phone through the `MediaElement` control include WAV, MP3, WMA, 3GP, 3G2, MP4, M4A, WMV, and M4V.

> **TIP** Not all devices support the same media codecs. For the full list of containers and decoders supported by Windows Phone and the emulator, see the official Microsoft documentation at http://mng.bz/3wQW.

`MediaElement` itself isn't what many users would call a media player. It's a surface for displaying video. `MediaElement` doesn't provide any user interface to control playback such as VCR-like buttons for play, pause, and stop. `MediaElement` does provide methods and properties to enable you to build your own media player user interface.

In this section you learn how to open and play media files with `MediaElement`. We show how to play files locally and from the internet, how to implement common player controls, and how to control volume. Let's jump right into code by showing you how to create a media player application.

15.2.1 Adding the MediaElement

Before we discuss how to use `MediaElement` to play audio and video files, you'll add a `MediaElement` control to the skeleton user interface you started in the last section. The application's screen displays a `MediaElement`, along with a few status controls hosted inside the `ContentPanel`. The following listing shows the starting XAML for the `ContentPanel`.

Listing 15.4 User interface skeleton

```
<Grid x:Name="ContentPanel" Grid.Row="1" Margin="12,0,12,0">
    <Grid.RowDefinitions>
        <RowDefinition Height="*" />
        <RowDefinition Height="40" />          ❶ Define four rows
        <RowDefinition Height="40" />
        <RowDefinition Height="80" />
    </Grid.RowDefinitions>
    <MediaElement x:Name="mediaElement" Source="Assets/sample.wmv" />    ❷ Media player
    <TextBlock x:Name="sourceTextBlock" Text="video from install"
       TextAlignment="Center" Grid.Row="1" />         ❸ Display media source
</Grid>
```

Divide the `ContentPanel` into four rows, allowing the first row to use up all the available space ❶. A `MediaElement` is defined to live in the first grid row and defaults to using a video deployed as content in the Assets folder of the application's install folder ❷. You also add a `TextBlock` to the second row ❸ to display the selected source option. You'll add controls to the other rows as you work through the chapter.

You'll now add playback controls for the play, pause, stop, and mute operations. The playback controls will be placed on the `ApplicationBar`. The XAML for the `ApplicationBar` is shown in the next listing.

Listing 15.5 MediaPlayback's `ApplicationBar` Buttons

```
<phone:PhoneApplicationPage.ApplicationBar>
   <shell:ApplicationBar IsVisible="True" IsMenuEnabled="True">
      <shell:ApplicationBarIconButton Text="play"
         Click="Play_Click"
         IconUri="/Assets/AppBar/transport.play.png" />
      <shell:ApplicationBarIconButton Text="pause"
         Click="Pause_Click"                               ❶ Playback controls
         IconUri="/Assets/AppBar/stop. png" />
      <shell:ApplicationBarIconButton Text="stop"
         Click="Stop_Click"
         IconUri="/Assets/AppBar/transport.pause.png" />
      <shell:ApplicationBarIconButton Text="mute"
         Click="Mute_Click"
         IconUri="/Assets/AppBar/minus.png" />
      <shell:ApplicationBar.MenuItems>
         ...
      </shell:ApplicationBar.MenuItems>
   </shell:ApplicationBar>
</phone:PhoneApplicationPage.ApplicationBar>
```

ApplicationBarIconButtons are used to control media playback. Following the style guide, the button text is a single lowercase word ❶. You'll implement the menu item click event handlers in the next few sections.

> **TIP** The images used in this sample are available in the Windows Phone SDK and can be automatically added to your project by selecting them from the visual application bar editor.

Let's see how to implement the Click event handlers for the buttons. You can start a playback using the Play method exposed by MediaElement control:

```
void Play_Click(object sender, EventArgs e)
{
    mediaElement.Play();
}
```

In a similar way, you can use the Pause and Stop methods to control playback:

```
void Pause_Click(object sender, EventArgs e)
{
    mediaElement.Pause();
}
void Stop_Click(object sender, EventArgs e)
{
    mediaElement.Stop();
}
```

You've seen how to control the playback. Now let's see how to show the playback progress. The MediaElement's Position property reports the playback time in terms of hours, minutes, and seconds. You can present the current progress by binding the MediaElement's Position property to a TextBlock's Text property:

```
<TextBlock Name="positionTextBlock"
    Text="{Binding ElementName=mediaElement, Path=Position}"
    TextAlignment="Center" Grid.Row="2" />
```

The positionTextBlock is added to the third row of the ContentPanel, right below the TextBlock that displays the current source option.

> **TIP** When you display the value of the Position property in your user interface, you should be aware that the Position property can change hundreds of times per second. In a production application, you should avoid databinding the property and implement another mechanism that updates the user interface less frequently.

We've assumed that the sample video you added to your sample project and that launches when the application starts is a WMV file. You could choose a file in any of the supported formats, and your code would be exactly the same (except for the filename). The MediaElement discovers the format when it loads the media. You've seen how to load a video by specifying a relative URI when declaring the MediaElement control in XAML, which is one of several methods you can use to load media files.

15.2.2 Loading media files

MediaElement can load files using relative or absolute URIs or can play media directly from a file stream. Relative URIs, such as Assets/sample.wmv, used in the previous section, refer to files (and folders) deployed in the application's install file. Absolute URIs are used to load media files located on the internet. Media files can also be stored in local storage.

You instruct MediaElement to load a file from a URI by setting the Source property. When you set the Source property, MediaElement locates the file and opens the corresponding file stream. You'll use the Source property to re-implement the VideoFromInstall_Click event handler for the Video from Install menu option:

```
void VideoFromInstall_Click(object sender, EventArgs e)
{
    mediaElement.Source = new Uri("Assets/sample.wmv", UriKind.Relative);
    sourceTextBlock.Text = "video from install";
}
```

In addition to setting the source element to a relative Uri, you update sourceTextBlock to display which option was selected. Loading a file from the internet is nearly the same:

```
void VideoFromWeb_Click(object sender, EventArgs e)
{
    mediaElement.Source = new Uri(
        "http://www.windowsphoneinaction.com/sample.wmv",
        UriKind.Absolute);
    sourceTextBlock.Text = "video from web";
}
```

The main differences between VideoFromInstall_Click and VideoFromWeb_Click are the Uri and UriKind used for the Source property and the text used to update sourceTextBlock. MediaElement will download the specified media file before starting playback. The download process may take some time, and the MediaElement doesn't provide any indication that it's waiting for the download. In the next section we discuss how you can use MediaElement events to determine when a file is fully loaded from a Uri.

Introducing the IsolatedStorage APIs

In chapter 7 we introduced the StorageFolder and StorageFile classes in the Windows.Storage API for reading and writing data to local storage. The Windows .Storage API is part of the Windows Phone Runtime and is new to Windows Phone 8. Prior to Windows Phone 8, files in local storage were accessed with the IsolatedStorage API. Although superseded by the Windows.Storage API, the IsolatedStorage API is still available for Windows Phone 8 applications.

Instead of accessing the file system with the StorageFolder and StorageFile classes, developers use IsolatedStorageFile, found in the System.IO.IsolatedStorage

(continued)

namespace. `IsolatedStorageFile` is a file system for an application and provides a basic file system API for managing files and directories. The file system methods provided by `IsolatedStorageFile` allow you to create, open, and delete files and folders. Only one instance of `IsolatedStorageFile` exists on the Windows Phone. It's accessible via the `GetUserStoreForApplication` static method.

Loading media files from local storage isn't as simple as specifying a `Uri` for the `Source` property. You must use `MediaElement`'s `SetSource` method instead, as shown in the following listing. Instead of using a `Uri`, `SetSource` takes a `Stream`.

Listing 15.6 Loading media files from local storage

```
using System.IO;
using System.IO.IsolatedStorage;
void VideoFromStorage_Click(object sender, EventArgs e)
{
    mediaElement.Source = null;                          <-- Close current media
    using (var store = IsolatedStorageFile.GetUserStoreForApplication())
    {
        if (store.FileExists("sample.wmv"))
        {
            var fileStream = new IsolatedStorageFileStream(   <-- 1 Open media file
                "sample.wmv", FileMode.Open, store);
            mediaElement.SetSource(fileStream);          <-- 2 Pass stream to media player
            sourceTextBlock.Text = "video from storage";
        }
    }
}
```

In the `VideoFromStorage_Click` event handler, start by opening isolated storage and confirming that the target media file already exists. Open an `IsolatedStorage-FileStream` for the file ❶ and pass the stream to the `MediaElement` ❷.

NOTE The `MediaElement` for Windows Phone supports only `Isolated-StorageFileStreams`.

One more `MediaElement` property is important when the `source` is set or changed. The `AutoPlay` property determines whether media playback is automatically started when the source changes. `AutoPlay` defaults to `true`, meaning the media will begin playing as soon as it's opened by the `MediaElement`. A good practice is to explicitly set the `AutoPlay` before setting the `Source` property to ensure the `MediaElement` behaves as you expect.

We've shown you how to use various methods to load media files. Loading files isn't instantaneous—for example, when loading files from the internet. When `Media-Element` is loading a file, it doesn't provide any progress or wait indicator to the user. Fortunately, `MediaElement` reports its current status so that you can build your own progress indicators.

15.2.3 MediaElement states

MediaElement contains properties and events that can be used to determine the current status of media playback and exert control over the user experience. The MediaOpened event can be used to determine when the MediaElement is ready to start playing. An application can be notified when media has stopped playing with the MediaEnded event. The BufferingProgress or DownloadProgress properties and their related changed events can be used to identify situations when you might display a wait indicator to the user.

Many of MediaElement's events and properties are low-level and require the programmer to track various properties and events in order to determine when media is playing and when it's stopped or paused. MediaElement exposes the CurrentState property so that user interface code can easily determine the playback state. The CurrentState property is of type MediaElementState, and the possible values are detailed in table 15.1.

Table 15.1 MediaElement states

State*	Description
Buffering	Media frames are being loaded and prepped for playback. During buffering, the Position property doesn't change, and if the media type is video, the current frame continues to be displayed.
Closed	The media source hasn't been set or has been cleared.
Opening	The media stream is being downloaded and opened, and the media type discovered as the MediaElement prepares to play.
Paused	The currently playing media is paused, and the Position property doesn't change. If the media type is video, the current frame continues to be displayed.
Playing	Media is being played, and the Position property is changing.
Stopped	Media is loaded but isn't being played. The Position property isn't changing and has the value 0. If the media type is video, the first frame is displayed.

* Two other states, AcquiringLicense and Individualizing, apply to digital rights management and are beyond the scope of this book.

You're going to use the CurrentState property to update the sample application's user interface with some helpful media playback hints. While waiting for video to load, the system progress indicator will be displayed (figure 15.6). This provides feedback to the user when the media file takes a while to load, such as when opening a file from the internet. Add the ProgressIndicator to MainPage.xaml but initialize it in an invisible state so that it's hidden from the user. Add the following code below the application bar markup in MainPage.xaml:

```
<shell:SystemTray.ProgressIndicator>
    <shell:ProgressIndicator x:Name="mediaProgress" IsIndeterminate="True"
        IsVisible="True" Text="Loading..."/>
</shell:SystemTray.ProgressIndicator>
```

Figure 15.6 Showing the system progress indicator when a video is loading. The system progress indicator appears at the top of the screen with a label. The indeterminate version of the progress bar consists of a series of small balls or dots moving from left to right.

You should also set the `IsIndeterminate` property to `True`, because download size and detailed opening progress aren't tracked and there's no need for a percentage-based display. The `ProgressIndicator` will be made visible from an event handler called when the `MediaElement` is opening a media file. Add a `TextBlock` to display the value of the `CurrentState`:

```
<TextBlock x:Name="stateTextBlock" Grid.Row="1"
    HorizontalAlignment="Right" />
```

The `TextBlock` should be added to the `ContentPanel` and will be displayed in the same row as and to the right of the `TextBlock` that displays the current source option. The text displayed in the new `TextBlock` should be updated whenever `MediaElement`'s `CurrentState` property changes. Code to update the `TextBox` can be placed in an event handler for `MediaElement`'s `CurrentStateChanged` event. Start by updating MainPage.xaml:

```
<MediaElement x:Name="mediaElement" ...
    CurrentStateChanged="mediaElement_CurrentStateChanged" />
```

Implement `mediaElement_CurrentStateChanged` in MainPage.xaml.cs:

```
using System.Windows.Media;
void mediaElement_CurrentStateChanged(object sender, RoutedEventArgs e)
{
    stateTextBlock.Text = mediaElement.CurrentState.ToString();
    if (mediaElement.CurrentState == MediaElementState.Opening)
        mediaProgress.IsVisible = true;
    else
        mediaProgress.IsVisible = false;
}
```

Update the `stateTextBlock` with the value of `CurrentState`. Because the `ProgressIndicator` should only be displayed when the media source is being opened, check for the `Opening` state and make the `ProgressIndicator` visible. For all other states, hide the `ProgressIndicator`.

What happens if there's an error during load or playback? There's no `MediaElementState` for error. Instead, there's a `MediaFailed` event that can be used to report errors to the user. Wire up the `MediaFailed` event in MainPage.xaml:

```
<MediaElement x:Name="mediaElement" ...
    MediaFailed="mediaElement_MediaFailed" />
```

The implementation of the `mediaElement_MediaFailed` event handler in MainPage.xaml.cs shows the error to the user:

```
void mediaElement_MediaFailed(object sender, ExceptionRoutedEventArgs e)
{
    MessageBox.Show(e.ErrorException.Message,
        "Media Failure", MessageBoxButton.OK);
}
```

The error message from the `Exception` is displayed in a `MessageBox` (figure 15.7). The `MediaFailed` event represents a generic failure, so it can relate either to the file location or to media content not properly understood by the `MediaElement`. Usually, this message is an error code, so you may consider inspecting the exception and building a more user-friendly message in your code.

Figure 15.7 A example error code returned by the `MediaFailed` event

You now know how to load media files and have looked at some of the methods and properties provided by `MediaElement` to control playback. One of the features we haven't looked at yet is controlling sound volume.

15.2.4 Controlling volume

Your media player application would be incomplete without controls to adjust the volume or mute all sound. The `MediaElement` control provides the `Volume` and `IsMuted` properties to support these desired features. The `Volume` property is represented by a `double` value in the range between `0` (silent) and `1` (maximum volume). If you implement the volume adjustment user interface with a `Slider` control, it can be configured to have a range between `0` and `1`, with resolution for changes of `0.1`:

```
<Slider x:Name="volumeSlider" Width="300" Grid.Row="3" Minimum="0.0"
    Maximum="1.0" SmallChange="0.05" LargeChange="0.1" Value="0.85"/>
```

Initialize the `Slider` control's `Value` property to `0.85`, which is the default value for the `MediaElement`'s `Volume` property. The `Slider` is added to the fourth row of the `ContentPanel` grid. Element-to-element data binding is used to connect the `Slider`'s `Value` to the `MediaElement` `Volume` property:

```
<MediaElement x:Name="mediaElement" ...
    Volume="{Binding ElementName=volumeSlider, Path=Value}" />
```

The user can now silence the media player by dragging the slider all the way to zero (figure 15.8).

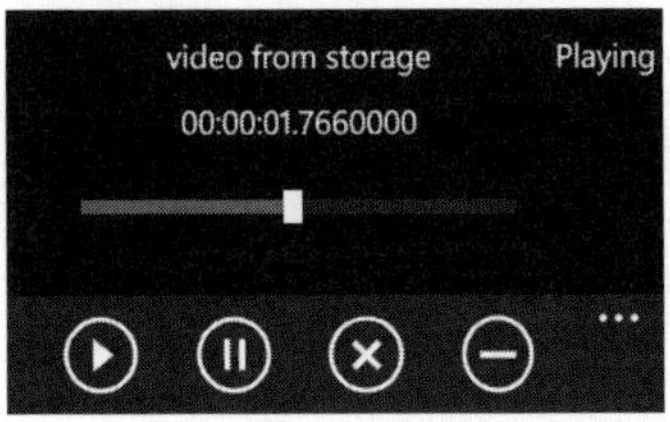

Figure 15.8 A slider control is used to control the sound volume of the media player. Dragging the slider all the way to the left silences the player.

A quicker method for silencing the media player is with the `IsMuted` property. Setting the `IsMuted` Boolean property to `true` will instantly silence the media player. When you first created the sample application in this chapter, you added a Mute button to the `ApplicationBar`. Now you'll implement the click event handler of the Mute button to toggle the `IsMuted` property:

```
void Mute_Click(object sender, EventArgs e)
{
    mediaElement.IsMuted = !mediaElement.IsMuted;
    mutedTextBlock.Text = mediaElement.IsMuted ? "muted" : string.Empty;
}
```

The event handler code also updates a `TextBlock` to provide the user with feedback when the media player is muted. The `mutedTextBlock` doesn't exist yet, so add a new `TextBlock` control to MainPage.xaml:

```
<TextBlock x:Name="mutedTextBlock" Grid.Row="3"
    HorizontalAlignment="Right" VerticalAlignment="Bottom" />
```

Add the `TextBlock` to the bottom row of the `ContentPanel`, to the right of the volume control. When the media player is muted, the control displays the word *muted* and displays nothing otherwise.

With the mute feature implemented, you're finished with the MediaPlayback sample application. Run the application and play with the volume slider and Mute button to make certain they work as expected. Though not quite as powerful and feature-rich as its WPF and Silverlight for the browser cousins, the `MediaElement` in Windows Phone should meet most of your media playback needs.

15.3 Summary

`MediaElement` allow Windows Phone developers to create cool multimedia applications incorporating audio and video, whether building a full media player or incorporating clips into a game or application.

Windows Phone supports a wide variety of audio and video containers and decoders but does have its limitations. Knowing the limits of the phone platform and of each of the media elements is important when working with your application teams. You don't want to find out that the media clip your animators and designers built is in a format that won't work on the phone.

In this chapter we looked at `MediaElement`, one of XAML's advanced controls. In the next chapter we take a deep dive into another advanced XAML control: the `Map` control.

16 Using Maps

This chapter covers

- Launching the built-in Maps application
- Determining device location
- Drawing movement on an embedded map
- Querying an address for a location

One of the appealing features of a smartphone like the Windows Phone is the ability to quickly discover your location or the location of nearby landmarks, especially when it's paired with features that provide directions between your location and a destination. Such location-aware features are made possible by two related technologies essential for mobile platforms: Map Services and Location Services. *Map Services* provide the user with maps, directions, and searches for nearby businesses and landmarks. *Location Services* can be used to determine the device's current location based on input from the cellular and Wi-Fi networks and the Global Positioning System (GPS). The Windows Phone SDK enables developers to access these technologies from within their applications.

The built-in Maps application can be started from within an application using tasks that launch the native application and push the running application to the background. When a more integrated user experience is desired, the developer can embed a map into an application using XAML controls provided in the SDK and the Windows Phone Toolkit.

In this chapter we demonstrate how to use Location Services to pinpoint a device's position on the globe inside a location-aware application. In addition to providing latitude and longitude, Location Services can also provide altitude, speed, and heading. Location Services are more than a simple GPS sensor. They combine GPS, Wi-Fi, and cellular network data with a web service to provide location information. You'll combine Location Services with the XAML `Map` control and explore how to display an embedded map pinpointing the user's location and tracking their movements. We also discuss in detail how to use the Maps API to determine the user's physical address using their current location.

Bing Maps and the GeoCoordinateWatcher

There are two different sets of Map APIs and Location Services for Windows Phone. One set is new to the Windows Phone 8 SDK and is covered in this chapter. The older set, originally part of the Windows Phone 7 SDK, is maintained in Windows Phone 8 for backward compatibility but isn't covered in this chapter.

The older set of Maps APIs uses the Bing `Maps` control, `BingMapsTask`, and `BingMapsDirectionsTask`. The Bing `Maps` control, from the `Microsoft.Phone.Maps.Controls` namespace, is deprecated and shouldn't be used in new Windows Phone 8 applications. If you use the Bing `Maps` control, you must manually reference the Microsoft .Phone.Maps.Controls.dll assembly found in the Windows 8 SDK libraries folder (C:\ProgramFiles(x86)\MicrosoftSDKs\WindowsPhone\v8.0\Libraries).

The `GeoCoordinateWatcher` is a .NET Framework Location Service component in the `System.Device.Location` namespace. Although the `GeoCoordinateWatcher` isn't covered in this chapter, you'll use other classes from the `System.Device.Location` namespace.

Version 8 of the Windows Phone SDK added four new Maps launchers to provide developers with an easy way to integrate maps into an application. The new launcher tasks are as follows:

- `MapsTask` launches the Maps application.
- `MapsDirectionsTask` launches the Maps application and displays driving directions between two points.
- `MapDownloaderTask` opens the Maps Settings application and allows the user to download offline map data.
- `MapUpdaterTask` opens the Maps Settings application and allows the user to update offline map data.

To highlight the Maps and Locations APIs, you're going to build two different sample applications. First, we introduce you to maps by showing you how to build a sample that launches two of the Maps tasks.

16.1 Introducing Maps

Applications can include mapping features by either launching the native Maps application or by embedding the XAML `Map` control into the application user interface. In this section you'll build a simple application to demonstrate how to use the `MapsTask` and `MapsDirectionsTask`. The sample application, shown in figure 16.1, prompts the user to enter a search term or two locations. It lets the user launch the native Maps application to show the specific location and driving directions.

You'll get started by preparing a new project with the basic user interface controls and buttons required to allow the user to interact with Maps.

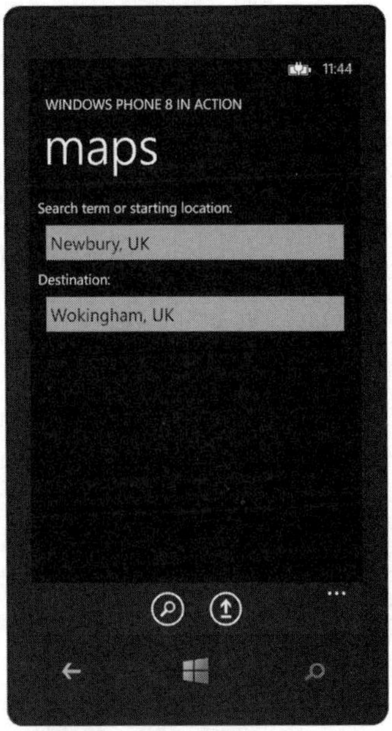

Figure 16.1 The MapsTasks sample application

16.1.1 Preparing the application

Your first sample application is named MapsTasks and is based on the Windows Phone App project template. Open Visual Studio and create the new project. The main user interface prompts the user to enter a search term or starting location and a destination location. These locations aren't necessarily full addresses and are passed to the launchers as search terms. Open MainPage.xaml and add a `StackPanel` with two `TextBlocks` and two `TextBoxes` to the `ContentPanel`:

```
<StackPanel>
    <TextBlock Text="Search term or starting location:" />
    <TextBox x:Name="departureTerm" />
    <TextBlock Text="Destination:" />
    <TextBox x:Name="destinationTerm" />
</StackPanel>
```

The `TextBoxes` should be named `departureTerm` and `destinationTerm` to allow you to access their `Text` properties from code-behind in MainPage.xaml.cs.

The application also needs two buttons to enable the two different features in the application. The first feature opens the native Maps application with the starting location centered in the map. The second feature opens the native Maps application showing driving directions between the starting and destination locations:

```
<phone:PhoneApplicationPage.ApplicationBar>
   <shell:ApplicationBar>
      <shell:ApplicationBarIconButton Text="map task" Click="mapTask_Click"
            IconUri="/Assets/AppBar/feature.search.png" />
      <shell:ApplicationBarIconButton Text="directions"
            Click="directionTask_Click"
            IconUri="/Assets/AppBar/upload.png" />
   </shell:ApplicationBar>
</phone:PhoneApplicationPage.ApplicationBar>
```

The images used for the buttons come from the Windows Phone SDK. Go ahead and create empty `Click` event handlers for both buttons. You'll add implementations for each `Click` event handler as you progress through the section. The first `Click` event handler will launch the built-in Maps application using the `MapsTask`.

16.1.2 Launching the Maps application

The built-in Maps application can be launched from any third-party application using the `MapsTask` launcher class. You learned how to use launchers and choosers in chapter 5. The `MapsTask` launcher exposes three properties to determine its behavior: `Center`, `SearchTerm`, and `ZoomLevel`.

Use the `Center` property to determine where the map is to be centered. If no value is specified for the `Center` property, the map will attempt to center itself at the device's current location. The centering behavior is influenced by the search term and zoom level values specified when the task is launched, as well as locations used in previous searches.

The optional `SearchTerm` property is a string used to highlight specific points on the map. The search term might contain a full or partial address, a city name, or the name of a landmark. The `SearchTerm` might specify other type of searches as well. For example, the user could type *pizzeria* to find the closest restaurant serving pizzas. Locations matching the search term are identified on the map with a labeled or numbered pushpin, as shown in figure 16.2.

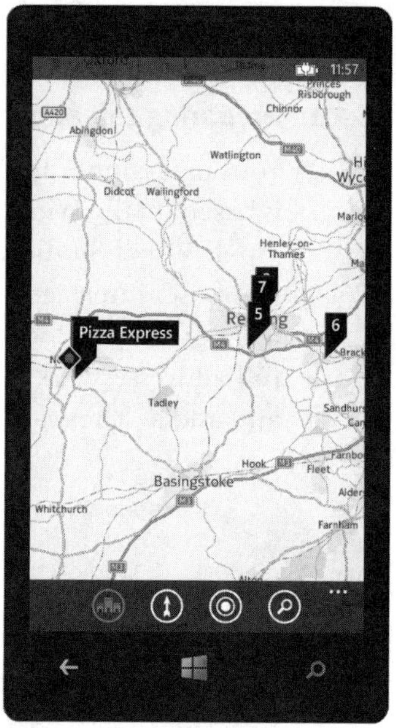

Figure 16.2 Searching for a local pizzeria with the MapsTask. The current location is shown on the map as a black diamond with a dot in the center, colored with the system's theme accent color. Locations or landmarks matching the search term are marked with labeled and numbered pushpins.

The `ZoomLevel` controls the initial zoom level to be used to display the map. The `MapsTask` documentation doesn't clarify what the appropriate values are for a zoom level, but our experimentation suggests that reasonable values are between 10 and 20.

The MapsTasks sample application uses the `MapsTask` when the user taps the first button in the application bar. The following listing shows the implementation of the button's `Click` event handler.

Listing 16.1 Launching Maps

```
using Microsoft.Phone.Tasks;
void mapTask_Click(object sender, EventArgs e)
{
    if(string.IsNullOrEmpty(departureTerm.Text))
```

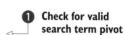

❶ Check for valid search term pivot

```
    {
        MessageBox.Show("Please enter a start location.");
        return;
    }
    var task = new MapsTask
    {
        SearchTerm = departureTerm.Text,
        ZoomLevel = 15,
    };
    task.Show();                                    ❷ Launch Maps
}
```

Before doing any work, the code checks whether the user has entered a valid search term ❶. The MapsTask requires either the Center property or the SearchTerm property to be set and will throw an InvalidOperationException if both are empty. If the search term is valid, construct a new instance of the MapsTask and set the SearchTerm property to the value of the departureTerm.Text field. The ZoomLevel is hardcoded to 15. The Maps application is launched with a call to the Show method ❷.

The application is now ready to test your first feature. Run the application on either your device or the emulator, enter a search term, and tap the Map task button.

Now let's move on to implementing the second feature: displaying directions between two locations.

16.1.3 Finding directions

MapsTask doesn't come alone. A second Maps launcher called MapsDirectionsTask provides an easy way to get directions from Maps. MapsDirectionsTask can be customized using two properties called Start and End. Both these properties are of the type LabeledMapLocation, and at least one of the two must be set or MapsDirectionsTask will throw an InvalidOperationException when launched. When the MapsDirectionsTask is launched, and either the Start or End property isn't set, the map will use the device's current position in place of the missing property.

The LabeledMapLocation class is used to provide a geographic coordinate along with a label for the location. If a GeoCoordinate isn't specified in the LabledMapLocation's Location property, MapsDirectionsTask interprets the Label property in much the same way that MapsTask interprets its SearchTerm property.

The MapsTasks sample application uses the MapsDirectionsTask when the user taps the second button in the application bar. The button's Click event handler is shown in the following listing.

Listing 16.2 Launching Maps to calculate directions

```
void directionTask_Click(object sender, EventArgs e)
{
    LabeledMapLocation start = null;
    LabeledMapLocation end = null;
    if (!string.IsNullOrEmpty(departureTerm.Text))
        start = new LabeledMapLocation { Label = departureTerm.Text };

    if (!string.IsNullOrEmpty(destinationTerm.Text))
```

❶ Did user input search term?

```
        end = new LabeledMapLocation { Label = destinationTerm.Text };
    if (start == null && end == null)
    {
        MessageBox.Show("Please enter start and/or end locations.");
        return;
    }
    var task = new MapsDirectionsTask { Start = start, End = end };
    task.Show();
}
```

Check for valid locations ❷ (points to `if (start == null && end == null)`)

❸ Launch Maps (points to `task.Show();`)

The listing begins by declaring two `LabeledMapLocation` variables, one for the departure location and the other for the destination location. The `LabeledMapLocations` are constructed only when the user has entered a term in the related `TextBox` controls ❶. To avoid an `InvalidOperationException`, the code checks to see that at least one valid location was created ❷. Finally a `MapsDirectionsTask` is constructed and launched to show the built-in Maps application ❸. You can see an example of the Maps application displaying turn-by-turn directions in figure 16.3.

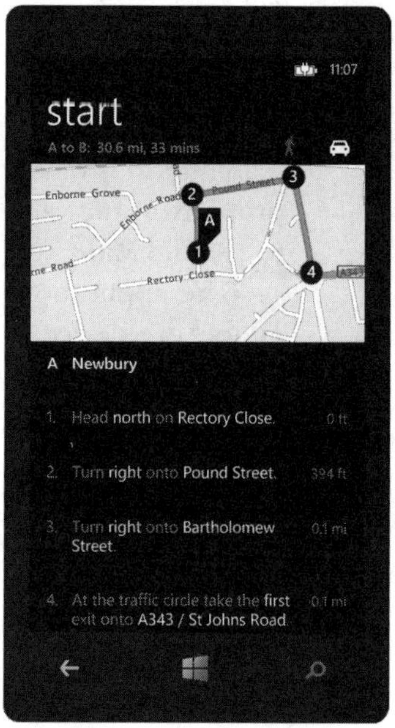

Figure 16.3 Turn-by-turn directions as displayed in the Maps application. The starting point is labeled with a lettered pushpin, and each turning point in the list is marked on the map with a numbered dot. The route is also marked as a line between each of the turning points.

Test your second feature by running the application, entering two search terms, and tapping the Directions task button. Press the Back button to return to the application, delete one of the terms, and tap the Directions task button again. Continue to return to the application to enter different search terms until you're comfortable with how the `MapsDirectionsTask` works with various combinations of search terms.

The Maps tasks are ideal for adding simple mapping features to your application that match the look and feel the user expects from a mapping application. The downside of using the Maps tasks is that your application becomes dormant when the Maps application is launched. You can keep your application alive—and more importantly keep the user in your application—by embedding a `Map` control right into your application.

The next sample application shows how to combine the Windows Phone 8 XAML `Map` control with Location Services to provide a rich map experience inside an application.

16.2 Embedding a Map control

Earlier in the chapter you learned how to use the Maps tasks to display maps to a user. What if you want a `Map` control inside your application, instead of launching out to the native Maps application? Have no fear: you can embed a map right inside your application.

The XAML `Map` control, found in the `Microsoft.Phone.Maps.Controls` namespace, performs most of the work necessary to render a map. This means you don't need to write any code to interact with a web server to download tiles, manage zooming animations, or respond to user-initiated touch events. The `Map` control is extensible and allows the application to layer custom elements on top of the rendered map.

Although a map by itself can be fascinating, mobile phone users expect a map to provide additional features, such as tracking their position and providing a physical address for their current location. These map-related features are exposed to a developer in the form of Map and Location Services, as we've mentioned.

The Map Service provides a number of different APIs exposing a variety of data. These include APIs for converting an address into latitude and longitude (*geocoding*) and from latitude and longitude into an address (*reverse geocoding*), as well as an API that returns driving directions. These APIs are implemented in the `GeocodeQuery`, `ReverseGeocodeQuery`, and `RouteQuery` classes found in the .NET Framework namespace `Microsoft.Phone.Maps.Services`.

Location Services are made up of different bits of hardware, software, and web services. The hardware includes a built-in GPS receiver, the cellular radio, and the wireless network adapter. The web service fronts a database that records the coordinates of wireless access points. The data from the web service, GPS, and cellular radio is analyzed to calculate the phone's current longitude, latitude, and altitude. All this complexity is hidden behind the interface of a single Windows Phone Runtime class called `Geolocator`, found in the `Windows.Devices.Geolocation` namespace. `Geolocator` provides the properties, methods, and events that an application uses to read location data.

> **NOTE** The `ID_CAP_MAP` capability must be declared in the WMAppManifest.xml when using the `Map` control or the Map Service. Likewise, the `ID_CAP_LOCATION` capability must be declared in order to use the `Geolocator`.

To learn how to use the `Map` control, query the Map Service, and retrieve location from the `Geolocator`, you'll build a new sample application called LocationAndMaps.

16.2.1 Building the LocationAndMaps sample application

Start the new sample application by creating a new Windows Phone App named LocationAndMaps. This project will use the Windows Phone Toolkit, so go ahead and use the NuGet Package Manager to add a reference to the toolkit assembly. The application is fairly simple, displaying two `TextBlocks` and a `Map`. The application is shown in figure 16.4.

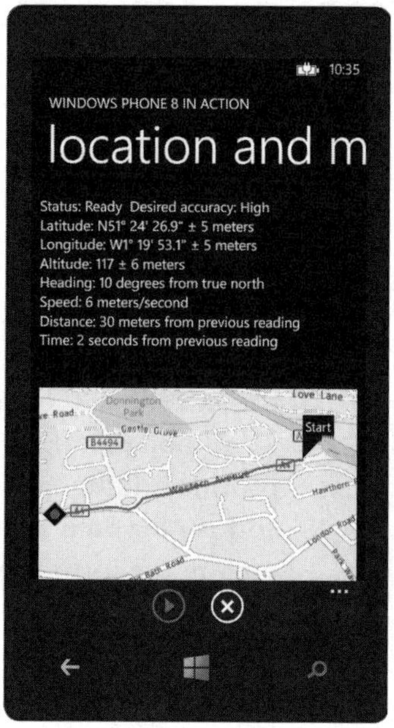

Figure 16.4 The LocationAndMaps sample application

The first `TextBlock` displays the `Status` reported by the `Geolocator`, and the second `TextBlock` displays information about the current location. The two `TextBlocks` are placed in a `StackPanel`, which is placed in the `ContentPanel` in MainPage.xaml, as shown in the following listing.

Listing 16.3 The XAML markup for the LocationsAndMaps main page

```
<phone:PhoneApplicationPage ...
  xmlns:maps="clr-namespace:Microsoft.Phone.Maps.Controls;
  ➥ assembly=Microsoft.Phone.Maps"
...
  <Grid x:Name="ContentPanel" Grid.Row="1" Margin="12,0,12,0">
    <Grid.RowDefinitions>
      <RowDefinition />
      <RowDefinition />
    </Grid.RowDefinitions>
    <StackPanel>
      <TextBlock x:Name="status" Text="Loading..."/>
      <TextBlock x:Name="position" />
    </StackPanel>
    <maps:Map x:Name="mapControl" Grid.Row="1" />
  </Grid>
```

1 Add maps and maps toolkit names

2 Add map to content panel

As we mentioned, the `Map` control is located in the `Microsoft.Phone.Maps.Controls` namespace. The XAML compiler doesn't automatically recognize this namespace, so you need to add an `xmlns` attribute to the top of the MainPage.xaml file **1**. The sample application displays the `Map` control in the second row of the `ContentPanel Grid` control **2** in the LocationAndMaps project's MainPage.xaml file.

TIP The maps xml namespace is added automatically if you use the Visual Studio Toolbox to drag and drop a `Map` control onto the Visual Studio Designer.

Drag, pinch, and other gestures supported in the native Maps application are supported in the `Map` control. The application generated from listing 16.3 is shown in figure 16.5.

If you run the application now, you should see the `Map` control displayed in the bottom half of the phone's screen. But the device's current location isn't represented on the map. The `Map` control doesn't know how to obtain the device's current location. You must determine the device's coordinates programmatically and assign them to the map's `Center` property. For the LocationAndMaps sample application, you'll determine the device's current coordinates with the `Geolocator`.

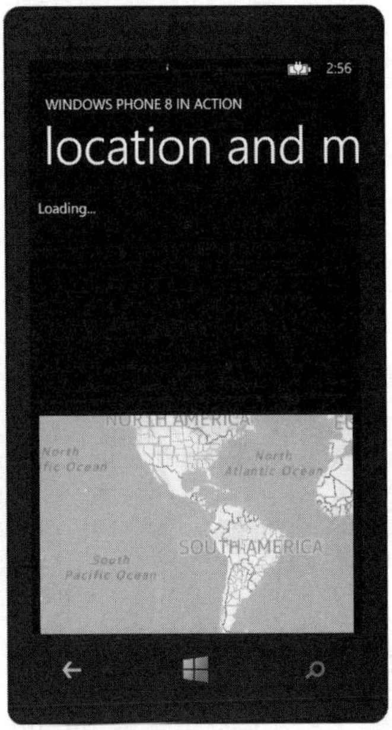

Figure 16.5 The LocationAndMaps sample application displaying a map

16.2.2 Centering on your current location with the Geolocator

The `Geolocator` is a Windows Phone Runtime class that reports location in two different ways: as a one-time asynchronous request and continuously via an event handler. If you expect that users will be relatively stationary while using your application, consider using `GetGeopositionAsync`. But if your use cases involve a highly mobile user—such as a tracking a daily jog or updating driving directions as the user approaches the destination—use the `PositionChanged` event. Let's look at the `GetGeopositonAsync` first. We'll look at continuous tracking later in the chapter.

`GetGeopositionAsync`, as the name implies, is an asynchronous operation that may take several seconds to complete. The `Geolocator` may need to turn on the cellular radio, Wi-Fi network adapter, and/or GPS receiver—which all take time. `Get-GeopositionAsync` returns a `Geoposition` object containing the device's current coordinate in its `Coordinate` property.

Remember that you want to query for the current device location when the application first starts up so that you can center the map and mark the user's position. You want to do this only after the `Map` control has been loaded. Wire up the loaded event handler in MainPage.xaml:

```
<maps:Map x:Name="mapControl" Grid.Row="1" Loaded="mapControl_Loaded" />
```

The `Geolocator` is found in the Windows Phone Runtime namespace called `Windows.Devices.Geolocation`. Include the `Geolocation` namespace along with the .NET

System.Device.Location namespace at the top of the MainPage.xaml.cs file, as shown in the following listing detailing the loaded event handler implementation.

Listing 16.4 Reading the device's current location

```
using System.Device.Location;                     // Include location namespaces
using Windows.Devices.Geolocation;
...
async void mapControl_Loaded(object sender, RoutedEventArgs e)
{
   status.Text = "querying for current location...";
   Geolocator locator = new Geolocator();
   Geoposition geoPosition = await locator.GetGeopositionAsync ();          // 1 Asynchronously request location
   GeoCoordinate coordinate = geoPosition.Coordinate.ToGeoCoordinate();     // 2 Convert Geocoordinate to GeoCoordinate
   mapControl.Center = coordinate;
   mapControl.ZoomLevel = 10;                                               // 3 Zoom in map

   position.Text = string.Format("Latitude: {0}\nLongitude: {1}\n",
       FormatCoordinate (coordinate.Latitude, 'N', 'S'),                    // 4 Display longitude and latitude
       FormatCoordinate (coordinate.Longitude, 'E', 'W'));
   status.Text += "complete";
}
```

Reading a device's location is as easy as constructing a Geolocator and asynchronously calling its GetGeopositionAsync method ❶. There's a slight incompatibility between the Windows Runtime Geolocator and the .NET API Map control—they use different classes to represent a coordinate. Geolocation uses a Geocoordinate from the Windows.Devices.Geolocation namespace. The Map control uses GeoCoordinate from the System.Device.Location namespace. Fortunately, the Windows Phone Toolkit provides an extension class to help convert one to the other. In listing 16.4 the toolkit's ToGeoCoordinate method ❷ is used to convert the Geolocator-provided coordinate before assigning it to the map's Center property. The Map's ZoomLevel property is changed ❸, giving the user a closer look at their location. The coordinate's Longitude and Latitude properties are displayed in the position TextBlock ❹, making use of a new method called FormatCoordinate (figure 16.6).

The ZoomLevel controls the zoom level to be used to display the map. As with the MapsTask, the Map control's documentation doesn't clarify what the appropriate values are for a zoom level, and the ZoomLevel property in listing 16.4 is hardcoded to level 10.

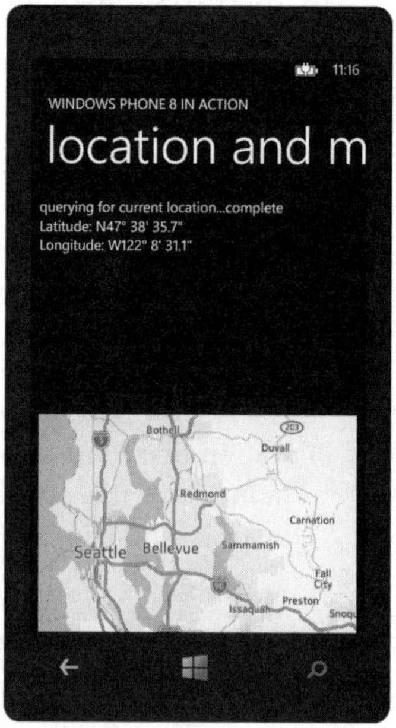

Figure 16.6 After calling Get-GeopositionAsync, the Map control's Center property is assigned to the retrieved coordinate. The longitude and latitude are also displayed in the sample application.

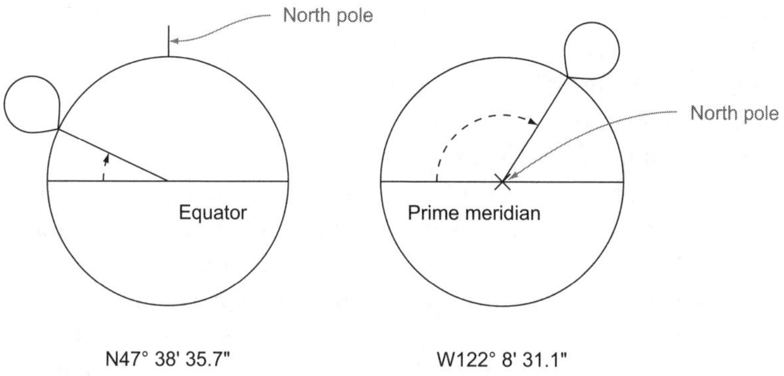

Figure 16.7 Latitude is the angle measured from the equator to a particular location, as shown in the left image. The right image demonstrates how longitude is measured as the angle from the prime meridian to a particular location.

FORMATTING LONGITUDE AND LATITUDE

`Geolocator` reports longitude and latitude as floating-point numbers representing the number of degrees east or west of the prime meridian and the number of degrees north or south of the equator, as shown in figure 16.7. Positive latitude values represent a position north of the equator. Positive longitude values represent a position east of the prime meridian. A few common formats are used to display degrees, and the sample application uses a format that breaks the number into degrees, minutes, and seconds:

N47° 38' 35.7"
W122° 8' 31.1"

The `FormatCoordinate` method accepts an angle measurement in degrees, along with the characters to display for positive and negative values, and returns a string displaying direction, degrees, minutes, and seconds. The following listing shows the implementation of `FormatCoordinate`.

Listing 16.5 Formatting longitude or latitude

```
string FormatCoordinate (double coordinate,
    char positive, char negative)
{
    char direction = coordinate >= 0 ? positive : negative;
    coordinate = Math.Abs(coordinate);
    double degrees = Math.Floor(coordinate);
    double minutes = Math.Floor((coordinate - degrees) * 60.0D);
    double seconds = (((coordinate - degrees) * 60.0D) - minutes) * 60.0D;
    string result = string.Format("{0}{1:F0}° {2:F0}' {3:F1}\"",
        direction, degrees, minutes, seconds);
    return result;
}
```

❶ Determine character for direction

❷ Convert decimal portion into minutes

The listing starts by picking the character that should be shown ❶. For example, the calling code should pass in `N` and `S` for latitude, and if the coordinate value is negative,

S should be shown. Next, the value is broken up into whole degrees, minutes, and seconds, using the Math.Floor method to return the whole part of a number. To calculate the number of minutes ❷, you subtract out the whole part of the coordinate value and multiply by 60. You do a similar operation to calculate the number of seconds. Finally, the numbers are formatted into a string.

By default, the Geolocator uses the most efficient mechanism for determining the current location. When a device's location is calculated (possibly even in another application), it's cached by the operating system. GetGeopositionAsync returns the cached location, if it isn't too stale, eliminating the need to turn on hardware and query remote devices for information. If the device doesn't have a location cached, the Geolocator uses location data calculated from nearby cellular towers or the Wi-Fi network. Usually the GPS receiver isn't turned on unless you specifically ask for highly accurate position data. We discuss position accuracy in more depth later in this chapter.

NOTE By default, the emulator believes that it's located at Microsoft's Redmond campus.

Now that you have the map centered, it would be nice to display a widget on it that represents the device's location. That way, if the user scrolls the map (using gestures), they'll still know where they are in relation to what's shown on the screen.

16.2.3 Marking the current location on the map

One beneficial feature of the Map control is that it allows the user to change the view with pinch, zoom, and drag gestures. When the view changes, so does the programmatically assigned Center point, and the user may lose track of their current position. Adding a widget to the map that represents the current location will keep the user grounded. Because the Map control is a UI element, you could always overlay another widget over the top of it, but then you'd have to worry about converting UI coordinates to the geographic coordinates where the widget should appear and how to keep the Map and widget in sync as the user zooms and scrolls.

To deal with this scenario, the Map control acts as a container that hosts content objects and controls. The content object or control is placed into a MapOverlay, which is itself placed into a MapLayer. As shown in figure 16.8, multiple overlays can be placed into the same layer, and the Map control supports multiple layers.

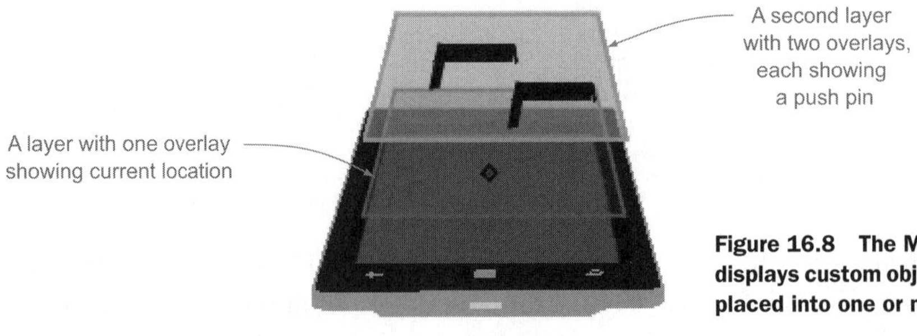

Figure 16.8 The Map control displays custom objects as overlays placed into one or more layers.

A MapLayer is nothing more than a collection of overlays, and overlays are dependency objects that contain content, content templates, and positions. MapOverlay positions are specified as GeoCoordinates. The Map then handles the conversion of GeoCoordinate to screen coordinate and determines whether the overlay's position is currently scrolled into view.

The Windows Phone Toolkit simplifies working with map overlays through the MapExtensions.GetChildren custom dependency property. The children collection allows you to add and remove any DependencyObject to/from the map. Behind the scenes, the toolkit creates the appropriate layers, overlays, and, where necessary, a content presenter.

The sample application will use MapExtensions to add a marker to the map at the device's current location. To keep your application consistent with the look and feel of the Windows Phone, you want your widget to look as much as possible like the widget used by the built-in application. Once again the Windows Phone toolkit comes to the rescue by including UserLocationMarker, a XAML control specifically designed to show the device's current location exactly as the native Maps application does. UserLocationMarker is derived from the toolkit's MapChildControl, which in turn is derived from the XAML ContentControl. The following listing demonstrates how to use MapExtensions.GetChildren to add a UserLocationMarker to the map.

Listing 16.6 Add a UserLocationMarker

```
using Microsoft.Phone.Maps.Toolkit;
UserLocationMarker marker;                                        // (1) Add field for marker control pivot

async void mapControl_Loaded(object sender, RoutedEventArgs e)
{
   ...
   marker = new UserLocationMarker();
   marker.GeoCoordinate = coordinate;
   MapExtensions.GetChildren(mapControl).Add(marker);             // (2) Add marker to Map

   status.Text += "complete";
}
```

After providing a using statement to include the toolkit's namespace, add a field to reference the UserLocationMarker instance ❶. In the Map's loaded event handler, which was created in the last section, new code is added to instantiate a UserLocationMarker and assign to the marker field. UserLocationMarker's GeoCoordinate property identifies exactly where the marker should be located on the map. The marker is added to the map by adding it to the collection found in the Children attached property provided by the toolkit's MapExtensions class ❷.

Run the application. You should now see a marker situated right in the center of the map, as shown in figure 16.9.

Use a variety of pinch, zoom, and drag gestures to enlarge and scroll the map. The marker's position should adjust to the changes to the Map's view, appropriately redrawing at the screen coordinate representing the marker's GeoCoordinate. The Map's ability to convert screen coordinates into GeoCoordinates is showcased again in the next section, where you add a new feature to the application that allows a user to look up an address by tapping a location on a map.

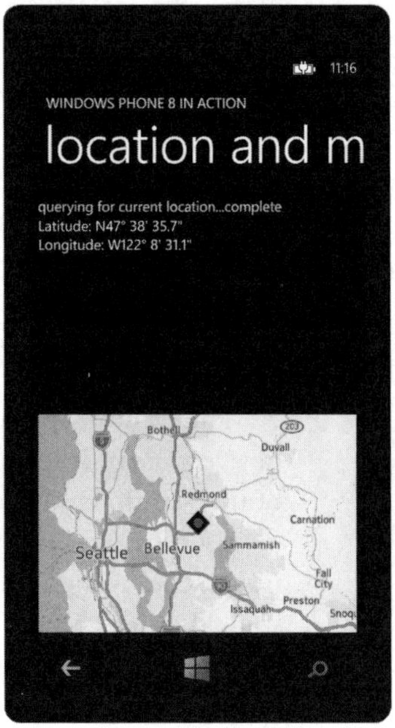

Figure 16.9 The LocationAndMaps sample application with a `UserLocationMarker` centered on the device's current location.

16.3 Reverse geocoding—looking up an address

Map Services provide a few different APIs exposing a variety of data. Some of these APIs convert an address into latitude and longitude (*geocoding*) and from latitude and longitude into an address (*reverse geocoding*). Map Services also perform *route calculation*, returning walking or driving directions from one location to another. Each of these requests is executed using a Microsoft.Phone.Maps.Services.Query<T> object. There are three different implementations of Query<T> in the Microsoft.Phone.Maps.Services namespace:

- RouteQuery class calculates directions and returns a Route.
- GeocodeQuery searches for GeoCoordinates of an address or search term and returns a list of MapLocations.
- ReverseGeocodeQuery looks up an address for a given GeoCoordinate and returns a list of MapLocations.

The LocationAndMaps sample application will use a ReverseGeocodeQuery to look up an address when the user performs a tap-and-hold gesture over a location on the Map control. This code will be added to an event handler for the Map's Hold event.

Start by wiring up the Hold event in MainPage.xaml:

```
<maps:Map x:Name="mapControl" Grid.Row="1"
     Loaded="mapControl_Loaded" Hold="mapControl_Hold" />
```

Before calling the reverse geocode service, you must create and populate a ReverseGeocodeQuery. The query requires a GeoCoordinate, which is populated with the coordinate corresponding to the location tapped by the user. The following listing demonstrates how to create and execute a ReverseGeocodeQuery in the Map's Hold event handler.

Listing 16.7 Executing a ReverseGeocodeQuery

```
using Microsoft.Phone.Maps.Services;
...
int pinNumber = 0;
async void mapControl_Hold(object sender, GestureEventArgs e)
{
   status.Text = "querying for address...";

   var point = e.GetPosition(mapControl);
   var coordinate =
      mapControl.ConvertViewportPointToGeoCoordinate(point);

   var pushpin = new Pushpin
   {
      GeoCoordinate = coordinate,
      Content = ++pinNumber
   };
   MapExtensions.GetChildren(mapControl).Add(pushpin);

   position.Text = string.Format("Latitude: {0}\nLongitude: {1}\n",
       FormatCoordinate (coordinate.Latitude, 'N', 'S'),
       FormatCoordinate (coordinate.Longitude, 'E', 'W'));

   ReverseGeocodeQuery query = new ReverseGeocodeQuery ();
   query.GeoCoordinate = coordinate;
   IList<MapLocation> results = await query.GetMapLocationsAsync();
   position.Text += string.Format("{0} locations found.\n", results.Count);

   MapLocation location = results.FirstOrDefault();
   if (location != null)
   {
      position.Text += FormatAddress(location.Information.Address);
   }
   status.Text += "complete";
}
```

❶ Convert screen coordinates to GeoCoordinate

❷ Mark location with pushpin

❸ Asynchronously execute query with Toolkit extension

The method starts out by reading the tapped screen position from the GestureEventArgs instance. The screen position is converted to a GeoCoordinate with the Map's ConvertViewportPointToGeoCoordinate method ❶. A Pushpin control ❷ is constructed with the specified coordinate and the value of pinNumber, a field created expressly for counting the number of pins added to the map. Pushpin, another control from the Windows Phone Toolkit, can be seen in figure 16.10. The Pushpin is added to the Map's Children attached property, and the longitude and latitude are displayed in the user interface.

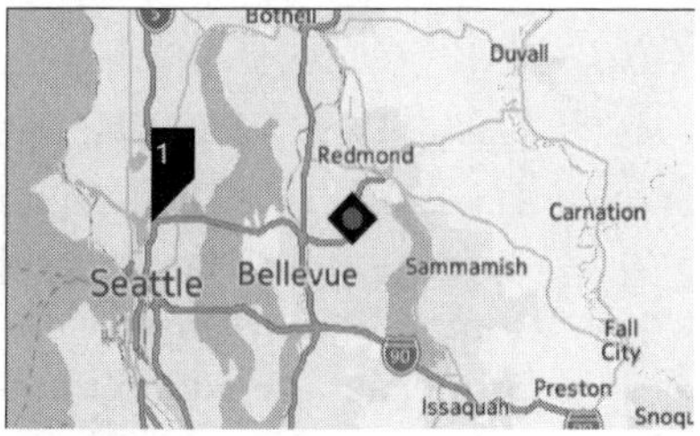

Figure 16.10 A Map control displaying a numbered Pushpin and a UserLocationMarker

One more Windows Phone Toolkit feature is used to asynchronously execute the `ReverseGeocodeQuery`. `GetMapLocationsAsync` is an extension method provided by the toolkit's `QueryExtensions` class that allows you to use the `async/await` pattern to query the Map Service ❸. The result of the query is a list of `MapLocation` objects, and the user interface is updated to show the count of `MapLocations` returned, as well as the address of the first location. The address is formatted in a new `FormatAddress` method.

> **NOTE** If you choose not to use the `async/await` support provided by the Windows Phone Toolkit `QueryExtensions` class, you can execute a query by subscribing to the `Query<T>.QueryCompleted` event and then calling `DoQueryAsync`.

FORMATTING REVERSE GEOCODING QUERY RESULTS

Found in the `Microsoft.Phone.Maps.Service` namespace, the `MapLocation` class declares `BoundingBox`, `GeoCoordinate`, and `Information` properties. In our testing, the `BoundingBox` property in the `MapLocations` returned by `ReverseGeocodeQuery` is always `null`. We also noticed that the `Information` class was only sparsely populated and that its `Name` and `Description` properties, as well as most of its `Address` properties, are empty. The `FormatAddress` method, shown in the following listing, accepts a `MapAddress` parameter and examines its properties before adding them to a formatted string.

Listing 16.8 Formatting the query results for display

```
using System.Text;
string FormatAddress(MapAddress address)
{
   StringBuilder b = new StringBuilder();
   if (!string.IsNullOrWhiteSpace(address.HouseNumber))      <- Add only if not empty pivot
      b.AppendFormat("{0} ", address.HouseNumber);

   if (!string.IsNullOrWhiteSpace(address.Street))
      b.AppendFormat("{0}\n", address.Street);

   if (!string.IsNullOrWhiteSpace(address.City))
      b.AppendFormat("{0}, ", address.City);

   b.AppendFormat("{0}  {1}", address.State, address.PostalCode);
   return b.ToString();
}
```

`FormatAddress` incrementally builds an address using a `StringBuilder`. The `MapAddress` properties `HouseNumber`, `Street`, and `City` are added to the builder only if they contain a non-empty value. The `State` and `PostalCode` properties are added to the builder, and the whole string is returned. The resulting user interface is shown in figure 16.11.

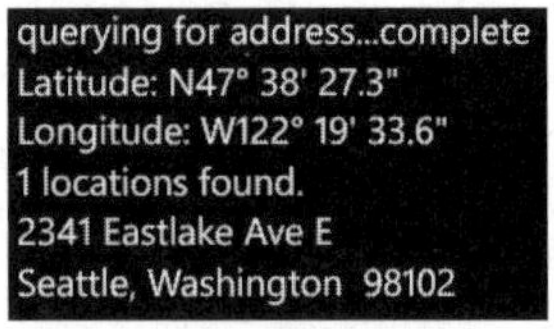

Figure 16.11 The address retrieved by reverse geocoding a coordinate

Run the LocationAndMaps sample application now, performing tap-and-hold gestures at several locations on the map. Try to find your home, your favorite coffee shop, or a nearby landmark and see how accurately the Map Services report its address.

You now have two of the LocationAndMaps sample application features complete. The remaining feature requires continuously tracking the device location and recording the route taken on the `Map` control.

16.4 Continuous tracking with Geolocator

Continuous tracking is the process whereby, for one reason or another, the device's position is recorded every few seconds or minutes. One popular category of location tracking applications allows runners or cyclists to record routes and times of their practices and races. Another popular class of applications is used to record where a car was parked and trace the route traveled from the parking lot, so a user can quickly find their way back. Perhaps the best example of continuous tracking is voice-enabled GPS navigation—those handy applications that plot driving directions and tell you when to turn.

In this section, the LocationAndMaps sample application is enhanced to allow the user to start and stop continuous tracking and to trace the device's movements on a map. You can see an example of the route traced by continuous tracking in figure 16.12.

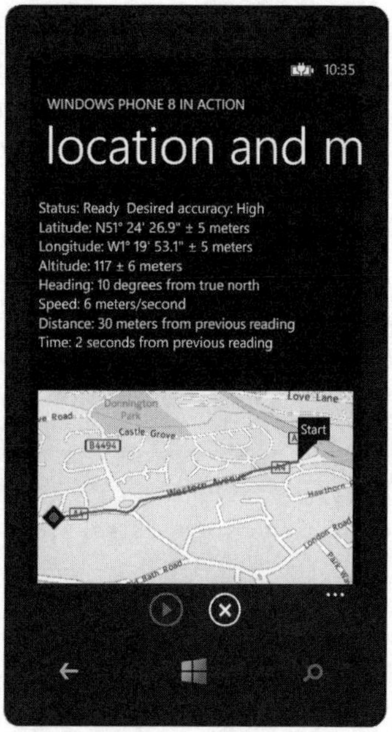

Figure 16.12 The LocationAndMaps application continuously tracking location. The start position is identified with a pushpin, the current position with a location marker, and the route from start to end drawn over the map. While tracking, the map appears tilted, and position information is displayed.

The sample application uses the `ApplicationBar` to present the user with two buttons. The first button starts the tracking with high accuracy. The second button stops continuous tracking:

```
<phone:PhoneApplicationPage.ApplicationBar>
   <shell:ApplicationBar>
      <shell:ApplicationBarIconButton Text="start" Click="start_Click"
            IconUri="/Assets/AppBar/transport.play.png" />
      <shell:ApplicationBarIconButton Text="stop" Click="stop_Click"
            IconUri="/Assets/AppBar/stop.png" />
   </shell:ApplicationBar>
</phone:PhoneApplicationPage.ApplicationBar>
```

The images for the buttons come from the icons library included with the Windows Phone SDK. The two `Click` event handlers are implemented in the next section. For now, add empty implementations of each method so that your code will compile.

You now have the skeleton in place for the continuous-tracking feature. In addition to implementing the `start_Click` and `stop_Click` methods, you need to create a member field for a `Geolocator` instance and hook it up to the rest of the application.

16.4.1 Working with high accuracy location data

The GPS receiver is the most accurate source of location data. This increased accuracy comes with a price, though. Activating the GPS receiver is an expensive operation, and the GPS uses a lot of battery power. Determining location from the cellular radio or the network adapter uses less battery power, with the tradeoff of decreased accuracy. The `Geolocator` allows the developer to specify the accuracy of location data with the `DesiredAccuracy` property. `DesiredAccuracy` can be set to one of the two values declared in the `PositionAccuracy` enumeration: `Default` or `High`. When reading data, the accuracy of the `GeoCoordinate` can be determined using the `IsUnknown`, `HorizontalAccuracy`, and `VerticalAccuracy` properties. Both the `HorizontalAccuracy` and `VerticalAccuracy` properties return the accuracy range in meters.

You've already learned how to construct a `Geolocator` and ask for a single position. This time when you construct an instance of the `Geolocator` in the `start_Click` method, you assign it to a member field. Instead of calling `GetGeopositionAsync`, you subscribe to two events that will report status and position. The `start_Click` implementation is shown in the following listing.

Listing 16.9 Initializing continuous tracking with high accuracy

```
Geolocator service;                                        <-- ❶ Declare member field
void start_Click (object sender, EventArgs e)
{
   ((ApplicationBarIconButton)ApplicationBar.Buttons[0]).IsEnabled = false;
   ((ApplicationBarIconButton)ApplicationBar.Buttons[1]).IsEnabled = true;
   service = new Geolocator();
   service.DesiredAccuracy = PositionAccuracy.High;
   service.MovementThreshold = 1.0;
   service.PositionChanged += service_PositionChanged;    ❷ Subscribe to
   service.StatusChanged += service_StatusChanged;           change events

   var startPin = new Pushpin
   {
      GeoCoordinate = marker.GeoCoordinate,
      Content = "Start"
   };
   MapExtensions.GetChildren(mapControl).Add(startPin);

   position.Text = string.Empty;
   status.Text = service.LocationStatus.ToString();
   mapControl.Pitch = 45.0;
}
```

Before adding code to the `start_Click` method, create a new class-level field named `service` ❶ to reference a `Geolocator` instance. Inside the `start_Click` method, change the `IsEnabled` properties of the two application bar buttons. Construct a new `Geolocator`, assigning it to the `service` field. Set the `DesiredAccuracy` to `High` and the `MovementThreshold` to `1.0` meter. Subscribe to the `PositionChanged` and `Status-Changed` events. The starting coordinate is read from the `marker` variable and marked on the map with a new `Pushpin` ❷. Update the user interface once everything is set up and ready to go: clear the position `TextBlock`, assign the `Geolocator` status to the `status TextBlock`, and change the `Map`'s `Pitch` property to `45`.

REPORTING GEOLOCATOR STATUS

The `Geolocator` reports its status via the `Status` property of the `StatusChanged` event. The status is reported as one of the values in the `PositionStatus` enumeration and is one of the following:

- `Disabled`
- `Ready`
- `Initializing`
- `NotInitialized`
- `NotAvailable`
- `NoData`

The sample application subscribes to the `StatusChanged` event and displays the current status and accuracy to the user in the `service_StatusChanged` method:

```
void service_StatusChanged(Geolocator sender, StatusChangedEventArgs args)
{
   Dispatcher.BeginInvoke(() =>
   {
      status.Text = string.Format("Status: {0}  Desired accuracy: {1}",
           args.Status, service.DesiredAccuracy);
   });
}
```

After the event handler executes, the user sees a message similar to that shown in figure 16.13.

Figure 16.13 The status message

The `Geolocator`'s continuous-tracking mode is enabled once an application subscribes to the `PositionChanged` or `StatusChanged` event. The `Geolocator` continues to monitor and report the device's location until the event subscriptions are removed or the application is exited or pushed to the background.

> **NOTE** Location-tracking applications can continue to run in the background if they're designed with background operation in mind and adhere to a few constraints. Background tracking applications must extend the `DefaultTask` element in WMAppManifest.xml and subscribe to the `PhoneApplication-Service.RunningInBackgroud` event. Background tracking applications can't update the user interface while in the background. For more information,

refer to the MSDN article "How to run location-tracking apps in the background for Windows Phone 8," located at http://mng.bz/gWWn.

At this point, the LocationAndMaps application only reports changes in the `Geolocator`'s status. This is useful because it may take a little while for the GPS receiver to be turned on and find a signal. If the GPS satellites can't be reached (for example, when the device is surrounded by materials that block the airwaves), it's a good idea to inform the user. It's not enough to report the `Geolocator`'s status. A continuous-tracking application needs to also report changes in position.

16.4.2 Reporting changes in position

When a devices position changes, the `Geolocator` raises the `PositionChanged` event, reporting the new `Geoposition`. In this section, the LocationAndMaps application is updated to display information about the new position in the user interface. In addition to reporting the current change, it would be nice to report how much it changed—how far the device traveled, how much time elapsed, and so on. Reporting changes in position is done in the `service_PostionChanged` method, shown in the following listing.

Listing 16.10 Handling the `PositionChanged` event

```
GeoCoordinate previous = new GeoCoordinate();         <-- ❶ Remember previous coordinate
DateTime previousTime = DateTime.Now;
void service_PositionChanged(Geolocator sender,
      PositionChangedEventArgs args)
{
   GeoCoordinate location = args.Position.Coordinate.ToGeoCoordinate();
   UpdateMap(location);
   UpdatePositionText(location);                 <-- ❷ Update user interface
   previous = location;
   previousTime = DateTime.Now;
}
```

Start by creating a new class-level `GeoCoordinate` field named `previous` ❶ to remember the last position reported by the `Geolocator` and a new `DateTime` field named `previousTime` to record the time. These new fields are used to inform the user how much distance was covered and how much time elapsed between the current reading and the previous reading. Implement the `service_PostionChanged` event handler. Read the current `Coordinate` from the `PositionChangedEventArgs`, converting from a `Geocoordinate` to a `GeoCoordinate`. Update the position of the user location marker by calling a new `UpdateMap` method. The text message in the user interface is updated ❷ by calling another new method named `UpdatePositionText`.

`UpdateMap` is responsible for updating the current position as the user moves, and, eventually, drawing the user's route on the map. The initial implementation of `UpdateMap` assigns the reported location to the `marker`'s `GeoCoordinate` property:

```
void UpdateMap(GeoCoordinate location)
{
```

```
    Dispatcher.BeginInvoke(() =>
    {
        marker.GeoCoordinate = location;
    });
}
```

The implementation of `UpdatePositionText` is shown in the next listing.

Listing 16.11 Display location in the user interface

```
private void UpdatePositionText(GeoCoordinate loc)
{
    StringBuilder b = new StringBuilder();
    b.AppendFormat("Latitude: {0} ± {1:F0} meters\n",
        FormatCoordinate (loc.Latitude, 'N', 'S'),          ❶ Format coordinate
        loc.HorizontalAccuracy);
    b.AppendFormat("Longitude: {0} ± {1:F0} meters\n",
        FormatCoordinate (loc.Longitude, 'E', 'W'),
        loc.HorizontalAccuracy);
    b.AppendFormat("Altitude: 0:F0} ± {1:F0} meters\n",
        loc.Altitude, loc.VerticalAccuracy);
    b.AppendFormat("Heading: {0:F0} degrees from true north\n",loc.Course);
    b.AppendFormat("Speed: {0:F0} meters/second\n", loc.Speed);
    double distance = Double.NaN;                           ❷ Calculate distance traveled
    if (!previous.IsUnknown)
        distance = loc.GetDistanceTo(previous);
    b.AppendFormat("Distance: {0:F0} meters from previous reading\n\n",
        distance);
    Dispatcher.BeginInvoke(() =>
    {
        position.Text = b.ToString();
    });
}
```

The location properties are read from the `GeoCoordinate` and appended along with message text to a `StringBuilder` instance. When writing the longitude and latitude, call the `FormatCoordinate` method ❶. In the middle of creating the message text, use the `GetDistanceTo` method ❷ to calculate the distance traveled since the previous value was read. Update the `position TextBlock`'s `Text` property on the UI thread. The updated user interface is shown in figure 16.14.

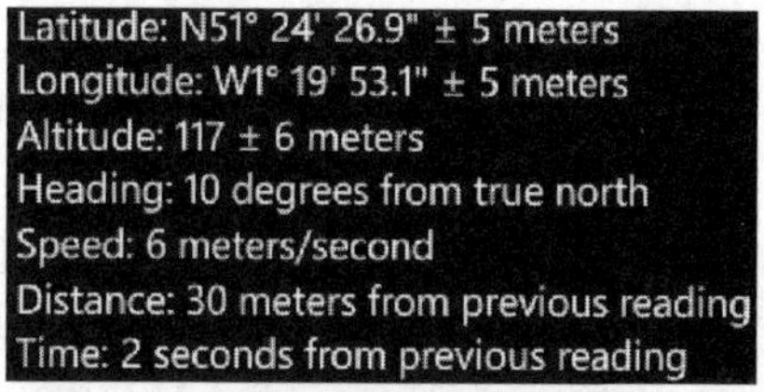

Latitude: N51° 24' 26.9" ± 5 meters
Longitude: W1° 19' 53.1" ± 5 meters
Altitude: 117 ± 6 meters
Heading: 10 degrees from true north
Speed: 6 meters/second
Distance: 30 meters from previous reading
Time: 2 seconds from previous reading

Figure 16.14 The position information displayed in the user interface includes altitude, heading, speed, and distance traveled, along with the estimated accuracy of the position and the length of time elapsed since the last update.

If you have a Windows Phone device handy, deploy the LocationAndMaps sample and run the application. Start continuous tracking and experiment by walking several yards in a variety of directions. Now change the `DesiredAccuracy` property to `Default` in the `start_Click` method, redeploy, and run the application again. How do the numbers compare between the High and Default accuracy modes? How do the numbers change as you move around? The Geolocator provides the data to pinpoint a user's location and track a user's movement. In the next section, you'll extend the sample application to show the user's movements on the Map control.

16.4.3 Displaying a route on the map

Your sample application already detects when the current position changes by subscribing to the Geolocator's PositionChanged event. The Windows Phone Maps API makes it simple to use position data to record a device's movement and display a route on the Map control. A route can be displayed with the MapPolyline class, found in the Microsoft.Phone.Maps.Controls namespace. A polyline is a shape made of a number of points, with a line segment drawn between each pair of points. A MapPolyline is a form of polyline that specifies its points with its Path property, which contains a collection of GeoCoordinates. The style of the line segments is specified with the MapPolyline properties called StrokeThickness, StrokeColor, and StrokeDashed.

In this section you'll see how easy it is to work with a MapPolyline. Start by adding a new MapPolyline member field:

```
using Microsoft.Phone.Maps.Controls;
using System.Windows.Media;
MapPolyline routeLine;
```

The routeLine is created when continuous tracking is started. Add the following code to the bottom of the start_Click method:

```
routeLine = new MapPolyline
{
   StrokeColor = (Color)Resources["PhoneAccentColor"],
   StrokeThickness = (double)Resources["PhoneStrokeThickness"]
};
routeLine.Path.Add(marker.GeoCoordinate);
mapControl.MapElements.Add(routeLine);
```

The routeLine will display its line segments using the XAML resource for the system accent color. The user specifies the system accent color in the operating system settings. The thickness of the line is specified using the XAML resource called PhoneStrokeThickness. The first point added to the routeLine is the current location as specified by the location marker. After the routeLine is initialized, it's added to the Map control's MapElements collection. Additional points are added to the route when the UpdateMap method is called from the PositionChanged event handler, as demonstrated in the following listing.

Listing 16.12 Updating the route shown in the map

```
void UpdateMap(GeoCoordinate location)
{
   Dispatcher.BeginInvoke(() =>
   {
```

```
        marker.GeoCoordinate = location;
        routeLine.Path.Add(location);    #1
        mapControl.SetView(LocationRectangle
            .CreateBoundingRectangle(routeLine.Path));
    });
}
```

1 Add new location to route

2 Center and zoom map

As with the initial position, the new position is added to `routeLine`'s `Path` property **1**. The next line instructs the `Map` control to zoom and scroll the route into view by calling the `SetView` method. `SetView` is passed a `LocationRectangle` constructed from the coordinates in `routeLine`'s `Path` property **2**. `SetView` changes the `Map`'s zoom level to ensure that the entire route is displayed. Figure 16.15 shows a polyline on a `Map` control with the view adjusted to show the entire route.

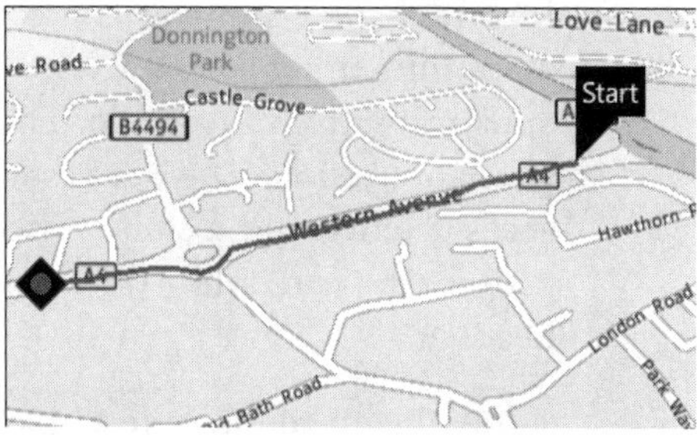

Figure 16.15 A `MapPolyline` drawn on a Map control. When using the polyline's collection of points as input into the Map's `SetView` method, the Map will ensure the entire route is displayed.

Once again, deploy the application to your Windows Phone, launch the application, and start continuous tracking. Walk around for a while and watch as your route is drawn on the screen. With continuous tracking implemented, you're almost finished with the LocationAndMaps application.

16.4.4 Stopping continuous tracking

Continuous tracking is enabled whenever an application subscribes to either the `PositionChanged` or `StatusChanged` `Geolocator` event. While continuous tracking is enabled, the device will consume battery power at a faster-than-normal rate. Applications should give the user the ability to stop continuous tracking. Before you can finish the LocationAndMaps application, you need to disable continuous tracking in the `stop_Click` method. The `stop_Click` method, shown in the following listing, stops continuous tracking and disposes of the `Geolocator`.

Listing 16.13 Stopping continuous tracking and releasing the `Geolocator`

```
void stop_Click (object sender, EventArgs e)
{
   ((ApplicationBarIconButton)ApplicationBar.Buttons[0]).IsEnabled = true;
   ((ApplicationBarIconButton)ApplicationBar.Buttons[1]).IsEnabled = false;
   service.PositionChanged -= service_PositionChanged;
   service.StatusChanged -= service_StatusChanged;
   service = null;
   status.Text += "\nContinuous tracking has been stopped.";
   mapControl.Pitch = 0;
   previous = new GeoCoordinate();
}
```

1 Unhook events

2 Update user interface

Before releasing the service, unhook the event handlers ❶ and set the `service` field to `null`. Before exiting the method, update the user interface ❷ to inform the user that the service has been stopped, and reset the `previous` coordinate.

16.5 Summary

In this chapter you learned how to use launchers and a XAML control to integrate maps into an application. The `MapsTask` and `MapsDirectionsTask` launch the Maps application from your code. The XAML `Map` control enables you to embed maps inside your application. The `Geolocator` uses data from the GPS, cellular network, wireless access points, and a web service to report the phone's longitude and latitude. The `Geolocator` can optionally report additional information such as altitude, speed, and heading.

> **TIP** If you're interested in location-based and mapping technologies, we recommend reading the book *Location-Aware Applications* by Richard Ferraro and Murat Aktihanoglu (Manning Publications, 2011). You can learn more about the book at www.manning.com/ferraro.

In addition to the Maps tasks and the `Map` control, we looked at how to use the Map Web Services. You learned how to use one of the available Maps APIs for reverse geocoding. The Windows Phone SDK provides other Map Services to geocode an address and calculate directions between two different addresses. The built-in Map Services aren't the only location and mapping services available to developers. Yahoo!, Google, and several other organizations provide free and fee-based mapping services.

In the next chapter we show a few techniques that use the `WebBrowser` control and allow you to build HTML 5 plus JavaScript applications.

17

Building HTML applications

This chapter covers

- Launching Internet Explorer
- Hosting the `WebBrowser` control
- Building HTML5 with JavaScript applications
- Bridging JavaScript and C#

The web browser is an essential application for mobile platforms, and the web browser available on Windows Phone 8 is Internet Explorer 10. Internet Explorer 10 for the Windows Phone is a version of the same Internet Explorer 10 that ships with Windows 8 for tablets and the desktop. The mobile edition of Internet Explorer 10 supports hardware-accelerated graphics and HTML5, the newest version of HTML. The Windows Phone SDK enables developers to launch Internet Explorer as well as embed a web browser into their applications.

Internet Explorer can be started from within an application using the `WebBrowserTask` task that launches the native web browser, pushing the running application to the background. `WebBrowserTask` allows the developer to start Internet Explorer and specify the `Uri` of a web page to be loaded into the browser. When a more integrated user experience is desired, the developer can embed a browser into an application using the XAML `WebBrowser` control provided in the SDK. We'll discuss both the rendering of HTML5 within an application and how C# code in the application can interoperate with JavaScript in the web page. To highlight Internet Explorer you're going to build a sample application that demonstrates how to use the `WebBrowser` control to build an HTML5- and JavaScript-based application. The sample application will start with the Windows Phone HTML5 App project template, but the generated web page will be replaced with markup using several of the new HTML5 tags, along with a bit of JavaScript.

NOTE Windows 8 allows developers to build HTML with JavaScript applications that use the Windows Runtime APIs and proprietary JavaScript libraries to provide a true Windows Store look and feel. The Windows Phone 8 SDK doesn't provide the APIs and integration points to enable a truly native HTML with JavaScript application.

The release of Windows Phone 8 was the first time mobile phones were able to use Internet Explorer 10. Internet Explorer 10 for mobile includes several new features, such as hardware acceleration and support for HTML5, ECMAScript 5, CSS3, and Scalable Vector Graphics (SVG). HTML5 includes several new tags and features to support web storage, geolocation, audio, and video. The sample application you're going to build in this chapter, shown in figure 17.1, will use HTML, JavaScript, and Cascading Style Sheets (CSS) to render the user interface.

Throughout this chapter we'll look at how Windows Phone applications can use Internet Explorer. We start by showing how to use the `WebBrowserTask` launcher to start Internet Explorer from within an application. Then we show how to use a browser embedded inside a XAML application. To make starting HTML5 plus JavaScript applications easier, Visual Studio ships with the Windows Phone HTML5 App project template.

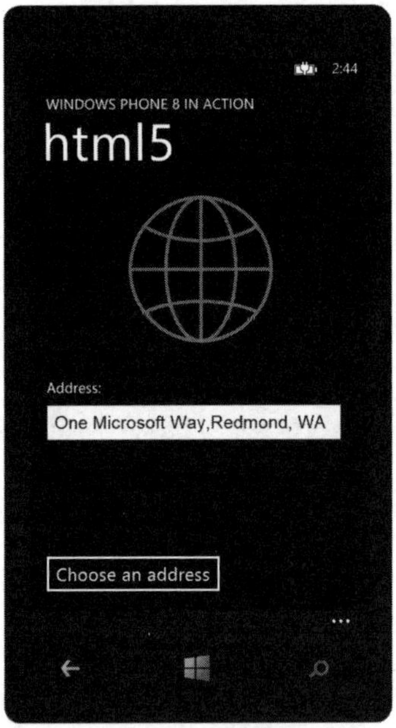

Figure 17.1 The completed HTML5 sample application

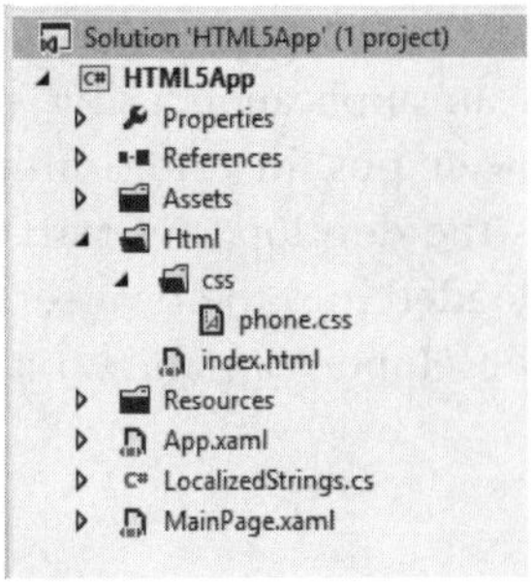

Figure 17.2 The generated Html5App project files as seen in the Visual Studio Solution Explorer. As with any other application, the project contains App.xaml and MainPage.xaml.

17.1 Introducing Windows Phone HTML5 App projects

The Html5App sample application runs from HTML files included in the application's XAP file using the XAML `WebBrowser` control. The browser loads the files directly from the install folder. The Windows Phone HTML5 App project template generates a simple application, complete with an Html folder containing a starting page named index.html and a default CSS file called phone.css, shown in figure 17.2. To see the generated project files, create a new Visual Studio project called Html5App using the Windows Phone HTML5 App project template. Later in the chapter, you'll add a Scripts folder to the project to contain a few JavaScript files.

COMPARING AN HTML5 APP WITH A STANDARD APPLICATION

The difference between an HTML5 app and a standard Windows Phone app is that MainPage.xaml hosts a `WebBrowser` control in the `LayoutRoot`, doesn't have a `ContentPanel`, and contains an `ApplicationBar` control with standard web navigation buttons, as shown in figure 17.3.

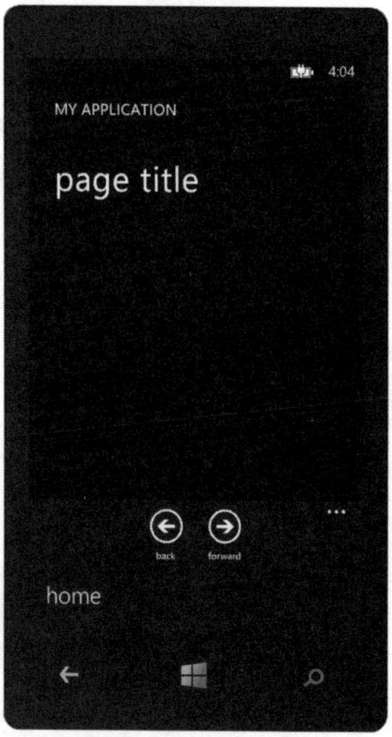

Figure 17.3 The user interface generated by the Windows Phone HTML5 App project template, including forward and back navigation buttons and a menu item that takes the user back to a home page

Other than the application bar, the entire user interface is built using HTML. The generated `LayoutRoot` and `ApplicationBar` markup is shown in the following listing.

Listing 17.1 MainPage.xaml markup generated by the project template

```
<Grid x:Name="LayoutRoot" Background="Transparent">
   <phone:WebBrowser x:Name="Browser" HorizontalAlignment="Stretch"
      VerticalAlignment="Stretch"
      Loaded="Browser_Loaded"
      NavigationFailed="Browser_NavigationFailed" />
</Grid>
<phone:PhoneApplicationPage.ApplicationBar>
   <shell:ApplicationBar IsVisible="True"
         IsMenuEnabled="True" Mode="Minimized">
      <shell:ApplicationBarIconButton IsEnabled="True" Text="back"
            IconUri="/Assets/AppBar/appbar.back.rest.png"
            Click="BackApplicationBar_Click"/>
```

❶ WebBrowser control named Browser

❷ Wire up Loaded event

```
    <shell:ApplicationBarIconButton IsEnabled="True" Text="forward"
          IconUri="/Assets/AppBar/appbar.next.rest.png"
          Click="ForwardApplicationBar_Click"/>
    <shell:ApplicationBar.MenuItems>
       <shell:ApplicationBarMenuItem Text="home"
             Click="HomeMenuItem_Click" />
    </shell:ApplicationBar.MenuItems>
  </shell:ApplicationBar>
</phone:PhoneApplicationPage.ApplicationBar>
```

The generated `WebBrowser` control is given the name `Browser` ❶, and will be used in the code-behind to call methods and set properties on the `WebBrowser` control. The generated markup also wires up the `Loaded` event ❷, which is how the index.html page is loaded into the browser.

LOADING A WEB PAGE

Open up MainPage.xaml.cs and take a look at the generated event handler named `Browser_Loaded`:

```
private string MainUri = "/Html/index.html";

void Browser_Loaded(object sender, RoutedEventArgs e)
{
   Browser.IsScriptEnabled = true;
   Browser.Navigate(new Uri(MainUri, UriKind.Relative));
}
```

The path to index.html web page is stored in the field `MainUri`, which is used to construct a `Uri` that's passed to the `Navigate` method. A `Relative UriKind` is a hint to the browser that it should look in the install folder or local storage for the web page. When `Navigate` is called, `WebBrowser` first looks in local storage for the specified file and, if it isn't found, then looks in the install folder. If the `Uri` is an absolute path to an internet resource, the browser will download the files from the web and display them.

> **TIP** The Windows Phone HTML5 App project template automatically adds the ID_CAP_WEBBROWSERCOMPONENT capability to the project's WMAppManifest.xml file. If you choose to use `WebBrowser` in an application not generated by the HTML5 App project template, you'll need to manually add this capability to your project.

`WebBrowser` supports loading web pages using three different APIs. In the preceding snippet, you specify the address of the web page to display in the `WebBrowser` control using the `Navigate` method. The `WebBrowser` control provides a `Source` property, which is handy if you prefer setting the `Uri` in XAML instead of code. You can also load dynamically built HTML with the `NavigateToString` method. The `NavigateToString` displays the HTML markup contained in the string passed to the method.

When loading a web page, the `WebBrowser` control raises three different events during normal navigation:

- `Navigating`–Raised when the page is loading
- `Navigated`—Raised when navigation to the page has succeeded
- `LoadCompleted`—Raised when page has been loaded

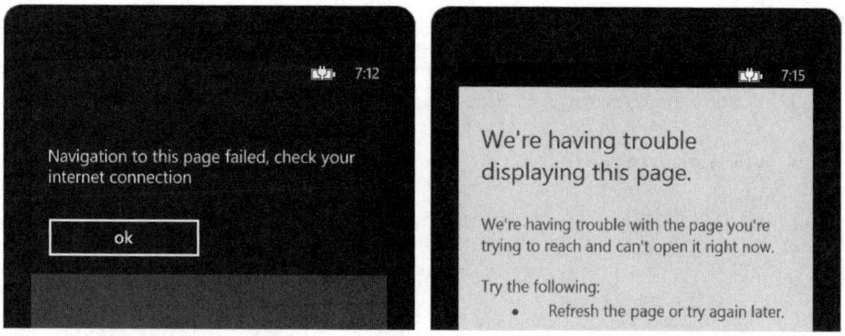

Figure 17.4 The navigation failed error message, shown in a message box by the Html5App sample application, appears on the left. On the right you see the navigation failed message shown by the `WebBrowser` control when the `NavigationFailed` event isn't handled.

Each of the `WebBrowser` navigation events may be called more than once when navigating to a web page. The number of events raised depends on the content of the page. Redirects and frames are a couple of the elements that may cause multiple navigation events to be raised for a page. The `Navigating` event has a particularly useful function, because you can interrupt the navigation by setting the `Cancel` property to `true` while handling the event.

HANDLING NAVIGATION FAILURES

`NavigationFailed` is another event raised by `WebBrowser`. As you would suspect, the `NavigationFailed` event is raised when the browser is unable to load a page. The HTML5 App project template captures the event and displays a generic error message. If your code doesn't handle `NavigationFailed`, the `WebBrowser` control will display an error message of one form or another, depending on the type of error. Examples of these error messages are shown in figure 17.4.

That's enough discussion about the boring application generated by the project template. We're going to replace the generated index.html with markup using several of the new HTML5 tags, including inline Scalable Vector Graphics (SVG). But the first feature of the sample application shows you how to launch Internet Explorer from within a XAML application.

17.2 Launching Internet Explorer

You can launch Internet Explorer from any third-party application using the `WebBrowserTask` launcher class. You learned how to use launchers and choosers in chapter 5. The `WebBrowserTask` launcher exposes a single property called `Uri`, which accepts a standard `Uri` object. In this section you'll launch Internet Explorer using `WebBrowserTask` when a user taps a new application bar menu item in the sample application.

Open MainPage.xaml and add an `ApplicationBarMenuItem`:

```
<shell:ApplicationBarMenuItem Text="about" Click="about_Click" />
```

Internet Explorer is launched from the button's `Click` event handler:

```
using Microsoft.Phone.Tasks;
void about_Click(object sender, EventArgs e)
{
    var task = new WebBrowserTask
    {
        Uri = new Uri("http://www.manning.com/binkley", UriKind.Absolute)
    };
    task.Show();
}
```

When you run the application and tap the About menu item, Internet Explorer is launched. Assuming the device has a network connection, the browser will load this book's page on the Manning website, as shown in figure 17.5. The drawback to using the `WebBrowserTask` is that the application is pushed to the background and the user leaves the application.

If you want to display a web page without leaving your application, you can add a new XAML page to the application that uses a `WebBrowser` control. You can use the `WebBrowser` control in any Windows Phone App, not just those created by the Windows Phone HTML5 App project template. If you're displaying web pages inside your application, you likely want to use the latest, greatest features found in HTML5.

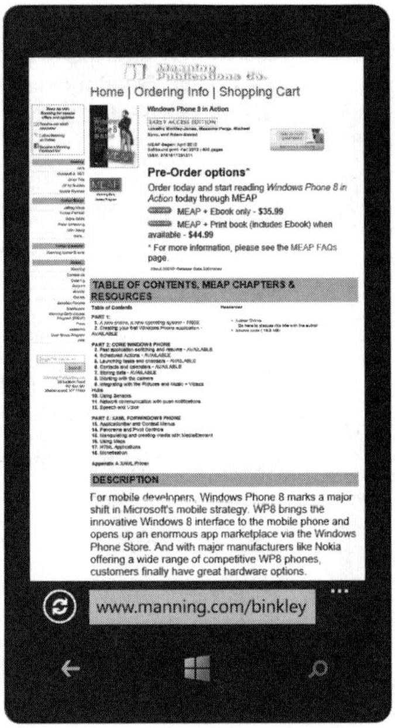

Figure 17.5 This book's page on the Manning website, shown in Internet Explorer launched by `WebBrowserTask`

17.3 Using HTML5

HTML originated as a markup language for publishing, sharing, and linking scientific papers to allow the world's physicists to collaborate with other researchers located around the world. Since its inception, HTML has evolved to power blogs, newspapers, online commerce sites, and browser-based applications of all categories. Many of the original HTML tags aren't used or have been adapted to fit situations different from their original purpose.

HTML5 is a new version of HTML that adds several new tags and features. New tags have been added to facilitate the structure of many web pages—a navigation section at the top of the page, another at the bottom, and various independent sections or articles throughout the remainder of the page. HTML5 also makes audio and video first-class elements of language.

NOTE This chapter isn't intended to be a full introduction to HTML5 and related technologies. Instead, we want to show how to create an HTML5 with

JavaScript application that uses a few of the HTML5, features. For a complete introduction to HTML5, consider reading *Hello! HTML5 and CSS3* by Rob Crowther (Manning Publications, 2012). You can view more details about the book at http://www.manning.com/crowther.

The index.html file generated by Visual Studio consists of a couple of `div` elements in the body of the document and doesn't make use of any of the new HTML5 elements. In this section you're going to change index.html to use `header`, `section`, and `footer` elements.

17.3.1 Marking up index.html with HTML5

The Html5App's main page, shown in listing 17.2, looks a lot like the main page of the Hello World application you built in chapter 2. The page has the standard Windows Phone application and page titles and asks the user to input an address. The application also allows the user to click a button and choose an address from the phone's address book.

Listing 17.2 HTML5 for the application's main page

```
<body>
   <header>
      <h2>WINDOWS PHONE 8 IN ACTION</h2>
      <h1>html5</h1>
   </header>
   <section>
      <label for="address">Address:</label>
      <input id="address" />
   </section>
   <footer>
      <button id="chooseButton">Choose an address</button>
   </footer>
</body>
```

1 Typical Windows Phone page titles

2 Styled to look like button

The updated index.html is a standard HTML5 page that uses the new `header`, `section`, and `footer` elements. The standard application and page titles are contained in the `header` element **1**. In the `footer` you add a `button` **2**. Later in the chapter you'll learn how to launch an `AddressChooserTask` when the button is clicked. The new user interface is shown in figure 17.6.

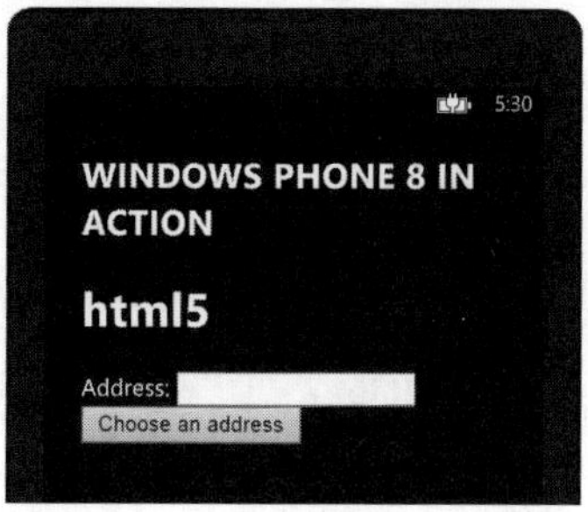

Figure 17.6 The user interface built by the updated index.html. Notice that this doesn't match the Windows Phone style, and the application title doesn't fit on a single line.

The new user interface doesn't look like a Windows Phone application. For starters, the application title wraps across two lines. In every other sample application you've built, the string "Windows Phone 8 in Action" fit nicely across the top of the screen. It seems like the screen is too narrow. This is due to the browser viewport settings.

17.3.2 Setting the browser viewport

By default, Internet Explorer 10 sets the viewport width to 1024 and adjusts the viewport height to be big enough to contain the page when rendered at 1024. The viewport is then scaled so that the entire viewport fits in the browser window. If the viewport defaults to 1024, the application should appear to be too small, not too big. The answer lies in the phone.css file generated by the project template.

The phone.css file contains a CSS rule that sets the portrait viewport width to 320px. It may seem odd to set the viewport width to 320px when XAML scales everything to 480px, but previous versions of mobile Internet Explorer used a 320px-wide screen, and defaulting to 320px maintains backward compatibility. The goal of the HTML5App sample application isn't backward compatibility but compatibility with the Windows Phone look and feel. Open phone.css, find the `@-ms-viewport` rule, and change the portrait viewport width to 480px:

```
@media all and (orientation:portrait) {
    @-ms-viewport {
        width:480px;
        user-zoom: fixed;
        max-zoom: 1;
        min-zoom: 1;
    }
}
```

With the viewport width corrected, the user interface no longer wraps the application title, as shown in figure 17.7.

Even though the application width is improved, the application still doesn't look like a Windows Phone application. A few more styles need to be added to phone.css to match the Windows Phone look and feel.

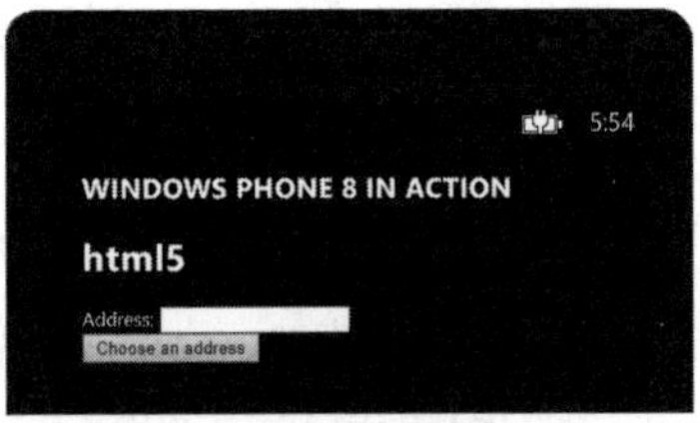

Figure 17.7 After correcting the viewport width, the application title no longer wraps.

17.4 Matching the Windows Phone style

If you're building an HTML with JavaScript application to look like a native application, you should consider trying to match the Windows Phone look and feel. How can you build CSS to match Windows Phone? What colors, fonts, and sizes should be used? You can find this information in the ThemesResources.xaml and System.Windows.xaml files included in the Design folder of the Windows Phone 8 SDK (C:\Program Files (x86)\Microsoft SDKs\Windows Phone\v8.0\Design).

Let's add a few styles to phone.css to make the Html5App match the Windows Phone style. The project template created a default `body` style, but the `font-size` isn't quite right. Update the `body` style to use a `font-size` of 20px:

```
body body {
   font-size: 20px;
...
}
```

The application title is placed in an `h2` element, and the page title uses an `h1` element. Both titles are contained in a `header` element. The following listing shows the `header` style properties.

Listing 17.3 CSS styles for the application and page titles

```
header {
    margin-top: 17px; margin-bottom: 43px;
}
h1 {
   font-size: 72px; font-weight: normal;
   margin-top: -5px; margin-left: -6px; margin-bottom: -10px;
}
h2 {
   font-size: 20px; font-weight: normal;
   margin-top: 0px; margin-bottom: -10px;
}
```

❶ Style for page title

❷ Style for application title

In the sample application, the page title appears in the second row of the `header` and uses the `h1` element ❶. In a XAML application, the page title is assigned the `PhoneTextTile1` style, which uses a font size of 72px, so the `h1` element font size is set to the same value ❷. The application title, using `h2`, is assigned a font size of `20px`. The two headers also change the margins to resemble the layout seen in a XAML application.

You'll also define a `button` style to make input buttons look like native XAML buttons:

```
button{
  color: white; background: transparent; text-decoration: none;
  border-style: solid; border-color: white; border-width: 3px;
  font-size:25.33px; font-family:Segoe WP Semibold;
  padding-left: 10px; padding-top: 3px;
  padding-right: 10px; padding-bottom: 5px;
}
```

The `button` style uses the Segoe WP Semibold font, a solid white border, and a transparent background.

The `input` text box is similar to the XAML `TextBox` and uses a font size of 25.333px. Add an `input` style to ensure the text box has the correct height, margins, and padding, and appears below its label text:

```
input {
    display: block; font-size: 25.333px; width: 400px;
    margin-top: 12px; padding: 9px;
}
```

Finally, add a `section` style so that the `header`, `section`, and `footer` aren't squashed up against each other:

```
section {
   height: 250px;
}
```

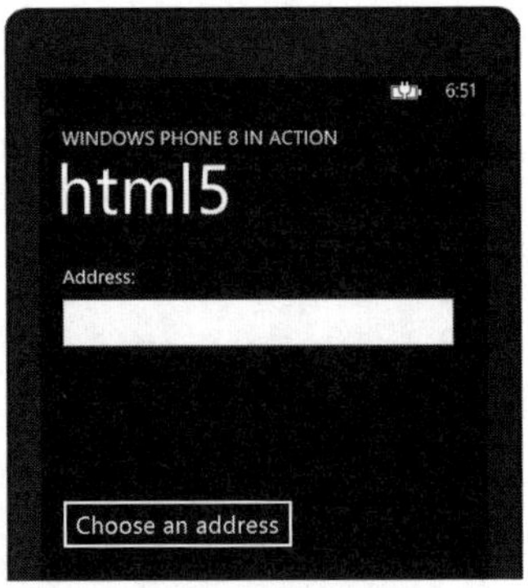

Figure 17.8 The Html5App sample application styled to resemble a standard Windows Phone XAML application

With all the new styles added to phone.css, the sample application now looks like a proper Windows Phone application. A screenshot of the user interface with the new styles appears in figure 17.8.

Run the application now to make sure everything appears as expected. Now that you have the basic layout working as desired, it's time to draw the globe using Scalable Vector Graphics (SVG).

17.5 Using Scalable Vector Graphics

The Hello World application from chapter 2 used XAML drawing primitives from the `System.Windows.Shapes` namespace to display a globe. Internet Explorer 10 and the `WebBrowser` control support SVG elements that are similar to XAML's `Shape` classes. The following listing demonstrates how to use SVG to replicate the Hello World globe.

Listing 17.4 SVG markup for a globe

```
<section>
    <svg xmlns="http://www.w3.org/2000/svg" version="1.1">
        <ellipse cx="100" cy="100" rx="100" ry="100" />
        <ellipse cx="100" cy="100" rx="50" ry="100" />
        <path d="M100 0 L100 200" />
        <path d="M0 100 L200 100" />
        <path d="M20 40 A100 50 0 0 0 180 40" />
        <path d="M20 160 A110 50 0 0 1 180 160" />
    </svg>
</section>
```

Add the `section` containing the globe immediately following the `header` element in index.html. The sphere of the globe and the two arced meridians are drawn with `ellipses`. The straight meridian and the three parallels are drawn with `paths`.

To display the globe properly, apply some CSS. Add the following styles to phone.css:

```
ellipse, path{
    fill: transparent; stroke: #1BA1E2; stroke-width: 5px;
}
svg{
    margin-left: 120px; margin-right: 160px;
}
```

The style specifies a transparent fill and a 5-pixel-wide blue stroke. The color value used matches the color used in the operating system's blue theme.

Run the application and you should see a friendly Hello World page written in HTML5. But nothing happens when you tap the Choose an Address button. HTML by itself isn't dynamic—to create an interactive user interface, you need to code up some JavaScript.

17.6 Executing JavaScript

The `WebBrowser` control supports JavaScript the same as Internet Explorer does, by embedding script into a .html file or by loading JavaScript from an external .js file. By default, the `WebBrowser` control disables JavaScript execution, and any application that uses JavaScript must enable JavaScript by setting the `IsScriptEnabled` to `true` before navigating to a page containing JavaScript.

Fortunately, the Windows Phone HTML5 App project template sets the `IsScript-Enabled` property before loading index.html. You can verify this by opening Main-Page.xaml.cs and looking at the `Browser_Loaded` method:

```
void Browser_Loaded(object sender, RoutedEventArgs e)
{
   Browser.IsScriptEnabled = true;
   Browser.Navigate(new Uri(MainUri, UriKind.Relative));
}
```

With scripts enabled, you're almost ready to write some JavaScript. Before adding code to handle the button click, let's install jQuery, a popular third-party JavaScript library.

17.6.1 Installing jQuery

Installing and using jQuery in a Windows Phone HTML project is simple, thanks to the NuGet Package Manager. We showed how to add NuGet packages in chapter 2 when you added the Windows Phone Toolkit to the Hello World sample project. Even though jQuery is a JavaScript library and not a .NET assembly, adding jQuery works the same way.

From Visual Studio's Project menu, select Manage NuGet Projects. When the dialog appears, select the Online category and enter *jQuery* in the search box. The search results are shown in figure 17.9. Select jQuery from the list and click the Install button.

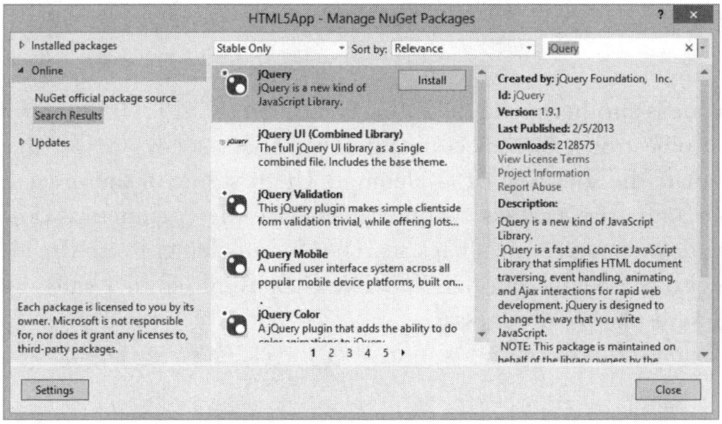

Figure 17.9 Adding jQuery to the sample application project. At the time of this writing, the latest version of jQuery is 1.9.1.

When the NuGet Package Manager adds jQuery to your project, it creates a new project folder called Scripts. The content of the Scripts folder is shown in figure 17.10. jQuery adds a few .js files and a .map file. The intellisense.js and .map files provide information to the editor and debugger and are beyond the scope of this book. The jquery-1.9.1.min.js file is a *minified* version of jquery-1.9.1.js—the code in the two files is identical, but the minified file has had all extraneous comments, linefeeds, and whitespace removed. Use only the minified version in a production application and change the build action for the other three files to None so they aren't copied into the application's XAP file during the build process.

Figure 17.10 The Scripts folder containing the jQuery JavaScript library

The next step is to update index.html to include the jQuery library. Open index.html and add a new `script` tag immediately following the closing `body` tag. Set the `src` attribute for the `script` tag to the relative path in the install folder to the minified jQuery file:

```
<script type="text/javascript" src="/Scripts/jquery-1.9.1.min.js"></script>
```

The Html5App project is finally ready for you to add a JavaScript `Click` event handler.

17.6.2 Adding a Click event handler.

One thing that makes jQuery so popular is how easy it is to keep your HTML markup separate from your JavaScript code. Throughout the remainder of the chapter, index.html is only modified to add one more `script include` tag. Instead of placing JavaScript inside index.html, all your code will be added in a file named html5app.js. Create this new file in the Scripts folder of the Visual Studio project. You can use the Add New Item Wizard to create a text file while specifying the name as html5app.js. Open the file and add the following snippet:

```
$(document).ready(function() {
    $("#chooseButton").click(function() {
        alert("Hello from javascript!");
    });
});
```

The `$` in this code is another name for a function called `JQuery`. The `JQuery` function accepts a DOM object or a CSS selector and constructs a `JQuery` object that can be used to manipulate the specified DOM element. The first line of the preceding snippet registers an anonymous callback to be called once the document is downloaded and ready. The document-ready callback searches for an element with the id `chooseButton` and registers a click event handler. The click event handler calls the built-in `alert` method to display a hello message.

Include the new script file in index.html after the closing `body` tag:

```
<script type="text/javascript" src="/Scripts/html5app.js"></script>
```

Run the application and click the button. The `WebBrowser` control displays the alert message in a message box, shown in figure 17.11.

Figure 17.11 The `WebBrowser` control displays an alert message in a message box.

Displaying an alert message isn't the same thing as choosing an address from the address book. To choose an address you need to use the `AddressChooserTask` from the Windows Phone .NET API, which is only callable from C# (or Visual Basic) code. How do you access an API that's not automatically exposed to JavaScript? The `WebBrowser` allows you to bridge JavaScript and C# to access almost any API in the Windows Phone SDK.

17.7 Bridging C# and JavaScript

As you already know, the Windows Phone SDK includes several launchers and choosers that developers can use to interact with native applications. You first learned about launchers and choosers in chapter 5 and have used them throughout the book. Using features of the `WebBrowser` control, you're going to learn how to use the `AddressChooserTask` to display an address in the index.html web page.

The two features of the `WebBrowser` control that enable C# to interoperate with JavaScript are the `ScriptNotify` event and the `InvokeScript` method. As shown in figure 17.12, the workflow started by a user clicking an HTML button flows through the `ScriptNotify` event handler, where the `AddressChooserTask` is constructed and shown. When the task is complete, code execution flows back to the web page through the `InvokeScript` method.

17.7.1 Wiring up the ScriptNotify event

Wire up the `ScriptNotify` event of the `browser` control declared in MainPage.xaml:

```
<phone:WebBrowser x:Name="Browser" HorizontalAlignment="Stretch"
        VerticalAlignment="Stretch" Loaded="Browser_Loaded"
        NavigationFailed="Browser_NavigationFailed"
        ScriptNotify="Browser_ScriptNotify" />
```

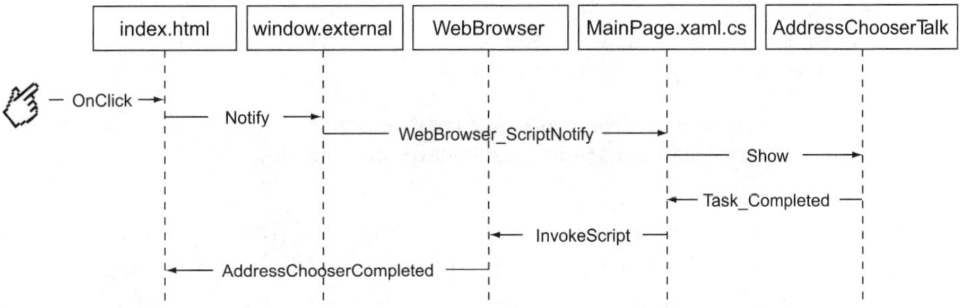

Figure 17.12 A sequence diagram showing the code execution from JavaScript to C# and back

WebBrowser adds a JavaScript function named Notify to the browser DOM. When JavaScript code calls the Notify function, the ScriptNotify event is raised. You'll see this in action by replacing the call to the alert function with a call to window.external.Notify. Change the Click event handler in html5app.js:

```
$("#chooseButton").click(function() {
    window.external.Notify("chooseAddress");
});
```

Inside the Click event handler, call the Notify function, passing a hint to the C# code informing it that you want the AddressChooserTask launched. The Notify function accepts a single string. When the Notify function is called, WebBrowser creates an instance of the NotifyEventArgs class and sets its Value property to the string sent to the Notify function. WebBrowser then raises the ScriptNotify event, passing the NotifyEventArgs instance to the event handler.

LAUNCHING THE ADDRESSCHOOSERTASK

Inside your implementation of the ScriptNotify event handler, examine the Value property for the string "chooseAddress" and (if you find it) instantiate an AddressChooserTask. Subscribe to the task's Completed event and launch the chooser by calling the Show method:

```
void Browser_ScriptNotify(object sender, NotifyEventArgs e)
{
    if (e.Value == "chooseAddress")
    {
        var task = new AddressChooserTask();
        task.Completed += task_Completed;
        task.Show();
    }
}
```

HANDLING THE COMPLETED EVENT

When the address chooser returns, it may have a valid address or it may have an error. The user may have canceled the task by pressing the Back button without selecting an address. You need to account for each of these scenarios in your Completed event handler:

```
void task_Completed(object sender, AddressResult e)
{
    string message;
    if (e.Error != null || e.TaskResult != TaskResult.OK)
        message = "No address chosen";
    else
        message = e.Address.Replace("\r\n", ",");
    Browser.InvokeScript("addressChooserCompleted", message);
}
```

The InvokeScript method accepts the name of the JavaScript method to invoke, and zero or more additional string parameters that will be passed along to the specified function. In this sample application, you tell WebBrowser to call a function named addressChooserCompleted, passing either an error message or the value of the AddressResult's Address property passed to the task's Completed event handler.

The last thing you need to do is create the JavaScript function addressChooser-Completed in html5app.js.

```
function addressChooserCompleted(address) {
    $("#address").val(address);
}
```

The function implementation copies the provided address, which may be an error message, into the Value property of the address Input control using jQuery's val function. The address input control is retrieved using a jQuery selector that returns the element with the id address.

Now that you're displaying an address chosen by the user, you've completed the HTML5 sample application. Run the application and experiment with choosing an address.

17.8 Summary

In this chapter you learned how to use WebBrowserTask and the WebBrowser XAML control to embed Internet Explorer into an application. WebBrowserTask can be used to launch Internet Explorer 10, whereas the XAML WebBrowser control allows you to embed Internet Explorer 10 into your application.

We showed you a few techniques that use WebBrowser and allow you to build HTML5 plus JavaScript applications. You learned how to install and use jQuery, a popular third-party JavaScript library. If you decide to build HTML5 plus JavaScript applications, you may consider using other third-party frameworks like Apache Cordova (PhoneGap). Apache Cordova is an HTML5 framework that allows you to build native applications for Windows Phone and several other mobile devices using the same code base.

In the next chapter we look at one last XAML control: the AdControl.

18 Releasing and monetizing apps

This chapter covers

- Submitting ad-supported apps
- Submitting paid and trial apps
- Implementing in-app purchases
- Testing in-app purchases

As developers, we code to learn, to have fun, and most importantly to make money. Without money, we wouldn't be able to support our families, let alone pursue our goals. In this chapter we explore the various options for monetizing your Windows Phone 8 applications. Whether you're a hobby developer looking to turn your efforts into additional income or a professional developer working for yourself or an employer, Windows Phone offers a variety of options to monetize the apps you produce.

Free apps are good for building your portfolio but do little to put money in your pocket and pay the bills. The time and effort you put in to writing your apps is valuable. Although it may not make your rich, it can help with some extra money. The strategy you choose will determine the potential payoff.

There are three major strategies for monetizing Windows Phone apps:

- Ad-supported apps
- Paid and trial apps
- In-app purchases

Each has its level of effectiveness, with ads on the low end, paid and trial apps in the middle, and in-app purchases at the high end. The level of effort required to implement each strategy follows the same order. The greater the effort you put into your monetization strategy, the bigger the payoff may be.

The next section looks at ad-supported apps, and includes a discussion of the Microsoft Advertising pubCenter and implementing the `AdControl` control in your apps. Then we'll look at selling your apps in the Windows Phone Store and implementing trial functionality. In the last part of the chapter we take a look at in-app purchases and their implementation.

18.1 Ad-supported apps

One of the simplest ways to derive revenue for your apps is by making them ad-supported. This way, you can offer your app for free, which means getting it on more devices. Many small, single-purpose apps don't offer enough functionality to prompt users to pay for them. In such a case, putting ads in the app may be the only way to monetize it. In other cases, you may want to take a trial app and put ads in it, but also make an ad-supported version and offer it for free. That lets you have the app appear in both the free and trial app lists. Figure 18.1 shows a paid app with a trial option as well as its free version, found via a search.

In Windows Phone 7 using ads in your app required installing the Microsoft Advertising SDK for Windows Phone. In Windows Phone 8 the Advertising SDK is included in the Windows Phone SDK, so no additional software is required to use it.

Figure 18.1 An app with both free and paid versions

> **About the samples**
>
> The samples in this chapter aren't complete. They are, however, part of the downloadable code for this chapter, which is complete and functional. Please download the code samples to see these examples in action.

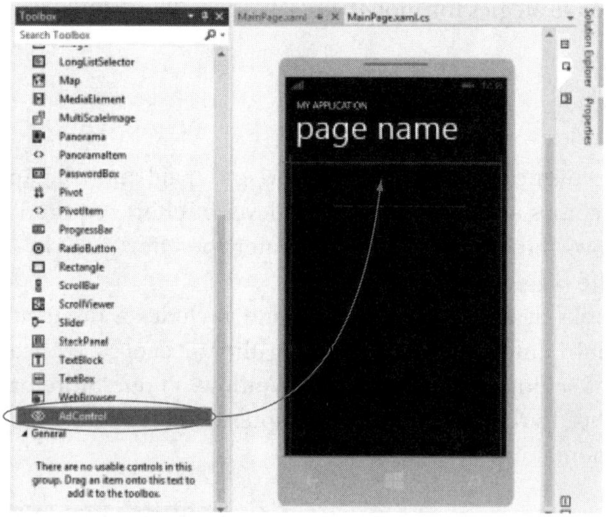

Figure 18.2 Adding `AdControl` to a page using drag-and-drop

To add the correct references, drag and drop the `AdControl` control onto a page in your project (figure 18.2). All required references will be added automatically.

18.1.1 Microsoft Advertising pubCenter

To display ads in your app, you need an account with Microsoft Advertising pub-Center. Go to http://pubcenter.microsoft.com and click the Sign Up Now button. Once you sign in with your Microsoft account, confirm your information and click the Continue button, as shown in figure 18.3. After a moment, registration is complete.

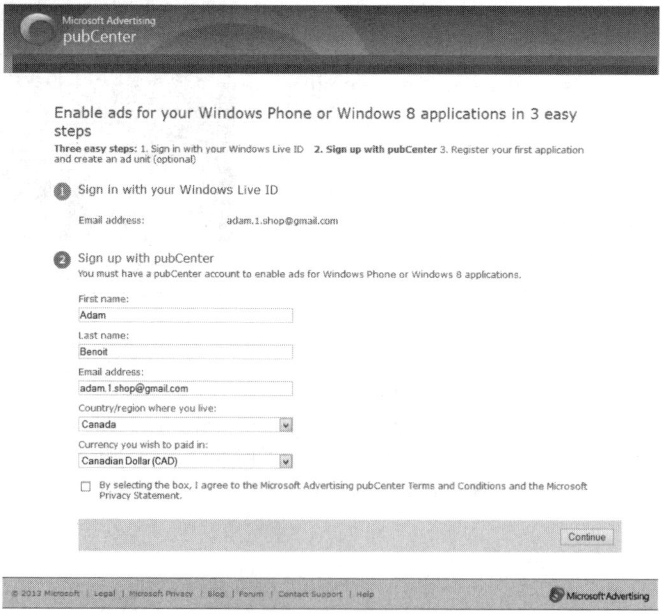

Figure 18.3 pubCenter Registration screen

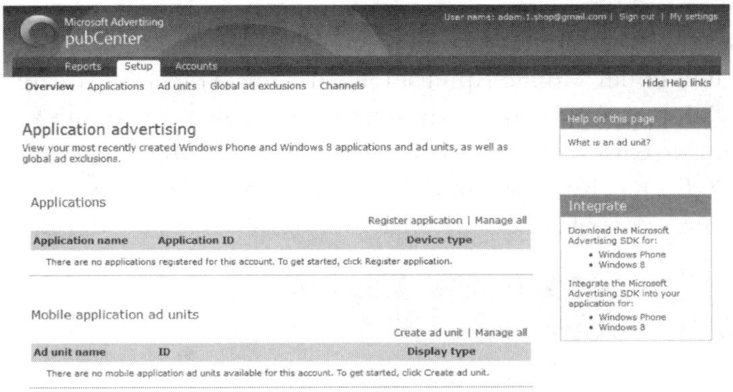

Figure 18.4 pubCenter Overview page

After your registration is complete, you're taken to the Confirmation screen, where you'll find everything you need to get started configuring one app with one ad unit. We cover that later in this section, so you can skip this page using the Skip and Enter pubCenter button at the bottom of the page.

REGISTERING AN APP IN PUBCENTER

To register an app after account creation, log in to your pubCenter account and select the Setup tab at the top of the screen, shown in figure 18.4. Then click the Register Application link, also shown in the figure.

On the Applications page, shown in figure 18.5, give your app a name, choose Windows Phone as the device type, and click the Save button. You'll be provided an Application ID you use in the `AdControl` in your app. A pubCenter account can have up to 10 applications, but you can have multiple accounts within your pubCenter account.

Once you've registered an app in pubCenter, you can create an ad unit for it. Ad units represent an ad configuration and can be reused across multiple apps, but are typically used for a single app only. Because you can edit an ad unit, it can be tweaked until you're satisfied with the ads served to app users.

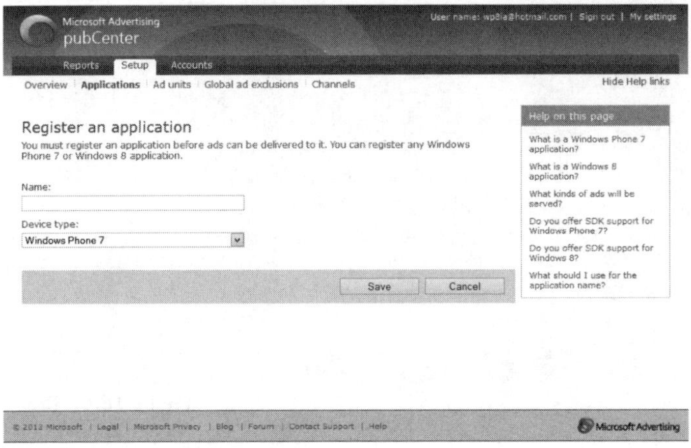

Figure 18.5 Registering an app in pubCenter

CREATING AD UNITS

To create a new ad unit, in the Setup tab at the top of the pubCenter site, click the Create Ad Unit link under Mobile Application Ad Units. Once the Create a Mobile Application Ad Unit page loads, as shown in figure 18.6, give the ad unit a name and select an ad size. Currently, only two sizes are offered for mobile apps: 480 * 80 and 300 * 50. 480 * 80 fits nicely across the width of the screen. We recommend that you use this size whenever possible to ensure all ads can displayed no matter their size.

Figure 18.6 Creating a mobile ad unit in pubCenter

Select the categories of ads to be displayed. You can select up to three Tier 1 and Tier 2 categories per ad unit. Tier 1 contains main categories, and Tier 2 is subcategories. You can change these after creating them, meaning you can tweak the ads displayed after the app is in the store.

In the Excluded URLS section, you can specify URLs that may lead to competitors. If an ad would send a user to one of these addresses, the ad won't display in your app. You can specify a full URL or only the domain. If you enter a domain, all pages within the domain will be blocked. Enter the URLs, one per line, up to 250 total.

Once you save the ad unit, you get an ad unit id. This is the second piece of info needed to implement an `AdControl` in your app.

Be sure to visit the Accounts tab and click the Tax Information link at the top of your pubCenter account. From there you create a tax profile. Without a tax profile, you can't be paid. When creating a tax profile you'll be asked a few questions, and based on your answers you'll be presented with the appropriate tax documents to electronically sign. During verification, you may be contacted to provide additional documentation, depending on your situation. Once your info is validated, you'll be eligible to be paid by check or electronic funds transfer.

Now that you've created a pubCenter account and created and registered an app and ad unit in it, you can use the identifiers provided to add ads to your app.

18.1.2 Implementing ads

At the heart of in-app ads for Windows Phone Silverlight apps is the `AdControl` control. The `AdControl` item can be found in the Visual Studio Toolbox under the All Windows Phone Controls header. You can add it to your apps by either dragging and dropping it onto the desired XAML page or manually adding it yourself. We tend to use the drag-and-drop method because doing so automatically adds all references needed and sets the `ApplicationId` and `AdId` parameters with test values. Once you've created a pubCenter account, you'll replace these test values with real ones. Using real values in the emulator causes an error to be silently thrown that can be caught using the `ErrorOccurred` event.

Required capabilities

For the `AdControl` to work correctly, you need to enable the following capabilities in the app manifest. Failing to add these capabilities will cause the `AdControl` to fail silently:

ID_CAP_USER_IDENTITY
ID_CAP_MEDIALIB_PHOTO
ID_CAP_PHONEDIALER
ID_CAP_WEBBROWSERCOMPONENT

To enable them, expand the Properties node in the Solution Explorer and double-click the WMAppManifest.xml file. Once the file is open, click the Capabilities tab. Find ID_CAP_SPEECH_RECOGNITION and check its check box. Save and close WMAppManifest.xml.

As we mentioned, two sizes of ads can be served to a Windows Phone App: 480 * 80 and 300 * 50. In the following listing, you can see the XAML needed to add `AdControl` to your page in both available sizes.

Listing 18.1 `AdControl` use in XAML

```
<StackPanel  x:Name="AdsStackPanel">
        <UI:AdControl Width="480"
                        Height="80"
                        ApplicationId="test_client"
                        AdUnitId="Image480_80"
                        IsAutoCollapseEnabled="True"
                        IsAutoRefreshEnabled="True"
                        ErrorOccurred="AdControl_OnErrorOccurred"
                        AdRefreshed="AdControl_OnAdRefreshed"
                        IsEngagedChanged="adcontrol_IsEngagedChanged"
        />
        <UI:AdControl Width="300"
                        Height="50"
                        ApplicationId="test_client"
                        AdUnitId="Image300_50"
                        IsAutoCollapseEnabled="True"
                        IsAutoRefreshEnabled="True"
                        Margin="10"
                        ErrorOccurred="AdControl_OnErrorOccurred"
                        AdRefreshed="AdControl_OnAdRefreshed"
                        IsEngagedChanged="adcontrol_IsEngagedChanged" />
</StackPanel>
```

Identify app in pubCenter (ApplicationId)

Ad configuration (AdUnitId)

If no ad, collapse ad to recover space (IsAutoRefreshEnabled)

Events triggered by AdControl

You can also add `AdControl` to a page programmatically in C#. The next listing shows a typical implementation of an ad in C# as opposed to XAML.

Listing 18.2 Adding `AdControl` in C#

```
using System.Globalization;
using Microsoft.Advertising;
using Microsoft.Advertising.Mobile.UI;

AdControl adcontrol = new AdControl()
{
        ApplicationId = "test_client",
        AdUnitId = "TextAd",
        Width = 480,
        Height = 80,
        IsAutoRefreshEnabled = true,
        IsAutoCollapseEnabled = true,
        CountryOrRegion =
        CultureInfo.CurrentCulture.TwoLetterISOLanguageName
};
adcontrol.ErrorOccurred += AdControl_OnErrorOccurred;
adcontrol.AdRefreshed += AdControl_OnAdRefreshed;
adcontrol.IsEngagedChanged += adcontrol_IsEngagedChanged;

this.AdsStackPanel.Children.Add(adcontrol);
```

Identify app in pubCenter (ApplicationId)

Ad configuration (AdUnitId)

If no ad, collapse ad to recover space (IsAutoCollapseEnabled)

Localize ads to phone's country (CountryOrRegion)

Events triggered by the AdControl

Add AdControl to StackPanel defined in XAML

In listings 18.1 and 18.2, you may have noticed that three events have handlers. The `AdRefreshed` event is triggered every time the ad is updated with a new ad. The `IsEngagedChanged` event is triggered when the user interacts with `AdControl`. The `ErrorOccurred` event occurs when an error happens. Depending on your error-handling implementation, you can use this event to log issues and report them back to you to take action to ensure the ads continue to generate revenue.

`AdControl` is capable of serving ads that are specific to the user's location using the `Latitude`, `Longitude`, and `PostalCode` properties. The `Keywords` property is used to provide `AdControl` with words to target the user, such as search terms or other contextual information.

Alternate ad options

Although the Microsoft Advertising pubCenter is the primary ad provider for Windows Phone apps, other companies offer SDKs for implementing ads for their respective ad networks. Here's a short list of alternate ad networks that may be useful:

- *Nokia Ad Exchange*—www.developer.nokia.com/Distribute/NAX/
- *AdMob by Google*—www.google.com/ads/admob/
- *AdDuplex*—www.adduplex.com
- *TapJoy*—www.tapjoy.com

As far as complexity goes, `AdControl` is a simple control to implement. The next section discusses a few best practices to follow to ensure the best experience for users.

18.1.3 Best practices

Here are a few things to remember when implementing ads in your apps:

- Position the ad control at the top or bottom of the screen. This is less obtrusive and distracting.
- When using a `Panorama` or `Pivot` control, place the `AdControl` outside the `Panorama` or `Pivot`. This keeps the ad in place when horizontally scrolling.
- When using a `ScrollViewer` control, place the `AdControl` outside the `ScrollViewer`. This keeps the ad in place when vertically scrolling.
- Using the 480 * 80 ad size is recommended for these scenarios. The 300 * 50 is best used in scrolling lists or where space is limited.
- The ad unit size must be at the same size or smaller than the `AdControl` size or no ad will display. For example, an `AdControl` of 300 * 50 configured with an ad unit set to 480 * 80 won't display any ads.
- Set the `IsAutoCollapseEnabled` property to collapse the control in case no ad is available.
- Unless you have a good reason, don't change any of the `AdControl` colors. If you do, make sure the border is visible to define the boundary of the ad.

Although ad-supported apps have some potential to generate income, due to low click rates and the large number of ad impressions needed, the potential to generate substantial income is low unless you have a popular app. If you want more income potential, the next monetization strategy to look at is that of paid and trial apps.

18.2 Paid and trial apps

The Windows Phone Dev Center and Store are where you submit and sell apps and games. Once you've built and tested your Windows Phone application, you want to get it into the hands of users and start earning some money. The Dev Center is where you submit your application to the Store. The Store, shown in figure 18.7, is the only place a user can install your application.

The Store was built to provide Windows Phone users with a single source for downloading and purchasing applications. Microsoft wanted to make it easy for developers to connect with users, get paid for their applications, and license their applications. Microsoft also wanted Windows Phone users to feel safe and secure, knowing that the applications they download have been tested and are free of malware.

The steps necessary for publishing an application are register, build, and submit. Once submitted, Microsoft will put the application through a series of certification tests. If your application doesn't pass certification, it won't be made available to Windows Phone users. The Windows Phone Developer Tools come with a helpful tool that walks you through automated and manual certification tests. You can track the certification status in your Dev Center Dashboard.

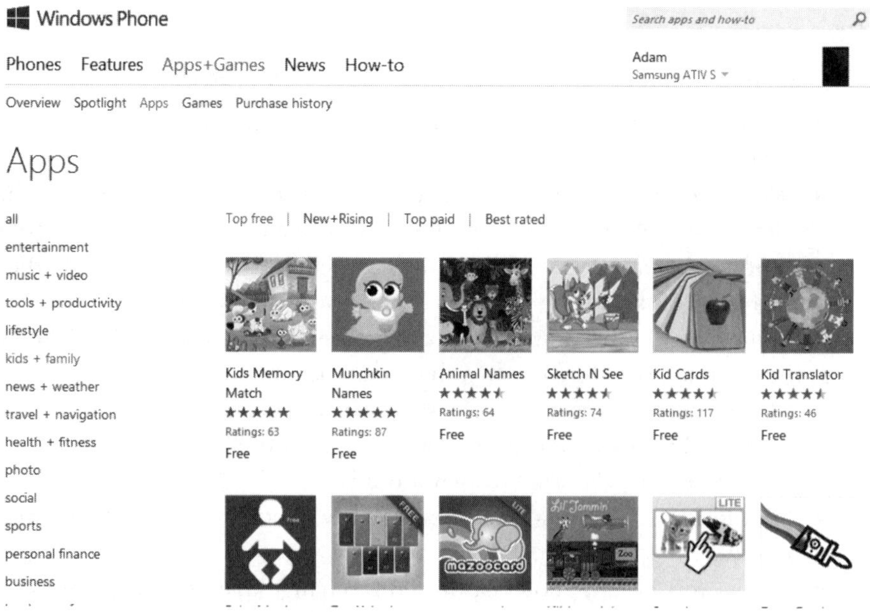

Figure 18.7 The Windows Phone Store

The Dev Center Dashboard is where you review the progress of your application. The Dashboard shows the certification status. Once your application passes certification and is made available to users, you can track downloads, money earned, and user reviews.

If you've come this far in this book, you're likely getting ready to release an app or two to the Store and start making some money. The first step to getting this ball rolling is to sign up for a Windows Phone Dev Center account.

18.2.1 Registration

If you haven't already signed into the Windows Phone Dev Center located at http://dev.windowsphone.com, head there now, click the Sign In link in the upper-right corner of the page, and sign in using your Microsoft account. Once in, click the Dashboard menu item at the top of the page. Without a paid subscription, you're presented with information on the benefits of a subscription, as shown in figure 18.8.

18.2.2 Subscriptions

A paid subscription not only lets you submit up to 100 free and unlimited paid apps, but it also lets you unlock three Windows Phone devices for testing your app through Visual Studio. The annual subscription price is $99, although there are a few ways to get a code for an account for free or almost free:

- *Students*—If you're a student with a school email address, you can join the DreamSpark program at www.DreamSpark.com. This program provides development tools and training for students. To get a Windows Phone Dev Center subscription with this program, be sure to use the same account to log in to both sites.

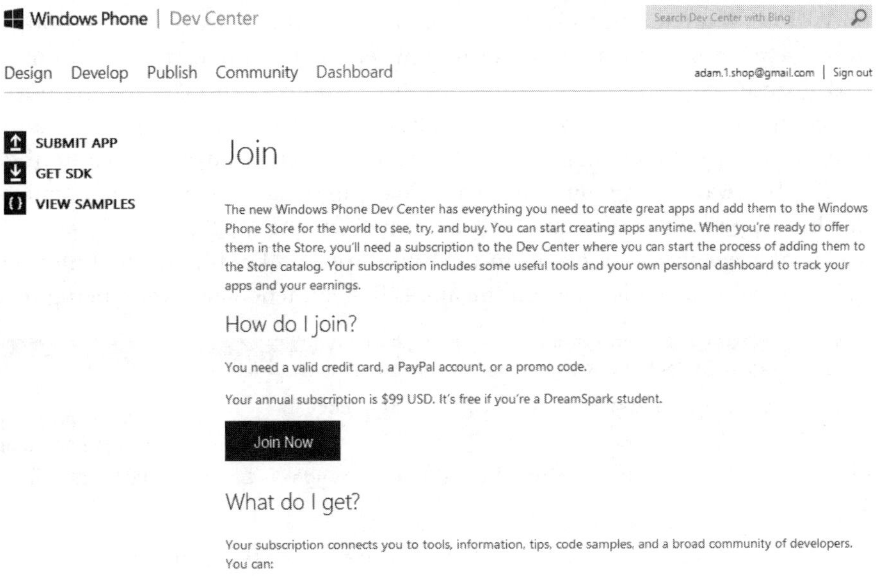

Figure 18.8 The Windows Phone Dev Center benefits page

- *Startups*—If you're a startup or an individual developer, you may be eligible to join the BizSpark program for software startup companies (www.BizSpark.com). One of the benefits of the BizSpark program is an MSDN subscription that includes a code you can enter on signup.
- *Promotions and contests*—Occasionally, promotions and app development contests are held to encourage developers to give Windows Phone development a try. Many times the events offer registration keys to developers who are ready to release their first app to the store. Both Microsoft and Nokia have offered these promotions through their MVPs (https://mvp.support.microsoft.com). You can also check the Dev Center for programs such as Generation App (U.S.) and Developer Movement (Canada) because they can make the $99 registration fee worth paying by offering prizes and rewards that can offset its cost.

18.2.3 Markets

Microsoft has expanded the number of markets (countries) in which Windows Phone apps can be distributed. At launch, Windows Phone 7 apps could be released only to about 40 markets, with an additional 13 markets added soon after. With the launch of Windows Phone 8, apps can be released to 191 countries, with 44 having some restrictions on app content. You can still release apps to these 44 countries, but you have the option of declining to do so if you know your app may not meet the restrictions. Details of these restrictions are available at http://mng.bz/n1lY.

18.2.4 Trial apps

Before committing hard-earned money to a purchase, many users like to use a demonstration or trial version of an application, and the Windows Phone Store provides support for limited trials. Applications use the `IsTrial` method of the `LicenseInformation` class to determine whether the application is running under a trial license. When calling this method, its response can take a short but undetermined amount of time to return a result. For this reason, it's a good idea to get this value as the app is loading and keep this value accessible anywhere within the app.

The best way to implement this trial-checking behavior is to create a static property in the App.xaml.cs file and set its value in the `Application_Launching` and `Application_Activated` events in the same App.xaml.cs file. In the following listing, the `IsTrial` property is set when the app is first launched and when being reactivated.

Listing 18.3 App.xaml.cs caching `isTrial` status

```
public static bool IsTrial { get; private set; }        // Static property available anywhere in app

private void Application_Launching(object sender, LaunchingEventArgs e)
{
        var licenseInfo = new
                Microsoft.Phone.Marketplace.LicenseInformation();
        IsTrial = licenseInfo.IsTrial();
}
```

```
private void Application_Activated(object sender, ActivatedEventArgs e)
{
        var licenseInfo = new
                Microsoft.Phone.Marketplace.LicenseInformation();
        IsTrial = licenseInfo.IsTrial();
}
```

Setting the property as static allows its value to be accessed as `App.IsTrial` from anywhere. Using it is as simple as this:

```
if (App.IsTrial)
{
    // implement trial mode logic here...
}
```

Developers should always test their applications in both trial and unlimited modes. Testing can be problematic because the `IsTrial` method always returns `false` when running in the emulator. Conditional compilation techniques can be used to test trial licensing. The following listing shows the same code as listing 18.3 with additional conditional compilation flags to allow setting the `IsTrial` property as needed during testing.

Listing 18.4 App.xaml.cs caching `isTrial` status with conditional compilation

```
public static bool IsTrial { get; private set; }          <-- Static property available anywhere in app

private void Application_Launching(object sender,
                                        LaunchingEventArgs e)
{
#if TRIAL_LICENSE
        IsTrial = true;                    <-- Trial mode when TRIAL_LICENSE flag enabled
#else
        var licenseInfo = new
                Microsoft.Phone.Marketplace.LicenseInformation();
        IsTrial = licenseInfo.IsTrial();                  <-- Check Store for license information
#endif
}

private void Application_Activated(object sender,
                                        ActivatedEventArgs e)
{
#if TRIAL_LICENSE
        IsTrial = true;
#else
        var licenseInfo = new
                Microsoft.Phone.Marketplace.LicenseInformation();
        IsTrial = licenseInfo.IsTrial();
#endif
}
```

To use the conditional compilation flag `TRIAL_LICENSE` for testing trial mode, double-click the Properties node in the Solution Explorer. Under Build, add *TRIAL_LICENSE;* to the Conditional Compilation Symbols field. Figure 18.9 shows how this should look.

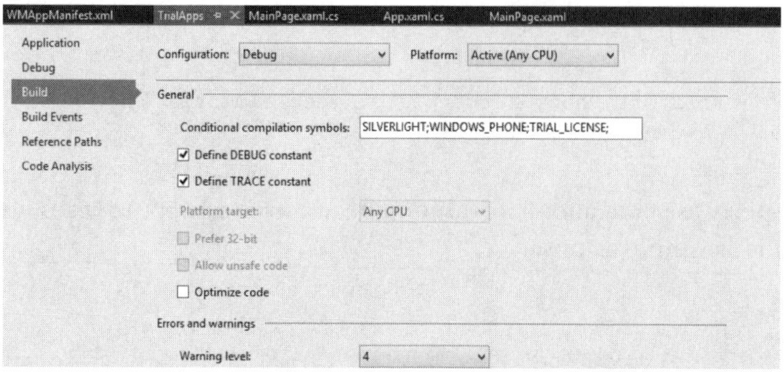

Figure 18.9 Setting a conditional compilation symbol

These custom conditional compilation flags can be safely left in your code. When you create the final build to submit, you set the configuration to Release so any code wrapped in them will not be in the Release build.

The Store trial licensing makes it easy for potential customers to preview your app or game, while eliminating the need to maintain and publish a separate free or light version of your product. Before you submit your first paid or trial app, you need to do one last thing in order to get paid.

18.2.5 Getting paid

In order to submit paid apps and in-app products that aren't free, you need to provide Microsoft with the same tax information required by pubCenter, as outlined at the end of section 18.1.1. Once you're logged into the Dev Center, click your email address in the upper-right corner to bring up your account. Click Edit under Tax Profile to fill in the required documents. Once verified, you'll be able to submit paid apps and receive your part of the sales.

18.2.6 Windows Phone Store Test Kit

Once an application has been developed, it must go through a Microsoft approval process before being published to the Windows Phone Store. This process ensures that the application conforms to Microsoft requirements for a Windows Phone application. Microsoft's requirements are detailed in App Certification Requirements for Windows Phone, available from MSDN at http://mng.bz/L8fH.

The Store Test Kit includes a series of automated, monitored, and manual tests you can use to ensure your application meets Microsoft requirements. The Store Test Kit also helps you assemble the graphics and screen shots that should be submitted along with the application's XAP file. The Store Test Kit is installed when you install the Windows Phone Developer Tools and is shown in figure 18.10. The Kit is an extension to Visual Studio and is accessed from the Open Store Test Kit option in the Visual Studio Project menu.

If your application violates any of the tests, it will be rejected during the submission process. Nobody likes to receive rejection letters. Though you should run the ingestion tool before you submit your application, you may also choose to run it periodically during development so that you can detect and fix issues as early as possible.

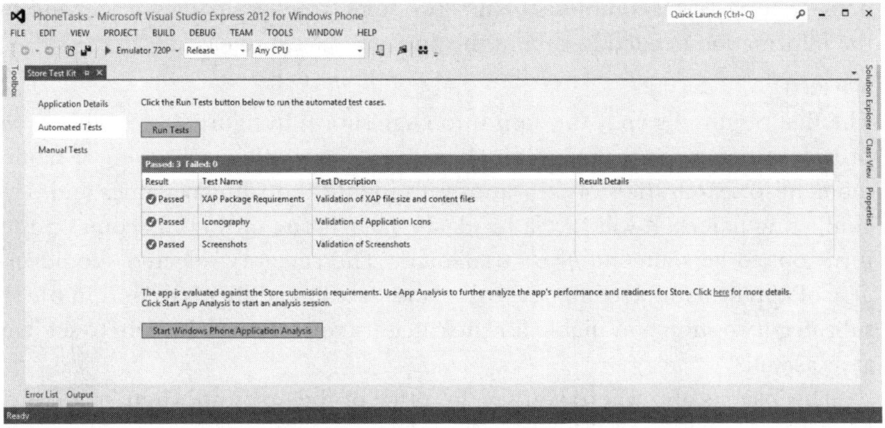

Figure 18.10 The results of automated tests performed by the Store Test Kit, including a list of security capabilities used by the application

18.2.7 App submission and certification

Once your application is finished and tested and your subscription is in order, you're ready to submit it to the Windows Phone Store. This is the final step before the general public can find and install your app. Head over to http://dev.windowsphone.com and sign in. Once you've signed in, click the Submit App link to get to the Submit App page, shown in figure 18.11. This page contains two required steps and three optional

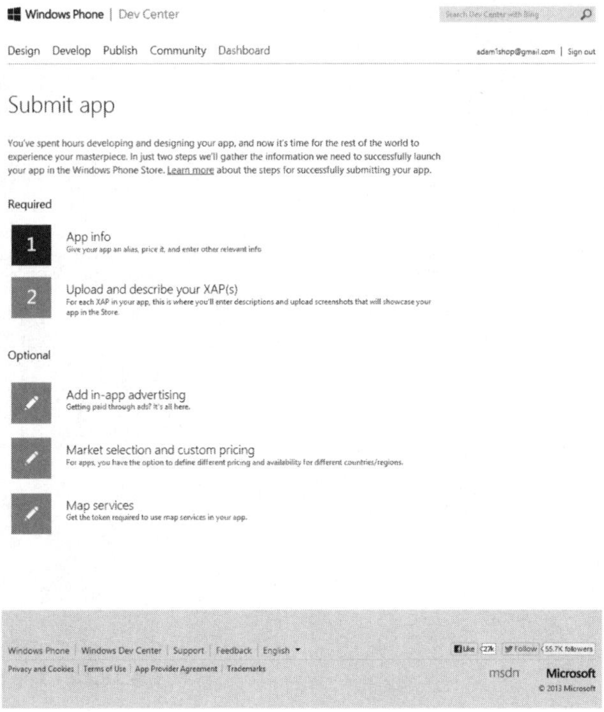

Figure 18.11 Submit App page

ones. As long as you complete the first two steps, you'll upload your app and submit all the information needed to submit the app and have it released into the store.

APP INFO

The first required step is the App Info page shown in figure 18.12. This is where you provide a name for your app and set its category. When choosing a name, take a moment to search the store for apps with identical or similar names and try to avoid conflicting names. It will save a headache later if one of them becomes popular or it turns out to be someone else's trademark. The category selected should match the type of app or its subject matter—otherwise it will be difficult to find in the store. If a subcategory option is available for the category you selected, be sure to set it appropriately as well.

This page is also where you set the price of the app and whether it contains trial features. If you haven't filled out the required tax documents, you can only submit free apps; otherwise you can submit apps priced from U.S. $0.99 to $499.99. If you implemented trial detection as described in this chapter, check the "Offer free trials of this app" check box to have the Try option appear in the Store.

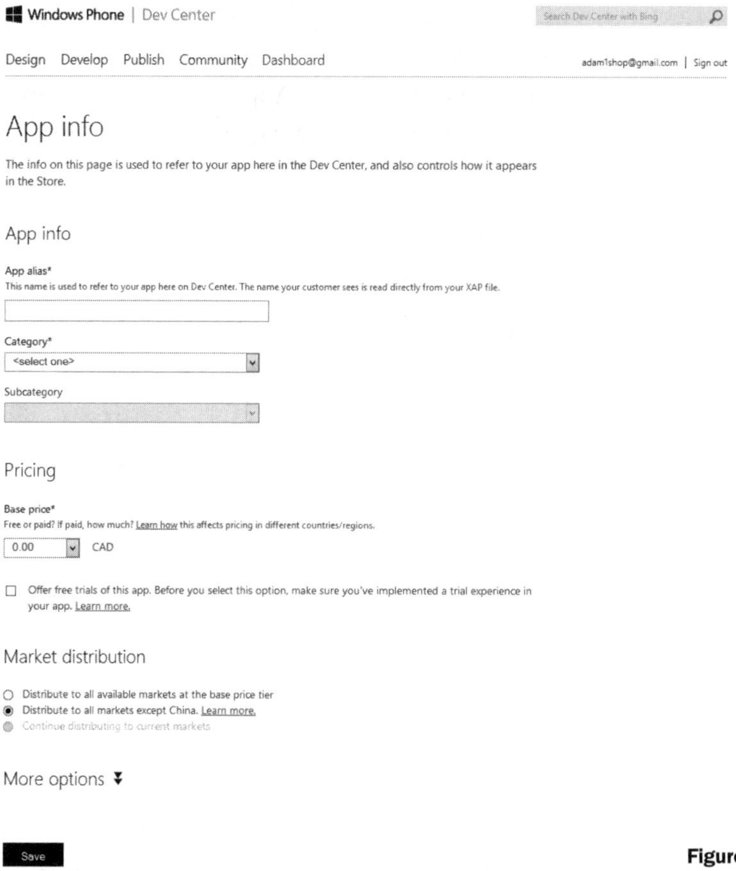

Figure 18.12 App Info page

> **Acceptable app content**
>
> Before submitting your first app, take a few minutes to read the content policies found on the Windows Phone Dev Center website (http://mng.bz/jU0q) to ensure your app doesn't contain any prohibited content. Additionally, some regions may have additional restriction on content. Section 3.10 (Country/Region Specific Requirements) of the content policy on the Windows Phone Dev Center website describes some of these additional restrictions. When submitting, you have the choice to submit to all regions or to all markets except those with stricter content rules.

Clicking More Options displays the last set of options on this page. The Distribution Channels option lets you control how people get your app. Selecting Public Store allows the general public access to your app through the Store. Checking the Hide from Users Browsing or Searching the Store option does exactly that: it hides the app so that the only way to download the app is a direct link to it (available from the Details page for the app in the Dev Center). This is useful for a soft launch, where you have a list of interested users but don't want to attract the general public quite yet. Selecting Beta allows you to give access to selected users to facilitate testing with devices. If you go the Beta route, you'll have to resubmit your app when you're ready to release it to the public Store. You can choose to release immediately after passing certification or wait to do it manually and provide a certificate for push notifications if you have one. Once you've filled in all the required details, click the Save button.

UPLOAD AND DESCRIBE YOUR XAP

The second required step is the Upload XAP page. On the Submit App page shown previously in figure 18.11, click the Upload and Describe Your XAP(s) item. Once the page loads, click the Browse link and select your XAP file. Uploading will take a few

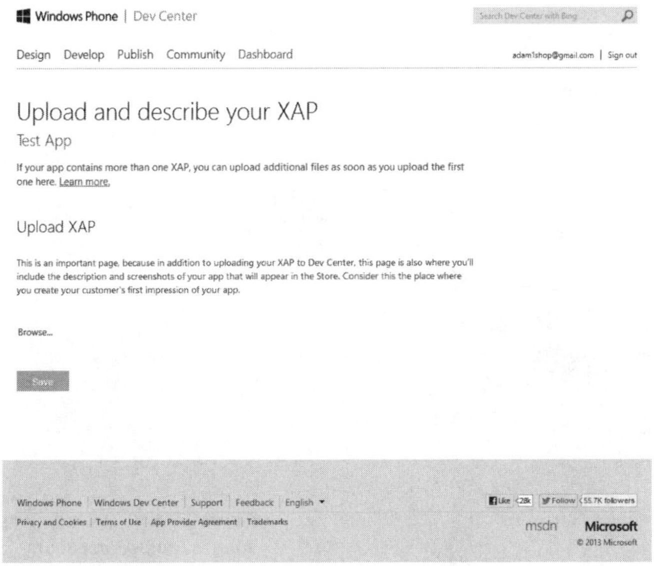

Figure 18.13 Upload and describe your XAP

minutes, depending on the size of your XAP file. When it's finished, you're presented with the remaining required info for app submission, shown in figure 18.13, including description, keywords to help users find your app, and images such as icons, background, and screenshots for the Store.

> **App description**
>
> Although the name of your app can make it stand out in the list, it's the description that convinces users to install it. Your description should be long enough that the user understands what your app is about, but not so long as to make them lose interest. Be descriptive, but don't write a manual.

After entering the app name and description, provide up to five keywords. Think of a few generic terms that users might use to find your app while searching. Because your app will be searchable by name and by publisher name as well, you don't need to enter those as keywords.

The rest of this page relates to application icons, background images for the store, and application screenshots. In the WMAppManifest.xml file, you can select the screen resolutions your app supports. When you submit the application, the supported resolutions are detected, and screenshots are required for each supported resolution shown in figure 18.14. Although you can upload each image one at a time, the quickest way is to copy all required images to a folder and use the Upload All link shown in the figure to select them all. They will be automatically set in the correct places, in order. After double-checking all values on the page, click Save.

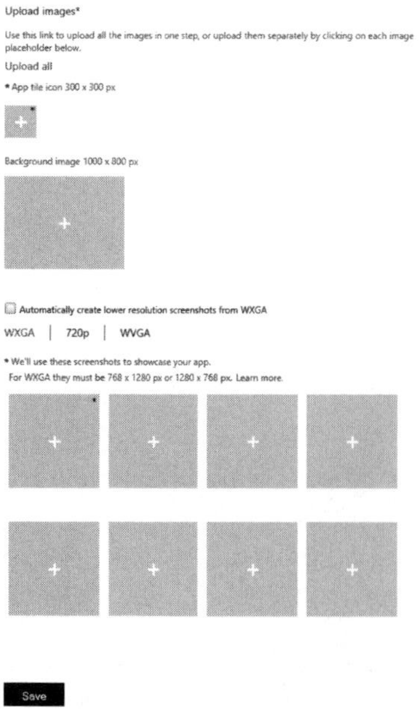

Figure 18.14 Uploading app icons, images, and screenshots

OPTIONAL STEPS

Optional steps during app submission include advertising, custom market pricing, and map services. If you implemented ads and did not create an `AppId` or `AdUnitId` in the process, now is your last chance before submission. Doing this step now may require re-uploading the XAP if you need to add these values to your code.

When you set the price, the submission process sets the price to the equivalent local currency for each region. If you want to adjust the price for specific regions, now is your chance. If you selected to submit only for less restrictive regions, some regions will be unchecked. This is also where you can choose to release to some restrictive regions but not others.

As with advertising, if you somehow missed getting a token to use Bing maps in your app, this is your chance to fix that. Again, you may need to rebuild and re-upload to the Dev Center.

Once you have apps in the Windows Phone Store, you're likely going to need to know some stats about downloads, app crashes, and earnings. That information is found in the Dev Center, in the Reports menu item in the sidebar of the Dev Center website.

18.2.8 Reports

The Reports section of the Dev Center, shown in figure 18.15, allows you to see the daily and cumulative download counts of your apps, as well as in-app purchases. The reports can be narrowed down to a single app or region and to a specific date range.

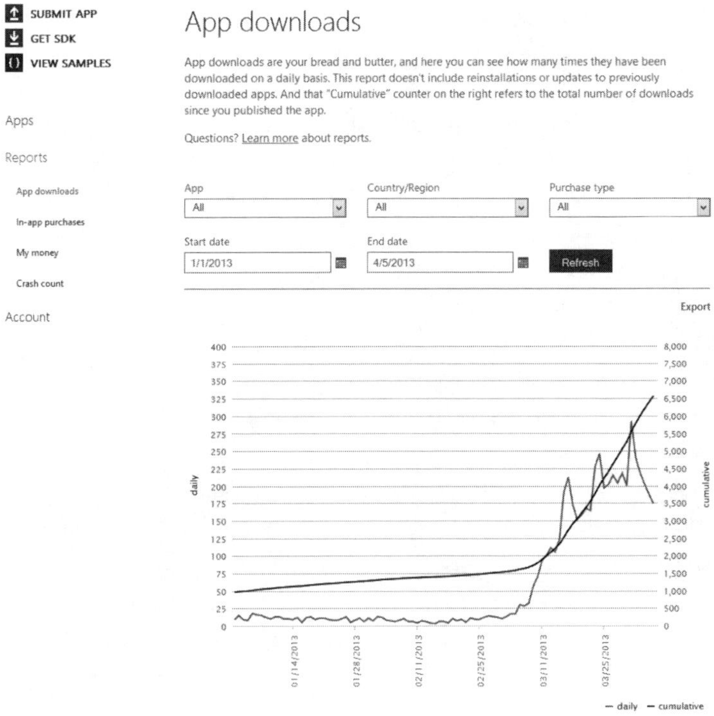

Figure 18.15
App download report

These reports are delayed several days, so you'll have to wait a couple of days to see launch-day stats.

The My Money report shows proceeds, payout, and withholding tax information. Payout reports can take up to 10 days to populate and can take varying amounts of time depending on the payment method. For example, payments made by the mobile operator (a list of supported mobile operators can be found at http://mng.bz/ep6y) can take up to 120 days to settle.

Crash reports, shown in figure 18.16, are important to keep an eye on. Apps that crash too much may be removed from the Store at Microsoft's discretion. Exporting stack traces will provide you with an Excel document containing the top issues where each row in the spreadsheet is a single issue, not an instance of an issue. The 30 Day Crash Count column reports the number of times a crash happened.

Although paid apps have more potential for making money than ad-supported apps do, most users don't buy large numbers of apps. The monetization strategy that has the most potential for making money is in-app purchases.

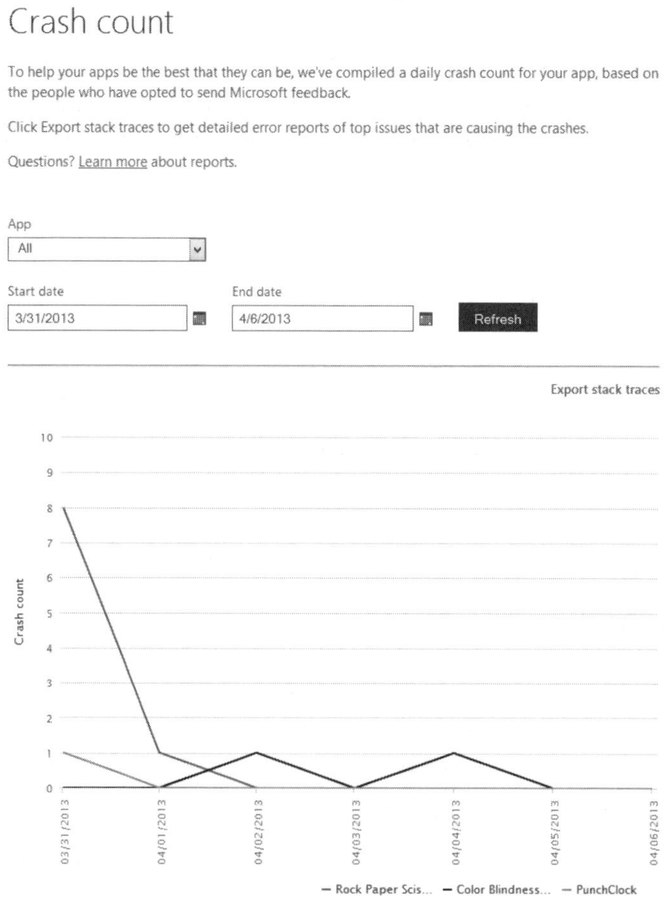
Crash count
To help your apps be the best that they can be, we've compiled a daily crash count for your app, based on the people who have opted to send Microsoft feedback.
Click Export stack traces to get detailed error reports of top issues that are causing the crashes.
Questions? Learn more about reports.
App
All
Start date
3/31/2013
End date
4/6/2013
Refresh
Export stack traces
Crash count
03/31/2013
04/01/2013
04/02/2013
04/03/2013
04/04/2013
04/05/2013
04/06/2013
— Rock Paper Scis... — Color Blindness... — PunchClock

Figure 18.16 Crash count report

18.3 In-app purchases

So far in this chapter, we've looked at several monetization strategies that, although able to generate income, are either passive with ads or are one-time sales with paid apps. In-app purchases (IAPs) allow you to sell additional items to users of your games or apps. This additional income stream is usually more lucrative, because you can continue to add new items for users to buy.

18.3.1 Why in-app purchases?

IAPs are estimated to have generated over $1 billion in revenue in 2012 across all mobile platforms and are expected to surpass $4 billion by 2016. Giving the app away for free but selling add-ons has become the most profitable business model for most top-grossing apps on the iOS platform. Users tend to resist paying for apps, but once they like them, they're often willing to pay for more.

In addition to lowering the cost of getting users to use your app, making in-app purchases is easy for users. Users have multiple options for making payments, including credit cards, PayPal, and mobile operator billing.

With mobile operator billing, Microsoft discovered that revenue increased significantly, with 75% of users choosing it over using a credit card. Mobile operator billing is available in 191 countries and is accessible to those without a credit card. Mobile operator billing gives you the chance to capture some revenue that you may not otherwise have been able to. A list of supported mobile operators can be found at http://mng.bz/ep6y.

18.3.2 Who provides what piece?

One of the great things about IAP is that you don't need to build a billing system in order to sell additional items to users. Microsoft provides the entire financial-related back end; all you need to do is implement the user experience.

In order to use IAP, you must provide the following:

- Rating-appropriate products
- Clear and accurate product listings
- The user experience to offer products
- Product fulfillment and downloads/delivery
- Testing

When you provide these, Microsoft provides the rest of the pieces needed:

- Product-management tools in the form of the Dev Center website
- Geo-distributed services
- The purchase user experience
- Payment system
- Purchase authenticity verification
- Testing tools and infrastructure

Between the parts you and Microsoft provide, your app will have the ability to generate revenue by selling users items that can be consumed such as coins and durables such as maps.

18.3.3 Types of IAP items you can sell

There are two types of IAP items you can sell: consumables and durables.

Consumables are items that are consumed in your app, such as gold coins or credits. Consumables can be purchased more than once. It's up to you to keep track of consumable items purchased by the user. If you're selling tokens or other spendable items, it's a good idea to keep good records of transactions outside of the handset—in an Azure Mobile Service table, for example. Doing so protects everyone if any disputes arise due to misuse or coding errors.

In figure 18.17 the screen on the left is an information screen in the app created to show the user what they're buying. The screen on the right is part of the Windows Phone 8 operating system and is provided by Microsoft.

Durables are items that are purchased once and are owned forever. These can include additional features, levels, maps, weapons, and armor. You can check the

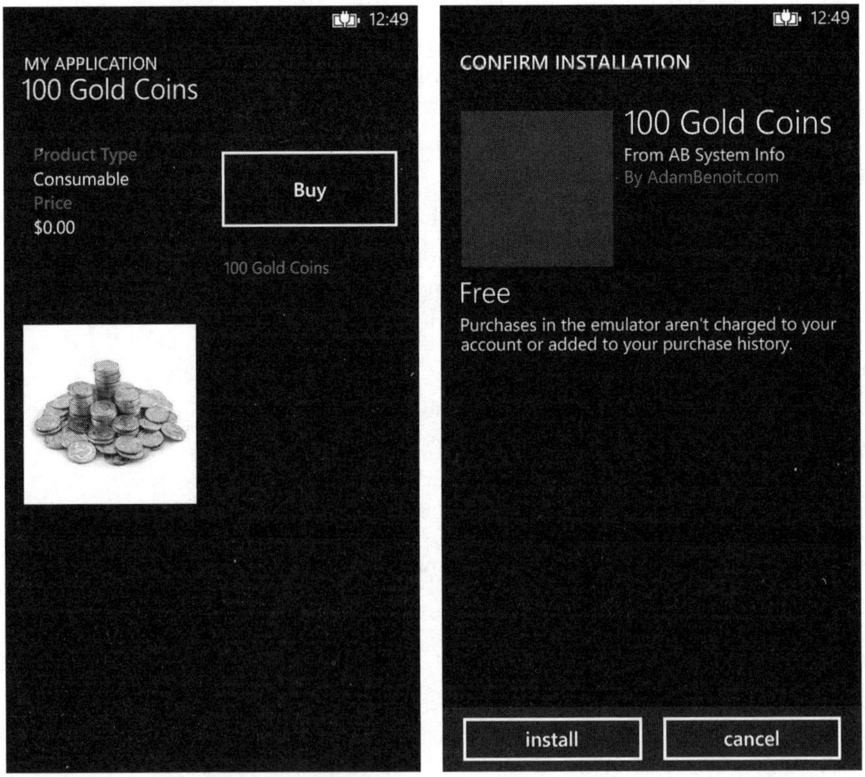

Figure 18.17 A consumable product

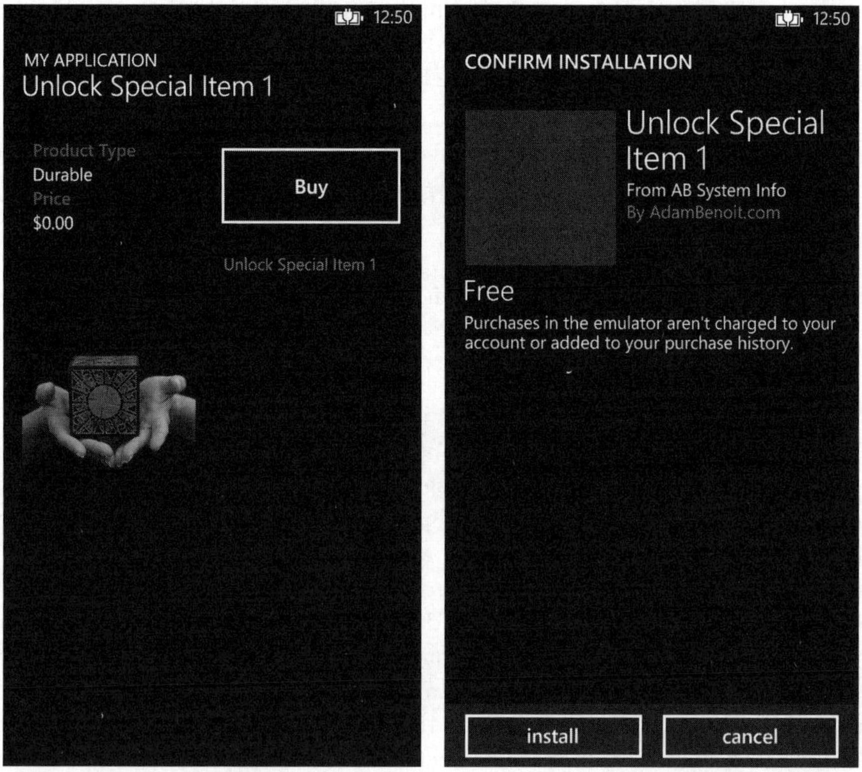

Figure 18.18 A durable product

license status of durables anytime using the `CurrentApp.LicenseInformation.ProductLicenses` collection.

In figure 18.18 the screen on the left is a purchase screen in the app created to show the user what they're buying. The screen on the right is part of the WP8 operating system and is provided by Microsoft. When you implement a purchase screen in your app, you first need to get the product details from the Store to display to the user and to initiate the purchase.

18.3.4 Getting products from the Store

Each application can contain as many in-app products, both durable and consumable, as you need. The `CurrentApp` class provides several methods to retrieve a collection of products:

- `LoadListingInformationByKeywordsAsync` accepts a `string[]` array of keywords you provide when you submit the product to the Store.
- `LoadListingInformationByProductIdsAsync` accepts a `string[]` array of `ProductIds`, again provided by you during product submission.
- `LoadListingInformationAsync` returns all products for the app.

Getting the product info and binding it to a control is demonstrated in the following listing. The first two lines load the `Listing` info for the current app and save the products in a `List<>`. This `List` is then bound to the `ItemsSource` of a `ListBox`.

Listing 18.5 Getting all products for the current app

```
using Windows.ApplicationModel.Store;

var Listing = await
        Store.CurrentApp.LoadListingInformationAsync();     <-- Load app's listing info
var Products = Listing.ProductListings.ToList();            <-- Get products from listing info
InAppItemsListBox.ItemsSource = Products;    <-- Assign products to data-bound ListBox
```

18.3.5 Implementing consumables

You implement consumables by initiating the purchase of a consumable item and processing the results after the purchase is complete. Because consumable items are consumed—they go away—you need to keep a record of consumable purchases and when they're spent. In a game, for example, after loading a `Player` data model, any in-app purchases could be saved to the `Player` data model and persisted to local storage or some other store mechanism. In the downloadable sample code for this chapter, a `Player` data model is updated after purchase. Listing 18.6 shows `RequestProductPurchaseAsync` being called using `await` to pause for the results. After returning from the purchasing screen, check the license using the `CurrentApp.LicenseInformation .ProductLicenses` collection. If the `IsActive` property is `true` for your consumable item, you have a license and can increment its value. Then you must report its fulfillment by calling the `ReportProductFulfillment` method. The item can't be purchased until you do so.

Listing 18.6 Processing an in-app purchase

```
using Windows.ApplicationModel.Store;

var receipt = await Store.CurrentApp
                .RequestProductPurchaseAsync(
                        Product.ProductId, true);      <-- Request product purchase using
if (Store.CurrentApp.LicenseInformation
                .ProductLicenses[Product.ProductId].IsActive)   <-- Check IsActive property for true value
{
        if (Product.ProductType == ProductType.Consumable)   <-- Process consumables, update local storage, report fulfillment
        {
                if (Product.ProductId == "GoldCoins100")
                {
                        App.Player.Gold += 100;
                        Store.CurrentApp
                                .ReportProductFulfillment(
                                        Product.ProductId);
                }
        }
```

```
        else if (Product.ProductType == ProductType.Durable)
        {
                var item = App.Player.Items.Single(
                        i => i.ProductId == Product.ProductId);
                if (item != null)
                {
                        item.Purchased = true;
                }
        }
}
ProcessPurchaseReciept(receipt);
```

Process durable, save in local storage

Do something with purchase receipt

18.3.6 *Implementing durables*

Durable items are implemented in much the same way, except you can check the license anytime you want. In listing 18.6, when a durable item is purchased, the data model (called `Player` because it represents a game player) is updated to indicate that the item was purchased. In a real-world situation, the licenses should be saved so the purchased item can be used offline (if applicable) and checked when the app is loaded, if possible.

If your durable item requires the app to download additional content, that should happen only after verifying the item's license and as you would download any other item. The delivery of additional content is the responsibility of nobody but you, the developer. Once the license has been verified, you can download files from network locations using the `WebClient` class and save them to local storage. Information on both can be found in chapters 11 and 7, respectively.

18.4 *Testing*

No app should be released without proper testing, and apps that implement IAP should be tested thoroughly. There are two simple ways to test IAP during the coding and QA (quality assurance) stages of development: local testing and beta testing.

LOCAL TESTING

Local testing is the best choice if you're still developing your app and will need to purchase the same durable item repeatedly to test various scenarios. This is facilitated using the mock in-app purchase library.

The mock in-app purchase library was designed to completely emulate the purchase process without making any calls to the Store. Download the mock in-app purchase library and sample app from http://mng.bz/fKYF. Once it's downloaded and unzipped, open the solution and build the solution. Then go back to your app and include a reference to the MockIAPLib.dll you built. You should find it in the bin folder within the MockIAPLib in the Mock solution folder.

With the reference added, you need to add it to each code file that uses IAP features. Conditional compilation helps you switch between the real Store and the mock library. The next listing shows this in action.

Listing 18.7 Using conditional compilation

```
#if DEBUG
using MockIAPLib;
using Store = MockIAPLib;
#else
using Windows.ApplicationModel.Store;
#endif
```

The mock library should be configured when the app needs to use it. Again using conditional compilation, you set up the mock at the end of the constructor in the App.xaml.cs file. The next listing shows how to load an XML file of mock products.

Listing 18.8 Using the mock purchase library in debug mode

```
using System.Windows.Resources;
using System.Xml.Linq;

#if DEBUG
    MockIAP.Init();

    MockIAP.RunInMockMode(true);
    MockIAP.SetListingInformation(1, "en-us",
                                "A description", "1", "TestApp");     <-- Configure details of current app
    StreamResourceInfo  xml = Application.GetResourceStream(
                        new Uri("MockProducts.xml", UriKind.Relative));
    XElement  appDataXml = XElement.Load(xml.Stream);
    MockIAP.PopulateIAPItemsFromXml(appDataXml.ToString());     <-- Load products from XML file

    MockIAP.ClearCache();     <-- Clear purchase cache for testing all durables
#endif
```

The XML document you load contains the details of the product you're selling. Ideally these products will match any you submit to the Store, so no code changes are necessary when you've finished testing and are ready to release your app. The next listing shows a single product MockProducts.xml file. The `Purchased` and `Fulfilled` properties of `ProductListing` allow you to set up various test cases to mimic.

Listing 18.9 MockProducts.xml

```
<?xml version="1.0"?>
<ProductListings>
  <ProductListing Key="GoldCoins100" Purchased="false"
Fulfilled="false">
    <Name>100 Gold</Name>
    <Description>A sample product listing</Description>
    <ProductId>GoldCoins100</ProductId>
    <ProductType>Consumable</ProductType>
    <FormattedPrice>$1.00</FormattedPrice>
    <ImageUri></ImageUri>
    <Keywords>test;product</Keywords>
```

```
    <Tag>Additional text</Tag>
  </ProductListing>

</ProductListings>
```

TIP As you test durables, you may come across a situation where you need to repurchase an item. To do that, call `MockIAP.ClearCache()` to clear previous purchases and receipts, allowing you to retest.

BETA TESTING

To test a beta app, you submit your app to the store as a beta. You can then submit in-app items under this beta app. If your app isn't ready to be submitted as a beta, you can submit in-app items under another published app. Beta is done once you're ready for testing by testers. Beta testing doesn't require every device to be developer-unlocked, but testing locally does. Local testing is typically used while the app is still under active development.

Once your items have been approved by Microsoft (it usually takes about 24 hours), open the Details page shown in figure 18.19 in the Dev Center site for the app. Under the Details link, find and copy the App ID. Open the WMAppManifest.xml file in Visual Studio, and, under the Packaging tab, set the Product ID to match the App ID (don't forget to surround it with curly braces [{}] as shown in figure 18.20). Now when you call the `LoadListingInformationAsync` method, you'll get products from the store.

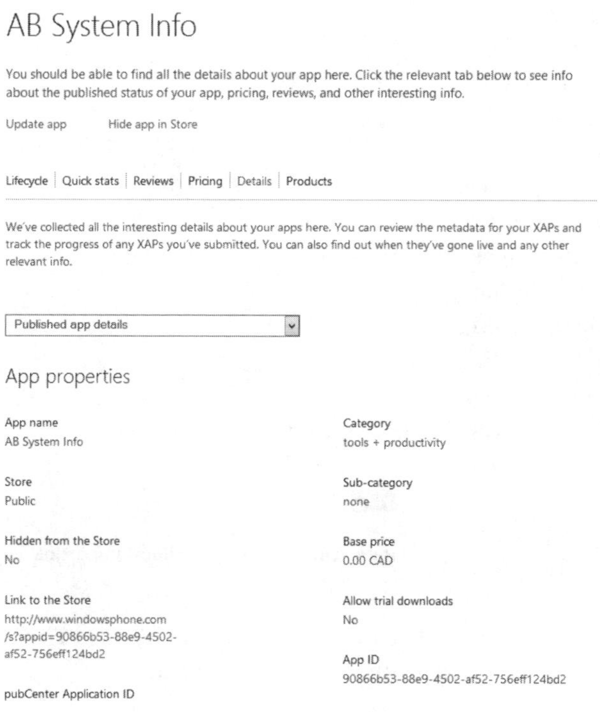

Figure 18.19 App Details page

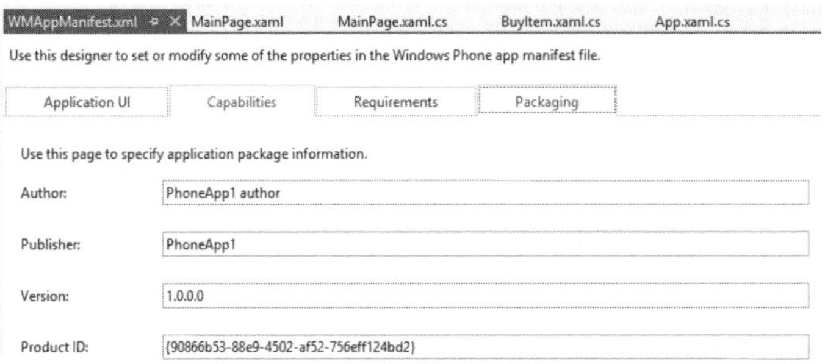

Figure 18.20 Product ID of an app

The downside to testing this way is that, once a product has been purchased, you can't purchase it again. Using the mock library doesn't have this limitation, which is why it's the preferred way to test.

18.4.1 Submitting your in-app items

Submitting in-app products to the store is quick and easy, with a short time for approval into the Store—typically 24 to 48 hours. To add an in-app product, log in to the Windows Phone Dev Center, click Apps in the sidebar menu, and select the app you're submitting products for. Once the App properties page loads, click the Products link (refer back to figure 18.19). Then click the Add In-App product link.

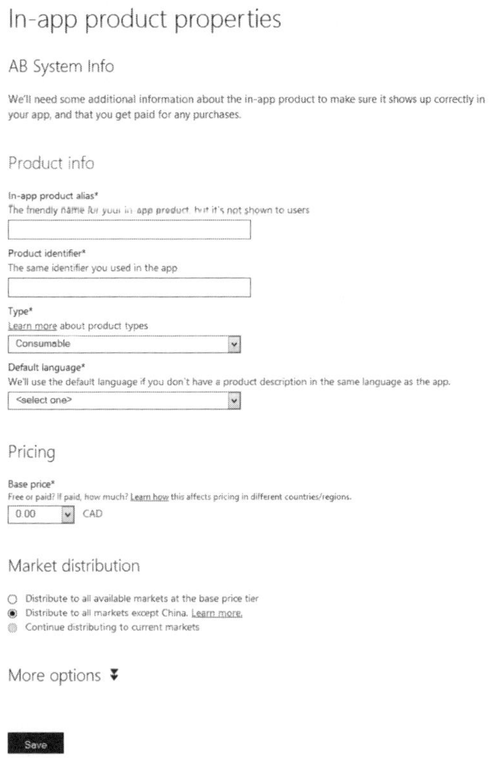

Figure 18.21 In-app product properties

The In-App Product Properties page shown in figure 18.21 allows you to set the in-app product alias, product identifier, type, default language, and market distribution. Tags and keywords can be configured in the More Options section. The product identifier is the `ProductId` you use within your code to refer to this product.

The Description page shown in figure 18.22 lets you set the product's public name, description, and image. Be sure to make all three indicative of what the user is buying. The user must understand the benefit of the purchase or they may not make it.

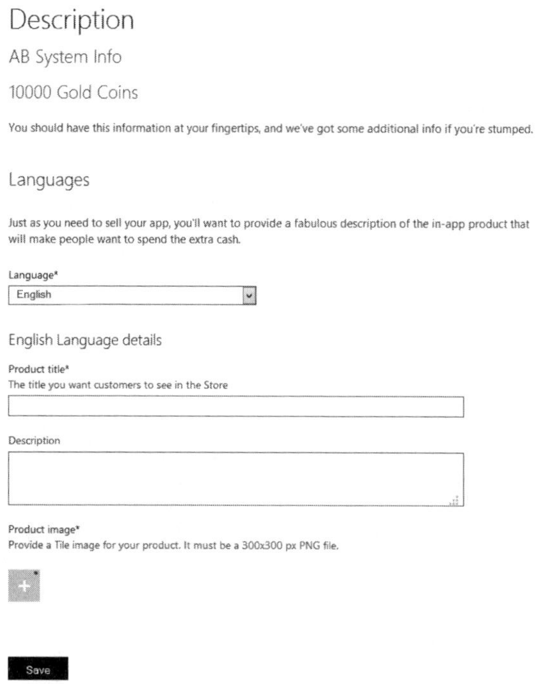
Description
AB System Info
10000 Gold Coins
You should have this information at your fingertips, and we've got some additional info if you're stumped.
Languages
Just as you need to sell your app, you'll want to provide a fabulous description of the in-app product that will make people want to spend the extra cash.
Language*
English
English Language details
Product title*
The title you want customers to see in the Store
Description
Product image*
Provide a Tile image for your product. It must be a 300x300 px PNG file.
Save

Figure 18.22
In-app product Description page

Once you submit the in-app product, it will take a day or two for approval, but once the approval comes through, you can use it in your app.

18.5 Summary

The different monetization strategies available for Windows Phone 8 have different levels of effectiveness, depending on the effort required to implement them. Ads are the easiest to implement, but require enormous amounts of impressions to make good money. Trial and paid apps are more complex to implement, but the payoff can be higher than with ads. In-app purchases are the most complex strategy to implement, but the payoff is almost always better than any of the other strategies. In-app purchases also have the advantage over the paid-app strategy due to the potential for ongoing income.

A mixture of these strategies can also be a good way to go. Putting ads in trial apps and removing them in the paid version is one mixed strategy we've used with some success. Having ads removed from an app via an in-app purchase is another idea worth looking into.

appendix A: XAML, the Extensible Application Markup Language

What's XAML? XAML is Microsoft's XML-based markup language for building stunning user interfaces. XAML was first introduced as part of the Windows Presentation Foundation, which Microsoft included as part of version 3.0 of the .NET Framework as a replacement for the two-decades-old graphics device interface (GDI)-based technology. XAML excels as a user interface markup language, separating the user interface design from the code-behind implementing an application's business logic. XAML not only defines WPF and Silverlight UIs, but is also one of the options when building Windows Runtime applications for the Windows 8 operating system. If you're coming from a web development background, you can think of XAML as similar to HTML, which you use to create UIs for your web pages. XAML is an XML document that represents the hierarchical structure of an application's user interface.

This appendix serves as a quick introduction to XAML. We cover basic UI layout and the available UI controls, and then move on to an introduction to the data-binding features built into XAML. We wrap up by using `DataTemplates` to create a user interface for a domain model object.

Let's start by examining the default XAML generated when you create a new application with the Windows Phone App project template. Figure A.1 shows the application generated by the project template.

Figure A.1 The default application

The default application generates a page that contains a `Grid` layout control, a `StackPanel` layout control, and two `TextBlocks`. The XAML markup for the form is shown in the following listing. We'll refer back to this listing several times in the next few pages.

Listing A.1 XAML generated by the Windows Phone Application project template

Root element ❶

```
<phone:PhoneApplicationPage x:Class="Primer.MainPage"
    xmlns="http://schemas.microsoft.com/winfx/2006/xaml/presentation"
    xmlns:x="http://schemas.microsoft.com/winfx/2006/xaml"
    xmlns:phone=
       "clr-namespace:Microsoft.Phone.Controls;assembly=Microsoft.Phone"
    xmlns:primer="clr-namespace:Primer"
...
    >
    <Grid x:Name="LayoutRoot" Background="Transparent">
        <Grid.RowDefinitions>
            <RowDefinition Height="Auto"/>
            <RowDefinition Height="*"/>
        </Grid.RowDefinitions>
        <StackPanel x:Name="TitlePanel" Grid.Row="0" Margin="12,17,0,28"
           Orientation="Vertical" >
           <TextBlock Text="MY APPLICATION"
                Style="{StaticResource PhoneTextNormalStyle}"/>
           <TextBlock Text="page name" Margin="9,-7,0,0"
                Style="{StaticResource PhoneTextTitle1Style}"/>
        </StackPanel>
        <Grid x:Name="ContentPanel" Grid.Row="1" Margin="12,0,12,0"/>
    </Grid>
</phone:PhoneApplicationPage>
```

The root of the XAML document is an element of type `PhoneApplicationPage` ❶. Elements in a XAML document must be matched with a class name from either the .NET class libraries or the application's code. The root element also contains a `Class` attribute that declares the full name of the C# class containing the code-behind for the user interface. The class named in the `Class` attribute must be derived from the class used as the root element. In this listing, the class `MainPage` is derived from the class `PhoneApplicationPage`.

You may have noticed that the root element uses the XML namespace `phone`. In XAML, *namespaces* can be declared with an assembly name or with a URI. An example of the URI version can be seen in the third line of the listing, declaring the `x` namespace. The fourth line of the listing shows the assembly name version declaring the `phone` namespace. We added the fifth line to the generated XAML; it's a declaration for the `Primer` namespace, which is part of the application and doesn't need to specify an assembly name.

Most XAML documents you create for Windows Phone will derive from either `PhoneApplicationPage` or `UserControl`. Both `PhoneApplicationPage` and `UserControl` expect to have a single child control. In most cases the child control will be a layout control derived from the `Panel` class.

A.1 Layout controls

Layout controls are containers of other controls and are responsible for automatically positioning their children on the screen. The Windows Phone SDK includes three different layout controls named `StackPanel`, `Grid`, and `Canvas`.

The `StackPanel` control lays out its children in a horizontal or vertical stack, depending on the value of its `Orientation` property. The `StackPanel` in listing A.1 specifies an orientation of `Vertical`, which is the default value if an `Orientation` attribute isn't declared. A vertical `StackPanel` stacks controls one on top of the other and ensures that all child controls have exactly the same width. A horizontal `StackPanel` stacks controls side by side and ensures that all controls have exactly the same height.

The `Grid` control lays out its children in a series of rows and columns. By default, a `Grid` has only one row and one column. Additional rows and columns are specified with the `Grid.RowDefinitions` and `Grid.ColumnDefinitions` properties, respectively. The `Grid` control called `LayoutRoot` in listing A.1 has two rows and a single column. The first row is given a height of `Auto` and uses as much height as needed. The second row is given a height of `*`, which tells the `Grid` to give the row a height that fills all of the remaining space. Child controls specify their rows and columns with the zero-based `Grid.Row` and `Grid.Column` attributes. For example, the `Grid` named `ContentPanel` specifies that it should be placed in the second row. Row and column indexes are zero-based. A control can span multiple rows and columns using the `Grid.RowSpan` and `Grid.ColumnSpan` attributes. If a child control doesn't specify its row and column values, it's placed in the first row and first column.

The `Canvas` control lays out its children using absolute positioning. The positions of child elements are declared using `Canvas.Left` and `Canvas.Top` properties. If a child doesn't declare its position, it's placed at coordinate (0,0).

A.2 Interacting with XAML controls

XAML for Windows Phone contains many of the common controls you'd expect in a user interface library. You should be aware that some of the controls present in WPF and Silverlight for the browser aren't supported on Windows Phone. Check the MSDN documentation for a full list of controls supported by Windows Phone, found at http://mng.bz/tl47.

Let's look at how to declare a simple form with a few controls and how to interact with the controls from code. The form will contain a `TextBlock` to display a label, a `TextBox` to receive input from the user, and a `Button`:

```
<StackPanel>
    <TextBlock Text="Please enter your name" />
    <TextBox x:Name="nameTextBox" />
    <Button Content="Save" Width="150" Click="Button_Click" />
</StackPanel>
```

You've given the `TextBox` a name using the `x:Name` attribute. The compiler will automatically generate a field for named controls, allowing you to easily access the control from code-behind. The Button control is defined with a Width value of 150 pixels. When the button is tapped by the user, a Click event is raised, and a custom event handler method named Button_Click is called:

```
private void Button_Click(object sender, RoutedEventArgs e)
{
    string name = nameTextBox.Text;
    MessageBox.Show("You entered : " + name);
}
```

In the Button_Click method, the generated field nameTextBox is used to retrieve the text entered by the user. The MessageBox class's Show method displays a message to the user with a popup window.

A.3 Styles and resources

Specifying individual properties for every control can become onerous and error-prone. Suppose a form contains five buttons, and each button specifies a width of 150 pixels. If you want to change the width from 150 pixels to 155 pixels, you must make the change five times. *Styles* allow you to set properties on multiple controls at the same time. Styles are declared inside the Resources property of a XAML element. The following snippet declares a Style with the key NarrowButton that applies to Button controls:

```
<Grid.Resources>
    <Style x:Key="NarrowButton" TargetType="Button">
        <Setter Property="Width" Value="150" />
    </Style>
</Grid.Resources>
```

The NarrowButton Style will set a Button's Width property to 150 pixels. Styles are explicitly set on controls using the StaticResource markup extension:

```
<Button Content="Save" Click="Button_Click"
    Style="{StaticResource NarrowButton}" />
```

Back in listing A.1, you can see two other examples of setting a Style with the StaticResource markup extension. The Styles named PhoneTextNormalStyle and PhoneTextTitle1Style are two of a number of different styles provided by the Windows Phone SDK to allow you easily build applications that match the operating system's look and feel. You can read more about built-in styles in chapter 2.

Styles can also be automatically applied to a set of controls. These automatic styles, called *implicit styles*, are activated by creating a style without a key.

A.4 Binding controls to model objects

One of the more powerful aspects of XAML is its ability to separate user interface markup from code logic. Data binding is one of the underlying features that enable UI separation. In the Button_Click method discussed earlier, the code-behind needs to know that a TextBox control named nameTextBlock exists in the UI markup. This knowledge links the UI markup to code-behind. If the TextBox is renamed, or if another type of control is used instead of a TextBox, the code will have to change as well.

Data binding enables you to write code-behind that's unaware of the names and types of input controls used in the user interface. Let's say there's a C# domain model object with a UserName property:

```
public class SampleModel
{
    public string UserName { get; set; }
}
```

In the page constructor, a new instance of the model object is constructed and assigned to the page's DataContext property:

```
DataContext = new SampleModel();
```

The DataContext property is used by the binding system as the data source when resolving data binding requests made in XAML markup. A data binding request is declared with the Binding markup extension:

```
<TextBox x:Name="nameTextBox" Text="{Binding UserName, Mode=TwoWay}" />
```

In this snippet, the markup declares that the TextBox should get its value from a property named UserName that exists on the model object referenced by the DataContext. Setting the binding Mode to TwoWay tells the TextBox to write any changes back to the UserName property as well. Now the Button_Click method can be updated by replacing knowledge of the TextBox with code that uses the DataContext:

```
private void Button_Click(object sender, RoutedEventArgs e)
{
    SampleModel model = (SampleModel)DataContext;
    MessageBox.Show("You entered : " + model.UserName);
}
```

Using plain C# objects works well if data binding is only writing to the model object. If portions of your user interface read from the model object as well, you can help out the data-binding system by implementing *property change notifications.*

A.5 Property change notifications

When a model object is used as a binding source, the binding system checks whether the model object implements the INotifyPropertyChanged interface. The INotifyPropertyChanged interface declares a single member—an event called PropertyChanged. The binding system subscribes to the PropertyChanged event and tells the user interface controls to update the values they're displaying when the event is raised. A sample model object that implements INotifyPropertyChanged is shown in the following listing.

Listing A.2 Implementing `INotifyPropertyChanged`

```
using System.ComponentModel;
public class SampleModel : INotifyPropertyChanged
{
    public event PropertyChangedEventHandler PropertyChanged;    <-- (1) Define event handler
    string userName;
    public string UserName
    {
        get { return userName; }
        set
        {
            userName = value;
            if( PropertyChanged != null)
                PropertyChanged(this,                             (2) Raise event
                    new PropertyChangedEventArgs("UserName"));
        }
    }
}
```

To implement `INotifyPropertyChanged`, an event called `PropertyChanged` ❶ is added to the class. The event should be raised whenever a property is changed. Inside the property setter, the code determines whether any listeners are subscribed to the event by checking whether the `PropertyChanged` event is `null`. If the event isn't `null`, the event is raised and sent a new instance of the `PropertyChangedEventArgs` class ❷. The name of the changed property is specified when constructing the event args.

In addition to binding user interface controls to model objects, the data-binding system also supports binding the property of one control to the property of another control. Binding one control to another is called *element-to-element binding*.

A.6 Element-to-element binding

When designing user interfaces, you'll often come across usability features that have little to do with the business logic implemented in a model object. For example, a button might be disabled or hidden if the value in a `TextBox` is empty. The model object shouldn't care whether a button is enabled.

Let's see how to use element-to-element binding to echo the value entered into a `TextBox` in another control, in this case a `TextBlock`:

```
<TextBlock Text="{Binding Text, ElementName=nameTextBox,
    StringFormat='You entered: \{0\}'}" />
```

The `Binding` markup extension binds the `Text` property of the `TextBlock` to the `Text` property of a `TextBox`. The `ElementName` attribute identifies which `TextBox` to use—in this example, the `TextBox` called `nameTextBox`. Finally, the `StringFormat` markup extension is used so that the value isn't merely echoed in the `TextBlock` but is a formatted message.

Let's return to the example of disabling a `Button` when a `TextBox` is empty. There's no automatic way to bind a `Button`'s Boolean `IsEnabled` property to the length of the `TextBox`'s `Text` string. You need a way to convert data during data binding.

A.7 Converting data during data binding

Data binding connects the property in a source object with a property in a target object. Sometimes the source property's type doesn't match the target property's type. XAML's data-binding system knows how to automatically convert certain types of data. For example, the data-binding system will automatically convert the string entered in a TextBox to an integer property in a bound object. XAML provides a mechanism called *value converters* as a way to convert data types that can't be automatically converted.

At the heart of the value conversion process is the IValueConverter interface, which is found in the System.Windows.Data namespace. IValueConverter defines two methods: Convert and ConvertBack. The Convert method is called when copying the source property into the target property. The ConvertBack method is used in Two-Way binding when the target property's value is copied back to the source property. A sample value converter, called StringLengthToBooleanConverter, transforms a string into a Boolean value, based on the length of the string. If the string is empty, the converter returns false:

```
using System.Globalization;
public object Convert(object value, Type targetType,
    object parameter, CultureInfo culture)
{
    string text = value as string;
    return string.IsNullOrEmpty(text) ? false : true;
}
```

To use a value converter in a XAML document, first declare an instance of the converter as a resource:

```
<Grid.Resources>
    <primer:StringLengthToBooleanConverter x:Key="stringLengthConverter" />
...
</Grid.Resources>
```

Value converters are specified using the Converter attribute of the Binding markup extension:

```
<Button Content="Save" Click="Button_Click"
    Style="{StaticResource NarrowButton}"
    IsEnabled="{Binding Text, ElementName=nameTextBox,
    ➥ Converter={StaticResource stringLengthConverter}}" />
```

We've scratched the surface of the features built in to the data-binding system and shown how to use data binding to separate user interface code from business logic. DataTemplates are another feature of XAML that enables the designer/developer workflow.

A.8 Using templates to build data model UI

DataTemplates allow application code to manage domain model objects without regard for the user interface used to display them. LongListSelectors, ContentControls, and other content-based controls are designed to display generic objects. By default, a content-based control will call the `ToString` method of its contained object and display the result in the user interface. The default presentation can be replaced using a `DataTemplate`. The following listing shows how to create a `DataTemplate` for a `ContentControl` bound to a sample model object.

Listing A.3 Creating a `DataTemplate` for a `ContentControl`

```
<ContentControl Content="{Binding}" HorizontalContentAlignment="Stretch">
    <ContentControl.ContentTemplate>
        <DataTemplate>
            <StackPanel Orientation="Horizontal">
                <Polygon Width="50" Height="60" Points="10,0 50,25 10,50"
                    Fill="{StaticResource PhoneAccentBrush}"/>
                <StackPanel>
                    <TextBlock Text="User Name:"
                      Style="{StaticResource PhoneTextGroupHeaderStyle}" />
                    <TextBlock Text="{Binding UserName}"
                      Style="{StaticResource PhoneTextLargeStyle}" />
                </StackPanel>
            </StackPanel>
        </DataTemplate>
    </ContentControl.ContentTemplate>
</ContentControl>
```

❶ Declare content template

❷ Bind to model property

Note that the `ContentControl`'s `Content` is using an empty `Binding` expression. An empty `Binding` expression causes the template to use the current binding context, which in this case is the page's `DataContext`. The `ContentTemplate` property of the `ContentControl` ❶ is set by declaring a `DataTemplate`. The `DataTemplate` uses nested `StackPanels` to display a triangle, a label, and the value of the model's `UserName` property ❷.

Although we haven't covered them here, templates are also used to customize the look and feel of controls. A designer can use templates to completely change the way a `Button`, `TextBox`, or other `Control`-derived class appears in the user interface.

A.9 Summary

XAML is a powerful application-development platform, and we've merely scratched the surface in this appendix. It has built-in support for transforms, animations, commands, custom controls, and more. Many XAML developers have adopted the Model-View-ViewModel (MVVM) pattern that uses XAML's features to further separate user interface code from business logic. You can read more about the MVVM pattern in appendix B.

There are plenty of good references for learning XAML:

- *Windows Store App Development* by Pete Brown (Manning Publications, 2013)
- Silverlight.net, a Microsoft portal with links to tools, tutorials, and forums
- "Microsoft Domain-Specific Languages and XAML Specifications," an MSDN page listing the published XAML specifications (see http://mng.bz/rede)

appendix B: Model-View-ViewModel (MVVM)

What is Model-View-ViewModel (MVVM)? MVVM is one of the design patterns that help developers define a clear separation between the user interface and application logic. Having this clear separation helps improve the testability of applications and allows developers and UI designers to work together on the application. This pattern is a variation of the Model-View-Controller (MVC) and Model-View-Presenter (MVP) patterns. MVVM got a lot of attention in the WPF and Silverlight world a few years ago because it works best with the core features of WPF/Silverlight, such as data binding, XAML markup extension, and so on. It's now widely adapted in other development platforms. We understand that you may not fully understand how this pattern improves the testability and developer/designer collaboration at this point. We'll give you detailed explanations with examples later in this section.

First, let's look at the main components of MVVM. MVVM consists of three main components: Model, View, and ViewModel.

B.1 The Model class

Responsibility—The Model is a class that encapsulates the business logic and data of your application. It has the responsibility of validating the business logic and managing the data flow. Say you're developing a contacts-management application. The Model class for your application will be a class called `Contact` that has properties like `First Name`, `Last Name`, `Phone Number`, and so on. It should have some validation logic such as checking the required field and phone number format. You can also put the logic for saving new contacts and updating and retrieving the existing contacts in that model class.

Management—The model classes should be managed by developers.

Variation—Some developers want to keep separate classes for domain data structure and the data flow. It's totally dependent on the developers' preferences, but we recommend that if you have very thick logic in your model, it's best to split it into small model classes.

B.2 The View class

Responsibility—The View is responsible for managing the appearance of your application. In XAML development, the View is usually a user control, data template, window, or page that contains the structure of UI elements you want to show your user, based on the requirements of the application.

Management—The View is created by UI designers (not developers), but they need to get the model contract from developers and create the mock while they're designing the View, using tools like Expression Blend. Ideally, the View shouldn't have any coding except the defaults, but there are scenarios where the UI logic you want is very difficult to achieve by using attached properties or binding. In those cases it's OK to have the UI logic in a code-behind file of the View.

Variation—None.

B.3 The ViewModel class

Responsibility—The responsibility of the ViewModel is to handle all presentation logic required for the View. The presentation logic includes the validation of inputs entered by the user in the ViewModel. It has the responsibility of coordinating between the View and the Model. We'll talk about how the Model, View, and ViewModel interact with each other later in this appendix.

Management—The developer implements all required logic in ViewModel and handles the interaction between the View and the Model.

Variation—You may or may not want to have a View reference in the ViewModel. Some developers believe that the View and ViewModel should communicate via binding, but others say that having a weak/strong reference of the View in the ViewModel makes things a lot easier. In our opinion, we don't think there's anything wrong with either approach, but having a reference of the View in the ViewModel is like using MVVM and MVP together.

Now that you know what the Model, View, and ViewModel are, let's see how these components communicate with each other.

B.4 Interaction between the Model, View, and ViewModel

The interaction between each component is shown in figure B.1. The View and ViewModel communicate via data binding, and the ViewModel talks to the Model, but there's no direct communication between the View and the Model.

Let's talk more about the details and responsibilities of each component and their interactions, using a very simple MVVM example. Create a new Windows Phone

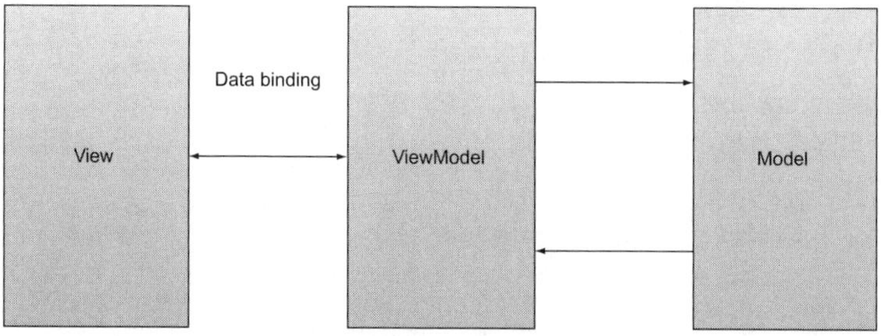

Figure B.1 The interactions between the View, Model, and ViewModel

project called MvvmSample in Visual Studio 2012. To make the sample as simple as possible, you're not going to use any database, service, or validation. It will be just an application that can show the list of contacts and allow a user to add new contacts.

Note that we're assuming you're already familiar with data binding, the `ICommand` interface, and the `INotifyPropertyChanged` interface. If not, you should read about them before starting to work on this example. If you have additional questions after reading about data binding, please post your questions to the *Windows Phone 8 in Action* Manning author forum at http://mng.bz/FiU4. Here are some other resources:

- Data binding overview (http://goo.gl/S7FFG)
- Data Binding (WPF) (http://goo.gl/dCUxE)
- How to Implement Property Change Notification (http://goo.gl/ClbNl)
- INotifyPropertyChanged Interface (http://goo.gl/0GYJp)

B.4.1 Adding the Model class

You'll start by adding a new Model class called `ContactModel` to your project. Do you recall the responsibilities of the Model class? The Model encapsulates the structure of your business object and holds the business logic. Because this is just a sample to show how to use the MVVM pattern, you're not going to add the validation or business logic inside, but remember that the Model is a class where you can put business logic when developing a real-life business application. You'll implement the `INotifyProperty-Changed` interface because the Model is a very simple one, and you don't need any presentation logic that requires an additional ViewModel, so you can simply bind the Model with the View via the ViewModel class. The `ContactModel` will be like that shown in the following snippet. We add only one property called `Id` to make the code short, but you should add three more properties such as `FirstName`, `LastName`, and `PhoneNumber` to the Model class. The data type of those three properties should be `string`. You can also download the full example from the source code that comes with this book. The implementation of `ContactViewModel` is as follows:

```
using System.ComponentModel;

public class ContactModel :  INotifyPropertyChanged
    {
```

```
        private int _id;
        public int Id
        {
            get { return _id; }
            set
            {
                _id = value;
                NotifyPropertyChanged("Id");
            }
        }
        public event PropertyChangedEventHandler PropertyChanged;
        private void NotifyPropertyChanged(string propertyName)
        {
            if (PropertyChanged != null)
            {
                PropertyChanged(this, new
    PropertyChangedEventArgs(propertyName));
            }
        }
    }
```

B.4.2 Adding the ViewModel class

You're going to add a ViewModel called `ContactViewModel` to your project. The ViewModel needs to handle all logic related to the UI and communicates between the Model and the View. Because it's a ViewModel, you need to implement the `INotifyPropertyChanged` interface, and you can use the same code you used in the Model class. You may be thinking, "Why do we need to duplicate the code?" If you were working on a real-life business application, you'd probably create an abstract base class and make that implementation as a common function. Also, do you see the magic string in the `Id` property? You're using it because it's just a sample project, but there are several ways to eliminate those magic strings by using lambda expressions or Aspect Oriented Programming (AOP). If you'd like to know more, enter the keywords "`INotifyPropertyChanged` implementation with lambda expression" or "AOP `INotifyPropertyChanged` implementation" into your favorite search engine.

Let's discuss what you're going to have in the ViewModel. The implementation for the ViewModel is totally dependent on the View, so we need to discuss how the View will look. You'll display the list of existing contacts at the top and the entry form at the bottom of the View. The entry form will have a button that can add new contacts to the list. In the ViewModel class you'll need three properties: `Contacts`, `Contact`, and `SaveCommand`:

```
using System.Collections.ObjectModel;
using System.Windows.Input;

    private ObservableCollection<ContactModel> _contacts;
        public ObservableCollection<ContactModel> Contacts
        {
            get { return _contacts; }
            set
            {
```

```
                _contacts = value;
                NotifyPropertyChanged("Contacts");
            }
        }
        private ContactModel _contact;
        public ContactModel Contact
        {
            get { return _contact; }
            set
            {
                _contact = value;
                NotifyPropertyChanged("Contact");
            }
        }
        public ICommand SaveContactCommand { get; private set; }
```

Because you're not going to have any persistence layer for the project, put some mock data in the constructor of the ViewModel class. Initialize the `Contacts` property with a list of mock data. Then initialize the `Contact` property and `SaveCommand`. The `ActionCommand` that you see in the sample is a simple implementation of the `ICommand` interface. If you're looking for a proper implementation of the `ICommand` interface, we recommend you use the `DelegateCommand` from the Prism framework, `RelayCommand` from MvvmLight, or any command implementation from other mature MVVM frameworks. The implementation of `ContactViewModel` is as follows:

```
public ContactViewModel()
       {
           Contacts = new ObservableCollection<ContactModel>
           {
               new ContactModel() { Id = 1, FirstName = "Tifa", LastName =
     "Lockhart", PhoneNumber = "91988872" },
               new ContactModel() { Id = 2, FirstName = "Aerith", LastName =
     "Gainsborough" , PhoneNumber = "87366790"},
               new ContactModel() { Id = 3, FirstName = "Cloud", LastName =
     "Strife" , PhoneNumber = "46738633"},
               new ContactModel() { Id = 4, FirstName = "Aki", LastName =
     "Ross" , PhoneNumber = "776463839"},
           };
           Contact = new ContactModel();
         SaveContactCommand = new ActionCommand(() =>
         {
               Contacts.Add(new ContactModel() { Id = Contacts.Count() + 1,
     FirstName = Contact.FirstName, LastName = Contact.LastName, PhoneNumber
     = Contact.PhoneNumber });
               Contact = new ContactModel();
           });
       }
```

B.4.3 Adding the View class

You've now added one Model class and one ViewModel class to the project. Next you'll add a View called `ContactView`. As mentioned, the View can be a data template, user control, window, or page. You'll choose a user control as the View in this sample.

You'll show the list of contacts at the top, so you can add the ListBox control, LongListSelector control, or an itemcontrol to the View. Add the entry form where users will enter new contact information. To avoid lengthy code, you're not going to add the whole XAML code here. You can refer to the View in the sample project for this appendix, which you can download with the source code for this book.

Add the ContentControl where you want to display the View in MainPage.xaml. You'll bind the ViewModel and View in the next snippet in the code-behind of MainPage. You can display the View by setting the View to the Content of ContentControl:

```
var view = new ContactView();
view.DataContext = new ContactViewModel();
ContentControl.Content = view;
```

NOTE You may not control the logic for showing the View from MainPage in a real-life project. You should create a controller (for example, a Navigation controller) to handle that navigation logic.

When you run the sample, you should see a screen like that shown in figure B.2.

That's all. You've successfully created your very first MVVM Windows Phone application. As you can see, the MVVM pattern is totally dependent on data binding, XAML markup extension, behavior, attached property, and the command pattern, so you need to master those things before learning about the MVVM pattern.

Figure B.2 View of the MVVM sample

B.5 Patterns as solutions to common problems

Patterns were created to solve problems. Did you notice which problem you could solve by using the MVVM pattern? When you were working on the sample, you may have noticed that you didn't need to write any code in the View. In the View, data binding and XAML cover everything. That's why the View can be managed by the designers who are familiar with XAML and expression blend. In typical application development, developer and designer collaboration can be difficult. The designers used to create the application UI design with Photoshop or other graphics tools. Then they would send those images to developers. But the developers always had problems creating the actual UI based on the images they received from the designers. That's why Microsoft came up with the idea for developers and designers to work together, so both parties are more productive and can produce better output.

We also mentioned that the MVVM pattern improves the testability of the application. If you're coming from a Web Form or WinForm background, you already know how difficult it is to write the unit test for UI logic. But with the MVVM pattern, all presentation logic is separated from the UI, so you can easily write the unit test or practice Test-Driven-Development (TDD) in your development.

B.6 Summary

In this appendix, you've learned about the MVVM pattern, but you can't use one pattern to do everything in real-life application development. You need to know a few patterns that work well with the MVVM pattern:

- *Event Aggregator pattern/Mediator pattern*—You know how to communicate between View, ViewModel, and Model. What about communicating between ViewModel and ViewModel? What if you wanted to link from one View to another? This is where the Event Aggregator or Mediator pattern comes in. The pattern sits between Views and ViewModels to communicate with each other using push.
- *Dependency injection/Ioc*—These patterns help manage object creating and the object lifetime. You can refer to a mature dependency injection framework, such as Unity (from Microsoft) or Autofac. If you're looking for a book about dependency injection, we recommend *Dependency Injection in .NET* by Mark Seemann (Manning Publications, 2001) and *Dependency Injection* by Dhanji R. Prasanna (Manning Publications, 2009). Links to those books are at www.manning.com/seemann/ and www .manning.com/prasanna/.
- *Repository pattern*—You can use this pattern to have one abstraction layer between your application logic and a persistence layer.

Those are the most common patterns developers use in applications that are heavily based on the MVVM pattern. We understand that MVVM is a big topic and you won't fully understand it in one example. Practice with a few more examples and feel free to ask any questions in our forum at http://mng.bz/FiU4.

index

Symbols

Numerics

A

B

C

D

E

F

J

K

L

Q

R

S

T

U

V